WORKERS COMPENSATION

THE FIRST ONE HUNDRED YEARS

CERTIFICATION PROGRAM

WCP®

Copyright © AMCOMP 2011
Fourth Edition 2021
The American Society of Workers Compensation Professionals, Inc.

Copyright © AMCOMP 2011
Fourth Edition 2021
The American Society of Workers Comp Professionals, Inc.

Publisher
The American Society of Workers Compensation Professionals (AMCOMP)
Indianapolis, Indiana

Copyright   AMCOMP 2011
All rights reserved.

Library of Congress Cataloging-in-Publication Data

DeCarlo, Donald T. and Thompson, Roger
Workers Compensation: The First One Hundred Years

ISBN: 979-8-9858499-0-5

No part of this publication may be reproduced, distributed, or transmitted in any form or by any means, or stored in a database or retrieval system, without the prior written permission of the authors.

Copyright © AMCOMP 2011
Fourth Edition 2021
The American Society of Workers Comp Professionals, Inc.

Copyright © AMCOMP 2011
Fourth Edition 2021
The American Society of Workers Comp Professionals, Inc.

Acknowledgements

Many people have shared their advice and information in developing the text and content covering the broad aspects of the workers compensation program which is greatly appreciated. The authors would especially like to acknowledge the AMCOMP board of directors for their support and advice throughout the process.

A special thank you is extended to Lucy DeCaro, vice president of operations of the New York Workers Compensation Insurance Rating Board, John Leonard, president of the Maine Employers Mutual Insurance Company (MEMIC), and Dana Kerr, professor of economics at the University of Southern Maine for the numerous hours providing input, reviewing, and commenting on the initial versions of both the text and course guide. Their beneficial contributions, along with members of their staff, have been invaluable in producing the current edition of the text.

Special thanks is also extended to Dr. Peter Barth, retired economics professor at the University of Connecticut; Warren Heck, former chairman and CEO of GNY Insurance Companies; Richard W. Palczynski, principal and founder of Sea Tower Insurance Consulting; Mike Stinziano, senior vice president of Demotech, Inc.; Greg Krohm, former executive director of the International Association of Industrial Accident Boards and Commissions (IAIABC); Carole Banfield, independent consultant; and to many others who have provided their input, suggestions, and chapter reviews that are so important to the project.

A special thank you to the assistance provided by Tonya Suits, CAE, IOM, association director; Taylor Meyers, communications coordinator; Dreyson Boyd, WCP®, WCP® credentialing staff; and the rest of the NAMIC team. As well as the members of the AMCOMP Education Committee – Jeffrey Fenster Esq., EVP, head of North American specialty risk for AmTrust Financial Services, Inc.; Thomas J. Phelan, CPA, CEO of Chesapeake Employers' Insurance Company; Bonnie Piacentino, WCP®, SVP and COO of PA/DE Compensation Rating Bureaus; Barry S. Lovell, president of Lovell Safety Management, Co.; Thomas Nowak, WCP®, principal of Strategy Conversations, LLC; and Brian Reardon, MBA, ARM, AIS, WCLS, with Maiden Global Service Company, LLC. All those mentioned above have aided in the improvement of the text as it has gone through its various revisions.

Copyright © AMCOMP 2011
Fourth Edition 2021
The American Society of Workers Comp Professionals, Inc.

About the Authors

Donald T. DeCarlo, Esq., WCP®

Donald T. DeCarlo, Esq. is the principal of an independent law firm in Lake Success, NY, which focuses on mediation/arbitration and regulatory and insurance counseling. Before establishing the firm in 2005, Mr. DeCarlo was a partner at Lord Bissell & Brook LLP and headed its New York office. Formerly, he was senior vice president and general counsel of The Travelers Insurance Companies, Deputy General Counsel for its parent corporation Travelers Group, Inc. and executive vice president and general counsel for Gulf Insurance Group.

Mr. DeCarlo is a certified ARIAS-US arbitrator and umpire, a master arbitrator for the NYS Insurance Department, and an arbitrator for the American Arbitration Association and Center for Dispute Resolution. Mr. DeCarlo is also the founder, chairman, and president of The American Society of Workers Compensation Professionals, Inc. (AMCOMP). In addition, Mr. DeCarlo is a director of 17 companies in the insurance industry.

Mr. DeCarlo has authored numerous scholarly articles in legal and trade journals and is a co-author of three books on workers compensation insurance, *Workers Compensation Insurance & Law Practice – The Next Generation, Stress in the American Workplace – Alternatives for the Working Wounded*, and his latest work, *Workplace Stress: Past, Present, and Future*. He chairs an Advisory Committee of the World Trade Center Captive Insurance Company, and formerly served as vice chairman and commissioner of the New York State Insurance Fund (NYSIF) for 10 years. He also served as an inspector for the NYS Athletic Commission.

In communal life, Mr. DeCarlo is a Knight of Malta and a former trustee of Mount St. Michael Academy. He recently received a Humanitarian Award for his efforts with the Judio-Christian tradition by the development Corporation of Israel. He has been honored by numerous major academic institutions such as Mount St. Michael and the College of Mount St. Vincent. He has also been honored by the Long Island Chapter of the Cystic Fibrosis Foundation and received AMCOMP'S certified Workers Compensation Professional (WCP®) designation in 1999.

Mr. DeCarlo graduated from Iona College with a major in economics and earned his Law Degree at Saint John's University Law School. He and his wife MaryAnne, an artist, reside in Douglaston, NY.

Roger Thompson, WCP®

Roger Thompson is a retiree from Travelers Insurance following 30 years of service in the area of workers compensation. Prior to his retirement, Mr. Thompson was director for Worker's Compensation Legislative and Regulatory Issues. A graduate of the University of California, Santa Barbara, he began his career with Travelers in Des Moines, Iowa in 1969 and subsequently transferred to the home office in Hartford, Connecticut in 1976.

During his career with Travelers, Mr. Thompson worked with various trade associations including the American Insurance Association (AIA), The International Association of Industrial Accident Boards and Commissions (IAIABC), and served on the Research Committee at the Workers Compensation Research Institute (WCRI).

Mr. Thompson is married and the father of two sons and has four grandchildren.

Copyright © AMCOMP 2011
Fourth Edition 2021
The American Society of Workers Comp Professionals, Inc.

Copyright © AMCOMP 2011
Fourth Edition 2021
The American Society of Workers Comp Professionals, Inc.

Copyright © AMCOMP 2011
Fourth Edition 2021
The American Society of Workers Comp Professionals, Inc.

WORKERS COMPENSATION
The First One Hundred Years

TABLE OF CONTENTS

Introduction

Chapter One	Workers Compensation History and Workplace Safety	Page 1
Chapter Two	Employers and Employees Subject To the Workers Compensation Law	Page 42
Chapter Three	Security Arrangements and Underwriting	Page 83
Chapter Four	Standard Workers Compensation Policy, Endorsements and Federal Coverages	Page 126
Chapter Five	Covered Occupational Events	Page 169
Chapter Six	Mandated Benefits	Page 215
Chapter Seven	Cost Containment Strategies and Other Medical Issues	Page 258
Chapter Eight	Claims Handling, Fraud and Subrogation	Page 297
Chapter Nine	Program Administration	Page 338
Chapter Ten	The Rate-Making Process	Page 376
Chapter Eleven	Exclusive Remedy and Bad Faith	Page 414
Chapter Twelve	Economic Security Programs	Page 458

Copyright © AMCOMP 2011
Fourth Edition 2021
The American Society of Workers Comp Professionals, Inc.

Copyright © AMCOMP 2011
Fourth Edition 2021
The American Society of Workers Comp Professionals, Inc.

WORKERS COMPENSATION
The First One Hundred Years
INTRODUCTION

This 12-chapter course is designed to develop a basic foundation of knowledge of the various aspects of workers compensation so that individuals who have taken the course will have a better understanding and appreciation of how the various pieces of the workerscompensation program (e.g. claims, risk management, pricing, etc.) work together in order to make the greater whole. Where appropriate, the material examines the pertinent approaches that have evolved since the first state workmen's compensation law was introduced in 1902 in this country.

The materials for this course have been developed from multiple sources and the text for the course is found in the book entitled *Workers Compensation: The First One Hundred Years.* This text was developed specifically for this course of study.

This course guide contains an introduction to each chapter along with a chapter outline. The following serves to highlight the material covered in each of the 12 chapters:

Chapter One – The early development of workmen's compensation laws (later to transition to workers compensation laws) in Europe is traced along with its subsequent development in the United States. With the passage of time, certain shortcomings of the program were recognized, and in 1972, a national commission was created to study the program and make recommendations for improvement. In response to these recommendations, states enacted substantial reforms in subsequent years. Issues continue to arise and are being addressed by state legislative bodies. The chapter concludes with a discussion about workplace safety and the role of the Occupational Safety and Health Administration (OSHA) at the federal and state level.

Chapter Two – The intended scope of workers compensation protection was universal coverage. Notwithstanding this intent, there are certain types of work activity (e.g., farm labors and domestics) that may, under certain circumstances, be difficult to cover. Additionally, many states originally had numeric exceptions to coverage along with other exceptions based on business type. The chapter examines the scope of workers compensation coverage along the issues associated with independent contractors, statutory employees, and professional employee organizations (PEOs). The impact of injuries occurring to out-of-state workers and to workers engaged in employment outside of their usual state of jurisdiction is also examined.

Chapter Three – Benefit security, and the various forms of that security, is examined in this chapter. Benefit security takes the form of insurance or individual or group self-insurance. Within the insurance mechanism, one finds private insurance, competitive or monopolistic state funds, and the residual market or assigned risk pools. While benefit security is a critical component of the program, responsible employers focus on workplace safety as the primary approach for purposes of reducing work-place injuries. The chapter concludes with an examination of the role of the underwriter along with the core elements associated with individual risk underwriting.

Chapter Four – Following an examination of the forms of benefit security covered in the previous chapter, the focus now shifts to an examination of the standard Workers Compensation and Employers Liability policy. Each section of the policy is reviewed with a copy of the policy available for purposes of perusal. The chapter includes a review of some of the more frequently used policy endorsements, along with an explanation of the situations in which the endorsements should be included with the policy. The chapter concludes with an examination of some of the various federal compensation programs involving the payment of benefits.

Chapter Five – The almost universal test for compensability of a workplace injury or death is that it must arise out of and in the course of the employment. While the two phrases arising out of and in the course of the employment appear fairly straight-forward in actual terminology, these phrases have been the subject of extensive litigation and expansion since their first enactment. While many of the states originally required a workplace injury to be a personal injury by accident, with the passage of time, this restrictive interpretation has evolved and today, the workers compensation program includes not only an expanded scope of covered injuries, but also a broad array of occupational diseases along with heart conditions and mental stress claims. Presumptions for coverage of certain conditions associated with employment exposures have also come to be recognized.

Chapter Six – The fundamental concept behind workers compensation is that the employer is responsible for certain benefits to an employee injured on the job without consideration for the issue of fault. These mandated benefits include the furnishing of medical care necessary for recovery and the payment of a portion of lost income in the instance of injury or death resulting from a work-related cause. Chapter six examines the various types of benefits afforded through the workers compensation program along with the different forms of income replacement benefits that may be available to a worker who receives a work-related injury. Certain prescribed benefits are also payable to surviving dependents in the event of a work-related death.

Chapter Seven – Claims management and accident investigations are topics covered in this chapter. Claims management begins with a review of the role of the case manager along with the various functions associated case management. An important role for the claims adjuster is the timely and thorough conducting of an accident investigation. With the increasing cost associated with claims, there is also the rising concern for workers compensation fraud. Fraud can be associated with virtually any party to the program including injured workers, employers, medical providers, attorneys, and benefit administrators. Claims management also involves the recognition of subrogation potential and the way recoveries are handled in various jurisdictions.

Copyright © AMCOMP 2011
Fourth Edition 2021
The American Society of Workers Comp Professionals, Inc.

Chapter Eight – The discussion of medical benefits available to injured workers under the workers compensation program is continued through a review of the factors influencing current medical cost increases. To address these increasing costs, several cost containment strategies have been developed which include legislation regarding the choice of medical provider, the application of physician and hospital fee schedules, the development of treatment protocols, and the introduction of utilization review. The subject of managed care at the state level is reviewed and the chapter concludes with an examination of the issue of medical records privacy and the Affordable Care Act (ACA).

Chapter Nine – Workers compensation program administration is performed at the state level through a board, bureau, commission or other administrative state agency, usually associated with the state's Department of Labor. Functions performed by these agencies include the promulgation of forms and regulations, the development of a dispute resolution process, along with functions designed to expedite and ensure the accuracy of benefit payments by insurers. The chapter concludes with an examination of the role of state second injury funds and special funds in terms of their original purposes(s) and the impact these funds have on overall program costs.

Chapter Ten – The method for determining workers compensation rates – the manual rating system – and an examination of the subjects of experience rating and retrospective rating are covered in this chapter. The method of classification of risks is reviewed in some detail since the classification system is the cornerstone of the rating process. Both experience rating and retrospective rating are programs available to employers of a certain size and are designed to make the cost for insurance more reflective of the employer's actual experience.

Chapter Eleven – A central feature of the workers compensation program is the exclusive remedy doctrine. The *quid pro quo* of workers compensation calls for the employer to be responsible for wage replacement and the offering of necessary medicalcare in exchange for the injured employee foregoing any right to bring a direct action for damages against his/her employer. The limits of the exclusive remedy bargain are constantly being challenged and tested in the courts. Some of the more prevalent theories and situations under which these challenges are being brought today areidentified in this chapter.

Chapter Twelve – While the workmen's compensation laws represent this country's initial foray into social insurance in the early 19th century, subsequent economic events prompted the introduction of additional forms of income replacement and medical care protection. Led first by the enactment of the Social Security Act and later followed with the adoption of Unemployment Insurance, Medicare and Medicaid, social insurance came to be a safety net for members of the working class. These new programs required efforts directed at appropriate coordination to preclude duplication of benefits. Other programs also developed to greater protection to those less advantaged. A number of these major programs are reviewed in this final chapter to afford a better glimpse of how the various programs are integrated.

In addition to the above noted text, an AMCOMP Code Ethics has been developed that sets forth the minimum standards of individual conduct expected of those certified as Workers Compensation Professionals (WCP). A copy of the AMCOMP Code of Ethics is included when ordering the course material.

The material covered in this 12-chapter course is intended as a major building block in the creation of a foundation of a better understanding of workers compensation. The intent of the course of study is not to furnish a definitive answer on any of these topics, but rather to continue to put forth the best and freshest ideas that come to AMCOMP's attention so that those who have taken the course of study will understand the many sides associated with each of these developing issues.

Upon completion of the first six chapters in the text and course guide, applicants seeking certification as a Workers Compensation Professional (WCP) are required to take a home study exam (based on the honor system). The exam is to be requested when the applicant has completed study of the first six chapters of the course guide. Following completion of the home study exam, the exam should be submitted for grading.

Upon completion of all twelve chapters, applicants are required to sit for a written, proctored exam. This exam is inclusive of all material covered in the text along with the AMCOMP® Code of Ethics. The exam will be administered in conjunction with AMCOMP educational forums, seminars, and conferences, and other times arranged by AMCOMP.

Successful completion of the exam will enable AMCOMP to recognize an individual as a certified Workers Compensation Professional. Individuals will be issued a certification certificate and a WCP lapel pin. Ongoing educational opportunities will be available for WCP's at regular forums and educational seminars.

DISCLAIMER: The information contained in the course material is intended for informational purposes only and should not be construed as legal advice. The reader should seek competent legal counsel for advice on any legal matter.

Chapter One

WORKERS COMPENSATION HISTORY AND WORKPLACE SAFETY

WORKERS COMPENSATION HISTORY

The American workers compensation program represents a unique form of social justice. It represents the means by which income replacement benefits and medical care are provided to workers who sustain a work-related injury or death. In exchange for these benefits and medical care, the injured worker is precluded from suing the employer for damages under the theory of negligence. The program also serves to place the cost of these injuries ultimately on the consumer through the medium of insurance as the premiums are passed on to the consumer through the cost of the product.

> The terms workers compensation and workmen's compensation refer to the same program. The use of workers was intended to replace the sexual connotation of workmen's. Workmen's compensation is generally associated with reference to the program prior to the Report of the National Commission in 1972 and workers compensation is used after that date.

The typical workers compensation law is comprised of the five following features:

1. A worker is entitled to certain benefits whenever he/she suffers a "personal injury by accident arising out of and in the course of employment."

2. Issues of negligence and fault are largely immaterial – negligence on the part of the worker does not lessen the extent of entitlement, and complete freedom of fault on the part of the employer does not eliminate the employer's responsibility.

3. Benefits to covered workers include cash benefits to replace a portion of lost earnings, medical care including entitlement to vocational rehabilitation, and, in the case of death, income replacement benefits for the spouse and/or dependents.

4. Benefit administration resides with a state board, bureau, or commission where adopted regulations expedite the accurate delivery of benefits, and relaxed rules of evidence facilitate the timely resolution of disputes.

5. Employers are required to secure their liability through one of several means including: private insurance, self-insurance, or through state insurance – either a competitive or monopolistic state fund – in certain states.

The combination of these features is a system that is neither a branch of tort law nor social insurance, but a blending of the characteristics of each. Like tort law, it places complete responsibility for the cost of the program with the employer with no contribution for that cost coming from the worker. Like social insurance, the right of entitlement is based largely on the social theory of providing support and preventing destitution. The program is not based on the theory of settling accounts between two parties based upon their respective degrees of fault.

SOCIAL RESPONSIBILITY UNDERLYING WORKERS COMPENSATION

As stated frequently by Dr. Arthur Larson, author of the well-known treatise entitled *The Law of Workmen's Compensation*, "the ultimate philosophy behind workers compensation rests with the wisdom of providing, in the most efficient and most certain means, income replacement and medical benefits for the victims of work-related injuries that an enlightened society should feel obligated to provide."

Dr. Larson frequently utilized the following example to illustrate the social philosophy underlying workers compensation. Suppose an employee had worked for 15 years at a punch press at wages that were not adequate for that individual to accumulate savings sufficient to care for his family should the employment cease. Rules posted by the employer required employees to wear a safety device, and, although it was a hot and uncomfortable appliance, the worker had worn it faithfully until the day of the injury. Then, in a moment of carelessness, the worker operated the machine without the safety device and crushed one of his hands.

A system of law, based upon any degree of individual fault at the time of the accident, would find only one result – non-liability on the part of the employer. The employee was not only negligent in not wearing the safety device, but had violated a posted rule specifically designed to prevent such an injury. The employer on the other hand had provided a safety appliance and had attempted to enforce its use. To now require that employer to pay the guilty worker would appear to flaunt the moral premise of any fault-based system of recovery.

In an entirely individualistic society this outcome might be considered acceptable. However, there may be a different result if the same situation is examined in the light of social responsibility. The society surrounding the disabled worker could do one of three things: First, it could refuse all aid and let the individual starve in the street or let him squat on the sidewalk and beg from those who were yesterday his equals. Our modern society no longer considers this approach as a morally acceptable solution.

An alternative to begging rests with placing the injured worker on relief or some other form of direct welfare. This approach – while an obvious improvement over the first - is a poor solution from at least two perspectives. Welfare serves to stigmatize the individual as a pauper and it also serves to place the cost on the political jurisdiction where the individual happens to reside, although that community may have had no connection with the injury.

The third and more enlightened alternative rests with the granting of certain wage replacement and medical care benefits to the injured worker without consideration for the element of fault. Through the granting of such benefits, the dignity and self-respect of the injured worker are preserved while the associated resulting costs are placed where they rightly belong – through the employer unto the consumer of the product whose manufacturer played an instrumental part in the injury.

Through this simple display of alternatives, it can be demonstrated that workers compensation, far from being a violation of moral principle is, in fact, the only morally responsible solution of the problem of the injured worker, once it is conceded that morality has a social as well as an individual aspect.

RECOVERY UNDER COMMON LAW

In attempting to deal with the consequences of personal injury, modern society developed a code of legal recourse where an injury resulted through the fault of another. In England, the remedies of an individual, injured through the fault of another, were originally those provided by common law. This common law had its origin with the Royal Courts of England at a time when there was little statutory law and when questions of right and of duty commonly rested upon custom and usage. Courts not only had to ascertain the customs but also had to seek out underlying reasons for these customs and then interpret the facts to establish a rule commensurate with the case at hand. From early on, decisions were recorded in the rolls of the court and each decision served as a stepping-stone to the next. Thus it was established, stone-upon-stone, never losing touch with the past and continuing to adjust to the needs of the present. The common law that developed was the work of no one mind and not a single instance, but was rather a continuous organic development growing simultaneously with the society to which it administered.

Recovery under common law was based upon the simple premise of fault. Under the law of negligence, failure to use a degree of care reasonably necessary to protect another from injury constituted a cause of civil action. To sustain this action, the injured party had to prove damage and establish a natural and continuous sequence between the cause and effect. Around 1700, this concept of common law negligence was extended to include the doctrine of "vicarious liability." This doctrine refers to the substitution, for legal reasons, of one person's liability for that of another. For instance, it was held from early on that a husband would be liable for the harm to another caused by his wife.

The doctrine of "vicarious liability" was shortly extended to the master-servant relationship wherein the doctrine came to be recognized as the principle of *respondent superior,* which literally means, "let the master answer." The logical basis for its application was found in the belief that the master controlled the acts of the servant, and should be responsible for any injury or harm resulting from their actions.

As claims by injured workers (servants) against the employer (master) came before the courts, the actual duties and responsibilities of the employer became crystallized in a few general principles. These principles centered on the duty of the employer to furnish a certain working environment that included:

1. A reasonably safe place within which to work.

2. Safe and suitable tools with which to work.

3. Supporting the individual with an adequate number of reasonably competent co-workers.

4. Offering proper instructions as to how and when the work should be conducted.

Violation of any of the above noted duties on the part of the employer could result in recovery for the injured worker for an injury sustained during the course of employment. However, there were other elements that arose to impede the opportunity for injured workers to recover damages. When the first cases involving the master-servant relationship were decided, the doctrines of individualism and *laissez-faire* (a minimum of government interference) were widely accepted. Courts, alarmed by the possible consequences of workers recovering damages against their employer while at the same time seeking to encourage industrial development by reducing any legal burdens facing employers, devised a number of defenses for use by the employer. Over time, the following three defenses, which proved to be quite effective in limiting the recovery available to injured workers, evolved:

Contributory Negligence - Under the doctrine of contributory negligence, the slightest lack of ordinary care on the part of the injured worker, which served to contribute to the injury, barred the worker from recovering any damages. While this doctrine existed before the period of industrial development, it was applied with severity in the case of workers. An example can be found in a United States Supreme Court decision involving a conductor who was injured when he fell off his train.[1] Although a loose handrail was found to be the cause of the fall, Martin's injuries were held to be not compensable because inspecting the train for faulty equipment was one of his job duties. Even a one percent degree of fault was sufficient to preclude payment under this doctrine.

Fellow-Servant Rule - The common employment or fellow-servant rule had its genesis in the *Priestly case* in England in 1837.[2] In that decision, a butcher's boy sued his master for an injury when an over-loaded cart collapsed. When it was proven that the over-loading was due to the negligence of a fellow-servant, the injured employee was barred from a recovery. The associated doctrine of common employment set forth that fellow workers are the best judge of the ability of another to perform an assigned task. An employee discovering a lapse on the part of another was responsible for notifying the employer. It was considered appropriate that where the employer failed to rectify the situation, the worker should seek

---

[1] *Martin v. Wabash Railroad*, 142 F. 650 (1905)
[2] *Priestley v. Fowler*, 3 Mees & Wels. 1, 150 Eng. Rep. (1837)

employment elsewhere from an employer who would heed his concerns. In either instance, it was held that the employer could not be responsible for injuries resulting from the acts of fellow-servants.

Assumption of Risk - The third and final defense available to the employer for avoiding liability resided with the doctrine of assumption of risk. This doctrine stemmed from the same decision as the fellow-servant rule and was based on the assumption that, where the employee freely accepted the employment, that employee assumed certain risks. These risks included the ordinary risks of the employment; the extraordinary risks of the employment if he knew or could reasonably be expected to know of them; and the risks arising from the carelessness, ignorance or incompetence of his fellow-servants.

The development of common law was not always as refined as we might consider it in light of current knowledge. The legal principal governing master-servant liability was relatively late in arriving with some of the more characteristic features not appearing until well into the 18th century. This later development was due in part because labor and employment were of a very different style. Basically, labor fell into one of three categories:

- Agricultural labor was for a long time a class of inferior civil rights. Slavery existed and for several hundred years, the characteristic status of agricultural labor was that of serfdom. Wages payable to a servant were restricted by statute and the liberty to change masters was limited. This was a situation subject to great abuse.

- Prior to the Industrial Revolution, trade and industry centered in towns and these affairs were conducted under the guild system that began in Europe. A youth entered industry as an apprentice and was bound to the master by indenture (normally a period of seven years). Following this apprenticeship period, the individual became a journeyman working for wages and might, in due course, become a master. The guild regulated all things including wages, hours of labor, prices, methods and the duties of the master toward the apprentice.

- The final category of labor, the seaman, constituted from the beginning duties and rights dependent upon maritime law in force by the Courts of Admiralty. The customary right of the injured seaman for care, maintenance, and wages to the end of the journey is said to predate the time of Christ. The right of action for personal injuries sustained by reason of the unseaworthiness of the vessel had its development in more modern times.

These classes of labor were for many years subject to independent peculiarities that tended to limit suits for damages against the master based on personal injury to the servant. With the dawn of the Industrial Revolution there arose a completely new economic philosophy - the cardinal points being freedom of contract, freedom of competition, and freedom of motion and action. As a result of these changes, labor found its status altered as there came to be an abundance of jobs along with the opportunity to pick and choose between employers.

There were also disadvantages associated with this new development. Industrial towns were unsanitary and the crowding of too many poorly built tenements gave rise to unspeakable social conditions. New forms of industry also brought together large numbers of untrained and often undisciplined workers who had been selected without regard as to their background or character. In addition, workers were exposed to new hazards such as rapidly moving power belts, rotating shafts, moving machine parts, and on occasion hot or molten metals, gases, or chemicals.

This new "industrialization" placed workers in peril both from their environment and from each other. The master no longer exercised personal oversight and direction but rather relied upon a staff of managers or supervisors. In many instances, the master was no longer a single person but rather a corporate entity operating through directors and officers. The relationship of master and servant was no longer a personal relationship and had become one of pure contract. Wages, conditions of labor, and other employment issues came to be matters of private negotiation.

Insofar as injuries were concerned, the master denied any responsibility other than that imposed by common law. The worker should have anticipated the possibility of injury and made any necessary allowance when negotiating for wages. If the worker failed to do this, it was not the employer's fault. The reasoning at that time followed that courts were open to the worker and questions of employer's liability were to be determined by the courts.

In addition to the three defenses available to the employer noted above, the employee's common law remedy was far from uniform in all jurisdictions. There was a wide degree of variation in procedures under different systems and in different jurisdictions. At best, redress under common law was not a simple matter. The indictment against the common law system of recovery could be summarized under four general headings:

1. The delay inherent in any enforcement of a claim in the courts.

2. The uncertainty as to the basis of a claim for damages under the common law.

3. The uncertainty as to the amount of damages that might be awarded.

4. The uncertainty as to the ability to collect a judgment after one had been obtained and sustained.

To these indictments could also be added the fact that an action for damages could be sustained only if the injured worker survived the accident. Claims under common law were held to die with the injured person. Finally, there was uncertainty of legal remedy and the employee was responsible for proving the necessary facts to defeat the employer defenses. This included the worker having to secure the evidence of witnesses who were frequently reluctant to testify because of their relationship with the employer.

EMPLOYERS' LIABILITY LAWS

Enactment of some of the early versions of employers' liability statutes was in response to public agitation for the removal of certain of the defenses available to the employer. With the growth of industrialization, the inequities of the common law principles of employer's liability became evident. Certain groups, pressuring for reform, noted that the philosophy of *laissez-faire* represented simple exploitation of the working class.

Efforts to enact employers' liability laws were not intended to create a new system of liability for the employer. Rather, they were based on the theory that the employee must bear the economic consequences of an industrial injury unless the employee could show that some other person, either through a negligent act or omission, was directly responsible for the accident. These acts were intended – through modification of certain of the employer defenses - to restore the worker to a position no worse than that of a stranger injured by the negligence of the employer or one of his employees.

Many of the early employers' liability acts were extremely narrow in scope confining their modifications to a specific industry or a particular defense. For example, in 1855 **Georgia** enacted the first such statute in this country whereby it abolished the fellow-servant rule for railroad companies only. By 1907, twenty-six states had enacted employers' liability acts with most of those laws abolishing the fellow-servant rule while a few limited or made adjustments to the assumption of risk and contributory negligence doctrines.

The Federal Employers' Liability Act of 1908, which covered all employees of common carriers engaged in interstate and foreign commerce, was the high point in this phase of worker protection. Taking its lead from many of the more advanced state laws, the federal law provided that contributory negligence should only mitigate damages, and that neither contributory negligence nor assumption of risk should apply in the case of violation of safety requirements set forth in the law. Finally, it made the railroad liable for the negligence of its officers, agents and employees, and for defects due to negligence in track, equipment, engines, and cars, that resulted in injury to an employee.

Although the enactment of state employers' liability laws represented a step forward, they remained inadequate as a viable remedy for workplace injuries and death in the developing age of industrialization. Even with a lowering of the threshold for recovery, injured workers or their dependents had to rely on the courts for any award of damages. Studies made in a number of states prior to the enactment of compensation laws illustrate this point quite explicitly. A report compiled in 1907 by an **Illinois** Commission concluded that of 614 death cases, the survivors received nothing in 214 cases and were engaged in pending litigation in another 111 cases. The remaining cases were settled for small sums averaging a few hundred dollars.

A similar review done in **New York** found that in 74 death cases where the disposition was known, there was no compensation paid in 32 and compensation under $500 was paid in 30 cases. Only 12 cases resulted in a recovery between $500 and $5,000.

In 1910, Crystal Eastman authored a book entitled *Work-Accident and the Law* where she presented the findings of the first systematic investigation of all cases for a representative period in a representative American district. The investigation consisted of a study of the work fatalities of which there was a public record in a given year, the indications as to the party responsible for causing the fatality, and the recovery of any income lost as a result of the accident.

While Ms. Eastman's book contains many examples of judicial outcomes, the following is just one – In October 1906, a Russian laborer employed at $1.60 a day was sent with two other men to an adjoining building used by the employer for storage. In the building, on the floor above, grain was stored in bags. The supports in the floor gave way and the floor collapsed. One worker escaped, one worker was injured, and the Russian laborer was killed. The victim had a wife and four children, but no savings. The claim agent for the employer offered a settlement of $400 but the widow refused. The widow put the claim in the hands of an attorney and suit was filed for $20,000. Six months after the accident the widow delivered another baby. It was the end of that year before the case came to trial. The court instructed the jury to return a verdict for the defendant. The widow had lost her case.[3]

Even those situations where a recovery was realized failed to reflect the complete story. Attorney fees, averaging a quarter to one-third of the recovery, would have to come out of any settlement amount. When funeral and other related expenses were also deducted, it became quite clear that system of recovery under the employers' liability laws was a complete failure, and, in most instances, left the workers family destitute where the workplace injury resulted in death or long-term disability.

WORKMEN'S COMPENSATION LAWS IN EUROPE

While much of the case law affecting workers' rights to recovery came from England, it was Germany that took the lead in offering protection for injured workers. In 1838 Germany enacted a law making railroads liable to their employees, as well as passengers, for all actions except those due to "acts of God" and those involving negligence on the part of the plaintiff. In 1884 Germany adopted the first modern workmen's compensation law – the Accident Insurance Law. This came 13 years before England, 25 years before the first American jurisdiction, and 65 years before the last American jurisdiction.

Workmen's compensation had its genesis in the notion that families of working people should not be crushed by industrial misfortune. German chancellor Otto Von Bismarck, while no great humanitarian, co-opted the key features of the Social Democratic Party that included the idea that Germany should provide for working people a system of insurance that would protect workers against the economic consequences resulting from sickness, accident, or death. Building upon existing sickness insurance societies, the new German Accident Insurance Law required workers to insure against disability.

Bismarck's first foray into the field was through the Employers' Liability Laws of 1971 that provided limited protection to workers in certain factories, quarries, railroads and mines. Later, and far more importantly, he pushed through Workers' Accident Insurance in 1884 creating the first modern system of workers compensation. This first compensation law covered all employees engaged in manufacturing, mining and transportation. Benefits included medical treatment and compensation for lost earnings up to two-thirds of the workers' pay. This first law

---

[3] Eastman, Crystal, *Work Injury and the Law (The Pittsburgh Survey),* New York Charitable Committee pgs. 3&4 (MCMX)

was noteworthy from the perspective of its method of funding. Contributions from the worker were an integral part of the system and the system itself was composed of three separate parts. The Sickness Fund (financed by employer contribution of one-third and employee contribution of two-thirds) paid for the first 13 weeks for sickness or disability due to an accident. The Accident Fund (completely financed by the employer) paid for disabilities extending beyond 13 weeks. The Disability Insurance Fund (the employer and the employee each contributed one-half of the cost) provided for disability resulting from old-age and other causes not specifically covered elsewhere.

The program was based on the employer deducting from the workers' wages the contributions to be made to the Sickness Fund and the Disability Insurance Fund, and the employer was to contribute his appropriate share to each Fund. The theory upon which the employer was to contribute one-third of the cost for the first 13 weeks of disability, was that industrial injuries, and to a certain extent occupational diseases, contributed to nearly one-third of the entire number of injuries and illnesses.

Very soon after Germany introduced their system of worker protection, Austria took action along similar lines. It was in 1880 that the British Prime Minister Gladstone pushed through the Employers' Liability Act which abolished the old common law defenses. Norway was the first of all countries to adopt the state insurance system. At the same time, Denmark introduced its plan for holding the employer liable and permitting the employer to insure or to self-insure. To ensure uniform adjustment of claims, Denmark also introduced a commission that was appointed by the state to resolve disputes.

In response to agitation to remove the defenses under the employers' liability law, Great Britain adopted its first workmen's compensation law in 1897. This law provided that the employer should be directly liable and that, in the event of injury to an employee, the employer would be required to pay compensation at the rate of fifty percent of the wages; subject to modification for high wages in certain situations. In the event of the death of a worker, the employer was obligated to pay three years of wages.

Later France also took action and introduced a system similar in nature to that of Great Britain. There then followed Finland, Sweden, Holland, Italy, Luxemburg, Russia, Spain, and Switzerland. Each of these countries made some provision for state insurance or supervised mutual insurance. Russia originally established a system similar to Great Britain under which the employer was directly liable for any injury or death. Prior to the 1918 Russian revolution, this approach was abandoned in favor of state insurance.

DEVELOPMENT OF WORKMEN'S COMPENSATION IN THE UNITED STATES

As early as 1891, serious interest in this country had been expressed in the European experiments with compensation for injured workers. In response to that interest, many states and the federal government established investigatory commissions to study the European systems. Populist sentiment for organized worker movements began to also grow during this early period.

After 1900 the slow stream of labor legislation quickened to a torrent and a drive for compensation laws began to move forward. This was due in part to the rise of labor unions which had achieved a position of effectiveness following a stormy and erratic history. An additional force behind workmen's compensation legislation was the rising middle class. This group had become increasingly aware of the plight of the worker because of personal experience and studies based on facts, figures, and to some extent, the emotions of social reformers, journalists, and government agencies.

Furthermore, social reformers such as Crystal Eastman, a labor lawyer, suffragist, socialist, and journalist played an important role in raising awareness concerning workplace conditions. Born in Marlborough, Massachusetts, in 1907 Ms. Eastman was hired by the editor of a social work magazine to investigate labor conditions. Over the next year she published the first in-depth sociological investigation of industrial accidents ever undertaken. In June 1909 New York Governor Charles E. Hughes appointed Ms. Eastman to become the first woman member of the Employer's Liability Commission. In this role she drafted New York State's first workmen's compensation law and in 1910 published her book *Work Accidents and the Law* (referenced earlier) that served to describe the financial hardships realized by families where the breadwinner had sustained a serious or fatal workplace injury.

In conjunction with the efforts of social reformers to address the subject of workplace accidents, there was the separate issue concerning child labor. As the demand for additional cheap labor increased during the early period of the Industrial Revolution, young children representing cheap labor were being hired to work in factories and mines. In the 1900s, over two million children were employed to help their families – often under dirty and unsafe working conditions. The photographer Lewis Hines used his photographs of children as young as seven working in cotton mills and coal mines to campaign for social reform. Over the course of a decade he took thousands of photographs that helped convince lawmakers to introduce new industrial regulations to protect children.

Following many years of efforts by the social reformers, the Keating-Owen Child Labor Act of 1916 was enacted by the United States Congress. This Act sought to address child labor by prohibiting the sale in interstate commerce of goods produced by factories that employed children under 14, mines that employed children younger than 16, and any facility where children under 16 worked at night or more than eight hours a day.

The Act was signed into law by President Woodrow Wilson – who had lobbied heavily for its passage – and went into effect September 1, 1917. Nine months later the Act was ruled unconstitutional by the Supreme Court of the United States.[4] It was not until 1938 that the Fair Labor Standards Act (FLSA) was enacted by Congress. The FLSA introduced a maximum 44-hour seven-day work week, established a national minimum wage, guaranteed "time-and-a-half" for overtime in certain jobs, and prohibited most employment of minors in "oppressive child labor."

---

[4] *Hammer v. Dagenhart*, 247 U.S. 251 (1918)

During this intervening period, action was being taken at the state level concerning workmen's compensation legislation. **Maryland** passed the first state workmen's compensation law in 1902. This law applied only to coal and clay mining, operations of steam and street railways, and to certain construction work done for municipalities. Benefits were granted only in the case of death and benefits were limited to $1,000. Other injuries were mentioned in the new law, but no benefits were conferred and the result was that workers lost their common law rights in many cases without an adequate substitution in the form of compensation benefits. In 1902 this law was declared unconstitutional on grounds that it deprived the parties of the right to trial by jury.

In 1903 a special five-member commission was appointed in **Massachusetts** to study the issue of compensation benefits for work-place injuries. This was followed by the establishment of similar commissions in **Illinois** (1905), **Connecticut** (1906), and numerous additional states beginning in 1909. By 1916, a total of 31 states had appointed commissions to investigate and report on conditions under employer's liability laws and to recommend changes with the law.

In January of 1908, President Theodore Roosevelt outlined in a message to Congress the need for government employees to be compensated for injuries occurring in government services. Acting upon this recommendation, Congress enacted in 1908 the first federal workmen's compensation law that provided a limited scale of benefits to certain government employees. In 1916, this Federal Employees Compensation Act (FECA) was expanded to encompass all civil service employees in the United States government.

It should be noted that the federal government played a limited role during the early part of the 20th century in advocating for rights and benefits to injured workers at the state level. It was not until the 1930's – with the introduction of Social Security and unemployment insurance – that the federal government began to take a more prominent role in providing for comprehensive schemes of economic security. Much of the change that did occur during this initial period was deliberated and enacted at the state level.

Illinois and **Massachusetts** enacted limited compensation laws in 1907 and 1908 respectively. It was in 1910 that **New York** enacted two workmen's compensation laws. The first of these was a compulsory law that applied to certain specified hazardous employments (e.g., structural iron works, the operation of hoisting machines, scaffolding work at an elevation of 20 feet or more, and work with explosives). This law also contained the features of other early laws that permitted the worker to maintain an action under the employer's liability law or to claim compensation benefits under the new law. The second law provided for voluntary agreement to compensation between the employer and the worker in those industries not covered by the compulsory law. The benefits were the same under both laws and the laws became effective on the same date.

Neither of the New York laws were successful. The voluntary law failed for lack of interest on the part of employers and workers. On March 24, 1911, the New York Court of Appeals declared in the *Ives* decision the compulsory law unconstitutional. The Court of Appeals was unanimous in concluding that *"this is a liability unknown to the common law and we think it plainly constitutes a deprivation of liberty and property under the Federal and State Constitutions unless its imposition can be justified under the police power. . . ."*[5] The court's analysis went on to add that it viewed this attempt to provide workmen's compensation benefits as nothing more than taking the property of the employer and giving it to employees without due process.

In 1911, **Wisconsin** became the first state in the nation to put a broad, constitutionally valid workmen's compensation system into operation. On May 3, 1911, Governor McGovern gave executive approval to the first state workmen's compensation law. It was published officially on the same day and went into immediate effect.[6] The constitutionality of the law was upheld by the Wisconsin Supreme Court on November 14, 1911.[7]

New Jersey approved its workmen's compensation law April 4, 1911 with an effective date *"the fourth day of July next succeeding its passage and approval,"* making the effective date for the New Jersey law July 4, 1911. In terms of states where the law was ultimately upheld as constitutional, New Jersey was the first state to enact such a law and Wisconsin was the first state in which such a law went into effect.

State Enactments of Workmen's Compensation Laws

State	Date	Type
Alabama	January 1, 1920	Elective
Alaska	July 28, 1915	Elective
Arizona	November 3, 1925	Compulsory
Arkansas	December 5, 1940	Elective
California	January 1, 1918	Elective
Colorado	May 1, 1919	Elective
Connecticut	January 1, 1914	Elective
Delaware	January 1, 1918	Elective
District of Columbia	July 1, 1928	Elective
Florida	May 25, 1935	Elective
Georgia	March 1, 1921	Elective
Hawaii	July 1, 1915	Elective
Idaho	January 1, 1918	Compulsory
Illinois	July 1, 1913	Elective
Indiana	September 1, 1915	Elective
Iowa	July 1, 1914	Elective
Kansas	June 30, 1927	Elective
Kentucky	August 1, 1916	Elective
Louisiana	January 1, 1915	Elective
Maine	January 1, 1916	Elective
Maryland	November 1, 1914	Elective
Massachusetts	July 1, 1912	Elective

---

[5] *Ives v. South Buffalo Railroad* 201 N.Y. 271 (1911)
[6] Wisconsin State Journal Madison, Wisconsin May 3, 1936
[7] *Borgnis v. Falk Co.* 133 N.W. 209 (1911)

Michigan	September 1, 1912	Elective
Minnesota	October 1, 1913	Elective
Mississippi	January 1, 1949	Elective
Missouri	November 2, 1926	Elective
Montana	July 1, 1915	Elective
Nebraska	December 1, 1914	Elective
Nevada	July 1, 1913	Elective
New Hampshire	January 1, 1912	Elective
New Jersey	July 4, 1911	Elective
New Mexico	June 7, 1929	Elective
New York	July 1, 1914	Compulsory
North Carolina	May 1, 1929	Elective
North Dakota	July 1, 1919	Compulsory
Ohio	January 1, 1912	Elective
Oklahoma	September 1, 1915	Compulsory
Oregon	June 30, 1914	Elective
Pennsylvania	January 1, 1916	Elective
Rhode Island	October 1, 1912	Elective
South Carolina	June 1, 1936	Elective
South Dakota	July 1, 1917	Elective
Tennessee	April 15, 1919	Elective
Texas	September 1, 1913	Elective
Utah	July 1, 1917	Compulsory
Vermont	July 1, 1915	Elective
Virginia	January 1, 1919	Elective
Washington	October 1, 1911	Compulsory
West Virginia	October 1, 1913	Elective
Wisconsin	May 3, 1911	Elective
Wyoming	April 15, 1915	Compulsory

In a somewhat ironic twist of fate, precisely one day following the March 24, 1911 decision by the **New York** Court of Appeals in *Ives* declaring the compulsory workmen's compensation law unconstitutional, a devastating fire occurred at the Triangle Shirtwaist factory in New York City that resulted in the death of 146 workers. The accident happened on a Saturday inside the Asch Building (located at the northwest corner of Washington Place and Greene Streets and today a part of New York University). About 500 women, mostly young immigrant women, were nearing the end of their 6 day, 52 hour work week. The women were working on the top three floors of the ten-story building behind locked doors making shirtwaists (blouses of lightweight fabric). By the time that someone screamed fire, flames were already coming up from the cutting room one floor below.

Within the next 15 minutes, nearly a third of all Triangle Shirtwaist workers were killed. Fire truck ladders could reach only the seventh floor. Firefighters held nets below but so many women were jumping at the same time that the nets tore and could not hold them. Others rushed to the elevator shaft, hoping to escape by sliding down the cables, only to lose their grip. Most of those who lost their lives had worked on the ninth floor. The Fire Marshal later concluded that the likely cause of the fire was the disposal of a still-lit match or cigarette butt in the scrap bin, which held two months' worth of accumulated cuttings at the time of the fire.

Later inquiries found that the doors leading from the shop areas had been locked, presumably to keep the women at their sewing machines. The owners, who were tried for manslaughter, were later acquitted when the jury could not establish whether the owners had ordered the doors locked or were not aware that they were locked. But in 1914, civil suits brought by relatives of 23 victims ended with payments of $75 to each of the families.

In response to the tragedy, the city of New York established the Bureau of Fire Investigations. Shortly thereafter, the New York legislature proposed a state constitutional amendment permitting the enactment of a compulsory workmen's compensation statute. This constitutional amendment was submitted to a popular referendum and adopted on November 4, 1913. This was followed by passage of a compulsory workmen's compensation law that was upheld by the Court of Appeals the following year.

Shortly following events in New York, the United States Supreme Court held in *Southern Pacific Co. v. Jensen* that the public welfare was certainly promoted by a compulsory scheme of insurance to secure injured workmen in hazardous employments and their dependents from becoming objects of charity.[8] The new thinking began to see workmen's compensation laws as a fair bargain between the employer and the employee. The court concluded that the state could require workers and employers each to yield something for a plan of compensation that would be for their mutual benefit and protection.

This foundation for the constitutionality of the law was seen to rest upon the exchange of rights between the employer and the employee; specifically, the exclusive remedy protections provided to employers in exchange for the guaranteed "no fault" benefits available to the injured employee. This exchange of rights is referred to as the *quid pro quo* lying at the heart of the American system of workmen's compensation.

The *quid* for the employer rests with the limitation on liability found in the compensation laws. This potential liability exposure can be significant when considering what a potential liability award in a case of negligence has versus the recovery available to the injured worker under the workmen's compensation law. The *quo* is equally significant because the injured worker is entitled to adequate compensation benefits even where the injury is the result of the employee's own fault so long as the resulting injury is found to be work-related.

During the corresponding period, the *Ives* decision by the New York Court of Appeals that had held the law enacted in 1910 to be unconstitutional had its impact on similar legislation in other states. Serious questions were raised as to the constitutionality of compulsory acts under both state and federal constitutions. Two courses of action were seen to follow. A minority of states, – such as **New York** - enacted compulsory laws, amending their constitutions where necessary. A larger number of states passed laws elective in form with provisions designed to make election to stay outside of the act as difficult as possible.

---

[8] *Southern Pacific Co. v. Jensen*, 244 U.S. 205 (1917)

The mechanisms of the elective laws differed in detail, but in the main consisted of two distinct parts – an employer's liability section and a compensation section. The employer who came under the compensation section was relieved of all other liability with respect to personal injury to an employee, being responsible only to pay compensation benefits. The employer who failed to bring himself under the compensation section became subject to employer's liability and was not permitted access to the three principal common law defenses of contributory negligence, assumption of risk, and the fellow-servant rule.

THE FORMATIVE YEARS

Characteristics of the early workmen's compensation laws reflected the environment that produced them. Despite the widespread dissatisfaction with employer's liability laws, workmen's compensation laws were a new venture and it was considered advisable to proceed with caution. Liberalization would come later. Consequently, the original laws frequently excluded many employments, were elective in many instances, applied only to "accidental injuries," imposed waiting periods of two weeks or more, limited medical recovery, and set the compensation rate at one-half of wages and further established a maximum weekly benefit amount. The following serves to trace a few of those characteristics and follow their expansion from the early stages of enactment of compensation laws through the early 1970's.

> **Covered Workers** - From the beginning there were those who believed that the compensation system should comprise all industries and all employers. However, the reality was that many forms of employment (e.g., domestics, agricultural laborers and casual workers) were excluded from coverage under the early laws. In addition, a few states limited coverage to only extra-hazardous employments.
>
> Many of the states continued this exclusion for domestics, farm workers and casual workers through the 1940's. In 1940, 25 of the 47 state laws contained a stipulation exempting employers of less than a specified number of employees. Seven laws exempted those with less than three workers, four states with less than four workers and six states with less than five. At the other extreme, **Alabama** covered only employers with 16 or more workers and **South Carolina** covered only employers with 15 or more workers.
>
> Continuing through 1970, the vast majority of states continued to exclude coverage for domestics, farm laborers and casual workers. By 1970, coverage was compulsory in 30 states and the general trend was toward those employers with three or more employees.
>
> **Waiting Periods** - Nearly all of the original compensation statutes included a 14-day waiting period requirement that had to be satisfied before compensation for disability could be paid. The purpose of the waiting period was twofold – to exclude minor injuries the cost of which could be borne by the worker, and to minimize the danger of fraudulent claims. Originally, most laws stipulated a waiting period but made no allowance for a retroactive period (a period after which compensation benefits would be paid from the first day of disability).

By 1940, the majority of states had reduced the waiting period to seven days and had established a retroactive period that ranged between 14 and 42 days. By 1970, 31 states had a seven day waiting period while the remaining states had a waiting period of lesser duration. **Hawaii** stood alone with a two day waiting period.

Medical Protection – Of 24 laws in effect on January 1, 1915, six failed to provide any medical benefits except in fatal cases. Of the remaining 18 states, 13 limited the period during which such benefits could be provided (generally 60 days) and ten limited the total dollar amount (generally $100).

By 1940, out of a total of 47 states with compensation laws – **Mississippi** was the last state to enact a workmen's compensation law in 1949 – 24 continued to establish a time limitation (ranging from 14 to 180 days), 25 states had dollar amount limitations (ranging from $100 to $800), and 12 states had neither time nor benefit amount limitations.

By 1970, 15 states continued to impose a time limitation but in all but nine of the states, extension of benefits could be granted upon application to the appropriate administrative board or commission. Nine states continued to place dollar limitations (between $5,000 and $35,000) on the amount of medical that could be paid.

Disability Benefits – From the beginning, compensation benefits were not designed or intended to replace the full extent of lost income. It had been observed with other forms of social insurance that the payment of full wages or an amount approximating the full wage, frequently resulted in malingering. Full replacement of wages would also have made the program cost prohibitive for employers. Most of the original laws calculated the weekly benefits at 50% of the pre-injury wage and further established maximum weekly compensation amounts in the range of $10. Of the original laws, most established a maximum duration for total disability benefits of 300 weeks, while a few states like **Kansas** and **Kentucky** allowed for a maximum duration of eight years.

By 1940, the majority of states had moved to replacing two-thirds of the workers' wages and increased the maximum weekly benefit amount to the range of $20. Maximum benefit durations had moved to 500 weeks while **Rhode Island** had a 1,000 week limitation. 1970 saw the percentage of replacement remain at two-thirds of prior wages and the maximum weekly benefits ranged between $40 in **Mississippi** and $150 in **Arizona**. In the case of benefit duration, nearly one-half of the states had enacted laws that paid benefits for the entire period of disability.

Death Benefits – A Conference of Commissioners on Compensation of Industrial Accidents recommended in 1910 that the death benefit equal 60% of the wages lost – subject to a maximum weekly benefit of $10 – to continue for a period of 300 weeks. Legislatures gravitated toward this scale of benefits, partly based on the fear of the potential cost to employers, and partly because of concern over the possibility that industries in states without workmen's compensation laws would gain a decided economic advantage. While there was variation among approaches, most of the original laws closely approximated the recommended amounts.

By 1940, the percentage of wage replacement in the case of death was moving toward two-thirds and the maximum weekly benefit followed that of disability benefits. In most states, the maximum duration ranged between 300 and 400 weeks. Benefits payable for death continued to improve through the ensuing period and by 1970, 35 states continued to have a maximum benefit amount payable in the case of death that ranged between $12,500 to $37,500 for a surviving spouse.

While states continued to make improvements in terms of the workers covered by compensation laws and the amount of benefits available to injured workers and their survivors, there were many who were critical of state laws that were not perceived as "progressive" as those in adjoining states. Notwithstanding the expansion of compensation laws during the formative years, there continued to be a perception that the program did not provide an adequate remedy for all work-related injuries. In response to these concerns, a national commission of experts was convened to make recommendations as to how to improve the program.

1972 NATIONAL COMMISSION ON STATE WORKMEN'S COMPENSATION LAWS

By the late 1960's, serious questions had arisen concerning the fairness and adequacy of existing workmen's compensation laws. A listing of problems included the continuing gaps in coverage; the few states that retained elective laws; states that continued to distinguish between hazardous and non-hazardous employment; common exclusions for agricultural workers, domestics, and small employers; limitations as they applied to compensable occupational diseases; and restrictive schedules of occupational diseases. However, an even larger problem was related to the perceived inadequacy of benefits for income replacement, medical, and rehabilitation.

Questions arose as to the adequacy and equity of workmen's compensation laws in the light of the growth of the economy, the changing nature of the labor force, increases in medical knowledge, increases in the general level of wages and the cost of living, and the onset of new technology bringing with it new risks to health and safety. For those reasons the United States Congress established the National Commission on State Workmen's Compensation Laws to undertake the study and evaluation of state laws in order to determine if such laws provided an adequate, prompt, and equitable system of compensation.

On June 15, 1971, President Richard Nixon appointed a fifteen-member Commission composed of representatives from state administrative agencies, business, labor, insurance carriers, medical professionals, educators and the general public. In addition, three members of the President's Cabinet were designated as members of the Commission. The Chairman of the National Commission was Professor John Burton from Cornell University, Executive Director was Professor Peter Barth, and John Lewis served as Associate Executive Director and Chief Counsel.

Following a year of intensive hearings and the compilation of numerous studies, the National Commission issued its critique of the state workmen's compensation program to the President in July of 1972. Their report began with a statement of the five major objectives for a modern workmen's compensation program. These objectives determined that workmen's compensation laws should:

(1) Provide broad coverage of employees and work-related injuries and diseases.

(2) Provide substantial protection against interruption of income,

(3) Provide sufficient medical care and rehabilitation services.

(4) Encourage safety.

(5) Be an effective delivery system.

The National Commission report included a total of 82 recommendations. The Commission identified 19 of these recommendations as the essential elements of a modern workmen's compensation program. The Commission further recommended that compliance of the states with these essential recommendations be evaluated on July 1, 1975, and, if necessary, Congress should enact federal legislation that would "guarantee compliance" with these standards.

Nineteen Essential Recommendations

R2.1 (a) Coverage by workmen's compensation laws is to be compulsory and (b) no waivers are to be permitted.

R2.2 Employers are not to be exempted from workmen's compensation coverage because of the number of their employees.

R2.4 A two-stage approach to the coverage of farm workers is recommended. First, as of July 1, 1973, each agriculture employer who has an annual payroll that in total exceeds $1,000 is to be required to provide workmen's compensation coverage to all his employees. As a second stage, as of July 1, 1975, farm workers are to be covered on the same basis as all other employees.

R2.5 As of July 1, 1975, household workers and all casual workers should be covered under workmen's compensation at least to the extent they are covered by Social Security.

R2.6 Workmen's compensation coverage is to be mandatory for all government employees.

R2.7 There is to be no exemption for any class of employees, such as professional athletes or employees of charitable organizations.

R2.11 An employee or his survivor is to be given the choice of filing a workmen's compensation claim in the state where the injury or death occurred, or where the employment was principally located, or where the employee was hired.

R2.13 All states should provide full coverage for work-related diseases.

R3.7 Subject to the state's maximum weekly benefit, temporary total disability benefits are to be at least 66 2/3 percent of the worker's gross weekly wage.

R3.8 As of July 1, 1973, the maximum weekly benefit for temporary total disability is to be at least 66 2/3 percent of the state's average weekly wage, and that as of July 1, 1975, the maximum is to be at least 100 percent of the state's average weekly wage.

R3.11 The definition of permanent total disability used in most states may be retained. However, in those few states which permit the payment of permanent total disability benefits to workers who retain substantial earning capacity, we recommend that our benefit proposals be applicable only to those cases which meet the test of permanent total disability used in most States.

R3.12 Subject to the state's maximum weekly benefit, permanent total disability benefits are to be at least 66 2/3 percent of the workers gross weekly wage.

R3.15 As of July 1, 1973, the maximum weekly benefit for permanent total disability is to be at least 66 2/3 percent of the state's average weekly wage, and that as of July 1, 1975, the maximum is to be at least 100 percent of the state's average weekly wage.

R3.17 Total disability benefits are be paid for the duration of the workers disability, or for life, without any limitation as to dollar amount or time.

R3.21 Subject to the state's maximum weekly benefit, death benefits are to be at least 66 2/3 percent of the workers gross weekly wage.

R3.23 As of July 1, 1973, the maximum weekly death benefit is to be at least 66 2/3 percent of the state's average weekly wage, and that as of July 1, 1975, the maximum is to be at least 100 percent of the state's average weekly wage.

R3.25 (a) Death benefits are to be paid to a widow or widower for life or until remarriage, and (b) in the event of remarriage, two years' benefits are to be paid in a lump sum to the widow or widower. (c) Benefits for a dependent child are to be continued at least until the child reaches 18, or beyond such age if actually dependent or at least until age 25 if enrolled as a full-time student in any accredited educational institution.

R4.2 There is to be no statutory limits of time or dollar amount for medical care or physical rehabilitation services for any work-related impairment.

R4.4 The right to medical and physical rehabilitation benefits should not terminate by the mere passage of time.

Federal legislation designed to ensure compliance with the 19 essential recommendations was never enacted. However, the potential for federal legislation led to many years of fairly proactive efforts on the part of states to move toward compliance. These efforts included expansion of the employers and employees subject to coverage, and particularly in the area of the level and duration of weekly compensation benefits.

ACTIVITY FOLLOWING THE NATIONAL COMMISSION RECOMMENDATIONS

The last quarter of the 20th century saw a great deal of activity at the state level directed toward the implementation of the recommendations set forth by the National Commission. While it is difficult to summarize all of the activity that took place at the state level during this period, there is a benefit to acknowledging the major activity that took place between pre and post year 2000. This effort is intended to capture the "highlights" of activity that can be identified as one examines the periods in retrospect. It should also be noted that early on during this period many states began to make the change in their statutes from "workmen" to "workers" in an effort to remove the previous "sexist" connotation.

> The Council on State Governments proposed a model workers' compensation act that incorporated all of the National Commission's recommendations.

Activity between 1970 and 2000 – The post-1972 period, following the issuance of the National Commission recommendations, saw a proliferation of legislative activity addressing virtually every area of the workers compensation program. In the area of required coverage for workers, as of 1970, nearly half of the states continued to have elective laws for coverage but by 1975, only three states (**New Jersey, South Carolina** and **Texas**) continued to have elective laws. Even in New Jersey there was some question as to whether the law was elective or compulsory and while the law was vague, the intent of the state regulatory authorities was to require coverage for all employers.

During this period, many states increased the level of weekly benefits. By 1975, nearly all of the states provided wage replacement rates of two-thirds or more for temporary total disability compared with only 29 states with that level of benefits in 1972. By 1977, nearly half of the states had made the maximum weekly benefit for temporary total disability 100 percent of the statewide average weekly wage, or higher, as compared with only a single state in 1972.

One of the most significant changes that took place during the latter half of the 1970s was the enactment of laws that allowed for an automatic annual increase in the maximum level of weekly compensation benefits. This approach tied the maximum weekly benefit amount to a percentage of the statewide average weekly wage thereby permitting the maximum amount payable weekly to increase each year. Rather than having to negotiate each time for an increase in the maximum weekly benefit level, the law now allowed the maximum weekly benefit to rise automatically each year for newly arising claims so that benefits for newly arising claims continued to remain adequate based on changes in wages and inflation.

A further facet of the benefit adequacy issue was the adjustment of benefits over time for those with injuries of long duration. Where benefits were not adjusted to reflect the impact of inflation, weekly benefits frequently became inadequate with the passage of time. A number of states began to enact laws that adjusted for inflation by increasing weekly disability benefits by the percentage change in the statewide average weekly wage during the prior year for those claimants with disability that extended beyond two years from the date of injury. Referred to as a Cost of Living Adjustment (COLA), this benefit change will be described more fully in Chapter Six under the subject of Disability Benefits.

In 1970, 22 states continued to impose a maximum amount payable for medical services or a maximum duration to medical entitlement. However, nearly half of these states permitted the amount or duration to be extended by application to the applicable board or commission. During the ensuing decade, laws were enacted removing these forms of limitations so that by the end of the decade, only **Georgia** continued to prescribe a medical dollar limit of $5,000 with the provision that this amount could be increased upon application.

During the 1980s, one of the perplexing issues for the program was identifying an equitable system of compensating for permanent partial disability. During the 1979 legislative session, **Florida** addressed the issue with the introduction of a "wage loss" format for compensating permanent partial disability based on the extent of actual wage loss. This approach was intended to reduce litigation through the elimination of scheduled or unscheduled payment periods for such disability. In 1983, both **Minnesota** and **Louisiana** also enacted provisions designed to modify the method for compensating for permanent partial disability.

A further development in determining the extent of permanent partial disability also took place during the 1980s. Rather than relying upon the subjective determination of what constituted permanent partial disability, legislation began to require that ratings for disability be based upon the *American Medical Association's Guides to Rating Permanent Impairment*. A number of states set forth the requirement by statute while many others adopted the guidelines through the adoption of rules and regulations.

The providing of rehabilitation benefits received increased attention during this period and a number of states enacted provisions mandating rehabilitation services where the disability continued beyond a specified number of weeks. A few states also established rehabilitation departments within the administrative agency to both monitor the delivery of rehabilitation services, and in some instances to provide such services.

Prompted by interest in controlling costs, twenty-four hour coverage became a subject for study and debate as the 1980s came to a close. Studies were conducted and a number of states (e.g., **Florida, Oregon**, and **Maine**) approved legislation permitting pilot programs that were designed to facilitate experiments with the "blending" of benefits between workers compensation and other non-occupational programs of economic security. Variations of certain of these pilot programs continued through the 1990s. None of these pilot programs managed to take form due to the obstacles imposed by the regulations required to establish such experimental projects.

The decade of the 1990s closed with a period of rapidly rising workers compensation costs which were a reflection of the benefit increases enacted during the previous decades. State funds were considered a less expensive alternative to insurance companies. In 1983, **Minnesota** became the first state in more than 40 years to establish a competitive state fund. In 1985, **Hawaii** took similar action. Through the 1990s, numerous states created study commissions to review the subject of state funds and make recommendations to their legislatures. As a result, in1991 **Louisiana, Maine** and **Texas** established competitive state funds. In 1992, **Tennessee** followed, and in 1993 **Missouri** created a competitive state fund.

Another approach designed to address rising workers compensation costs was the "opt- out" program first adopted in the state of **Texas.** The Texas law was an elective law so employers were not required to obtain workers compensation coverage or to self-insure. Enacted in 1993, the "opt-out" program permitted employers to offer alternative schemes of benefit security in lieu of statutory workers compensation benefits. **Oklahoma** adopted an "opt-out" program in 2013 but this law was invalidated by the Oklahoma Supreme Court. A number of other southern states have studied the approach but have declined to enact specific legislation.

Following the significant rising costs that were experienced at the end of the 1980s and the beginning of the 1990s, there was a dramatic change by the mid-1990s. Through the combination of reform, improved administrative oversight of the benefit delivery system, greater education of workers and employer efforts to contain costs, the last half of the decade saw workers compensation costs stabilize and employers in many states began to see rates for insurance actually decline.

The Twenty-First Century - The economic crises that followed the opening of the twenty-first century and repeated itself again eight years later, brought a halt to much of the attention that had been directed at the workers compensation program. While new forms of self-insurance (group self-insurance), along with insurer-provided large and small insurance deductible programs, all evolved near the end of the prior century, a number of competitive state funds were also formed in response to the uncertainty of insurance rates and the difficulty in finding insurance in the voluntary market.

In a change in direction, in 2006 W**est Virginia** abolished their monopolistic state fund (the Workers Compensation Commission) and replaced it with a new private competitive market named BrickStreet Mutual Insurance Company. Following the successful change over in West Virginia, several other states including **Arizona, Colorado, Maine,** and **Oklahoma**, all with competitive funds, began looking into some form of privatization. During this same period, more and more of the competitive state funds moved in the direction of becoming domestic mutual insurance carriers.

Taking its cue from the **Texas** "opt-out" program adopted in 1993, in 2013 **Oklahoma** enacted legislation permitting employers to provide an alternate benefit program in lieu of the standard workers compensation benefit system. The new law required the level of benefits available through the alternate program to be at least equal to those available through the administered workers compensation program. In 2016, the Oklahoma Supreme Court held that the core provision of the Act "creates impermissible, unequal disparate treatment of a select group of injured workers" thereby rescinded the law.[9]

Administrative oversight of the program was also addressed in a number of states. In 2005, **Texas** transferred responsibility for workers compensation administration from a commission to the Texas Insurance Department. **Tennessee** enacted sweeping reforms in 2013 that included the transfer of all oversight functions from the courts to a single independent state agency. These reforms also created an ombudsman, tightened the definition of a work-related injury, and established medical treatment guidelines.

The most recent debates and reforms occurring at a national level have involved the classification of workers (such as Uber drivers) as independent contractors. Following the lead of at least 11 other states, in 2018, the **California** Supreme Court's decision in *Dynamex* brought California in line with several other states that had already enacted identical, if not similar, independent contractor laws classifying these workers as employees.[10] Using the commonly called "ABC Test," the Supreme Court held that a worker is an independent contractor only if *all* of the following three elements were satisfied:

A. The person is free from the control and direction of the hiring entity in connection with the performance of the work, both under the contract for the performance of the work and in fact.

B. The person performs work that is outside the usual course of the hiring entity's business.

C. The person is customarily engaged in an independently established trade, occupation, or business of the same nature as that involved in the work performed.

Further legislative changes followed this decision and in November of 2020, California voters approved Proposition 22 that reversed the previously adopted changes that classified Uber, Lyft, DoorDash, InstaCart, and Postmates drivers as independent contractors. A recent attempt by some of these "gig" drivers to invalidate Prop. 22 was not successful. It is likely that further litigation over the subject will continue and that similar propositions and legislative proposals will be attempted in other states.

In response to the growing liberality of compensation laws during the 2000s, states began to adopt language designed to restrict access by legislating that an accident was only compensable if the workplace incident was the major contributing cause or was the prevailing (primary) factor in causing both the resulting condition and the disability. A

---

[9] *Vasquez v. Dillard, Inc.*, 2016 OK 89 (Sept. 13, 2016)
[10] *Dynamex Operations West, Inc. v. Superior Court of Los Angeles* (2018)

number of the changes made in occupational disease legislation during this period also sought to change the standards of proof in occupational disease claims. Generally, these tended either to clarify or to tighten those standards, making it somewhat less likely that claims would be accepted.[9]

DEVELOPING ISSUES FOR THE WORKERS COMPENSATION PROGRAM

Two big issues have attracted the attention of legislators toward the end of the second decade of the twenty-first century. These issues involved the legalization of marijuana for medical and/or recreational use along with the establishment of presumption of compensability for certain cancers and other diseases, as well as compensability for post-traumatic stress disorder (PTSD). With **New York, New Mexico** and **Virginia** being the most recent, there are now a total of 17 states along with the **District of Columbia** that have enacted, either through the legislative process or through a ballot initiative, laws that legalize marijuana for adults. In addition, 18 states have approved the use of medical marijuana.

Case law is also beginning to evolve around the use of marijuana in the treatment of workers compensation cases. For example, marijuana has been legal in **Massachusetts** since 2012. A recent decision by the Supreme Judicial Court held a workers compensation insurer may not be ordered to reimburse an employee for medical marijuana expenses.[11] The Court based its decision on the fact that the Massachusetts Medical Marijuana Act explicitly alleviated insurers from the burden of reimbursing for medical marijuana expenses. This decision is likely to draw attention in other jurisdictions where marijuana has been recently legalized for medical and/or recreational use.

During the 2019 legislative session, at least 26 states considered legislation addressing coverage for mental-mental injuries such as PTSD for first responders. And then came the COVID-19 pandemic in early 2020. The COVID-19 pandemic and the follow-up variants, the likes of which the United States had not seen for more than a century, prompted lawmakers in numerous states to consider broad protections for workers.

One of the major regulatory and legislative stories beginning in 2020 was following those states where workers compensation COVID-19 presumptions were either being enacted or were at least being considered. It began with states taking action to extend coverage to include first responders and health care workers impacted by COVID-19. A common approach was to amend state policy so that COVID-19 infections in certain workers are presumed to be work-related and covered. This presumption places the burden on the employer and insurer to prove that the infection was not work-related, making it easier for those workers to file successful claims.

- **Alaska, California, Illinois, Minnesota, New Jersey, Utah, Vermont, Wisconsin,** and **Wyoming** all passed presumptions that provide workers' comp benefits to specific employee populations that contract COVID-19.

---

[11] *Wright's Case*, 2020 Mass. LEXIS 658 (Oct. 27, 2020)

- Regulatory activity, like executive orders and emergency rules, also extended coverage to workers' in some states. **Connecticut, Florida, Kentucky, Michigan, Missouri, New Hampshire,** and **New Mexico** all extended coverage for COVID-19 to certain workers through regulatory activity.

It is anticipated that unless and until the country controls the spread of COVID-19, legislators will continue expanding benefits for frontline workers who will face greater exposure to the coronavirus as cities, counties and states reopen. The fragile state of financial budgets at the state level will likely encourage more states to strive to ensure workers compensation responds for employees exposed to the coronavirus. Future challenges will include retroactivity of the presumption, the scope of workers eligible for expanded benefits, and the duration of compensability presumptions enacted.

In addition to the looming concerns associated with the use of marijuana along with COVID-19, there are additional concerns facing the workers compensation program as it enters into the third decade of the twenty-first century. Some of the more prominent of these issues include:

- The gig economy, which includes temporary drivers, laborers and independent professionals, is transforming the workforce. Some suggest that in the foreseeable future, two-fifths of all workers will be gig workers or independent contractors. This trend carries benefits and risks. Gig workers and independent contractors can e ercise e ibility in their schedules and workload however, ambiguity in terms of workers compensation coverage for injuries occurring on the job is a long-standing discussion.

- COVID-19 has forced a change in terms of the location of a workers employment. With more people working from home during the pandemic, questions arise regarding workers compensation liability for injuries occurring in a "workplace" that is outside the employer's control. These are unprecedented times with no direct authority addressing this precise issue.

- As has been recognized for some time, there is also the aging workforce, putting a strain on skilled workers and resulting in increased severity and duration of care. While many older workers may not want to work longer, they often need to continue working for economic reasons. While not applicable in all cases, older workers have longer periods of disability, higher medical costs, and have greater difficulty becoming re-employed or finding a new occupation following a serious workplace injury.

- In the not too distant future, large and small trucks, buses, and taxis will become self-driving vehicles. At the same time, many delivery services will have been replaced by drones with self-service equipment. These dramatic changes in transportation along with the automation of manufacturing plants and construction sites will serve to replace human workers with robotic technology. While these changes will result in fewer work-related injuries and deaths, there will be the accompanying reduction in the need for workers. The effects will be felt industry wide including declining payroll-based premium for insurers, and fewer claims within the medical and legal systems due to the lower frequency of losses.

Workers compensation has stood the test of more than one hundred years, but must establish its relevancy in an ever-changing environment every day. The question is whether workers compensation will continue to evolve so as to remain relevant, or will it be subsumed by one of the existing – or perhaps some new – form of economic security. Only time holds the answer to the long-term future of the program.

WORKPLACE SAFETY AND LOSS PREVENTION

As noted by the 1972 National Commission on State Workmen's Compensation Laws, one of the five major objectives for a modern workers compensation program is the encouragement of safety in the workplace. Appropriate attention to workplace safety results in the elimination or at least reduction in workplace accidents. Without workplace accidents there would be no need for workers compensation coverage. However, we know that in reality, workplace injuries and deaths are a frequent occurrence.

In gauging the extent of the issue, the United States Bureau of Labor Statistics (BLS) reported that in 2019, nearly 2.8 million non-fatal workplace injuries and illnesses were reported by private industry employers. This represented an incidence rate of 2.8 cases per 100 equivalent full-time workers, according to estimates from the Survey of Occupational Injuries and Illnesses (SOII), unchanged from 2018. For the same period, the BLS also reported a preliminary total of 5,333 fatal work injuries in private industry. This number was up two percent from the total of 5,250 fatal work injuries in 2018. The rate of fatal work injury for workers during 2019 was 3.5 per 100,000 full-time equivalent workers, the same rate as it was in 2018.

Based on these numbers, on average, more than 9,000 workers are injured every day in this country and nearly 12 workers lose their life because of workplace exposure or accidents. From these statistics, it is important to recognize that, no matter how well a factory or workplace is managed, attention to injury and illness prevention must be one of management's primary focuses. Unfortunately, developing and maintaining a loss control or safety program in an era of corporate re-engineering and downsizing creates significant challenges.

In a strapped economy, companies are often reluctant to invest in departments or programs that do not represent a return of investment to the bottom line. In addition, in many companies, the safety director must wear multiple hats. To be effective, it is important that the loss control program occupy its rightful place in the organizational structure along with the resources necessary to achieve its bottom-line goal – reducing workplace accidents and illnesses.

Those responsible for handling and reporting claims, including lower-level managers and supervisors, are in a unique position to promote workplace safety. In order to be effective, they need to be aware of the locations where accidents are occurring and the most prevalent type of accidents. It is also important for those individuals to understand and be aware of what types of accidents are most costly. The attention of lower-level managers and supervisors needs to be directed to accidents and illnesses with a focus that middle and upper management cannot hope to match. To be effective, companies should link claims and safety on their organization charts as elements of risk management.

DEVELOPING AN EFFECTIVE LOSS CONTROL PROGRAM

The most important ingredient in an effective loss control program is management commitment and direction. A good loss control program requires not merely support, but strong direction from upper management. If that support is merely verbal and not backed by action, the program's effectiveness will be compromised. When workplace injuries are accepted as a normal or even an inevitable cost of doing business, that attitude will quickly permeate to all levels of management. At that point, loss control becomes little more than an exercise in tracking numbers and monitoring claims once they occur. Workplace safety requires a continuous effort to create an environment where accidents don't happen. This can occur only in a workplace where the emphasis is on education, training, and awareness.

Research supports the findings that injury prevention involves more than removing workplace hazards. The traditional approach to workplace safety tracks the following pattern: The worker suffers a physical injury from an identifiable hazard, the injury is treated, the workplace hazard that caused the injury is either altered or replaced the worker recovers from the injury, and returns to his/her regular employment. This alteration or removal of the workplace hazard is akin to locking the barn door after the horse has gotten out. The time to take action is before the accident occurs.

Loss prevention is complex and should involve not only the employer but also the insurance carrier. The insurance carrier, through its safety department and safety professionals, can lend technical support to the employer in identifying and eliminating workplace hazards. Familiarity with the type of business places the insurance carrier in a unique position to offer guidance and direction to an individual employer.

Employers frequently prepare a safety program in order to be in compliance with state or federal laws. However, a good safety program can do far more than simply keep an employer on the right side of the law. By helping ensure that an employer has the right systems and programs in place, a proactive safety program can help to ensure a reduction in the number of on-the-job injuries. Because they are probably an employer's greatest asset, and are critical to meeting the needs of customers, keeping employees safe and healthy also keeps the business safe and healthy.

The type of programs a business requires depends on the industry and the type of work the employer does. The first step in developing a safety program is for the employer to understand the rules or standards that apply to the specific industry. To illustrate, if a contractor is in construction, the Occupational Safety and Health Administration (OSHA) published CFR Part 1925 Safety and Health Regulations for Construction contains the federal laws related to worker safety. Most other industrial companies can look to CFR Part 1910 for regulations applicable to the safety of their employees.

These regulations contain the minimum standards that the employer needs to comply with federal laws in order to establish a solid foundation for a safety program. Along with those minimum standards, the employer needs to add their own standards and opinions about safety. Through this process, a well-crafted policy serves as a written explanation of the employer's safety culture and the mission of its safety-related efforts. It may also outline minimum requirements for contractors who work on the employer's sites along with their subcontractors.

Having the plan in writing serves several purposes beyond meeting regulatory requirements. It says that the employer is serious about safety. It is a constant reminder that the employer conducts their business only in a safe manner. In addition, it provides benchmarks against which safety performance can be measured and evaluated. Issues employers need to address in their safety program policies include the following:

- **Roles and responsibilities** – It is important to clearly define everyone's responsibilities where safety is concerned in order to prevent misunderstandings and omissions due to uncertainty about who is responsible for what.

- **Orientations** – In addition to understanding what the employer does, it is important to ensure that everyone working on the site understands the employer's expectations and philosophy regarding safety.

- **Safety inspections** – Safety-related aspects of the inspection should be conducted in order to ensure that everyone on the site is following the standards that have been established.

- **Personal protective equipment** – A safety plan should spell out the personal protective equipment that will be required with specific tasks on the jobsite and ensure that workers receive appropriate training that will allow the equipment to be used properly.

- **Hazardous materials communications** – Steps should be taken to ensure that workers are aware of the hazards involved with the chemicals they'll handle or may come in contact with.

- **Investigations** – A pre-determination should be made as to what steps will be undertaken to determine the cause of any accident, and the identification of any steps necessary to prevent a reoccurrence.

Employers can develop their own safety programs, but there are numerous well-documented advantages to turning to outside expertise. First, a safety professional will have a solid understanding of state-of-the-art safety practices and will bring that level of knowledge and understanding to the process. Second, developing an effective safety policy is a time-consuming effort that can take someone away from other work that needs to be done.

With state law mandates in many jurisdictions, developing a written safety manual has become a matter of urgency for many employers. Claims management plays an integral role in developing safety policies and keeping the written safety manual up to date. The place to begin is with a written statement setting forth the employer's policy on safety and loss control.

The Sample Corporate Safety Policy set forth below focuses on accident prevention as part of an overall quality effort. This sample is also effective inasmuch as it sets out the safety policy itself and goes on to summarize the responsibilities of management.

SAMPLE CORPORATE SAFETY POLICY

Our company regards accident prevention as a primary corporate objective, which can be realized only through proper planning, clearly defined safety responsibilities, and appropriate steps to ensure a safe work environment. Accident prevention is a management responsibility equally as important as quality and production.

The following are elements of a loss control program which senior management considers necessary to provide a safe work environment for its employees:

Organization and Responsibilities

The highest level of management at each site is responsible for implementing and sustaining a safety program and ensuring that all safety and health policies are applied uniformly across the site. Division and plant managers are obligated to ensure that all operations in their area of responsibility are conducted within safety standards and regulations.

The supervisor has direct responsibility for the safety of employees under his or her supervision, for developing safety awareness, and for eliminating conditions which might endanger personnel or property.

Each employee is responsible for observing safety instructions and warning signs and for following safe practices at all times. Individuals should report all accidents causing injury, regardless of the severity, to the medical or human resource department. They must also report to their supervisor all unsafe acts or conditions which come to their attention so that appropriate action can be initiated.

To be successful, a safety program requires the cooperation of all concerned. Accident prevention must be the goal of everyone, regardless of their job or responsibilities. A conscientiously followed safety program will help prevent injury to employees.

Safety Committees - Each location is responsible for establishing a safety committee, whose function is to create and maintain an active interest in safety and to reduce and prevent future accidents by formulating safety, health, and accident prevention policies.

Pre-employment Screening - Each location will have either in-house medical personnel or a contract with a local medical facility to provide pre-employment screening for prospective employees. Health history forms should be carefully reviewed, and pre-employment physical exams should be required. Consideration should be taken to assure that an employee's physical capabilities meet those of the job he or she is hired to perform.

New Employee Safety Orientation - Safety should play an important role in the orientation of new employees, as well as employees returning to work after layoff. Employees should clearly know what safety requirements apply to their particular position. This will include instructions on machine operation, proper lifting techniques, chemicals, material handling, and personal protective equipment. Reporting procedures on unsafe conditions or operations should also be addressed.

Return-to-Work Programs - The appropriate human resources or medical representative at each location will maintain contact with individuals who have sustained lost-time injuries to assure that proper medical attention is being received. An employee's supervisor should also make direct communication to emphasize the employer's concern for the injured worker and his or her family and to ease their concerns over health, income, and job status. Every effort should be made to return injured employees to full or light duty employment as soon as possible.

Simple math tells one that fewer workers compensation insurance claims translate into lower costs and culminate in a healthier workforce and a stronger bottom line. It is therefore obvious that it is in the best interest of both the employer and the insurance carrier to reduce the frequency and severity of workplace injuries and deaths.

A reduction in losses can be accomplished by coordinating efforts on risk management and loss control. The better workers compensation insurance carriers emphasize risk management, and offer a variety of tools to help insureds control their losses, the better will be the result in reducing workplace injuries. Likewise, it's up to the employer to understand what's available and take steps toward implementing these resources.

Following are some of the tools that an insurance carrier or third party administrator can offer to accomplish that end:

- **Loss control surveys.** These surveys are frequently provided by safety professionals employed by or assigned by the insurer or benefit administrator. They're in-depth, on-site, consultative evaluations of a workplace that identify uncontrolled hazards and offer suggestions for protecting employees, business assets and insurance policies from loss. Not all sizes of businesses qualify for this assessment as a free service, but nonetheless it's one worth considering.

- **Web-based safety training and educational materials.** Insurance carriers and benefit administrators may provide technical guidance and general safety and training resources in the form of handouts and safety videos specific to common job functions and workplace situations. The materials are designed to support safety initiatives in place at the insured's workplace. Examples can range from first aid to slips/trips/falls, burns, lifting, ladder safety, lockout/tagout, driving safety and many others.

- **Technical loss analysis.** For those employers with a history of higher-volume claims, this can include an in-depth study of loss drivers, as well as a comparison of current and past results. The end result would be the identification of cost-reduction opportunities and development of a customized plan of action.

- **Designing of a Return-to-Work Program** – While most think of a return-to-work program as a post-loss strategy, an effective program starts before the injury occurs. The job assessments used for the post-offer/pre-employment testing gives the employer the starting point by accurately identifying the physical requirements of each task. From there, a determination of what reasonable modifications could be made to the work site in order to meet potential work restrictions.

- **Underwriting support.** Finally, having underwriters on staff who are active and engaged in assessing a particular risk can help minimize the potential for accidents. An underwriter needs a true picture of the business operation, and loss control accomplishes that most optimally through on-site interviews, walk-throughs of work spaces and detailed reporting forms to accurately evaluate the potential for loss, confirm pricing and provide an overall picture of a risk.

Running a successful business relies on controlling costs; workers compensation insurance costs definitely among them. It has been observed that the cheapest workers compensation claims are always the ones that never occur. Working with their insurance carrier or benefit administrator, employers can adjust its operations to help strengthen both its financial position and operations through a reduction in workplace injuries.

FEDERAL EFFORT TO IMPROVE WORKPLACE SAFETY AND HEALTH

The late 1960s were an interesting yet turbulent period in America history. The nation faced serious concerns both abroad and at home. Civil rights, women's rights, Vietnam, and the environment all demanded the country's attention. At the same time, occupational injuries and illnesses were increasing in both number and severity. Disabling injuries increased 20 percent during the decade, and 14,000 workers were dying on the job each year. One of the first workplace areas to receive attention was the coal mining industry. The United States Department of Labor reported that while annual coal mining deaths numbered more than 1,000 a year in the early part of the 20th century, by the 1950s, the average number of annual coal mining fatalities had decreased to 450. This number of fatalities continued to represent a serious issue for the coal industry.

In December of 1969, President Nixon signed into law the Federal Coal Mine Health and Safety Act creating the Mining Enforcement and Safety Administration (MESA), later renamed the Mine Safety and Health Administration (MSHA). This law was primarily designed to establish nationwide health and safety standards for the coal mining industry. The new law, generally more comprehensive and stringent than previous federal laws governing the mining industry, required two annual inspections of every surface coal mine and four at every underground coal mine.

Since its original enactment, the Federal Coal Mine Health and Safety Act has been the subject of further amendments designed to improve mine safety and reduce the number of mine workers injuries and fatalities. In 2020, the U.S. Department of Labor's Mine Safety and Health Administration reports there were 29 mining fatalities, making it the sixth consecutive year that mining fatalities were below 30.

At the same time, there was similar interest in improving workplace safety in areas external to the mining industry. In pressing for prompt passage of workplace safety and health legislation, attention was directed to the need to protect workers against such hazards as cotton dust, noise, and asbestos. Conditions all now covered by Occupational Safety and Health Administration (OSHA) standards. In the House of Representatives, William A. Steiger (R. WI), working for the passage of that same piece of legislation, observed that, *"In the last 25 years, more than 400,000 Americans were killed by work-related accidents and disease, and close to 50 million more suffered disabling injuries on the job."* He went on to point out that, *"Not only has this resulted in incalculable pain and suffering for workers and their families, but such injuries have cost billions of dollars in lost wages and production."* [12]

On December 29, 1970, President Richard M. Nixon signed the Occupational Safety and Health Act of 1970, also known as the Williams-Steiger Act in honor of the two congressional members who pressed diligently for its passage. The Act established three permanent agencies:

- The **Occupational Safety and Health Administration (OSHA)** within the Labor Department to set and enforce workplace safety and health standards;

- The **National Institute for Occupational Safety and Health (NIOSH)** in what was then the Department of Health, Education and Welfare to conduct research on occupational safety and health; and

- The **Occupational Safety and Health Review Commission (OSHRC)**, an independent agency to adjudicate enforcement actions challenged by employers.

Known initially as "the safety bill of rights," the Act charged OSHA with assuring safe and healthful conditions for working men and women. From its earliest days, OSHA was a small agency with a big mission. OSHA was created because of the public outcry against rising injury and death rates on the job. Through the years the agency has responded to that challenge.

OSHA MISSION AND STRATEGY

Through the years the agency has focused its resources where they can have the greatest impact in reducing injuries, illnesses, and deaths in the workplace. Over the past decades, agency strategies have evolved in keeping current with events and needs of the times. In response to specific tragedies, OSHA established a standard to prevent grain elevator explosions and published a process safety management standard to forestall chemical catastrophes caused by inadequate planning and safety systems. OSHA has also focused on emerging health issues such as blood-borne pathogens and musculoskeletal disorders.

OSHA's enforcement strategy has evolved from initially targeting a few problem industries to zeroing in on high-hazard industries and more recently, pinpointing specific sites with high injury rates. OSHA published its first consensus standards on May 29, 1971. Some of those standards, including permissible exposure limits for more than 400 toxic substances, remain in effect today. Others have been updated or expanded through public rulemaking, dropped as unnecessary or overly specific, or amended to clarify their intent.

During the early years, OSHA was frequently criticized for the development and promulgation of confusing and burdensome regulations. A good deal of the early conflict arose because of arbitrary and inconsistent enforcement. In addition, businesses were expected to retrofit guards

---

[12] Fleming, Susan Hall, *OSHA at 30: Three Decades of Progress in Occupational Safety and Health*, Spring 2001 edition of Job Safety & Health Quarterly

and other safety devices on existing equipment and to implement other hazard controls, often at considerable expense, to bring them in line with then-current best safety practices. Other requirements, such as mandated training, communication, and extensive documentation were seen as even more difficult and expensive.

Over time, manufacturers of industrial equipment have included OSHA-compliant safety features on new machinery. Enforcement has become more consistent across jurisdictions, and some of the more outdated or irrelevant rules have been repealed or are not enforced. In the 1980s, OSHA began to focus on minimizing regulatory burdens. The agency relied more on computers to track its activities and provide accountability. Its goal was to provide a balanced mix of enforcement, education and training, standard-setting, and consultation activities.

Major new health standards introduced during OSHA's second decade included requirements to provide employees access to medical and exposure records maintained by their employers; hazard communication; and more stringent requirements for asbestos, ethylene oxide, formaldehyde, and benzene. Safety standards covered a wide range of issues such as updated fire protection and electrical safety, field sanitation in agriculture, grain handling, hazardous waste operations and emergency response, and lockout/tagout of hazardous energy sources.

During the Reagan administration and the first Bush administrations, several important rules were issued including hazard communication (right-to-know requirements about chemical exposures) and the blood-borne pathogens (to protect workers against illnesses such as hepatitis and AIDS).

In 1982, OSHA initiated a program entitled the Voluntary Protection Program (VPP). The VPP recognizes employers and workers in the private industry and federal agencies who have implemented effective safety and health management systems and maintain injury and illness rates below national Bureau of Labor Statistics averages for their respective industries. The program is a cooperative compliance program designed to allow companies that met certain criteria the ability to be exempt from unannounced OSHA inspections by regulating their own safety in accordance with OSHA guidelines. VPP is a way of encouraging companies to exceed minimum OSHA safety requirements and is designed to recognize and promote effective safety and health management

The VPP concept recognizes that enforcement of safety regulations alone can never fully achieve the objectives of the Occupational Safety and Health Act. Good safety management programs that go beyond OSHA standards can protect employees more effectively than simple compliance.

VPP represents a process that defines a single system and structured approach to help achieve the goal of working more safely. The program has been described as both an "umbrella" and as a "roadmap," focusing on four key areas necessary to have a comprehensive safety and health program. Those key areas are:

- Management Leadership and Employee Involvement

- Worksite Analysis

- Hazard Prevention and Control

- Safety and Health Training

Participants in VPP are selected based on their written safety and health management system and ongoing performance. OSHA also conducts a thorough on-site evaluation to judge how well the site's protective system is working, including a review of site injury/illness rates. Continuous improvement is expected.

- The Star Program is designed for exemplary worksites with comprehensive, successful safety and health management systems. Companies in the Star Program have achieved injury and illness rates at or below the national average of their respective industries. These sites are self-sufficient in their ability to control workplace hazards. Star participants are reevaluated every three to five years, although incident rates are reviewed annually.

- Merit is an effective stepping stone to Star. Merit sites have good safety and health management systems, but these systems need some improvement to be judged excellent. Merit sites demonstrate the potential and the commitment to meet goals tailored to each site and to achieve Star quality within three years. However, each Merit site is limited to one three-year term unless a second term is approved by the Assistant Secretary of Labor for Occupational Safety and Health. Onsite evaluations occur every 18 to 24 months.

Statistical evaluation of the program is calculated annually by the Office of Partnership and Recognition and is based upon the injury and illness data submitted every year by the VPP participants. Results for the program are impressive inasmuch as the average participating worksite has a Days Away Restricted or Transferred (DART) case rate of 52 percent below the average for its industry. Typically these sites do not start out with such reduced rates but experience such results when the site commits to the VPP approach to safety and health management.

Fewer injuries and illnesses in turn mean greater profits to the company as workers compensation premiums and other costs associated with workplace injuries drop. Entire industries benefit as these sites evolve into models of excellence and influence practices industry-wide.

In its third decade, OSHA re-examined its goals as part of the overall government reinvention process, looking for ways to leverage its resources and increase its impact in reducing workplace injuries, illnesses, and deaths. The "New OSHA" focused on reducing red tape, streamlining standard setting, and inspecting workplaces that most needed help in protecting employees.

OSHA broke new ground in 1991 by introducing a blood-borne pathogens standard to address biological hazards. During the 1990s, the agency also updated its asbestos, formaldehyde, methylene chloride, personal protective equipment, and respiratory protection standards; developed a standard covering lead exposure in construction; and issued rules to protect laboratory workers exposed to toxic chemicals. The agency also issued guidelines for preventing workplace violence in health care and social services work and in late-night retail establishments.

During the mid-1990s, OSHA began collecting data annually from about 80,000 employers in high-hazard industries to identify sites with high injury and illness rates. In 1999, the agency adopted the Site Specific Targeting Program, which for the first time directed inspections to individual workplaces with the worst safety and health records. Injury and illness rates and fatalities declined significantly during this decade.

Emphasis on partnerships increased dramatically in the 1990s, and participation in the agency's premier effort, the VPP, increased eight-fold. OSHA also formed partnerships with companies that wanted to improve their safety and health records, beginning with the Maine 200 program, which encouraged employers with many injuries at their sites to find and fix hazards and establish safety and health programs.

As the new century began, OSHA broadened its out-reach efforts, with new compliance assistance specialists slated to join every area office to provide safety seminars, training, and guidance to employers and employees upon request. More and more the agency used its website to provide information to its customers. The agency added an improved small business page, a partnership page, and a workers page to its website to make its information more readily available and easily accessible. The workers page enables concerned employees to file complaints online. Along with its counterparts in the European Union, OSHA set up a joint website on job safety and health issues of concern to many countries.

The second Bush administration largely replaced the process of issuing mandatory regulations with voluntary guidelines and put additional resources into other, previously existing voluntary programs. In 2004, the General Accounting Office (GAO) issued a report recommending that the agency collect more data from participants in order to better ascertain the benefits of the program. An earlier GAO report released in 1992 concluded that employers participating in the program benefited from significant cost reductions in workers compensation premiums while improving labor productivity.

Despite OSHA's somewhat "checkered" history over the years, progress has been made in the area of reducing workplace injuries and deaths. The occupational injury rate is 40 percent lower than when OSHA opened for business in 1971. Deaths from occupational injuries are at an all-time low – 60 percent lower than 30 years ago. The agency has made great progress, but its work is far from done.

As OSHA looks to its future, it continues to focus its attention on reducing injuries, illnesses, and fatalities in traditional industries. At the same time, it looks ahead to the challenges of the future that include: new chemicals and other hazards in the workplace, growing service sector industries, and changing work force needs. OSHA remains a small agency with a big mission.

Major Industrial Safety Regulations Promulgated by OSHA

1. **Guards on All Moving Parts** – By 1970, there were guards to prevent inadvertent

contact with most moving parts that were accessible in the normal course of operation. With OSHA, use of guards was expanded to cover essentially all parts where contact is possible.

2. **Permissible Exposure Limits (PEL)** – Maximum concentrations of chemicals stipulated by regulation for chemicals and dusts. They cover around 600 chemicals. Most are based on standards issued by other organizations in 1968 or before.

3. **Personal Protective Equipment (PPE)** – Broader use of respirators, gloves, coveralls, and other protective equipment when handling hazardous chemicals; goggles, face shields, ear protection in typical industrial environments

4. **Lockout/Tagout** – In the 1980s, requirements for locking out energy sources (securing them in an "off" condition) when performing repairs or maintenance

5. **Confined Space** – In the 1990s, specific requirements for air sampling and use of a "buddy system" when working inside tanks, manholes, pits, bins, and similar enclosed areas

6. **Hazard Communication (HazCom)** – Also known as the "Right to Know" standard, was issued as 29CFR1910.1200 on November 25, 1983 (48 FR 53280), requires developing and communicating information on the hazards of chemical products used in the workplace.

7. **Process Safety Management (PSM)** – Issued in 1992 as 29CFR1910.119 in an attempt to reduce large scale industrial accidents. Although enforcement of the standard has been spotty, its principles have long been widely accepted by the petrochemical industry.

8. **Blood-Borne Pathogens (BBP)** – In 1990, OSHA issued a standard designed to prevent health care (and other) workers from being exposed to blood-borne pathogens such as hepatitis B and HIV.

9. **Excavations and Trenches** - OSHA regulations specify that trenches and excavations wherein workers are working 5 feet or more down must be provided with safeguards in addition to proper sloping and storage of excavated material in order to prevent collapses/cave-ins.

10. **Exposure to Asbestos** - OSHA has established requirements in 29 CFR 1910.1001 for occupational exposure to asbestos. These requirements apply to most workplaces - most notably excepted is construction work. "Construction work" means work for construction, alteration, and/or repair including painting and decorating.

OSHA AND CDC RESPONSE TO COVID-19 PANDEMIC

At the onset it is important to recognize that the COVID-19 pandemic has altered the reality of workplace safety and corresponding industry standards. Employers face dramatically different workplace challenges and new obligations regarding safety precautions and workplace protections. OSHA has advised that employers should direct their efforts toward developing and implementing effective COVID-19 safety policies for the workplace.

OSHA, along with the Centers for Disease Control and Prevention (CDC), released the following list of safety protocols for all employers in response to COVID-19:

- **Social Distancing:** Employers should implement policies to practice social distancing when possible. This includes staying six feet apart and avoiding "large gatherings," which is not defined by the CDC.

- **Implement Flexible Sick Leave Policies:** Employers should ensure that sick leave policies are flexible and consistent with public health guidance. Policies should also permit employees to stay home to care for a sick family member. Employers that do not offer sick leave should consider implementing a non-punitive "emergency sick leave" plan.

- **Institute an Employee Training Program to Educate Employees About Reducing the Spread of COVID-19:** CDC guidance states that employers should set clear expectations with their employees when it comes to illness and personal hygiene. Employees should stay home if they are sick, should wash their hands with soap and water for at least 20 seconds or use a hand sanitizer with at least 60 percent alcohol if soap and water is not available, and should avoid touching their eyes, nose, and mouth with unwashed hands.

In January of 2021, OSHA implemented a coronavirus prevention program that was intended to provide an effective way for employers to reduce the spread of the virus. The guidance recommended several essential elements to be included in a prevention program:

- Conduct a hazard assessment.

- Identify control measures to limit the spread of the virus.

- Adopt policies for employee absences that don't punish workers as a way to encourage potentially infected workers to remain home.

- Ensure that coronavirus policies and procedures are communicated to both English and non-English speaking workers.

- Implement protections from retaliation for workers who raise coronavirus-related concerns.

The use of Personal Protective Equipment (PPE) has become commonplace in most workspaces in response to COVID-19. Employers are under an obligation from OSHA to properly train employees in the proper use of PPE. The CDC recommends that any time an individual is in public (including the workplace if interacting with other individuals), the individual should wear cloth face coverings in public settings where other social distancing measures are difficult to maintain. The CDC continues to modify its recommendations for safety and social distancing as preventive measures and vaccinations are implemented. Prior recommendations have included that the public use cloth face coverings and not surgical masks or N95 respirators, which should be reserved for healthcare workers and other medical first responders.

Due to the fluctuating COVID-19 landscape, employers are advised to continue to monitor developments in the law and in agency guidance. Establishing effective workplace safety plans during this pandemic requires employer diligence and flexibility.

OSHA PENALTIES AND CITATIONS

To enforce its standards, OSHA is authorized under the Act to conduct workplace inspections. Every establishment covered is subject to inspection by OSHA compliance safety and health officers who are chosen for their knowledge and experience in the occupational safety and health field. These safety and health officers are thoroughly trained in OSHA standards and in the recognition of safety and health hazards. Similarly, states with their own occupational safety and health programs conduct inspections using qualified state safety and health officers.

OSHA conducts two general types of inspections: programmed and unprogrammed. There are various OSHA publications and documents which describe in detail OSHA's inspection policies and procedures. Unprogrammed inspections respond to fatalities, catastrophes, and complaints. The following are the types of violations that may be cited and the penalties that may be proposed:

- **Serious Violation**: A violation where there is substantial probability that death or serious physical harm could result and that the employer knew, or should have known, of the hazard. The charge involves a minimum penalty of $975 per violation and a maximum penalty of $13,653 per violation. The maximum penalty for a serious violation may be adjusted downward based on the employer's good faith, history of previous violations, the gravity of the alleged violation, and size of business.

- **Other-Than-Serious Violation**: A violation that has a direct relationship to job safety and health, but probably would not cause death or serious physical harm. The penalty for an other-than-serious charge ranges from a minimum of $0 to a maximum of $13,653 per violation. The penalty amount for an other-than-serious violation may be adjusted downward by as much as 95 percent, depending on the employer's good faith (demonstrated efforts to comply with OSHA), history of previous violations, and size of business. When the adjusted penalty amounts to less than $50, no penalty is proposed.[13]

- **Willful or Repeated Violation**: A violation that the employer intentionally and knowingly commits. The employer either knows that what he or she is doing constitutes a violation, or is aware that a hazardous condition exists and has made no reasonable effort to eliminate it. The OSH Act provides that an employer who willfully or repeatedly violates the OSH Act may be assessed a maximum penalty of not more than $13,653 per violation to a minimum of $9,753 per violation.

- **Posting Requirement:** Penalties for posting requirements are set at a minimum of $0 per violation to a maximum of $13,653 per violation.

The gravity of a violation is defined by the Gravity Based Penalty (GBP). A high gravity violation is one with a GBP of $13,653; a moderate gravity violation is one ranging between $7,780 and $11,703; and a low gravity violation is one with a GBP of $5,851.

STATE OSHA PROGRAMS

Section 18 of the Occupational Safety and Health Act encourages states to develop and operate their own job safety and health programs. OSHA approves and monitors state plans and provides up to 50 percent of an approved plan's operating costs. OSHA approved the first state plans for **South Carolina, Montana,** and **Oregon** in late 1972.

There are currently 21 states and **Puerto Rico** operating complete state plans (covering both the private sector and State and local government employees). The states of **Connecticut, Illinois, New Jersey, New York** along with the **Virgin Islands** cover public employees only. Eight other states were approved at one time but subsequently withdrew their programs.

To gain OSHA approval for a developmental plan – the first step in the state plan process – a state must assure OSHA that within three years it will have in place all the structural elements necessary for an effective occupational safety and health program. These elements include: appropriate legislation; regulations and procedures for standards setting, enforcement, appeal of citations, and penalties; a sufficient number of qualified enforcement personnel.

Once a state has completed and documented all its developmental steps, it is eligible for certification. Certification renders no judgment as to actual state performance, but merely attests to the structural completeness of the plan. At any time after initial plan approval, when it appears that the state is capable of independently enforcing standards, OSHA may enter into an "operational status agreement" with the state. This commits OSHA to suspend the exercise of discretionary federal enforcement in all or certain activities covered by the state plan.

---

[13] For a repeated other-than –serious violation that otherwise would have no initial penalty, a GBP penalty of $390 shall be proposed for the first violation; $975 for the second repeated violation; and $1,950 for a third repetition.

The ultimate accreditation of a state's plan is called final approval. When OSHA grants final approval to a state, it relinquishes its authority to cover occupational safety and health matters covered by the state. After at least one year following certification, the state becomes eligible for final approval if OSHA determines that it is providing, in actual operation, worker protection "at least as effective" as the protection provided by the federal program. The state also must meet 100 percent of the established compliance staffing levels (benchmarks) and participate in OSHA's computerized inspection data system before OSHA can grant final approval.

States with their own OSHA programs conduct inspections to enforce health and safety standards and provide occupational safety and health training and education. In addition, they provide free onsite consultation to help employers identify and correct workplace hazards. OSHA approves and monitors state plans and provides up to 50 percent of an approved plan's operating costs.

States must set job safety and health standards that are "at least as effective as" comparable federal standards. (Most states adopt standards identical to federal ones.) States have the option to promulgate standards covering hazards not addressed by federal standards.

Employees finding workplace safety and health hazards may file a formal complaint with the appropriate state plan or with the appropriate OSHA regional administrator. Anyone finding inadequacies or other problems in the administration of a state's program may file a complaint with the appropriate OSHA regional administrator as well. The complainant's name is kept confidential. OSHA investigates all such complaints, and where complaints are found to be valid, requires appropriate corrective action on the part of the state.

Chapter Two

EMPLOYERS AND EMPLOYEES SUBJECT TO THE WORKERS COMPENSATION LAW

Under the workers compensation program, employment is generally viewed as a contractual relationship between two parties: one being the employer and the other being the employee. In this regard, an employer is generally described as one who hires another, has the right to direct and control the activities undertaken by that person, and provides that person with some form of remuneration for the services provided. In the same regard, an employee can be defined as *"A person in the service of another under any contract of hire, express or implied, oral or written, where the employer has the power or right to control and direct the employee in the material details of how the work is to be performed."*[14] Note that this definition makes no mention of remuneration.

All state compensation laws include a description of what employees are covered by the Act. For example, in **Wisconsin** the term "employee" is defined to include –

> *"Every person in the service of another under any contract of hire, express or implied, all helpers and assistants of employees, whether paid by the employer or employee, if employed with the knowledge, actual or constructive, of the employer, including minors, who shall have the same power of contracting as adult employees . . ."* [15]

As found in most states, the statute then goes on to enumerate a listing of occupations that are not covered. This list may include such occupations as domestic servants, farm workers, those persons selling or distributing newspapers or magazines on the street or from house to house, and so forth.

When considering what employers and employees are subject to a state's workers compensation law, it is important to keep in mind the first of the five basic objectives identified by the 1972 National Commission on State Workmen's Compensation Laws. That objective is to "provide broad coverage of employees and work-related injuries and diseases." This broad approach to coverage was intended to relieve public welfare programs and private charities of the financial burden associated with uncompensated industrial accidents.

---

[14] Black's Law Dictionary page 471 (5th ed. 1979)
[15] Wis. Stat. § 102.07 (4)

COVERAGE OF EMPLOYEES

To accomplish the basic objective as set forth by the National Commission, workers compensation coverage is generally described as universal. Most employers and employees in the United States are covered by a state statutory workers compensation system. According to the estimate of the numbers of covered workers developed by the National Academy of Social Insurance (NASI) in 2020, in 2018 the workers compensation program covered an estimated 139.8 million workers. The number of jobs covered by workers compensation continued to grow, with that growth moving slightly from 2.8 percent between 2014 and 2016 to 3.0 percent between 2016 and 2018.[16]

From the beginning there were those who believed that the workmen's compensation system should include all industries and extend coverage to all employees. However, the reality was that many forms of employment (e.g., domestics, agricultural laborers, and casual workers) were excluded from coverage under early compensation laws. In addition, a few states initially limited coverage to only extra-hazardous employments. For example, mining operations, construction, those engaged in electrical work, etc. Today, **Wyoming** and **Illinois** are the only two states that continue to make reference to coverage of extra-hazardous employments. Notwithstanding this apparent coverage limitation, the statutory list of extra-hazardous employments in Wyoming and the definition of "extra hazardous" in Illinois are sufficiently broad so as to cover virtually every type of employment.

As noted in the prior chapter, the early compensation laws were elective rather than compulsory. An elective law permits the employer to make a decision as to whether or not to insure their workplace exposure. In states where the law was compulsory, all employees as defined by statute were required to be covered. In **New York**, the first serious attempt in that state at a statutory workmen's compensation program had been declared unconstitutional because it made coverage compulsory for certain hazardous employments. The finding of unconstitutionality in the *Ives* decision was based on the theory that requiring employers to purchase workmen's compensation insurance, especially in those cases where the employer was not at fault for the injury or death, was to deprive the employer of "life, liberty or property without due process of law."[17]

Under an elective law, the employer had the right to accept or reject coverage. Where the employer rejected coverage, the employer was not able to assert any of the three common law defenses: contributory negligence, fault or negligence on the part of a fellow-employee, or assumption of risk. As recently as 1972, 18 jurisdictions continued to have laws that were elective. Members of the 1972 National Commission on State Workmen's Compensation Laws set forth the recommendation that *"coverage by workmen's compensation laws be compulsory and that no waivers be permitted."*[18]

Today, every state, with the exception of **Texas,** mandates coverage under their workers compensation program for almost all private employers. In Texas, coverage is elective, and an

---

[16] https://www.nasi.org/sites/default/files/Sources%20Methods%20and%20State%20Summaries%202018(1).pdf
[17] *Ives. V. South Buffalo Railway co.* 94 NE 431 (1911)
[18] National Commission Recommandation 2.1

employee not covered under workers compensation is permitted to pursue an action against the employer based upon fault of the employer for his or her work-related injury or illness. In Texas, employers who forego coverage are referred to as "non-subscribers." While later attempted in **Oklahoma** in 2013, the "opt-out" program legislatively enacted was later ruled unconstitutional by the Oklahoma Supreme Court.

In response to the rising cost of workers compensation insurance during the 1990s, a number of state legislative bodies introduced alternative benefit schemes in lieu of the traditional workers compensation program. Carve-out programs, applicable for contractors and unions, were first introduced in **Massachusetts** and have since expanded to additional states.

Notwithstanding these alternative schemes, the general purpose and scope of the workers compensation program remains universal coverage. Nonetheless, there are certain situations where employees may be exempt from coverage. The following describes in more detail a number of the more common employment situations that are subject to exemption from state workers compensation laws:

> **Numeric Exceptions** – One of the major exceptions to workers compensation coverage has been the exclusion of employers with a small workforce from the requirement of compulsory coverage. The rationale historically expressed for states not extending coverage to all employers without regard for the number of employees was two-fold. The first was concern for the ability of small employers to bear the financial cost associated with compensation coverage. The second reason was associated with the administrative cost of providing that coverage through the mechanism of insurance. (The costs associated with issuing the policy would be more than the cost of the insurance coverage.)
>
> In January of 1972, nearly one-half of the states had some form of numerical exception. This ranged from one employee before coverage was required in **Nevada** and **Oklahoma** to nine employees in **Georgia** and fourteen employees in **South Carolina**. In response to these situations, the National Commission on State Workmen's Compensation Laws included the recommendation that *"employers not be exempted from workmen's compensation coverage because of the number of their employees."* [19]
>
> Today, despite the recommendation of the National Commission that coverage not be precluded based on the number of employees, several states continue to utilize numerical exemptions. Depending upon the state, the law does not require an employer of between three to five employees to buy workers compensation insurance. However, it should be noted that the employer with fewer than the stated minimum number of employees may voluntarily purchase coverage for those employees.
>
> Although numerical exemptions have over the years been disappearing, they continue to have considerable significance. Currently, twelve states exempt those employers with less than a specified number of regular employees.

---

[19] National Commission Recommandation 2.2

- The states of **Alabama, Mississippi, Missouri,** and **Tennessee** require coverage for those employers with five or more employees. In both **Missouri** and **Tennessee** there is an exception for those in the construction industry where employers with one or more employees are required to obtain coverage, and in Tennessee, the same type of exception applies to those engaged in mining operations.

- **South Carolina** requires coverage for those employers with four or more employees.

- The states of **Arkansas, Georgia** and **Virginia** require employers with three or more employees to obtain coverage. The same criteria applies to private employers in **New Mexico**, with the exception that all employers licensed under the Construction Industries Licensing Act must secure coverage for their employees. **North Carolina** also requires coverage where three or more employees are involved, but the compensation law is compulsory for all employers with radiation exposure. **Michigan** law is compulsory as to all employers with three or more employees, or less than three employees if one is employed for 35 hours per week for 13 weeks by the same employer. **Wisconsin** requires coverage where the employer has three or more full-time or part-time employees or where the employer has one or more full-time or part-time employees who have combined gross wages of $500 or more in any calendar quarter for work done at one or more locations in Wisconsin.

Coverage requirements in the state of **Florida** are broken down by industry. For example, in the construction industry, an employer with even one employee must obtain coverage. In the non-construction industries, coverage is required where there are four or more employees. In the agricultural industry, an employer with five or more regular employees and/or 12 seasonal employees must carry coverage. It should also be noted that in **California**, not only must employers carry workers compensation if they have even one employee, but roofers must insure themselves even if there are no other employees.

Again, it is important to re-emphasize that numeric exceptions to coverage are not meant to imply that employers may not provide workers compensation coverage to such workers. With the exception of **Wyoming**, a monopolistic fund state, an employer may generally elect to purchase workers compensation coverage for such employees even though the law does not require same.

Agricultural Laborers – Agricultural or farm workers historically constituted one of the largest blocks of exempt employees. Originally it was thought that agricultural pursuits were excluded from coverage because, at the time, farming was a family affair with relatively few occupational hazards. Actually, farm work was particularly hazardous, especially with the transition to mechanical equipment. The farm worker exemption was probably due more to the fact that farm owners carried considerable weight in the earlier legislative arenas and did not want to have to provide workmen's compensation coverage any more than they wanted other forms of labor legislation. Thus it was that from early on, permitting an exemption for agricultural workers was one of the prices paid for enacting workmen's compensation laws for industrial workers.

While agricultural work has always been hazardous, replacement of the family farm with commercial operations has only served to make the occupation more hazardous in many respects. To offer more protection to certain categories of agricultural workers, in 1986 the federal government passed the Migrant and Seasonal Agricultural Worker Protection Act (MSAWPA)[20]. Even though a small percentage of farmers did provide workers compensation coverage for their migrant and seasonal workers, the law was designed to provide for the protection of virtually all migrant and seasonal agricultural workers and for the registration of contractors of these workers. The protection afforded under the new law included the right for farm workers to sue for damages when injured or killed as a result of workplace incidents.

In 1990, the United States Supreme Court in *"Adams Fruit Co. V. Barrett"*[21] permitted workers covered by MSAWPA to sue their employer for injuries caused by significant safety violations even where the worker was eligible for workers compensation benefits. The Federal Act was amended in 1995 to preclude this form of double recovery.[22] These amendments to the original MSAWPA worked to encourage employers to protect migrant workers through the purchase of workers compensation insurance.

Today, in 12 states plus the **District of Columbia**, farm workers are covered the same as all other employees. In one-half the states, the law requires some coverage of agricultural workers. The following provides a few examples of states that have enacted provisions establishing some criteria for determining which farm workers are covered and under what conditions:

- Coverage is required in **Florida** for agricultural labor performed on a farm in the employ of a bona fide farmer, or association of farmers, that employs six or more regular employees and that employs 12 or more other employees at one time for seasonal agricultural labor.

- In **New York**, coverage is required for farm laborers if the payroll during the prior year was greater than $1,200.

- A **Pennsylvania** employer employing agricultural labor is required to provide workers compensation coverage for such employees if during the calendar year such employer pays wages to one employee for agricultural labor totaling $1,200 or more or furnishes employment to one employee in agricultural labor on 30 or more days.

---

[20] Federal Law 29 USC 1801, et seq
[21] 494 U.S. 638 (1990)
[22] Sec.504. (d) (1) Notwithstanding *any* other provision of this Act where *a* State workers compensation law is applicable and coverage is provided for a migrant or seasonal agricultural worker the workers compensation benefits shall be the exclusive remedy for loss of *such* worker under this Act in the case of bodily injury or death in accordance with such State's workers' compensation law.

- Under the **Vermont** workers compensation law, a covered worker includes a person engaged in agriculture or farm employment for an employer whose aggregate payroll is greater than $2,000 in a calendar year.

Casual Workers – Another class of exempt employees are "casual" workers – those workers who work only occasionally or intermittently for a given employer. Casual labor is generally defined as work that is not in the usual course of the trade, business, occupation, or profession of the employer (contracting party). This could include relationships such as a manufacturer hiring a landscaping company to maintain the grounds or the owner of an insurance agency hiring a carpenter to upgrade the office. The contractor hired is not performing duties that would normally be considered as part of the work of the employer and is being conducted outside the normal operational requirements. Essentially, a casual laborer is one that does not directly promote or advance the employers' business.

Another way to look at casual employees is that a casual employee is a worker hired on a short-term basis to perform services which are not in the normal course of the employer's business. While the precise definition of what constitutes casual employment varies from state to state, the following provides a number of examples:

- In **Arkansas**, the term "employee" is defined to mean *"any person, including a minor, whether lawfully or unlawfully employed in the service of an employer under any contract of hire or apprenticeship, written or oral, expressed or implied; but excluding one whose employment is casual and not in the course of the trade, business, profession, or occupation of his employer."*[23]

- **Texas** law stipulates that a *"casual worker engaged in employment incidental to a personal residence"* is not subject to the Act.[24]

- In **Wisconsin**, any person whose employment is not during a trade, business, profession, or occupation of the employer is not covered unless the employer has elected to include them. But, that provision *"shall not operate to exclude an employee whose employment is in the course of any trade, business, profession, or occupation of the employer, however casual, unusual, desultory, or isolated the employer's trade, business, profession, or occupation may be."*[25]

Two-thirds of the states and the **District of Columbia** exempt "casual" employees or *"any employee whose employment is not in the trade, business, profession or occupation of the employer."* This exclusionary provision applies in nearly every state with each applying different requirements to the exception. It could therefore happen that a worker considered a casual employee in one jurisdiction might be considered an employee subject to the workers compensation law in another. The following illustrates some of those potential differences:

---

[23] Ark. Code Ann. § 11-9-102.(9)(A)
[24] Tex. Code Ann. § 406.091(A)(1)
[25] Wis. Stat. § 102.7 (4)(a)

- States may simply define casual labor and exclude the requirement to provide protection. Some states apply subjective terms to this definition such as "brief," "occasional," "irregular," "sporadic," or "infrequent" which may require arbitration or litigation to arrive at what the legislature intended.

- Some states assign a maximum dollar limit that can be paid or a maximum number of days the job can last before the work is no longer considered "casual."

- A few states establish the number of casual employees allowed.

Domestics – One early argument raised in opposition to providing coverage for domestic workers was that such workers were not engaged in the usual course of the employer's trade or business. With respect to industrial employment, the cost of the product was to cover the cost of workplace injuries. It was argued that employers of domestics had no product to sell. In addition, there were practical problems in the way of providing protection to those employed sporadically, irregularly, and for brief periods of time. Again, like agricultural employment, the administrative cost in issuing workers compensation policy was not sufficient to cover the potential exposure.

In the majority of states, domestic workers are exempt from workers compensation coverage but the employer may choose to provide coverage. In some states, domestic workers are covered where employed by the same employer for a certain number of hours per week or month or where the worker earns more than a certain amount of money. For example, in **California**, any domestic workers, including workers who care for and supervise children, who are employed 52 hours or more, or who earn $100 or more during 90 calendar days, are required to be covered.[26]

In **Massachusetts**, domestic workers must be covered if they work more than 16 hours a week for a single household. There are 12 other states with some level of time requirements or earnings.[27]

Two states provide for an alternative means to cover domestic workers. In **New Hampshire** and **New Jersey**, all homeowners' and tenants' insurance policies are required to include an endorsement for workers compensation insurance for occasional domestic service workers.

- In **New Hampshire**, all insurance companies authorized to provide comprehensive personal liability, tenant's or homeowner's insurance are required to provide workers compensation insurance covering domestics unless the employer has a separate policy of workers compensation insurance covering domestics.[28]

---

[26] Cal. Labor Code § 3351 (d)
[27] Colorado, Connecticut, Delaware, Hawaii, Illinois, Iowa, Maryland, Michigan, Minnesota, Ohio, South Dakota and Utah.
[28] N.H. Rev. Stat. § 281-A:6

- In **New Jersey**, *"Every homeowners' policy or other policy providing comprehensive personal liability insurance . . . shall afford coverage against liability for the payment of any obligation which the policyholder may incur to an injured domestic servant or household employee or the dependents thereof pursuant"* to the Workers Compensation Act.[29]

Family Members – Workers compensation laws in the majority of jurisdictions are silent regarding the status of family members as "covered" employees. Therefore, it is assumed in those jurisdictions that family members are "covered" employees under the respective laws. State workers compensation laws in **California**, **Hawaii**, **Idaho,** and **Kansas** specifically exempt certain family members from coverage. In California and Kansas, household employers may not elect to provide coverage for exempt family members; however, in Hawaii and Idaho, household employers may elect to cover exempt family members.

A number of jurisdictions have specific provisions addressing coverage for certain types of family members:

- In **Connecticut**, if the wages or salary of a member of the employer's family dwelling in his or her home is included in the payroll on which the premium is based, then that person will be deemed an employee and compensated in accordance with the statute if they sustain an injury arising out of and in the course of their employment.[30]

- **Iowa** exempts "members of the household" from coverage. A *"member of the household is defined as a spouse or relative of the employer, or a relative of the spouse residing in the household of employment.'"*[31]

- **Missouri** provides that *". . . an employee who is a member of the employer's family within the third degree of affinity or co-sanguinity shall be counted in determining the total number of employees of such employer."*[32]

- **Vermont** does not consider members of the employer's family dwelling in his/her house to be employees under the state's workers compensation law. However, *"if in any contract of insurance, the wages or salaries of a member of the employer's family dwelling in his house is included in the payroll on which the premium is based, then such person must, in the event of his or her sustaining injury arising out of and in the course of his/her employment, be deemed an employee and compensated accordingly."*[33]

Sole Proprietors and Partners – The simplest form of business entity is the sole proprietorship. A sole proprietor operation is one in which there is only a single owner of the

---

[29] N.J. Stat. Ann. § 17:36-5.29
[30] Conn. Gen. Stat. § 31-275 (9)(b)(iii)
[31] Iowa Code Ann. § 85.3 (b)(1)
[32] Mo. Rev. Stat. § 287.030 (3)
[33] Vt. Stat. Ann. § 601 (14)

business. In a partnership arrangement which involves two or more owners, the employer is the business entity, not the individual partners.

In the vast majority of jurisdictions, sole proprietors may elect to be covered under the workers compensation law. Election of coverage means that the individual is not covered but may elect to be covered through proper notification of the insurer. An endorsement is available to be added to the standard workers compensation policy extending coverage to sole proprietors and partners where such persons are excluded from coverage by law. A separate endorsement is available to exclude coverage in those states where the sole proprietor or partner is covered by law but elects to be excluded from coverage.

In the states of **Arkansas, New Mexico, Texas, West Virginia,** and **Wyoming,** sole proprietors are covered by law but may elect to be excluded from coverage. In those jurisdictions, the election not to be covered requires completion of the proper notification form. **Pennsylvania** and **Rhode Island** include sole proprietors in coverage but do not permit rejection of such coverage.

Similar to coverage for sole proprietors, partners may elect to be covered under the workers compensation law of a large majority of jurisdictions. For example, in the states of **Arkansas, Connecticut, Michigan, West Virginia,** and **Wyoming,** individual partners are covered by law and may elect to be excluded. Again, **Pennsylvania** and **Rhode Island** include partners in coverage and do not permit rejection of such coverage.

A number of jurisdictions base coverage requirements on the percentage of the business owned by the partner. Partners in **Louisiana** and **Oklahoma** are not required to purchase coverage if they own at least 10 percent of the company. In **Minnesota**, partners who own at least 25 percent of the corporation are exempt from the requirement to be insured.

Executive Officers – Where a workers compensation policy is issued to insure a corporation, the policy is designed to cover and insure all the corporation's executive officers. Executive officers of a corporation include the president, vice president(s), secretary, treasurer, and other executive officers elected or appointed in accordance with the charter or by-laws of the organization. Most state laws treat executive officers as employees, but others provide that they are not covered unless they elect to be covered.

In a significant number of jurisdictions, executive officers are covered and may, in certain jurisdictions, elect to be exempted from such coverage. Similar to coverage for sole proprietors and partners, an endorsement is available to be added to the standard workers compensation policy extending coverage to executive officers where such persons are excluded from coverage by law. A separate endorsement is available to exclude coverage in those states where the executive officer is covered by law but elects to be excluded from coverage.

Seventeen jurisdictions permit executive officers to be exempt from coverage. **Virginia** also permits executive officers to exclude themselves from coverage except for occupational disease benefits. In **North Dakota** and **Wyoming**, executive officers are exempt from coverage but may elect to be covered.

Certain jurisdictions utilize different criteria for determining when executive officers may be excluded from coverage. In the jurisdictions of **Colorado, Idaho** and **Oklahoma**, executive officers who own 10 percent or more of the corporation are exempt from coverage. In **Minnesota** and **Nebraska**, the level of business ownership is 25 percent at which point such executive officers are exempt from coverage. In **New York**, coverage is required for all corporate officers if the corporation has more than two officers and/or two stockholders and for officers of one or two person corporations if there are other individuals in employment. In **New Hampshire**, once a corporation has four executive officers, all are considered employees but three of such officers may elect to be excluded from coverage. In **Florida**, no more than three corporate officers within a construction company are allowed to be exempt from coverage.

The foregoing provides just a limited number of examples of the variety of criteria used in determining whether executive officers are required to be covered or are exempt from coverage. Rules regarding the coverage criteria are subject to change and a review of a jurisdiction's statute, along with related insurance regulations, is recommended when considering coverage for or exclusion of executive officers in a particular jurisdiction.

Non-Citizens – There is an inherent tension between state workers compensation laws and federal immigration laws with regard to the treatment of undocumented or non-citizens (formerly referred to as illegal aliens). On one hand, state workers compensation laws are designed to provide wage replacement and medical care to those who sustain injury arising out of and in the course of their employment. On the other hand, under federal immigration law, undocumented or non-citizens cannot lawfully work in the United States, and it is illegal for employers to knowingly hire such workers.

The statutes in about one-third of the states have been expressly designed to provide coverage for non-citizens. This is accomplished through language that specifically defines an "employee" as any person whether lawfully or unlawfully employed in the service of an employer. In the majority of the remaining states, the statute defines the term "employee" to include any person, but is silent as to the inclusion or exclusion of non-citizens. A few states reference coverage for aliens but make no distinction for legal or illegal non-citizens.

It is to be noted that **Wyoming** is the only state that expressly denies workers compensation benefits for non-citizens by limiting coverage to those legally employed. Wyoming defines a covered "employee" as "*any person engaged in any extra-hazardous employment under any appointment, contract of hire or apprenticeship, express or implied, oral or written, and includes legally employed minors, aliens authorized to work by the United States department of justice, office of citizenship and immigration services, and aliens whom the employer reasonably believes, at the date of hire and the date of injury based upon documentation in the employer's possession, to be authorized to work by the United States department of justice, office of citizenship and immigration services.*"[34]

---

[34] Wyo. Rev. Stat. § 27-14-102 (a) (vii)

Statutes like the one found in **New York** address aliens separately from the statute defining an employee. In New York, the workers compensation law states: *"Compensation under this chapter to aliens not residents or about to become nonresidents of the United States or Canada, shall be the same in amount as provided for residents..."*[35] While the statute does not specifically address non-citizens, the New York courts, noting that workers compensation is given without reservation and wholly regardless of wrongdoing of any kind, have construed the statute to permit payment to non-citizens.[36]

Courts in states with similar statutes, which include "aliens" in their definition of employee, have generally come to the conclusion that non-citizens should be covered for those injuries or diseases that arise out of their employment. Absent statutory language addressing an alien's right to compensation, a different result may occur. The **Virginia** Supreme Court considered a state statute which defined an employee as someone working under a contract of hire but which did not mention "aliens." In that case, the court concluded that non-citizens would not qualify, since they could not legally enter into a contract of hire in this country.[37] The Virginia legislature subsequently amended the statute to include "aliens and minors."

Another statutory approach addressing the issue of illegal aliens' right to workers compensation benefits can be found in **Florida** where the law defines obtaining employment under false pretenses as fraud and disqualifies the claimant from receiving compensation benefits. The law provides that:

"an employee shall not be entitled to compensation or benefits under this chapter if any judge of compensation claims, administrative law judge, court, or jury convened in this state determines that the employee has knowingly engaged in any of the acts described in sec. 440.105 or any criminal act for purposes of securing workers compensation benefits."[38]

(Sec. 440.105 provides that *"It shall be unlawful for any employer to knowingly participate in the creation of the employment relationship in which the employee has used any false, fraudulent, or misleading oral or written statement as evidence of identity."*)

Where the statute is silent on the subject, case law often holds that non-citizens are covered employees and entitled to workers compensation benefits. Decisions in **Maryland**,[39] **Massachusetts**,[40] **Nebraska**,[41] **New Jersey**,[42] **Oklahoma**[43] and **Pennsylvania**[44] have all

---

[35] Workers' Compensation Article 2 - (9 - 35) COMPENSATION 17 - Aliens.
[36] *Testa v Sorrento Restaurant*, 10 AD2d 133 (1960)
[37] *Granados v Windsor Development Corp.* 509 S.E.2d 290 (1999)
[38] Fla. Stat. Ann. § 440.09 (4)(a)
[39] *Design Kitchens and Bath v. Lagos* 882 A. 2d 817 (2005)
[40] *Medellin V. Cashman KPA, etal, Mass. Dept. of Industrial Accidents* (2003)
[41] *Isaac Ortiz v. Cement Products* No. S-05-437 (2005)
[42] *Mendoza v. Monmouth Recycling Corp.* 672 A. 2d 221 (1996)
[43] *Cherokee Industries, Inc. v. CNA Insurance Company* 84 P3 798 (2004)

ruled such persons to be covered. The courts in **California, Nebraska,** and **Oregon** have upheld decisions to deny vocational rehabilitation benefits to undocumented workers while the statute in **Virginia** precludes non-citizens from receiving vocational rehabilitation benefits.

The Supreme Court of **Iowa** recently held that undocumented workers are not excluded under the Iowa Workers Compensation Act's definition of "employee" and that the contract of employment between an undocumented worker and the employer is not void. Following the lead of other states, the Iowa court favorably cited case law from **Connecticut** and further indicated that the purpose of the federal Immigration Reform and Control Act (IRCA) was to inhibit employment of undocumented workers, not to diminish labor protections for undocumented workers.

The Immigration Reform and Control Act (IRCA) prohibit employers from hiring illegal aliens, as well as using fraudulent documents to obtain employment. In 2002, a **North Carolina** Appeals Court decision cited a report from the United States House of Representatives which expressly explained that it was not the intention of the Committee that the employer sanctions provisions of the bill be used to undermine or diminish in any way labor protections in existing law,...[45] The court further concluded that federal law does not prevent illegal aliens, based solely on immigration status, from receiving workers compensation benefits. In 2011, the United States Supreme Court denied a petition for writ of certiorari to address the issue of whether the IRCA may be used to deny workers compensation benefits to injured non-citizens.[46]

Real Estate Agents or Brokers – Most state workers compensation laws address directly coverage for real estate agents or brokers. In a small number of states - **Florida**, **Hawaii**, **Idaho, Illinois,** and **Oklahoma** - the compensation law does not apply to services performed by an individual for a real estate broker as an associate real estate broker or as a real estate salesman, if all such services performed by such individual person are performed for remuneration solely by way of commission.

- In **Massachusetts**, every person in the service of another under any contract of hire, express or implied, oral or written, is covered with the exception of *"a salesperson affiliated with a real estate broker pursuant to an agreement which specifically provides for compensation only in the form of commissions earned from the sale or rental of real property."*[47]

Going one step beyond the criteria established above, the states of **Delaware, Maine,** and **South Carolina** define the term "employee" so as <u>not</u> to include *"a real estate broker or salesperson whose services are performed for remuneration solely by way of commission if*

---

[44] *Reinforced Earth Company v. Workers Compensation Appeal Board* 749 A 2d 1036 (2000)
[45] *Ruiz v. Belk Masonry Co.* 559 SE 2d 249 (2002)
[46] *Vaughan Roofing & Sheet Metal, LLC v. Rodriquez* 131 S. Ct. 1572 (2011)
[47] Mass. Gen. Laws Ann. Ch. 152 § 1

the broker or salesperson has signed a contract with the agency indicating the existence of an independent contractor relationship."[48]

A significant number of states exclude coverage for licensed real estate agents or brokers where:

(1) Substantially all of the sales agent's or associated broker's remuneration from real estate brokerage is derived from real estate commissions.

(2) The services of the sales agent or associated broker are performed under a written contract specifying that the sales agent or associated broker is an independent contractor.

(3) Such contract provides that the sales agent or associated broker shall not be treated as an employee for federal income tax purposes.

Iowa utilizes a similar approach except that in order to require coverage for real estate personnel, the law requires that *"Seventy-five percent or more of the remuneration, whether or not paid in cash, for the services performed by the individual as a real estate sales person is derived from one company and is directly related to sales or other output, including the performance of services, rather than to the number of hours worked."*[49] The **Michigan** law contains similar criteria.

California requires real estate brokers to provide workers compensation coverage for their real estate sales agents. The California Labor and Workforce Development Agency considers a real estate salesperson to be an employee for the purposes of workers compensation insurance. In **Texas**, an employer may elect to provide workers compensation insurance coverage for persons licensed by the Texas Real Estate Commission and who are compensated solely by commission. *"If coverage is elected by the employer, the insurance policy must specifically name the salesperson or broker. The coverage continues while the policy is in effect and the named salesperson or broker is endorsed on the policy."*[50]

Other Exempt Employees – In addition to the employees previously described that may be subject to exemption under state workers compensation laws, there are a number of other employment forms that are frequently the subject of questions as to whether coverage is required. In many instances, these situations involve close questions between whether the worker is an employee or an independent contractor or a gig employee.

Questions frequently arise as regards the coverage status of taxicab drivers and newspaper vendors. In both instances, these tasks are generally viewed as being filled by independent contractors and therefore not subject to state workers compensation coverage. However, a small number of states have enacted legislation designed to either specifically include or

---

[48] Del. Code § 2316
[49] Iowa Code Ann. § 85.61
[50] Tex. Code Ann. § 406.094

exclude such workers from coverage. States enacting laws excluding taxicab drivers from coverage under certain conditions include:

- **Alaska** – The following persons are not covered: *"an individual who drives a taxicab whose compensation and written contractual arrangement is as described in AS 23.10.055(13), unless the hours worked by the individual or the areas in which the individual may work are restricted except to comply with local ordinances."* [51]

- **Florida** – "Employee" does not include *"A taxicab, limousine, or other passenger vehicle-for-hire driver who operates said vehicles pursuant to a written agreement with a company which provides any dispatch, marketing, insurance, communications, or other services under which the driver and any fees or charges paid by the driver to the company for such services are not conditioned upon, or expressed as a proportion of, fare revenues."* [52]

- **Massachusetts** – "Employee" does not include *"a person who operates a taxicab vehicle which is leased by such person from a taxicab company pursuant to an independent contract which specifically provides for a rental fee or other payment to the owner of such taxicab vehicle which is in no way related to the taxicab fares collected by such person; and provided, further, that such person is not treated as an employee for Federal tax purposes."* [53]

- **Virginia** – "Employee" does not include *"Any taxicab or executive sedan driver, provided the Commission is furnished evidence that such individual is excluded from taxation by the Federal Unemployment Tax Act."* [54]

New York approaches coverage for taxi cab drivers differently by making the question of coverage contingent on the status of the employer. Under the compensation law, "employer" means:

"A person, partnership, association, or corporation who leases or otherwise contracts with an operator or lessee for the purpose of driving, operating or leasing a taxicab as so defined in section one hundred forty-eight-a of the vehicle and traffic law, except where such person is an owner-operator of such taxicab who personally regularly operates such vehicle an average of forty or more hours per week and leases such taxicab for some portion of the remaining time. For the purposes of this section only, such an owner-operator shall be deemed to be an employer if he controls, directs, supervises, or has the power to hire or terminate such other person who leases the vehicle." [55]

---

[51] Alaska Stat. § 23.30.230 (a) (7)
[52] Fla. Stat. Ann. § 440.02 (15)(d)10
[53] Mass. Gen. Laws Ann. Ch. 152 § 1 (4)(e)
[54] Va. Code Ann. § 65 - 201
[55] N.Y. Con. Law Art. 3 § 2. 3

The situation in **California** of coverage for "gig economy" workers such as Uber, Lyft, and similarly situated taxi drivers, delivery workers, etc. will be addressed in the following section that looks at coverage for independent contractors.

As regards the situation with newspaper vendors, a few states have enacted laws designed to exclude newspaper vendors from coverage under the workers compensation law.

- **Arkansas** – Employment does not include *"Any person engaged in the vending, selling, offering for sale, or delivery directly to the general public of any newspapers, magazines, or periodicals, or any person acting as sales agent or distributor as an independent contractor of or for any newspaper, magazine, or periodical."* [56]

- **Missouri** – Covered employment does not include *"a person performing services as a newspaper carrier or free-lance correspondent if the person performing the services or a parent or guardian of the person performing the services in the case of a minor has acknowledged in writing that the person performing the services and the services are not covered."*[57]

- **North Carolina** – It is a rebuttable presumption that the term "employee" does not include *"any person performing services in the sale of newspapers or magazines to ultimate consumers under an arrangement whereby the newspapers or magazines are to be sold by that person at a fixed price and the person's compensation is based on the retention of the excess of the fixed price over the amount at which the newspapers or magazines are charged to the person."* [58]

Oregon takes a somewhat more benevolent approach in determining whether newspaper vendors are subject to coverage. An exemption to coverage is available to the newspaper publishing company or independent newspaper dealer or contractor where the employer (a) encourages any minor so utilized to remain in school and attend classes; (b) encourages any minor so utilized to not allow newspaper carrier duties to interfere with any school activities of the individual; and (c) provides accident insurance coverage for the individual while the individual is engaged in newspaper carrier duties: [59]

Two states, **New York** and **Wisconsin**, specifically provide for the inclusion of newspaper vendors. Again, New York, through the term "employer" accomplishes that result with the following: *"For the purposes of this chapter only "employer" shall also mean a person, partnership, association, corporation, and the legal representatives of a deceased employer, or the receiver or trustee of a person, partnership, association or corporation who delivers or causes to be delivered newspapers or periodicals for delivering or selling and delivering*

---

[56] Ark. Code Ann. § 11-9-102 (1)(vii)
[57] Mo. Rev. Stat. § 39-71-401 (k)
[58] N.C. Gen. Stat. § 97-2 (2)
[59] Or. Rev. Stat. § 656.075

by a newspaper carrier under the age of eighteen years as defined in section thirty-two hundred twenty-eight of the education law."[60]

In **Wisconsin**, the term "employee" includes *"Every person selling or distributing newspapers or magazines on the street or from house to house. Such a person shall be deemed an employee of each independent news agency which is subject to this chapter, or (in the absence of such agencies) of each publisher's (or other intermediate) selling agency which is subject to this chapter, or (in the absence of all such agencies) of each publisher, whose newspapers or magazines the person sells or distributes. Such a person shall not be counted in determining whether an intermediate agency or publisher is subject to this chapter."*[61]

In addition to those exclusions described above, there are other exemptions unique to particular states. In **Nevada,** the term "employee" excludes *"Any person engaged as a theatrical or stage performer or in an exhibition."*[62]

Review of a particular state's workers compensation law will indicate the forms of employment that are subject to exemption. Due to the uncertainty some employers face in determining whether certain employees are truly exempt from the law, all states and territories, with the exception of **Wyoming**, allow employers to elect to provide coverage for employees who are considered exempt. **California** and **Kansas** do not permit household employers to provide coverage for exempt family members. When an employer elects to provide coverage, states may require coverage be provided for all employees and that the employer formally notify the jurisdiction's workers compensation administrative agency of his/her intent to provide or terminate coverage for exempt employees.

INDEPENDENT CONTRACTORS

The most basic question about the employment relationship is whether a worker is, in fact, an employee or an independent contractor. As with many employment law issues, the answer is, it depends, and often falls to, who is asking. The answer may differ among the Federal Internal Revenue Service (IRS), the United States Department of Labor (DOL), and a workers compensation hearing officer and so on. Within the workers compensation program, the difference may occur even between states where courts have admitted that the distinction is not always clear.

In the workers compensation program, employment is generally viewed as a contractual relationship between two parties – one being an employer and the other being an employee. In this regard, under **Wisconsin** compensation law, an employee is defined as: *"Every person in the service of another under any contract of hire, express or implied, all helpers and assistants of employees, whether paid by the employer or employee, if employed with the knowledge, actual or*

---

[60] N.Y. Con. Law Art. 3 § 2
[61] Wis. Stat. § 102.07 (6)
[62] Nev. Rev. Stat. § 616A.110

constructive, of the employer, including minors, who shall have the same power of contracting as adult employees, but not including the following: 1. Domestic servants. 2. Any person whose employment is not in the course of a trade, business, profession or occupation of the employer, unless as to any of said classes, the employer has elected to include them."[63]

The question of whether a worker is an employee of independent contractor results in significant disputes, litigation, and ensuing case law. The proper classification of workers can be a complex task for any business as the potential exists for impacting company expenses. The general rule is that if the one who pays for the labor and services of another has the right to control what will be done and how it will be done, the person supplying the labor or service is an employee. This will be so even though the employee has been given some degree of freedom of action in terms of how the work is to be done. In many instances, the key determinant is the existence of the right to control the details of how any work is done. Whether such control is actually exercised is irrelevant.

On the other hand, as a general rule, if the one paying for the work does not have the right to control the day-to-day activity but is merely in a position to direct the desired outcome or result, the person supplying the labor is an independent contractor. A good example of this is found with the business of home construction. If a builder uses in-house employees for basic construction but hires outside experts for electrical, plumbing, and decorating work as and when the work is required, these outside experts are likely to be considered independent contractors. Usually, one clear sign as to whether there is an independent contractor relationship is whether such individuals are entered in the payroll system and paid as other employees, or paid when the work contracted for is completed and certified of satisfactory quality.

Beyond their role in construction, independent contractors are common in a number of other industries including trucking, real estate transactions, computer technology, and the performing arts. Within these industries there is a greater likelihood that businesses may misclassify these workers as independent contractors. With some employers, it is not uncommon to find secretaries, clerks, managers, janitors, nurses, machine operators, and a multitude of other workers being classified as independent contractors. What was at one point a less distinct area of coverage has now become, as a result of legislative changes and case law, more defined where clearly most of these workers are employees and not independent contractors.

At first glance, it appears that the use of independent contractors for some operations may be an effective avenue to reduce expenses, while at the same time bypassing the need to engage in certain administrative practices and record-keeping. However, this method of controlling expenses merits considerable study and an examination of the potential disadvantages and possible penalties associated with such action. Any decision to classify a worker as an independent contractor should be made with full knowledge of the potential legal, financial and practical consequences if that worker is later held to be an employee.

The following lists some of the more prominent advantages and disadvantages associated with classifying workers as independent contractors.

---

[63] Wis. Stat. § 102.07 (4)(a)

Potential Advantages for the Employer

Withholding of Federal Taxes and Payments for Social Security – Withholding of federal income taxes and payments for Social Security is required when the employer makes payment to an employee for labor or services rendered. When the worker is an independent contractor, the employer is not responsible for withholding income taxes or Social Security payments. The independent contractor receives annually a Form 1099 from the employer and the independent contractor is then responsible for paying any taxes or Social Security payments due.

Reduction in Insurance Premium – The use of independent contractors may produce two areas of premium savings. In the first instance, workers compensation premium charges may be reduced because payments made to independent contractors are not payroll and are not used in determining workers compensation premium charges. In the same way, an employer's responsibility of funding for unemployment compensation is eliminated where the worker is classified as an independent contractor.

Company-Provided Benefits – Beyond not including independent contractors for purposes of workers compensation coverage, many businesses provide a number of other important benefits to their employees. For example, employers frequently pay a portion of the cost of health or medical insurance, life insurance, retirement or 401k plans, paid vacations, sick days, and holidays. Independent contractors are not eligible for and do not receive such benefits. For the user of independent contractors, these represent major savings.

Tools, Equipment, and Supplies – Independent contractors normally provide and maintain their own tools, supplies and equipment, including vehicles. Depending on the nature and extent of a particular operation, use of independent contractors to perform certain operations may be an extremely valuable method of expense reduction.

Potential Disadvantages for the Employer:

Federal Income Tax and Social Security Withholding Penalties – If a worker is determined to be an employee and not an independent contractor, federal taxes and payments for Social Security that have not been properly withheld are due and payable immediately. In addition, potential penalties and fines can be substantial for both the employee and the employer. In some instances, fines and penalties can range from 20 percent to 40 percent of the employee's portion of the tax.

Collection of Previously Due Insurance Premiums on Audit – If it is found that the employer understated payroll, the business owner may, depending on the terms of the insurance contract, be required to pay the premium due in cases where an independent contractor is misclassified and is actually an employee. The amount of premium involved in these cases with workers compensation coverage can be significant and the insurance company has the right in these situations to go back several years for the purpose of doing revised audits and charging additional premiums for prior policy periods.

Loss of Workers Compensation Protection – Employees of a business are eligible for workers compensation coverage. Where an independent contractor is used to perform some or all of the business operations, the owner may be subject to a direct action for damages based on negligence, without benefit of the defenses available under the workers compensation law.

From a listing of the possible advantages and disadvantages associated with the classification of employees as independent contractors, it is quite evident that the issues extend beyond that of simply workers compensation coverage. While the issue of improper independent contractor classification is a significant problem for workers compensation, it is also a significant issue of concern at the federal level (Social Security, the Internal Revenue Service, and the federal unemployment program) as well as for the state unemployment benefit program.

Early on the United States Supreme Court weighed in on the issue of whether a person was an employee or an independent contractor.[64] In the *Silk* decision, a case dealing with whether an employer owed Social Security taxes on certain workers, the Supreme Court determined the following factors to be important:

1. The degree of control exercised by the alleged employer.

2. The extent of the relative investments of the [alleged] employee and employer.

3. The degree to which the "employee's" opportunity for profit and loss is determined by the "employer".

4. The skill and initiative required in performing the job.

5. The permanency of the relationship.

A subsequent 1987 decision rendered by the Fifth Circuit Court of Appeals, served to further clarify that in determining an employee versus an independent contractor relationship, that the *"focus is whether the employees as a matter of economic reality are dependent upon the business to which they render service"*. In the same case it was also noted that *"it is dependence that indicates employee status...the final and determinative question must be whether the total of the testing establishes the personnel are so dependent upon the business with which they are connected"* that they are employees.[65]

Taken literally, this emphasis on dependence and economic reality appears to require nothing more than a common sense approach. An employee who has nothing to invest in an enterprise beyond the time he/she puts in and who sells his/her services to only one "customer", the employer, is economically dependent upon that work. An independent contractor, on the other hand, is not normally dependent upon only one customer, but rather, being in business for

---

[64] *United States v. Silk*, 331 U.S. 704 (1947),
[65] *Brock v. Mr. W Fireworks, Inc.*, 814 F.2d 1042 (5th Cir. 1987

oneself and with an investment in their own equipment and supplies and has an entire customer base upon which to fall back.

Today, the economic reality or case law (CL) test remains in use by the United States Department of Labor (DOL) and the Social Security Administration (SSA). But other federal and state agencies use other criteria or "tests" for purposes of determining an independent contractor relationship. For example, the Internal Revenue Service (IRS) uses a so-called "Eleven Factor" test (formerly the "Twenty Factor" test) for determining the coverage of various federal employment tax laws. The 11 factors are all based upon the common law, economic reality, and other tests and represent their various criteria either reorganized or broken down into more detail. The 11 factors include:

Behavioral Control – The factors that show whether the business has a right to direct and control how the worker does the task for which the worker is hired include the type and degree of control: Common examples of behavioral control can include where the work is done, when the work is done, and how the work is done, especially when it comes to a code of conduct.

- Instructions the business gives the worker
- Training the business gives the worker.

Financial Control – A factor showing whether the business has a right to control the business aspects of the worker's job include: Financial control is also determined by how readily available your worker provides the same services on the open market. In other words, is your employee performing the same functions for multiple clients at once?

- The extent to which the worker has unreimbursed business expenses.
- The extent of the worker's investment.
- The extent to which the worker makes services available to the relevant market.
- How the business pays the worker.
- The extent to which the worker can realize a profit or loss.

Type of Relationship – Ways in which the relationship is determined comes through:

- Written contracts or statements of work describing the intended relationship.
- Whether the business provides benefits, such as sick pay, vacation, pension, equity, etc.
- The terms of the employment (how long is the contract for?)

As regards the question of independent contractors at the state level for purposes of workers compensation and unemployment compensation, several different approaches have been adopted. One approach is called the "ABC" test, or variation thereof, which is used for purposes of determining whether a worker is an employee or independent contractor for state unemployment tax purposes. In order to be considered an independent contractor, a worker must meet three separate criteria (some states require that only two criteria be met):

> A. The worker is free from control or direction in the performance of the work. Minor exception to this test may exist where, for example, the hiring organization may set some hours because of access restrictions.
>
> B. The work is done outside the usual course of the company's business and is done off the premises of the business. For example, an attorney working for a restaurant as outside counsel would be an independent contractor, since the work is unusual compared to the restaurant's regular business and performed off-site at the attorney's office.
>
> C. The worker is customarily engaged in an independent trade, occupation, profession, or business. Various professions and trades are customarily independent contractors available on a per job basis since they have their own business identity and engage in business for profit on the open market.

Nearly two-thirds of the states use the ABC test in establishing the employment relationship. Eight states use some variation of the ABC test. Those states using a variation of the ABC test (e.g., AB or AC) include: **Colorado, Idaho, Montana, Oklahoma, Pennsylvania, Virginia, Wisconsin,** and **Wyoming**. The remaining states continue to use the CL test.

It is somewhat ironic that those working in certain high risk occupations (e.g., construction, transportation, roofing, etc.) often find themselves without workers compensation coverage because of their independent contractor status. Prior to the occurrence of a workplace injury, a worker will frequently be satisfied to be classified and paid as an independent contractor instead of an employee. As an independent contractor, the worker will not have money withheld for state and federal taxes, payments for Social Security, and other similar expenses associated with a traditional employer-employee relationship.

However, when this same worker sustains a serious work-related injury, often their only recourse to disability benefits and medical care is to claim an employment relationship with the employer operating the site where they were injured. In response, the employer will frequently respond that the worker is not his/her employee because the employer does not control the work. At the same time, the worker will claim that the contractor does control the work and hence, there is an employer-employee relationship. The determination of whether the worker is an employee or an independent contractor will oftentimes be the determining factor as to whether workers compensation benefits are payable.

In addition to the tests for employment relationship described above, a number of states have enacted specific legislation to further clarify what is required to establish an independent contractor relationship. Effective in 2011, in **Pennsylvania** the Construction Workplace

Misclassification Act was enacted to define an "independent contractor" for purposes of workers compensation, unemployment compensation, and worker classification. The Act prohibits construction employers from classifying as independent contractors workers who do not satisfy all of the definitional criteria. These criteria require the independent contractor to: have a written contract to perform construction services with the business or person, carry at least $50,000 in general liability coverage for the duration of the job, document a proprietary interest in their business, and realize a profit or loss for the project.

Like Pennsylvania, a few other states provide guidance for purposes of determining who is an employee and who is an independent contractor. A significant number of states either define the term "independent contractor" or list the criteria used in making a determination of independent contractor status. While perhaps not as binding as statutory language, a few states address the subject through the promulgation of rules or regulations.

An interesting aspect of the **Arizona** statutes is that an independent contractor that performs work different from the client's normal work and who is not supervised by the client during the execution of that work is considered a true independent contractor and not an employee of the client for purposes of workers compensation coverage. There is a significant difference between Arizona rules and those rules pertaining to independent contractors found in many other states. The Arizona statute also requires there be a written agreement signed by both parties establishing the independent contractor relationship.

With a law effective in 2009, **Minnesota** requires individuals who work as independent contractors in the building construction industry to obtain an Exemption Certification from the Minnesota Department of Labor and Industry. This certificate exempts these individuals from workers compensation coverage of those who hire them along with exempting them from unemployment, wage and hour, and occupational and safety and health laws. The certification application includes a Declaration by the applicant that reads as follows:

> **This is to certify that the individual or business making this application as a residential building contractor, residential remodeler, or residential roofer claims an exemption from licensure pursuant to Minnesota Statutes § 326B.805. Subd. 6(5), because they do not expect to exceed $15,000 in gross annual receipts derived from their contracting, remodeling or roofing activities during this calendar year.**
>
> - **I understand a certificate of exemption shall not be issued unless and until a signed and notarized Affidavit in Support of Certificate of Exemption Application is filed with the application, which shall be signed by an identified owner, partner, member, or corporate officer.**
>
> - **I understand that a Certificate of Exemption must be applied for each year and that this certificate expires March 31 of each year.**
>
> - **I understand that if I exceed $15,000 in gross annual receipts, regardless of where the activities are performed, during any calendar year, that I must**

- **immediately surrender the Certificate of Exemption and apply for the appropriate license.**

- **I understand that if I am exempt from the licensure requirements, I may be required by a municipality to obtain a local license prior to becoming eligible to obtain a building permit.**

- **I understand that a Certificate of Exemption is NOT a license and that I am prohibited from advertising as a licensed contractor unless I or my company holds a municipal license.**

- **I understand that I am required and may be requested to provide the Department of Labor and Industry with additional information to verify qualification for this Certificate of Exemption.**

- **I hereby declare that any statements herein are true and complete, with the same force and effect as though given under oath.**

A similar approach is accomplished by a number of other states where guidance or position papers are issued by the administrative agency or other appropriate state office that prescribes the conditions to be met in order for an applicant to attain independent contractor status.

There are numerous court decisions addressing the subject of independent contractors. A **South Carolina** Supreme Court decision, reversing a decision by the state's Court of Appeals, held that direct evidence supported the Workers Compensation Commission's original determination that a certified registered nurse anesthetist (CRNA), who sustained injuries when she fell during a surgical procedure, was an employee of the hospital where the surgery took place, and not an independent contractor.[66]

Citing *Larson's Workers Compensation Law* §§ 61.01 and 61.04, the South Carolina Supreme Court indicated that the evidence of the hospital's control of the CRNA weighed heavily in favor of an employment relationship, that immediately upon assignment to the hospital by a medical staffing firm, the CRNA signed multiple documents indicating the hospital's right to control details such as where she could park and to whom she should report upon arriving each work day, and that the hospital's contention that its control over the CRNA was merely linked to governmental regulations was not persuasive. For example, the court observed that the hospital subjected the CRNA to a dress code that was more stringent than the legal requirement that she merely wear sterile clothing.

In a case that drew a great deal of national attention some years ago, three FedEx Ground employees brought a class action suit in **California** contending that they were employees and not independent contractors. While not directly a workers compensation case, the case did involve an interpretation as to who was an employee. The drivers won at the initial trial and also won on

---

[66] *Shatto v. McLeod Regional Med. Ctr.*, 2013 S.C. LEXIS 339 (2013)

two appeals.[67] In affirming the major portion of the decision rendered at the trial court level, the Court of Appeals included the statement of the trial court that had concluded *"if it looks like a duck, walks like a duck, swims like a duck, and quacks like a duck, it is a duck."*[68] The case was remanded back to the trial court with directions to conduct such further proceedings as were necessary to determine the amounts to which the drivers were entitled for out-of-pocket expenses.

A more recent California Supreme Court decision brought the state in line with at least a number of other states that had enacted identical, if not similar, independent contractor laws. Using the commonly called "ABC Test," the Supreme Court in Dynamex held that a worker is an independent contractor only if all of the three elements of the test were satisfied.[69]

Dynamex, the employer and a same-day courier service, initially classified all of its drivers as employees and compensated them pursuant to applicable wage and hour laws. Then, in 2004, in an effort to reduce operating costs, the company converted all of its drivers to independent contractors requiring them to provide their own vehicles, pay for all of their transportation expenses (i.e., fuel, tolls, vehicle maintenance, and vehicle liability insurance), as well as all taxes and workers compensation insurance. The workers were also required to wear Dynamex shirts and badges, paid for out of their own pockets.

Two delivery drivers sued individually and on behalf of a class of allegedly similarly situated drivers, alleging Dynamex failed to pay overtime, provide itemized wage statements, and failed to compensate the drivers for business expenses, as required for *employees* under the California Labor Code. Rather than follow the prevailing law in California, however, the California Supreme Court adopted the ABC Test to "streamline" and clarify the distinction between employees and independent contractors. In applying the ABC Test to the Dynamex drivers, the Court found the drivers were employees.

Subsequently, Assembly Bill 5 (AB5) was signed into law. This law change then became the subject of criticism, litigation, and lobbying efforts from a number of "gig" industries, freelancers, and independent contractors that did not find the legislation workable for their industries. Follow-up legislation in AB 2257 addressed the grievances that many industries and freelance workers had with AB 5. Still not satisfied with the status of the classification issue, Uber, Lyft, DoorDash, InstaCart, and Postmates spent more than $200 million in lobbying efforts for a ballot initiative that would override AB 5 and AB 2257, and classify drivers as independent contractors. The ballot initiative, Proposition 22, and was approved by California in November 2020 creating a third category of worker for those in the gig economy, neither full-time employees nor independent contractors. These workers are not eligible for state unemployment insurance, a guaranteed state minimum wage, overtime pay, sick leave, and no right to collectively bargain.

---

[67] *Estrada v. Fedex Ground Package System, Inc.,* 154 Cal. App. 4th 1 (2007)
[68] Ibid.
[69] *Dynamex Operations West, Inc. v. Superior Court of Los Angeles* (2018)

Upset as the loss of these protections, some gig drivers filed a lawsuit requesting to be classified as employees on the grounds that it defies state legislators' constitutional authority to implement a workers compensation system. On February 10, 2021 the Supreme Court dismissed their petition. It is likely more litigation will follow. It is also likely that propositions and legislative efforts aimed at a similar outcome will take root in other states.

THE GIG ECONOMY

Once regarded as those in need of temporary employment on the periphery of the American workforce, today it is difficult to imagine a world without the gig economy's ever-expanding services. The gig economy is commonly defined as digital platforms that allow freelancers to connect with potential clients for short-term jobs, contracted work, or asset-sharing. Statistics provided by the Bureau of Labor show there were 55 million gig workers in 2017.[70]

The COVID-19 pandemic, and the negative impact it has had on the economy, has pushed more and more Americans into the gig economy as they seek to make ends meet. While many gig economy employees provide single-use, unskilled labor for ridesharing services and peer-to-peer car or apartment rentals, the gig economy also includes such diverse professionals as licensed massage therapists, car mechanics, attorneys, and doctors. These and other gig economy workers can perform functions peripheral to a company's core operations and products, such as building maintenance, food service, or IT management, as well as other services that require sought-after skillsets.

Today it is estimated that gig economy freelancers make up 36 percent of the American workforce.[71] The gig economy has created many opportunities for companies to utilize the cost savings, efficiency, and availability of an on-demand workforce. In addition, an increasing number of virtual marketplace companies are providing digital platforms to connect independent workers with a wide range of end-market consumers, from large companies to individuals seeking to staff urgent project needs with independent workers.

The basic question comes down to whether the gig worker fits the definition of an employee or an independent contractor. For those who have read the preceding section, these are questions similar to those that need to be asked and are the building blocks of whether or not a person is considered an employee or an independent contractor. Unfortunately, our criteria for approaching the employee-versus-independent-contractor question for workers compensation imposes 20th century constraints on a 21st century labor model.

Laws vary, but most states have strict rules requiring employers to provide workers compensation coverage. But, there is a loophole. The gig economy refers to employment that is outside a permanent job, often through short term engagements, and without labor protections such as unemployment compensation, workers compensation, and a plethora of so-called wage and hour provisions such as overtime. While some app-based temporary staffing models may

---

[70] https://www.smallbizgenius.net/by-the-numbers/gig-economy-statistics/#gref
[71] Ibid.

suggest that workers compensation coverage isn't provided, it might be helpful to verify coverage as lawmakers continue to take notice and investigate ways to regulate workers and companies in this growing sector.

As noted previously, the legal definition of an independent contractor changes depending on the jurisdiction and between federal statutes, such as Title VII of the Civil Rights Act and the Fair Labor Standards Act (FLSA), and federal agencies, such as the Internal Revenue Service (IRS), the Equal Employment Opportunity Commission (EEOC), involved. Differences also exist depending on the state and local agencies involved. Consequences for misclassifying an employee as an independent contractor can be severe — back pay for overtime wages, liquidated damages, federal income tax liability and IRS penalties, FICA contributions, and interest.

The existence of an "Independent Contractor Agreement" or an IRS 1099 form is not dispositive of whether a worker is an independent contractor or an employee. Generally, gig economy independent contractors exercise independent business judgment over how to complete their work and are paid by completed task, instead of by hours worked. As applied to the rideshare and taxicab industry, the Department of Labor (DOL) imposed an "Economic Realities Test" in April 2019 to determine whether a gig economy worker is properly classified as an independent contractor. The test considers:

- The employer's degree of control over the work performed.

- The permanency of the relationship.

- The relative investment of the worker in the project.

- The worker's opportunity for profit/loss.

- The integration of the worker into the employer's workplace.

As these factors emphasize, the DOL test focuses on the extent to which a worker is economically dependent on the employer. It is no secret that traditional employers often benefit from non-traditional workplace arrangements available in the gig economy, such as relief from paying unemployment insurance and workers compensation insurance or being exempt from many minimum wage or overtime laws that apply to the traditional employer-employee relationship. Companies also can save in traditional training costs since temporary gig workers do not require the same level of training or retention efforts.

The experience from the passage of Proposition 22 in California in 2020 will be a telling experience for many gig workers. It has been observed by some that Uber, Lyft, and DoorDash will benefit most from the new law change, but companies beyond the gig economy have also seen the opportunity to get in on the low-cost labor pool. In early 2020, grocery giants Vons, Pavilions, and Albertsons announced that they'd be firing their full-time, benefits-receiving delivery staff and replacing them with subcontractors from DoorDash, which has secured a nationwide deal to take over the service. That move is a sign of things to come as companies realize that Proposition 22 allows them to subcontract the same labor at a lower cost.[72]

Proposition 22 is also likely to be the forerunner of activity in other states where employers are looking for means to reduce their payroll expenses and shift cost through other employment relationships.

STATUTORY EMPLOYEES

Most people are familiar with the two common types of employment relationships: a common-law employee relationship and an independent contractor relationship. There is also a third type of relationship that lies somewhere between an independent contractor and an employer/employee type of relationship. This is a statutory employee relationship.

According to the Internal Revenue Service (IRS), if a worker is an independent contractor under common law rules, such a worker may nevertheless be treated as an employee by statute (statutory employee) for certain employment tax purposes. They will be considered a statutory employee if they fall within any one of the following four categories below and are in compliance with the three conditions that follow:

- A driver who distributes beverages (other than milk) or meat, vegetables, fruits, or bakery products; or one who collects and delivers laundry or dry cleaning, if the driver is an agent of an employer or is paid on commission.

- A full-time life insurance sales agent whose principal business activity is selling life insurance or annuity contracts, or both, primarily for one life insurance company.

- An individual who works at home on materials or goods that you supply and that must be returned to you or to a person you name, if you also furnish specifications for the work to be done.

- A full-time traveling or city salesperson that works on your behalf and turns in orders to you from wholesalers, retailers, contractors, or operators of hotels, restaurants, or other similar establishments. The goods sold must be merchandise for resale or supplies for use in the buyer's business operation. The work performed for you must be the salesperson's principal business activity.

One of the best examples of a statutory employee under workers compensation is an employee that is hired to do the same work that the company employees regularly do. The *Bass* decision from the **Missouri** Supreme Court sets forth a four-prong test to determine whether an employee is a statutory employee or not.[73] The four prong test is centered on the activities of the possible statutory employee in question:

---

[72] https://prospect.org/labor/prop-22-is-here-already-worse-than-expected-california-gig-workers/
[73] *Bass v. National Super Markets, Inc.*, 911 S.W.2d 617 (1995)

1. Activities that are routinely done.

2. On a regular and frequent schedule.

3. Contemplated in the agreement between the independent contractor and the statutory employer to be repeated over a relatively short span of time.

4. The performance of which would require the statutory employer to hire permanent employees absent the agreement.

A statutory employer can best be illustrated where there is a general contractor and subcontractor arrangement. In the instance of a work-related injury to an employee of the subcontractor, that employee would first seek workers compensation benefits from their direct employer, the subcontractor. If the subcontractor has workers compensation insurance, the insurer of the subcontractor will be responsible for the benefits. However, there is the second possibility where the subcontractor does not have insurance or denies that the claim is compensable. Under this scenario, the general contractor may be held to be a "statutory employer" (also referred to as a "principal employer") and required by law to pay the injured employee's workers compensation benefits.

The importance of the statutory relationship for the employer (general contractor) becomes evident when considering the issue of exclusive remedy. In keeping with the *quid pro quo* of workers compensation, the application of the exclusivity remedy rule is usually limited to the direct employer of the injured worker. Therefore, except in a limited number of states, the exclusivity rule does not preclude an injured worker from filing a negligence lawsuit against an employer other than his/her direct employer, such as a project owner, general contractor, or other entity purportedly responsible for the injury. Likewise, these non-exempt entities are not subject to the "no-fault" rule imposed under workers compensation laws and therefore can raise defenses as to responsibility for the alleged injuries.

The statutory employer defense originated at a time when employers were permitted to elect whether to purchase workers compensation coverage for their employees. Employers who failed to purchase such coverage remained subject to suit in tort. Under this original statutory system, when a construction subcontractor elected not to purchase workers compensation coverage, and one of its employees was injured on a job, the general contractor was conclusively determined to be the employer of the injured employee of the subcontractor and was responsible for the payment of workers compensation benefits.

When a general contractor assumes responsibility for workers compensation payments, thus becoming the statutory employer, it likewise receives those protections associated with the exclusive remedy rule. There is a certain logic behind the extension of this entitlement insofar as the company that provides the injured employee with workers compensation benefits receives the right of exclusivity, thereby maintaining the purpose of the *quid pro quo*. Conversely, and consistent with this reasoning, a direct employer that neglects to obtain the required workers compensation typically surrenders the right of exclusivity and is thereby exposed to tort liability.

PROFESSIONAL EMPLOYER ORGANIZATIONS (PEOs)

There is an additional employer/employee relationship that merits consideration. This is the Professional Employer Organization (PEO) relationship. A PEO is an entity that contractually assumes various employer rights and human resources responsibilities through the undertaking of an "employer relationship" with workers either assigned to or hired by its clients (employers). In short, the PEO and the employer/client share an employment relationship that allows the PEO to handle and manage employee-related matters such as payroll, benefits, tax matters, and, in many cases, workers compensation programs. According to the National Association of Professional Employer Organizations (NAPEO) there are 907 PEOs in the United States providing services to 175,000 small and mid-sized businesses that employ 3.7 million people.[74]

While PEOs have served to rescue employers from certain costs associated with the running of a business, it is important to recognize that their very existence has also set the stage for the emergence of PEO-related workers compensation fraud. With acknowledgement for the fact that the overwhelming majority of PEOs are legitimate, law abiding companies, the emergence of fraud in this arena should put employers on alert when contemplating entering into a PEO arrangement.[75]

This co-employment relationship has been summarized by NAPEO, in part, as a contractual relationship whereby the PEO:

- Co-employs workers at the client locations and assumes responsibility as an employer for specified purposes;

- Reserves a right to direct and control these employees;

- Pays wages and employment taxes of the employee out of its own accounts;

- Reports, collects and deposits employment taxes with the state and federal authorities;

- Establishes and maintains an employment relationship with its employees that is intended to be long-term and not temporary; and

- Retains the right to hire, re-assign and fire the employees.

When an employer outsources its workers compensation coverage responsibility to a PEO, it is entrusting that all insurance requirements will be fulfilled by the PEO. This means that the PEO

---

[74] https://www.napeo.org/about-napeo
[75] Natale, Anthony III, *PEOs: A New Potential for Workers' Comp Fraud*, National Underwriter Property & Casualty, October 2013

will be responsible for classifying employees, communicating payroll to insurers, selecting appropriate coverage and paying premiums. This also presupposes that the PEO is familiar with the local workers compensation statutes and regulations.

Unknowingly, some employers may willingly shift this burden to the PEO without securing contractual evidence of the PEO's rights and duties. These same employers may rely on an ambiguous contract drafted by the PEO which does nothing to protect the employer's interests. Unfortunately, the lack of a clearly defined, written contract between the PEO and employer can not only lead to fraud or misrepresentation by the PEO, but also can negate the existence of a valid PEO relationship in states that require a written PEO contract.

When an employer contracts with a PEO and a workers compensation claim is filed, questions often arise as to whether appropriate insurance has been maintained, if there is documentary evidence available to support the PEO's responsibility to defend the workers compensation claim, and even, sometimes, whether the PEO is fiscally solvent. There have been cases where a "fly by night" PEO is saddled with liability by a workers compensation judge and simply fails to pay benefits. Under such circumstances the employer would likely be liable for the injury and could be put into a situation where no insurance exists, thus exposing employers to criminal liability in certain states.

The fact that the PEO and its employer-client are viewed as co-employers in the workers compensation system has a perceived advantage. From a theoretical standpoint, an employer can farm out its workers compensation coverage while keeping the protection of tort immunity. It follows that in the PEO relationship, where the PEO and the employer both share the right to control the worker, both technically possess the right to assert tort immunity. However, this has not stopped a number of lawsuits naming the employer as a third party tortfeasor following a work-related injury.

The emergence of incidents of PEO fraud in relation to workers compensation matters provides a cautionary warning for employers considering entering into a PEO arrangement. Employers should be aware of statutes in certain states that require a PEO to define its contractual obligations and the protocols by which the PEO is to be managed. For employers operating in states without such legislation, it is important to insist on a written contractual agreement with the PEO, drafted in unambiguous language that is understood and agreed upon by both parties at the start of the co-employment relationship.

A new development in the area of PEOs is the arrival of Administrative Services Organizations (or sometimes Administrative Services Outsourcing.) These ASOs provide services somewhat similar to those of a PEO but different in some key aspects. Generally, an ASO will handle certain human resources tasks such as tax filing and payroll. For workers compensation purposes, the key distinction between an ASO service and PEO is that the ASO may or may not offer workers compensation insurance to clients. When the ASO offers such coverage, it will be offering individual policies to each client company. In a PEO, compensation coverage is provided to client companies via a master policy negotiated by the PEO, although some states require the insurance company to issue a separate policy for client companies. If the PEO loses its compensation coverage, coverage is lost for all client companies.

Under an ASO format, each client company has its own separate policy direct with the insurance company and independent of the ASO. The ASO handles billing that is coordinated with other payroll services but is not a co-policyholder with the client company. This means that the client company retains all the legal rights a policyholder has in relation to the insurance company. In a PEO relationship, the policyholder is technically the PEO, and the client company may well not have the same protections that are provided to the policyholder.

EXTRATERRITORIAL COVERAGE

In today's mobile society, employment can take place either in one principal location, or may involve travel between locations, including travel outside the state of primary employment. With recognition for the fact that injuries and accidents may occur outside an employee's principal location, one of the nineteen essential recommendations of the 1972 National Commission on State Workmen's Compensation Laws provided that *"An employee or his survivor is to be given the choice of filing a workmen's compensation claim in the state where the injury or death occurred, or where the employment was principally located, or where the employee was hired."*[76]

When a worker is principally employed in one state, and sustains a work-related injury in another state, that worker may have the option of claiming benefits under the law of the state where the injury occurred, depending on the law in the state of injury. Extraterritorial coverage, as it applies to workers compensation, could be described as a provision in workers compensation insurance under which an employee who incurs an injury in another state, and elects to come under the law of his/her home state, will retain coverage under the workers compensation coverage of his/her home state.

To provide coverage for an employee claiming benefits under the law of another state, either the workers compensation policy must be amended to include coverage in that other state, or another policy must be obtained in the other state. One can easily see the problem when an employer sends an employee to another state to attend a meeting or conference for a few days or an employer who operates close to a state border has the opportunity to compete for a short-term project in an adjoining state. Does the employer have to go to the expense of adding that other state to their insurance policy to ensure compliance?

In addition to the more obvious situations, there are also situations where an injured worker can seek workers compensation benefits based on the state where the contract of employment was entered into. There is also the rarer situation where the residence of the employee can play a part in determining whether an injured worker is entitled to workers compensation benefits following a work-related injury in some other state. For example, a recent **Massachusetts** Supreme Judicial Court decision dealt with case involving a Commomwealth resident who entered into an

---

[76] National Commission recommendation 2.11

employment contract, performed much of the work, and was injured all outside the Commonwealth.

Following protracted administrative and appeal proceedings, the denial of benefits was appealed to the Appeals Court, at which time the Supreme Judicial Court granted an application for direct appellate review. Considering the foregoing, the Court held there were sufficient significant contacts between Massachusetts and the claimant's employment such that the employment relationship was located in Massachusetts. Accordingly, the Court vacated the Board's decision and remanded the case to the department for further proceedings consistent with the Court's opinion.[77]

While states have a very real interest in ensuring that employers and employees working in their state are properly covered in the case of a work-related injury or death, the insurer has an equally high concern that employers are properly protecting their employees. Employers without proper insurance coverage (be it workers compensation, unemployment compensation, state disability benefit programs, etc.) are at a competitive advantage when bidding on a work project. Such action similarly places the employer "who plays by the rules" at a tremendous competitive disadvantage when bidding on any work project. Furthermore, from the insurer perspective, proper rating of the work classification for pricing purposes requires that the total payroll in that classification includes the entire payroll in that state.

Another issue for insurers is the employer who is insured for workers compensation in one state but fails to notify the carrier when that employer becomes involved in a work project in another state. With states abutting each other and especially for smaller size states it is a common occurrence for those employers engaged near a state border to have work projects in multiple states. While perhaps insured for workers compensation in one state, the coverage does not always extend to projects in an abutting state. Likewise, exposure to an injury associated with travel or limited activity in another state for a conference or convention may expose the insurer to a risk that the company was not aware of.

It is important to recognize that there exists little uniformity among the state statutes as regards their approach to extraterritorial coverage. While case law continues to evolve in an effort to provide guidance to the jurisdictions in terms of which injured workers may apply for workers compensation benefits, a number of states have enacted specific statutory provisions dealing with coverage for in-state workers who sustain an out-of-state injury, while a much larger number of states address both the issue of in-state coverage for workers who sustain an out-of-state injury and those out-of-state workers who sustain an in-state injury.

Because workers compensation law differs by state, it is often unclear as to which state's workers compensation benefits might apply. Although this issue has been litigated heavily, firm rules do not exist, and each situation needs to be evaluated on its own merits. At least one general conclusion can be reached, however. An employee hired in one state and injured in another may obtain benefits in the other state. In practical terms, this means that any business

---

[77] *Mendes's Case*, 2020 Mass. LEXIS 661 (2020).

sending an employee to another state could conceivably have an incidental workers compensation exposure in that state.

For purposes of this section, the two different aspects of this issue will be examined. In this first place, the examination will address those states where an in-state worker sustains an out-of-state injury. In the second case, the review will examine how states address the situation where an out-of-state worker sustains an in-state injury.

IN-STATE WORKER/OUT-OF-STATE INJURY

One may say that in general, the workers compensation law in at least one-third of the states will apply whether the injury occurred in that state or outside the state so long as the employee or employer meet certain requirements. These requirements vary by state but some of the more common requirements include: (1) the employee having been hired in the state; (2) the employer conducting business in the state; and (3) the employee being a resident of the state.

A fairly precise example of this legislative approach is found in the state of **North Carolina** where the law addresses three criteria regarding the employment relationship. The statute also recognizes the fact that a recovery may be realized under the laws of another jurisdiction, but such an award should not result in a double-recovery for the injured worker or his dependents.

> *Where an accident happens while the employee is employed elsewhere than in this State and the accident is one which would entitle him or his dependents or next of kin to compensation if it had happened in this State, then the employee or his dependents or next of kin shall be entitled to compensation (i) if the contract of employment was made in this State, (ii) if the employer's principal place of business is in this State, or (iii) if the employee's principal place of employment is within this State; provided, however, that if an employee or his dependents or next of kin shall receive compensation or damages under the laws of any other state nothing herein contained shall be construed so as to permit a total compensation for the same injury greater than is provided for in this Article.*[78]

Effective July 1, 2011, a new law went into effect in **Florida** which serves to exempt certain employees and employers working in Florida from the compensation law under certain conditions. The law requires the establishment of prima facie evidence that the employer carries certain compensation insurance and requires the courts to take judicial notice of the construction of certain laws. It further establishes requirements for claims made in other states and provides criteria for employees to be considered temporarily working in Florida.

While driven in part by interest in conforming to the approach found in the majority of states, the Florida law change was also driven in large part by professional athletic teams domiciled in Florida. Professional players on those teams play games in many different jurisdictions resulting in the potential exposure to serious injury in any number of jurisdictions. During the past decade,

---

[78] N.C. Gen. Stat. § 97-36.

this has become a growing problem with many professional players, formerly associated with one or more of the Florida teams, filing claims for cumulative injury in **California.** These claims have generally been resolved through the payment of a lump-sum settlement entered into following the conclusion of the player's professional career under the auspices of the California Workers Compensation law.

In light of certain ongoing litigation in California and elsewhere, it is anticipated that the Florida approach will serve to preclude certain of these claims from being recognized in California. The new statute reads as follows: *(1) If an employee in this state subject to this chapter temporarily leaves the state incidental to his or her employment and receives an accidental injury arising out of and in the course of employment, the employee is, or the beneficiaries of the employee if the injury results in death are, entitled to the benefits of this chapter as if the employee were injured within this state.*

> *(2) An employee from another state and the employer of the employee in the other state are exempt from this chapter while the employee is temporarily in this state doing work for the employer if:*
>> *(a) The employer has furnished workers 'compensation insurance coverage under the workers compensation insurance or similar laws of the other state to cover the employee's employment while in this state;*
>> *(b) The extraterritorial provisions of this chapter are recognized in the other state; and*
>> *(c) Employees and employers who are covered in this state are likewise exempted from the application of the workers 'compensation insurance or similar laws of the other state.*
>
> *(3) The benefits under the workers compensation insurance or similar laws of the other state, or other remedies under similar law, are the exclusive remedy against the employer for any injury, whether resulting in death or not, received by the employee while temporarily working for that employer in this state.*
>
> *(4) A certificate from the duly authorized officer of the appropriate department of another state certifying that the employer of the other state is insured in that state and has provided extraterritorial coverage insuring employees while working in this state is prima facie evidence that the employer carries that workers 'compensation insurance.*
>
> *(5) Whenever in any appeal or other litigation the construction of the laws of another jurisdiction is required, the courts shall take judicial notice of such construction of the laws of the other jurisdiction.*
>
> *(6) When an employee has a claim under the workers 'compensation law of another state, territory, province, or foreign nation for the same injury or occupational disease as the claim filed in this state, the total amount of compensation paid or awarded under such other workers 'compensation law shall be credited against the compensation due under the Florida Workers Compensation Law.*
>
> *(7) For purposes of this section, an employee is considered to be temporarily in a state doing work for an employer if the employee is working for his employer in a state other than the state where he or she is primarily employed, for no more than 10 consecutive days, or no more than 25 total days, during a calendar year.*
>
> *(8) This section applies to any claim made on or after July 1, 2011, regardless of the date of the accident.*[79]

---

[79] Fla. Stat. Ann. § 440.094

In addressing the subject of an in-state worker sustaining an injury in another jurisdiction, a number of the statutes attempt to restrict coverage for in-state workers who sustain out-of-state injuries by restricting coverage to those only "temporarily" out of state. In addressing the issue, **Colorado** utilizes a six month limitation for coverage but permit the employer to file for an extension prior to the end of that six month period.

> *If an employee who has been hired or is regularly employed in this state receives personal injuries in an accident or an occupational disease arising out of and in the course of such employment outside of this state, the employee, or such employee's dependents in case of his death, shall be entitled to compensation according to the law of this state. This provision shall apply only to those injuries received by the employee within six months after leaving this state, unless prior to the expiration of such six-month period, the employer has filed with the division notice that he has elected to extend such coverage for a greater period of time.*[80]

While the extraterritorial provisions found in the workers compensation laws of the majority of states extends coverage to workers temporarily working in another state, such provisions do not serve to restrict injured workers to the compensation benefits of their home state.

The key phrase identified in the majority of the state extraterritorial provisions is that the injured party *"shall be entitled"* to the benefits or compensation payable under this article, chapter, etc. The extraterritorial provisions do not mandate that the injured party accept the compensation payable from that state. The laws only indicate that if the injured party is willing to accept those benefits, and all other criteria for a compensable claim are fulfilled, then workers compensation benefits will be payable.

OUT-OF-STATE WORKER/IN-STATE INJURY

While coverage for an in-state worker who sustains an out-of-state injury represents one side of the coverage equation, there is another side, and certainly more complex side to the subject of benefit entitlement. One-half of the states have enacted statutory provisions that address the situation both where an in-state worker sustains an out-of-state injury and also, where an out-of-state worker sustains an in-state injury.

Probably one of the more straight-forward approaches to this subject is found in the state of **Missouri** where the law provides for the following –

> *This chapter shall apply to all injuries received and occupational diseases contracted in this state, regardless of where the contract of employment was made, and also to all injuries received and occupational diseases contracted outside of this state under contract of employment made in this state, unless the contract of employment in any case shall otherwise provide, and also to all injuries received and occupational*

---

[80] Colo. Rev. Stat. Ann. § 8-41-204

diseases contracted outside of this state where the employee's employment was principally localized in this state within thirteen calendar weeks of the injury or diagnosis of the occupational disease.[81]

Another state with a direct approach is found in **California** where the law addresses the two distinct situations of domestic and foreign coverage's':

(a) Domestic employment; foreign policy. If an employee who has been hired or is regularly employed in the state receives personal injury by accident arising out of and in the course of such employment outside of this state, he, or his dependents, in the case of his death, shall be entitled to compensation according to the law of this state.
(b) Foreign employment; domestic injury. Any employee who has been hired outside of this state and his employer shall be exempted from the provisions of this division while such employee is temporarily within this state doing work for his employer if such employer has furnished workers compensation insurance coverage under the workers compensation insurance or similar laws of a state other than California, so as to cover such employee's employment while in this state; provided, the extraterritorial provisions of this division are recognized in such other state and provided employers and employees who are covered in this state are likewise exempted from the application of the workers compensation insurance or similar laws of such other state. The benefits under the Workers Compensation Insurance Act or similar laws of such other state, or other remedies under such act or such laws, shall be the exclusive remedy against such employer for any injury, whether resulting in death or not, received by such employee while working for such employer in this state.[82]

The clarity with which the second provision – addressing a domestic injury to a worker from out of state – leaves little question that those working temporarily in the state and are covered through a workers compensation policy in the state of their principal employment, are exempt from coverage in California. However, in the past, California courts have frequently relied heavily upon the "state of interest" doctrine whereby an injury occurring in the state of California makes California the "state of interest."

Perhaps the most comprehensive approach found in the statutes that addresses both the subject of in-state injury to an out-of-state worker and the lack of workers compensation coverage in the state of injury is found in the jurisdictions of **Alaska, Delaware, Idaho, Kentucky, Pennsylvania** and **Washington.** These jurisdictions have statutorily addressed the issue of out-of-state coverage when an employee sustains a work-related injury or death within their state and the employer has failed to secure compensation coverage in that state. The statutory language found in each of these jurisdictions is remarkably similar and provides as follows:

(a) If an employee, while working outside the territorial limits of this State, suffers an injury on account of which he, or in the event of his death, his dependents, would have been entitled to the benefits provided by this act had such injury occurred within this

---
[81] Mo. Rev. Stat. § 287.110 2
[82] Cal. Labor Code § 3600.5.

State, such employee, or in the event of his death resulting from such injury, his dependents, shall be entitled to the benefits provided by this act, provided that at the time of such injury:

(1) His employment is principally localized in this State, or

(2) He is working under a contract of hire made in this State in employment not principally localized in any state, or

(3) He is working under a contract of hire made in this State in employment principally localized in another state whose workers compensation law is not applicable to his employer, or

(4) He is working under a contract of hire made in this State for employment outside the United States and Canada.

(b) The payment or award of benefits under the workers compensation law of another state, territory, province or foreign nation to an employee or his dependents otherwise entitled on account of such injury or death to the benefits of this act shall not be a bar to a claim for benefits under this act; provided that claim under this act is filed within three years after such injury or death. If compensation is paid or awarded under this act:

(1) The medical and related benefits furnished or paid for by the employer under such other workers compensation law on account of such injury or death shall be credited against the medical and related benefits to which the employee would have been entitled under this act had claim been made solely under this act.

(2) The total amount of all income benefits paid or awarded the employee under such other workers compensation law shall be credited against the total amount of income benefits which would have been due the employee under this act, had claim been made solely under this act.

(3) The total amount of death benefits paid or awarded under such other workers compensation law shall be credited against the total amount of death benefits due under this act. Nothing in this act shall be construed to mean that coverage under this act excludes coverage under another law or that an employee's election to claim compensation under this act is exclusive of coverage under another state act or is binding on the employee or dependent, except, perhaps to the extent of an agreement between the employee and employer or where employment is localized to the extent that an employee's duties require him to travel regularly in this State and another state or states.

(c) If an employee is entitled to the benefits of this act by reason of an injury sustained in this State in employment by an employer who is domiciled in another state and who has not secured the payment of compensation as required by this act, the employer or his carrier may file with the director a certificate, issued by the commission or agency of such other state having jurisdiction over workers compensation claims, certifying that such employer has secured the payment of compensation under the workers compensation law of such other state and that with respect to said injury such employee is entitled to the benefits provided under such law.

In such event:

(1) The filing of such certificate shall constitute an appointment by such employer or his carrier of the Secretary of Labor and Industry as his agent for acceptance on the

service of process in any proceeding brought by such employee or his dependents to enforce his or their rights under this act on account of such injury;

(2) The secretary shall send to such employer or carrier, by registered certified mail to the address shown on such certificate, a true copy of any notice of claim or other process served on the secretary by the employ or his dependents in any proceeding brought to enforce his or their rights under this act;

(3)(i) If such employer is a qualified self-insurer under the workers compensation law of such other state, such employer shall, upon submission of evidence, satisfactory to the director, of his ability to meet his liability to such employee under this act, be deemed to be a qualified self-insurer under this act;

(ii) If such employer's liability under the workers compensation law of such other state is insured, such employer's carrier, as to such employee or his dependents only, shall be deemed to be an insurer authorized to write insurance under and be subject to this act: Provided, however, That unless its contract with said employer requires it to pay an amount equivalent to the compensation benefits provided by this act, its liability for income benefits or medical and related benefits shall not exceed the amounts of such benefits for which such insurer would have been liable under the workers compensation law of such other state;

(4) If the total amount for which such employer's insurance is liable under clause (3) above is less than the total of the compensation benefits to which such employee is entitled under this act, the secretary may, if he deems it necessary, require the employer to file security, satisfactory to the secretary, to secure the payment of benefits due such employee or his dependents under this act; and

(5) Upon compliance with the preceding requirements of this subsection (c), such employer, as to such employee only, shall be deemed to have secured the payment of compensation under this act.

(d) As used in this section:

(1) "United States" includes only the states of the United States and the District of Columbia.

(2) "State" includes any state of the United States, the District of Columbia, or any province of Canada.

(3) "Carrier" includes any insurance company licensed to write workers compensation insurance in any state of the United States or any state or provincial fund which insures employers against their liabilities under a workers compensation law.

(4) A person's employment is principally localized in this or another state when (i) his employer has a place of business in this or such other state and he regularly works at or from such place of business, or (ii) having worked at or from such place of business, his duties have required him to go outside of the State not over one year, or (iii) if clauses (1) and (2) foregoing are not applicable, he is domiciled and spends a substantial part of his working time in the service of his employer in this or such other state.

(5) An employee whose duties require him to travel regularly in the service of his employer in this and one or more other states may, by written agreement with his employer, provide that his employment is principally localized in this or another

such state, and, unless such other state refuses jurisdiction, such agreement shall be given effect under this act.
(6) "Workers compensation law" includes "occupational disease law[83]

Washington, one of the states noted immediately above, is a monopolistic fund state. Monopolistic fund states create some unusual problems inasmuch as private insurers cannot write workers compensation coverage in the four monopolistic fund states – **North Dakota, Ohio, Washington** and **Wyoming**. In addition, self-insurance is not permitted in the state of North Dakota and Wyoming.

In addition to the two scenarios described above, there are also other approaches that merit consideration. The first is the use of written agreements to establish, prior to the occurrence of a workplace incident, the state law under which workers compensation benefits will be payable in the case of a workplace accident. Another subject, more prominently found with the states in the Northwest portion of the country, is the use of reciprocal agreements to establish state of entitlement. Reciprocal agreements, while in some instances referred to in the statute, are not creatures of statute, but are the result of negotiations between insurance regulators between states.

EXPRESS WRITTEN AGREEMENTS

Express written agreements between the employer and employee establishing that benefits of a particular state to be payable in the case of a work-related injury, are generally considered ineffective either to enlarge the applicability of that state's statute or to diminish the applicability of the statutes of other states. This is most obvious when such an agreement purports to deny jurisdiction where it otherwise exists. This is specifically addressed in *Larson's Workers Compensation* § 143.07 [1] *–"Express agreement between employer and employee that the statue of a named state shall apply is ineffective either to enlarge the applicability of that states' statute or to diminish the applicability of the statutes of other states. Whatever the rule may be as to questions involving commercial paper, interest, usury, and the like, the rule in workers compensation is dictated by the overriding consideration that compensation is not a private matter to be arranged between two parties: the public has a profound interest in the matter which cannot be altered by any individual agreements."*

Notwithstanding the above, a number of states have enacted provisions permitting the employer and employee to enter into a written or contractual agreement to select the jurisdiction where benefits are to be provided. If both parties (the employer and the employee), preceding the occurrence of a work-related injury, agree to accept the benefits as provided in the agreement, then there is nothing that would forestall its application.

The statutes in **Alabama, Alaska, Delaware, Kentucky, New Mexico, Pennsylvania,** and **Washington** contain a concise provision recognizing the right of the employer and employee to enter into such an agreement. To illustrate their approach, the Alabama statute provides for the

---
[83] Pa. Stat. Ann. Title 77 § 411.2

following: *"An employee whose duties require him to travel regularly in the service of his employer in this and one or more other states may, by written agreement with his employer, provide that his employment is principally localized in this or another state; and, unless the other state refuses jurisdiction, the agreement shall be given effect under this section."*[84]

However, it is interesting to read a recent decision from the **Alabama** appellate court, where an Alabama resident had sustained injuries in a work-related vehicular accident in Alabama. The court held that in spite of a broad provision in her employment agreement that indicated her employment was principally localized in Tennessee, and that jurisdiction for disputes related to her employment would be determined in Tennessee, she could seek workers compensation benefits before an Alabama court. The appellate court also stressed that, as a general rule, an employee may not validly contract away the employee's right to seek workers compensation benefits under the Act for a covered accident.[85]

RECIPROCAL AGREEMENTS BETWEEN STATES

While negotiated agreements between the employer and an employee are generally not recognized as binding on the parties or the jurisdiction, agreements relative to which jurisdiction should provide benefits may be negotiated between states. These agreements are referred to as reciprocal agreements.

Not every state will recognize another state's extraterritorial provision. Essentially, some states don't care what another state law provides; employees working in their jurisdiction will abide by and be subject to the law of the state in which the employee is working, allowing the employee more benefit selection options. Reciprocal agreements are generally negotiated between states, most often insurance regulator to insurance regulator. The agreement will say something to the effect that, "*We will not fine companies insured in your state when they have a worker who is injured in our state if it is just temporary work under a specified set of conditions, if you will do the same for us.*"

To illustrate how a reciprocal agreement might operate, we can use the states of **Washington** and **Oregon**. Our example begins with an employer based in Washington with all of the employees working in Washington. There is a conference in Portland, Oregon and the employer decides to send a number of employees to Oregon for the conference. While at the conference, one of the employees is injured and files a claim in Oregon for Oregon workers compensation benefits. The employer does not have Oregon coverage.

The injured worker insists that they be provided Oregon benefits and complains to the regulator. (This is assuming that the claim meets all the requirements for compensation in both Oregon and Washington.) The regulator has two choices. First, the regulator can send the claim to the uninsured employer pool and fine the employer for failure to secure workers compensation coverage in Oregon. On the other hand, the regulator can say to the injured worker, we have a

---

[84] Ala. Code § 25-5-35 (c)
[85] *Sellers v. Venture Express, Inc.*, 2021 Ala. Civ. App. LEXIS 9 (2021)

reciprocal agreement with the State of Washington, your claim comes under the jurisdiction of that agreement, your employer has coverage in Washington, and we are therefore denying your claim for Oregon benefits. Under the second scenario, the injured worker would not be entitled to Oregon benefits and would be directed to file for benefits in the state of Washington.

If we use the same example as above, but the work performed in Oregon was not just attending a conference, but the worker had been sent there to do work for a week or two and the work was outside the limits of the reciprocal agreement, the worker injured in Oregon could now file for Oregon benefits and the insurance carrier would accept the claim as an Oregon claim and pay Oregon benefits. If the employer's workers compensation policy did not have an extraterritorial rider providing coverage in the state of Oregon, then the insurer would deny acceptance of the claim for Oregon benefits, and the Oregon regulator would come after the employer for failure to secure Oregon insurance for work the employer was performing in Oregon.

Since **Washington** is an exclusive fund state, the problem arises frequently. Employers insured by the state fund must purchase separate coverage for exposures in other states, unless the Washington worker injured in another state comes under any reciprocal agreement that might be in place with the regulators in the other state. It is also to be noted that many reciprocal agreements exclude construction activities and construction employers. In those situations, those employers must purchase coverage for any construction work from carriers admitted to write workers compensation insurance in that state.

Reciprocal agreements differ between states. Many of them are very old and updating them may be difficult to achieve legislatively. According to a former industrial accident board administrator, sometimes there exists what appears to be a valid agreement with another state and a new regulator comes into office and will no longer honor the agreement arranged by the former regulator. Because of all of the confusion and inconsistency, many employers wind up paying fines or forced to buy duplicate coverage.

Being aware of the reciprocal status between states will allow better decisions when considering the need to extend standard workers compensation policy coverage to a particular state. The difficulty lies in the fact that the states do not have relatable reciprocal agreements. For instance, **Oregon** fully reciprocates with 24 states according to the Oregon state web site while **Idaho** lists seven states with whom they reciprocate. **Washington** has reciprocal agreements with **Idaho, Montana, Nevada, North Dakota, Oregon, South Dakota, Utah,** and **Wyoming.** The agreements with Montana and Nevada do not include construction work. (Note that the majority of states with reciprocal agreements are located in the Northwest section of the country.)

Each state develops and adopts its own reciprocal agreements. States that mutually honor the other's extraterritorial provisions limit the injured employee's choice of jurisdictional benefits to those of the home state or state to which the employee is primarily assigned. Employees injured while working in a non-reciprocating state may have their choice of any of the four employee options discussed previously.

Chapter Three

SECURITY ARRANGEMENTS AND UNDERWRITING

WORKERS COMPENSATION SECURITY ARRANGEMENTS

The need for a fair and equitable system of workers compensation evolved out of the industrial revolution. As economic and industrial activities flourished, the number of worker injuries also grew. The increasing use of machinery, new concepts of producing goods, and the pressure of increased demand for products resulted in a greater number of industrial injuries without solutions for employers and employees. Only a few large employers had sufficient resources to guarantee injured employees these mandated benefits without endangering their solvency. For those employers not large enough to self-insure, the vast majority purchased insurance protection against these mandated liabilities.

Depending upon the state in which an employer conducts its business, the employer must either apply for authorization to self-insure, purchase insurance from a private insurer, or in certain states, obtain coverage through a state insurance fund. There are two types of state funds: competitive state funds that compete with private insurers, or monopolistic state funds that serve as the sole provider of workers compensation in the particular jurisdiction. For employers unable to purchase insurance either through the voluntary market, in most states, there are residual market mechanisms known as assigned risk pools that serve as a last resort for employers who have been rejected by the voluntary market.

Except for the state of **Texas** where the workers compensation law is elective, employers who fail to purchase insurance or qualify for self-insurance are subject to fines or penalties for non-compliance. Should an injury occur to an employee of an employer without insurance, most states provide that such employer is liable to a direct action for damages without benefit of the three common law defenses.

The following provides an overview of the primary forms of security available through the mechanism of insurance whereby the employer purchases a policy of protection either from an agent, broker or through the direct sale of the product from the insurer.

EXCLUSIVE STATE FUNDS

The first type of compulsory workmen's compensation insurance provided by statute was in Washington in 1911 through a state fund created exclusively for that purpose. **Michigan**, **Nevada, Oregon, Wyoming,** and **North Dakota** followed, in that order. By the end of 1916, six states had established exclusive (monopolistic) state funds. Contributions to such a fund were in the nature of taxes rather than premiums, and it was perhaps for this reason that the systems were adopted.

Exclusive funds were established on the assumption that: (1) these funds would have low expenses, permitting them to return the bulk of monies collected in the form of benefits; (2) all employers in the jurisdiction would be certain of a market to purchase insurance; and (3) private insurers would not be in a position to make a profit on this mandated form of social insurance.

As of January 1, 2021, four states continued to rely upon an exclusive state fund for the offering of workers compensation insurance. These states include **North Dakota, Ohio, Washington,** and **Wyoming.** Effective July 1, 1999, **Nevada** no longer provided insurance through a state fund. On January 1, 2006, **West Virginia** abolished its monopolistic state fund (the Workers Compensation Commission) and replaced it with a newly formed insurance company called BrickStreet Mutual Insurance Company. In the November 2010 election, the state of **Washington** had an initiative on the ballot which was intended to open up the workers compensation market to private competition. This initiative was defeated by the voters.

The following provides a brief description of the operations and coverage afforded through the four remaining exclusive state funds:

North Dakota has its own dedicated rating organization that handles and administers its workers compensation insurance arrangement. With limited exception, North Dakota law requires all employers to secure workers compensation insurance to cover their full-time, part-time, seasonal, or occasional employees at the time of hire. Out-of-state employers with full-time employees working in North Dakota must secure workers compensation insurance on those workers in North Dakota unless the employer's home state is one having a reciprocal agreement with North Dakota. If the employer's workers compensation insurance extends into North Dakota, and any one employee earns 25 percent or more of his or her gross annual wage in the state, or 25 percent or more of the employer's total payroll is for employees working in the state, coverage is required and the employer must report all payroll generated in the state.

Ohio has two separate and distinct operations in its state organization to handle and administer its workers compensation insurance arrangement. The Bureau of Workers Compensation handles the day-to-day operations, other than legal issues. The Industrial Commission is the organization that resolves legal issues. This includes, but is not limited to, contested or disputed claims, publishing rates and assigning classifications.

Employers that are required to provide workers compensation coverage may select from one of two available options. The first option is to purchase workers compensation insurance from the state fund. The second is to self-insure within the state rules and guidelines for doing so. All private and public employers that have at least one employee must purchase workers compensation coverage. This requirement also applies to employers of domestic employees whose earnings exceed a stated minimum amount or threshold.

Washington handles and administers its workers compensation arrangement through the Department of Labor and Industries. All employers, both public and private, are required to provide coverage for all employees with a few exceptions. Coverage is not mandatory for corporate officers, partners, sole proprietors, and domestic workers. However, coverage is required for domestic workers when two or more are employed on a full-time basis. Washington also law provides for self-insurance to a limited extent, but it is subject to a number of narrow and strict requirements and involves a substantial financial commitment by the employer who seeks to self-insure.

Wyoming has a Workers Compensation Division that administers the state insurance system. Workers compensation coverage is mandatory in the state program for hazardous operations as defined, as well as for other specific and defined operations. Employers engaged in operations other than those in hazardous occupations have the option of not providing workers compensation coverage at all or of purchasing coverage from private insurance companies. While workers compensation coverage is available through private insurance companies for certain employers, the state establishes the rates for each industry or business classification.

Exclusive state funds are largely subject to the same regulatory requirements as private companies, in terms of surplus and reserves. Major independent accounting and actuarial firms validate the funds' financial position and reserves. Like private insurance carriers, exclusive funds maintain unearned premium reserves reflecting the obligation of the fund to provide protection in the future because of premiums or deposits in hand.

Loss reserves are established on the basis of individual or average case cost estimates. The funds employ accredited actuaries to establish these estimates. Where loss reserves are found to be inadequate, the state fund has the authority to increase insurance rates to remedy the problem of rate inadequacy. An exclusive state fund has the advantage that it can increase premiums in order to avert insolvency without fear of losing its customers because employers have only the single source of the state fund for coverage.

In exclusive fund states, it should be noted that although workers compensation insurance is generally considered to be the exclusive remedy for injury to employees, in some cases an employer may be held liable (and sued) for injuries to his/her employees. These cases include consequential injury (loss of consortium, loss of services, etc.) to an injured employee's family members, dual capacity claims, intentional tort claims, and claims for injury or disease not covered by workers compensation laws. (The final chapter in this text is devoted to exceptions to the exclusive remedy in the workers compensation program.)

To obtain coverage for these exposures – all of which are also specifically excluded under commercial general liability insurance – the employer needs employer's liability insurance. Standard workers compensation policies include this coverage in addition to coverage for the payment of statutory workers compensation benefits. Employer's liability insurance is not offered by monopolistic fund states. Employers operating in these states need insurance protection for those claims or suits by employees that fall outside the immunity provided to employers under workers compensation statutes. To fill that gap in coverage, "stop gap" coverage, available from private insurance companies, has been developed in which coverage for defense costs is typically included.

Employers can buy stop gap coverage from private insurers. A common way to provide stop gap coverage is to add it as an endorsement to a commercial general liability policy. If an employer operates in several states, in one or more of which a standard workers compensation policy applies, employer's liability coverage for operations in the monopolistic state may be obtained through the purchase of a stop gap endorsement and adding it to the workers compensation policy.

All employers who apply to a monopolistic state fund for coverage must be accepted. This inability to select risks affects the loss experience of the fund. Rating factors to increase the rates may be applied by the fund where the employer has a poor loss history. These rating factors may also decrease the rates for employers with better than average claim experience, and higher rates for those employers with worse than average claim experience. Because the fund must accept all risks that apply for coverage, there is no residual market or market of last resort in monopolistic fund states.

COMPETITIVE STATE FUNDS

A competitive state fund is a state-owned and operated fund that provides workers compensation insurance to employers operating in that state. Competitive state funds compete directly with private insurance carriers for business in the state where the state fund was organized. Competitive state funds were established with a number of the same underlying assumptions that applied to the establishment of exclusive state funds, but with the added assumption that competition with private insurers would result in the best combination of both service and pricing. It was also felt by many that a competitive state fund would serve to enhance competition among private insurers.

During the 1990s, competitive state funds were often created as a means to gain some control over the rising cost of workers compensation insurance for employers. In other words, in many instances they were formed to address a unique crisis in accessing affordable workers compensation insurance. Typically these funds were formed through the action of the state legislature who established the fund, provided initial start-up capital and provided a level of initial fund management.

In 1912, **Michigan** established the first state fund in which employers could be insured, and at the same time, private insurers were also permitted to compete for the business. Shortly thereafter, competitive state funds of a similar nature were established in **California, Colorado, Maryland, Montana, New York, Pennsylvania,** and **Utah.**

Oregon, which began initially as an exclusive state fund, converted to a competitive state fund in 1965. By 1970, there were 12 competitive state funds operating in the United States. With upward pressure on insurance rates that occurred during the middle to latter part of the 1980's, a number of additional states created competitive state funds for the purpose of stabilizing the workers compensation market.

The following lists the current competitive state along with the year the fund was established:

Arizona - State Compensation Fund	(1925)
California - State Compensation Insurance Fund	(1913)
Hawaii - Hawaii Employers Mutual Insurance Company	(1985)
Idaho - State Insurance Fund	(1918)
Kentucky - Kentucky Employers' Mutual Insurance Authority	(1994)
Louisiana – Louisiana Workers Compensation Corporation	(1991)
Minnesota - State Fund Mutual Insurance Company	(1983)
Missouri - Missouri Employers Mutual Insurance Company	(1993)
Montana- Montana State Fund	(1915)
New Mexico – New Mexico Mutual Casualty Company	(1991)
New York – The State Insurance Fund	(1913)
Oregon - State Accident Insurance Fund Corporation	(1965)
Pennsylvania - State Workmen's Insurance Fund	(1915)
Rhode Island – The Beacon Mutual Insurance Company	(1990)
Utah - Workers Compensation Fund of Utah	(1917)

In the life cycle of a competitive state fund, it is not unusual to find that at some point, managers of the fund will attempt to establish a separation from its state affiliation. A number of the funds originally established as competitive funds have subsequently reorganized in order to become mutual insurers. For example, in 2001, the **Texas** Workers Compensation Insurance Fund became the Texas Mutual Insurance Company and in 2002, the **Colorado** fund became Pinnacol Assurance Fund.

Another example is found in the state of **Maine**. Maine Employers' Mutual Insurance Company (MEMIC) is a competitive state fund that opened for business in January 1993 as a private mutual insurance company. In 2000, MEMIC formed MEMIC Indemnity Company, a subsidiary based in Manchester, New Hampshire. Today, MEMIC Indemnity Company is licensed to serve employers in 46 states with a focus on territories across the Eastern Seaboard from Maine to Florida. In 2012, MEMIC acquired a Vermont-based insurer and created MEMIC Casualty Company to provide greater flexibility in pricing.

Along with Maine, two states that have recently changed their competitive state funds to mutual companies include **Maryland**, where in 2012 the legislature converted the Maryland Injured Workers Fund to the newly named Chesapeake Employers Insurance Company. In 2013, the **Oklahoma** legislature converted CompSource Oklahoma (which was formerly the Oklahoma State Insurance Fund) into the CompSource Domestic Mutual Insurance Company. The new company is independent of the state of Oklahoma and began its operations January 1, 2015.

With these changes occurring within the competitive state fund environment, it is sometimes difficult to differentiate between a competitive state fund and a private insurance carrier. One distinction being that these companies originally began as competitive state funds and monies from the state were used in creating these funds. In all instances, this original source of financing has been reimbursed to the state. A second means to continue to distinguish between these two types of entities is to identify those insurers required to pay federal taxes. If the insurer is not required to pay federal taxes, it would be categorized as a competitive state fund.

PRIVATE INSURANCE

With the exception of the four exclusive state funds, private insurance carriers are permitted to underwrite workers compensation coverage in the remaining states plus the **District of Columbia**. Private insurers can be classified according to their legal form of organization and their marketing methods. Insurers may be classified as either stock companies or mutual insurers.

- Stock companies have owners who bear the risk of the insurer and whose representatives manage the day-to-day operations of the company. The typical example is the stock insurer that is owned by stockholders who operate through a board of directors.

- Mutual insurers have no owners other than their policyholders. A mutual is represented by a board of directors that is elected by policyholders exercising their right to vote. Unlike stock companies, a mutual does not have capital stock. The distinct feature of mutual insurers is that retained earnings, also known as policyholder surplus, serve as the capital structure of the company and is returned in the form of dividends to policyholders based on good performance.

Private insurers market their services through independent agents and brokers, or in the case of direct writers, through their own employees. Independent agents typically represent several different insurance carriers, receive a commission for the business they place with an insurer, and as the representative of the insured retain the right to renew a customer's insurance contract with the same or another insurer. The typical commission is based upon a percentage of the premium for the insurance coverage provided.

In March of 2020, the National Association of Insurance Commissioners (NAIC) released the names and market share of the top 25 workers compensation company's direct written premium for 2019. Total direct written premium for the 25 companies was $56,132,546,749.

The top five companies include:

Company	Direct Written Premium	Market Share
Travelers	$4,211,528,800	7.5%
Hartford Fire	$3,365,297,798	6.0%
Zurick Ins. Group	$2,640,320,129	4.7%
Liberty Mutual Group	$2,447,305,755	4.35%
Chubb Ltd. Group	$2,430,117,636	4.33%

In each state in which private insurers operate, they are subject to insurance regulation at the state level. State insurance departments are the principal regulators with respect to the formation and approval of new insurance companies, licensing of foreign insurers, oversight of the continued solvency of insurers, and their business practices; particularly as such practices apply to rates and forms of coverage.

State workers compensation industrial accident boards, bureaus or commissions are mostly concerned with the claims handling practices of an insurance carrier. These state administrative agencies monitor the reporting of claims, ensure timely payment of benefits by the insurer, and provide for the initial levels of dispute resolution. These agencies have become more involved in the collection of statistical data for purposes of monitoring insurer performance and in identifying cost-drivers in the system.

Insurer solvency is regulated primarily by the state insurance department by checking on the valuation of an insurers liabilities and the nature and valuation of their assets. Insurance departments check on these two aspects of insurer operations primarily through annual statements that furnish detailed information on premiums, losses, expenses, assets, and liabilities, and conduct in-house examinations of insurer assets, financial records and operations.

The assets of insurers are regulated to some extent in how the insurer invests its funds, the valuation of its assets, and whether such assets are admitted or non-admitted. Although insurers invest some funds in real and personal property required to transact their business, the bulk of their assets are invested in bonds or stocks. State laws vary in their regulations and restrictions on these investments.

In most states today, filed rates used by insurers incorporate the loss costs approved by the state insurance department along with the insurer's administrative expenses. These administrative expenses include a small factor for profit. Looking at the premium dollar, it is generally recognized that approximately 64.5 cents of each premium dollar goes toward actual claim expenses while the balance – 35.5 cents – goes toward an insurer's administrative expenses. The following reflects a typical example of how the administrative expenses of an insurer are divided:

State Premium Tax Expense	3.5%
Loss Adjustment Expense	8.5%
Acquisition Expense	13.5%
General Expenses	7.5%
Profit and Contingency Expense	2.5%
Total Expense Loading	35.5%

It is important to recognize that these expense loadings are merely an example and vary from state to state and insurer to insurer. These figures also do not reflect premium discounts, reduced acquisition expenses, and in some states, premium taxes, residual market charges, administrative agency surcharges, assessments for second injury funds, rehabilitation funds, etc.

Individual private insurers underwrite their business and are free to reject any applicant they consider to be a poor or undesirable risk. An employer may be considered an undesirable risk because of a poor loss record or the employer may be engaged in hazardous operations or has a catastrophic exposure that the insurance company does not wish to cover. In states where the residual market is not handled by a competitive state fund, private insurers share in the financial obligations that stem from the residual market, known as the assigned risk plan.

Because workers compensation insurers may be exposed to a catastrophic loss when a large number of employees are injured in a single incident, most insurers shift some of the risk associated with a catastrophic loss by purchasing reinsurance against some portion of the loss in excess of a stated amount. Reinsurance is insurance that is purchased by an insurance company (the ceding company) from one or more insurance companies (the reinsurer) in order to manage its risk exposure

On a less frequent basis, insurers may also purchase aggregate excess insurance that protects against aggregate losses in a single year that exceed a specific portion of their premiums or dollar amount. Through the mechanism of reinsurance, insurers reduce their risk by sharing it with one or more reinsurers for a ceding reinsurance premium.

RESIDUAL MARKETS

With the exception of **Texas** where the purchase of workers compensation coverage is optional, in all other jurisdictions workers compensation is mandatory depending upon the eligibility requirements of the state. Depending upon the state, employers can purchase workers compensation insurance from a private insurance company, a competitive state fund, a monopolistic state fund, or self-insure. Because workers compensation insurance is a mandatory coverage in essentially every state, some type of market of last resort or "residual market" mechanism (in some states referred to as the assigned risk plan or pool) must exist so as to ensure coverage for any employer not able to secure coverage in the voluntary market.

There are multiple reasons why an employer may have difficulty obtaining insurance coverage in the voluntary market. Some of the more prominent include:

- A poor loss history with many small losses may raise questions as to management's commitment to safety.

- A new business often lacks a track record of claim experience for purposes of assessing exposure.

- A very small business may not generate sufficient premium to cover the administrative cost in issuing a policy along with the risk of claims.

- Hazardous occupations like logging, trucking, and roofing often find it difficult to obtain coverage in the voluntary market.

The way the residual market is handled varies from state to state. All states have designated an administrator that operates the assigned risk plan and oversees the issuance of policies. In most states, the administrator is one of the following: (1) the National Council on Compensation Insurance (NCCI); (2) the state competitive insurance fund; or (3) The state rating organization or some other third party.

The NCCI administers plans on behalf of 22 jurisdictions. Each of these states requires all workers compensation insurers that operate within its borders to participate in the assigned risk plan. Insurers may either join a multi-state reinsurance pool or serve as a "direct assignment" carrier. When an insurer participates in a pooling arrangement, it may act as a servicing carrier (issuing policies and paying claims) or provide reinsurance to servicing carriers. If an insurer chooses the direct assignment option, it must agree to accept and retain all risks assigned by the NCCI. The direct assignment insurer pays all losses incurred by the assigned employers and is not reimbursed by reinsurance.

In 14 states, the assigned risk plan is administered by the state competitive fund. Examples are **California, New York**, and **Montana.** Most of the remaining states have designated their rating organization or an insurer as their plan administrator.[2]

In states administered by the NCCI, the general requirement is that the employer must be rejected for coverage by at least three private insurers before qualifying for placement with the residual market mechanism.

The residual market population ebbs and flows depending upon general market conditions. In any given state, when market conditions are favorable and rates are adequate, insurers are more likely to voluntarily write business. This is described as a "soft market" that creates a competitive environment for employers and the residual market is generally at its lowest level. However, when market conditions are unfavorable due to inadequate rates, scarce or expensive reinsurance or other factors, the market is described as a "hard market" and insurers tighten up their underwriting standards and become more selective. Under these conditions, availability for insurance becomes constricted and the pool residual market begins to grow.

If the residual market becomes too large in a state, this is generally a sign that the voluntary market has essentially evaporated. This occurred in the late 1980s when the residual market burgeoned. In **Massachusetts** for example, the residual market grew to the extent that it accounted for more than 65 percent of the entire premium in the Commonwealth and more than 80 percent of all employers were in the assigned risk pool. Over time, through a combination of rate stabilization and the introduction of an innovative credit program – the Qualified Loss Management Program (QLMP) which was designed to de-populate the pool by offering a credit to employers who successfully improved the safety of their operations thereby controlling losses – thousands of employers improved their loss experience and were able to exit the residual market.

The same market constriction occurred in **Maine** at nearly the same time which culminated in the creation of the Maine competitive state fund, the Mutual Employers Insurance Company (MEMIC).

When an employer is in a competitive market, that employer has some leverage in terms of price and service. Employers in the residual market enjoy no such advantages and the cost of coverage is frequently higher than in the voluntary market. Employers that find themselves in an assigned risk pool may be: (1) subject to costly surcharges and significantly higher rates; (2) ineligible for premium discounts or schedule- credits; (3) limited in terms of available loss control services; and (4) have little or no choice in terms of their servicing carrier.

SELF-INSURANCE

Alternate methods to finance workers compensation exposures become more attractive when the traditional insurance market hardens. Workers compensation, in particular, lends itself to self-insurance due to several aspects inherent in its nature.

- There is a statutory cap on loss wage benefits payable that brings an element of certainty to the severity of losses to be expected.

- The payment of large claims is spread over time providing cash-flow advantages to the self-insuring employer.

- Typically, workers compensation loss patterns are high volume, low severity, which translates to a fairly predictable loss forecasting analysis.[86]

Self-insurance is a risk managing method by an employer or member employers in a group self-insurance program, in lieu of purchasing workers compensation insurance, of setting aside an actuarially calculated amount of funds to pay losses to injured employees. These self-insured employers are financially responsible for the losses and expenses associated with their workers compensation program. Self-insurance can be an attractive alternative to traditional insurance because it may be less costly for the employer by eliminating the private insurer's profit margin, so long as the program is managed in a professional manner.

To successfully manage a self-insurance program, it is necessary to implement a quality safety program as well as claims services provided through an insurer or third party claims administrator. Further, it is important to analyze the tax considerations, and the "opportunity cost" of paying an insurer a premium instead of directly paying losses and expenses, and the expertise required to set adequate loss reserves for the unpaid claims as they occur. With the introduction of deductible programs, many large employers are reviewing their options in terms of insurance versus self-insurance. Through a greater focus on loss control, self-insurers may realize an improved loss experience which translates into a less costly form of providing workers compensation benefits.

---

[86] https://www.irmi.com/articles/expert-commentary/the-workers-compensation-self-insurance-decision

In the case of a self-insurance program – individual or group – regulation generally resides with the workers compensation administrative agency in the state or jurisdiction. In a few states (e.g., **Iowa, Maine, Minnesota, Nevada, North Carolina,** and **Tennessee**) the responsibility for regulating self-insurance resides with the insurance department. Notwithstanding the location of regulatory oversight, statutory provisions along with adopted administrative rules are the common vehicles for setting forth the threshold of requirements in order to qualify for self-insurance.

There are numerous issues for the employer to consider when contemplating self-insurance. While there is no single approach applicable to all employers, experts in the field indicate that a feasibility study for self-insurance should be undertaken when an employer has about $150,000 of premium in one state or $250,000 of premium when operating in multiple states.

Once a decision has been made to consider the feasibility of self-insurance, it is necessary to review the filing requirements in the state in which the employer operates. Approval must be obtained from the appropriate regulatory agency in each state or jurisdiction in which the employer seeks to be self-insured. While the requirements for approval vary from state-to-state, the following lists some of the more pertinent points for consideration.

Filing Fee – The filing fee for self-insurance is an incidental expense required to cover the administrative costs of the regulatory agency to review and act on an application for self-insurance. About a quarter of the states have no filing fee and the remainder have fees that vary between $100 and $4,000.

Minimum Net Worth – In most instances, employers are not of a sufficient size to consider self-insurance. Some states have established minimum net worth thresholds as guidelines for approving self-insurance. These minimum thresholds of net worth are as low as $250,000 in **Arkansas** and rise to the level of $10 million in **Arizona**. In many instances, the question of minimum net worth is determined by the regulator on a case-by-case basis in conjunction with other financial considerations made as part of the application. **Minnesota**, in a somewhat unique approach, establishes the minimum net worth at 10 times the selected retention limit. The retention limit is that portion of the total losses that the employer is responsible for before ceding the loss to the reinsurer.

Security Deposit – In order to ensure that a self-insured employer can meet their financial obligations, the state regulator will typically require the posting of a surety bond for collateral. Not all states require the posting of security, but for those that do, the amount of security varies from $100,000 (**Arkansas, Florida, Louisiana, Maryland,** and **Mississippi**) to $500,000 in **Indiana** and **Kentucky**. **Minnesota** again is somewhat unique in requiring a security deposit of 110 percent of all outstanding workers compensation liabilities.

Reinsurance Requirements – In select states, a self-insured employer may decide to purchase insurance against a loss or losses in excess of a certain dollar threshold – their retention limit. Many states require the purchase of reinsurance or excess insurance and most indicate the minimum amount to be purchased. In the case of **Utah**, reinsurance or excess insurance is required with unlimited coverage. In certain states, reinsurance or excess insurance is not required by statute, but the regulatory agency recommends the need for such coverage as part of the approval process.

Taxes, Fees and Assessments – Moving from an insurance program to self-insurance may reduce costs in certain instances, but will not eliminate responsibility for certain taxes, fees, and assessments. Assessments necessary to fund the administrative agency and second injury funds will continue even though the assessment base may shift from a percentage of premiums to a percentage of the compensation payments made during the preceding calendar year. While in certain states the premium tax is not applicable for self-insured employers, a number of states (e.g., **Delaware, Georgia, North Carolina, Texas,** and **Utah**) have enacted specific taxes for self-insurers in lieu of the traditional insurance premium tax. A number of states have also established self-insurance guaranty funds – as a protection against default on the part of a self-insured employer – in which all self-insurers must participate.

Reporting Requirements – Financial reporting to the state regulatory agency is part of the filing requirements when seeking approval to self-insure. This reporting of annual financial information and conducting of audits continues after approval has been granted. The purpose is to ensure the financial viability of any organization that has taken on the obligation to pay compensation benefits to the employees of the organization.

There is an additional consideration for employers contemplating self-insurance. The more states an organization operates in, the greater the administrative costs associated with the self-insurance program since the organization must file its plan for approval in each state where it hopes to operate as a self-insurer. Additionally, state requirements for self-insurance vary and should be carefully reviewed so that the administrative burden for self-insurance does not become overwhelming or cost prohibitive. When an organization has some of its operations in states that do not allow self-insurance, arrangements must be made to handle these states separately through workers compensation insurance. This can also increase the administrative workload.[87]

It is important to note that individual and group self-insurers are not required to participate in the residual market for employers unable to otherwise purchase insurance. Also, individual and group self-insurers may obtain claims and other administrative through the establishment of in-house operations, or may elect to obtain these services from a third party administrator (TPA).

Individual Self-Insurance - An individual employer who provides compensation protection by furnishing proof of financial ability to pay compensation benefits is identified as a self-insurer. In all jurisdictions with the exception of **North Dakota** and **Wyoming** employers are permitted under certain conditions to self-insure for workers compensation. To qualify as a self-insurer, the employer must deposit with the appropriate regulatory agency such securities as may be required by law. In some instances, this security may be in the form of a bond purchased from a surety company authorized to transact business in the state.

---

[87] Ibid.

In all states where employers are permitted to self-insure their workers compensation obligations, the standards for qualification vary considerably from state to state moving from the very general to the very specific. The qualifying procedures for individual self-insurance are generally not overly complicated, but it is necessary that a separate application be filed and approved for each state where operations are to be self-insured. It is the responsibility of the state's administrative agencies to make certain that employees will be paid for compensable injuries, both currently and for many years in the future in the case of a catastrophic or fatal injury.

The application form for self-insurance includes a request for information on loss control activities which describe the specific organization of the safety program, recordkeeping procedures, training programs, safety-related incentive programs, loss history, etc. Specifications are often required as to how claims will be administered and what firm or individuals will be responsible for investigating and handling claims. While each state adopts its own application form, it is important to bring to the attention of the approving authorities any factors that will favorably influence the regulators opinion of the employer's ability to fulfill workers compensation obligations in future years.

It may take anywhere from one to six months to receive approval or disapproval of an application. Some states will schedule hearings on an individual basis; others will consider applications only during specified times. Unless an applicant for workers compensation self-insurance is a veritable giant, the entity will be required to secure its obligation to pay benefits through one or more forms of security. Surety bonds are acceptable in all states. Most states accept cash escrow accounts or certificates of deposit. Some accept debt obligations of the state or federal government, and others will accept letters of credit. It is also becoming increasingly popular to use several forms of collateral to satisfy a security obligation.

The adoption of stricter capital requirements for banks by the Federal Reserve Corporation in 1989 had an adverse effect on the availability and cost of letters of credit. This has influenced the decision-making process for methods of financing risks. Specifically, paid-loss retrospective rating and other cash-flow plans developed to compete with self-insurance, including the more recent large-deductible plans, require the use of collateral to support the deferred premium or deductible elements. The most common form of collateral has been a letter of credit.

A surety bond is a financial guarantee or a promise by the insured (principal) to reimburse the surety (the insurer) should there ever be a payment made under the bond. Letters of credit are not necessarily required to secure surety bonds, but can be depending upon the amount of the obligation under bond.

Whether required by law, regulatory authority, or good risk management judgment, any program of self-insurance is almost certain to be dependent on an insurer providing some form of reinsurance or excess protection. A number of states require specific excess coverage with minimum limit requirements. In some cases, excess coverage is required only for certain businesses or under certain circumstances. There are two basic types of excess coverage, specific and aggregate:

- **Specific Excess Coverage** – With specific excess coverage, the self-insurer assumes a pre-determined amount of the loss arising out of any one occurrence, and the insurer (or reinsurer) is responsible for any losses in excess of this sum, up to the limit of the policy. A typical arrangement is to have a per-occurrence limit ranging from $1 million to $5 million in excess of a self-insured retention of $250,000 or $500,000. As the first million dollars of specific excess insurance will cover most exposures, increasing the limit to $2 million or $5 million to take care of a catastrophic loss is generally a practical consideration. Obviously, the increase in cost will reflect the amount of the self-insured retention, type of business, etc. Each additional $1 million of coverage will generally cost much less than the first $1 million, as only a small number of losses would be expected to exceed the first $1 million.

  Another option, which has become increasingly available in the marketplace, is to purchase specific excess coverage on a "statutory" basis. With this option, the reinsurer covers each occurrence from the attachment point (for example, $250,000) for whatever additional sums are required by statute in the jurisdiction in which the employer is self-insuring

- **Aggregate Excess Coverage** – Aggregate excess coverage is generally written to cover losses which exceed some percentage of the normal premium. Typically, the normal premium is the standard premium an insurer would charge before discounts, dividends, or participation, but this may be calculated differently from one insurer to another. It may or may not reflect experience rating charges or credits.

  Aggregate coverage is generally written by the same insurer providing specific excess coverage. Often, this is done through the use of a single policy that provides both types of stop loss insurance, but separate policies are also commonly used. Obviously, the retention and limits of the specific coverage will be reflected in the underwriting and rating of the aggregate excess insurance. In some states, aggregate excess coverage is not considered in determining financial stability or the amount of security required. Administrative authorities may require an applicant to purchase excess coverage of a particular type and amount, even though it is not mandated by law.

It is important to keep in mind that the standard workers compensation policy does not contain any specific limit of liability with respect to the workers compensation obligations of an employer, although specific limits are applicable to the employer's liability portion of the policy. While it is possible to write specific excess coverage to provide indemnification for the full benefits payable under a workers compensation law, it is common for both specific excess and aggregate excess coverage to be subject to a limit of liability. In case of a catastrophic accident or a series of losses, it is possible to exhaust all of the excess coverage and pay losses far higher than ever contemplated.

To a large extent, the success of any self-insured plan will depend on how effectively the employer manages loss prevention and loss control activities. Different types of servicing agencies are willing and able to act as a third party administrator (TPA) or provide a wide variety of services for self-insured companies. Some of the services available through various vendors include: occupational safety training; occupational disease control; air and water pollution surveys; claims investigation, settlement, and defense; loss statistical reporting; Occupational Safety and Health Administration (OSHA) surveys; physical and vocational rehabilitation; product safety consultation; and industrial hygiene surveys. Each of the noted services may not be required by the self-insured, but every self-insurer needs some of these services; even those that have the apparent capabilities to administer a self-insured program in-house.

Because workers compensation protection is closely regulated, self-insured programs have legal requirements that impose special responsibilities on a firm. Effective service is crucial – not only to handle claims and control losses, but also to assure that the firm is complying with workers compensation laws. Qualifying for self-insurance is not an overly complicated process, but it does require a certain amount of involvement in government regulations. Many service organizations are available to assist an employer in designing a program of self-insurance to satisfy the requirements of the law.

Self-Insurance Groups (SIGs) – Self-Insurance Groups (SIGs) represent a pooling arrangement wherein a number of employers come together for the purpose of insuring their workers compensation exposure. SIGs are permitted in a total of 39 states. Again, in addition to **North Dakota** and **Wyoming** where self-insurance is not permitted, SIGs are not permitted in 11 states.

Employers that are not large enough to self-insure on their own may consider forming a group in order to pool their workers compensation losses and expenses. By doing so, an employer may be able to take advantage of the benefits of self-insurance, gaining more control over claims and costs much as an individual self-insured can. While many of the pros and cons are the same for a self-insurance group as for an individual self-insured, there are distinct pros and cons to pooling risk as a member of a group.

As a member of a SIG, the employer pays premiums into a trust or corporation based on classification codes, payrolls, rates, and experience modifications developed by, or in accordance with, the state's rate-making bureau. Those premiums pay for claims administration, covered losses, reinsurance, and any other costs pertaining to the management of the group (legal, actuarial, etc.). Surplus premiums are returned to members based on the group's yearly loss experience. Unlike individual self-insurance, where reserves are not tax deductible, with a SIG, the reserves are part of the premium paid to the group – often a nonprofit corporation established by the group for the sole purpose of orchestrating insurance for the group. The premium is fully deductible as a business expense. Of course, the surplus refunds (e.g., dividends) are taxable, as are any other insurance dividends.

Without question the most critical aspect of a SIG is that all group members are in good financial condition. Some states require that the entire group have a net worth to premium ratio of, for example, at least four to one. The state may not necessarily impose the same requirement on individual group members. The group should consider requiring each individual member to have at least the same ratio as is required by the state to assure that each member will be able to meet the member's financial obligations should joint and several liability become a factor due to a catastrophic loss or other unanticipated contingency.

Some states allow heterogeneous (mixed type of industries) groups of employers to pool for purposes of forming a SIG, but most states require homogeneous (a single type of industry) groups. The reason that homogeneous groups are favored is because it is easier to predict losses for companies with similar industrial exposures. If all members belong to a single industry type or class, they will obviously have much in common, enabling them to better predict future exposure to losses.

With a decision that a SIG is a viable option, the next step for the employer is finding other employers who share an interest in forming a SIG. Trade associations often serve to identify other employers with a similar interest. However, just because other companies operate similar businesses does not mean they would be interested in forming a SIG or would be a good risk to include in the SIG.

Another issue is the number of members required to form a SIG. State regulations generally specify the minimum number of members required to form a SIG in a given state. In most instances it is better to have more than the minimum number of members to assure the tax deductibility of premiums and more accurate predictability of losses. Also, the more members in a group, the less devastating is the loss if a single member decides to withdraw from the group. At the same time, the more members in a group also increase the potential for a catastrophic loss that must be shared by all members.

After obtaining a sufficient number of employers interested in forming a SIG, a temporary board is usually selected to undertake a feasibility study. Regulations regarding the composition of the board also vary from state to state. The board is responsible for developing the group's by-laws and adopting written policies. It must also select the group's administrator. Most states require the administrator to be bonded.

The role of SIG administrator is a crucial consideration. The administrator should conduct the preliminary investigation so as to make certain that all potential members have similar operations and loss experience. Once the SIG is established, the administrator supervises the daily activities and operations of the group including such responsibilities as selecting the appropriate service providers, purchasing excess insurance, distributing dividends, and selecting new members.

The group must be able to administer and pay claims through adequate funding. The administrator should be familiar with the funding, excess insurance and historical loss requirements as well as retention limitations. From there, the appropriate data is collected from each potential member. Historical data is necessary to establish prior losses and project future losses. Loss forecasting is an extremely important element of this step in the analysis.

There are sometimes events that precipitate a member leaving a SIG. For example, a SIG member might be acquired by another entity with a different workers compensation arrangement, or a change in market conditions might lure a SIG member back to the private insurance market. To address that concern, many SIGs have membership contracts that require as much as six or more months' notice that a member is leaving.

There are other considerations that mitigate leaving a viable SIG. For example, in states where the SIG's individual members' payroll and loss information is not required to be filed with the rating organization, the departing member may have lost its experience rating in the commercial insurance market, requiring that member to start fresh with an experience modification of 1.00. Some states even consider adding 10 percent to the experience modification of any former SIG members that wants to become insured in the commercial market.

An important aspect peculiar to SIGs is joint and several liability. All SIG members are jointly and severally liable for any workers compensation and employer's liability losses suffered by any member, as well as all of the reinsurance premiums, administrative expenses, and management fees. Even if one member files bankruptcy or is terminated from the group, the remaining group members are still liable for their portion of that member's losses as well as other expenses that occurred during the period the departing member was in the group. The same holds true for a catastrophic loss that wipes out the SIG's retention funds and excess insurance.

Members are responsible for paying their pro rata share of the total loss. As a consequence, it is important for the group as a whole, and each group member individually, to take loss control and loss prevention seriously. One group member, with a commitment to cost containment that is perhaps not as solid or serious as the remaining members can cause the entire group to fail.

To illustrate the importance of the joint and several liability issue, it is beneficial to look at events that occurred in **New York** regarding their self-insurance trusts. The workers compensation law includes a provision which requires the Workers Compensation Board (WCB) to assess all self-insured employers (individual and group self-insureds) for all expenses incurred by the WCB relative to self-insured business. It has been the WCB's interpretation that these expenses include administrative and regulatory costs along with the costs of any unmet obligations incurred by an insolvent individual or group self-insurer.

Prior to the 2006/07 fiscal year there had never been a trust default in New York. In that fiscal year several groups were closed due to financial concerns. In the following fiscal year those groups, plus several additional groups became insolvent. In all, a total of 15 self-insurance trusts were shut down by the state. The trusts ran out of money because they underpriced their premiums and under reserved claims. While the scheme lasted, the administrators paid themselves handsomely for their work. The cost of the insolvency of these trusts rose to a level between $500 million and $600 million.

In response to the growing level of unfunded costs related to these insolvent groups, the provision of the law which applied to all individual and groups self-insured programs in the state came into effect. Like a stack of dominoes, as additional groups defaulted, and as the projected costs of under-reserved claims continued to grow, this assessment grew ever higher. In order to ensure that all of the obligations to injured workers would be met, the WCB began to impose assessments against all individual self-insured employers as well as members of all of the group self-insured trusts

In 2009, the New York Supreme Court declared that requiring solvent trusts to pay for the sins of insolvent trusts was a violation of the United States Constitution's "taking" clause.[88] The ruling of the Supreme Court was subsequently overruled by a four judge panel, which reinstated the assessments on the solvent trusts.[89] In 2011, the New York legislature adopted new regulations for the troubled self-insured groups that included a strengthening of the financial requirements to be a member of a group.

The situation in New York continues to be played out, but in the opinion of many, the liabilities associated with operating or being a member of a group or trust is uncontrollable and virtually unlimited.

ALTERNATIVE BENEFIT SCHEMES

When workmen's compensation laws were first being crafted, because the concept was new, a number of states included a provision permitting substitute benefit systems. For example, the **Indiana** law provided: *"Subject to the industrial board, any employer may enter into or continue any agreement with his employees to provide a system of compensation, benefits, or insurance in lieu of the compensation and insurance provided by this act. No such substitute system shall be approved unless it confers benefits upon injured employees at least equivalent to the benefits provided by this act, nor if it requires contributions from the employees unless it confers benefits in addition to those provided under this act at least commensurate with such contributions."*[90]

These provisions were intended to permit substitute systems so long as the benefits available were at least equal to those available under the workmen's compensation law. Because many of these newly enacted workmen's compensation laws were elective – permitting employers to

---

[88] *Held v. New York State Workers Compensation Board* 58 A.D.3d 971 (2009)
[89] *Held v. New York State Workers Compensation Board* 85 A.D.3d 35 (2011)
[90] Indiana Acts of 1915 Part IV. Sec. 44

forego coverage if they so choose – in order to pass constitutional muster, there was little reason for employers to consider developing substitute programs.

It was during the late 1980s that attention was drawn to the idea of a new form of an alternative benefit scheme. The general concept of 24-hour coverage was to integrate workers compensation and other employee benefits, such as employer-provided health care coverage and disability income benefits. In the initial approach, the idea was to combine into a single package coverage for work-related and non-work-related illnesses and injuries. It later evolved into a plan whereby coverage could be defined as the joint issuance of a workers compensation policy with a disability insurance policy or other medical coverage addressing both occupational and non-occupational injuries and illnesses. While the 1972 National Commission had considered the possibility of combining workers compensation with other benefit systems, writers of the report concluded that the need for some form of benefit security combination did not exist at that time.

Initially described as 20-hour coverage in the 1980s, the idea for an alternative benefit scheme sprang from the premise that there existed a patchwork of economic security programs (e.g. group health, short and long term disability, state disability insurance, workers compensation, Social Security, and Medicare, etc.) that could be addressed by creating a single program designed to create a seamless economic security program for the whole individual. The fundamental thought behind going in this direction was to reduce the administrative costs associated with these multiple programs plus reducing the friction costs and litigation related to the determination as to who was responsible for what payments.

This initial interest in twenty-four hour coverage was focused on addressing employee health and disability outcomes while at the same time realizing costs savings, or at least stabilizing costs, for employers. In an October 1991 report entitled, "Understanding 24-Hour Coverage," the American Legislative Exchange Council (ALEC) stated the concept most simply by noting, "At its broadest, 24-hour coverage would ignore causation in compensating for medical care or lost wages."[91]

The difficulty experienced in promulgating the regulations necessary to initiate these proposals, along with the dearth of interested participants, culminated in the missed opportunity to study the concept in-depth. Time will only tell whether more effort should have been directed to test the feasibility of the idea.

When considering alternative benefit schemes, it is well to include the state of **Texas**. As noted previously, Texas is unique among the states in that it maintains a traditional workers compensation system but does not require employers to participate. While the workers compensation law in Texas requires public entities to provide workers compensation insurance, coverage is voluntary for most employers. In 2019, the state's Division of Workers Compensation (DWC) reported that, "about 28 percent of private, year-round employers do not have workers compensation, and they employ about 18 percent of the private workforce in Texas."[92]

---

[91] https://www.leg.state.nv.us/Division/Research/Publications/Bkground/BP97-05.pdf
[92] https://www.employers.com/resources/blog/

Texas employer have three options for addressing work related injuries and death. The employer may insure their workers compensation exposure through the traditional medium of insurance or qualify to self-insure. Secondly, under what is frequently referred to as the "opt-out" program, the employer – referred to as a non-subscriber under the opt-out program – may forego traditional coverage and elect to provide some form of occupational injury coverage where the benefits provided may be the same, greater, or less than under traditional coverage.

Or finally, the employer, because the law is elective, may forego completely any type of coverage and thereby permit an injured worker to seek recovery through a liability action based on the theory of negligence. Under this final approach, the Texas employer forfeits the exclusive remedy protection and foregoes the three common law defenses of comparative negligence, assumption of risk and the fellow-servant rule.

Non-subscribers in Texas must comply with certain requirements as set forth by the Texas DWC. In the first place, the employer must post written notice at their workplace notifying their employees that they do not have workers compensation insurance. This notice must be in English, Spanish, and any other language that is appropriate. The non-subscribing employer must also provide written notice of non-coverage to new employees at the time of hire. The notice may be signed and dated by the employer and the new employee. Non-subscribing employers with more than four employees are required to report to the DWC any work related injuries that cause an employee to miss more than one day of work, along with all occupational illnesses, and all fatalities that occur at the work place.

Non-subscribers frequently purchase a comprehensive occupational benefit plan that provides certain income replacement and medical benefits to their employees in the case of an occupational injury or death. In today's market, there are multiple insurance plans to choose from that provide some level of medical benefits, wage replacement benefits, and death and dismemberment benefits. However, these occupational benefit plans contain dollar limits and time duration in terms of the length of time for which medical coverage and disability benefits are payable. While difficult to generalize, the following illustrates some of the possible contents of an occupational benefit plan:

Death or Dismemberment Benefits – In the event of an occupational death, the plan typically pays up to a certain dollar amount to the dependents of the deceased along with a burial benefit. Dismemberment benefits are generally payable in accordance with a policy schedule delineating the amount payable for the complete or partial loss of a body member.

Disability Benefits – Following a waiting period (generally seven days), income replacement benefits are payable based on two-thirds to 75 percent of the workers pre-injury earning, subject to a weekly maximum benefit. The duration of disability benefits is generally limited to a specific time period. While the duration period may be longer, many plans terminate disability benefits after two years.

Medical Coverage – Plans frequently pay for a range of medical services, after a deductible, based on usual and customary charges for medically necessary treatment ordered by a physician. Medical coverage is also limited to a maximum dollar amount and/or time duration.

The opt-out program has proven very popular in Texas and by some estimates, one-third of Texas employers are non-subscribers. Through the coordination and efficiencies that these non-subscription programs provide, millions of dollars in savings realized by these businesses can, in turn, be invested in their employees, their operations, and their communities. While a valuable outcome for the employer, this does not reflect the significant potential loss to the severely injured where occupational benefits are concluded before complete recovery is realized, or where any recovery through a tort action must demonstrate negligence on the part of the employer.

With legislation enacted in 2013 creating the Oklahoma Employee Injury Benefit Act (OEIBA), **Oklahoma** attempted to follow the Texas approach. This new act provided Oklahoma employers with two options. Either the employer could continue to insure his/her exposure through the traditional medium of insurance or self-insurance thereby providing benefits and processes as found in the Oklahoma Workers Compensation Act, or the employer could qualify to purchase or provide coverage under the newly created OEIBA.

The OEIBA provided for payment of the same form and level of disability, medical and rehabilitation benefits as found in the Act. There were three features built into the new law that were intended to serve as an incentive for employers to forego the traditional workers compensation program. Under the OEIBA, the employer was granted discretion in terms of what injuries are to be covered; employers were in a stronger position to select the treating provider and managed care was open to innovations outside of the regulated environment; and the new law set forth an expedited approach to resolve disputes.

Litigation concerning the constitutionality of the new law followed its enactment. In 2016, the Oklahoma Supreme Court held that the core provision of the Act "creates impermissible, unequal disparate treatment of a select group of injured workers" thereby rescinded the law.[93]

A final alternative program that merits a brief examination developed in response to increasing workers compensation insurance rate increases and eroding employee health care benefits during the early 1990s. This alternative program began in **Massachusetts** in 1992 when the legislature approved a program permitting contractors and unions to enter into a special arrangement frequently referred to as a "carve-out". The Bechtel Company and the Pioneer Valley Building and Construction Trades Council were the first companies to negotiate such an arrangement permitting them to operate outside the Massachusetts Workers Compensation Act.

The immediate results from the carve-out arrangement in Massachusetts exceeded expectations. The incidence of claims fell by 80 percent and litigated cases dropped to zero, with overall costs falling by more than 50 percent. Not surprisingly, the experience with the Bechtel arrangement attracted the attention of other states. **California**, one of the more litigious workers compensation systems, adopted enabling legislation in 1993.

---

[93] *Vasquez v. Dillard, Inc.*, 2016 OK 89 (Sept. 13, 2016)

Currently, nine additional states permit collectively bargained "carve–outs": **Maine** [1993]; **Florida** [1993]; **Kentucky** [1994]; **Hawaii** [1995]; **Minnesota** [1995]; **New York** [1995]; **Pennsylvania** [1996]; **Maryland** [1997]; and **Nevada** [2009].

Stripped to the bare essentials, a carve-out is a special agreement between unions and contractors. The main feature of the program is the emphasis on alternate dispute resolution (ADR) and the central role of the ombudsman in reducing attorney involvement and corresponding litigation. These arrangements permit industry representatives to set-up tailored programs that serve the needs and interests of their workforce and their businesses. A carve-out program may also call for replacing attorneys and litigation with an ombudsman as part of an ADR process. In addition to the principal feature of ADR, carve-out programs may also include:

- Special medical arrangements such as allowing the employer to require that injured workers be directed for an indefinite time period to a network provider.

- A light duty, modified job, or return-to-work program.

- Agreed upon medical providers to conduct permanent disability evaluations.

- A vocational rehabilitation or retraining program.

- Worker injury and illness prevention programs.

Along with those items permitted under a negotiated arrangement, it is important to recognize that the program does not permit any deviation from the benefit structure as set forth in the workers compensation law. Disability benefits are not subject to negotiation but, in return for certain concessions from the union, the carve-out program may offer enhanced disability benefits to injured workers.

These carve-out programs are an alternative to, but not independent of, the state supervised insurance program. Statutes commonly impose reporting requirements and authority over appeals and final determination of claims may reside with state officials. The state's role is primarily to provide oversight of the alternative process – to act more as watchdog than governing body.

Cost reductions and savings for the employer are most likely to result from the use of an ADR program because of lowered legal expenses. Other benefits of a carve-out program include:

- Fostering a more cooperative and less adversarial employer/employee relationship.

- Expediting of the claims process and promoting administrative efficiency.

- Reduction in the number of lost-time injury days and enabling the injured worker to return-to-work quicker.

- Providing immediate information and prompt, appropriate care to the injured worker.

In most states that allow the carve-out program, with the notable exception of **California**, the program is limited to those in the construction industry. The reasons why are because the construction is a particularly dangerous industry and workers compensation rates are correspondingly high. The risks are inherent in the work and compounded by the presence of multiple contractors and crafts on the site at a given time.

WORKERS COMPENSATION UNDERWRITING

An article in the Wall Street Journal once described economics as a science when things worked out as the textbook predicted and an art when they did not. Of course, what the writer was trying to say was that when things "go right," the tendency is to view it as arising out of a very orderly process, but when things go wrong we see that things are not all that certain. In those cases where we admit we do not have all the answers, the inclination is to be less certain of the underlying structure.

As respects that observation, the very same thing could be said about insurance underwriting. The following looks at the subject of workers compensation underwriting which has often been described as a deceptively simple process – receive the application, classify the risk, and price the business. However, in many respects it is a science because it has a limited number of relatively uncomplicated general rules. If these rules are followed, they will likely produce a profitable result, but if ignored, the likelihood is that the business will not be profitable.

> A large portion of the material covering the subject of underwriting was taken from an article originally written by John Richmond (retired Vice President from Zenith Insurance Company). The article contains the basic principles of workers compensation underwriting and has been modified to reflect elements that have changed since the article was first written.

When considering the subject of underwriting – whether it is for the purpose of workers compensation or any other line of insurance – attention is directed to the role of the underwriter.

In the early days of marine underwriting, the underwriter was an individual known as "names" who was often the guarantor of the risk he accepted. His personal net worth guaranteed the endeavor by signing his name at the bottom of the insurance contract; hence the term "underwriter" developed. Today, there are few, if any, individual underwriters at Lloyd's of London that take the entire risk upon themselves. In the case of Lloyd's, the business is placed through brokers and underwritten by syndicates of many individuals who bear the risk, and most of the syndicates today are incorporated which limits their liabilities.

As business and insurance became more complex, corporate underwriters – most commonly insurance companies – came to be the guarantor of risk operating through their representative underwriters. These underwriters decide for their corporate principals what risks to assume and under what terms and conditions. The underwriter, whether working for his own account or acting for a principal, is essentially involved in the risk selection and pricing process. In this capacity the individual determines what coverage will be offered and the conditions under which a risk will be written.

Today, many insurance companies invest millions of dollars into "smart systems" designed by actuaries tasked to identify target areas for acceptability of risk. Smart systems and predictive modeling are reflective of how many insurance companies decide whether a workers compensation risk is eligible for coverage. It's these systems that decide whether or not they want to insure the company or business and provide coverage for their operations.

Predictive models incorporate many of the mundane risk assessment items that previously underwriters had to consider on each and every risk presented. For many workers compensation insurance companies today, it is now more of a numbers game with hands on underwriting taking a backseat to actuarially developed insurable models. It is less about knowing the company or business and more geared toward predicting profit.

The following is provided for those with an interest in understanding the fundamentals of the underwriting process and how it can be used to identify profitable risks. The principles of workers compensation underwriting are not complicated; however, the losses can be significant if not practiced in a disciplined manner.

ROLE OF THE UNDERWRITER

The first thing that a workers compensation insurance underwriter needs to understand is that workers compensation is different from all other insurance. As will be covered in the following chapter, the standard workers compensation policy is only 6-8 pages long and wording in the policy refers back to the workers compensation laws of the states where the policy applies. Thus, coverage is subject to an individual states workers compensation act for guidance. It is in the act that an individual state defines "employee" and "who must be covered" and "exempted employments." It is in the act where the "benefits to be provided" and "medical benefits" and "indemnity (lost wages) benefits" and "death benefits" are also set forth.

While a small employer may only be subject to the jurisdiction of a single state, other employers may have exposure to more than a single legal jurisdiction when it comes to their workers compensation obligations. Beyond other states, federal workers compensation laws, including Maritime coverage, are treated differently than under state laws. The underwriter must first know how state and federal laws affect the policy, secondly be able to identify an employers' exposure to these different legal jurisdictions and finally be able to attach required endorsements, identify and use the correct classifications and properly calculate the appropriate premium for the exposure.

Underwriting involves all of the aspects of workers compensation coverage from the selection and pricing of the risk, the role of loss control, the premium audit function, the relationship with the producer and the employer policyholder, and of course having a close relationship with the claims department in helping interpret policy coverage and respond to inquiries from employers and employees concerning rules and procedures of the boards and commissions in the various states.

Workers compensation is an integrated program, dependent on the smooth functioning of a number of component parts. These include, first of all, the level of benefits provided by the state's workers compensation laws. If benefits are not adequate in terms of replacing a substantial portion of lost wages, the program will not operate effectively and will be subject to substantial external pressures. Conversely, if benefits are set at too high a level, the system will be extremely costly and employers who pay the bill will look for corrections or seek other sources for insurance.

While some business enterprises may have sufficient resources to guarantee that workers compensation benefits will be available when required through self-insurance, most businesses turn to insurance to fulfill their workers compensation obligation. The insurance mechanism is another integral part of the total workers compensation program.

The insurance company's assignment of losses incurred by insured employers to any one of several hundred individual risk classifications permits the system to allocate to a given type of employer the costs incurred in that particular type of business. Workers compensation insurance not only provides a method whereby employers can fund their obligations to injured workers, but it makes possible an equitable distribution of costs.

In the 1980's, the debate over whether the regulatory process for workers compensation should move from an administered rate mode to one of manual rate competition, the statement was often made that workers compensation insurance is different and, as such, entitled to a different treatment. Whether this perspective was correct depends upon one's viewpoint as there are many scholars who did not see any significant difference between workers compensation insurance and other lines of insurance. In the end, the majority of states moved in the direction of manual rate competition or open rating.

However, when one moves beyond the limited insurance-related functions and sees workers compensation insurance as a part of an overall social benefits delivery system, it does in fact become something quite different. It has a relationship to a total system that makes it unique. Because of this, there are a number of constraints that are imposed upon the insurer and the underwriter. Underwriters must be aware of the wider implications of their actions. They must understand that their activities do not occur in a vacuum and that to the degree any action taken on their part causes damage to the total workers compensation system, these activities will be harmful.

There is a definite need for the underwriter to be concerned with protecting the right of the company to continue to write this line of insurance. The United States is one of a number of major industrialized nations that have a private enterprise system of workers compensation insurance. It should be noted that several Australian states, some European countries, and several

South American countries have private insurance companies similar to those found in the United States.

For insurers to be able to continue to offer this insurance they must fulfill the obligations assigned to them by the system. At the same time underwriters must be concerned with availability of workers compensation insurance at equitable costs and they must be concerned that they generate a return on investment sufficient to attract and maintain capital.

Insurers today offer a variety of services to injured workers and have as a primary objective the rehabilitation and early return-to-work of the injured worker. In most instances, these services are provided efficiently and effectively. Accordingly, a delicate underwriting balance is required. In conducting underwriting activities, the workers compensation underwriter must be mindful of the obligations and responsibilities that are associated with this market base. The underwriter must always remember that he is only one part of a total system that functions because all of the parts mesh. The underwriter must not engage in activities that might undermine the effectiveness and efficiency of the total workers compensation program.

THE WORKERS COMPENSATION APPLICATION

The major function within the underwriting process involves the gathering of information about a risk to be considered for insurance coverage, a determination and understanding of the exposures to loss which often requires physical inspection of the risk and obtaining information about the risk from the internet, analyses of the applicants financial statements, and an analysis of the past loss record of the insured including the workers compensation experience rating data which is usually available from the workers compensation rating bureaus in the various states and/or the National Council on Compensation Insurance (NCCI).

The entire process begins with the application for insurance. The workers compensation application contains a series of questions aimed at uncovering exposure related to potential loss or employee injury. It also provides a source for classification, pricing and acceptability of the risk. A copy of the application is included on the following two pages.

The application contains the critical information as to the name and location of the applying employer. The Policy Information section of the application identifies any Other States and Other Coverages requested by the applying employer.

After reviewing the application, the underwriter makes a determination about whether the risk meets the eligibility requirements outlined in the underwriting guideline along with the risk appetite of the insurer. Another consideration is whether there are any catastrophic exposures associated with the risk.

For example, a catastrophic exposure may be an employer applicant that has a thousand employees in a single office skyscraper building in midtown Manhattan with a high terrorism exposure. Upon completion of the underwriting evaluation and a determination that the risk is in a class of business that meets the underwriting requirements of the insurer, the next step is to establish a premium for the risk based upon the analysis of the exposures performed, and based upon the estimated annual payroll of the employer applicant for the year of coverage.

While workers compensation is essentially a self-administering system, legitimate disputes do occur. Accordingly, workers compensation laws contain provisions for administrative mechanisms to handle adjudication of disputed cases. The statutes generally establish a body to oversee the benefit delivery function. The activities of such bodies – usually known as industrial commissions or boards – often affect underwriting results. The underwriter must know whether these administrative bodies and the courts are fairly interpreting the workers compensation law. Only when there is fair and equitable interpretation along with an even handling and timely resolution within the adjudicatory process, will the benefits being awarded be commensurate with premium.

WORKERS COMPENSATION APPLICATION

DATE (MM/DD/YYYY):

AGENCY NAME AND ADDRESS:

COMPANY:
UNDERWRITER:
APPLICANT NAME:
OFFICE PHONE: **MOBILE PHONE:**
MAILING ADDRESS (Including ZIP + 4 or Canadian Postal Code):
YRS IN BUS:
SIC:
NAICS:
WEBSITE ADDRESS:

PRODUCER NAME:
CS REPRESENTATIVE NAME:
OFFICE PHONE (A/C, No, Ext):
MOBILE PHONE:
FAX (A/C, No):
E-MAIL ADDRESS:
CODE: **SUB CODE:**
AGENCY CUSTOMER ID:

E-MAIL ADDRESS:

☐ SOLE PROPRIETOR ☐ CORPORATION ☐ LLC ☐ TRUST
☐ PARTNERSHIP ☐ SUBCHAPTER "S" CORP ☐ JOINT VENTURE ☐ OTHER

CREDIT BUREAU NAME: **ID NUMBER:**
FEDERAL EMPLOYER ID NUMBER **NCCI RISK ID NUMBER** **OTHER RATING BUREAU ID OR STATE EMPLOYER REGISTRATION NUMBER**

STATUS OF SUBMISSION
☐ QUOTE ☐ ISSUE POLICY
☐ BOUND (Give date and/or attach copy)
☐ ASSIGNED RISK (Attach ACORD 133)

BILLING / AUDIT INFORMATION
BILLING PLAN **PAYMENT PLAN** **AUDIT**
☐ AGENCY BILL ☐ ANNUAL ☐ AT EXPIRATION ☐ MONTHLY
☐ DIRECT BILL ☐ SEMI-ANNUAL ☐ SEMI-ANNUAL
 ☐ QUARTERLY % DOWN: ☐ QUARTERLY

LOCATIONS
LOC #	STREET, CITY, COUNTY, STATE, ZIP CODE

POLICY INFORMATION
PROPOSED EFF DATE **PROPOSED EXP DATE** **NORMAL ANNIVERSARY RATING DATE**
☐ PARTICIPATING ☐ NON-PARTICIPATING **RETRO PLAN**

PART 1 - WORKERS COMPENSATION (States)
PART 2 - EMPLOYER'S LIABILITY
$ EACH ACCIDENT
$ DISEASE-POLICY LIMIT
$ DISEASE-EACH EMPLOYEE
PART 3 - OTHER STATES INS
DEDUCTIBLES (N/A In WI) ☐ MEDICAL ☐ INDEMNITY
AMOUNT / % (N/A In WI)
OTHER COVERAGES ☐ U.S.L. & H. ☐ VOLUNTARY COMP ☐ FOREIGN COV
MANAGED CARE OPTION

DIVIDEND PLAN/SAFETY GROUP **ADDITIONAL COMPANY INFORMATION**

SPECIFY ADDITIONAL COVERAGES / ENDORSEMENTS (Attach ACORD 101, Additional Remarks Schedule, if more space is required)

TOTAL ESTIMATED ANNUAL PREMIUM - ALL STATES
TOTAL ESTIMATED ANNUAL PREMIUM ALL STATES	TOTAL MINIMUM PREMIUM ALL STATES	TOTAL DEPOSIT PREMIUM ALL STATES
$ 0.00	$ 0.00	$ 0.00

CONTACT INFORMATION
TYPE	NAME	OFFICE PHONE	MOBILE PHONE	E-MAIL
INSPECTION				
ACCTNG RECORD				
CLAIMS INFO				

INDIVIDUALS INCLUDED / EXCLUDED
PARTNERS, OFFICERS, RELATIVES (Must be employed by business operations) TO BE INCLUDED OR EXCLUDED (Remuneration/Payroll to be included must be part of rating information section.) Exclusions in Missouri must meet the requirements of Section 287.090 RSMo.

STATE	LOC #	NAME	DATE OF BIRTH	TITLE/ RELATIONSHIP	OWNER-SHIP %	DUTIES	INC/EXC	CLASS CODE	REMUNERATION/PAYROLL

ACORD 130 (2009/09) Page 1 of 4 © 1980-2009 ACORD CORPORATION. All rights reserved.
The ACORD name and logo are registered marks of ACORD

STATE RATING SHEET # 1 OF 1 SHEETS   AGENCY CUSTOMER ID: _____

STATE RATING WORKSHEET

FOR MULTIPLE STATES, ATTACH AN ADDITIONAL PAGE 2 OF THIS FORM

RATING INFORMATION - STATE:

LOC #	CLASS CODE	DESCR CODE	CATEGORIES, DUTIES, CLASSIFICATIONS	# EMPLOYEES FULL TIME	# EMPLOYEES PART TIME	SIC	NAICS	ESTIMATED ANNUAL REMUNERATION/ PAYROLL	RATE	ESTIMATED ANNUAL MANUAL PREMIUM

PREMIUM

STATE:	FACTOR	FACTORED PREMIUM		FACTOR	FACTORED PREMIUM
TOTAL	N/A	$			$
INCREASED LIMITS		$	SCHEDULE RATING *		$
DEDUCTIBLE *		$	CCPAP		$
EXPERIENCE OR MERIT MODIFICATION		$	STANDARD PREMIUM		$
		$	PREMIUM DISCOUNT		$
		$	EXPENSE CONSTANT	N/A	$
ASSIGNED RISK SURCHARGE *		$	TAXES / ASSESSMENTS *	N/A	$
ARAP *		$			$

* N/A in Wisconsin

TOTAL ESTIMATED ANNUAL PREMIUM	MINIMUM PREMIUM	DEPOSIT PREMIUM
$	$	$

REMARKS (Attach ACORD 101, Additional Remarks Schedule, if more space is required)

ACORD 130 (2009/09)   Page 2 of 4

AGENCY CUSTOMER ID: _____

PRIOR CARRIER INFORMATION / LOSS HISTORY

PROVIDE INFORMATION FOR THE PAST 5 YEARS AND USE THE REMARKS SECTION FOR LOSS DETAILS | LOSS RUN ATTACHED

YEAR	CARRIER & POLICY NUMBER	ANNUAL PREMIUM	MOD	# CLAIMS	AMOUNT PAID	RESERVE
	CO:					
	POL #:					
	CO:					
	POL #:					
	CO:					
	POL #:					
	CO:					
	POL #:					
	CO:					
	POL #:					

NATURE OF BUSINESS / DESCRIPTION OF OPERATIONS

GIVE COMMENTS AND DESCRIPTIONS OF BUSINESS, OPERATIONS AND PRODUCTS: MANUFACTURING - RAW MATERIALS, PROCESSES, PRODUCT, EQUIPMENT; CONTRACTOR - TYPE OF WORK, SUB-CONTRACTS; MERCANTILE - MERCHANDISE, CUSTOMERS, DELIVERIES; SERVICE - TYPE, LOCATION; FARM - ACREAGE, ANIMALS, MACHINERY, SUB-CONTRACTS.

GENERAL INFORMATION

EXPLAIN ALL "YES" RESPONSES	Y/N
1. DOES APPLICANT OWN, OPERATE OR LEASE AIRCRAFT / WATERCRAFT?
2. DO / HAVE PAST, PRESENT OR DISCONTINUED OPERATIONS INVOLVE(D) STORING, TREATING, DISCHARGING, APPLYING, DISPOSING, OR TRANSPORTING OF HAZARDOUS MATERIAL? (e.g. landfills, wastes, fuel tanks, etc)
3. ANY WORK PERFORMED UNDERGROUND OR ABOVE 15 FEET?
4. ANY WORK PERFORMED ON BARGES, VESSELS, DOCKS, BRIDGE OVER WATER?
5. IS APPLICANT ENGAGED IN ANY OTHER TYPE OF BUSINESS?
6. ARE SUB-CONTRACTORS USED? (If "YES", give % of work subcontracted)
7. ANY WORK SUBLET WITHOUT CERTIFICATES OF INSURANCE? (If "YES", payroll for this work must be included in the State Rating Worksheet on Page 2)
8. IS A WRITTEN SAFETY PROGRAM IN OPERATION?
9. ANY GROUP TRANSPORTATION PROVIDED?
10. ANY EMPLOYEES UNDER 16 OR OVER 60 YEARS OF AGE?
11. ANY SEASONAL EMPLOYEES?
12. IS THERE ANY VOLUNTEER OR DONATED LABOR? (If "YES", please specify)

ACORD 130 (2009/09)   Page 3 of 4

AGENCY CUSTOMER ID: _____

GENERAL INFORMATION (continued)

EXPLAIN ALL "YES" RESPONSES	Y/N
13. ANY EMPLOYEES WITH PHYSICAL HANDICAPS?	
14. DO EMPLOYEES TRAVEL OUT OF STATE? (If "YES", indicate state(s) of travel and frequency)	
15. ARE ATHLETIC TEAMS SPONSORED?	
16. ARE PHYSICALS REQUIRED AFTER OFFERS OF EMPLOYMENT ARE MADE?	
17. ANY OTHER INSURANCE WITH THIS INSURER?	
18. ANY PRIOR COVERAGE DECLINED / CANCELLED / NON-RENEWED IN THE LAST THREE (3) YEARS? (Missouri Applicants - Do not answer this question)	
19. ARE EMPLOYEE HEALTH PLANS PROVIDED?	
20. DO ANY EMPLOYEES PERFORM WORK FOR OTHER BUSINESSES OR SUBSIDIARIES?	
21. DO YOU LEASE EMPLOYEES TO OR FROM OTHER EMPLOYERS?	
22. DO ANY EMPLOYEES PREDOMINANTLY WORK AT HOME? If "YES", # of Employees: _____	
23. ANY TAX LIENS OR BANKRUPTCY WITHIN THE LAST FIVE (5) YEARS? (If "YES", please specify)	
24. ANY UNDISPUTED AND UNPAID WORKERS COMPENSATION PREMIUM DUE FROM YOU OR ANY COMMONLY MANAGED OR OWNED ENTERPRISES? IF YES, EXPLAIN INCLUDING ENTITY NAME(S) AND POLICY NUMBER(S).	

REMARKS (Attach ACORD 101, Additional Remarks Schedule, if more space is required)

APPLICABLE IN TENNESSEE AND VERMONT: IT IS A CRIME TO KNOWINGLY PROVIDE FALSE, INCOMPLETE OR MISLEADING INFORMATION TO ANY PARTY TO A WORKERS COMPENSATION TRANSACTION FOR THE PURPOSE OF COMMITTING FRAUD. PENALTIES INCLUDE IMPRISONMENT, FINES AND DENIAL OF INSURANCE BENEFITS.

ANY PERSON WHO KNOWINGLY AND WITH INTENT TO DEFRAUD ANY INSURANCE COMPANY OR ANOTHER PERSON FILES AN APPLICATION FOR INSURANCE OR STATEMENT OF CLAIM CONTAINING ANY MATERIALLY FALSE INFORMATION, OR CONCEALS FOR THE PURPOSE OF MISLEADING INFORMATION CONCERNING ANY FACT MATERIAL THERETO, COMMITS A FRAUDULENT INSURANCE ACT, WHICH IS A CRIME AND SUBJECTS THE PERSON TO CRIMINAL AND [NY: SUBSTANTIAL] CIVIL PENALTIES. (Not applicable in CO, DC, FL, HI, MA, NE, OH, OK, OR, VT or WA; in LA, ME, TN and VA, insurance benefits may also be denied)

IN THE DISTRICT OF COLUMBIA, WARNING: IT IS A CRIME TO PROVIDE FALSE OR MISLEADING INFORMATION TO AN INSURER FOR THE PURPOSE OF DEFRAUDING THE INSURER OR ANY OTHER PERSON. PENALTIES INCLUDE IMPRISONMENT AND/OR FINES.

IN MASSACHUSETTS, NEBRASKA, OREGON AND VERMONT, ANY PERSON WHO KNOWINGLY AND WITH INTENT TO DEFRAUD ANY INSURANCE COMPANY OR ANOTHER PERSON FILES AN APPLICATION FOR INSURANCE OR STATEMENT OF CLAIM CONTAINING ANY MATERIALLY FALSE INFORMATION, OR CONCEALS FOR THE PURPOSE OF MISLEADING INFORMATION CONCERNING ANY FACT MATERIAL THERETO, MAY BE COMMITTING A FRAUDULENT INSURANCE ACT, WHICH MAY BE A CRIME AND MAY SUBJECT THE PERSON TO CRIMINAL AND CIVIL PENALTIES.

IN WASHINGTON, IT IS A CRIME TO KNOWINGLY PROVIDE FALSE, INCOMPLETE, OR MISLEADING INFORMATION TO AN INSURANCE COMPANY FOR THE PURPOSE OF DEFRAUDING THE COMPANY. PENALTIES INCLUDE IMPRISONMENT, FINES, AND DENIAL OF INSURANCE BENEFITS.

APPLICANT'S SIGNATURE (Must be Officer, Owner or Partner)	DATE	PRODUCER'S SIGNATURE	NATIONAL PRODUCER NUMBER

ACORD 130 (2009/09)

A final element of the underwriting environment is the competitive situation. Sound and informed competition is an indication of a healthy condition. But at the same time, during periods of intense competition, there is the potential for the underwriter to make concessions on business being submitted in order to maintain market share. Lack of competition may be an indication that certain elements in the system may not be in balance. While desirable, there can be no doubt that serious price competition increases the degree of underwriting skill required.

Evaluation of Individual Risk – With the application in place, it is appropriate to consider the evaluation of individual risks. This activity, as has been described, consists of gathering, analyzing and acting on a set of facts that pertain to the account in question. While these facts may vary from risk to risk, there is generally a set of core elements involved in most cases the underwriter confronts. Differences may arise out of varying types of operation or from the coverages requested. United States Longshoremen and Harbor Workers Compensation Act (USL&HW) coverage is an example of the latter. The underwriter has to rely on experience and may need the assistance of more experienced insurance experts or senior underwriters to determine what data beyond the core elements will be required.

The core elements normally include the type of operations being undertaken by the risk (the risk classification), the business expertise of the risk, the financial condition of the risk, the safety attitude of management, the extent and control over the hazards in the workplace, and the loss history of the risk.

Risk Classification – In considering the operation of the risk, the underwriter needs to know what the risk does, what is used and how the operation is done. The purpose is to determine the correct classification for the particular account. It is axiomatic for most lines of insurance, but especially for workers compensation, that when a classification is established a rate is established also. Each particular classification has a corresponding rate and by making a classification assignment, a rate is determined.

The National Council on Compensation Insurance (NCCI), the rating organization for the insurance industry, produces a manual that details what is to be included in each classification code. There are more than 600 different classification codes. This manual is *The Scopes® of Basic Manual Classifications*, or the "Scopes® Manual" for short.

Risks may be assigned to a classification based on their operation. Thus, an operation where the predominant activity is metal stamping may be assigned to the machine shop classification. Alternatively, a classification may be established based on the end-product produced. Accordingly, the manufacturer of wooden chairs may be assigned to furniture manufacturing. Because a product might be made in several ways or from different kinds of material that may require different processes, the end-product means of classifying risks is often times inappropriate.

A third way to classify workers compensation operations is by analogy. This method of classification is appropriate when the operation could be described by an end-product type of classification, but the particular classification does not accurately reflect the operations of the risk. One of the key questions that the underwriter needs to ask is whether the operations of the risk being evaluated are generally consistent with the operations of others assigned to the same classification.

The NCCI does not operate as the rating organization for the industry in all states. In a number of states, the rating bureau that is normally an insurer-sponsored organization, maintains classifications on many of the risks operating in its jurisdiction. In a few states, the rating bureaus undertake comprehensive examinations of the operations of these risks and are quite thorough in classification assignments. In these jurisdictions, the classification assigned by the local rating bureau usually will be the proper one.

However, the underwriter's job in every jurisdiction is to verify the correctness of the classification being used and change it if it is determined to be incorrect. To perform this function, the underwriter needs to be alert. The underwriter must study the risk operations and classification assignments for each piece of business being evaluated. By so doing, the underwriter increases his/her knowledge of industrial processes and will also be able to detect potential classification problems. The underwriter must be sure that all of the pertinent information concerning the operations of a risk has been compiled in order to arrive at a proper conclusion on classification assignment.

Proper classification is very important to successful underwriting. The classification carries with it a cost per hundred dollars of payroll. The underwriter's action in pricing business can be a major factor in attaining company objectives and maintaining company profitability. If the wrong classification is selected and the risk is priced too low, there may be no profit. On the other hand if the risk is priced too high, growth objectives may not be reached or business may be lost to competition. The underwriter must strive to achieve a rate which is adequate, but not excessive. Stated another way, the rate, as determined by the classification, must be commensurate with the hazard(s) involved.

When the underwriter concludes that a classification change that produces a higher rate is required, the underwriter must be able to convince the insured of the need to change the classification and the rate. If the insured and the producer will not accept the change, the underwriter has to elect to continue the same classification or withdraw from the risk. Requests to a rating bureau to allow a reclassification which results in a higher rate should not be made without the concurrence of the producer and the insured.

Risk Conditions and Attitude – To determine whether a prospective employer knows the business, the underwriter will examine the work history of the account. Attention will be directed to the length of time the employer has been in business, what operations have been conducted during that time, and what is the experience of management. Desirable risks know their business.

The employer must be able to demonstrate competency in his/her own field. This is customarily measured by the aggregate experience of the management and the supervisory staff in the field of work. A residential plumbing contractor is likely to have poor injury experience if the contractor takes occasional sewage treatment, plant, or water main jobs.

Additionally, the employer must have the proper attitude. Does the employer wish to create a safe place to work for the employees? Is workers compensation viewed as an easy answer to employee injuries? And is the employer safety minded and willing to undertake necessary hazard-control activities?

An equally important aspect of the process is examining the financial condition of a risk to determine whether the insured has the resources to make changes that may be necessary to assure that loss-causing hazards are eliminated or controlled. The financial condition of a prospective account is also important because a determination has to be made as to whether the insured will be able to pay the premium for the policy. Even risks with the best experience, ones with no losses, are undesirable accounts if they cannot pay their premium, for the insurer will lose money because of expenses incurred

An essential characteristic of the desirable risk is a positive employer attitude with respect to work injuries. Cooperation and assistance after the loss and in the reporting, investigation, and adjustment of any claim is imperative. Similarly, management attitude as respects preventive or control measures before the loss is equally important. The classical definition of "moral hazard" in the sense of the insured's causing a loss does not directly apply to workers compensation. However, the chance of having a work injury due to management indifference is a form of moral hazard.

Hazards Control – A point that has caused much of the difficulty in arriving at sound underwriting decisions is the acceptability of the physical hazard(s) that the risk presents. There is no definition of what represents the average, better than average, or worse than average risk. Therefore, to make some judgments about these conditions, the underwriter must determine what average means. There are an infinite number of features which enter into the make-up of each individual account and any average used will vary according to the nature and number of these conditions.

It is not necessary for the underwriter to know the average of every characteristic of each risk in the classification considered. However, the underwriter must analyze the features of the risk that will influence the volume of its losses and expenses. Each hazard must be analyzed separately and the results combined to produce a composite evaluation. There are a number of clues that can be followed that will lead to the desirable risk.

The control exercised over the hazards, which are inherent in the operations being considered, is most important. The quality of a risk is more dependent upon the extent to which its hazards are controlled than it is upon the severity of those hazards. In most cases the hazards, which a particular risk faces, do not determine its quality. Instead, the quality of the risk is determined by the extent to which its hazards are controlled.

Accordingly, the best risk is the one that has the best balance between hazards and control. Conversely, the worst risk is one which does nothing to control its hazards. All of the other risks in any classification lie somewhere on a line between those two. Hence, by evaluating the particular facts, the underwriter is able to make a judgment as to whether the risk in question is acceptable. The fact that the underwriter is able to do this rests on the premise that, within any group of risks with similar hazards, the best risks are the ones which provide the best control over their hazards without consideration for what those hazards may be.

There are certain general features that exist in varying degrees in every risk which have a marked effect on the loss experience encountered. These are the ones which result from management's applied attitude toward housekeeping, maintenance, and hazard control. The quality of risk conditions on these points will alleviate or intensify all other risk hazards. Unfavorable conditions may, in fact, actually create additional hazards. There are a number of items that fall into each of these categories that the underwriter can use to evaluate the quality of any workers compensation risk.

Housekeeping – Housekeeping describes the qualities of planned arrangement, cleanliness, and efficiency. It is more than just house cleaning. For instance, sweeping accumulated chips from a woodworking machine would be house cleaning, while the installation of an exhaust system to keep them off the floor in the first place would be housekeeping. The quality of general housekeeping is judged by the overall appearance of arrangement, cleanliness, and efficiency. A number of specific items should be considered in evaluating this feature. Among these are:

Floors and stairways – Poor conditions in these areas may either be a cause of accidents or may intensify the hazards of adjacent machinery. Good conditions are necessary to prevent losses.

Aisle layout – The adequacy and arrangement of aisles has a substantial bearing on the quality of every risk. Narrow or crooked aisles increase the materials handling hazard.

Equipment layout – There must be sufficient space around machines and equipment to permit safe and efficient performance of work. Congestion at these points is a contributing factor in many accidents.

Storage of material – Materials should be stored in an orderly fashion. Adequate space and facilities should also be provided.

Flow of materials – Proper planning will result in the right quantity of the right material in the right place at the right time. In turn, this will increase efficiency and reduce hazards caused by re-handling and congestion.

Handling of waste – Almost every industrial process produces waste that must be removed from the point where it is created. A regular disposal program is necessary in order to prevent excessive accumulations of waste material that results in congestion and cluttered floors and work areas.

Control of traffic – Planned control of the movement of employees and materials eliminates congestion and cross-traffic and will increase efficiency and reduce hazards.

Maintenance – The second general feature, maintenance, is equally important. Again, there are a number of specific situations that the underwriter must examine. Among these are:

Buildings – Buildings must be maintained in good condition if safe and efficient operations are to result.

Floors and Stairways – Poor conditions in these areas create hazards in and of themselves.

Machines and Equipment – Employee's place reliance on the proper operation of the machinery they operate. The failure of some part of a machine can easily result in serious injury to the operator or to fellow employees. Proper maintenance is not limited to repair of equipment that has failed, but rather must include a continual maintenance program in order to locate potential trouble before breakdown occurs.

Hand Tools – While few hand tools are inherently hazardous when properly used, they are dangerous when defective.

Lighting – Lighting intensifies or reduces all other risk hazards.

LOSS CONTROL

The workers compensation insurance program generates abundant safety and health data through its underwriting, claims, and risk control functions. Underwriters begin the insurance coverage process, which includes evaluating the risk for injuries associated with current or potential policyholder operations. Loss control consultants employed by the insurance carrier conduct employer site visits to collect necessary underwriting information including data on workplace processes, exposures and controls, and safety and return-to-work programs. Loss control (sometimes referred to as hazard control) is often the key determinate in the risk selection process.

This information is used by the underwriter to establish coverage terms including the types and extent of losses that will be covered by the insurance carrier along with the premium to be charged. Loss control consultants can also use this information to guide policyholder safety improvement and risk reduction efforts. When an injury occurs and a policyholder files a claim, the claims adjuster collects information from the policyholder about the nature of and the events related to the injury/illness. This enables a determination of whether the insurance policy covers the loss and, if so, the amount of compensation due to the policyholder.

A primary prerequisite in any loss control program is the interest and participation by management. Without this, little can be accomplished. Management should be encouraged constantly to take an active part in loss control activities. Ultimately, this will reduce the cost of insurance through the reduction or elimination of losses.

Loss control begins with awareness as to potential hazards. According to the Occupational Safety and Health Administration (OSHA), the leading causes of death in the construction industry – known widely as the "fatal four" – are falls, struck by an object, caught-in/between, and electrocution. Awareness of the hazards in the various work classifications places the underwriter in a position to identify risks and assist the employer in implementing a safety plan that can lead to a safer workplace.

There are two fundamental methods by which a worker can be protected from injurious contact with hazardous machines and equipment. The first is to guard the hazards so that they cannot reach the worker. Examples are machine guards and exhaust systems. The second is to guard the worker from the hazards that reach him. Examples are respirators and gloves. The provision of protective equipment to control hazards will have a positive effect on the quality of the risk.

It is not enough, however, to merely supply protective equipment. The equipment must be used. Often there is a reluctance to make use of equipment because it may be cumbersome or considered unnecessary. However, protective equipment that is provided but not used is no better than no protective equipment. Firm enforcement rules requiring the use of such equipment can ensure its use.

It is also necessary that the protective equipment be adequately maintained. The underwriter should ask about this during risk evaluations. Inasmuch as workers come to rely on the efficiency of the equipment provided to them, failure of such equipment to function properly may result in serious injury. A thorough program of preventive maintenance is essential.

Although many plants are one-story units, a number of multi-story industrial buildings still exist. Some of these are quite old and may be in a weakened condition. Since a structural failure can produce a major catastrophe, the underwriter should consider the possibility of reinsurance.

The underwriter also needs to be concerned with exit facilities. In the event of fire or explosion, building evacuation will be required. This should be accomplished speedily and completely. There should be two or more exits from every floor of every building or section. These minimum requirements may be inadequate under some conditions or in the presence of special hazards.

All of these conditions have an effect on safety and efficiency of the risk. The two can never be separated. Safety is an integral part of efficient operations. The same conditions, which create accident hazards, delay the smooth, efficient flow of production. Safety and efficiency are inseparable and the applied attitude of top management towards efficiency as reflected in these general conditions might be used as an indication of management's attitude towards employee safety. If high grade housekeeping, maintenance, and hazard control programs have not been instituted as a matter of efficient operations, there is little hope that they will be established for the purposes of increasing the safety of working conditions.

Specific Hazards – In addition to the general conditions that apply to all types of risks, most risks have specific hazards that arise from their individual operations. These involve the machinery, equipment, materials and processes used. The specific hazards require specific controls designed to fit the individual situation. The underwriter needs to determine the severity of each of the specific hazards and evaluate the degree of control exercised over them. Often, loss control technicians can supply this information. A determination of the quality of a given risk depends upon the balance between the severity of the hazards encountered and the degree of control exercised over these hazards. Although there are many ways in which a worker can be injured, the specific hazards can be grouped into a few very basic categories. These include:

- Machines and equipment
- Material-handling hazards
- Electrical hazards
- Occupational disease hazards
- Fire and explosion hazards
- Slips, falls, collisions
- Burns, heat, and chemicals
- Flying materials
- Miscellaneous injuries

The material-handling hazard is especially noteworthy, for it is a hazard which just about every risk encounters. It also is responsible for the majority of back injuries, the costliest type of workers compensation loss. This hazard is so universal that it often is overlooked. The underwriter must be constantly alert to its existence and controls.

Catastrophe Hazards – The underwriter must also evaluate the potential exposure to catastrophe hazards. A catastrophic event would be illustrated by the roof collapse resulting in multiple injuries or deaths, or the catastrophic losses caused by terrorism in the Oklahoma City blast and the events of 9/11. In underwriting workers compensation insurance, the underwriter is concerned with both the potential for serious injury to a single employee and the potential for multiple injury accidents. Long-term latency diseases which arise from industrial exposures require that the underwriter also evaluate the potential for multiple injuries arising from industrial diseases. Although most risks do not have a real catastrophe hazard, any risk may suffer a serious loss to an individual employee. What the underwriter needs to examine is the chance of this occurring. On the other hand, there are some risks, such as structural steel erectors, that have an inherent catastrophic exposure.

Whether or not a particular risk does have a catastrophe exposure is a judgment decision on the part of the underwriter. In reaching this decision, the underwriter must weigh the premium that will be received for the risk against the potential losses. For some risks or types of risk, there may be catastrophic exposures that are so severe that they outweigh all other conditions.

In all probability, the underwriter will find it helpful to review a list of all major accidents that have occurred over the past several years. A review of the operations themselves should be conducted to determine whether there is a possibility for serious injury to a single employee or the potential for multiple injury accidents. Evaluation of this exposure should be measured as being slight, moderate, or severe. The underwriter might then review the controls that are exercised over the catastrophe hazard and determine whether they do, in fact, control the hazard to an adequate degree.

In respect to industrial diseases, the underwriter will need to evaluate operations that have taken place in the risk's locations over an extended period of time. In this evaluation the underwriter will want to know what raw materials have been used and what products have been produced. There will also need to be a "state of the art" reading on the particular industry and operations being evaluated. In all of this, a large amount of informed judgment may be required.

Hazard Information – It is important for the underwriter to obtain substantial and detailed hazard information. In doing this, the underwriter will have to know what is being looked for. Experience and knowledge of the operation in question will be very helpful. Underwriters should visit their insured's operations in order to develop a complete understanding of industrial and construction processes. However, the underwriter will need to rely on the expertise of others. In most cases, this will be a loss control technician or other professional in the safety field whose job is to supply information about the risk to the underwriter and to describe and evaluate the hazards and their control.

There was a time when loss control and inspection reports were provided by the Engineering Department and were among the primary tools that an underwriter used in evaluating a risk. Many insurance companies have cut back on the level of engineering and loss control professionals on staff. Because of the extreme importance that these documents had, it is important that, where appropriate, risk information be obtained from alternate sources in a manner that can be understood and readily used.

Loss History – An important source of information that provides a basis upon which to judge the desirability of an account is the company's loss history. The experience developed by any risk over a period of time is unquestionably an excellent indication of its desirability. However, past experience is a reliable guide to future expectations only if future risk conditions will be essentially the same as those under which the experience was developed. Hence, when examining past loss histories, the underwriter should determine the cause of losses and whether the conditions that produced those losses remain the same or have been corrected. If conditions have substantially changed either because operations have been changed or because action has been taken to correct the conditions that caused the losses, judgments based on the loss history should be adjusted accordingly.

There are other considerations when examining a company's loss history. In the case of the employer with no claims in their loss history, the question must be asked if the employer would know what to do in case a work-related injury occurred. Would the employer know how important it is to report the injury promptly? Is the employer aware of the need for immediate quality medical attention and how to ensure proper care following the injury? Has the employer considered a program of light duty work to facilitate an early return-to-work for the injured employee?

There is also the challenge associated with an employer who demonstrates a loss history with none or only a few minor losses. A company with a good loss history is often paying less for workers compensation insurance coverage than a similar employer with average loss experience. The employer with good experience may be receiving a credit experience modification which serves to lower the premium paid by that employer when compared to that paid by a competitor with a history of losses. In addition, as a result of premium discounts and adjustments designed to attract better businesses, the insurance company may be collecting substantially less premium which serves to allow a smaller margin for profit should a claim occur.

On the other hand, employers with a loss history that demonstrates more claims than average may not necessarily be a reflection of a poor risk. The important thing to consider is whether the employer has learned from the events and has taken steps to prevent injuries of that type in the future. Also, frequency is generally worse than severity. An employer with many claims may involve an employer with little or no interest in workplace safety while the employer with a single substantial loss may have taken steps to correct the situation. Additionally, in the case of an employer with a frequency of small claims, the clock may simply be ticking until one of those small claims becomes a catastrophic injury.

With the employer with a poor loss history, there is the likelihood that that employer is not receiving any premium discounts and is likewise not receiving any type of experience modification credit. Thus, because the employer is not subject to any credits or discounts, there may be a greater margin for profit for the insurer. If the employer is willing to take steps to reduce workplace injury hazards, it may be beneficial for the insurer to "ride the high mod" and write the account.

All the above are considerations that the underwriter must factor into any decision when deciding whether to write or renew an account. Factors that require experience and judgment developed over time.

RISK PRICING

This section is prefaced with the acknowledgement that the entire subject of ratemaking and the insurance pricing mechanisms will be discussed more fully in Chapter Ten. Stated briefly, establishing a classification for a workers compensation risk establishes the manual rate. However, manual rates often are only the starting point in the workers compensation costing process. The workers compensation insurance costing process makes use of mandatory experience rating programs that provide an adjustment factor based on the particular risks past experience. These programs, which apply to risks employing the vast majority of the insured work force, follow the insured regardless of carrier. As such, they provide a large incentive for safe operations. The programs which apply on a single or multi-state basis are primarily frequency sensitive, but as a risk grows in size, severity is increasingly reflected.

For many accounts there are "size of risk" credits known as premium discounts that are normally applied subsequent to experience rating. These recognize that as the size of a risk grows, the expenses necessary to handle that risk decrease on a proportional basis. In most states today, carriers can elect either of two systems of expense gradation that are commonly known as the stock and non-stock premium discount plans. Stock premium discounts are greater and thus produce a lower discounted premium. Non-stock premium discounts, however, are normally used in connection with dividend programs and thus contemplate the existence of policyholder dividends. In a competitive workers compensation market, dividend programs may also be offered in conjunction with stock premium discounts.

Other costing programs applicable to larger-sized risks which gear the cost of a particular policy to the experience incurred under the policy include retrospective rating and large and small deductible programs. A retrospective rating program provides that the insured's final cost will be determined by adding required insurer expenses to losses incurred. This premium is then limited to certain predetermined minimum and maximum amounts. Because of this limitation, a charge known as the insurance charge is included in the insurer expenses. The large and small deductible programs are designed to permit the employer to essentially self-insure a portion of the employer's potential exposure.

Retrospective rating programs and large and small deductible programs should not be viewed as a substitute for competent underwriting. While they are legitimate underwriting tools, especially in the costing area, they should not be used with the expectation that, somehow, they will turn a poor risk into a good one.

Policyholder dividend programs are another workers compensation loss-sensitive costing method. While policyholder dividend programs may return a portion of the premium to the insured much as retrospective rating programs do, they differ in one very important respect. They differ in that they are not contractual programs and policyholder dividends can be paid only after they are declared by the insurer's board of directors. There are three general types of policyholder dividend program.

The first is the flat or level dividend. In this type of program the insurer determines that a given rate of dividend will be applied to qualifying policies without regard to the loss experience of the individual policies. In determining what the rate of dividend will be, the insurer most likely takes into consideration the experience on all of the policies subject to the program.

A second kind of policyholder dividend is the sliding scale program. Under this type, the amount of dividend is normally determined from a table that shows the dividend payable according to size of risk and loss ratio. There are no rules, however, as to when an insurer must compute the dividend or at what date losses will be evaluated.

A final type of policyholder dividend program is the retention program. Here, a factor much like the insurer expense factor under a retrospective rating plan is computed and is used to determine the amount of the dividend. These factors include a charge to recognize that since, in most states, dividends are payable in addition to premium discount, the maximum premium payable by the insured will be the discounted premium even if the loss experience may be poor.

The underwriter can make use of all of these various pricing programs either alone or in combination to present a net cost pricing program to the insured. In developing such programs the underwriter must be aware of past experience of the insured and should tailor the program to individual risk characteristics. To do otherwise would leave the account open to more competitive pricing programs submitted by another insurer.

At the end of a year, or at some other periodic interval, when the underwriter takes the time to look at the business that has been written, there will be concern if the aggregate results incurred are adverse. While this may be a chance occurrence, such a condition calls for an analysis of the business written. Occasionally the underwriter may find that a small number of extremely large losses have caused the adverse result. If this is the case, the underwriter will want to evaluate the likelihood of similar losses reoccurring. However, the underwriter must not rationalize that large losses will not occur. One of the biggest mistakes underwriters make is to conclude that their book is sound because there were only a limited number of large losses.

Alternately, the underwriter's initial analysis may indicate that the poor experience is principally found in certain geographic areas or in certain classifications. There are two possible approaches an underwriter may take toward an adverse book. The first involves a review of each and every account in order to ensure that the poorer risks are "weeded out." This review may take place on the normal anniversary date of the policies or some method can be devised to conduct the review at one point in time. The former method is probably less disruptive but requires the time of an entire renewal cycle.

In order to make the review more manageable, the underwriter will normally break risks down into segments. The most logical division is by producer which is the second approach to a poor book. Probably the initial action of the underwriter will be to segregate results by producer so that attention maybe directed to those that have had poor loss experience. Then an individual risk review of all of the given producers business will be conducted. Finally, after problem areas have been identified, the underwriter needs to develop and implement a corrective action plan.

It is difficult to define a good risk and it is the task of the underwriter to do his or her best in trying to sort out the good risk from the bad risk. However, there are a few characteristics that are generally common to good risks. These include:

- An experienced and competent workforce where the employees feel that they are a valued part of the organization.

- Adequate pay and compensation to ensure that good employees are not being lost to the competition.

- Planned growth with minimal fluctuations in the workforce.

- A sense of shared pride among all of the workers.

- A fundamental focus on the basics that include: good housekeeping, attention to detail, a continual focus on safety, and high standards in every aspect of the work and work environment.

ADDITIONAL UNDERWRITING FUNCTIONS

The underwriting operation is often described as the hub of the insurance operation. While other activities may also claim this position, the fact is that many things revolve around the underwriting process. Not only is the underwriter concerned with individual risk evaluations and in managing books of business, but the underwriter is also involved in other internal and external company activities.

Underwriting responsibilities are much broader than just gathering information and making decisions regarding risk desirability. The underwriter must see that the insurance policy is issued and must provide instructions as to how this is to be done. Additionally, the underwriter must monitor the services that the company provides to be sure that the producer and insured customers receive the attention desired and promised.

The underwriter must also recognize that nothing happens until a sale is made. Hence, while the sales operation might not be the direct responsibility of the underwriter, the underwriter must take an interest in sales and production activities.

Within the company, the underwriter will have management responsibilities that include the preparation of reports for management. As a part of this process, the underwriter should be prepared to suggest how problem areas might be addressed. In large companies, the underwriter may also have some responsibilities relating to personnel and training. No paper on workers compensation underwriting would be complete without acknowledgment of the training process. While an underwriter's career is one of constant learning, it is also one of continuous training of others.

With respect to underwriting generally, a person can be taught the basic tenets but, in the final analysis, it comes down to individual judgments. The underwriting process is a multi-faceted one. It stretches far beyond individual risk underwriting although that activity is the one around which all of the other activities revolve.

Although workers compensation underwriting may seem on the surface to be a mundane operation, it is an extremely fascinating and rewarding vocation. It exposes the individual to all types of business, to a discipline that is both a science and an art, and to a line of insurance that is almost totally and uniquely American. In performing his/her duties, the workers compensation underwriter must recognize that these activities comprise but one part of a total benefits delivery system whose purpose is to provide medical and wage loss benefits to workers injured on the job. To take any other view, subjects the company to the danger of losing the ability to write workers compensation insurance.

Chapter Four

THE STANDARD WORKERS COMPENSATION POLICY, ENDORSEMENTS AND FEDERAL COVERAGES

STANDARD WORKERS COMPENSATION POLICY

The predominant means of insuring an employer's obligation against injury or disease arising out of and in the course of employment is through the medium of insurance. The standard Workers Compensation and Employers Liability Insurance Policy (hereinafter referred to as the workers compensation policy or the policy) (WC 00 00 00A) developed by the National Council on Compensation Insurance (NCCI), provides insurance coverage for the statutory liability under the state's workers compensation law for medical treatment and indemnity

The workers compensation policy is designed to accomplish two purposes. The first purpose is to pay the statutory benefits specified by the compensation law of those states listed on the Information Page (formerly referred to as the Declaration Page). The listing of states in item 3 A. of the Information Page delineates only those states in which coverage applies. The policy is not designed to extend coverage to every state automatically. Part One of the policy covers the insured employer for those benefits mandated by those states listed in 3 A. which must be paid to an employee, or dependents of an employee in the case of death, who sustains a workplace injury.

The second purpose of the policy is to cover the liability arising from a workplace injury when legal action is brought seeking damages other than the benefits provided under the compensation law. Part Two of the policy covers tort actions by an employee including third party claims for contribution or indemnification arising out of a claim by an employee. Oftentimes these actions will be barred by the exclusive remedy doctrine, but Part Two of the policy will, in the majority of instances, provide defense protection for the employer.

As underwriter of the policy, the insurer has an obligation to both the employer and the covered workers. When the insurance carrier has a policy that provides compensation coverage to the employer for the operation in which the employee was working at the time of the injury, this is referred to as statutory coverage. When there is statutory coverage and there has been some breach of the policy by the employer, the carrier must provide to the covered employee whatever compensation benefits are payable and then resolve the coverage issue(s) with the employer.

The current workers compensation policy is referred to as the "standard policy" because the majority of insurance carriers use the prescribed policy form and language. Prior to the current form of the policy first adopted in 1954, there was a policy form that, while universally used, did not provide coverage for any specific state without modifying endorsements. Under that scenario, for an employer conducting operations in multiple states, it was necessary to attach several state laws or modifying endorsements to complete the coverage. The result was a voluminous document that was neither simple to understand nor easy to handle.

In 1954, the policy form was modified so that coverage was provided for all operations and locations of the insured within the scope of any state listed on the Declaration Page (currently referred to as the Information Page). A further simplification of the 1954 Policy was inclusion of the reference to "manuals in use by the company" in lieu of including a series of endorsements that detailed how premiums were to be computed.

In 1984, the policy was further modified by simplifying the language and putting the policy into a "plain English" format. The essential nature and intent of the 1954 policy was retained in the 1984 revised policy. Under the changes adopted in 1984, the insurer is now referred to as "we" or "us," and the insured employer is referred to as "you." It is also stated that the insurance policy constitutes the entire agreement between the insurer and the insured, and that there are no other agreements relating to the insurance. Any changes to be made in the insurance contract must be in the form of an endorsement issued by the insurer and made a part of the policy. The intent of this approach is to prevent any oral agreements, or any agreements not put into the form of an endorsement, from becoming part of the insurance contract. In addition to language simplification, a third form of coverage – "Other States Insurance" – was incorporated into the 1984 policy.

The most recent changes to the policy included minor technical amendments adopted in 1992. Many of the changes adopted in 1992 were designed to replace the need for certain endorsements. The 1992 policy by intent excludes all federal laws thereby removing the need for specific endorsements excluding federal coverages. These excluded federal coverages include: the Longshore and Harbor Workers Compensation Act, the Black Lung Benefits Act of 1972, the Federal Employer's Compensation Act, the Federal Employer's Liability Act, the Merchant Marine Act of 1920 (known as the "Jones Act"), and the Federal Coal Mine Health and Safety Act of 1969. Any of the excluded coverage's may be added to the policy by endorsement.

With the exception of the four monopolistic fund states (**North Dakota, Ohio, Washington,** and **Wyoming**) where coverage is afforded through a certificate of insurance, the standard workers compensation policy is used in every other jurisdiction. In the majority of jurisdictions, the National Council on Compensation Insurance (NCCI) files the policy for approval by the state insurance department. In a number of states with independent rating bureaus (e.g., **California, Massachusetts, New York**), the rating bureau files the policy with the state for approval. Consequently, except for the monopolistic fund states, the workers compensation policy is in use on a national basis and those subject to state workers compensation laws and insurance generally utilize this policy.

Since the policy was last revised in 1992, it has been the subject of numerous summaries designed to explain the content of the various parts of the policy. Little effort has been expended to examine the case law that has arisen concerning policy issues and interpretations of the coverage and duties under the contract. The following is designed to examine the policy in terms of both its structure and some of the case law that has arisen offering form and shape to the coverage.

GENERAL SECTION

It is important to remember that the Workers Compensation and Employers Liability Insurance Policy is subject to the same rules of construction as any other form of insurance contract. For example, the policy must be considered as a whole instead of taking individual provisions and attempting to interpret their literal meaning. Likewise, where the policy is issued pursuant to state law, it is to be interpreted in the light of the states' workers compensation statute. Thus, the policy is to be read as though the exact terms of the statute were expressly incorporated into the contract.

In view of the fact that the parties to the policy may ordinarily establish terms of their own choosing, the insurer and employer are free to provide for broader coverage of employees than would otherwise be required by law. For example, there is nothing that precludes the parties from providing coverage of exempt employees in which case the insurer is liable for compensation benefits following a work-related injury. The extension of benefits to those not covered under the law is strictly a matter of contract between the insurer and the employer. Consequently, the compensation law has no governing effect over such contracts, although the amount of compensation and other benefits payable are determined by statute.

The policy is composed of three separate and distinct parts. Coverage's available under the policy are set forth in the Information Page. The policy itself opens with a General Section which is really an introduction to the main points of the policy. The General Section contains five clauses.

- The first clause identifies the policy as a contract of insurance between the employer (named on the Information Page) and the insurer. The benefits paid under a workers compensation claim may go to an injured worker, a spouse, or dependent in the case of death, but the insured is the employer. The first clause also specifies that the Information Page is part of the overall policy.

- The second clause confirms that an employer named in the Information Page is the named insured under the policy. The insured can be an individual, a partnership, a corporation, or some other entity.

- The third clause notes that the coverage and benefits paid to the injured workers are based on the workers compensation law of each state or territory named in the Information Page. Where the insured is conducting operations in multiple states and faces multiple state exposures, it is important that all of the states are listed in the Information Page. Since the insured is charged with the responsibility of listing the appropriate state(s) or territory so that the proper benefits can be paid to injured employees, understanding and complying with this clause is crucial.

This clause also emphasizes the point that workers compensation coverage is applicable under and in accordance with state law, not federal compensation law. Prior to the changes adopted in 1992, the policy did not exclude coverage for maritime exposures or federal laws, but it was common for insurers to exclude maritime coverage by endorsement when a Longshore and Harbor Workers Compensation Act coverage exclusion endorsement was added to the policy. Under the current policy, the definition of "workers compensation law" has been changed to state that *"The workers compensation law does not include any federal workers or workmen's compensation law, any federal occupational disease law, or the provisions of any law that provide non-occupational disability benefits"*. Also, the "non-occupational disability benefits" phrase shows that coverage is meant for injuries arising out of and in the course of employment, not disabilities that have no connection with the employment.

- The fourth clause defines "state" as *"any state of the United States of America, and the District of Columbia."* State is defined here simply to clarify other references and phrases found throughout the policy. For example, if an employee is traveling or working temporarily in a foreign country on business, benefits for injuries suffered will be based on the workers compensation law of one of the states listed on the Information Page.

- The final clause in the General Section declares that the policy *"covers all of your workplaces listed in Items 1 or 4 of the Information Page; and it covers all other workplaces in Item 3.A. states unless you have other insurance or are self-insured for such workplaces."* If the insured has a single workplace or multiple workplaces, this policy can apply. Coverage exists so long as the insured lists all the states(s) where workplaces are located on the Information Page and, of course, pays the premium. This coverage would not apply if the insured has other insurance or is self-insured for such other workplace accidents.

PART ONE – WORKERS COMPENSATION INSURANCE

Part One of the policy represents the focal point of the coverage - the pledge on the part of the insurer to provide the statutory benefits available for work-related bodily injury by accident or disease, including death resulting from such injury. Provisions in the policy call for the insurer to pay promptly when due all compensation and other benefits required of the employer by the workers compensation law. The term "workers compensation law" is defined to mean the workers compensation and occupational disease laws of each state or territory listed in item 3 A. on the Information Page. Part One contains eight clauses.

How This Insurance Applies – Workers compensation insurance applies to bodily injury by accident or by disease. Bodily injury includes resulting death. The clause attaches stipulations to this declaration. First, bodily injury by accident must occur during the policy period. Secondly, bodily injury by disease must be caused or aggravated by conditions of the employment, with the employee's last exposure to the conditions causing or aggravating the bodily injury occurring during the policy period.

There are several items to note concerning this clause. First, the insurance applies to "bodily injury." The states, through case law, determine what constitutes a bodily injury and the workers compensation policy responds to what the law has determined to be a bodily injury. Finally, the clause certifies that coverage is provided if the bodily injury occurs during the policy period. This makes the workers compensation policy an occurrence-type policy, similar to the commercial general liability occurrence policy.

We Will Pay – In this clause the policy specifies that the insurer will *"pay promptly when due the benefits required ... by the workers compensation law"* – a very simple and straightforward insuring agreement. Whatever the state workers compensation law declares the benefit to be, that is what the insurer is responsible to pay. A complication can arise over the fact that an employee who is injured while working in a certain state can claim the compensation benefits of the state where the injury occurred regardless of the fact that the employer is based in another state. (This addresses the situation of extraterritorial coverage that was covered in a previous chapter.)

A case with an unusual result occurred in **Tennessee** where the claimant worked for a Tennessee company but was injured while on business in **Maryland.** He filed for benefits in Maryland, but the claim was held to be non-compensable. He then filed a claim for benefits in Tennessee, but the court declared that the election of remedies rule barred the Tennessee claim since the employee had *"affirmatively acted"* to get benefits in another state. Just because that other state denied his claim, the employee could not then seek the benefits in Tennessee. He had made his choice (Maryland) and to allow a second choice (or a third or fourth) would be unfair to the workers compensation system and a burden to the legal system.[94] (It should be noted that another state adjudicating the same set of facts may arrive at a different conclusion.)

It is important to recognize that due to the nature of state workers compensation laws, the dollar amount of coverage granted under Part One B is literally unlimited, both with respect to any particular accident, and with respect to any number of accidents occurring during the policy period. There is another point to consider: The insurer has agreed to pay the benefits required by the workers compensation *law*, a phrase defined in the policy as the *"workers compensation law . . . of each state or territory named in Item 3.A. of the information page."* This makes it important for the insured employer to specifically list those states in which the employer has a workers compensation exposure.

We Will Defend – With this clause, the insurer promises to defend, at its expense, any claim, proceeding, or suit against the insured for benefits payable by the workers compensation policy. It is important to recognize that the insurer reserves the right to settle claims or lawsuits, so the insured has no veto power over the matter. For example, if the employer does not want to pay benefits to an injured employee because the employer believes the claim is of a questionable nature, the insurer need not obtain the permission of the employer in order to pay the claim if the insurer determines the claim to be compensable.

---

[94] *Bradshaw v. Old Republic Insurance Company*, 922 S.W. 2d 503 (1996)

The usual rule to the effect that "*the duty to defend is broader than the duty to indemnify*," has application for the workers compensation policy. Unless the allegations on which a claim is based clearly takes it outside the scope of the coverage, the insurer has a duty to defend until such time as the remaining allegations could no longer be the basis of a covered claim. Inclusion of this language is necessary for those courts that would say that if a clear denial of the duty to defend under certain circumstances is not included in the policy language, then the insurer must defend any and all claims or lawsuits.

We Will Also Pay – The insurer agrees to pay certain enumerated costs as part of any claim, proceeding, or lawsuit that is defended. The listed costs are: reasonable expenses incurred at the insurer's request (but not loss of earnings), premiums for bonds to release attachments and for appeal bonds, litigation costs taxed against the insured, interest on a judgment as required by law, and expenses incurred by the insurer. These payments are in addition to the amounts payable as workers compensation benefits, so any of these costs that are paid by the insurer will not diminish the amounts available for workers compensation benefits.

Other Insurance – A separate provision under both Parts One and Two of the policy addresses the situation of Other Insurance. The basic purpose of this section is to ensure that different insurers or self-insured's will pay losses in equal shares. This provision addresses the possibility that there may be more than one workers compensation policy applicable to a particular accident or occupational disease, or that some self-insurance may apply together with the insurance provided by the policy. The sharing is to be accomplished on an equal basis until the loss is paid. Since the benefits paid under workers compensation are set by state law and not subject to the vagaries of a jury, there is no specified limit of liability on the workers compensation policy; however, any amounts to be paid as benefits will be split equally among affected insurers and self-insured's.

Payments You Must Make – This clause details when the insured, instead of the insurer, has to make payments arising out of an injured worker's claim. Here the policy points out that the insured is responsible for any payments in excess of the benefits regularly provided by the workers compensation law. This excess is usually the result of the insured's violating workers compensation laws, such as: knowingly employing someone in violation of law, failure to comply with a health or safety law, or discharging or discriminating against any employee in violation of law.

Recovery From Others – This is the subrogation provision of the policy. Prior to the redrafting of the policy in 1984, the policy made reference to the right of subrogation. The 1984 Policy, applying simplified language, achieves the same result without the need to use the term subrogation. Subrogation refers to the right of the payer of compensation benefits to collect from a negligent third party an amount equivalent to the compensation it has paid and/or will be required to pay under the terms of the policy. The language adopted in 1984 reads that the insurer has the *"right and rights of persons entitled to the benefits of this insurance, to recover our payments from anyone liable for the injury."* Furthermore, the insured is to do what is necessary to protect those rights and to help enforce them.

Under the statutory provisions found in the majority of states, the payer of compensation benefits is entitled to reimbursement for the amount of its expenditures as a first claim upon the proceeds of any third-party recovery. The employee is entitled to any excess. Some states, for reasons of incentive, have varied this approach slightly. In **Massachusetts**, the employee receives only four-fifths of the excess on the theory that the subrogee (the one subrogating against another) will have a greater incentive to seek to recover more than the bare minimum necessary to cover the compensation expenditure.

The Waiver of Our Right to Recover from Others Endorsement, WC 00 03 13, may be used to waive the insurer's right of subrogation against named third parties who may be responsible for an injury. The endorsement provides a schedule to list the person or organization to which the benefit will inure. The insurer will usually charge for adding this endorsement to the policy.

Statutory Provisions – Where required by law, workers compensation insurance is subject to several statutory provisions. These clauses provide that: notice to the insured of an injury constitutes notice to the insurer; default, bankruptcy, or insolvency of the insured does not relieve the insurer of obligations under the policy (the insurer states that it is directly and primarily liable to any person entitled to payable benefits); and, jurisdiction over the insured is jurisdiction over the insurer for purposes of the workers compensation law – that is, the state law that decides if and what compensation is to be paid to the injured employee is the guide for both the insured and the insurer.

The statutory provisions also note that terms of the insurance coverage that conflict with the workers compensation law are changed to conform to the law. In other words, state statutes and case law takes precedence over the wording of the insurance policy. Workers compensation coverage is guided by state law, not by an insurance policy and not by federal law.

PART TWO – EMPLOYERS LIABILITY INSURANCE

The second part of the policy is the Employers Liability insurance portion of the policy which covers the legal liability of the employer separate and apart from any legal obligation to pay workers compensation benefits because of a work-related injury to a covered employee. It should be noted that many of the suits introduced under Part Two of the policy result in a defense verdict because the exclusive remedy provisions of the state law will generally prohibit any recovery. Part Two coverage protects the insured against liability imposed by law for injury to employees in the course of employment that is not compensable as an obligation imposed by a state's workers compensation, occupational disease, or any similar laws.

Despite the fact that workers compensation is usually considered to be the exclusive remedy for covered employees for work-related injuries and occupational diseases claims, there are several reasons why employer's liability coverage is a necessary form of protection. There may be instances when an on-the-job injury or disease is not considered to be work-related and therefore not compensable under the statutory coverage. Nevertheless, the employee may still have reason to believe that the employer should be held accountable, and proceed with a direct action for damages. Additionally, the workers compensation laws of some states have been interpreted as permitting lawsuits and recovery against employers by spouses and dependents of injured workers, even though the workers are compensated for their injuries. The basis of such lawsuits is loss of consortium – loss of companionship, comfort, and affection.

For a short period, one of the primary coverage's available under Part Two was for suits against the employer by third parties who have paid damages to an employee of the insured and are seeking to recover all or a portion of that payment in a contribution or indemnification action. These types of suits are referred to as "third party action-over." A fairly common basis for the third party action over against the employer arises from product liability cases. For example, an employee may sustain a workplace injury when caught in a machine and bring an action for damages against the manufacturer for designing or selling a defective product. The manufacturer may then bring a third party action (action-over) against the employer alleging that the employer's negligence in some way (e.g. machine maintenance or alteration) was the cause of the employee's injuries.

Probably the most significant ruling falling within the category of action-over cases involved the **New York** decision in *Dole v. Dow*[95]. The worker (Dole) died after being exposed to the poison methyl bromide when he was ordered by his employer (Dow) to clean a storage bin. Following Dole's death, his wife sued the manufacturers of the substance for negligently causing the death of her husband. The manufacturer sued the employer alleging that the employer was primarily negligent in their handling of the methyl bromide. Following a number of lower court reversals, the New York Court of Appeals held that where a third party was found to be responsible for part, but not all, of the negligence, the responsibility for that part was recoverable by the prime defendant (the manufacturer of the substance) against the third party (the employer). The court held that an apportionment of responsibility between those parties had to take place.

The case confirmed that an employee could not directly sue his/her employer, but did expand the liability of the employer by permitting a defendant in an action by the employee to implead the employer to share in the third party's liability based upon the alleged negligence of the employer. In 1996, after many proposals before the New York legislature, the liability of an employer for contribution or indemnity created by the *Dole* decision was limited to apply only where the suit against the third party was for a "grave injury" thereby significantly reducing that type of exposure under Part Two of the policy.

Since Part Two of the policy specifically provides coverage for civil actions seeking damages for bodily injuries by accident or disease caused by or aggravated by the conditions of the employment, it is a reasonable assumption that this coverage will be triggered in an employee's discrimination case. More specifically, when an employee pleads intentional injury or tort in conjunction with a claim of discrimination, then that pleading will avoid the exclusivity of workers compensation and trigger Part Two coverage.

---

[95] *Dole v. Dow Chemical Company*, 30 N.Y. 2d 143 (1972)

In 1984, two additions to the policy were adopted in response to evolving case law. The first addition was coverage for *"consequential bodily injury to a spouse, child, parent, brother, or sister of the injured employee"* or loss of consortium, provided that the damages were the direct result of the bodily injury that arose out of and in the course of employment. To illustrate, this provision would at least afford a defense to the employer where a wife alleged bodily injury as a result of viewing the husband's work-related injury.

Loss of consortium cases had their genesis with a **Massachusetts** decision.[96] Following a compensable injury to a covered worker, his wife and children sued to recover from the employer under the negligence theory for loss of consortium (loss of services of the deceased) and for negligent infliction of emotional distress. The court held that the children's claim for loss of consortium was a claim upon which relief could be granted. The previous recovery of the injured worker did not serve to bar the claims of the wife and children. It is to be noted that loss of consortium claims where virtually eliminated in Massachusetts through the passage of legislation in 1985.

The second policy addition addressed claims brought against an employer *"claimed against you in a capacity other than as employer."* These types of claims are frequently referred to as "dual capacity" claims. Under the doctrine of dual capacity, the employer is the party who employs the employee but is also alleged to be another party - for example, the manufacturer of the product that injured the employee. The dual capacity doctrine had its genesis in **California** with the *Duprey* decision when a nurse, following a work-related injury, was permitted to sue her employer (a doctor) who treated her for her work injury, but in so doing, aggravated her original injury.[97] In holding for the employee, the court noted that the doctor had a "dual legal personality," that of a doctor and that of an employer. Where the claim alleges a dual capacity exposure, Part Two of the policy is available to respond. Part Two of the policy contains nine clauses.

> **How This Insurance Applies** – Employers Liability insurance applies to bodily injury by accident or by disease. The bodily injury must arise out of and in the course of employment, and the employment must be necessary or incidental to the named insured's work in a state or territory listed in Item 3.A. of the Information Page. The same issues regarding the naming of states in 3.A. that were described in Part One of the policy are applicable here.

> **We Will Pay** – Under Part Two of the policy, the insurer promises to pay all sums that the insured legally must pay as damages because of bodily injury to employees. The covered damages, where recovery is permitted by law, include: (1) the insured's liability for damages claimed against a third party by one of the insured's employees (third-party-over actions); (2) damages assessed for care and loss of services (loss of consortium); and (3) consequential bodily injury to a spouse, child, parent, or sibling of the injured employee. In addition, the employer's liability insurance applies to damages assessed against the insured in a capacity other than as an employer (e.g., a dual capacity action).

---

[96] *Ferriter v. Daniel O'Connell's Sons, Inc.*, 413 N.E. 2d 690 (1980)
[97] *Duprey v. Shane*, 241 P. 2d 78 (1951)

Exclusions – Employers liability coverage is subject to twelve exclusions that highlight the nature of this coverage. As found in most policies of insurance, Part Two excludes coverage for any action based upon the insured's contractual promise to be liable for damages. A common assumption of liability by contract is an indemnification contract or hold-harmless agreement. Whereas express indemnity contracts are excluded from coverage, implied indemnification (indemnity by operation of law) or warranty that work will be performed properly are covered in the majority of states. An exception is **California** which specifically excludes coverage for an implied warranty.[98] In other states, this warranty of workmanlike performance is a contractual obligation that is covered because it is an exception to the exclusion. Whether the insured is liable on this basis, where the exclusive remedy provision does not bar recovery, is a question of liability and not of coverage.

There is also a specific exclusion under Part Two for coverage of punitive or exemplary damages. The exclusion is restricted to claims based on illegal employment. Many jurisdictions do not permit insurance to cover punitive damages since the purpose of awarding punitive damages is to punish the wrongdoer. If insurance allowed for the payment of punitive damages, the employer who performed the illegal action would suffer no financial punishment.

Other exclusions apply to intentional acts and violations of laws showing that this coverage is meant for accidental incidents. Employers Liability insurance does not cover liability assumed under a contract (note that liability assumed by the insured under an insured contract is covered by the Comprehensive General Liability (CGL) policy form – another example of one coverage form complementing the other).

Employers Liability insurance does not cover fines or penalties imposed for violation of federal or state law. It does not cover punitive or exemplary damages because of bodily injury to an employee who is employed in violation of law. Most insurance policies exclude coverage for intentional acts, as does Part Two of the policy.

A further exclusion added to the 1984 Policy was the exclusion of coverage for suits arising out of certain illegal actions. With the growing number of discrimination lawsuits filed in the preceding decades, many insurers attempted to insert a specific exclusion for an insured employer's personnel policies and practices including discrimination and harassment. Developed as part of the 1992 Policy revision, this standard policy exclusion provides that there is no coverage for *"damages arising out of coercion, criticism, demotion, evaluation, reassignment, discipline, defamation, harassment, humiliation, discrimination against termination of any employee, or any personnel practices, policies, acts or omissions."*

Finally, the policy contains an exclusion for bodily injury occurring outside the United States, its territories or possessions, and Canada. This exclusion could pose a huge problem in today's

---

[98] California 3864. *"If an action as provided in this chapter prosecuted by the employee, the employer, or both jointly against the third person results in judgment against such third person, or settlement by such third person, the employer shall have no liability to reimburse or hold such third person harmless on such judgment or settlement in absence of a written agreement so to do executed prior to the injury."*

business world since many companies do business on an international scale. However, the exclusion has an exception for bodily injury to a citizen or resident of the United States or Canada who is temporarily outside these countries. For example, if an employee of the named insured company is in Japan on a business trip and is injured, Employers Liability insurance is available to the insured if needed.

We Will Defend – The policy gives the insurer the right and duty to defend the insured against any claim, proceeding, or lawsuit for damages payable by the Employers Liability insurance. Part One of the standard policy includes a section addressing the insurer's duty to defend. Under Part One, the provision reads that *"We have the right and duty to defend at our expense any claim, proceeding or suit against you for benefits payable by this insurance. We have the right to investigate and settle these claims, proceedings or suits. We have no duty to defend a claim, proceeding or suit that is not covered by this insurance."*

Part Two includes the same language and adds a final sentence stating that – *"We have no duty to defend or continue defending after we have paid our applicable limit of liability under this Policy."* This provision is added in light of the policy limits applicable under Part Two coverage in the majority of states. Recall that there are no policy limits under Part One of the policy.

These provisions clearly indicate that there is no intent to defend a suit that is not covered by the policy. In a liability case, the standard measure of the insurer's obligation to defend is whether the allegations in the complaint state a claim for relief under the provisions of the policy. If they do, there is an obligation to defend – if they do not, there is no obligation to defend.

We Will Also Pay – This provision is the same as that found under Part One as described previously. The payments promised here by the insurer are similar to the supplementary payments that are offered under the Commercial General Liability (CGL) coverage form, and do not diminish the limits of liability as shown on the Information Page.

Other Insurance – This provision is again like the Other Insurance clause found under Part One. Other insurance addresses the possibility that there may be more than one workers compensation policy applicable to a particular accident or occupational disease, or that some self-insurance may apply together with the insurance provided by the policy. The fact that Part Two coverage has limits that are applicable in some states also may serve to raise this provision. In either case, each participant pays its equal share of the loss until its policy limits are exhausted.

Limits of Liability – In the majority of states, the insurer's liability to pay for damages is limited. The limits of liability are shown on the Information Page and are broken down as follows:

- A dollar limit for bodily injury per accident.

- A dollar limit for bodily injury by disease for any single employee.

- A dollar limit for bodily injury by disease for the entire policy.

The "per accident" limit is based on each accident so that the insurer will pay no more than the listed amount in any one accident regardless of how many employees are injured. For example, if three employees are injured in the same accident and the bodily injury by accident limit is $100,000, then that is the total amount payable by the insurer. This is not to say that all three employees will receive equal amounts – that is to be decided by the facts of the case – but, in total, they will divide a total of $100,000.

The "by disease" limit has an aggregate limit and an "each employee" limit. The aggregate limit shown on the Information Page is the total amount payable by the insurer for all bodily injuries arising out of a disease, regardless of the number of employees who suffer from the disease. So, for example, if 30 employees suffer injury from a disease for which the employer is legally liable, the total amount available for all the injured employees is the amount listed as the policy limit for bodily injury by disease. How the amount is split up is again decided by the facts of the case. The disease limit is also subject to an "each employee" limit in that, regardless of the aggregate limit, each employee injured by disease can collect only an amount up to the dollar limit listed on the Information Page.

Part Two benefits are generally limited to $100,000 for each accident or disease, with a disease aggregate of $500,000. These limits may be increased for an extra charge. Additional or "excess" Employers Liability insurance may also be provided under an excess or umbrella policy, separate from the Workers Compensation and Employer's Liability policy.

Two states, **Massachusetts** and **New York**, require unlimited Employers Liability insurance. For these states, special endorsement forms are mandatory. Payments under Part One are guided by the state workers compensation law and not the policy itself. In this respect, Part Two coverage is more like a Commercial General Liability policy.

Recovery from Others – This is the subrogation clause for Part Two coverage and is again similar to, but more limited than, the clause found in Part One. Unlike Part One, coverage under Part Two of the policy does not give the insurer the injured employee's rights, but only the rights of the employer against third parties. This difference is necessary because contractually the insurer can only acquire rights from the employer with whom it is in "*privity of contract*". (A doctrine of contract law that prevents any person from seeking the enforcement of a contract or suing on its terms, unless they are a party to that contract.) Under Part Two coverage, the employer and not the injured worker are a party to the contract.

Actions Against Us – This provision spells out a bit of the contractual relationship between the insured and the insurer. The insured has agreed not to exercise a right of action (file a lawsuit) against the insurer unless certain things have occurred. Basically, the insured agrees not to sue the insurer unless a claim has been filed against the insured, all the provisions of the policy have been followed by the insured, a definite amount of liability has been assessed against the insured, and then, the insurer has, for whatever reason, refused to pay the amount due.

This clause makes the point that the policy is a contractual agreement between the insured and the insurer and so, no outside party (one not a party to the contract) has the right under the policy to sue the insurer to enforce the provisions of the policy. The insurer agrees through this provision not to abandon its contractual commitments under the policy to the insured even if the insured goes bankrupt or becomes insolvent. Existing claims will still be paid even if the insured is no longer in business.

PART THREE – OTHER STATES INSURANCE

Coverage under Parts One and Two of the policy are applicable only to claims made under the compensation laws of the states listed under 3.A. on the Information Page. Part Two coverage applies to operations in the same designated states and also covers operations in other states, but only to the extent such operations are *"necessary and incidental"* to operations in the designated states.

Because of the potential for gaps in coverage, Other States Insurance is provided through Part Three. This coverage is intended to provide only temporary coverage for new exposures. The conditions of the policy require the employer to notify the insurance carrier if work is begun in any state to which the Other States Insurance coverage applies. Once notified of this new exposure, the insurer can make the necessary filings required by the state regulatory authorities in order to provide permanent coverage.

A key point in this part of the policy is the importance of giving notice to the insurer. The policy emphasizes that if the insured already has ongoing work on the effective date of the policy in any state not listed in Item 3.A. of the Information Page, *"Coverage will not be afforded for that state unless we (the insurer) are notified within 30 days."* For example, if the insured has employees working in **Wisconsin** at the time the workers compensation policy renews, and Wisconsin is not listed under Item 3.A. on the Information Page, the insured must notify the insurer of the Wisconsin exposure within thirty days or there is no coverage for claims that may arise after that time period expires.

Note that this 30 day time period is, presumably, 30 days after policy inception, but the policy's wording is not clear on that point. In order for the insured to be safe, the insurer should be notified of work begun in states other than those listed in Item 3.A. as soon as such work begins, and not wait for any 30 day time period to go by. In support of this immediate notice requirement, the policy has another paragraph that reminds the insured to, *"Tell us (the insurer) at once if you begin work in any state listed in Item 3.C. of the Information Page."* Through these measures, the insurer is simply trying to exercise a degree of control over their loss exposure.

PART FOUR – YOUR DUTIES IF INJURY OCCURS

This part of the policy sets forth the duties that the named insured must perform if an injury occurs lest the insured breach contractual obligations, thereby making the insurance contract voidable. Part Four lists seven duties that the insured is to undertake in the event of an injury occurring to an employee.

- First and foremost is the duty of the insurer to notify the insurer if an injury that may be covered by the policy occurs. The obvious reason for this is so that the insurer can investigate and accept or deny an injury claim promptly. Such promptness can aid the insured, the insurer, and the injured employee.

- Following notification of the injury to the insurer, the next listed duty of the insured is to provide for immediate medical and other services required by the workers compensation law. This serves to minimize the extent of any workplace injury.

- The insured is to give the insurer or the agent the names and addresses of the injured persons and of witnesses, and other information needed by the insurer.

- The insured is to promptly provide the insurer with all notices, demands, and legal papers related to the injury, claim, or lawsuit. This aids the insurer to process the claim as soon as possible, and to plan for any future legal action on behalf of or against the insured.

- The insured is to cooperate with the insurer and to assist in the investigation, settlement, or defense of any claim, proceeding, or lawsuit.

- This duty deals with the insurer's right of subrogation. The insured must do nothing after an injury occurs that would interfere with the insurer's right to recover from others.

- The final duty of the insured is to refrain from making any voluntary payments, assume any obligations, or incur any expenses associated with the claim. These are the responsibilities of the insurer and any action on the part of the insured may jeopardize proper claims-handling processes.

PART FIVE – PREMIUM

Part Five of the policy is an important part of the policy for the insured and agent since it describes how premiums are determined. To assist the insurer in arriving at accurate information, the employer is obligated to maintain necessary records and the insurer has the right to audit records of the employer that relate to the policy. Similarly, even when accurate information is furnished timely by the insured, the final premium determination is not made until the end of the policy period. The estimated premium already paid to the insurer will be adjusted up or down and the insured will owe the insurer the difference if the final premium is an increase over the estimate, or the insurer will refund any difference where the final premium is lower.

Certain workers compensation policies provide for the retroactive computing of premiums. The NCCI rating plan manual requires an employer to have an estimated standard annual premium in excess of $25,000 to qualify for retrospective rating. In those cases, an estimated premium is made at the time the policy is issued with the final computation of premium based upon the actual claims experience during the policy period. Disputes between the insured and insurer may arise relative to the claims process inasmuch as an improperly handled claim may result in a higher final premium.

In a 2003 decision from the **New York** Supreme Court, the ruling addressed the situation where the carrier sought premium reimbursement long after the policy had expired. The court found the claim for reimbursement not to be time-barred.[99]

State insurance commissioners have administrative authority to approve or disapprove filed rates. In states such as **California**, where rates are subject to "file and use," the insurance commissioner does not approve rates, but may disapprove rates only if they are *"inadequate, unfairly discriminatory, tend to create a monopoly, or threaten the solvency of the insurer."*

To preclude a long delay in the establishment of new rates, states may require action by the commissioner within a specified period of time. The factors taken into consideration for purposes of setting the rates for a particular industry or type of employment include the estimated payouts to workers engaged in such work, the expenses of the insurer, and the profit to be made by the insurer in writing such policies. In addition, a particular employer's premium may be reduced or increased according to that employer's past experience of compensable workplace injuries. An insurer who increases an insured's premiums due to the settlement of a claim must demonstrate that the settlement was reasonable and entered into in good faith.[100]

In accordance with the general rule that no premium is due unless risk attaches, an insurer cannot recover premiums based upon compensation paid to employees for which it was not liable under its contract. An insurer may, however, recover from an insured amounts representing the difference between premiums paid by the insured and premiums actually earned by the insurer, due to its exposure to greater risk then it had contemplated when estimating the premiums the insured was to pay, where the policy stated that the premium charged was an estimated premium only, that upon termination a final earned premium would be computed, and that the insured would be liable for any excess of the final premium over the estimated premium.[101]

Judicial review of rate-making is limited because rate-making – a technical and complex function requiring much expertise – is not a judicial function.[102] As a general rule, the courts will not set aside compensation premium rates fixed by an administrative body unless the rates do not comport with applicable standards and are "excessive, inadequate, or unfairly discriminatory." There are seven clauses under Part Five of the policy.

- The first clause notes that the premium for the policy is determined by the insurer's manuals of rules, rates, rating plans, and classifications. The insurer claims the role as guide for determining premiums that will be paid by the insured. The insured can affect the premium by

---

[99] *Commissioners of State Insurance Fund v. Photocircuits Corp.*, N.Y. Misc. LEXIS 1388 (2003)
[100] *Deerfield Plastics Co. v. Hartford Insurance Co.*, 536 N.E. 2d 322 (1989)
[101] *Nationwide Mutual Insurance Co. v. Ed Soules Construction Co.*, 397 So. 2d 775 (1981)
[102] *Attorney General v. Insurance Commissioner of Michigan*, 323 N.W. 2d 645 [Footnote 3]

risk management efforts, loss claims history, deductibles, and other methods, but it is the insurer that ultimately determines the premium charged for the policy exposures presented by the insured.

- The second clause establishes that classifications are categories into which the insurer puts the insured to properly gauge the risks of workers compensation losses that the insured will face over the policy period. The classification is based on information supplied mainly by the insured. This clause tells the insured how the insurer classifies the business of the insured, and how that classification leads to the premium charge.

- The remuneration clause tells the insured what the basis is for the premium charge. The premium is determined by multiplying a rate times a premium basis, which is remuneration. This term includes payroll and all other remuneration paid or payable during the policy period for the services of all the officers and employees engaged in the work of the insured that is covered by the policy and all other persons engaged in work that could make the insurer liable under the policy. The rate is charged per $100 of remuneration.

- The premium payments clause notes that the insured named in Item 1 of the Information Page is required to pay all premium when due. In the event of multiple named insured's, the first named insured has the responsibility for the payment.

- The fifth clause addresses final premium. The premium shown on the Information Page is an estimate. The final premium is determined after the policy ends by using the actual, not the estimated, premium basis and the proper classifications and rates that lawfully apply to the work covered by the policy. This clause also determines the amount of premium in case the policy is cancelled. If the insurer cancels the policy, the final premium is calculated on a pro rata basis, based on the time the policy was in force. If the insured cancels the policy, the final premium is based on the time the policy was in force plus the short-rate cancellation table and internal procedures of the insurer. Note that a final premium figured on the basis of an insured-cancelled policy will be more than one figured on an insurer-cancelled basis.

- The sixth clause relates to the responsibility of the insured to maintain records. The insurer needs certain information concerning the risk to charge a proper premium, and the insured is required to help in this endeavor. This clause requires the insured not only to keep records, but also to provide copies of those records to the insurer upon request.

- The final clause deals with the right of the insurer to conduct audits. The insurer is given the right to examine and audit all the records of the insured that relate to the policy. Such records include ledgers, journals, registers, vouchers, contracts, tax reports, payroll and disbursement records, and programs for storing and retrieving data.

PART SIX – CONDITIONS

There are five conditions listed in the workers compensation policy that address the issues of administration. These issues include: dealing with inspections, long term policies, the transfer of the named insured's rights, cancellation of the policy, and just who acts as the sole representative on behalf of all the insured's.

- The inspections clause gives the insurer the right to inspect the workplace *"at any time."* This condition has given rise to a theory that would allow the injured employee to maintain an action for negligence against the workers compensation insurer for failure to inspect a workplace. However, the current policy contains a specific disclaimer about the inspection of the workplace and the duty such an inspection places on the insurer. In the inspection condition of the policy, the insurer declares that inspections it may carry out are not safety inspections but relate only to the insurability of the workplaces and the premiums to be charged. Furthermore, the insurer states that it does not undertake to perform the duty of any person to provide for the health or safety of the employees, and does not warrant that the workplace is safe or healthful, or that they comply with laws, codes, or standards. Thus, the insurer strives to intentionally limit its duty under the workers compensation policy to both the insured and any of the insured's employees.

- The long term policy clause notes that, if a policy is written for longer than one year and sixteen days – for example, a two or three year policy – then all the provisions in the existing policy apply as if under a brand new policy. In other words, the annual renewal is treated as an automatic rewrite of the existing policy, though both the insured and the insurer should reexamine the exposures in order to get proper premium for proper coverage.

- The transfer of rights clause acts to prevent the insured from transferring his or her rights or duties to another party without the written consent of the insurer. This is meant to protect the insurer from insuring an employer that it neither contracted for nor would want to insure in any instance. An exception is made, of course, for the legal representative of the insured in case the insured dies – notice must be given to the insurer within 30 days after the insured's death.

- The cancellation clause details how the insured or the insurer can cancel the policy. The clause allows the insured to cancel the policy at any time, even with only one day notice, as long as written notice is mailed to the insurer in advance of the cancellation date. The conditions for cancellation are frequently quite explicit in terms of statutory requirements. For example, in a number of states the workers compensation act provides that cancellation is not effective absent notice to the state agency charged with administering the compensation law, or the statute may require notification of the employer by registered mail rather than ordinary mail.

- The final policy condition makes the first named insured the sole representative to the insurer, so that important items such as changing the policy provisions or cancelling the policy can be dealt with without having the insurer sort through possibly conflicting statements or wishes from the various insured's. This is simply a common sense business practice.

INFORMATION PAGE

In addition to the contents of the standard workers compensation policy, the employer is provided with an Information Page which describes the scope of the contractual agreement between the insured and the insurer. The Information Page includes the name of the insurer and the name and address of the insured along with the period of time covered by the policy. Limits as regards coverage under the policy are defined in Item 3 along with a listing of the states where the policy is applicable. Any policy endorsements are also listed under Item 3.

Because the standard policy does not provide blanket coverage for all states in which the insured may have operations, it is important to fully understand how the policy affords coverage for various states. The two items which reference what states are covered are 3 A. and 3 C. Item 3 A. is fairly straight-forward and simply has the insurer list the states the insured operates in or expects to operate in at the inception of the policy. If an insured has work or employees residing (since an employee may be able to choose his state of residence when claiming benefits) on the effective date of the policy in any state not listed in Item 3 A. of the Information Page, coverage will not be afforded for that state unless the insurer is notified within 30 days.

Item 3 C. represents a safety net. In Item 3 C., states are listed where an insured expects it may have employees working in but the work in those states will begin after the effective date or renewal date of the policy, with some exception noted below. The policy requires that the insured notify the insurer at once if the insured begins any work in any state listed in Item 3 C.

"At once" is not defined when looking for coverage under Item 3 C. of the policy. However, it is clear that if work is taking place in a state when the policy goes into effect or renews, that state needs to be listed in Item 3 A. The following suggested wording should be used in 3 C., whenever possible: *"All states, U S territories and possessions except Washington, Wyoming, North Dakota, Ohio, Puerto Rico and the U.S. Virgin Islands and states designated in Item 3A of this Information Page."* However, this approach is only applicable if the insurer is licensed to write workers compensation coverage in "all states" except for the four monopolistic fund states.

This broad wording denoted above assures coverage in most jurisdictions even in unforeseen circumstances. In addition to those situations noted above, other exceptions to the general rule include the following:

- The employer is insured with a state fund that only writes in their state and are precluded by law from extending coverage to other states. Many state funds have made arrangements with other insurance carriers to address this situation.

- The insurer is not licensed to write workers compensation insurance in all states. Many regional insurers are licensed in a handful of states while other insurers may be licensed in only a single state for strategic reasons. Insurers are precluded from writing insurance in a state where they are not licensed.

- A number of insurers are not willing to provide the broad wording denoted above because the insurer may want to ensure that they know those locations where their insured is operating. This may be because the insurer does not want to provide coverage in certain states where they feel that rates may be inadequate or where they may be hesitant to write because rates in a particular classification are perceived inadequate for the exposure. Another reason may be that the insurer wants certain states of operation specifically listed as a "red flag" for their auditor to look for potential payroll in those states at audit.

The final item found on the Information Page is Item Four. This item contains a listing of work classifications used in the computation of the employer's premium. A rate per $100 of remuneration is included along with the estimated annual premium. As described in Part Five of the policy, the final premium will be determined following the conclusion of the policy period using the actual premium basis and the proper classifications and rates that lawfully apply to the work covered by the policy. The minimum premium for the policy is also included in Item Four.

BINDERS, RENEWALS AND CANCELLATIONS

A binder may be issued for workers compensation insurance. Generally, a binder is issued for a short period (e.g., 15, 20, 30, or 60 days) in order to provide the insurer with an opportunity to determine the characteristics of the risk and exercise its underwriting judgment. The binder is subject to the same rules and premium charges as policies. Every binder must show clearly the term for which the risk is covered and indicate that it is subject to the standard provisions contained in the policy. A binder is also subject to the same cancellation provisions and rules that pertain to the policy.

When a policy expires, it may be renewed by a new policy or by a renewal agreement. This renewal agreement refers specifically to a designated policy. The term of the renewal agreement may be one year or three years, at the option of the insurance carrier. A renewal agreement must be issued prior to the stated expiration date in the policy or in the latest renewal agreement which it renews.

The use of a renewal agreement eliminates the necessity for issuing a complete new policy. However, a renewal agreement is regarded as a separate policy subject to the rules applicable to the type of policy being renewed, (e.g., one-year, three-year fixed-rate, and three-year variable rate.)

Every policy or renewal agreement must afford coverage for a continuous period. If a policy has been terminated by cancellation, it may not be reinstated after the effective date of cancellation. Subsequent coverage must be afforded under a new policy. However, it is permissible to reinstate a policy prior to the effective date of cancellation. In all cases after a policy has expired, a renewal may be obtained only by means of a new policy.

The method of policy cancellation is set forth in the policy. A workers compensation policy may be canceled by either the insurance carrier or the insured. All cancellations, regardless of the reason, whether initiated at the request of the insured or initiated by the insurance carrier, must be affected by the insurer in accordance with the laws and regulations of each state. The period required for notice of cancellation differs by state, but the most common period for cancellation is 30 days.

WORKERS COMPENSATION AND EMPLOYERS LIABILITY INSURANCE POLICY WC 00 00 00 A

1st Reprint   *Effective April 1, 1992*   Standard

WORKERS COMPENSATION AND EMPLOYERS LIABILITY INSURANCE POLICY

In return for the payment of the premium and subject to all terms of this Policy, we agree with you as follows:

GENERAL SECTION

A. The Policy

This Policy includes at its effective date the Information Page and all endorsements and schedules listed there. It is a contract of insurance between you (the employer named in Item 1 of the Information Page) and us (the insurer named on the Information Page). The only agreements relating to this insurance are stated in this Policy. The terms of this Policy may not be changed or waived except by endorsement issued by us to be part of this Policy.

B. Who is Insured

You are insured if you are an employer named in Item 1 of the Information Page. If that employer is a partnership, and if you are one of its partners, you are insured, but only in your capacity as an employer of the partnership's employees.

C. Workers Compensation Law

Workers Compensation Law means the workers or workmen's compensation law and occupational disease law of each state or territory named in Item 3.A. of the Information Page. It includes any amendments to that law which are in effect during the Policy period. It does not include any federal workers or workmen's compensation law, any federal occupational disease law or the provisions of any law that provide nonoccupational disability benefits.

D. State

State means any state of the United States of America, and the District of Columbia.

E. Locations

This Policy covers all of your workplaces listed in Items 1 or 4 of the Information Page; and it covers all other workplaces in Item 3.A. states unless you have other insurance or are self-insured for such workplaces.

PART ONE
WORKERS COMPENSATION INSURANCE

A. How This Insurance Applies

This workers compensation insurance applies to bodily injury by accident or bodily injury by disease. Bodily injury includes resulting death.

1. Bodily injury by accident must occur during the Policy period.
2. Bodily injury by disease must be caused or aggravated by the conditions of your employment. The employee's last day of last exposure to the conditions causing or aggravating such bodily injury by disease must occur during the Policy period.

B. We Will Pay

We will pay promptly when due the benefits required of you by the workers compensation law.

C. We Will Defend

We have the right and duty to defend at our expense any claim, proceeding or suit against you for benefits payable by this insurance. We have the right to investigate and settle these claims, proceedings or suits.

We have no duty to defend a claim, proceeding or suit that is not covered by this insurance.

D. We Will Also Pay

We will also pay these costs, in addition to other amounts payable under this insurance, as part of any claim, proceeding or suit we defend:

1. reasonable expenses incurred at our request, but not loss of earnings;
2. premiums for bonds to release attachments and for appeal bonds in bond amounts up to the amount payable under this insurance;
3. litigation costs taxed against you;
4. interest on a judgment as required by law until we offer the amount due under this insurance-, and
5. expenses we incur.

E. Other Insurance

We will not pay more than our share of benefits and costs covered by this insurance and other

© 1991 National Council on Compensation Insurance.

WC 00 00 00 A	WORKERS COMPENSATION AND EMPLOYERS LIABILITY INSURANCE POLICY	
Standard	Effective April 1, 1992	1st Reprint

insurance or self-insurance. Subject to any limits of liability that may apply, all shares will be equal until the loss is paid. If any insurance or self-insurance is exhausted, the shares of all remaining insurance will be equal until the loss is paid.

F. Payments You Must Make

You are responsible for any payments in excess of the benefits regularly provided by the workers compensation law including those required because:

1. of your serious and willful misconduct;
2. you knowingly employ an employee in violation of law;
3. you fail to comply with a health or safety law or regulation; or
4. you discharge, coerce or otherwise discriminate against any employee in violation of the workers compensation law.

If we make any payments in excess of the benefits regularly provided by the workers compensation law on your behalf, you will reimburse us promptly.

G. Recovery From Others

We have your rights, and the rights of persons entitled to the benefits of this insurance, to recover our payments from anyone liable for the injury. You will do everything necessary to protect those rights for us and to help us enforce them.

H. Statutory Provisions

These statements apply where they are required by law.

1. As between an injured worker and us, we have notice of the injury when you have notice.
2. Your default or the bankruptcy or insolvency of you or your estate will not relieve us of our duties under this insurance after an injury occurs.
3. We are directly and primarily liable to any person entitled to the benefits payable by this insurance. Those persons may enforce our duties; so may an agency authorized by law. Enforcement may be against us or against you and us.
4. Jurisdiction over you is jurisdiction over us for purposes of the workers compensation law. We are bound by decisions against you under that law, subject to the provisions of this Policy that are not in conflict with that law.
5. This insurance conforms to the parts of the workers compensation law that apply to:
   a. benefits payable by this insurance;
   b. special taxes, payments into security or other special funds, and assessments payable by us under that law.
6. Terms of this insurance that conflict with the workers compensation law are changed by this statement to conform to that law.

Nothing in these paragraphs relieves you of your duties under this Policy.

PART TWO
EMPLOYERS LIABILITY INSURANCE

A. How This Insurance Applies

This employers liability insurance applies to bodily injury by accident or bodily injury by disease. Bodily injury includes resulting death.

1. The bodily injury must arise out of and in the course of the injured employee's employment by you.
2. The employment must be necessary or incidental to your work in a state or territory listed in Item 3.A. of the Information Page.
3. Bodily injury by accident must occur during the Policy period.
4. Bodily injury by disease must be caused or aggravated by the conditions of your employment. The employee's last day of last exposure to the conditions causing or aggravating such bodily injury by disease must occur during the Policy period.
5. If you are sued, the original suit and any related legal actions for damages for bodily injury by accident or by disease must be brought in the United States of America, its territories or possessions, or Canada.

B. We Will Pay

We will pay all sums you legally must pay as damages because of bodily injury to your employees, provided the bodily injury is covered by this Employers Liability Insurance.

The damages we will pay, where recovery is permitted by law, include damages:

1. for which you are liable to a third party by reason of a claim or suit against you by that third party to recover the damages claimed

WORKERS COMPENSATION AND EMPLOYERS LIABILITY INSURANCE POLICY

against such third party as a result of injury to your employee;
2. for care and loss of services; and
3. for consequential bodily injury to a spouse, child, parent, brother or sister of the injured employee; provided that these damages are the direct consequence of bodily injury that arises out of and in the course of the injured employee's employment by you; and
4. because of bodily injury to your employee that arises out of and in the course of employment, claimed against you in a capacity other than as employer.

C. Exclusions

This insurance does not cover:
1. liability assumed under a contract. This exclusion does not apply to a warranty that your work will be done in a workmanlike manner;
2. punitive or exemplary damages because of bodily injury to an employee employed in violation of law;
3. bodily injury to an employee while employed in violation of law with your actual knowledge or the actual knowledge of any of your executive officers;
4. any obligation imposed by a workers compensation, occupational disease, unemployment compensation, or disability benefits law, or any similar law;
5. bodily injury intentionally caused or aggravated by you,
6. bodily injury occurring outside the United States of America, its territories or possessions, and Canada. This exclusion does not apply to bodily injury to a citizen or resident of the United States of America or Canada who is temporarily outside these countries,
7. damages arising out of coercion, criticism, demotion, evaluation, reassignment, discipline, defamation, harassment, humiliation, discrimination against or termination of any employee, or any personnel practices, policies, acts or omissions,
8. bodily injury to any person in work subject to the Longshore and Harbor Workers' Compensation Act (33 USC Sections 901-950), the Non-appropriated Fund Instrumentalities Act (5 USC Sections 8171-8173), the Outer Continental Shelf Lands Act (43 USC Sections 1331-1356), the Defense Base Act (42 USC Sections 16511654), the Federal Coal Mine Health and Safety Act of 1969 (30 USC Sections 901-942), any other federal workers or workmen's compensation law or other federal occupational disease law, or any amendments to these laws;
9. bodily injury to any person in work subject to the Federal Employers' Liability Act (45 USC Sections 51-60), any other federal laws obligating an employer to pay damages to an employee due to bodily injury arising out of or in the course of employment, or any amendments to those laws-,
10. bodily injury to a master or member of the crew of any vessel;
11. fines or penalties imposed for violation of federal or state law; and
12. damages payable under the Migrant and Seasonal Agricultural Worker Protection Act (29 USC Sections 1801-1872) and under any other federal law awarding damages for violation of those laws or regulations issued thereunder, and any amendments to those laws.

D. We Will Defend

We have the right and duty to defend, at our expense, any claim, proceeding or suit against you for damages payable by this insurance. We have the right to investigate and settle these claims, proceedings and suits.

We have no duty to defend a claim, proceeding or suit that is not covered by this insurance. We have no duty to defend or continue defending after we have paid our applicable limit of liability under this insurance.

E. We Will Also Pay

We will also pay these costs, in addition to other amounts payable under this insurance, as part of any claim, proceeding, or suit we defend:
1. reasonable expenses incurred at our request, but not loss of earnings;
2. premiums for bonds to release attachments and for appeal bonds in bond amounts up to the limit of our liability under this insurance-,
3. litigation costs taxed against you;
4. interest on a judgment as required by law until we offer the amount due under this insurance; and
5. expenses we incur.

F. Other Insurance

We will not pay more than our share of damages and costs covered by this insurance and other insurance or self-insurance. Subject to any limits of liability that apply, all shares will be equal until the loss is paid. If any insurance or self-insurance is exhausted, the shares of all remaining insurance and self-insurance will be equal until the loss is paid.

G. Limits of Liability

Our liability to pay for damages is limited. Our limits of liability are shown in Item 3.B. of the Information Page. They apply as explained below.

1. Bodily Injury by Accident. The limit shown for "bodily injury by accident—each accident" is the most we will pay for all damages covered by this insurance because of bodily injury to one or more employees in any one accident.

    A disease is not bodily injury by accident unless it results directly from bodily injury by accident.

2. Bodily Injury by Disease. The limit shown for "bodily injury by disease—Policy limit" is the most we will pay for all damages covered by this insurance and arising out of bodily injury by disease, regardless of the number of employees who sustain bodily injury by disease. The limit shown for "bodily injury by disease—each employee" is the most we will pay for all damages because of bodily injury by disease to any one employee.

    Bodily injury by disease does not include disease that results directly from a bodily injury by accident.

3. We will not pay any claims for damages after we have paid the applicable limit of our liability under this insurance.

H. Recovery From Others

We have your rights to recover our payment from anyone liable for an injury covered by this insurance. You will do everything necessary to protect those rights for us and to help us enforce them.

I. Actions Against Us

There will be no right of action against us under this insurance unless:

1. You have complied with all the terms of this Policy; and

2. The amount you owe has been determined with our consent or by actual trial and final judgment.

    This insurance does not give anyone the right to add us as a defendant in an action against you to determine your liability. The bankruptcy or insolvency of you or your estate will not relieve us of our obligations under this Part.

PART THREE
OTHER STATES INSURANCE

A. How This Insurance Applies

1. This other states insurance applies only if one or more states are shown in Item 3.C. of the Information Page.

2. If you begin work in any one of those states after the effective date of this Policy and are not insured or are not self-insured for such work, all provisions of the Policy will apply as though that state were listed in Item 3.A. of the Information Page.

3. We will reimburse you for the benefits required by the workers compensation law of that state if we are not permitted to pay the benefits directly to persons entitled to them.

4. If you have work on the effective date of this Policy in any state not listed in Item 3.A. of the Information Page, coverage will not be afforded for that state unless we are notified within thirty days.

B. Notice

Tell us at once if you begin work in any state listed in Item 3.C. of the Information Page.

PART FOUR
YOUR DUTIES IF INJURY OCCURS

Tell us at once if injury occurs that may be covered by this Policy. Your other duties are listed here.

1. Provide for immediate medical and other services required by the workers compensation law.

2. Give us or our agent the names and addresses of the injured persons and of witnesses, and other information we may need.

3. Promptly give us all notices, demands and legal

papers related to the injury, claim, proceeding or suit.

4. Cooperate with us and assist us, as we may request, in the investigation, settlement or defense of any claim, proceeding or suit.

5. Do nothing after an injury occurs that would interfere with our right to recover from others.

6. Do not voluntarily make payments, assume obligations or incur expenses, except at your own cost.

PART FIVE—PREMIUM

A. Our Manuals

All premium for this Policy will be determined by our manuals of rules, rates, rating plans and classifications. We may change our manuals and apply the changes to this Policy if authorized by law or a governmental agency regulating this insurance.

B. Classifications

Item 4 of the Information Page shows the rate and premium basis for certain business or work classifications. These classifications were assigned based on an estimate of the exposures you would have during the Policy period. If your actual exposures are not properly described by those classifications, we will assign proper classifications, rates and premium basis by endorsement to this Policy.

C. Remuneration

Premium for each work classification is determined by multiplying a rate times a premium basis. Remuneration is the most common premium basis. This premium basis includes payroll and all other remuneration paid or payable during the Policy period for the services of:

1. all your officers and employees engaged in work covered by this Policy; and

2. all other persons engaged in work that could make us liable under Part One (Workers Compensation Insurance) of this Policy. If you do not have payroll records for these persons, the contract price for their services and materials may be used as the premium basis. This paragraph 2 will not apply if you give us proof that the employers of these persons lawfully secured their workers compensation obligations.

D. Premium Payments

You will pay all premium when due. You will pay the premium even if part or all of a workers compensation law is not valid.

E. Final Premium

The premium shown on the Information Page, schedules, and endorsements is an estimate. The final premium will be determined after this Policy ends by using the actual, not the estimated, premium basis and the proper classifications and rates that lawfully apply to the business and work covered by this Policy. If the final premium is more than the premium you paid to us, you must pay us the balance. If it is less, we will refund the balance to you. The final premium will not be less than the highest minimum premium for the classifications covered by this Policy.

If this Policy is canceled, final premium will be determined in the following way unless our manuals provide otherwise:

1. If we cancel, final premium will be calculated pro rata based on the time this Policy was in force. Final premium will not be less than the pro rata share of the minimum premium.

2. If you cancel, final premium will be more than pro rata; it will be based on the time this Policy was in force, and increased by our short-rate cancelation table and procedure. Final premium will not be less than the minimum premium.

F. Records

You will keep records of information needed to compute premium. You will provide us with copies of those records when we ask for them.

G. Audit

You will let us examine and audit all your records that relate to this Policy. These records include ledgers, journals, registers, vouchers, contracts, tax reports, payroll and disbursement records, and programs for storing and retrieving data. We may conduct the audits during regular business hours during the Policy period and within three years after the Policy period ends. Information developed by audit will be used to determine final premium. Insurance rate service organizations have the same rights we have under this provision.

© 1991 National Council on Compensation Insurance.

WC 00 00 00 A **WORKERS COMPENSATION AND EMPLOYERS LIABILITY INSURANCE POLICY**

Standard *Effective April 1, 1992* 1st Reprint

PART SIX—CONDITIONS

A. Inspection

We have the right, but are not obliged to inspect your workplaces at any time. Our inspections are not safety inspections. They relate only to the insurability of the workplaces and the premiums to be charged. We may give you reports on the conditions we find. We may also recommend changes. While they may help reduce losses, we do not undertake to perform the duty of any person to provide for the health or safety of your employees or the public. We do not warrant that your workplaces are safe or healthful or that they comply with laws, regulations, codes or standards. Insurance rate service organizations have the same rights we have under this provision.

B. Long Term Policy

If the Policy period is longer than one year and sixteen days, all provisions of this Policy will apply as though a new Policy were issued on each annual anniversary that this Policy is in force.

C. Transfer of Your Rights and Duties

Your rights or duties may not be transferred without our written consent.

If you die and we receive notice within thirty days after your death, we will cover your legal representative as insured.

D. Cancelation

1. You may cancel this Policy. You must mail or deliver advance written notice to us stating when the cancelation is to take effect.

2. We may cancel this Policy. We must mail or deliver to you not less than ten days advance written notice stating when the cancelation is to take effect. Mailing that notice to you at your mailing address shown in Item 1 of the Information Page will be sufficient to prove notice.

3. The Policy period will end on the day and hour stated in the cancelation notice.

4. Any of these provisions that conflict with a law that controls the cancelation of the insurance in this Policy is changed by this statement to comply with the law.

E. Sole Representative

The insured first named in Item 1 of the Information Page will act on behalf of all insureds to change this Policy, receive return premium, and give or receive notice of cancelation.

WORKERS COMPENSATION AND EMPLOYERS LIABILITY INSURANCE POLICY WC 00 00 01 A

Original Printing *Issued May 1, 1988* Standard

INFORMATION PAGE

Insurer:

POLICY NO.
| | | | | | | | | | |

1. The Insured: _____ Individual

   Partnership

   Mailing address: _____ Corporation or

   Other workplaces not shown above:

2. The Policy period is from _____ to _____ at the insured's mailing address.

3. A. Workers Compensation Insurance'. Part One of the Policy applies to the Workers Compensation Law of the states listed here:

   B. Employers Liability Insurance: Part Two of the Policy applies to work in each state listed in Item 3.A. The limits of our liability under Part Two are:

   Bodily Injury by Accident $_____ each accident
   Bodily Injury by Disease $_____ Policy limit
   Bodily Injury by Disease $_____ each employee

   C. Other States Insurance: Part Three of the Policy applies to the states, if any, listed here:

   D. This Policy includes these endorsements and schedules:

4.

Classifications	Code No.	Premium Basis Total Estimated Annual Remuneration	Rate Per $100 of Remuneration	Estimated Annual Premium

Total Estimated Annual Premium $

Minimum Premium $

Expense Constant $

Countersigned by _____

i

© 1987 National Council on Compensation Insurance.

WORKERS COMPENSATION AND EMPLOYERS LIABILITY INSURANCE POLICY WC 00 00 01 A
Original Printing   *Issued June 1, 1991*   **Standard**

GENERAL INFORMATION PAGE NOTES

1. Insurance carriers may show a renewal agreement statement on the standard Information Page when a Policy is renewed. The carrier must show "Renewal Agreement" or a like heading along with the title "Information Page" if a renewal agreement statement is shown on the Information Page.

2. Insurance carriers showing a renewal agreement statement on the Information Page or entering into a renewal agreement not shown on the Information Page may list any or all endorsements in Item 3.D., elsewhere on the Information Page or in an Information Page Schedule. A carrier is not required to attach such listed endorsements to the Information Page and Policy if the endorsements have already been provided to the insured by that carrier.

3. These General Information Page Notes do not affect the standard Information Page entry requirements set forth in the Information Page Notes.

© 1988, 1991 National Council on Compensation Insurance.

WORKERS COMPENSATION POLICY ENDORSEMENTS

NCCI has developed and filed policy endorsement forms in eligible states. These forms are of two types – "Standard" and "Advisory." Standard forms allow only limited modifications which may be applied to the form or endorsement which are spelled out in detail. Advisory forms may be used and modified in almost any way the insurer feels necessary as long as appropriately filed with the proper state authorities.

The coverage forms and endorsements are designated with unique identification sequences that give clues to the type, usage, version, and applicable state in which the form or endorsement may be used. NCCI endorsements begin with the prefix "WC" to indicate that they are workers compensation endorsements, followed by eight and sometimes nine characters. They are arranged in three two-digit sequences, sometimes followed by a single letter of the alphabet. The first two digits indicate whether the form or endorsement is multi-state or state specific. If 00 is used, it is general. Any other two-digit combination except 89 and 99 indicates a state-specific endorsement. The number 89 means a miscellaneous endorsement, notice, or related transaction and the number 99 may be used by an insurer for their own company specific endorsements.

The following lists just a sample of the available endorsements to include with a policy and describes their content. It should be noted that there are also state-specific endorsements that are applicable only in that particular state named in the endorsement that bring the policy into conformity with state law or regulation. (Those state specific endorsements are too numerous to discuss in any detail here.) There are also endorsements that pertain to federal laws on the subject of workers compensation, such as the maritime coverage endorsement and the federal employer's liability coverage endorsement.

A brief description of the endorsements covered is presented in numerical order. This description includes the purpose and use of each of the endorsements. It is important to again reiterate that this is only a partial list of endorsements that are available for use and that individual states have also developed specific endorsements for use in that particular jurisdiction.

WC 00 03 01 – Alternate Employer Endorsement applies only with respect to bodily injury to the employees of the named insured who are in the course of special or temporary employment by the alternate employer listed on the endorsement. For example, this endorsement can be used when a supplier of temporary office help (the insured) is required by its customer (the user of the temporary office help, that is, the alternate employer) to provide this insurance to protect the customer from claims brought by the insured's employees against the alternate employer. If the named insured has an employee who is injured while working for the alternate employer listed on the endorsement, coverage will be provided for claims made by the employee against that alternate employer.

WC 00 03 03 B – Employers Liability Coverage Endorsement is generally used in monopolistic fund states where the workers compensation system is not open to coverage by private insurance companies. The endorsement is explicit that Part One of the workers compensation policy does not apply to work conducted in the monopolistic fund state. On the other hand, Part Two coverage applies to work in such states as though the states were shown in Item 3.A. of the Information Page. Basically, the endorsement provides "stop gap" coverage for employers in those states where the state fund provides Part One coverage but does not offer Employers Liability coverage.

WC 00 03 05 – Joint Venture as Insured Endorsement states, *"If the employer named in Item 1 of the information page is a joint venture, and if you are one of its members, you are insured, but only in your capacity as an employer of the joint venture's employees."* The workers compensation policy makes no mention of business arrangements such as joint ventures, but joint ventures can be employers. Large construction projects often are performed by joint venture contractors. This endorsement makes explicit that the insurance afforded by the policy is limited to that of the employer of those employees that are working for the joint venture. If an employer is involved in a joint venture but also has other business interests and operations, such employer will need a separate workers compensation policy to apply to injuries suffered by those employees working in the other businesses and operations.

WC 00 03 06 – Medical Benefits Exclusion Endorsement states that workers compensation medical benefits of a state listed on the endorsement are not covered. Some states permit insured's to pay medical benefits directly, instead of channeling them through the workers compensation insurer. Thus, the policy pays only indemnity benefits — often called an "ex-medical policy." At present, 17 states permit self-insurance of medical benefits: **Alabama, Colorado, Connecticut, Florida, Hawaii, Idaho, Indiana, Iowa, Kentucky, Louisiana, Minnesota, New Mexico, North Carolina, Rhode Island, South Carolina, South Dakota,** and **Vermont.** The endorsement directs that the insured employer pay medical benefits as required by law and to the satisfaction of the insurer. In **New York,** a related reimbursement endorsement (WC 31 03 10) applies to insured employers who operate licensed or authorized hospitals or medical facilities.

WC 00 03 08 – Partners, Officers and Others Exclusion Endorsement allows, in a number of states, partners and executive officers to choose to be subject to the workers compensation laws. If these individuals so choose the premium basis of the workers compensation policy includes their remuneration. However, where the individual partners or executive officers opt not to be covered, endorsement WC 00 03 08 should be attached to the policy. The endorsement states that the policy does not cover bodily injury to any person described in the schedule and that the premium basis for the policy does not include their remuneration. Individuals can be named on this endorsement only when the state workers compensation law allows it.

WC 00 03 10 – Sole Proprietors, Partners, Officers and Others Coverage Endorsement is in direct contrast with endorsement WC 00 03 08. This endorsement is used when partners and executive officers opt to be subject to the workers compensation laws. The endorsement notes that the individuals listed on the schedule have elected to be subject to the law and that the premium basis for the policy includes their remuneration. As with the previous endorsement, individuals can be named in this endorsement only when it is allowed by the state workers compensation law.

WC 00 03 11 - Voluntary Compensation and Employers Liability Coverage Endorsement can be used to cover employees such as domestics, farm workers or other employees who are not subject to the law in the state where the policy is written. This endorsement can be attached to an existing workers compensation policy that is in place for those employees that are required by state law to be covered.

Coverage provided under the Voluntary Compensation endorsement is identical to that for employees required to be insured under the law. WC 00 03 11 states that the insurer *"will pay an amount equal to the benefits that would be required of you if you and your employees described in the schedule were subject to the workers compensation law shown in the schedule. We will pay those amounts to the persons who would be entitled to them under the law."* In other words, benefits are provided for injuries that would have been compensable in the same manner as they would have been provided had the employment been subject to any applicable state workers compensation laws.

It is also to be noted that before any payments can be made to those entitled to such benefits, the beneficiaries must release the insured and the insurer, in writing, of all responsibility for the injury. Any right to recover from others who may be responsible for the injury must be transferred to the insurer, and the injured party must cooperate fully with the insurer in enforcing the right of recovery. If the persons entitled to the benefits of the insurance refuses to comply with the requirements, or if they claim damages from the insured or the insurer, the duty to pay under this endorsement terminates immediately.

WC 00 03 13 – Waiver of Our Right to Recover from Others provides that the insurer, through this endorsement, waives its right of subrogation against third parties who may be responsible for an injury if those third parties are named in the endorsement's schedule. In many instances, these named third parties include other companies under the same ownership as the insured.

WC 00 03 15 – Domestic and Agricultural Workers Exclusion addresses the fact that domestic, agricultural, and casual employees are not treated in a uniform manner under the workers compensation systems of the various states. Some states have written their workers compensation laws to include domestic and agricultural employees either on a compulsory basis, or to allow employees to provide coverage voluntarily. This endorsement can be used to deny workers compensation benefits coverage to any agricultural, domestic, or household worker as long as the state law allows this course of action. Those workers denied coverage have to be listed in the endorsement's schedule.

WC 00 03 19 – Employee Leasing Client Endorsement is attached to policies issued to labor contracting businesses. It specifies that coverage for leased workers will be provided by the business that is leasing the employees under contract (the client), not the labor contractor. The endorsement requires that the labor contractor provide its insurer with the following information within 30 days of entering a labor contract: contract effective date and term, client's name, client's federal employer identification number, client's mailing address, number of workers leased, description of duties of each, and work location for each. Clients of the labor contract must maintain workers compensation coverage for their direct and leased workers, and proof of that coverage must be submitted to the labor contractor's insurer. If proof is not submitted, the labor contractor must pay premium for the leased employees and the insurer may cancel the labor contractor's policy.

WC 00 03 20 A – Labor Contractor Endorsement is attached to policies issued to businesses that lease workers (the client) from a labor contracting business. It specifies that leased employees will be covered for workers compensation under the client's insurance policy. This endorsement is used in conjunction with WC 00 03 19, which is attached to the labor contractor's policy. If the client's insurer is not permitted to pay benefits directly, the insurer will reimburse the labor contractor for benefits it is required to pay for the leased employees. This endorsement does not satisfy the labor contractor's need to carry workers compensation coverage. It addresses only the employees leased by the client from the labor contractor specified in the schedule for the states listed. The coverage may be further restricted to a specific contract or project on which the leased employees are working.

WC 00 03 21 – Labor Contractor Exclusion Endorsement defines employee leasing as an arrangement in which a business engages a third party to provide it with workers for a fee or other compensation. The third party is referred to as the labor contractor. The entity leasing the employees is called the client. The endorsement excludes coverage for workers that the labor contractor leases to clients listed on the endorsement. Coverage must be provided by the client. The endorsement is attached to a labor contractor's policy. Temporary workers are not considered leased workers.

WC 00 03 22 – Employee Leasing Client Exclusion Endorsement limits coverage under the policy to employees of the insured who are not leased from third parties. It excludes coverage under the policy for workers that the insured leases from labor contractors. It defines labor contractor and client in the same way as does WC 00 03 21.

WC 00 04 02 - Anniversary Rating Date Endorsement. Most companies are subject to experience rating and the experience modification is subject to change on the anniversary rating date of the company. The anniversary rating date usually corresponds with the inception date of the policy. However, there are times when the anniversary rating date differs from the policy inception date. When this happens, WC 00 04 02 is attached. The endorsement states that the premium, rates, and experience modification used on the policy may be changed at the anniversary rating date that is shown in the endorsement.

WC 00 04 03 - Experience Rating Modification Factor Endorsement is attached when the experience modification that applies to the policy is not available when the policy is issued. The endorsement states that the factor will be endorsed onto the policy when it becomes available. The premium is subject to change if the modification differs from the one used when the policy was issued.

WC 00 04 05 - Policy Period Endorsement is used if the policy period is longer than one year and 16 days and does not consist of complete 12-month periods. It stipulates how the policy will be separated into premium periods.

WC 00 04 06 - Premium Discount Endorsement is used to show the application of a premium discount, or to identify the insured's policy that shows the application of the discount rule. The endorsement (or WC 00 04 06 A) may be used to outline the premium discount percentages that apply to the ascending premium amount.

WC 00 04 20 - Terrorism Risk Insurance Act (TRIA) Endorsement was developed by NCCI to fulfill a requirement of the TRIA to show the charge for terrorism coverage as a separate line item on the policy. The endorsement contains definitions based on TRIA, states the limit of liability on the insurer as stated in TRIA, states that the government will pay 90 percent of terrorism or war losses above the insurer's deductible, and shows the rate per $100 of remuneration for each applicable state.

On a federal level, in response to 9/11, Congress enacted and the President signed into law the Terrorism Risk Insurance Act (TRIA) of 2002. This law does not address the compensability of injuries arising from terrorist acts. Such injuries remain subject to state workers compensation laws. However, while it is in effect, TRIA requires property and casualty insurers to offer policyholders insurance for losses resulting from acts of foreign terrorism occurring within the United States or on an air carrier or vessel or on the premises of a U.S. mission. Acts of war as declared by Congress are expressly considered terrorist acts for purposes of workers compensation insurance. Insurance coverage offered for terrorist acts may not differ materially from the terms of coverage for losses from acts arising from events other than terrorist acts. In both instances, the U.S. government provides a backstop for a certain percentage of losses under the TRIA.

TRIA was initially created as a temporary three-year federal program allowing the federal government to share monetary losses with insurers on commercial property and casualty losses due to a terrorist attack. Since then, it has been renewed four times: in 2005, 2007, 2015, and 2019. The current reauthorization is currently slated to expire December 31, 2027. TRIA requires insurers to make terrorism coverage available to commercial policyholders but does not require insureds to purchase it.[103]

WC 00 05 03 A - Retrospective Premium Endorsement One Year Plan acknowledges that a one-year retrospective rating plan is in effect. The endorsement outlines the retrospective premium formula and program elements, including the policies subject to retro rating; loss limitation, if any; loss conversion factor; minimum and maximum premium factors; basic premium factors; and the tax multipliers, excess loss premium factors, and retrospective development factors as they apply in the states where retrospective rating is applicable.

---

[103] https://content.naic.org/cipr_topics/topic_terrorism_risk_insurance_act_tria.htm

FEDERAL COMPENSATION PROGRAMS

There are various federal laws pertaining to workers compensation that affect workers employed in areas that are beyond the authority of an individual state. As a way to comply with these federal coverage requirements, several endorsements are available for use with the workers compensation policy. Federal coverages include:

Federal Employees Compensation Act (FECA)[104]

The Federal Employees' Compensation Act (FECA) provides federal employees injured in the performance of their duties with benefits which include wage-loss benefits for total or partial disability, monetary benefits for permanent loss of use of a schedule member, medical benefits, and vocational rehabilitation. In addition, compensation benefits are payable to surviving dependents if a work-related injury or illness results in the employee's death.

As the name implies, the largest group of employees covered under FECA is the federal workforce. Eligible workers include all civilian executives, legislative and judicial branch employees as well as civilian defense workers, medical workers in veterans' hospitals, and employees of the U.S. Postal Service. Additionally, special legislation extends coverage to Peace Corps and other volunteers, federal jurors, Reserve Officer Training Corps (ROTC) cadets, and other groups working in some capacity as part of federal programs.

All injuries, including disease proximately caused by the employment, sustained while in the performance of duty by civilian employees of the Department of Defense (DOD) including volunteers and emergency hires are covered. It is the responsibility of the employee to provide medical and factual evidence to establish the essential elements of the claim – i.e., that the claim was filed within the statutory time requirements of FECA, the injured or deceased person was an employee within the meaning of FECA, the employee sustained an injury or disease, the employee was in the performance of duty when the injury occurred, and the condition found resulted from the injury.

The FECA disability benefit formula replaces two-thirds of the employee's pay rate if he/she has no dependents, or augmented to three-fourths of the pay rate if he/she is married or has one or more dependents. In addition to the payment of disability benefits, generally, all necessary hospital, physician and medication costs are covered as well as transportation costs to a medical facility for treatment. FECA is administered by the Office of Workers Compensation Programs (OWCP), U.S. Department of Labor, through district offices located throughout the United States.

---

[104] 5 USC Chapter 81

In FY2019, the FECA program paid out more than $2.7 billion in benefits to the survivors of federal employees killed on the job. In FY2019, administrative expenses totaled $177.4 million.[105]

Federal Employers Liability Act (FELA)[106]

No-fault workers compensation benefits available to injured workers in other industries are not available to railroad workers injured or killed on the job. To recover for an on-the-job injury or death, railroad workers or their dependents must prove their case under the Federal Employer's Liability Act (FELA), which was passed by Congress in 1907. FELA allows a railroad worker injured on the job to sue to recover damages for lost earning, both past and future; out-of-pocket medical expenses; any reduction in ability to earn wages because of the injury; and pain and suffering. This law requires proof that the injury to the worker was caused, in whole or in part, by the negligence of the railroad through the conduct of another railroad employee, agent, and/or contractor.

The legislative history of FELA and judicial decisions interpreting the law plainly indicate that Congress regards FELA as more than a compensation scheme for railroad workers, but also as an inducement to the railroad industry to promote safe work practices to reduce the number of injuries and deaths. Following enactment of the Act 1907, the United States Supreme Court recognized the Congressional intent to promote safety through the FELA when it opined: "*The Act ... is intended to stimulate carriers to greater diligence for the safety of their employees and of the persons and property of their patrons.*"[107] Clearly, Congress passed FELA to force the railroads to impose safe working conditions not just for the protection of the workers but also for the protection of the public at large.

In the 44 years immediately following the enactment of FELA, twenty-six bills were introduced to replace FELA with a traditional workers compensation program. In each instance, Congress refused to make the change. These attempts to change FELA have continued to the present, and in each instance they have been rebuffed by a Congress acutely aware of the need in the railroad industry for a law with the emphasis directed at the cause of safety for the public and for railroad workers exposed to the peculiar hazards of this industry on a daily basis.

Although FELA requires a showing of negligence or fault in the awarding of damages for a work connected injury or death, it employs the doctrine of *comparative negligence,* even in those jurisdictions that have adhered to the common law doctrine of contributory negligence. Negligence is generally defined as the doing of something that a reasonably prudent person would not do, or the failure to do something that a reasonably prudent person would do under the same or similar circumstances. In the context of FELA cases, the reasonably prudent railroad worker is substituted for the reasonably prudent person.

---

[105] https://www.dol.gov/sites/dolgov/files/owcp/OWCPAnnualReporttoCongressFY19_FINAL.pdf
[106] 45 U.S.C. §§ 51-60
[107] *Jamison v. Encarnacion,* 281 U.S. 635, 640 (1930)

In applying the doctrine of comparative negligence, if the injured employee was negligent, rather than strike out the entire award, the award in a FELA case would be reduced by the percentage that the employee's own negligence contributed to the injury. For example, if the employee was found to be 30 percent negligent and the railroad was held to be 70 percent negligent, the railroad workers damage verdict would be reduced by 30 percent.

Where the injured worker can show negligence on the part of the railroad, he or she can recover damages, generally payable in a lump sum award which would include payment for any wage loss, past and future medical expenses not covered by insurance provided by the railroad and not already paid by the railroad, along with damages awarded for pain and suffering, past and future, including damages for disfigurement from scarring, permanent injury, or emotional distress.

FELA claims may be pursued in a state or federal court and a jury trial is provided to the injured railroad worker. The jury determines whether there was negligence on the part of the railroad, whether there was any negligence of the injured worker, the percentage of comparative negligence contributing to the injury by each, and the amount of damages, if any.

The Federal Employers Liability Act Coverage Endorsement (WC 00 01 04) applies only to work subject to the Federal Employers Liability Act and any amendment to that Act in effect during the policy period. For example, FELA makes an interstate railroad liable for bodily injuries sustained by an employee if the injured employee can show any negligence on the part of the railroad. Due to the interstate nature of the employment, such employees are not subject to state workers compensation laws and this endorsement covers the liability of the railroad. The liability to pay for damages is limited and the limits are set forth in the schedule. The limits of liability for bodily injury by accident are on an each accident basis. The limits for bodily injury by disease are on an aggregate basis.

Coal Mine Health and Safety Act (CMHSA)

In 1891, the United States Congress passed the first federal statute governing mine safety, marking the beginning of what was to be an extended evolution of increasingly comprehensive legislation regulating mining activities. The 1891 law was relatively modest legislation that applied only to mines in U.S. territories and established minimum ventilation requirements at underground coal mines and prohibited operators from employing children under 12 years of age.

Following a decade in which the number of coal mine fatalities exceeded 2,000 annually, Congress established the Bureau of Mines in 1910 as a new agency in the Department of the Interior. The Bureau was charged with the responsibility to conduct research and to reduce accidents in the coal mining industry. In 1947, Congress authorized the formulation of the first code of federal regulations for mine safety. In 1966, Congress extended coverage of the 1952 Coal Act to all underground coal mines.

The Federal Coal Mine Health and Safety Act of 1969[108] included surface as well as underground coal mines within its scope, required two annual inspections of every surface coal mine and four at every underground coal mine, and dramatically increased federal enforcement powers in coal mines. The Coal Act also required monetary penalties for all violations, and established criminal penalties for knowing and willful violations. The safety standards for all coal mines were strengthened, and health standards were adopted.

Most importantly, the Coal Act of 1969 provided compensation for miners who were totally and permanently disabled by the progressive respiratory disease caused by the inhalation of fine coal dust pneumoconiosis or "black lung." In addition, miners became eligible for medical and disability benefits and the survivors of miners who died because of black lung disease became eligible for cash benefits. The medical benefits consist of diagnostic testing (available for all claimants) and services needed due to the disease, including drugs, durable medical equipment, home nursing visits, and hospitalization.

The base rate of the compensation benefit is set at three-eighths of the federal salary for an employee in grade GS-2, Step 1. The benefit is augmented if the miner or his or her survivor has dependents, up to double the base rate when there are three or more dependents. Black lung benefits are not subject to federal income tax but may be taxed by the states. The benefits may be subject to offsets, depending on when the initial claim was made, against various other support systems such as state workers compensation programs, private disability insurance, and Social Security Title II benefits.

In 2006, Congress passed the Mine Improvement and New Emergency Response Act (MINER Act) which amended the former law to require mine-specific emergency response plans in underground coal mines, added new regulations regarding mine rescue teams and sealing of abandoned areas, required prompt notification of mine accidents, and enhanced civil penalties.

The Federal Coal Mine Act is administered by the Federal Office of Workers Compensation Programs and is funded primarily by a tax on coal production. While dust control has yielded some success in reducing new cases, nearly 5,000 new black lung claims are still being received each year and more than 60,000 primary beneficiaries remain on the rolls, at a total cost of $400 million per year.

The Federal Coal Mine and Safety Act Coverage Endorsement (WC 00 01 01) is used when the workers compensation policy is to cover exposures subject to the Federal Coal Mine Health and Safety Act. The endorsement states that the definition of workers compensation law includes the Coal Mine Act and applies only to work in a state shown in the schedule. Under this endorsement, the insurance applies to bodily injury by disease that is caused or aggravated by the conditions of the employment and the employee's last day of exposure to the conditions causing or aggravating such bodily injury by disease must occur during the policy period.

---

[108] 30 U.S.C. § 901 et seq

Radiation Exposure Compensation Act (RECA)

The Radiation Exposure Compensation Act provides one-time benefit payments to persons who may have developed cancer or other specified diseases after being exposed to radiation from atomic weapons testing or uranium mining, milling, or transporting. Administered by the Department of Justice (DOJ), RECA has awarded over $2.4 billion in benefits to more than 37,000 claimants since its inception in 1990. RECA benefits are available to the following groups:

- Onsite participants — $75,000 to persons who participated onsite in the atmospheric test of an atomic weapon and developed one of the types of cancers specified in the statute.

- Downwinders — $50,000 to persons who were present in one of the specified areas near the Nevada Test Site during a period of atmospheric atomic weapons testing and developed one of the types of cancers specified in the statute.

- Uranium miners, millers, and ore transporters — $100,000 to persons who worked in mining, milling, or transportation of uranium between 1942 and 1971 and developed one of the types of diseases specified in the statute.

The RECA program is scheduled to sunset in July 2022.

Energy Employees Occupational Illness Compensation Program Act[109]

Congress passed the Energy Employees Occupational Illness Compensation Program Act in October of 2000. Part B of the EEOICPA, effective on July 31, 2001, compensates current or former employees (or their survivors) of the Department of Energy (DOE), its predecessor agencies, and certain of its vendors, contractors and subcontractors, who were diagnosed with a radiogenic cancer, chronic beryllium disease, beryllium sensitivity, or chronic silicosis, as a result of exposure to radiation, beryllium, or silica while employed at covered facilities.[110]

Part E of the EEOICPA (enacted October 28, 2004) compensates DOE contractor and subcontractor employees, eligible survivors of such employees, and uranium miners, millers, and ore transporters as defined by RECA Section 5, for any occupational illnesses that are causally linked to toxic exposures in the DOE or mining work environment.[111]

Employees (or their survivors) whose claims are approved under Part B of the program may receive a lump-sum payment of $150,000. Medical benefits are payable to eligible employees who have covered illnesses. Uranium workers who received compensation under

---

[109] 42 U.S.C. § 7384 et seq
[110] https://www.energy.gov/ehss/services/worker-health-and-safety/energy-employees-occupational-illness-compensation-program
[111] Ibid.

Section 5 of the RECA are eligible for an additional $50,000 in compensation under the EEOICPA. Eligible Part E recipients may be compensated up to $250,000 and medical benefits. Part E benefits were also made available to workers as defined under the Radiation Exposure Compensation Act (RECA).

Death on the High Seas Act[112]

Federal Maritime law governs deaths that occur on the high seas. The Death on the High Seas Act (DOHSA) is a wrongful death statute designed to protect the family of a seaman who died as a result of an employer's negligence or because of an unseaworthy vessel. The injury must occur three miles off the shore of any State, the District of Columbia, or United States territory. The beneficiaries of the DOHSA include the decedent's wife, husband, parent, child, or dependent relative. Congress amended the DOHSA to also include commercial aviation crashes that occurred beyond 12 nautical miles from the shore of the United States.

A claimant bringing a DOHSA lawsuit may be entitled to significant damages, including:

- Loss of Support

- Loss of Inheritance

- Loss of Services

- Loss of Nurture, Guidance, and Instruction

- Funeral Expenses

Importantly, DOHSA damages are limited to pecuniary damages. This means that grief, bereavement, and mental anguish damages are not compensable. Further, losses of society and consortium damages are prohibited. However, spouses can recover the monetary value of any household services the decedent would have provided throughout the remainder of his/her life. This is calculated using the number of anticipated hours of service the decedent would have provided multiplied by an hourly rate for those services.

Merchant Marine Act of 1929 (JONES ACT)[113]

Generally, seamen are not covered by state or federal workers compensation laws. Rather, they are compensated for employment-related injuries through the federal court system. For seamen, the Merchant Marine Act of 1920, commonly known as the Jones Act allows injured seamen to collect benefits for employment-related injuries. The United States Congress adopted the Merchant Marine Act in early June 1920 for the purpose of regulating

---

[112] **46 U.S.C. §§ 761 et seq**
[113] 46 U.S.C. § 688 et seq. and re-codified on October 6, 2006 as 46 U.S.C. § 30104

maritime commerce in U.S. waters and between U.S. ports. The Act was named after U.S. Senator Wesley Jones from Washington and was enacted in support of the U.S. Merchant Marine.

The Act addresses two issues. The first deals with *cabotage* (i.e., trade or navigation in coastal waters) and initially required that all goods transported by water between U.S. ports be carried in U.S.-flag ships, constructed in the United States, owned by U.S. citizens, and crewed by U.S. citizens and U.S. permanent residents. The second issue allows injured sailors to obtain damages from their employers for the negligence of the ship owner, the captain, or fellow members of the crew. It operates simply by extending similar legislation already in place that allowed for recoveries by railroad workers and providing that this legislation also applies to sailors.

Since the Jones Act deals with the recovery for injury to or death of a seaman, that term merits examination. The United States Supreme Court has attempted to clarify the definition of seaman. In 1995, the Supreme Court said that a seaman must contribute to the function of the vessel and that his or her connection to a vessel must be substantial in both duration and nature.[114] The Court added that as a rule of thumb, a seaman should spend more than 30 percent of his or her time on the vessel. Since that time, lower courts have tried to use this direction from the Supreme Court to determine just what a seaman is, on a case-by-case basis.

In 1997, the Supreme Court made another attempt to clarify the issue. In the latter case, a worker was injured while on a one day assignment obtained through the union hiring hall to paint a tug at dockside. This worker fell from a ladder and hurt his leg. He sued for benefits under the Jones Act and, after the trial court decided he was not a seaman and could not receive Jones Act benefits, an appeals court declared that he was a seaman. The Supreme Court took the case and agreed with the initial finding by the trial court. The Court said that defining a seaman under the Jones Act is a mixed question of law and fact, but that coverage under the act should be confined to those who face a regular exposure to the perils of the sea; land based employment is inconsistent with the Jones Act.[115]

In the early history of ocean marine insurance, an injured seaman could file an action *in rem* to seek compensation for his injury. In such an action, the seaman filed a suit directly against the ship and not the owner, thereby seeking compensation by claiming a property interest in the ship and bypassing the problem of whether or not the ship owner carried liability insurance. An endorsement did exist that provided coverage for such *in rem* lawsuits, but that endorsement is now obsolete since WC 00 02 01 A includes a statement that a suit or action *in rem* against a vessel owned by the insured is treated by the insurer as a suit against the insured requiring a defense by the insurer.

---

[114] *Chandris, Inc. v. Latsis*, 515 U.S. 347 (1995)
[115] *Harbor Tug & Barge Co.v. Papai*, 520 U.S. 548 (1997)

An endorsement, WC 00 02 01 A (the Maritime Coverage Endorsement) has been developed for attachment with the standard workers compensation policy and states that the insurance afforded by the Employers Liability insurance part of the workers compensation policy for bodily injury to a master or member of the crew of a vessel is changed by the provisions of the endorsement. The endorsement applies the insurance to bodily injury by accident or by disease arising out of and in the course of the injured employee's employment that is described in the schedule on the endorsement. The bodily injury must occur in the territorial limits of, or in the operation of a vessel sailing directly between the ports of, the United States of America or Canada.

Court decisions through the years have supported the proposition that federal and state courts have concurrent jurisdiction to enforce the right of action established by the Jones Act. However, since the act is a federal law, federal principles of law and rules of construction prevail if a conflict arises with a state law. As to the potential for dual recovery, in a precedent setting case in Louisiana, a federal court decided that a workers compensation action is not precluded under the Jones Act under certain circumstances. However, if a seaman receives compensation under the Jones Act for his injury, and then files a state workers compensation claim based on that same injury, a court may allow the workers compensation action as permitted by state law, but will offset any award by the amount already received.[116] Thus, the possibility of double recovery being an unlimited source of compensation is remote.

Longshore and Harbor Workers Compensation Act (LHWCA)[117]

Sixteen years after the first state workmen's compensation law was passed, the United States Longshore and Harbor Workers Compensation Act was enacted in 1927. The federal act was designed to provide medical and physical rehabilitation and compensation for lost wages to employees (other than seamen) who work in maritime employment upon the navigable waters of the United States and who were usually considered outside the scope of state compensation laws. Even so, the purpose of this federal compensation law is no different than that of a state compensation law – namely, to compensate workers for injuries that affect their wage earning capabilities and that arise out of the workers' employment.

The Longshore and Harbor Workers Compensation Act covers injuries that occur during maritime employment on "navigable waters" of the United States. Benefits are paid by the employers, with oversight by the OWCP in the U.S. Department of Labor rather than State governments. The program was originally established in response to a United States Supreme Court decision holding that state workers compensation laws did not apply on the nation's navigable waters.[118]

---

[116] *Dominick v. Houtech Inland Well Service, Inc.*, 718 F. Supp. 489 (E.D. La 1989)
[117] 33 U.S.C. §§ 901- 952
[118] *Southern Pacific Co. v. Jensen*, 244 U.S. 205 (1917)

One of the original problems that arose with the L&HWCA was that anyone performing work however remotely connected to maritime employment attempted to obtain the benefits of the Act. Therefore, in order to curb the jurisdictional scope of the Act, not only does the coverage paragraph of the L&HWCA contain certain exclusions, but the definition of "employee" has been limited to specific classes of workers.

The term "employee" means any person engaged in maritime employment, but this term does not include clerical, secretarial, security, or data processing work. It does not include individuals employed by a camp, restaurant, recreational operation, or retail outlet. Nor does it include individuals employed by a marina, aquaculture workers, individuals employed to build, repair, or dismantle any recreational vessel under 65 feet in length. Masters or members of a crew of any vessel or any person engaged to load or unload or repair any small vessel under 18 tons net are also not considered employees under the Act. Needless to say, disputes and legal challenges over what constitutes an "employee" continue.

Section 904 of the Act states that every employer is liable for and shall secure the payment to his employees of the compensation payable under the requirements of the Act. In the case of an employer who is a subcontractor, the contractor shall be liable for and shall secure the payment of such compensation to employees of the subcontractor unless the subcontractor has secured such payment.

This liability of the employer is exclusive and precludes all other liability of the employer to the employee, his legal representative, or his dependents. In other words, the exclusive remedy theory as applied to the employer. Of course, if the employer fails to secure payment of compensation, an injured employee can file suit at law or in admiralty for damages and the employer cannot use the defenses that were common prior to the enactment of state workmen's compensation laws: negligence of a fellow servant, the assumption of risk by the employee, or contributory negligence on the part of the employee to the employer.

L&HWCA insurance may be provided by attaching endorsement WC 00 0106 A to the standard workers compensation policy. The endorsement applies to work done in the states scheduled (including those states with a monopolistic state fund) and extends the definition of workers compensation law to include the L&HWCA. This is necessary because the policy declares in the General Section that the term "workers compensation law" does not include any federal workers compensation law. The statutory obligation of an employer to furnish benefits required by the L&HWCA is thus satisfied. The coverage, exclusions, and conditions of Part One of the workers compensation policy are applied to those parties involved under the L&HWCA.

This endorsement applies only to work subject to L&HWCA in a state shown in the schedule and provides compensation coverage to employees such as longshoremen, harbor workers, ship repairmen, and shipbuilders. The endorsement is attached to the workers compensation and Employers Liability insurance policy (WC 00 00 00) and expands the definition of workers compensation law to include the L&HWCA and any amendments to that Act that are in effect during the policy period.

WC 00 0106 A declares that exclusion 8 under the Employers Liability part of the policy (Part Two) does not apply to work subject to L&HWCA. This is, of course, similar to the wording found on endorsement WC 00 0101 A, as noted above. It is also stated on the L&HWCA coverage endorsement that the endorsement does not apply to the Defense Base Act, the Outer Continental Shelf Lands Act, or the Non-appropriated Fund Instrumentalities Act.

Under the Employers Liability portion of the policy, the insurance applies to bodily injury by accident or by disease arising out of and in the course of the injured employee's employment. The L&HWCA endorsement drops exclusion 8 of the Employers Liability insurance. For operations subject to the L&HWCA, the standard limits of liability under Part Two of the policy are: $100,000 per each accident for bodily injury by accident, $100,000 per each employee for bodily injury by disease, and a $500,000 policy limit for bodily injury by disease. Increased limits are available for an additional premium.

It is important to note that recent amendments to the L&HWCA require that a worker or dependent who is excluded from the definition of "employee" must first claim compensation under the appropriate state workers compensation program and receive a final decision on the merits of that claim before any claim may be filed under the L&HWC Act.

It is recognized that the L&HWCA covers more than maritime industry workers. Through a series of amendments, coverage was extended to include several miscellaneous classes of employees through the following extensions to the law:

Defense Base Act (DBA) – Established in 1941, the primary goal of the Defense Base Act was to cover workers on military bases outside the United States. The Act was amended to include public works contracts with the government for the building of non-military projects such as dams, schools, harbors, and roads abroad. A further amendment added a vast array of enterprises revolving around the national security of the United States and its allies. Today, almost any contract with an agency of the U.S. government, for work outside the U.S., whether military in nature or not, will likely require DBA coverage.

Defense Base Act coverage is accomplished through attachment of endorsement WC 00 01 01 A. This endorsement applies only to the work described in the schedule or described on the Information Page as subject to the Defense Base Act. Basically, WC 00 01 01 A modifies the workers compensation insurance policy by replacing the definition of "workers compensation law" found in the policy with the following meaning: *workers compensation law means the workers compensation law and occupational disease law of each state or territory named in Item 3.A. of the Information Page and the Defense Base Act (42 USC Sections 1651-1654).* The definition goes on to state that it does not include any other federal workers compensation law or federal occupational disease law.

Non-appropriated Fund Instrumentalities Act – enacted in 1952, this Act, which is an extension of the Longshore and Harbor Workers Compensation Act (LHWCA), provides workers compensation coverage to civilian employees of non-appropriated fund instrumentalities. The most common application of this Act is to civilian employees who provide services to the U.S. Armed Forces such as at a military post exchange. Like the LHWCA, the Non-Appropriated Fund Instrumentalities Act is administered by the Office of Workers compensation Program (OWCP).

The Non-Appropriated Fund Instrumentalities Act Coverage Endorsement (WC 00 01 08 A) applies only to the work described in the schedule as subject to the Non-Appropriated Fund Instrumentalities Act and the definition of "workers compensation law" is expanded by this endorsement to include the Non- Appropriated Fund Instrumentalities Act. WC 00 01 08 A also notes that exclusion 8 of the Employers Liability insurance part of the workers compensation policy does not apply to work subject to the Non-Appropriated Fund Instrumentalities Act.

Outer Continental Shelf Lands Act – enacted in 1953, the Outer Continental Shelf Lands Act[119] covers mineral exploration and production workers such as those on offshore drilling platforms. The 1953 statute defines the Outer Continental Shelf (OCS) as all submerged lands lying seaward of State coastal waters (three miles offshore) which are under United States jurisdiction. The statute authorized the Secretary of Interior to promulgate regulations to lease the OCS in an effort to prevent waste and conserve natural resources and to grant leases to the highest responsible qualified bidder as determined by competitive bidding procedures.

The Outer Continental Shelf Lands Act Coverage Endorsement (WC 00 0109 A) applies only to the work described in the schedule as subject to the Outer Continental Shelf Lands Act. The coverage will apply to that work as though the location shown in the schedule were a state named on the workers compensation policy. Therefore, the description of the work must show the state whose boundaries, if extended to the outer continental shelf, would include the location of the work.

---

[119] 43 U.S.C. §§ 1331 - 1356

Chapter Five

COVERED OCCUPATIONAL EVENTS

When state workmen's compensation laws were first enacted, most states modeled their laws after the English Workmen's Compensation Act of 1897. The opening provision of the English Act states, *"If in any employment personal injury by accident arising out of and in the course of the employment is caused to a workman, his employer shall, subject as hereinafter mentioned, be liable to pay compensation in accordance with the first schedule of this act."*[1]

Little has changed over the past century and today, the almost universal test for compensability of a workplace injury or death is that it must "arise out of" and "in the course" of the employment." Although this terminology appears to be fairly straightforward, these few words have been the subject of extensive controversy and litigation since their incorporation into the first workmen's compensation laws. This chapter begins with an examination of the first of those two critical phrases.

"ARISING OUT OF" THE EMPLOYMENT

The "arising out of" phrase is intended to convey that the injury must be work-related to the extent that there is a direct causal connection between the injury and the employment. In an often-quoted early **Massachusetts** decision, *"The causative danger must be peculiar to the work and not common to the neighborhood. It must be incidental to the character of the business."*[2] In determining the causal relationship, the "arising out of" concept is concerned with the type of risk to which a worker is exposed by reason of the employment.

As a starting point, it is important to recognize that all risks can be brought within one of three basic types: risks directly associated with the employment, risks personal to the employee, and "neutral" risks (i.e., risks having neither a particular employment nor personal character). In the first instance, risks normally associated with a particular employment are considered occupational and are in most instances held to be compensable. There is little room for question relative to the compensability of an injury where a maintenance worker falls from a ladder and breaks a leg while changing a light bulb at the employer's place of business. Similarly, there is little room for question

---

[1] Workman's Compensation Act, 1906, § 1 (Eng.)
[2] *In re McNicol's Case*, 102 N.E. 697 (1913)

where the type of risk is personal and not associated with the employment. For example, the worker who breaks a leg while on a winter skiing vacation. In such instance, the workers compensation program is not called upon to respond.

However, questions frequently arise in connection with the third type of risk where the injury occurs as a result of risks that are neither distinctly job-related nor personal. The usual answer under early compensation laws was to have these losses remain with the worker. Over time, the courts shifted their interpretation of the law, taking the position that where either the employer or the worker must bear the loss, the employer would be found responsible if some degree of connection could be established with the workplace. This shift in approach to compensability for such injuries or diseases came to be identified with the humanitarian aspect of compensation legislation insofar as it was intended to protect the worker and benefit society.

In some jurisdictions, it is through established case law that the scales were tilted in favor of the injured worker if certain criteria were met. This approach, stated by the courts in **Alabama**, is that the workers compensation law is to be liberally construed *"to accomplish its beneficent purposes,"* with doubts resolved in favor of the employee.[3] In **California,** the Labor Code calls for the workers compensation law to *"be liberally construed by the courts with the purpose of extending their benefits for the protection of persons injured in the course of their employment."*[4]

However, changes occurred with the passage of time and while the majority of states continue to rely upon the liberal construction of the law, in 2005 **Missouri** enacted a provision whereby, *"Administrative law judges, associate administrative law judges, legal advisors, the labor and industrial relations commission, and the division of workers compensation shall weigh the evidence impartially without giving the benefit of the doubt to any party when weighing evidence and resolving factual conflicts."*[5] Other states have attempted over time to enact similar provisions.

RISK DOCTRINES

To illustrate the evolution of thinking that resulted in the expansion of compensability for many neutral risks, it is beneficial to examine a number of tests or risk doctrines that have evolved for purposes of determining whether or not a sufficient causal connection exists between the work and the injury. Depending upon the state where the injury occurs, and in some instances the circumstances surrounding the injury, one of the following tests for compensability may be applied to injuries falling within that neutral category:

> **Peculiar or Increased-Risk Doctrine** – The majority of jurisdictions originally adopted the peculiar risk doctrine which provided that an injury is compensable

---

[3] *Holmes v. Gold Kist, Inc.* 670 So. 2d 449 (1995)
[4] Cal. Labor Code § 3202
[5] Mo. Rev. Stat. § 287.800

when caused by an increased risk from the employment that was greater than the risk held by the general public. The doctrine was originally designed to exclude injuries for which the employment offered no special exposure. This doctrine can be illustrated by an early **Massachusetts** decision where a town worker froze his foot while cleaning the streets on an extremely cold day. In rendering their opinion against the payment of benefits, the Massachusetts Supreme Judicial Court stated that the *"condition of his employment and its nature did not in fact expose him to a greater degree of danger of being frozen than the ordinary out of door worker."*[6]

Over time, the peculiar risk doctrine was modified or replaced by the increased risk doctrine. This test differs from the peculiar risk doctrine in that *"the distinctiveness of the employment risk can be contributed by the increased quantity of a risk that is qualitatively not peculiar to the employment."*[7] The increased-risk doctrine served to lower the bar a slight amount for purposes of establishing compensability. An early ruling from **Connecticut** held that an employee, who died of sunstroke after shoveling coal on a hot day in a building located about twenty feet above the ground, was entitled to compensation benefits. In rendering their decision the Connecticut Supreme Court noted, *"exposure in this employment was far greater than the exposure of the community and the effect of the sun was substantially greater than that on the community."*[8]

Minnesota and **New Hampshire** recently used the increased-risk test to determine whether an injury arose out of and in the course of employment. In 2013, the Minnesota Supreme Court explicitly adopted the increased-risk test in a case where a preventative maintenance coordinator, walking toward a conference room, fell to the marble floor of the hallway, dislocating her left knee. The compensation judge found that the employee was not able to prove that the floor was slippery. On appeal to the Minnesota Supreme Court, in overturning the compensation judge, noted that, *"The compensation judge did not apply the work-connection balancing test because she did not give consideration to the strength of the "in the course of" element. Where, as here, the strength of the in the course of element outweighs any deficiencies in the arising out of element, the injury is compensable."*[124]

In March of 2015, the New Hampshire Supreme Court overruled a denial of benefits by the state's Compensation Appeals Board to driver who was injured after he fell asleep behind the wheel of a company truck and struck a utility pole. The Supreme Court noted that, *"Although not all injuries resulting from mixed risks are compensable, the concurrence of a personal risk and an employment risk does not necessarily defeat compensability if the employment was also a substantial contributing factor to the injury . . . Even if we were to assume that the petitioner was negligent in choosing to drive and in falling asleep while doing so, barring recovery*

---

[6] *Robinson's Case*, 198 N.E. 769 (1935)
[7] *Larson's Workers' Compensation Law*, § 21.02 (1) (a) (2000)
[8] *Ahern v. Spier*, 105 A. 340 (1918)

on that basis would be contrary to the remedial purpose of the Workers Compensation Law."[125]

Actual Risk Doctrine – As a follow-up to the increased risk doctrine, a substantial number of states adopted the actual-risk doctrine which required only that the employment subject the worker to the actual risk that resulted in injury. It did not matter if the risk was common to the general public. For example, in a **Virginia** case, a store manager was called away from the entrance of the store to discuss a customer's bill. The discussion took place next to the customer's automobile and, after discussing the bill, the manager stepped back from the automobile and fell breaking his hip. The Supreme Court acknowledged and adopted the actual risk doctrine in ruling the claim compensable.[9] The doctrine permits recovery in most street risk cases and in a greater number of "act of God" cases.

Positional Risk Doctrine – Increasingly the positional risk doctrine is being used to support awards in those situations where the employment requires the claimant to be at a particular place at a particular time when the injury occurs. Under the positional risk doctrine, an injury arises out of the employment if the injury would not have occurred "but for" the fact that the obligations of the employment placed the worker in a position where he or she was injured. **Colorado** was the first state to recognize the positional-risk doctrine.[10] Today, nearly half of the states have accepted the doctrine

In many cases covered under the positional risk doctrine, the nature of the work is irrelevant to the injury. Workers have been awarded workers compensation benefits where the injury was caused by lightning, stray bullets, roving lunatics, and other situations in which the only connection to the employment with the injury is that its obligations placed the employee in the particular place at the particular time when the employee was injured by some neutral force. In a **New York** case, an employee was working as a printer when an explosion in an adjoining building caused that building to collapse on to the building where the printer was working. The printer was fatally crushed because of the collapse and the claim was subsequently ruled compensable.[11]

A classic illustration of the principle of positional risk is the **New Jersey** case of *Gargiulo v. Gargiulo*. A butcher's helper was on his way to empty the trash when he was struck in the eye by a stray arrow shot into the air by a child in the neighborhood. In awarding compensation, the New Jersey Supreme Court in finding the injury to be compensable said, "*It [the employment] brought him unwittingly into the line of fire of the arrow, where he would not have been except for his employment. But for the compliance with his allotted work directive requiring his*

---

[9] *Cohen et al. v. Cohen's Department Store, Inc.*, 198 S.E. 476 (Va. 1938)
[10] *Aetna Life Insurance Co. v. Industrial Comm'n*, 254 P. 995 (1927)
[11] *State Industrial Commissioner v. Leff*, 265 N.Y. 533 (1934)

presence at the particular time and place in question, the injury would not have been inflicted."[12]

A few examples of workplace situations that have a potential connection with the employment, yet are considered neutral risks, may serve to illustrate the concept that underlies these various doctrines. The decision on the part of a jurisdiction to either accept or reject a particular risk may make the difference between finding for or against the compensability for an alleged workplace injury.

Assault – From early on it was recognized that in the cases of assault, *"even when involving co-employees, liability is not conceded because the issue is considered personal rather than industrial."*[13] In the case of an assault by a third party, the general rule was also to deem the injury or death as non-compensable and to allow the injured party or survivors to pursue a direct action for damages against the wrongdoer. It is important to distinguish between the term "assault" which refers only to the threat of violence while the term "battery" refers to the actual contact associated with a violent act. For purposes here, the term assault is used in its generic sense which infers physical violence to the person from another party.

The attitude toward cases of assault has evolved markedly since those early holdings. Today, where it can be demonstrated that the employment involves an increased risk of assault due to the dangerous duties of the work or dangerous environment, courts have routinely held that injuries stemming from such assaults arose out of the employment. In the case of police, firefighters, prison guards, schoolteachers, and various other professions with exposure to assaults, virtually every jurisdiction holds in favor of compensation for injuries stemming from an unprovoked assault. The main points of consideration are whether the factors that prompted the assault were connected in some way with the employment, and whether the injured worker was one of aggressor or defender.

Where the assault has been of an unexpected nature, there has also been an evolution in thinking. Most jurisdictions formerly held such injuries to be non-compensable for lack of an increased employment risk. However, more recently, courts have applied a more liberal construction to the law so as to find for compensability where the injury results from an unexpected assault. In a **Pennsylvania** case, an injured employee who was fueling his truck was awarded benefits after being assaulted at a gas station by another patron. This other patron allegedly assaulted the employee for refusing to move his truck. Because the employee refused the request because of the size of the truck, the court found that the assault was not inflicted for personal reasons, but for reasons directly related to the employment.[14]

---

[12] *Gargiulo v. Gargiulo,* 97 A.2d 593 (1953).
[13] Reede, Arthur H., *Adequacy of Workmen's Compensation*, Harvard University Press (1947)
[14] *Bachman Co. v. WCAB*, 683 A. 2d 1305 (1996)

However, where the assault arises out of issues not connected to the employment and the motive is not associated with employment factors, the result in most instances has been to find such injuries non-compensable. For example, in an **Alaska** case, two individuals had a running personal dispute and one came to the other's place of employment and caused injury, the motive and cause were personal, and the resulting injury or harm was not deemed to have stemmed from the employment relationship.[15]

Horseplay – The difference between an injury stemming from an assault and one stemming from horseplay is that an assault involves the *"willful intent to injure"* whereas in horseplay, the injury is the result of an innocent prank which usually does not involve intent to cause injury or harm. It is generally recognized and accepted that employees participate in occasional practical jokes and frivolity or pranks at the workplace.

Early case law generally held that an employee injured by a practical joke or by horseplay with a fellow employee was not entitled to compensation benefits. In the Alaska case referenced above, it was held that such injury *"did not arise out of the employment because it bore no relation to the duties the employee was required to perform."*[16] In a case where the injured worker was an innocent victim, the **New Jersey** courts held that while an accident happening in such circumstances may arise in the course of the employment, it could not be said that it arose out of the employment.[17]

More recent case law holds that the victims of horseplay are entitled to benefits, but still not in all cases. If the instrument used by a practical joker to cause the injury or death is provided by the employer, there is a greater probability that the injury arose out of and in the course of employment. Administrative adjudicators and the courts are less inclined to award benefits to an employee who causes his or her own injury, than to a worker who was an innocent victim.

Recent cases have held that a non-participating victim or innocent victim who is injured as a result of horseplay is entitled to compensation benefits. For example, in an **Alabama** case, an employee, who had engaged in horseplay with a co-worker in the past, the court noted that the worker was not engaged in such horseplay at the time of the injury and held the claim compensable.[18] There is also a growing tendency on the part of adjudicators to view these acts as free-spirited fun during downtime. In a **New York** case, the decision of the Compensation Board was sustained at the appellate level when benefits were awarded to a claimant who attempted to do a handstand on the arms of a swivel chair. The Board noted that *"young men, whose jobs call for expenditure of physical energy, cannot be expected,*

---

[15] *Temple v. Denali Princess Lodge*, 21 P .3d 813 (2001)
[16] Ibid
[17] *Hulley v. Moosbrugger*, 95 A. 1007 (1916)
[18] *Gilbert v. Tyson Foods Inc.* , 782 So. 2d 786 (2001)

during slack periods, to sit in idleness and gossip: that the employer must expect that they will engage in some form of activity and that the risk was a risk of the employment."[19]

"Acts of God" – An "act of God" is an event that takes place solely through the effect of the forces of nature without benefit of human intervention. Floods, lightning, earthquake, tornadoes, landslides, and hurricanes are all considered "acts of God." For those jurisdictions that accepted the peculiar risk doctrine, injuries arising from "acts of God" were usually classified as risks to which the general public was equally exposed and therefore not compensable.

With the passage of time, a growing number of jurisdictions applied the increased risk doctrine and held claims resulting from "acts of God" to arise out of the employment if the working conditions – such as working at heights or in cold or damp environments – served to increase the chances of injury. The **North Carolina** Court of Appeals upheld benefits for a construction framer who suffered injuries as a result of a lightning strike that occurred while he was at work. The court concluded that the worker did not have to provide expert testimony to establish increased risk.[20]

Additionally, a number of jurisdictions have found such injuries to be compensable through acceptance of the positional risk doctrine. Under the positional risk doctrine, the injury is compensable if the employment placed the worker at the particular time and place where the injury was sustained, even though a member of the general public who was at the same place would have suffered the same injury. Probably the best examples of this would be workplace injuries sustained as a result of an earthquake or tornado that severely damages or destroys the building in which the employees were working.

But not all states accept the positional risk doctrine. In a recent decision by the **Virginia** Court of Appeals, a fall suffered by a school security guard in Virginia Beach, was held not to be compensable because the wind that allegedly caused a door to shut, which caused her to fall was considered an "act of God" and not within the scope of her employment.[21] Applying the "risk test," the Commission had earlier ruled that she did not face a risk that was any greater than the public at large. The fall was caused by a natural wind force which, standing alone, had to be considered an "act of God."

The State of **Texas** is somewhat unique since the workers compensation law contains a specific reference to "acts of God." Under the exception provisions of the law, an employer is not liable for compensation if the injury *"arose out of an act of God,*

---

[19] *Aucompaugh v. General Electric* 111 A.D. 2d 1073 (1985)
[20] *Heatherly v. Hollingsworth Co., Inc.*, No. COA10-994 (2011)
[21] *1632194* Sylvia Martin v. Virginia Beach (2020)

unless the employment exposes the employee to a greater risk of injury from an act of God than ordinarily applies to the general public."[22]

Suicide – In the majority of jurisdictions, the compensation law includes a provision whereby benefits are not payable where the injury or death occurs due to an employee's *"willful intent to injure himself."* However, in certain rare instances, suicide prompted by job-related stress may be compensable. For a suicide claim to be held compensable, the dependents of the deceased must generally establish a chain of causation that includes three elements: (1) there must be a work-related injury; (2) the injury must cause a mental disturbance in the employee to the extent that normal rational judgment is impaired; and (3) the disturbance must ultimately lead to suicide.

In 1915 the **Massachusetts** Supreme Court enunciated the majority rule. In that case the decedent, while in the course of his employment, had hot molten lead splashed into his eyes. While hospitalized and in a state of agonizing pain, he threw himself from a window to his death. The court upheld the decision of the Industrial Commission, allowing the claim.[23]

In a **Nevada** case, the Nevada Supreme Court awarded benefits where a sufficient chain of causation was established. The deceased was a bartender and suffered back injuries in a fall down stairs. He was awarded compensation benefits for his injuries. Thereafter, the claimant suffered relentless pain, could not keep food down, and spent his life in bed. Nearly three years after the accident the injured worker took his own life. Under the state's "willful intention" clause, his widow was denied benefits several times until the matter reached the Nevada Supreme Court where the precedent-setting determination of awarding benefits was made.[24]

In another **Massachusetts** case, the employee injured his back at work. When he tried to return to work on light duty, he was terminated. He then grew depressed and committed suicide a few weeks later. At the hearing, the claimant's attorney introduced medical evidence that the employee's back injury caused him to become clinically depressed, and that the termination exacerbated his depression to a degree that he was acting irrationally when he committed suicide. The justices concluded that the injury and termination were inextricably connected.[25]

A similar outcome was realized in **Iowa**. In this case the husband felt personally responsible when the businesses he was managing for his wife's family failed. He became withdrawn, depressed, and eventually killed himself. However, the court held that his work related depression wasn't severe enough to warrant killing himself. In other words, the decedent must have suffered from a mental disorder above and beyond the work related depression, and that was the ultimate cause of death.[146]

---

[22] Tex. Labor Code Ann. § 416.032
[23] *In re Sponatski,* 220 Mass. 526, 108 N. E. 466 (1915)
[24] *Sharon Vredenburg v. Sedgwick CMA and Flamingo Hilton-Laughlin.* (2008)
[25] *Dube's Case,* Mass. Ct. App., No. 06-P-728 (2007)

Under the **Pennsylvania** Workers Compensation Act, an employer is not liable for compensation when an employee's death is self-inflicted. There are, however, exceptions. If the claimant can prove 1) there was an initial work injury, 2) the injury caused the employee to be severely overcome with a disturbance of the mind as to override normal, rational judgment, and 3) the disturbance results in the employee's suicide, benefits may be awarded. In *Hansell v. Southeastern Pennsylvania Transportation*, a widow filed a fatal claim petition after her husband committed suicide. In this case, doctors' testimonies that the work injury had caused such pain and disturbance of rational thought that it lead to the suicide of the worker were credible and was therefore compensable.[26]

Suicides in the workers compensation program continue to be outliers, but state courts have shown sympathy to the idea that pain and depression can pierce a "willful intention" defense by the employer. The courts seem consistent from state-to-state in requiring a chain of causation. In addition, dependents may need to demonstrate that the decedent's working conditions were, in fact, abnormal, and not just perceived as abnormal by the decedent. Dependents are unlikely to receive benefits if the decedent suffered from a psychological disturbance prior to the workplace injury or if there was an intervening cause between the injury and the suicide.

Acts of Terrorism – Ongoing hostilities throughout the world, including terrorist activity in this country, have caused many employers uncertainty over possible workers compensation exposure. Examples of such activity in this country includes the 1995 Oklahoma City bombing, the events of 9/11, and the Boston marathon bombing. One may also include in this category the "storming of the Capitol" on January 6, 2021. Coverage for these events is a complex and evolving subject. Certainly these exposures were not considered for coverage when the original workmen's compensation laws were enacted.

Regarding terrorism activity in this country, the events that took place in Oklahoma City, New York, the Pentagon in Washington D.C and the national Capitol served to bring home the hard reality of terrorist attacks and the essence of war. While injuries or deaths resulting from war were not initially considered covered exposures, the positional risk doctrine serves to bring this type of risk under the umbrella of workers compensation coverage in states that have adopted that test for compensability. In the **Oklahoma** City Murrah Building bombing, three state employees were killed, and several other employees were injured. All of these claims were accepted by the Oklahoma State Insurance Fund.

The terrorist attack and collapse of the World Trade Center (WTC) on 9/11/2001 involved far more fatalities and injuries than the Oklahoma bombing. An earlier **New York** case established the precedent for determining compensability for injury or death resulting from such attacks. The case involved an outside worker in the

---

[26] https://www.rothmangordon.com/suicide-workers-compensation-claims-may-be-compensable/

printing business that was injured in the so called "1922 Wall Street Explosion." While the source of the explosion had no connection with the employer's business and the claimant was instead injured because of his location at the time, the court affirmed the finding of a compensable accident. The court noted that *"it best conforms to the spirit and purpose of the workmen's compensation law to hold that, when a man is injured by accident in the street while performing the services for which he was employed, he is covered by the statute."*[27]

As a result of the terrorist attacks on 9/11/2001, 2,977 people were killed and more than 6,000 injured. 344 firefighters and 71 law enforcement officers were killed and many more were injured. In addition, tens of thousands of workers participated in the subsequent rescue, recovery, and clean-up operations. Many of these workers became ill as a result of exposure to the toxic dust. In September 2020, New York Governor Cuomo extended the Sept. 11th Worker Protection Task Force for another five years. As a result, any public employee who suffered an injury or illness directly related to the terrorist attacks on 9/11/2001 is presumptively eligible for an accidental disability.

It is interesting to note that only one state, **Pennsylvania**, has enacted a statutory provision expressly addressing workplace injuries resulting from a hostile attack. The Pennsylvania law provides that *"no compensation shall be paid if, during hostile attacks on the United States, injury or death of employees results solely from military activities of the armed forces of the United States or from military activities or enemy sabotage of a foreign power."*[28]

"IN THE COURSE OF" THE EMPLOYMENT

In the context of most state workers compensation laws, "arising out of" the employment represents the first half in the test of compensability. In conjunction with this first step, "in the course of the employment" represents the second half of the equation. The determination of what constitutes "in the course of" the employment is rarely articulated in the statutory definition but is the subject of extensive controversy and litigation.

Taken in its literal sense, "course of employment" is concerned primarily with the time and the place of the injury along with the activity that the worker was engaged in when the injury occurred. Using the literal interpretation, workers compensation benefits would be payable only for those injuries sustained during working hours on the premises of the employer while engaged in activities that were unquestionably work-related. However, such a strict interpretation would not be consistent with the underlying philosophy of workers compensation laws. These laws were introduced as a no-fault replacement for the tort system to ensure workers adequate and timely compensation in

---

[27] *Roberts v. J.F. Newcomb & Co.*, 138 N.E. 443 (1922)
[28] Pa. Stat. Ann. Title 77 § 431

the case of a work-related injury or death. Each situation must be reviewed and considered on its own merit when determining whether an injury is compensable.

Concurrent with these changes is the recognition that certain work situations may also influence the compensability of an injury occurring in the workplace. The following describes some of the more troublesome aspects of "in the course of employment" determinations.

Employee Misconduct – Nearly every jurisdiction included in its original compensation statute a provision denying or reducing benefits for injuries or death resulting from employee misconduct. Misconduct takes the shape of either willful misconduct on the part of the employee, or intentional or self-inflicted injury. However, to preclude the payment of benefits, it was generally recognized that mere misconduct was not sufficient. An early **Massachusetts** decision held that *"Serious and willful misconduct is much more than mere negligence, or even gross or culpable negligence. It involves conduct of a quasi-criminal nature, the intentional doing of something either with the knowledge that it is likely to result in serious injury, or with a wanton and reckless disregard of its serious consequences."* [29]

While the meaning of the term appears quite clear, an interesting case regarding workplace misconduct occurred in **New York**. An employee sustained fatal injuries while in the course of stealing copper downspouts from the roof of a building. While awaiting materials to arrive at the worksite, the employee and a co-worker went to another part of the building to steal the downspouts for sale as salvage. While engaged in the theft, the employee slipped on a patch of ice and fell seven stories to his death. In awarding benefits to the surviving spouse, the Workers Compensation Board found that it was common practice in the industry for roofers to remove the downspouts and sell them for salvage. Moreover, the employer was aware of the practice but had neither disciplined nor discharged an employee for such thefts. This opinion was affirmed by the Court of Appeals.[30]

A common form of misconduct is the failure to follow established safety or work rules. In some jurisdictions, such failure on the part of the employee is a complete or partial defense to a claim, provided that the employer can demonstrate a direct causal link between the safety breach and the injury. For example, an employee who injured his ankle while "hitching a ride" on a forklift was not entitled to benefits because the employer had an explicit safety rule prohibiting such rides. In that case the violation of the safety rule had a clear connection to the resulting injury and benefits were denied by the court. [31]

A sizeable number of states have statutorily addressed the subject of safety rule violation. Thirteen states provide that no benefits are payable in the event of a safety

---

[29] *Nickerson*, 105 N.E. 602 (1906)
[30] *Richardson v. Fiedler Roofing, Inc.*, 502 N.Y.S. 2d 125 (1986)
[31] *Saunders v. Industrial Commission*, 727 N.E. 2d 247 (2000)

rule violation. Other states are less harsh in their approach. For example, **Colorado** calls for the reduction of compensation benefits by 50 percent, and **Florida** provides for a 25 percent reduction of compensation for injuries stemming from a safety rule violation. In **Kentucky, Missouri, Utah,** and **Wisconsin**, the law calls for a 15 percent reduction in compensation benefits. In the states of **New Mexico, North Carolina, South Carolina,** and **Washington**, the reduction in compensation is set at ten percent.

"Going and Coming" Rule – The general rule regarding claims arising from coming and going to the place of employment is that in most instances, employees are not considered within the course of their employment until they reach the employer's premises or after they leave such premises. The premises are generally considered to be the entire area devoted to the industry with which the employer is associated. Parking lots, stairs, elevators, lobbies, and hallways are all generally considered part of the premises, even if the employer does not own or lease the actual place where the injury occurred. In a **New Jersey** case, it was held that the course of employment includes the preparation necessary for beginning work after reaching the employer's premises.[32]

A subsequent **New Jersey** Supreme Court decision, in reversing the opinion of the Superior Court, held that an employee injured when he fell into a freight elevator shaft while on his way to his employer's place of business was injured "in the course of employment." In rendering its decision, the court recognized that the elevator was in a common area of a multi-tenant building that the employer did not control, and that the accident occurred nearly an hour before the employee was scheduled to arrive for work.[33]

The theory behind the "going and coming" rule is that the relationship of employer and employee is suspended from the time the employee leaves the premises to go home until they resume work. Injuries sustained while traveling to or from work normally do not demonstrate the required causal connection with the employment and therefore do not arise in the course of the employment. Despite the general rule of non-compensability for such injuries, there are numerous well recognized exceptions which depend upon the nature, circumstances, and conditions of the employment and the cause of the injury. One of the primary exceptions is the off-premises worker who does not have a regular place of employment. In the case of the off-premises worker, the work shift begins with the departure from the place of residence. The on-call worker is another whose work shift generally coincides with the call to report for duty.

Each case that deals with an exception to the general rule must be judged on its own merits and considering the specific state workers compensation law. Where the law calls for a "liberal construction" in favor of the injured worker, reasonable doubt as

---

[32] *Terlecki v. Strauss,* 89 A. 1023 (1914)
[33] *Ramos v. M&F Fashions,* 713 A. 2d 486 (1998)

to whether a trip comes within the exception to the general rule is usually resolved in favor of the employee. The common thread that runs through all of the exceptions to the general rule is a finding of benefits for the employee.

A further departure from the "going and coming" rule is identified with the "dual purpose doctrine." In most instances, where an employee is injured while performing some activity for the benefit of himself or a third person, the mere fact that the employer might incidentally receive some benefit from the performance of such an act does not necessarily bring the act within the scope of the employment so as to render the injury compensable. For example, a **Florida** grocery store assistant manager was injured in an automobile accident while on her way to work. At the time of the accident, the employee was bringing with her the weekly newsletter which the employer paid her to do at home and which was to be distributed with the weekly paycheck that day. The Florida Supreme Court held the accident to be non-compensable. [34]

The "dual-purpose" doctrine generally represents an exception to the "going and coming" rule when an employee is injured while taking work home. The doctrine may also be invoked when an accident occurs in the course of a business trip or errand during which the employee is injured while taking care of some personal business. If the deviation from work is slight, the injury is more likely to be considered work-related. In a **Maine** case, an employee was seriously injured in an automobile accident that occurred while proceeding to the dealership in the employer's vehicle to sign for the purchase of a personal car. Although the trip to the dealership was a deviation after making a delivery for the employer, the Maine Supreme Court held the claim compensable. [35]

Personal Comfort Doctrine – Simply stated, the personal comfort doctrine recognizes that certain on-the-job acts of personal comfort are "necessarily contemplated" to be incidental to the employment itself, blanketing any inevitably attendant danger with compensability. This doctrine contemplates employees attending to personal needs that include work-time breaks for eating, drinking, using the restroom, smoking, or otherwise seeking relief from discomfort. In this regard, the "personal comfort" doctrine was established to cover the situation where an employee is injured while taking a pause from normal work activities to minister to the various necessities of life.

Professor Arthur Larson sets forth the personal comfort doctrine in the following terms:
> *"Most courts have concluded that the unpaid lunch hour on the premises should be deemed to fall within the course of employment. One can arrive at this result by the following chain of arguments: If going to and from work on the premises is covered, then going to and from lunch on the premises must*

---

[34] *Gilbert v. Publix Supermarkets, Inc.,* 790 So. 2d 1057 (2001)
[35] *Cox v. Costal Products Company, Inc.,* 774 A. 2d 347 (2001)

be covered. If going to and from lunch on the premises is in the course of employment, then simply remaining on the premises for lunch must also be. The actual eating of lunch is no more remote from the employment than traveling to it." [36]

The personal comfort doctrine has been applied in the case of the use of restroom facilities during working hours, seeking protection from the heat or cold, or other activities associated with personal convenience. Although technically the employee may not be performing services that contribute directly to the business of the employer, this result is justified on the basis that the employer obtains an indirect benefit in the form of better work from a happy, rested, and relieved worker.

An interesting case from **Illinois** demonstrates how one of the "in the course of employment" doctrines may lead to a second coverage doctrine. An employee injured while attempting to dislodge a bag of Fritos stuck in a vending machine on the employer's premises was found to have sustained a work-related injury, notwithstanding the fact that the chips had been purchased by a co-worker. The Illinois Commission applied the personal comfort doctrine, in awarding compensation benefits. The Illinois Appellate Court affirmed the lower commission's award but modified the Commission's determination so as to reflect that the personal comfort doctrine applied in this case to establish the "in the course of" requirement was contrary to the law. Instead, the court found the "good Samaritan doctrine" satisfied the "in the course of employment" requirement.[37]

A recent case from **Kentucky** served to place limits on the personal comfort doctrine, especially for injuries occurring in that state. The Kentucky Supreme Court, in a split decision, reversed a decision of the state's Court of Appeals and held that a bank employee's injuries sustained when, during a paid break, she was struck by a car as she crossed a busy street to get a quick bite of lunch did not arise out of and in the course of her employment. The high court found that in jay-walking (crossing the street between intersections) and failing to yield to an oncoming vehicle, the bank employee "voluntarily exposed herself to a hazard so completely outside those normally encountered" as to negate any authority the bank had over her.[38]

Traveling Employees - Employees required to travel as part of their employment responsibilities are generally deemed to be in the scope of their employment at all times while they are on a business trip. In the case of travel, the compensability of injuries incurred is dependent upon whether the injury results from a risk that is inherent in the nature of the employment, is reasonably incidental to the employment, or is one to which the employee is specifically exposed because of the trip.

---

[36] *Larson's Workers' Compensation Law*, § 21.02 (1) (a)
[37] *Circuit City Stores v. Illinois Workers' Comp.* 391 Ill.App.3d 913 (2009)
[38] *US Bank Home Mortgage v. Schrecker*, 2014 Ky. LEXIS 617 (2014)

Injuries to employees while engaged in business travel may be compensable under various circumstances, as for example, when incurred while staying at hotels or motels; eating in restaurants; traveling by car, train or airplane; or engaged in social or athletic activities. Early case law on the subject typically addressed accidental deaths resulting from fire or asphyxiation in a hotel.[39] The rationale in awarding benefits was that there was no difference in principle between the employee who is housed upon the employer's own premises and the employee who is housed in an accommodation paid for by the employer.

A **Florida** case, however, reached the opposite conclusion. In this case, a construction worker was injured in an accident that occurred on a drive home from work after stopping in a bar to shoot pool with co-workers. The claim was initially denied, but on appeal, the appeals court reversed the decision and held that the employee's injuries were indeed incidental to employment because the worker was traveling for business. As discussed previously, in most instances, travel to and from work is not considered to be "in the course of employment," but in this case, the court took a very inclusive approach in evaluating circumstances because the employee was traveling overnight for business. [40]

A separate issue associated with traveling employees is the determination of the state of jurisdiction should a claim arise in a state or country different from that in which the worker's normal employment activities take place. Most compensation laws are extra-territorial, in effect permitting the local law to apply if the injury occurs within the state, if the contract of employment was entered into in that state; or if the work is normally conducted in that state.

Where the injury or death occurs while the worker is traveling temporarily out of the country on business, a state may extend coverage to persons working abroad under contracts entered into within the state. An employee, who signed an employment contract in **Texas** and subsequently contracted pleurisy on a job in Saudi Arabia, was entitled to Texas workers compensation benefits.

Telecommuting - The 21st century workplace is markedly different from the workplace at the turn of the 20th century and the recent COVID-19 pandemic has prompted a further dramatic shift as many employees transitioned to working remotely. Telecommuting, remote work, working from home, and telework are all fairly synonymous, but slight differences do exist between the terms. Remote work implies that the worker lives outside of the geographic area of the company's main headquarters or office. Telecommuting and telework can mean that there may (or may not) be some on-site work being done by the worker. Additionally, not all work done at a distance is done from home - workers may opt to sit with a laptop at a coffee shop or a satellite workspace. So, while telecommuting is a common phrase, it

---

[39] *Blake v. Grand Union Co.*, 98 N.Y.S. 2d 738 (1950)
[40] *Thompson v. Keller Foundations, Inc.*, 883 So. 2d 356 (2004)

might not actually be accurate in terms of describing exactly where an employee is actually working.

COVID-19 has introduced a notable impact on the workforce and has prompted companies and businesses to revisit their telecommuting protocols. Traditional safety measures had been put in place to mitigate and eliminate physical and ergonomic hazards generally encountered at the traditional worksite. An increase in telecommuting served to create new exposures. Office equipment, home office space, and ergonomic challenges have become broader telecommuting concerns. This may potentially contribute to an increase in the number of work-related slips and falls and repetitive-motion claims (e.g., exposed cords, distractions, and makeshift office arrangements). A potential offsetting consequence of increased telecommuting is a decrease in the number of work-related vehicular accidents, which tend to be more costly than other causes of injuries.[41]

Whether or not an injury occurring while telecommuting is compensable will be largely fact specific. However, when employees are directed to or required to telecommute or work from a satellite location, it is possible to speculate that some of these injuries will be considered to have arisen out of and in the course and scope of their employment. In making an ultimate determination, the Courts will normally examine all facts and circumstances before determining if the claim is compensable. The time of the event along with the specific location and the circumstances surrounding the event will be important in arriving at a determination.

In addition to employment status, a work-related injury must "arise out of and in the course of employment." A presumption usually exists that an employee injured during normal working hours, while at the usual place of employment, and while using equipment furnished by the employer, sustained a work-related injury. This presumption is difficult to apply to an at-home worker because the at-home employee may keep variable hours, parts of the home may not be considered the usual place of employment, and establishing what equipment was furnished by the employer may be difficult.

According to **South Carolina** appellate court, "*[t]he term "arising out of" refers to the origin of the cause of the accident. An accidental injury is considered to arise out of one's employment when there is a causal connection between the conditions under which the work is required to be performed and the resulting injury. An injury occurs within the course of employment when it occurs within the period of employment, at a place where the employee reasonably may be in the performance of his duties, and while fulfilling those duties or engaged in something incidental thereto.*" [42]

---

[41] www.ncci.com/Articles/Documents/Insights_COVID-19_Impact_Motor_Vehicle_Accidents-wc.pdf
[42] *McGriff v. Worsley Companies, Inc.*, 654 S.E.2d 856, 376 S.C. 103 (S.C. App. 2007).

In a **New York** decision, the court held that a compensable accident may result from either a specific work assignment or from a regular pattern of work at home.[43] In a **Utah** case, the claimant had been authorized to use his residence as his base of operations for work. In expectation of a package delivery, the claimant began spreading salt on his driveway to ensure safety for the postal worker delivering the package. While engaged in salting the driveway, the employee slipped on the ice, resulting in a neck injury. After reviewing the facts in the case, the court awarded compensation benefits.[44]

Recreational, Social and Athletic Activities - The subject of awarding compensation benefits for injuries occurring while engaged in recreational, social or athletic activities has gone through a transitional process since the compensation laws were first enacted. From an early point, injuries that occurred in the course of recreation, social or athletic activities were held not to have arisen out of the employment.[45] With the passage of time there came recognition that injuries arising from an employee's attendance at a company sponsored recreational, social or athletic activity may be so closely connected with the employment so as to create a compensable condition under most workers compensation laws. While not applicable in every jurisdiction, in most states, such activities were deemed to "arise out of and in the course of employment" when any one of the following criteria was met:

- The injury occurred on the employer's premises during lunch or recreation period as a regular incident of the employment.

- The employer, either expressly or implicitly, required participation or by making the activity part of the services of an employer.

- The employer derived substantial direct benefit from the activity over and above that of improving employee morale.

The most serious injuries associated with this type of activity stem from company sponsored athletic events. Company sponsored baseball, softball or bowling teams are typical examples of such activities. The degree of employer sponsorship may extend from furnishing team shirts with the company logo to affording practice time during working hours. Where the employer derives some benefit in the form of company publicity or advertising, injuries arising from such activities are often held to be compensable.

Whereas case law tended to favor compensability for injuries stemming from recreational, social, and athletic events where the employer derived some benefit, beginning in the 1980s, states began to enact specific statutory provisions designed

---

[43] *Fine v. S.M.C. Microsystems Corp.*, 553 N.E. 2d 1337 (1990)
[44] *Ae Clevite, Inc. v. Labor Comm'n*, 996 P. 2d 1072 (2000)
[45] Honnold, Arthur B. *A Treatise on the English and American Workmen's Compensation Laws* Vol. 1 page 323 (1918)

to limit compensability. These states followed the approach set by **California** where injuries arising out of voluntary participation in any off-duty recreational, social or athletic activity, not constituting part of the employee's work-related duties, were not compensable unless the activities were a *"reasonable expectancy of, or are expressly or impliedly required by the employment."* [46]

Colorado took a similar approach with the further requirement that the activity produce a *"substantial direct benefit to the employer beyond improvement in employee health and morale."* [47] Other states that enacted such legislation include **Kansas, New Jersey, New York, Oregon, Texas,** and **Wyoming.**

In an August 2014 decision, the **New York** Workers Compensation Board affirmed a decision denying benefits to a worker for injuries sustained while playing softball on company property with his coworkers. The players were all company employees, the equipment was provided by the employer and stored on the employer's property. In affirming the denial of benefits, the Board panel noted that when an employee is injured in a voluntary athletic activity which is not part of the employee's work-related duties, the New York law precludes the awarding of benefits unless one of three conditions is met. These conditions are *"the employer (1) required the employee to participate in the activity; (2) paid the worker to do so; or (3) sponsored the activity."*[48] The Board found that the employer did not require the employee to participate or pay the employee to participate, and there was no obvious benefit to the employer.[49]

A few states have taken a more deliberate approach to the question of the compensability of injuries arising from such activities by denoting that an injury does not arise out of the employment where it was caused by the voluntary participation in any activity that is mainly for social or recreational purposes, including athletic events, parties, and picnics *"even if the employer pays some or all of the costs."* **Maine** and **Rhode Island** preclude the payment of benefits where the participation is voluntary. Nevada has adopted perhaps the most restrictive approach by precluding coverage for employees engaged in an athletic or social event sponsored by the employer *"unless the employee receives remuneration for participation."* [50]

It is important to keep in mind that some of the principles concerned with determining whether a condition arose "in the course of employment" summarized above vary by degree from state to state, and adjudicators will occasionally find means to bend the facts in individual cases to either accept or reject a claim. In those cases where the claim is denied, there may be the potential for the injured worker to

---

[46] Cal. Labor Code § 3600 (a)(9)
[47] Colo. Rev. Stat. Ann. § 8-40-201 (8)
[48] N.Y. Workers Compensation Law Article 2 § 10 (1)
[49] *General Electric,* 114 NYWELR 142 (N.Y.W.C.B., Panel 2014)
[50] Nev. Rev. Stat. § 616A.265(1)

bring a direct action for damages against his/her employer based on the theory of negligence. This potential exposure for the employer will be addressed more fully in chapter covering the exclusive remedy of workers compensation.

COMPENSABILITY STANDARDS

The subject of compensability standards is one that has been in an evolutionary process since the first workmen's compensation laws were enacted. While some of the original laws did not require the occurrence of an "accident" for recovering compensation benefits, others, following early English law, required that there not only be an injury, but the injury had to result from an accident. In such cases, "accident" was used in its ordinary meaning indicating "a*n unlooked for mishap or untoward event which was not expected or designed by the workman himself*".[51]

Over time, states began moving away from that strict interpretation and adopted the approach where a sudden and unexpected breaking or wrenching of some portion of the body structure brought about by the normal exertions of the employee engaged in his or her normal work activities was compensable as an "injury by accident." Many legal battles were fought in this country - and the matter continues to be the subject of litigation - over the question of compensating injuries resulting from normal or usual exertion. The issue became one of whether an injury was accidental when it was the unexpected consequence of a usual exertion in the workplace or if it was necessary to demonstrate an unusual exertion or stress.

The following summarizes the two approaches as found in the majority of jurisdictions.

> **Usual Exertion Rule** - Jurisdictions that accept the "usual exertion" rule hold that a claim is compensable if the work-related stress or exertion was a substantial contributing cause of the injury, without consideration as to whether the stress or exertion was unusual or extraordinary. States that accept this rule recognize that usual work exertion can result in heart attacks, back injuries and other bodily "breakages." In a **Michigan** case, an employee who regularly performed clerical work was required to perform minor maintenance duties. After performing these duties the employee suffered a heart attack. The court held the claim compensable and noted that only a reasonable link between the work and the heart attack was necessary.[52]
>
> Notwithstanding application of the "usual exertion" rule, the injured party must still prove that the work exertion was a contributing cause of the harm. While under continual review and modification due to legislative activity and judicial interpretation, at present a majority of jurisdictions accept the usual exertion rule.

---

[51] Honnold, Arthur B. *A Treatise on the English and American Workmen's Compensation Laws* Vol. 1 page 276 (1918)
[52] *Farrington v. Total Petroleum, Inc.,* 486 N.W. 2d 677 (1992)

Only a few states have legislation addressing compensation for claims arising from "usual exertion," an example is found in the **Arkansas** where a, a "compensable injury" includes a *back or neck injury which is not caused by specific incident or which is not identifiable by time and place of occurrence.*[53]

Unusual Exertion Rule - Roughly a third of the jurisdictions reject the "usual exertion" rule and require a showing of "unusual exertion" in order to establish a heart attack or "breakage" claim was related to the employment. About one-quarter of the jurisdictions apply the "unusual exertion" rule. For example, in a **North Carolina** case, the employee was performing his normal duties when the tarp he was attempting to remove became stuck. The employee became frustrated because of this problem, and subsequently suffered a heart attack. The claim was held not compensable because the frustration was not considered an unusual strain or exertion sufficient for the heart attack to be considered an accident.[54]

In reviewing a disputed claim involving a back injury sustained by a worker while doing normal laundry activities with a co-worker, the **Maryland** Supreme Court overturned a long line of cases that had injected the "unusual activity" requirement into the definition of "accidental injury." The court noted, *"The 'unusual activity' requirement is not supported by the language of the Worker' Compensation Act, is contrary to other opinions by this Court, is a distinct minority view in the nation, and contravenes the liberal purposes of the Workers Compensation Act."*[55]

It should be noted that any hard-and-fast listing of jurisdictions that comply with this general rule is difficult to compile. The facts associated with an individual claim along with the specific statutory provision of the law at the time of the alleged injury are all factors to be considered in determining compensability.

In recent years, a number of states have moved away from the subjective test of whether or not the work exertion was "usual" or "unusual" and have introduced legal thresholds or standards for purposes of determining compensability. For example, in **Kentucky**, any work-related traumatic event or series of traumatic events is a compensable injury where the employment is the *"proximate cause producing a harmful change in the human organism evidenced by objective medical findings."*[56] **Mississippi** defines "injury" as *"an untoward event or events, if contributed to or aggravated or accelerated by the employment in a significant manner."*[57] And in **Missouri,** an "accident" means *"an unexpected or unforeseen identifiable event or series of events happening suddenly and violently, with or without human fault and producing at the time objective symptoms of an injury."*[58]

---

[53] Ark. Code Ann. § 11-9-102 (4)(A)
[54] *Cody v. Snider Lumber Co,* 399 S.E. 2d 104 (1991)
[55] *Harris v. Board of Education,* 825 A. 2d 265 (2003)
[56] Ky. Rev. Stat. Ann. § 342.0011
[57] Miss. Code Ann. § 71-3-3 (b)
[58] Mo. Rev. Stat. § 287.020 2

In a continuing attempt to define more clearly what constitutes a compensable injury, a number of jurisdictions have enacted provisions requiring the compensable injury to be the major cause of any resulting disability. In **Arkansas**, for injuries resulting from repetitive motion, back injury and hearing loss, the established burden of proof is a *preponderance of the evidence,* and the workers compensation law further provides that *"the resultant condition is compensable only if the alleged compensable injury is the major cause of the disability or need for treatment."*[59] The law in Arkansas goes on to explicitly define the term "major cause" to mean more than fifty percent of the cause.[60]

Similar to the approach found in **Arkansas,** a number of jurisdictions have enacted a provision requiring that the workplace injury rise to the level of the *"major contributing cause"* in order for the claim to be compensable. Examples of such an approach can be found in the laws in **Florida, Louisiana, Montana, Oregon**, and **South Dakota**. While not using the explicit term of "major contributing cause," provisions such as *"major cause," "predominate cause,"* or *"prevailing cause"* can be found in a number of other statutes.

In **Oregon** the adoption of the "major contributing cause" terminology has resulted in extensive litigation and several further amendments by the legislature. The process began in 1990 when, in response to rising workers compensation costs, the legislature enacted language whereby *"No injury or disease is compensable as a consequence of a compensable injury unless the compensable injury is the major contributing cause of the consequential condition."*[61] In litigation over that statutory change, a series of court decisions drew a great deal of attention to a separate but very important issue for employers: the exclusivity of the workers compensation remedy. Overturning prior opinions, the Oregon Supreme Court determined that the exclusive remedy provision of the revised Oregon law did not bar a tort claim against the employer for negligence when a medical condition was not compensable because work was a partial contributing cause of the injury but did not reach the level of "major contributing cause."[62]

Responding promptly to this decision, the Oregon legislature in 1995 amended the compensation law to make the act the exclusive remedy for all *"injuries, diseases, symptom complexes or similar conditions arising out of and in the course of employment, not just compensable injuries."*[63] In due course the issue of exclusive remedy was back before the Oregon courts. In May of 2001, the Oregon Supreme Court reversed a lower court opinion and held that the "major contributing cause" standard, combined with the exclusive remedy of the workers compensation law, violated the Oregon Constitution's "remedy clause," which provides that there must be a remedy for every harm recognized by the law. This standard, coupled with the exclusive remedy provision, created a

---

[59] Ark. Code Ann. § 11-9-102 (4)(A)
[60] Ark. Code Ann. §11-9-102 (14)
[61] Or. Rev. Stat. § 656.005 (7)(a)
[62] *Errand v. Cascade Steel Rolling Mills,* 888 P.2d 544 (1994)
[63] Or. Rev. Stat. §§ 656.012, 656.018

situation where workers were left without any remedy for injury to a constitutionally protected right. The court deemed this lack of redress to be unconstitutional and allowed the employee to proceed with an action for damages against his employer in court.

TYPES OF INJURIES COVERED

As observed at the outset of this chapter, when states began to enact workmen's compensation laws, these laws were modeled after the English Workmen's Compensation Act of 1897 which stated - *"If in any employment personal injury by accident arising out of and in the course of the employment is caused to a workman, his employer shall, subject as hereinafter mentioned, be liable to pay compensation in accordance with the first schedule of this act."*[64]

The particular reference to *"personal injury by accident"* was intended to ensure that employers were only responsible for unintended injuries stemming from a workplace incident. The term accident is commonly understood to mean an unintended mishap or an event which is not expected or designed.

Whether the language concerning "injury by accident" was expressly stated or not, the standard that the injury be accidental became a self-imposed requirement in the majority of the early state workmen's compensation laws. Consistent with the English interpretation, the purpose behind the injury requirement was to ensure that the employer was responsible only for unintended injuries that arose out of and in the course of employment. The "injury by accident" requirement was also seen as a means to prevent the compensation law from becoming a general health insurance plan. So long as the injury arose from an unintended incident in the workplace, it was clear that any resulting injury was directly associated with the employment.

From the outset, state compensation laws utilized essentially one of three different terms in denoting what work-related conditions were to be covered. These terms included "personal injury by accident," "accidental injury" and "injury" or "personal injury."

> **Personal Injury by Accident** – While the term "injury" was viewed as a broad term, the "by accident" requirement was intended to mean *"an unexpected or unforeseen event, happening suddenly and violently, with or without human fault, and producing at the time objective symptoms of an injury."*[65] It was intended that the injury be unexpected and traceable to a definite time, place and occasion or cause. Where the injury was both unexpected and traceable to a definite time, place and cause associated with the employment, there was clearly a work-related accident.
>
> In the course of employment, injuries may arise that lack the specificity of time and/or place needed to make the claim compensable. Many back injuries resulting

---

[64] Workman's Compensation Act, 1906, § 1 (Eng.)
[65] *Robbins v. Original Gas Engine Co.*, 157 N.W. 437 (1916)

from strain follow this pattern. For example, a worker may lift heavy bags of cement over an extended period of time without incident but experience severe back pains some morning upon awakening.

An early example upholding this approach comes from **Pennsylvania** where an employee worked in a woolen mill as a sewing machine operator for nearly three years until she became unable to continue working because of severe pain in both hands. The referee found that she had sustained work-related carpal tunnel syndrome because of which she was determined to be totally disabled. On appeal, the court affirmed compensation benefits, holding that it is well settled that for an injury to be compensable, it is not required that the injury result from a sudden occurrence or accident but instead, it may be due to daily trauma or a daily aggravation of a pre-existing injury. In determining that there was a causal relationship, the court relied on both the treating physician and the employer's medical witness who stated that *"repeated bending and twisting of the hands could cause the complaints and symptoms experienced by the claimant."*[66]

In the above case, using a literal interpretation of the "by accident" requirement would result in the injury being held to be non-compensable because no incident was specifically associated with the repetitive activity and the pain was first experienced while the employee was physically away from her place of employment.

Accidental Injury – A number of states like **Illinois** and **Oklahoma** initially limited their coverage to an "accidental injury" arising out of and in the course of employment. This wording served to provide a greater degree of latitude in concluding that only an accidental result was needed, rather than an accidental cause. Rather than moving down the path of "injury by accident," these jurisdictions moved directly to the position where it was necessary only to have an unexpected or unintended result in order to establish the compensability of a work-related incident.

Under an act that incorporated the "accidental injury" phrase, the worker in the lifting situation noted above would be compensated because the injury was an unexpected result. The worker would still have to demonstrate that the lifting occurred while at work and the attending physician would also have to verify the connection between the lifting process and the injury being alleged. The shift from a focus on a specific time, place or cause to one that focused on result also served to bring heart conditions and certain other health-related conditions within the parameters of workers compensation. The criteria would now shift to one of being able to medically verify that the work being performed was the producing cause of the injury that culminated in the worker's disability.

Personal Injury – The most liberal approach to coverage for workplace injuries was found in those states that employed the term "personal injury" or "injury" without reference to the requirement that the injury be accidental in character. The first

---

[66] *Oakes v. Workmen's Compensation Appeal Board,* 445 A. 2d 838 (1982)

Massachusetts Workmen's Compensation Act did not require that the injury also be an accident, differing in this respect from the English Act and most other states, and was thus more liberal for the employee. The standard of compensability established in Massachusetts was receiving a *"personal injury arising out of and in the course of employment."* It was intended for all work-related injuries to be compensated unless willfully incurred; disease was the only other exception.[67]

The passage of time has seen a nearly universal trend away from the more restrictive definition of a compensable workplace injury toward the more liberal interpretation associated with "accidental injury." In 1972, the National Commission recognized that all but six jurisdictions – **California, Iowa, Massachusetts, Minnesota, Rhode Island,** and **Texas** – required that the injury be accidental. About three-fifths of the states continued to use the phrase "injury by accident" and a number of other states used other terminology with the same effect. It was noted, *"Whatever the variations may be, the one basic and necessary element of 'accident' is that at least some part of the incident be unexpected."*[68]

The report compiled by the 1972 National Commission noted that the term "accident" had frequently operated as a bar to compensability because of the failure in a particular case to meet either the standard of a sudden, unexpected event, or not being identified with a particular time and place. The unanimous recommendation from the National Commission was that the "accidental" requirement be dropped as a test for compensability.[69]

Following the issuance of the National Commission report, a number of states dropped the particular reference to "accident." Other states held that the accidental requirement was satisfied if either the cause of the injury was unanticipated or the injury itself was the unexpected result of routine performance of the job. Dropping the accident requirement served to open the system to a greater number of back cases, heart attack claims, and claims associated with mental stress and cumulative injury.

Today, while the "by accident" requirement still exists on the books in some state laws, it is generally deemed satisfied where either the cause was of an accidental character or if the result was the unexpected result of routine performance of the workers' duties. In addition, the majority of jurisdictions interpret the accident requirements found in "injury by accident" and "accidental injury" in such a liberal fashion as to include repetitive physical trauma usual to the occupation or disability partially caused by occupational factors.

---

[67] Arthur B. Honnold, *A Treatise on the English and American Workmen's Compensation Laws* 274-75 (1918)

[68] Nat'l Commission on State Workmen's Compensation Laws, *Compendium on Workmen's Compensation* 182 (1973)

[69] Report of the National Commission on State Workmen's Compensation Laws, Recommendation 2.12 (1972)

GRADUAL OR CUMULATIVE INJURY

More than 50 years ago, the concept of gradual or cumulative injury began to be recognized as a number of jurisdictions awarded compensation benefits for conditions ranging from injurious exposures over a period of a few days to several decades. These conditions resulted typically from pulmonary or other illnesses due to exposures to toxic substances, repeated noises resulting in deafness, and repeated physical motions causing conditions such as bursitis and carpal tunnel syndrome.

In such cases, courts adopted various legal theories by which to find the occurrence of an "accident" in order to award benefits. For instance, under the repeated-impact theory, each impact, bump, jar, strain, or even breath was sufficient to be considered an accidental occurrence. A second approach was to consider the occurrence of pain as an unexpected result sufficient to supply the accidental component. It is clear that the compensability of these types of claims is well established regardless of the legal theory under which they are classified, and they will clearly continue as a significant part of workers compensation litigation.[70]

Florida addresses the situation where an employee sustained an injury over time but without a specific accident (i.e., "repetitive trauma") through development of a three-prong test for establishing compensability. To prevail under the "repetitive trauma" or "exposure theory" of an accident, an employee had to demonstrate: (1) prolonged exposure; (2) the cumulative effect of which is injury or aggravation of a pre-existing condition; and (3) that the employee has been subjected to a hazard greater than that to which the general public is exposed.

This three-prong test in Florida was affirmed in a 1980 case where the worker was employed as a maker of plastic plugs. For prolonged periods during the workday, the worker repeated the twisting and turning action of his wrist while exerting 30 to 40 pounds of pressure. He made from 500 to 900 plugs per work shift. Ordinarily two employees performed this task, but the employee worked alone for 45 days before his problems developed. Medical testimony established that he had developed carpal tunnel syndrome and that the primary cause was his work. The court found the claim compensable on grounds that it was sufficient that the claimant demonstrate a series of occurrences, whose cumulative effect resulted in a compensable injury.[71]

A number of states have specifically amended their statutes to address claims for carpal tunnel syndrome or repetitive trauma. In certain cases, such claims are included within the definition of injury. **Alabama, Arkansas,** and **Connecticut** are states that have incorporated coverage for carpal tunnel syndrome into their definition of a compensable injury. Another example is found in **Kentucky** where the term injury has been defined to

---

[70] Donald D. DeCarlo and Martin Minkowitz, *Workers Compensation and Law Practice* 266 (LRP Publications 1989)
[71] *Festa v. Teleflex, Inc.*, 382 S.E. 2d 122 (1980)

include *"any work-related traumatic event or series of traumatic events, including cumulative trauma arising out of and in the course of employment which is the proximate cause producing a harmful change in the human organism evidenced by objective medical findings."*[72]

A number of states include a reference to repetitive injury or cumulative trauma syndrome under the definition of occupational disease. In **Louisiana**, an occupational disease includes injuries due to work-related carpal tunnel syndrome.[73] **Missouri**[74] also recognizes repetitive motion injuries, and in **Texas,** the term occupational disease is defined to mean a disease arising out of and in the course of employment that causes damage or harm to the physical structure of the body, including a repetitive trauma injury. "Repetitive trauma injury" means damage or harm to the physical structure of the body occurring as the result of repetitious, physically traumatic activities that occur over time and arise out of and in the course and scope of employment[75].

After a long history of litigation over the subject of cumulative injury, **California** came to establish a different approach. Under its law, a covered injury may be "specific" or "cumulative." A cumulative injury is defined as one occurring as repetitive mentally or physically traumatic activities extending over a period of time, the combined effect of which causes any disability or need for medical treatment.[76] For purposes of clarity, California defines the date of injury for occupational disease or cumulative injuries as *"that date upon which the employee first suffered disability therefrom and either knew, or in the exercise of reasonable diligence should have known, that such disability was caused by his present or prior employment"*[77]

The Supreme Court of **Nebraska** held in a 2014 case that for purposes of assigning liability among several employers for a dental hygienist's repetitive trauma injury, the injury manifested itself on the day the claimant first missed work due to pain and not the date several years earlier when she first began to feel discomfort and sought medical treatment.[78] The court noted that the phrase "suddenly and violently" as found in the Nebraska statute (§ 48-151(2)) did not mean "instantaneously and with force," but rather, required only that the injury manifest itself at an identifiable point in time. The court acknowledged that other jurisdictions applied different tests, but indicated the test it applied was neither inconsistent with the statutory language nor was it unfair or unjust.

When a state draws any distinction between a cumulative injury and an event-specific injury for purposes of determining compensability, how the injury is characterized makes all the difference in whether benefits will be awarded. In a **Virginia** case, the court of appeals reversed an earlier award of compensation benefits to an airline reservation agent who began

---

[72] Ky. Rev. Stat. Ann. § 342.0011 (1)
[73] La. Rev. Stat. Ann. § 1031.1 B
[74] Mo. Rev. Stat. § 287. 067
[75] Tex. Code Ann. § 401.011 (34)
[76] Cal. Labor Code § 3208.1
[77] Cal. Labor Code § 5412
[78] *Potter v. McCulla,* 288 Neb. 741, 2014 Neb. LEXIS 124 (2014)

to suffer from photosensitivity after being moved to a work station equipped with fluorescent lighting. Presumably as a result of the lighting, the claimant's eyes began to burn, the mole on her arm darkened, her arms became speckled and colored, her joints were in pain, and her vision was impaired. The court of appeals reversed, however, finding that the claimant's condition of photosensitivity was the result of only a cumulative exposure to the lighting, and thus, as a cumulative injury, was not an industrial disease as defined by Virginia's Workers Compensation Act.[79]

PRE-EXISTING RISK AND INJURY AGGRAVATION

A fundamental principle among early workmen's compensation laws was that the employer took the employee subject to his/her physical condition when entering upon employment. In other words, the employer took the worker "as he found him." Hence, compensation coverage was not solely for the protection of employees in normal physical condition, but also extended to those with serious underlying health conditions such as those with tuberculosis or syphilis. It followed that neither a congenital weakness nor a pre-existing disease would render non-compensable an injury received under conditions which would otherwise make it compensable, even if the injury was made more severe because of the pre-existing weakness or would not have occurred but for the condition.

A vivid example of this interpretation comes from an early **Massachusetts** case where a middle-aged worker was furrowing posts in the employer's workshop. The furrowing operation required the worker to push the posts toward the knives using his abdomen. After finishing a number of posts, the worker sat down in obvious pain and died three days later from internal hemorrhage. The court held that, although the worker was suffering from internal cancer, the facts of the case warranted a finding that the unusual pressure exerted in pushing the posts with body parts weakened by disease was the proximate cause of the death.[80]

That philosophy continues to the present time. Where the injury is related to the personal condition of a worker, such as a pre-existing weakness or disease that leads to some injury or some resulting disabling condition, the issue is not whether the resulting injury – produced in part by the pre-existing condition – is an injury arising out of the employment, but rather, the general rule is that such injuries are compensable if the employment contributes to the final disability by placing the worker in a position where the condition is aggravated or worsened by factors in the workplace.

This general rule applies to claims stemming from idiopathic falls. Thus, a worker who suffers a heart attack or epileptic fit and falls from an elevated level or into a machine will generally be deemed to have sustained a work-related injury. However, benefits will be restricted to that portion of the disability associated with the employment hazard, not the original attack or stroke.

---

[79] *United Airlines v. Walter,* 482 S.E. 2d 849 (1997)
[80] *In re Madden,* 111 N.E. 379 (1916)

In similar fashion, a weak heart which is further weakened as a result of exertion or stress, or a diabetic condition that may have remained dormant if not provoked by the workplace exposure or event, are examples of accelerated injuries that are deemed to arise out of the employment. The same holds true for cancers, allergies, skin conditions, and other related disorders that are aggravated by the nature of the employment.

In the case of aggravation of a medical condition caused by a workplace injury, the majority of decisions follow the principle that where the original injury is proven to have arisen out of and in the course of the employment, every natural consequence that follows from that injury is likewise considered to be part of that injury, unless there is some intervening cause or event that is attributable to the conduct of the claimant. When an original injury or condition progresses into serious complications, or when the existence of a compensable injury in some way worsens the effects of an independent weakness or disease, the results are fully compensable. The typical example is where a pre-existing diabetic condition prevents the normal recovery from a workplace accident. The same rule applies where the aggravation is due to medical or surgical mistreatment that results in increased disability.

Questions surround the type of conduct on the part of the employee that would serve to break the chain of compensability. It has been suggested that when the subsequent injury is directly related to the compensable injury, such as an accident on the way to the doctor's office, only intentional misconduct should break the chain. Thus, when a claimant rashly engages in some activity such as disregarding medical orders, with knowledge of the risk associated with such action, the chain of causation is broken and any subsequent injury is generally deemed not to have arisen out of the employment.

OCCUPATIONAL DISEASE

In examining the subject of occupational disease, it is important to recognize the difference between a traumatic injury and an occupational disease. Several important differences distinguish an occupational disease from a traumatic injury. Traumatic injuries, for the most part, present few questions relative to their occurrence or their relationship to the employment. A fall or a severed limb occurring at work is readily apparent. In many instances there are witnesses to the event and evidence of the injury is observable. In the vast majority of cases, a traumatic injury can be associated with a specific time and/or event, and it is readily apparent whether the accident arose "out of and in the course of employment."

For occupational disease claims, these distinguishing characteristics are not always apparent. In large part, the difficulties associated with occupational diseases result from the interrelated issues of latency and causation. The interval between the first exposure to an injurious hazard and the manifestation of a resulting disease is referred to as the latency period. Not all occupational disease involves long periods of latency. Those for which the period of latency is short – for example skin rashes resulting from contact with a caustic agent – have an impact on the compensation system like those of traumatic injuries because of the clear connection between the exposure and the resulting condition.

There is considerable evidence, however, that many serious diseases or conditions suspected of arising from a workplace exposure to harmful substances require many years to develop. The following table illustrates the estimated latency periods for cancers due to the following known or suspected carcinogenic substances.[81]

Carcinogenic Substance	Range of Latency (in Years)
Arsenic	10 plus
Asbestos	4 to 50
Benzene	6 to 14
Chromium	15 to 25
Uranium/radium	10 to 15
Vinyl Chloride	20 to 30
X-rays	10 to 25

Establishing a causal connection between the workplace exposure and a worker's injury or disease is a basic requirement for establishing the compensability of a work-related event. Occupational diseases with a long latency period pose difficulties in this regard. The worker and/or the treating physician may not recognize the connection between an exposure that took place many years in the past and a current physical condition or disability. Even where such knowledge and awareness exists, the parties involved are frequently operating at a disadvantage because of the inability to obtain pertinent evidence regarding the type and extent of the original exposure.

In addition to the problems that stem from periods of extended latency, there are also issues associated with establishing medical causation. Determination of the medical causation of occupational disease claims involves three essential considerations.

- The first is whether the hazardous exposure can cause the disability. While for numerous occupational diseases (e.g., acute poisonings associated with toxic chemicals, certain chronic diseases such as asbestosis and silicosis, etc.) the conditions for which the connection to a particular hazard has been established with reasonable certainty, there are many other diseases where the evidence is of a less certain nature.

- A second consideration is the question whether the worker has the disorder or condition being claimed. Diagnostic issues are frequently resolved in an adversarial arena despite the no-fault intent of workers compensation administration and in some cases, physicians who testify do not have a specific interest in, specialized expertise about, or the time to delve into the occupational causes of certain diseases.

---

[81] *Workers Compensation: Exposures, Coverage, Claims* 5-19 (Standard Publishing Corporation 1994).

- The third and most complex component of establishing medical causation is whether the alleged occupational exposure was the sole or primary cause of the disease. For certain occupational diseases, this question is easily resolved, but for many there is the potential for dual causation. For example, in addition to certain known workplace hazards, smoking, alcohol consumption, poor diet, etc. along with possible exposure to other hazardous substances outside of the workplace may produce disabling conditions. The question becomes one relative to the extent and degree of the workplace exposure.

It should be noted that extended periods of latency only serve to add complexity and difficulty to each of the above considerations associated with the determination of medical causation.

By the beginning of the 20th century – concurrent with the original enactment of many of the first compensation laws in this country – a number of specific diseases or health-related conditions had come to be associated with exposure to certain hazardous substances. For example, for some time ptomaine poisoning or enteritis had been recognized as being contracted from continuous work around sewers or drains. Similarly, lead poisoning was a recognized hazard for painters and those who worked in lead mines. Notwithstanding this level of knowledge and the recognized connection between certain diseases and the employment, most early compensation laws did not provide coverage for occupational diseases.

For many reasons, drafters of the early compensation laws were reluctant to provide coverage for occupational diseases. The major reason was that, at that time, occupational diseases were thought to arise from ordinary, known risks of employment. As a result, occupational diseases were not viewed as being accidental or associated with an employer's fault or negligence. It was assumed that a painter, given sufficient exposure to lead paint, would ultimately come down with lead poisoning. Similarly, a worker in the coal mines was expected to eventually succumb to lung disease associated with exposure to coal dust.

Moreover, during the period prior to the enactment of the first compensation laws, claims for occupational disease did not form a basis for tort recovery. For this reason it was not considered part of the employer/employee bargain that ultimately served as the foundation for the first workmen's compensation laws. Other factors that served to keep occupational disease claims outside of these early laws were fears that full coverage would be too expensive for employers in certain industries and that there was insufficient scientific evidence linking specific diseases with certain employment hazards to justify broadened coverage.

In 1911, the State of **Michigan** enacted a workmen's compensation law. In one of the early decisions construing the new law, the court, following precedent established in English cases, held that lead poisoning was not an "accident" but rather an "occupational disease" and therefore not compensable. The case involved an employee who worked as a sifter in a red lead plant. In this position he came into contact with lead and after completing his day at work, he immediately became so ill that he was unable to return to his job. The employee died one month later of lead poisoning. In the opinion of the Michigan court, it was not a sudden event occurring at a fixed time but was a gradual and slow process and therefore not an accident.[82]

However, in a review of early case law, it is notable that a number of states considered infectious diseases to be compensable. In 1916, an employee who wore gloves and was required to handle dirty and diseased hides that contained wet salt recovered compensation benefits after he suffered an abrasion of the skin, came into contact with anthrax germs contained in the hides and developed the disease. The **New York** court considered the disease to be unexpected, unusual, and extraordinary and therefore compensable.[83]

Within two decades after the enactment of the original state workmen's compensation laws, a majority of the states' amended their statutes to extend compensation benefits to occupational diseases. By statutory and judicial action, the states of **California** and **Massachusetts** were the first to recognize occupational diseases as compensable. California enacted an amendment in 1918 to include any injury arising out of and in the scope of employment as compensable.

By July 1, 1940, 26 jurisdictions had made express provisions for diseases other than those resulting from accidents. Through the 1950s and 1960s, states began modifying their compensation laws to provide broader coverage for occupational disease by adopting a broad definition of occupational disease or by developing a schedule of covered diseases.[84]

Notwithstanding the expanded coverage for occupational disease claims, substantial criticism continued because many of these laws contained certain statutory restriction and procedures that operated to preclude the payment of compensation benefits even where the disease was clearly linked to the employment. Numerous observers noted the following principal limitations and restrictions:

- Continued use of the by accident phrase served to preclude compensation payments for diseases produced by regular, routine exposures to a hazard. Other compensability thresholds such as those requiring the injury to be "peculiar to the worker's employment," "independent of other cause," or "incidental to the character of the business" similarly served as barriers to the compensability of occupational disease claims.

---

[82] *Adams. v. Acme White Lead and Color Works,* 148 N.W. 485 (1914)
[83] *Heirs v. John A. Hull & Co.,* 164 N.Y.S. 767 (1917)
[84] Arthur Reede, *Adequacy of Workmen's Compensation,* Harvard University Press, pgs. 47-48 (1947)

- Claims could also be limited where compensable occupational disease cases were restricted to those listed in a schedule contained in the law. In 1970, 13 states[85] continued to use a statutory list or schedule of covered diseases.

- Statute of limitation provisions had been a part of workers compensation laws from the beginning. Generally, these statutes served to bar claims that were not filed within one or two years after an injury has occurred. Such restrictions failed to recognize the multi-year time lag (latency period) that can occur between the last injurious exposure and the resulting manifestation of an occupational disease.

- Several states used minimum exposure requirements to limit compensable claims to those where a worker was exposed to certain hazardous substances for a period of time sufficient to cause the occupational disease.

The 1972 National Commission addressed the subject of occupational disease claims. Recognizing that with advances in medical epidemiology and increased growing exposures to a growing number and combination of stresses, it was impractical to define work-related diseases by specific enumeration, the Commission recommended *"That all states provide full coverage of work-related diseases." (R2.13)*

With a similar recognition for the long latency period associated with certain occupational disease, the Commission recommended that *"The time limit for initiating a claim be three years after the date the claimant knew or, by exercise of reasonable diligence should have known, of the existence of the impairment and its possible relationship to his employment, or within three years after the employee first experiences a loss of wages which the employee knows or by exercise of reasonable diligence should have known, was because of the work-related impairment."*[86]

In response to the recommendations of the National Commission, all states have extended coverage to all occupational diseases, and many states removed any restrictive tests for compensability from their laws, either legislatively or through the judicial process. The most common test that remains, the arising out of and in the course of employment requirement found in most states has not proven to be an unrealistic threshold to obtaining coverage for occupational disease claims.

The most fundamental determination of workers compensation is whether a workers' injury or occupational disease is compensable. While a small number of states have incorporated occupational disease claims within the definition of injury, many states have legislated a separate chapter or section of the law that is devoted exclusively to claims arising as a result of occupational disease.

---

[85] Arizona, Colorado, Georgia, Idaho, Kansas, Louisiana, Montana, New Mexico, New York, Oklahoma, South Dakota, Tennessee and Texas.
[86] National Commission Recommendation 6.13

State definitions of an occupational disease vary widely. Probably the simplest approach is found in Mississippi where *"an occupational disease shall be deemed to arise out of and in the course of employment when there is evidence that there is a direct causal connection between the work performed and the occupational disease."*[87] Virginia follows a model that had been developed in a number of other states where the term is defined to mean *"a disease arising out of and in the course of the employment, but not an ordinary disease of life to which the general public is exposed outside of the employment. A disease shall be deemed to arise out of the employment only if there is apparent to the rational mind, upon consideration of all the circumstances:*

1. A direct causal connection between the conditions under which work is performed and the occupational disease;

2. It can be seen to have followed as a natural incident of the work as a result of the exposure occasioned by the nature of the employment;

3. It can be fairly traced to the employment as the proximate cause;

4. It is neither a disease to which an employee may have had substantial exposure outside of the employment, nor any condition of the neck, back, or spinal column;

5. It is incidental to the character of the business and not independent of the relation of employer and employee; and

6. It had its origin in a risk connected with the employment and flowed from that source as a natural consequence, though it need not have been foreseen or expected before its contraction."[88]

While a frequently adopted approach in the past had been to enact a schedule of covered occupational diseases, many states have moved away from that approach. Today schedules for occupational disease claims can be found in only a few states. All of the states that continue to utilize the schedule approach have amended their schedule in some fashion so as to include *"any other occupational disease related to the employment."* This catchall addendum essentially eliminates the need for the remainder of the schedule.

The concept of time limitations for the filing of a lawsuit was first codified in this country when legislative bodies adopted statutes of limitations to compel individuals to exercise a right of action against another party within a specified period of time. These laws are perceived as necessary to provide the opposing party with a fair opportunity to defend the claim. Knowledge and evidence relative to the circumstances of the claim could be lost where too much time had elapsed.

Following the recommendation of the National Commission, many states amended their workers compensation laws to start their statute of limitations when the worker had knowledge of the condition and its relationship to the employment. In these circumstances, knowledge is generally considered to take place when the treating physician communicates to the worker the diagnosis and its possible relationship to the employment. For example, In **California**, the date of injury in cases of occupational diseases or cumulative injuries is *"that date upon which the employee first suffered*

---

[87] Miss. Code Ann. § 71-3-7
[88] Va. Code Ann. § 65.2-400

disability therefrom and either knew, or in the exercise of reasonable diligence should have known, that such disability was caused by his present or prior employment"[89]

A minor variant to this approach can be found in those states where the statute of limitations begins to run following the first manifestation of the condition. States that rely upon manifestation include **Connecticut, Idaho, Kentucky,** and **Rhode Island**. A small number of states refer to the statute of limitations running from the date of disability.

It has always been generally accepted that the occupational disease provisions were not intended to cover ordinary diseases of life to which the general public was equally exposed. State workers compensation laws expressly generally exclude coverage for an *"ordinary disease of life"* to which anyone is susceptible, and as to which there is not necessarily a causal connection between the worker's employment and the disease. For example, in **South Carolina**, *"ordinary diseases of life"* are expressly excluded from the definition of an occupational disease.[90]

Cases involving employees sickened from infectious diseases, such as hepatitis B, were unsuccessful in seeking workers compensation benefits. In these cases, the courts ruled that the claimants had not met their burden of proving that the illness was an occupational disease to which the claimant's work caused a peculiar and heightened risk of exposure, as distinct from an ordinary disease of life to which members of the public are exposed generally. Two such decisions include a case of the West Nile virus in **Louisiana**[91] and a Florida case of fungal meningitis.[92]

The pandemic has altered that position in response to the COVID-19 virus. Many states have rapidly responded, either through enactment of legislation covering the virus through presumptions or through executive action by the program administrator to extent coverage for virus infections among hospital workers and others identified as "essential" employees.

As a final point, the basic goal of the workers compensation program is to promote safety by providing incentives to engage in safety and loss prevention activities, distribute compensation costs equitably among employers, and reflect the cost of the associated workplace injury in the price of goods and services. These goals are accomplished by internalizing the cost of workplace injury claims to the industries and employers who expose workers to hazardous conditions and substances that cause injury.

Because workers may be exposed to hazardous substances or conditions while working for multiple employers during their working life, a legitimate question may arise as to which employer is responsible. The majority of states have adopted the "last injurious exposure" rule, which places responsibility for benefits on the last employer where the

---

[89] Cal. Labor Code § 5412
[90] S.C. Code § 42-11-10(B)
[91] *Easly v. D&O Contractors*, 895 So.2d 23 (2005)
[92] *Taylor v. City of Titusville*, 288 So.3d 731 (2019)

claimant was "injuriously" exposed to the hazardous substance or condition. This approach attempts to strike a balance between equity and efficiency. Before liability can be imposed, employment at a specific employer must have exposed the worker to conditions, sufficient in dosage and toxicity, to have contributed to the disease. A problem associated with this approach is the fact that the question of what constitutes an injurious exposure is a highly technical judgment that often resides at the cutting edge of scientific knowledge.

To eliminate disputes over whether an exposure was injurious, several states removed that threshold and assigned liability to the employer who last exposed the individual to the harmful substance causing the disease. In this case, there is more emphasis on efficiency because no effort is made to determine whether the exposure to the hazardous substance was injurious. Any costs or delay associated with determining which exposure was the last injurious exposure are avoided. Examples of jurisdictions that utilize the last exposure rule include **Alabama, Iowa, Kentucky, Minnesota, Missouri,** and the **Federal Longshore Act.**

Many of the early occupational disease laws served to apportion liability among all employers who contributed to the exposure causing the disease by requiring each to pay benefits in proportion to their responsibility. While this approach was perceived as emphasizing fairness and equity by requiring payment from all responsible employers, it often resulted in substantial delay in determining who were the responsible parties and their relative share of the causation. This resulted in substantial "friction costs" for all parties involved. Today, only a few states – for example **New York** and **Rhode Island** – continue to apportion liability among all responsible employers.

California limits the apportionment rule among employers to cases involving occupational disease or cumulative injury. Prior to a reform enacted in 2004, in cases of aggravation of any disease existing prior to the compensable injury, compensation would be allowed only for the proportion of the disability due to the aggravation of such prior disease that was reasonably attributable to the injury. With the changes enacted in 2004, the employer is responsible only for the approximate percentage of injury caused by the present work-related injury.

MENTAL STRESS

Workers compensation claims for mental disorders have proliferated since the 1980s. The rise in mental health problems presents some exacting challenges for both the workers compensation programs and health care professionals. Mental health problems are associated with a multitude of conditions (e.g., stress, depression, work pressure) and for the workers compensation program, the challenge is to separate out the possible influence of the family, the community, and other social influences/actors from the work environment.

Professor Arthur Larson in his landmark treatise entitled *Larson's Workers Compensation Law*, separated workers compensation claims involving mental aspects into three categories that have been accepted almost universally by boards and commissions across this country and also in Canada. (For purposes here, the term mental is generally understood to include both psychological and emotional aspects.)

> A recently published book, authored by Don DeCarlo and David Torrey entitled *STRESS Past, Present and Future*, examines the modern-day stressors that serve to cause accidents, illnesses and even death. These stressors are reviewed in terms of their association both in and away from the workplace. The book includes a 50-state legal analysis of laws related law enforcement, first responders, firemen, and others.
>
> The book is published by The American Society of Workers Compensation Professionals (AMCOMP) Indianapolis, Indiana.

Physical-Mental claims involve the development of a mental disability related to a work-related physical injury. For example, a mental disability such as depression, anxiety or panic attacks, or a nervous breakdown following a work-related physical injury.

Mental-Physical claims arise when a work-related mental stimulus results in a disabling physical disability, such as ulcer, or suffered a heart attack, due to the mental stress associated with the employment.

Mental-Mental claims arise in which mental disability results from mental stress on the job where the disability is not tied to a physical event. For example, an employee forced to work long hours in a high-stress environment, or an employee who has been harassed, may develop an anxiety disorder or depression.

Subject to certain restrictions, physical-mental and mental-physical claims are generally held to be compensable in essentially every jurisdiction, although in certain jurisdictions it is more difficult than in others to convince the adjudicating body of the merits of such claims. The category of mental-mental claims proves far more controversial than the first two, and the subgroup of claims within the category of mental-mental arising from repeated stressful work-related stimuli (the often referred to chronic stress or cumulative psychiatric injury conditions) are the most controversial of all.

A significant number of states bar completely those claims resulting in mental injury unless produced or caused by some physical injury to the body. For example, **Kansas** case law requires that in order to establish a compensable claim for traumatic neurosis, the claimant must establish: a work-related physical injury, symptoms of the traumatic neurosis, and that neurosis is directly traceable to the physical injury. This type of injury would be classified as an injury-mental claim.[93] This approach may be identified with about a quarter of the states. In **Nebraska**, mental injuries are only compensable if the

---

[93] *Gleason v. Samaritan and Church Mutual Insurance Co.*, 926 P. 2d 1349 (1996)

psychiatric problem or depression is a product of a physical work-related injury (physical-mental injuries). An exception exists for first responders (sheriff, police, state patrol, firefighters, and EMT/paramedics) who may recover workers compensation benefits for mental-mental injuries.[94]

It is the third type of claim, the mental-mental, that is the most difficult to understand, analyze, and pass judgement on. These claims have also been the subject of a great deal of litigation and controversy. Most workers are not in physical danger while at work, nor are they typically exposed to the type of workplace event traumatic enough to induce a physical ailment. Yet, more and more, courts have begun to recognize mental-mental stress claims that were virtually non-existent in the past.

Throughout the decades before the 1970s, courts in many cases awarded compensation to workers disabled as a result of fright or shock. These cases were typically justified by holding that an injury or accidental injury cannot reasonably be limited to one's flesh and bones. It was not until the late 1970s and the early 1980s that change began to occur. Two cases are worth noting:

- In a 1975 **New York** decision, the Court of Appeals overturned a lower court decision denial of benefits where a key assistant to the security chief of a department store, discovered the body of the security chief who had committed suicide. Recognizing the mental-mental cause of action, the court remarked, poetically, that there is "nothing talismanic about physical impact,"[95]

- A **California** court in 1982 awarded benefits where a supermarket cake decorator, who suffered from significant pre-employment emotional problems, suffered a nervous breakdown. The worker accused her supervisor of a series of various harassments and eventually stopped work. During the proceedings, the credible evidence indicated that the claimant had in essence imagined the harassments while the same expert testimony certified that claimant was authentic in her imaginings. This fact was enough for the court to award benefits:[96]

It was during the subsequent decades, using the *Albertson* decision as the springboard, that California experienced an unequalled upsurge in claims, lawyer involvement, and fractious litigation. The acceptance of mental-mental claims spread and today, among the 50 states, 33 permit recoveries, under various tests, for mental-mental injuries. The **District of Columbia**, the Longshore Act, and FECA also allow recovery for mental-mental claims. Meanwhile, 17 states exclude such claims. While some states, either through statute or case law, serve to bar compensation benefits for mental-mental claims, other states have established various thresholds to compensability.

---

[94] Neb. Rev. Stat. § 616C.180
[95] *Wolfe v. Sibley, Lindsay & Curr Co.*, 36 N.Y.2d 505 (1975).
[96] *Albertson's Inc. v. WCAB (Bradley)*, 182 Cal. Rptr. 304 (1982).

States Allowing Recovery for Mental-Mental Cases

South Carolina has defined how claims for mental injuries, illness, or stress are to be compensated. *"Stress, mental injuries, and mental illness arising out of and in the course of employment unaccompanied by physical injury and resulting in mental illness or injury are not considered a personal injury unless the employee establishes, by a preponderance of the evidence: (1) that the employee's employment conditions causing the stress, mental injury, or mental illness were extraordinary and unusual in comparison to the normal conditions of the particular employment; and (2) the medical causation between the stress, mental injury, or mental illness, and the stressful employment conditions by medical evidence."* [97]

A **Pennsylvania** case exemplifies a claim where the claimant prevailed. There, three levels of adjudication all held that a case manager at the Community Empowerment Association had been exposed to abnormal work conditions after her employer had both sexually harassed her and pressured her to participate in Islamic religious rituals, including wearing special garb. [98]

In addition to the extraordinary or unusual stress, the states of **Alaska** and **Maine** require that the work stress be the predominant cause of the mental injury. In **Arizona,** mental claims require *"unexpected, unusual or extraordinary stress related to the employment, or some physical injury related to the employment to be a substantial contributing cause of the mental injury, illness or condition."*[99] In **Missouri,** the work stress is required to be e*xtraordinary and unusual,* and the amount of work stress must be measured by *objective standards and actual events.*[100]

Closely akin to those states requiring the workplace stress to be extraordinary or unusual are those states requiring some form of specific or traumatic event. For example, in **Colorado**, a "mental impairment" is a recognized permanent disability arising out of and in the course of employment when the accidental injury involves no physical injury and consists of *"a psychologically traumatic event that is generally outside of a worker's usual experience and would evoke significant symptoms of distress in a worker in similar circumstances"*[101] A few other states following this approach in some fashion.

In **New York, t**he New York Court of Appeals first recognized the compensability of mental-mental claims the *Wolfe* decision holding that psychological or nervous injury precipitated by psychic trauma is compensable to the same extent as physical

---

[97] S.C. Code Ann. § 42-1-160.(B)
[98] *Empowerment Association v. WCAB (Porch)*, 962 A.2d 1 (2008).
[99] Ariz. Rev. Stat. Ann. § 23-1043.01 B
[100] Mo. Rev. Stat. § 287.120
[101] Colo. Rev. Stat. Ann. § 8-41-301

injury.[102] New York's intermediate appellate courts have construed the decision in *Wolfe* as, at the least, requiring stress greater than that of day-to-day employment.

In **Texas**, mental trauma can produce a compensable injury, even without any underlying physical injury if it arises in the course and scope of employment and is traceable to a definite time, place, and cause.[103] In *Bailey,* the Texas Supreme Court held that neurosis suffered by a structural steel worker solely as a result of fright was an "injury" within the definition of the workers compensation law and was compensable. The neurosis suffered by the worker was prompted by seeing a co-worker fall to his death from a collapsing scaffold. The worker himself suffered only minor injuries.

California, with its long history with mental-mental claims, has tried to eliminate as much ambiguity in the law as possible through legislative changes that (a) allows a gradual stress mental-mental in employees with six months or more of employment; but (b) for newer workers, obliges the same to prove "a sudden and extraordinary employment condition"; and (c) in all cases, except those subject to violence, obliges claimant to prove that work stress is the predominant cause of the injury. As to (c), the statute is extraordinary in providing that, for victim of violence, only substantial cause must be shown, with that phrase meaning "at least 35 to 40 percent of the causation …."[104]

During the 2013 legislative session, **Minnesota** amended their workers compensation law so as to expand the definition of occupational disease to include mental impairment where a mental impairment is defined as a *"diagnosis of post-traumatic stress disorder by a licensed psychiatrist or psychologist."* Prior to the recent law change, the courts had declined to include 'mental/mental' injuries in the statutory definition of "personal injury." In a 1981 decision, the court held that the inability to discern whether the legislature intended to include such injuries in the statute precluded coverage.[105] The Minnesota legislature also included language whereby a mental impairment is not considered a disease if it results from a disciplinary action, work evaluation, job transfer, layoff, demotion, promotion, termination, retirement, or similar action taken in good faith by the employer.[106]

In **Connecticut,** the terms personal injury or injury do not include a mental or emotional impairment, unless the impairment arises from a physical injury or occupational disease; or a mental or emotional impairment resulting from a personal action, including a transfer, promotion, demotion, or termination. However, such

---

[102] *Wolfe v. Sibley, Lindsay & Curr Co.,* 369 N.Y.S. 2d 637 (1975
[103] *Bailey v. American General Insurance Company*, 279 S.W. 2d 315 (1955) and *Olson v. Hartford Accident and Indemnity Company*, 477 S.W.2d 859 (1972)
[104] CAL LABOR CODE § 3208.3(b)(3).
[105] *Lockwood v. Independent School Dist. No. 877* 312 N.W.2d 924 (1981)
[106] Minn. Stat. Ann. § 176.011 subd. 15

injuries may be covered in the case of police officers using deadly force in the line of duty, or in the case of firefighters diagnosed with post-traumatic stress disorder.[107]

States Barring Recovery for Mental-Mental Claims

Probably the clearest statement of legislative intent regarding claims for mental-mental injury can be found in the **Montana** workers compensation law where the following public policy statement was added - *"It is the intent of the legislature that stress claims, often referred to as "mental-mental claims" and "mental-physical claims", are not compensable under Montana's workers compensation and occupational disease law"*[108]

A complete denial of benefits is illustrated by a **Nebraska** case where the court denied benefits to the dependents of a state police trooper who committed suicide in response to alleged stress. The officer had detained and then released a motorist who shortly thereafter committed a murder during a robbery. The trooper's distress at contemplating that scenario led him to take his own life. Yet, as far as the court was concerned, mental-mental claims are not covered either as injuries or occupational diseases under the Nebraska Act.[109]

A final issue includes those states where, while recognizing mental-mental claims to be compensable, require neither the rule of extraordinary or unusual stress nor a specific or traumatic event. States falling into this category include **Delaware, Hawaii, Indiana, Michigan, New Jersey, New Mexico, North Carolina, Oregon,** and **Pennsylvania.**

In response to the subjective nature of the mental-mental type claim, a number of states have enacted legislation designed to bar benefits where the claim stemmed from good faith personnel actions. For example, **Massachusetts** has enacted a law that states that *"No mental or emotional disability arising principally out of a bona fide personnel action including a transfer, promotion, demotion, or termination except such action which is the intentional infliction of emotional harm shall be deemed to be a personal injury within the meaning of this chapter."*[110]

In addition to Massachusetts and Minnesota, another twelve states include a provision where compensation benefits are not payable for a psychiatric injury if the injury was substantially caused by a lawful, nondiscriminatory, good faith personnel action. These states include **Alaska, California, Colorado, Hawaii, Maine, Missouri, Nevada, New Mexico, New York, South Carolina, Texas,** and **Utah.**

---

[107] Conn. Gen. Stat. § 31-275 (16)(B)(ii)
[108] Mont. Code Ann. § 39-71-105
[109] *Zach v. Nebraska State Patrol*, 727 N.W.2d 206 (Neb. 2007)
[110] Mass. Gen. Laws Ann. Ch. 152 § 1(7A)

PRESUMPTION OF INJURY

At the core of the workers compensation program is the *quid pro quo* between employers and workers in which each side received and gave up something of value for a more streamlined system of providing protection to injured workers.[111] It must be recognized at the onset that the *quid pro quo* of workers compensation does not mean that there is an explicit balance between the two competing interests. Because of the remedial nature of workers compensation legislation, states have employed a wide range of presumptions to tilt the scales at least slightly in favor of the injured worker.

One of the basic presumptions identified with a number of states is technically not a presumption, but rather a doctrine of statutory construction. This liberal construction doctrine is intended to tilt the scales, in a small degree, in favor of the employee where certain criteria are met. This feature, sometimes explicitly contained in the statute is more frequently stated by the courts. An **Alabama** decision noted that the workers compensation act is to be liberally construed *"to accomplish its beneficent purposes" with doubts resolved in favor of the employee.*[112] There are a few other states that hold a similar opinion.

A number of states go a step beyond simply the liberal construction. The **Hawaii** law provides that in *"any proceeding for the enforcement of a claim for compensation under this chapter, it shall be presumed, in the absence of substantial evidence to the contrary, that the claim is covered for the injury."*[113] In **New York**, the law provides that once an employee has shown the employer-employee relationship exists and that there exists a causal connection or nexus between the accident and the employment, the Workers Compensation Board should apply a presumption that the claimed injury is compensable under the Workers Compensation Law insofar as the injury arose out of and in the course of the employment.[114]

> **Presumption for Unwitnessed Injury or Death** – A number of states provide certain presumptions once the essential parts of the claim have been established. A common presumption found in a number of jurisdictions is the presumption that an unwitnessed death occurring at a place where the employee might reasonably be in the course of their employment and during the time of their employment, arose out of and in the course of the employment. For example, the **Idaho** statute provides that *"In any claim for compensation, where the employee has been killed, or is physically or mentally unable to testify, and where there is unrebutted prima facie evidence that indicates that the injury arose in the course of employment, it shall be presumed, in the absence of substantial evidence to the contrary, that the injury arose out of the*

---

[111] Thomas A. Robinson, J.D., Feature National Columnist <u>LexisNexis Workers' Compensation eNewsletter</u>,
[112] *Holmes v. Gold Kist, inc.* 673 So. 2d 449 (1995)
[113] Hawaii Rev. Statute § 386-85(1)
[114] N.Y. Work. Comp. Law § 21(1)

employment and that sufficient notice of the accident causing the injury has been given."[115]

A similar example of presumptive coverage can be found in the **Maine** statute where *"In any claim for compensation, when the employee has been killed or is physically or mentally unable to testify, there is a rebuttable presumption that the employee received a personal injury arising out of and in the course of employment, that sufficient notice of the injury has been given and that the injury or death was not occasioned by the willful intention of the employee to injure or kill the employee or another."*[116]

Following a rather checkered history of denying benefits in the case of an unexplained injury without witnesses, **Virginia** enacted legislation designed to help workers injured in unwitnessed accidents who were unable to recall the circumstances of the incident. The newly enacted legislation provides that *"In any claim for compensation, where the employee is physically or mentally unable to testify as confirmed by competent medical evidence and where there is unrebutted prima facie evidence that indicates that the injury was work related, it shall be presumed, in the absence of a preponderance of evidence to the contrary, that the injury was work related."*[117]

For those situations involving an unwitnessed injury or death, the practical justification for the extension of coverage lies in the realization that, when the injury or death has removed the only possible witness who could testify to a causal connection, fairness suggests some softening of the rule requiring affirmative proof of each element of compensability.

Presumption for Heart and Cancers for Emergency Personnel – During the past several decades, there has been a plethora of statutes enacted granting special workers compensation coverage to police officers, fire fighters, and sometimes to others including first responders and emergency medical technicians (EMTs). This coverage extended primarily to coverage for respiratory and heart diseases associated with the exertions of the employment. In some instances, this coverage was also extended to certain medical conditions such as cancer of the testes, brain, and lymphohematopoietic systems. While there are 19 states with these statutory presumptions, **California, Florida, Michigan, Pennsylvania** and **Wisconsin** are examples of states where these special provisions can be found.

Presumption for Disabling Condition – A different form of presumption is found in a few states, particularly **Louisiana,** where an injured worker may be aided by the presumption that a disabling condition was caused by a work-related accident where the worker, who enjoyed good health prior to a work-related accident is disabled

---

[115] Idaho Code § 72-228
[116] Me. Rev. Stat. Ann. Title 39-A, § 327
[117] Va. Code Ann. § 65.2-105

following the accident and can show a reasonable possibility of causation.[118] Similar to the Louisiana approach, in **West Virginia,** injured workers are entitled to a presumption that if a disabling condition cannot be attributed to a cause other than the industrial injury, it must have resulted from the injury.[119]

Marriage/Dependent Presumption – Following the common law in effect in the majority of states, where marriage is an issue, there is a strong presumption or validity of the most recent marriage. In a number of states, there is a strong presumption, in some cases a conclusive presumption, that a surviving spouse (and/or/ children) living with the employee at the time of his or her work-related death to be dependent upon that deceased worker.

Presumption for PTSD Claims – It has been recognized that those engaged as first responders, such as police, firefighters, and emergency medical technicians (EMTs), have jobs that most agree are stressful. Many such workers have encountered difficulty following an incidence or event when exposed to the extreme violence and appalling tragedies which are so regretfully common in the present day. In response, in recent years, there has been a growing trend among states to recognize a presumption of injury for first responders (e.g. fire fighters, law enforcement officers, emergency personnel, etc.) affected by post-traumatic stress disorder (PTSD). In February 2020, the National Council on Compensation Insurance (NCCI), an industry association which monitors proposed and enacted workers compensation legislation, characterized the PTSD bills, including those featuring a presumption, to be the top trending issue for 2019.[120]

The idea behind such presumption laws is that when a first responder develops PTSD or other listed condition, he or she will no longer bear the burden of showing causation. Instead, the law presumes, or takes for granted, that work causation exists, and it is for the employing municipality to prove that the condition has its genesis in some non-work-related cause. **Maine** and **Vermont** were states which, in 2018, enacted such laws. Meanwhile, the NCCI identified **Idaho, California, Louisiana, New Hampshire, New Mexico, Nevada,** and **Oregon** as states which, during the first half of 2019, enacted laws establishing PTSD presumption laws for first responders. **Minnesota** and **Washington** also have first responder statutes that feature presumptions.

It is important to recognize that no two presumption laws are precisely alike. All feature PTSD as the malady covered, though **New Hampshire** and **Oregon** also include the diagnosis, "acute stress disorder." Meanwhile, the range of occupations is different for each jurisdiction. Oregon seems the most expansive, affording the PTSD presumption to full-time firefighters, emergency medical personnel, police

---

[118] *Burrough's v. LCR-M* 781 So. 2d 877 (2001)
[119] *Bias v. Workers' Compensation Comm'r*, 176 W. Va. 421 (1986)
[120] https://www.workcompwire.com/2020/02/ncci-releases-insights-2020-legislative-session-workers-comp-preview/

officers, correctional officers, parole and probation officers, emergency dispatch personnel, and 911 operators.

An example of a presumption statute for first responders is found in **Vermont** where the workers compensation law provides, "*In the case of police officers, rescue or ambulance workers, or firefighters, post-traumatic stress disorder that is diagnosed by a mental health professional shall be presumed to have been incurred during service in the line of duty and shall be compensable, unless it is shown by a preponderance of the evidence [by the employer] that the post-traumatic stress disorder was caused by nonservice connected risk factors or nonservice-connected exposure.*"[121] Notably, other mental conditions suffered by these Vermont workers are now covered as well, but in such cases the worker will bear the initial burden of proof of causation. And, notably, a statute of repose is a feature of the statute: "*A police officer, rescue or ambulance worker, or firefighter who is diagnosed with post-traumatic stress disorder within three years of the last active date of employment [in such occupation] ... shall be eligible for benefits under this subdivision.*"

While not a presumption law, **Minnesota**, a state which otherwise excludes mental-mental injury, enacted a unique law facilitating PTSD awards. The law was enacted in response to an extremely harsh denial of a claim by a police officer who had been mentally traumatized but was left without a remedy. The Minnesota law also extends such coverage to all workers. **Colorado** has also enacted a similar law covering claims for PTSD. The state is one of the shock or fright jurisdictions where compensability for mental-mental injury is highly restricted. After reports that first responders would routinely use group health insurance for such mental injuries, a lobby developed to amend the law. In the current version, all workers can potentially secure an award for PTSD.[122]

In total, nineteen states cover cancer for firefighters and nine currently cover PTSD for first responders. As indicated above, states continue to seek legislative presumptions to protect these workers. At the same time, several lobbying groups have been working to expand PTSD presumptions to other groups of workers such as health care workers and teachers.

COVID-19 Presumptions – The presumptions just described addressed injuries such as cancer or PTSD for firefighters or first responders since one could make the reasonable assumption that these conditions either developed or were sustained in their line of work. However, a key exclusion for nearly all presumption laws in the past was that they have not covered infectious diseases, since proving that a person was infected on the job is typically very difficult if not impossible. Infectious diseases such as the annual flu would fall under the category of ordinary disease of life and therefore would not be covered. This precedent changed with COVID-19.

---

[121] VT. STAT. § 601(11)(I)(i).
[122] COLO. REV. STAT. § 8-41-301(3).

According to the Centers for Disease Control, there have been more than 600,000 deaths as a result of the COVID-19 pandemic as of mid-year 2021. Analysis developed by The Guardian and Kaiser Health News, as of late April 2021, over 3,600 U.S. healthcare workers have died due to Covid-19. Frontline healthcare workers also felt the direct impacts of the pandemic on a personal level.

According to the National Council on Compensation Insurance (NCCI) data, nearly 75% of reported COVID-19 WC claims have so far involved workers at nursing homes, hospitals, and other healthcare settings, plus first responders. In all, data from NCCI states presented during the 2021 Annual Issues Symposium shows 45,000 COVID-19 claims and $260 million in workers compensation losses in Accident Year 2020, That is an average severity of nearly $6,000.

The COVID-19 pandemic has brought the discussion of presumption laws to the forefront, as states examine whether workers compensation should cover workers if they contract COVID-19 on the job. Many states have passed legislation or executive orders requiring insurers to cover essential workers who test positive for the virus. Depending on the state, the definition of "essential worker" might be limited to just healthcare and frontline workers, or it may include a wide range of occupations.

By the end of 2020, 19 states have expanded their presumption laws to include COVID-19. Some of these states, including **Alaska, Minnesota, Utah,** and **Wisconsin**, limit the coverage to healthcare workers and first responders, while other states such as **Illinois** and **Wyoming** have expanded their presumptions to include a wide range of workers. **California**'s presumption coverage created under the governor's executive order expands presumptions to a wide range of workers deemed "essential," including grocery store employees.

Alaska passed the only law to conclusively presume that firefighters, emergency medical technicians, police officers, and health care providers who are exposed to an individual with COVID-19 and are diagnosed with the virus within that exposure window acquired the virus on the job. Examples of other states and their particular approaches include:

- In **Arkansas**, the governor signed an executive order modifying the state's statutes to allow for the compensability of infectious diseases such as COVID-19. The order does not presume compensability

- In **Indiana**, the state's Workers Compensation Board in April urged employers of first responders and health care workers who were susceptible to contracting COVID-19 because of their job duties to presume that workers who acquired the virus were covered if directed to quarantine at the behest of the employer.

- **Kentucky**, which passed the first COVID-19 executive order relating to compensability in April, has required employers whose workers were removed from work on the directive of a physician for occupational exposure to pay temporary total disability to those employees. Workers covered under the Kentucky order include health care workers, first responders, grocery, and postal workers, as well as community-based and childcare workers permitted to operate during the pandemic.

- In **Missouri,** the state passed an emergency rule creating a presumption for first responders if they were required to quarantine by their employer, displayed symptoms, and were diagnosed with COVID-19.

Many of the COVID-19 presumption laws have an expiration date, but the sweeping adoption of these rules may usher in a reassessment of other diseases that could be presumed to have occurred at the workplace.

With the new year of 2021, legislators in two more states have introduced legislation that would make COVID-19 an occupational injury by presumption, potentially joining the wave of laws and executive orders currently in place in 19 states and introduced as legislation in 11 states so far. Lawmakers in **North Dakota** introduced a bill that would create a rebuttable presumption for 34 professions considered "essential," including transportation workers, government workers, school employees, and health care workers. That bill, which was sent to the Joint Industry, Business, and Labor Committee, would go into effect upon passage and would expire on July 31, 2023.

In **Virginia**, legislation was introduced and would apply the COVID-19 presumption to firefighters, emergency medical services personnel, law-enforcement officers, and correctional officers. The bill, which would provide presumption to workers infected between March 12, 2020, and Dec. 31, 2021, was sent to a House Labor and Commerce subcommittee.

These most recent endeavors indicate that enacting state presumptions for COVID-19 continues to receive legislative attention. It will be interesting to continue to follow the subject to see if the presumptions will be extended to other diseases that do not attain the level of a pandemic.

Chapter Six

MANDATED BENEFITS

State workers compensation programs mandate a broad range of benefits associated with employment related injuries, occupational diseases, and events resulting in death. These benefits include medical care related to the injury or illness, partial replacement of lost income during the period of recovery, compensation for long-term or permanent injuries, benefits to survivors of those fatally injured on the job, and certain costs associated with rehabilitation and/or retraining. This chapter will address in some detail each of the mandated benefits and offer a description of some of the variances that exist among the state programs.

Mandated coverage of medical treatment is intended to restore the injured individual to the state of health that existed prior to the injury. While medical benefits available to an injured worker are generally consistent across jurisdictional lines subject to an individual state utilization of a medical fee schedule, income replacement benefits vary considerably from one state to another with respect to both amounts payable and methods of computation. Income replacement benefits are subject to legislative, judicial, and administrative revisions. Therefore, careful review of the current law of the state having jurisdiction over a case is necessary in order to determine the specific level of income replacement benefits to which an injured employee may be eligible.

Stated another way, the typical workers compensation benefit structure consists of the following:

- **Medical and hospital benefits** necessary to furnish all appropriate care and treatment, including drugs and prosthetic devices, reasonably necessary to attain maximum medical improvement.

- **Vocational or physical rehabilitation benefits** designed to support the injured worker achieving his/her former level of employment or physical ability, or to retrain the individual for previous or new employment.

- **Income replacement benefits** designed to replace a portion of lost income during periods of work-related disability. Benefits include temporary total, temporary partial, permanent partial, permanent total, payments to the dependents of a deceased worker, and disfigurement benefits.

The following describes these mandated benefits in greater detail along with statutory provisions as they relate to benefit escalation and offsets.

MEDICAL AND HOSPITAL BENEFITS

In addition to the various types of income replacement benefits to which an injured worker may be entitled when a covered employee has suffered a work-related injury or occupational disease the employer or its insurer is required to promptly provide all medically necessary and appropriate medical care and treatment. Such care and treatment is to include all medical services and surgical care including hospital and nursing services, medicine, orthopedic appliances, prostheses and prescription and non-prescription medications.

Medical care costs in the workers compensation program have continued an upward trend, growing faster than the overall Consumer Price Index (CPI). According to the National Council on Compensation Insurance (NCCI), medical care costs accounted for 58 percent of total workers compensation claim costs in 2008, compared with 42 percent for lost income payments. In 1987 the medical component represented only 46 percent of total costs and in earlier years, the general break-down was two-thirds of the claim dollars for income replacement and one-third for medical.

Medical care and treatment is required from the time of the occurrence of a work-related injury or identification of an occupational disease, and such care and treatment is provided without the injured worker sharing in the cost of such services. Entitlement to such services may continue indefinitely or for whatever period is required by the nature of the accidental injury or occupational disease so long as there is evidence establishing that the need for such services is reasonable, necessary and causally related to the accidental injury or occupational disease. When state workmen's compensation laws were first enacted, it was not uncommon to have a prescribed maximum period (e.g., 50 weeks, 100 weeks, etc.) or some dollar limit for medical benefits. With the passage of time and following the recommendation of the 1972 National Commission, virtually all states moved to unlimited medical benefits in terms of duration or benefit amounts.

Today, with the exception of two states, all remaining states have unlimited medical benefits in terms of duration and dollar limit. In **Arkansas**, if no time is lost following a workplace accident, medical care is limited to six months or a maximum dollar limit of $10,000.[123] However, the workers compensation commission may intervene and extend the time and dollar limits. During the 2013 legislative session, **Georgia** amended their workers compensation law to cap medical benefits for non-catastrophic cases at 400 weeks from the date of accident. Formerly, Georgia medical coverage was lifetime.

Also, typically under the workers compensation program, there is no such thing as a medical deductible or co-insurance. While a few states introduced legislation designed to

---

[123] Ark. Code Ann. § 11-9-509

permit the introduction of a co-insurance program during the late 1980's and early 1990's, there was little interest on the part of either the employers or the insurance community. The administrative cost of attempting to recover the amount of the deductible or co-insurance prompted most carriers and benefit administrators to forego the application of these cost-sharers. **Florida** does have a law requiring a $10 co-payment after the injured worker reaches maximum medical improvement.[124] There is no available data to indicate how often that co-payment amount is applied.

COVERED MEDICAL EXPENSES

For the most part, the same basic benefits are covered in every state. Generally, covered medical benefits include all necessary treatment and physical rehabilitation. This includes podiatric, osteopathic, chiropractic, surgical, hospital, and dental care though limits may be imposed on the maximum utilization of some of these services. Psychotherapy and other psychiatric treatment may be included if regarded as necessary for the injured worker's rehabilitation. Chiropractic or podiatric treatments; prescription medications, supplies such as wheelchairs or wrist braces, orthopedic mattresses, and nursing services may also be specifically authorized. In some areas, the range of treatment may be even broader; for example, acupuncture is authorized in a few states, and several states provide for treatment by Christian Science practitioners or other spiritual healers. Most workers compensation statutes also provide for the reimbursement of the employee's travel expenses incurred in the process of obtaining medical services.

While care is provided for a work-related injury, a treating provider may be required to obtain prior authorization for referrals to specialists and, above a certain dollar amount, for tests, prosthetic devices, and incidental expenses.

Covered medical expenses commonly include any required prescription and non-prescription drugs, artificial members and attendant care. State compensation laws are generally specific in terms of the medical, hospital, surgical and medical treatment that is covered. For example, in **California**, the following are explicitly covered: *"medical, surgical, chiropractic and hospital treatment, nursing, medicines, medical and surgical supplies, crutches and apparatus (including artificial members) which are reasonably required to cure or relieve from the effects of the injury."*[125] **Florida** law requires an employer to furnish medically necessary remedial treatment and care *"including medicines, medical supplies, durable medical equipment, orthoses, prostheses, and other medically necessary apparatus".*[126]

Because of the significant increase in medical expenses, states have undertaken various approaches in an effort to control costs. Chapter Eight is devoted to a more extensive

---

[124] Fla. Stat. Ann. § 440.13 (14)(c)
[125] Cal. Labor Code § 4600 (a)
[126] Fla. Stat. Ann. § 440.13 (2)

review of covered medical expenses along with strategies that have been developed to contain these expenses.

The following describes in more detail some of the issues associated with four particular types of covered medical expenses or services:

Prescription Drugs – According to a 2020 study released by the National Council on Compensation Insurance (NCCI), prescription drug costs make up 13 - 14 percent of an overall workers compensation claim. Other notable conclusions by the authors of the NCCI study include:

- Prescription drug prices continue to rise, although at a slower rate than in recent years.

- The number of opioid prescriptions continue to decrease as doctors opt for alternative treatments.

- The top three drugs - Lyrica, Oxycontin, and Gabapentin - account for more than 15 percent of all prescription drug costs.

Another study showed the following are the top 10 drugs, ranked by dollars paid, during Service Year 2016:

- Lyrica
- Oxycontin
- Gabapentin
- Oxycodone HCL acetaminophen
- Lidocaine
- Oxycodone HCL
- Meloxicam
- Duloxetine
- Tramadol HCL
- Hydrocodone Bitartrate Acetaminophen

Although most prescription drugs associated with workers compensation cases are generic (76 percent of total prescriptions), the largest portion of the cost of drug prescriptions comes from brand names.

Artificial Members – Almost all laws require the employer to furnish artificial limbs and other prosthetic devices. Coverage includes those expenses necessary to replace, support or relieve a portion or part of the body resulting from an injury for a period as the nature of the injury or the process of recovery may require. Treatment for the fitting and training for use of prosthetic devices that are reasonably required and which arise out of or are necessitated by an injury are also included.

Attendant Care – Whether specifically provided by statute or implicit in the definition of reasonable medical expenses, the cost of attendant care is often a compensated medical expense. Some states specifically provide for this through the statute. For example, **Idaho** law states that an employee who is entitled to benefits must be paid an additional sum when the constant service of an attendant is necessary, if the employee *"is totally blind or has lost both hands and both feet or has lost the use thereof."*[127]

Most states specify that medical benefits be reasonable. Language such as *"reasonably required to cure or relieve from the effects of the injury must be provided by the employer"* or *"medically necessary remedial treatment and care"* is common. Because these are subjective terms, there is often disagreement about whether expenses are reasonable and/or necessary.

For example, a nursing assistant was entitled to payment of medical expenses for a work-related back injury despite an opinion from the judge of compensation claims that her chiropractor's services were unnecessary and unreasonable. The judge had concluded that the claimant's testimony of subjective pain was not believable, because she did not demonstrate observable physical discomfort at the hearing. However on appeal, it was ruled that the claimant had sought payment for treatment she received prior to the hearing and not for continuing treatment. Thus, it was irrelevant that she demonstrated no observable discomfort at the hearing.

In another case, the Supreme Court of **New Hampshire** reversed and remanded a denial of further medical benefits by the state compensation appeals board, which had denied the worker's treatments because they were palliative and not curative. The applicable statute, however, did not address palliative treatment. It merely required that (1) the treatment must be reasonable; and (2) the treatment may continue only so long as required by the nature of the injury. Following her injury, the claimant sought treatment from a number of doctors to determine the nature and extent of her injuries, and for pain management therapy. Her initial treating physician, at the time of her last appointment, concluded that she had reached "a point of maximum medical improvement."

While the claimant continued to seek diagnostic and rehabilitative treatment for continued pain in her elbow, the insurer refused to reimburse medical expenses incurred after her last appointment with her initial treating physician. The court ruled that a determination of the "reasonableness" of the treatment should not be outcome dependent. Rather, the proper analysis is whether the petitioner presented objective evidence showing, that at the time the tests were ordered, it was reasonable for her to seek further treatment, be it diagnostic or palliative. Therefore, the board's finding that reimbursement was not warranted because the tests yielded negative results was not sufficient to support their conclusion that the petitioner has failed to meet her burden of proof. The court vacated the ruling of the board with respect to

---

[127] Idaho Code § 72-432 (3)

reimbursement of the petitioner's medical costs and remanded for a determination of reimbursable medical costs consistent with the standards set forth in the opinion.[128]

INDEPENDENT MEDICAL EXAMINATION (IME)

During a workers compensation claim, an independent medical examination (IME) may be requested in order to introduce an impartial or independent expert medical opinion into some area of medical disagreement. The request for an IME may be made by either the injured employee or insurance carrier or benefit administrator. In most instances, it is the insurance carrier or case manager that makes the request for an IME. The IME is conducted by an independent third-party physician in order to ensure impartiality.

It is important to note that a physician performing an IME does not provide any medical services to the injured worker. The physician investigates the validity and/or severity of an injured worker's injuries and may request a wide range of tests to determine:

- Causality of the injury
- Medical necessity of care and reasonableness of treatment
- Maximum medical improvement
- Relevant pre-existing conditions
- Fitness for return-to-work
- Permanent impairment estimates for purposes of evaluating permanent disability

An IME is most generally requested when an injured worker's recovery from an injury takes longer than normal, or when the employee is released from medical care but receives a higher than expected disability rating by the treating physician requested by the judge or by the injured worker. While the majority of physicians treating workers compensation patients are reputable providers, some treating physicians rely on attorney or benefit administrator referrals for a sizeable portion of their business.

An injured employee who has selected the initial treating provider may select a provider who lacks experience in handling workers compensation claims and who may shape the initial medical findings in order to make the alleged condition work-related, may extend the period of lost time longer than medically necessary, and may have a tendency to overstate the injured worker's degree of permanent partial disability. Because of these factors, it is often necessary for the insurer or benefit administrator to obtain an IME in

---

[128] New Hampshire Supreme Court Appeal of Judy Lalime, 687 A. 2d 994 (1996)

order to document the current medical status of the injured worker in order to ensure a fair resolution of the claim.

If the injured worker has more than one aspect of their medical condition in question, more than a single IME may be necessary. For example, to properly evaluate an injured employee's claim for benefits, it may be necessary to have separate IMEs done by an orthopedic surgeon, a neurologist, and a physical rehabilitation specialist. Most states limit the number of IMEs to one, two or three in each area of medicine. While a few states allow the insurer or benefit administrator as many IMEs as they want, the cost of an IME can add a substantial amount to the overall cost of the claim.

An IME is frequently performed by a medical provider who specializes in the field of medicine routinely treating the type of injury the employee has incurred. In most states the insurer or benefit administrator selects the IME physician. In a few states, a petition must be filed with the workers compensation board or administrative agency to have the employee seen by an IME doctor while in other states the board/agency selects the IME doctor. Whether the doctor is insurer selected or board/agency selected, it is important that the doctor be a specialist in the field of medicine that involves the injury. The proper selection of the IME doctor results in high quality examinations that are both accurate and medically sound.

To insure the IME is accurate, it is necessary for the insurer to provide the IME doctor with all the employee's medical records and diagnostic tests results (x-rays, CT scans, MRI reports, EMG studies, etc.). This information needs to be provided to the IME doctor in advance of the injured worker's appointment in order to allow the doctor adequate time to review the employee's medical history. Also, a detailed job description obtained from the employer is often provided so that the IME doctor does not have to rely on the employee's description of the physical demands of the occupation.

During the IME the doctor conducts an interview of the employee, performs the appropriate medical examination, conducts various tests to verify the symptoms alleged, observes the employee's general appearance, the employee's gait, how the employee stands, whether or not the employee has any difficulty climbing onto the examination table, whether or not the employee shows any signs of distress and the employee's weight. The doctor evaluates the employee's subjective symptoms and determines if they are consistent with the manifestations of the injury claimed. The IME doctor looks for any signs of exaggeration or deception by the employee.

In addition, the doctor questions the employee about his/her ailment(s), the treatment the employee has had for the injury, whether or not the employee had a prior injury or an injury subsequent to the workers comp injury and discusses any underlying pathologies to the injury. The IME doctor determines if the employee smokes drinks, uses illicit drugs or has other health or lifestyle issues that will impact the employee's ability to recover from the injury or the employee's level of permanent disability.

The IME is used by the insurer or benefit administrator to document the medical status of the employee at that point in time. The information obtained from the IME is used either to establish whether further or additional medical care or treatment is needed, whether lost time benefits should be continued, or to determine the employee's level of disability.

MEDICAL MARIJUANA

We begin a discussion of medical marijuana with the recognition that under federal law, marijuana is illegal. The United States first regulated marijuana under the Marihuana Tax Act of 1937. The plant was subsequently subjected to country-wide prohibition under the Controlled Substances Act of 1970 (CSA), which established a scheduling system for substances regulated under federal law. Despite the restriction of marijuana under federal law, in 1996 California became the first state to pass legislation permitting a medical marijuana program.

Since that time more than 35 states and the **District of Columbia** have passed legislation permitting so-called comprehensive medical marijuana programs, which typically allow qualifying patients to access, possess, and use marijuana and marijuana-related products. An additional 13 states have passed legislation permitting so-called limited access programs, which restrict patient access to products with low levels of delta-9-tetrahydrocannabinol (THC), the active chemical that induces user intoxication, or to non-intoxicating cannabidiol-only (CBD) products.

With **New York, New Mexico,** and **Virginia** being the most recent, at the time this material is being written, a total of 17 states along with the **District of Columbia** have passed, either through legislation or through a ballot initiative, laws legalizing marijuana for adults. In addition, about one-third of the states have approved the use of medical marijuana.

At a time when marijuana was illegal under both state and federal law, employers would typically prohibit employees from using marijuana as a condition of employment. As states have begun to allow the medical and recreational use of marijuana, the situation has become more complicated. Thus, there are two basic workers compensation issues: (1) Does workers compensation cover a workplace injury in which the injured employee tested positive for marijuana, and (2) does workers compensation reimburse medical marijuana expenses incurred by an injured employee?

Some states protect patients from discrimination or adverse employment actions based solely on their off-duty marijuana use or on their status as medical marijuana cardholders. There can be exceptions if the employer would be violating federal law or if permitting off-duty marijuana use could cost the employer. About one-quarter of the states extend some employment protections to medical marijuana cardholders (either by statute or by court decision).

For example, **Arizona's** medical marijuana law prohibits employers from discriminating against job applicants and employees based on their status as medical marijuana cardholders or for testing positive for marijuana, unless the employee was also impaired during the scope of their employment. Some of these states also require employers to provide "reasonable accommodations" to medical marijuana cardholders. In **Nevada**, the medical marijuana law requires employers to make reasonable accommodations for the needs of a medical marijuana patient, as long as this accommodation does not pose any risk to persons or property, or places an "undue hardship" on the employer.

The workers compensation law in most states restricts benefits if an employee was intoxicated at the time of injury or if the intoxication was a "proximate cause" of the injury. Some states deny or limit compensation if an injured employee refuses to take a drug test. However, it is currently difficult to determine whether an injured worker was impaired by marijuana when an accident occurred. Unlike alcohol, tetrahydrocannabinol (THC), the intoxicant in marijuana, levels in a user's body may not be an accurate indication of impairment. THC and its metabolites can remain in a user's bloodstream or urine for days or weeks, long after intoxication has ended.

States have taken different stances on how THC persistence and marijuana impairment impact workers compensation benefits. For instance, many states will "presume" that a positive drug test indicates that an employee was impaired; however, some of these states will also allow employees to rebut the presumption with other evidence. An **Oklahoma** Court of Civil Appeals decision ruled in favor of an injured worker who tested positive for marijuana, writing that *"the presence of an intoxicating substance in the blood does not automatically mean that person is intoxicated."*[129] An earlier **Ohio** case came to a similar conclusion.[130]

The second issue concerns whether workers compensation covers medical marijuana expenses incurred by an injured employee. There is no simple question to this question. States, courts, and workers compensation authorities have differed significantly on how to treat medical marijuana reimbursement. And the regulatory and legal environment is evolving rapidly. The issue can change dramatically even within a state. In some cases, a workers compensation board will find that marijuana is reimbursable, only for that decision to be overturned by a court. This happened in **Maine** where the Supreme Court held that an employer was not required to reimburse for medical marijuana, since such a requirement could create a conflict between federal and state law.[131] In other cases, the opposite outcome occurs as happened in **New Hampshire**.[132]

The issue is continuing to evolve. In April 2021, the Supreme Court of **New Jersey** affirmed a decision of the state's Appellate Division that earlier held that an employer could be required to reimburse an injured worker for the cost of medical marijuana

---

[129] *Rose v. Berry Plastics Corp. et al.,* 2019 OK Civ. App. 55
[130] *Trent v. Stark Metal Sales, Inc.,* 2015-Ohio-1115, 2015 Ohio App. LEXIS 1070 (2015)
[131] *Gaetan H. Bourgoin v. Twin Rivers Paper Co. L.L.C., et. al.*36
[132] *Re Appeal of Panaggio,*

dispensed to him pursuant to the state's version of the Compassionate Use Act,[133] joining the states of **Connecticut, Minnesota, New Hampshire, New York,** and **New Mexico** which have all ruled that medical marijuana does qualify for reimbursement under workers compensation laws. **Florida, Maine, North Dakota**, and **Michigan** continue to exclude the substance from reimbursement

In **New York**, the state's Workers Compensation Board determined that medical marijuana is reimbursable if certain criteria are met.[134] In that decision, the board acknowledged that New York state law states that nothing requires *"an insurer or health plan under [the public health law] or the insurance law to provide coverage for medical marihuana."* The board found that this exemption only applied to health insurers and not workers compensation insurers. By contrast, in **California**, medical marijuana/cannabis has been legal for any patient since 1996, but only with a doctor's recommendation. However, it is not covered by the workers compensation system, so insurance companies usually deny reimbursements for cannabis-based treatments.

In a more recent decision by the **New York** appellate court, the court affirmed a decision by the state's Workers Compensation Board that allowed a variance to the state treatment guidelines for workers compensation claims and which ordered an employer's workers compensation carrier to reimburse an injured employee for medical marijuana expenses provided under New York's Compassionate Care Act[135].

Case law continues to evolve around the use of marijuana in the treatment of workers compensation cases. As another example, marijuana has been legal in **Massachusetts** since 2012. A 2020 decision by the Supreme Judicial Court held a workers compensation insurer may not be ordered to reimburse an employee for medical marijuana expenses.[136] The Court based its decision on the fact that the Massachusetts medical marijuana act explicitly alleviated insurers from the burden of reimbursing for medical marijuana expenses.

The most one can observe at this point is that the issue of coverage and reimbursement remains in a state of flux. Program administrators, legislators, and the courts are faced in many states with establishing a position on these issues. It is important for those engaged in the workers compensation arena to remain attentive to decisions adopted in these denoted areas.

VOCATIONAL AND PHYSICAL REHABILIATATION

Closely associated with the subject of medical costs is the issue of rehabilitation. Rehabilitation – physical and vocational - has three prime objectives. The first is to

---

[133] *Hager v. M&K Construction*, 2021 N.J. LEXIS 332 (April 13, 2021)
[134] *Matter of WDF Inc*, 2018 NY Wrk Comp G1403803 (2017)
[135] *Matter of Quigley v. Village of E. Aurora*, 2021 N.Y. App. Div. LEXIS 1223 (2021)
[136] *Wright's Case*, 2020 Mass. LEXIS 658 (Oct. 27, 2020)

eliminate the disability completely, the second is to reduce or alleviate the disability to the greatest degree possible, and the third is to retrain the injured worker to live and function within the limits of the disability but to the maximum of his or her capabilities. The first two objectives fall primarily within the realm of physical rehabilitation, whereas the third objective falls within the realm of vocational rehabilitation.

In the majority of instances, a work-related injury results in only one or two physician office visits, a few days of lost-time from work, and the worker is then able to return to his or her former level of employment without any form of outside intervention. Where the injury is of a more serious nature, the job site itself may require certain modifications to protect the worker from subsequent injury or to eliminate certain job functions until a complete recovery has been realized. Those are the simple cases. The more difficult cases involve those where the employee is hurt seriously enough to prevent the worker from returning to their regular occupation for an extended period of time, or perhaps forever. It is in those situations where vocational or physical rehabilitation can be an effective tool in reducing claim costs.

The ultimate goal of vocational rehabilitation is to return the injured worker back to work, preferably at or near the pre-injury wage level. In most instances, the injured worker will be assigned a rehabilitation counselor who will coordinate the rehabilitation program. As a first step in the rehabilitation process, the counselor evaluates the worker's current status and future potential with the help of specific rehabilitation services. The evaluation generally includes securing the following information:

- Medical information, particularly regarding functional restrictions and limitations; a thorough vocational history, including previous employment, skills, wages, reasons for leaving previous jobs, and possibilities for reemployment.

- An educational history, including any specialized training.

- An assessment of the worker's understanding and attitudes related to the diagnosis, prognosis, and treatment options.

The worker's expectations and understanding of the vocational rehabilitation process should also be explored, along with any personal goals for recovery. Aptitude and interest testing may be advisable, especially if a career change will be necessary.

After the initial evaluation phase is completed, the next step is frequently the development of a written rehabilitation plan. To be effective, the worker should be an active participant in developing this plan. The plan sets forth clear short-term and long-term objectives. The plan should identify who will be responsible for achieving each objective and should specify a time frame for completing each step. For example, the employer might be responsible for installing a ramp within 30 days to accommodate the worker, while the medical case manager would be responsible for obtaining and funding a motorized wheelchair within that time frame. The rehabilitation counselor is responsible for following up and making sure that goals are achieved in a timely manner.

With a plan in place, there are a variety of possible outcomes for an effective return-to-work rehabilitation plan. Working with both the employer and the injured worker, the vocational rehabilitation counselor will explore the possibilities for the worker's return to the former place of employment. The most desired outcome involves returning the worker to the same job with the same employer. In most instances, depending upon the severity of the initial injury and the extent of any resulting disability, that objective is achievable.

Even where there the initial injury results in some form of continuing disability that operates as an impediment to returning the worker to his or her former position of employment, minor modifications to the workstation may be sufficient to permit the worker to return. The Americans with Disabilities Act (ADA) – which will be discussed in the final chapter – requires employers to make such workplace accommodations. Even where not required by laws such as the ADA, it is in the interest of the employer to take such action.

An alternative to workstation modifications is locating a new position or new occupation with the same employer. This alternative will involve certain retraining for the employee and will require time for the employee to adapt to the new position. In many instances this will depend upon the size of the employer's operations and whether such openings are available consistent with the rehabilitated employees' skills and limitations.

When the opportunity to return to some level of employment within the original employers' workplace is not feasible, even with accommodations, employment opportunities with other employers may need to be explored. The vocational rehabilitation counselor may serve as mentor and coach at this level. The worker may not be aware of job-hunting resources such as the Internet and the worker's resume may need to be radically revised to focus on present skills. Depending upon the age of the client along with prior work experience, more supportive counseling may be needed in this phase.

The least desirable alternative is some form of self-employment. Here realistic job goals are an important consideration. The skills necessary for self-employment, including money management and business administration, are frequently not those identified with those formerly in a labor position. The real test of whether self-employment is a realistic goal is dependent on the workers' self-motivation and organizational skills.

Workers Compensation Benefits During Rehabilitation – Most states include some level of vocational rehabilitation benefits in their workers compensation laws. A number of states prescribe that the employer/insurer is responsible for vocational rehabilitation costs. In addition, several other states stipulate that the employer/insurer is responsible for board, lodging and travel expenses.

In many states, the employee must accept vocational rehabilitation services or face a termination or reduction of benefits. Some states require that employers and insurers provide services for a certain amount of time or up to a certain dollar limit, while in other states, program parameters are discretionary. **Iowa** and **Louisiana** require the employer/insurer to continue temporary total disability during the period of rehabilitation subject to a maximum of 26 weeks. In **Michigan,** such benefits for temporary total disability are to continue for a maximum of 104 weeks, and in Wisconsin such benefits are payable for a maximum of 80 weeks.

In a few instances, vocational rehabilitation costs are handled by the state. For example, in **Arizona**, a portion of the vocational rehabilitation costs are paid by the state fund. In **Florida**, the cost of board, lodging or travel are paid through the Special Disability Trust Fund. In **Texas**, employees eligible for vocational rehabilitation services are referred to the Department of Assistive and Rehabilitative Services.

In **Nebraska**, vocational rehabilitation training costs are paid from the Workers Compensation Trust Fund. In addition, when vocational rehabilitation training requires residence at or near a facility or institution away from the employee's customary residence, whether within or outside the state, the reasonable costs of board, lodging, and travel are to be paid from the Trust Fund.

In addition to the continuation of workers compensation benefits during the period when vocational rehabilitation is being offered, there are certain additional incentives for employers to hire or accommodate disabled workers. The federal government offers several tax incentives for employers that hire or accommodate disabled workers. If an employer hires a worker referred from a vocational rehabilitation program, it might qualify for a tax credit under the Work Opportunity Tax Credit Program. This program allows a tax credit of up to 40 percent of the first $6,000 or up to $2,400 in wages paid during the first 12 months for each new hire. For an employer to qualify, the employee must work at least 180 days or 400 hours. In addition for the employer to qualify, the worker must be certified by the state employment security agency.

In **Maine**, if an employer hires an employee after the employee has completed a rehabilitation program, that subsequent employer may apply for a wage credits from the Employment Rehabilitation Fund. Wage credits consist of a sum equal to 50 percent of the average weekly direct wages, not exceed the amount of workers compensation benefits that the employee did not receive because of the employment. Total wage credit payments may not exceed a period of 180 days. The Fund also pays benefits if that worker sustains a subsequent injury that results in a reduction in earning capacity

The **Oregon** Reemployment Assistance Program (RAP) has two programs designed to assist injured workers to go back to work. The first, the Employer-at-Injury Program (EAIP), offers incentives to employers to provide light-duty work during recovery process. Incentives may include three-month wage subsidy, work-site modification up to $2,500, and special purchases (such as tools) needed to perform the light-duty job. Workers compensation insurers administer EAIP and receive reimbursement of program costs from the Workers Compensation Division.

The second program, the Preferred Worker Program, offers incentives to Oregon injured workers and to the employers who hire them. Workers who have permanent disability and cannot return to regular work may be eligible for six-month wage subsidy, work-site modification up to $25,000, or obtained employment purchases (e.g., the worker's tools, clothing, moving expenses, etc.). Injured workers or their employers may initiate these return-to-work services. In addition, employers who hire Preferred Workers are exempt from workers compensation premiums for those workers for up to three years and their insurers are eligible for claims-cost reimbursement should the worker sustain a new injury during the premium exemption period.

INCOME REPLACEMENT BENEFITS

When a covered employee suffers a work-related injury or occupational disease, in addition to reasonable and necessary medical treatment required to cure and relieve the employee from the physical effects of the injury, the employee is entitled to the replacement of a portion of the wages lost because of the injury. In the case of the death of the employee, his or her dependents are entitled to dependency benefits based upon a portion of the wages lost along with payment for funeral expenses. In addition, as discussed above, most of these laws provide some vocational rehabilitation services for workers whose injury led to permanent physical limitations that prevent them from returning to the occupation they were engaged in at the time of their injury. However, the amount of all of these various forms of income replacement benefits and the period during which they will be paid differ greatly from jurisdiction to jurisdiction.

In the majority of instances, a work-related injury or occupational disease results in minimal amount of lost work-time with the worker needing some medical treatment and returning to work within the jurisdiction's disability benefit waiting period. A study conducted by the Workers Compensation Research Institute (WCRI) located in Cambridge, Massachusetts found, in their review of claims in twelve large states, the percentage of occupational injury and disease claims that resulted in the need for only medical treatment, with no compensable lost time, varied from a high of 88 percent in **Indiana** to a low of 72 percent in **Massachusetts**.

The more serious cases, where the lost time extends beyond the statutory waiting period, are those cases where the injured worker may become entitled to replacement of a portion of his/her pre-injury earnings. A separate category of benefits are available in the case of a work-related death. To adequately describe how and when these benefits may be payable requires a description of the various benefit features common to all workers compensation programs. These features include:

Jurisdictional Waiting and Retroactive Periods – Although medical treatment and related services are provided to an injured employee from the date of the injury, income replacement benefits are subject to a waiting period provided for in the state compensation law. The waiting period serves to reduce administrative costs by eliminating many small payments. Typically, an employee must be out of work due to an injury or illness that is work-related for three to seven days before payments begin. Twenty-three jurisdictions have a three-day waiting period while 22 have a seven-day waiting period. **Montana** has a four-day waiting period and **Idaho, Massachusetts, Mississippi, Nevada,** and **North Dakota** have a waiting period of five days.

Where the disability extends beyond the waiting period, disability benefits for that initial period of lost time are payable when the disability extends beyond a second specified time period known as the retroactive period. Nearly one-half of the jurisdictions have a 14-day retroactive period, meaning that if the disability extends beyond 14 days, the injured worker would be compensated for the benefits not paid during the waiting period.

This retroactive period is also subject to variation across jurisdictional lines. Seven states have a seven-day retroactive period, 24 jurisdictions have a 14-day retroactive period, and eight states have a 21-day retroactive period. The retroactive period in **Nevada** and **North Dakota** is five days, eight days in **Wyoming**, three days in **Hawaii**, and 10 days in **Minnesota**, 28 days in **Alaska** and **New Mexico**, and 42 days in **Louisiana** and **Nebraska. Montana, Oklahoma** and **Rhode Island** are unique in that benefits are payable from the date of injury or disability where the period of lost time extends beyond the waiting period.

The following from the **Texas** workers compensation law demonstrates the typical wording for a seven-day waiting period with a 14-day retroactive period – *"No compensation shall be allowed for the first seven (7) days of disability resulting from the injury, excluding the day of injury . . . but if disability extends beyond that period, compensation shall commence with the eighth day after the injury. In the event, however, that the disability from the injury exists for a period as much as fourteen (14) days, then compensation shall be allowed beginning with the first day after the injury."*[137].

In addition to specifying a waiting period prior to the payment of compensation benefits, many states further provide a specific time period for the continued payment of benefits. For instance, many compensation laws require that, after the initial payment of compensation, payments be continued on a weekly or biweekly basis until such time as the compensation payments are discontinued. In **Alaska,** for example, the employer or

---

[137] Tenn. Code Ann. § 50-6-205 (a)

insurer must send a check to the injured employee within 14 days of the check coming due. Where payment is not made within the prescribed time, a 25 percent penalty may be imposed.

Statutory Maximum and Minimum Compensation Benefits – In the majority of states, income replacement benefits for a totally disabled worker are based upon a portion of the weekly earnings – typically two-thirds of the worker's pre-injury weekly earnings – subject to a state maximum and minimum weekly compensation amount prescribed by statute. Frequently, the maximum weekly benefit payable for disability is tied to a percentage of the statewide average weekly wage.

It is helpful to use an example to illustrate how replacing a portion of the injured worker's pre-injury wage and a statewide maximum weekly benefit operate in tandem. We begin with the assumption that the state compensation law provides that benefit payments are be based on two-thirds of the employee's average weekly wage and the maximum weekly benefit is 100 percent of the statewide average weekly wage. For our example, we will use a statewide average weekly wage of $750. For an injured worker who had earned wages of $2,100 per week, that worker would receive only $750 per week in compensation benefits because, although two-thirds of $2,100 is $1,400, $1,400 is greater than the state average weekly wage and the weekly benefit is limited to the state's average weekly wage. However, if that same worker had earned only $600 per week, the worker's benefit payments would be $400 per week (two-thirds of $600 which is less than the state average weekly wage.)

The maximum weekly compensation rate in 45 jurisdictions is set as a percentage of the statewide average weekly wage. In those states, the maximum weekly benefits range from a low of 66 2/3 percent of the statewide average weekly wage in **New York** and **Delaware** to a high of 200 percent of the statewide average weekly wage in **Iowa**. In 36 of those 45 jurisdictions, the maximum replacement level is 100 percent of the statewide average weekly wage or higher. For example, the **Connecticut** law states that *"... the weekly compensation received by an injured employee under the provisions of this chapter shall in no case be more than one hundred percent, raised to the next even dollar, of the average weekly earnings of all workers in the state as hereinafter defined for the year in which the injury occurred."*[138]

Two states – **Georgia** and **Indiana** – continue to establish the maximum weekly benefit legislatively. In **Georgia**, effective July 1, 2015, the maximum weekly benefit for temporary total disability was increased to $550. This maximum amount was not increased after 2015. The maximum temporary total weekly benefit in **Indiana** was set at $780 for the period July 1, 2019 to June 30, 2020.

Similarly, states have all established a minimum weekly benefit which is either the legislated amount or the injured employee's actual wage, whichever is less.

---

[138] Conn. Gen. Stat. § 31-309 (a)

Minimum benefit levels are designed to protect low wage earners. In reality, however, minimum levels, regardless of the injured worker's pre-injury wage rate, are frequently inadequate to meet the living expenses of injured workers.

Disability Benefit Duration – In the majority of states, income replacement benefits continue during the period of total disability. Exceptions to this rule can be found in a number of states where a duration limit is applied to benefits payable for Permanent Total Disability (PTD). For example, in **Arkansas** and **Mississippi** entitlement to PTD benefits terminates following 450 weeks; in **Indiana** and **South Carolina** PTD benefits are terminated after 500 weeks. Quite a few states place a duration limit for Temporary Total Disability (TTD) but other forms of income replacement benefits may be payable once TTD benefits end.

A number of jurisdictions have enacted legislation designed to terminate entitlement to certain disability benefits following either the injured employee reaching retirement age or where the claim for benefits is filed following retirement. Probably the most explicit approach to benefit termination at the time of retirement is found in the **Kentucky** statute. For injuries occurring on and after December 12, 1996, *"All income benefits payable pursuant to this chapter shall terminate as of the date upon which the employee reaches the age of seventy (70), or four (4) years after the employee's injury or last exposure, whichever last occurs.*[139]

Florida has a similar provision terminating benefits after age 70 if the worker is entitled to social security benefits, unless the injury occurs after age 70 from which point the worker is entitled to five years of benefits following the determination of permanent total disability.[140] A number of states also tie benefits duration to entitlement to social security retirement.

DISABILITY BENEFIT COMPUTATION

Most states base temporary disability benefit determination on an average of two-thirds of the injured worker's pre-injury weekly earnings; a calculation that results in a reduced take-home amount for most workers. In addition, statutory provisions address the situation where wages are paid either by the hour, day, week, or some other time variable. Language as found in the **South Carolina** law is fairly typical.

"(A) When the incapacity for work resulting from an injury is total, the employer shall pay, or cause to be paid, as provided in this chapter, to the injured employee during the total disability a weekly compensation equal to sixty-six and two-thirds percent of his average weekly wages, but not less than seventy-five dollars a week so long as this amount does not exceed his average weekly salary; if this amount does exceed his average weekly salary, the injured employee may not be paid, each week,

---

[139] Ky. Rev. Stat. § 342.730
[140] Fla. Stat. Ann. § 440.15 (1)(b)

less than his average weekly salary. The injured employee may not be paid more each week than the average weekly wage in this State for the preceding fiscal year." [141]

Policymakers generally agree that workers compensation benefits should be set at a level that will not result in undue financial hardship on a recovering worker but that would also not be a financial disincentive to return to work. Limiting the amount of weekly benefit payments to a set percentage of the employee's average weekly wage can often result in a greatly reduced take-home amount for injured workers. In response to this problem, as well as suggestions for improvement of the workers compensation system, the 1972 National Commission issued the following recommendations:

- *Subject to the state's maximum weekly benefit, a worker's weekly benefit payment should be at least 80 percent of his spendable weekly earnings.*

- *Workers compensation should be the primary source of benefits for work-related injuries and illnesses. Therefore, the benefits of other public insurance programs should be coordinated with the workers compensation program.*

- *Workers compensation benefits should not be reduced by the amount of any payments from a welfare program or other program based on need.*[142]

It is to be noted that workers compensation income replacement benefits are not subject to federal or state income taxes or Social Security contributions. As such, some workers in higher income brackets currently have near to or in excess of 100 percent of their take home earnings replaced where the compensation benefits are based upon replacement of two-thirds of the workers pre-injury earning. Basing the income replacement rate at 80 percent of spendable income is designed to address this inequity.

Currently five jurisdictions – **Alaska, Connecticut, Iowa, Maine, Michigan,** and **Rhode Island** – compute compensation benefits based on spendable earnings. Spendable income being defined as gross earnings less the amount withheld for state and federal taxes as determined by the number of dependents. Connecticut and Rhode Island compute benefits on the basis of 75 percent of spendable income and the remaining states replace 80 percent. Iowa was the first state to adopt the concept of spendable income for computing benefits.

The amount of compensation an injured employee receives is generally based on the employee's average weekly wage. This is usually a percentage of the employee's weekly wage during a prescribed period. The term "average weekly wage" is generally defined as all remuneration received for services constituting employment. Therefore, in addition to wages and salaries, the reasonable value of board, rent, housing, bonuses, commissions, car allowances, and overtime pay may be included in the calculation of wages. The

---

[141] S.C. Code Ann. § 42-9-10
[142] National Commission Recommendation 3.18

Michigan law provides an example of such inclusions – *"As used in this act, 'average weekly wage' means the weekly wage earned by the employee at the time of the employee's injury in all employment, inclusive of overtime, premium pay, and cost of living adjustment, and exclusive of any fringe or other benefits which continue during the disability."*[143]

TYPES OF DISABILITY BENEFITS

In the typical workers compensation scenario, income replacement benefits are awarded – following a waiting period – during the period of disability and the incapacity to work. These benefits are designed to replace a portion of the injured workers' lost earnings while disabled. Four general categories of disability are identified with most state workers compensation laws.

> **Temporary Total Disability (TTD)** – In a typical case where the inability to work as a result of a work-related injury exceeds the statutory waiting period, the worker can receive a tax-free cash benefit that is linked to the worker's pre-injury average weekly wage. **New Mexico** defines temporary total disability to mean *"the inability of the worker, by reason of accidental injury arising out of and in the course of the worker's employment, to perform the duties of that employment prior to the date of the worker's maximum medical improvement."*[144]
>
> As described previously, weekly benefits for disability are linked to the worker's pre-injury weekly wage, based on a formula set out in the statute. As noted, a typical formula sets the benefit at two-thirds of the worker's average weekly wage, subject to a maximum weekly benefit while a small number of states compute TTD benefits as a percentage of the workers spendable income.
>
> TTD benefits generally cease when the worker has returned to employment at or near the pre-injury wage level. TTD benefits can be terminated when the worker is found medically able to return to work. Alternatively, if the worker's medical condition stabilizes and is unlikely to change, the temporary benefit may also be concluded. While state laws vary, this stage is generally described as one in which the condition of the injured worker has reached maximum medical improvement or has become permanent and stationary.
>
> In addition, some jurisdictions limit the payment of TTD benefits to a set number of weeks or a specific dollar amount. For example, in **Florida, Texas,** and **West Virginia**, temporary benefits are limited to 104 weeks; in **Massachusetts**, TTD is limited to 156 weeks; and in **Missouri, New Jersey,** and **Tennessee**, TTD is limited to 400 weeks. In **Kansas** TTD benefits are limited to $100,000. When temporary total benefits are discontinued because of the benefit duration limit or dollar

---

[143] Mich. Stat. Ann. § 418.371 (2)
[144] N.M. Stat. Ann. § 52-1-25.1 A

limitations, the worker may be entitled to receive benefits for continuing temporary partial or permanent partial disability.

The concept of replacing two-thirds of a person's gross wages or 80 percent of an injured worker's spendable earnings is fairly easy to understand and applied when the period of disability is of a short duration. However, in most jurisdictions, once the treating provider determines that additional medical treatment will not result in further physical recovery (maximum medical improvement or the end of the healing period), either further income replacement benefits terminate or the worker becomes eligible for another form of income replacement benefits. Each state program has a mechanism to determine what further benefits are due when a worker has a permanent loss of physical function and therefore will presumably have a continuing loss of earnings. As with TTD benefits, there are two separate types of permanent benefits available under most workers compensation statutes: permanent total disability and permanent partial disability.

Permanent Total Disability (PTD) – Permanent total disability (PTD) benefits are the less complicated of the two to explain and, in many respects, are similar to Social Security Disability Insurance (SSDI) benefits. The payment of PTD benefits in workers compensation cases reflects either a very severe injury or a very severe physical limitation for an employee disabled because of a workplace injury or disease. PTD benefits represent a wage replacement benefit and in most states are computed on the same basis as TTD benefits.

In many states, permanent total disability is a type of injury that meets certain specific criteria assigned to that phrase. In those states, the law enumerates certain body parts, the loss of which will be presumed to constitute a permanent total disability. The most common list of enumerated injuries includes *"the loss of both arms, both feet, both legs, both eyes, and any two thereof."* In addition, a number of states include injuries resulting in paralysis and incurable imbecility or insanity. Individuals with other conditions may be eligible if they have a specific percentage of disability as rated by a physician.

A number of examples serve to demonstrate various state approaches to defining what constitutes a permanent total disability. The first example is from **Virginia** and illustrates the brevity that may be used for purposes of defining a PTD case.

> *(2) "Compensation shall be awarded pursuant to sec. 65.2-500 for permanent and total incapacity when there is:*
> *1. Loss of both hands, both arms, both feet, both legs, both eyes, or any two thereof in the same accident;*
> *2. Injury for all practical purposes resulting in total paralysis, as determined by the Commission based on medical evidence; or*

3. Injury to the brain which is so severe as to render the employee permanently unemployable in gainful employment."[145]

The second example is from the state of **Florida** and illustrates a more comprehensive description of who may be presumed to be permanently and totally disabled.

(1) (a) In case of total disability adjudged to be permanent, 66⅔ or 66.67 percent of the average weekly wages shall be paid to the employee during the continuance of such total disability. No compensation shall be payable under this section if the employee is engaged in, or is physically capable of engaging in, at least sedentary employment.

(b) In the following cases, an injured employee is presumed to be permanently and totally disabled unless the employer or carrier establishes that the employee is physically capable of engaging in at least sedentary employment within a 50-mile radius of the employee's residence:

1. Spinal cord injury involving severe paralysis of an arm, a leg, or the trunk;

2. Amputation of an arm, a hand, a foot, or a leg involving the effective loss of use of that appendage;

3. Severe brain or closed-head injury as evidenced by:

a. Severe sensory or motor disturbances;

b. Severe communication disturbances;

c. Severe complex integrated disturbances of cerebral function;

d. Severe episodic neurological disorders; or

e. Other severe brain and closed-head injury conditions at least as severe in nature as any condition provided in sub-subparagraphs a.-d.;

4. Second-degree or third-degree burns of 25 percent or more of the total body surface or third-degree burns of 5 percent or more to the face and hands; or

5. Total or industrial blindness.

In all other cases, in order to obtain permanent total disability benefits, the employee must establish that he or she is not able to engage in at least sedentary employment, within a 50-mile radius of the employee's residence, due to his or her physical limitation. Entitlement to such benefits shall cease when the employee reaches age 75, unless the employee is not eligible for social security benefits under 42 U.S.C. s. 402 or s. 423 because the employee's compensable injury has prevented the employee from working sufficient quarters to be eligible for such benefits, notwithstanding any age limits. If the accident occurred on or after the employee reaches age 70, benefits shall be payable during the continuance of permanent total disability, not to exceed 5 years following the determination of permanent total disability. Only claimants with catastrophic injuries or claimants who are incapable of engaging in employment, as described in this paragraph, are eligible for permanent total benefits. In no other case may permanent total disability be awarded.[146]

---

[145] Va. Code Ann. § 65.2-503 C
[146] Fla. Stat. Ann. § 440.15 (1)(b)

In the majority of states, PTD benefits are paid at the same rate as those for temporary total disability, again subject to the state's maximum and minimum benefit provisions. In most states, permanent total disability benefits are payable until death or as long as the inability to work continues. In a number of states benefits may be capped at a dollar amount or a number of weeks or may be paid only until a certain age is reached. For example, **Mississippi** limits the duration of PTD benefits to 450 weeks while **Indiana** and **South Carolina** limit benefits to 500 weeks. **Michigan** has a limit of 800 weeks and **North Carolina** has a limit of 500 weeks, but in both cases, this period may be extended.

Minnesota law contains a rebuttable presumption that PTD benefits cease at age 67; and **West Virginia** stops paying PTD benefits when the employee reaches the age of eligibility for Social Security old-age and survivor benefits. **Kentucky** terminates entitlement to total disability benefits when there is an award based upon eligibility for old age Social Security benefits, or two years after the date of injury. In **Tennessee**, PTD benefits are to terminate at age 65, but if the injured worker sustains the injury after age 60, benefits are payable for a total of 260 weeks. As described on the preceding page, **Florida** law provides for the discontinuation of PTD benefits when the injured worker reaches age 70 unless the worker is not eligible for Social Security benefits. There is also recognition for injuries occurring after age 70 limiting PTD benefits to five years.

The assumption is frequently made that once entitlement to PTD benefits has been designated, that determination is definitive and permanent. In the case of an award for PTD, many state administrative agencies are open to reconsidering continued entitlement at periodic intervals during the worker's ongoing disability. In addition, most insurers will conduct periodic or annual activity checks to determine whether the employee is working or able to work. With today's technology and improved medical procedures, individuals who once may have been considered permanently and totally unable to work may be able to again return to gainful employment.

There is also an alternate means to become entitled to PTD benefits. The "odd-lot" doctrine is an avenue by which a worker may be found to be totally disabled based on unemployability rather than the extent of the workplace injury. The doctrine provides that, although a worker is not completely unable to work, the condition is such that the worker will not be regularly employed in any reasonably stable area of the labor market. The doctrine had its genesis in England where a claimant's search for work was fruitless since his physical defects in combination with his lack of skills made him an unmarketable unit.

Various states, including **New Jersey**, have embodied the concept statutorily. In New Jersey where at least seventy-five percent of total disability can be attributed to medical reasons, then the other personal handicaps may be considered in combination with the medical conditions in reaching a determination of unemployability.

Illinois, like many other jurisdictions, does not require an employee to show that he or she has been reduced to complete physical incapacity to be entitled to PTD benefits. In Illinois, a claimant ordinarily satisfies the burden of proving that he or she falls into the odd-lot category in one of two ways: by showing diligent but unsuccessful attempts to find work, or by showing that because of the claimant's age, skills, training, and work history, he or she will not be regularly employed in a well-known branch of the labor market.[270]

Today, virtually every state accepts, in some fashion, the "odd lot" doctrine. However, this doctrine took time to develop over the course of the 20th century, and in fact, the doctrine continues to evolve through considerable litigation. The history of the odd lot doctrine reflects judicial, legislative, and advocacy attempts to provide adequate compensation for those unusual situations where the injured worker, while not physically incapable of working, is unable to find adequate and continuous employment in the workforce. Age and education are frequently issues that lend themselves to this determination.

Temporary Partial Disability (TPD) – Following a work-related injury, a worker may be able to return to work for fewer days per week or fewer hours per day than before the injury, or at reduced earnings in the same or another place of employment. If the employee is earning less in this new position or is working fewer hours, he or she will have a continuing wage loss even while working and may be entitled to benefits for temporary partial disability following a period of temporary total disability.

Temporary partial benefits are generally calculated as a percentage of the difference between what the employee was making when originally injured and what he or she is able to earn with the physical limitations following maximum medical improvement. In general, TPD benefits under workers compensation and disability benefits under Social Security would generally not be paid simultaneously because the payment of temporary partial disability benefits indicates the employee is not totally disabled. SSDI requires the worker to be totally disabled in order to qualify for benefits and there is also a six month waiting period before SSDI benefits begin.

Both TTD and TPD benefits are generally paid while the employee is in active medical treatment and while recovering from the effects of a workplace injury or illness. Generally, entitlement to this type of benefit continues only until the worker reaches his or her pre-injury earning level or, the worker is found eligible to receive benefits for a permanent partial disability.

An example of an approach for TPD is taken from the statute in **California:**

> *"In case of temporary partial disability the weekly loss in wages shall consist of the difference between the average weekly earnings of the injured employee and the weekly amount which the injured employee will probably be able to earn during the disability, to be determined in view of the nature and extent of the*

injury. In computing such probable earnings, due regard shall be given to the ability of the injured employee to compete in an open labor market. If evidence of exact loss of earnings is lacking, such weekly loss in wages may be computed from the proportionate loss of physical ability or earning power caused by the injury."[147]

Permanent Partial Disability (PPD) – Permanent partial disability benefits represent the most complicated and diverse form of benefit both in terms of design and application. Peter Barth, member of the National Commission and retired University of Connecticut professor, wrote an article for the Social Security Bulletin in which he described the scope and purpose of PPD benefits.[148] In the article he noted that in the case of temporary disability or death, there is a clear rationale for the payment of workers compensation benefits, that is, to replace in some measure a worker's lost earnings. The reason for paying benefits for a permanent partial disability is, less clear, however, as is the scope of such benefits.

The uncertainty surrounding the rationale for paying permanent partial disability benefits is evident when one examines the different manner in which states assess the degree of disability and thereby the amount of compensation to be paid. One must presume that the estimation of future earnings that may be lost because of the condition is an important consideration in setting the amount of the benefit. Yet, other factors evidently serve as the basis for the amount of the benefits that a worker will receive. For example, in a few states, the amount of compensation for a permanent disability is not linked to the worker's pre-injury earnings level. And in some states, an older worker can retire and then seek and receive compensation for a permanent disability that is hardly likely to affect his or her future earnings.[149]

Barth observed that permanent partial disability benefits in the state programs can be sorted into two broad classes: individual justice and average justice. Under individual justice, the specific worker's circumstances are considered and are used in assessing what the economic impact of the permanent disability will be or has been on the individual. For reasons that are clear and will be more evident below, there are costs in assessing these losses, primarily from the potential for contention in arriving at such an estimate. In addition, one might question the accuracy of the estimates that emerge from a process in which the payer and the potential beneficiary have incentives to reach very different estimates. Moreover, the likely dispute is almost certain to delay determining an outcome for the parties as well as create backlogs in other areas of the dispute in the state's compensation system. Yet the individual justice approach is so fundamental in most parts of criminal and civil justice that some parties resist any effort to deny it.

---

[147] Cal. Labor Code § 4657

[148] *Permanent Partial Disability Benefits: Interstate Differences*, published by the Workers' Compensation Research Institute in 1999

[149] Barth, Peter, *Compensating Workers for Permanent Partial Disabilities,* Social Security Bulletin • Vol. 65 • No. 4 • 2003/2004 (pg. 18)

By contrast, in the second class the state uses an average justice approach in determining the level of compensation. This approach presumes that the law can estimate a fairly typical loss associated with a permanent disability and, by treating workers with similar losses the same, can avoid incurring the costs of the individual justice approach. Implicit in the average justice approach are two assumptions: first, that we know how to identify similar workers, that is, that we understand what variables are likely to affect future earnings losses and can measure them and their impact; and second, that the variance in the errors associated with this process is not large. Stated simply, supporters of this view seem likely to recognize that some degree of under-compensation or over-compensation will result in cases because of individual circumstances but that the errors will not be large.[150]

For the majority of states, permanent partial disability is awarded by using two principle forms of compensation. The first form involves those cases where the impairment is readily traceable to a specific part of the body (e.g., a finger, hand, arm, foot, leg). In this first form, compensation is payable in accordance with a schedule of benefits delineated in the statute and are commonly referred to as scheduled awards. The second form is the unscheduled award that includes injury to body parts not listed in the schedule (e.g., back or head injuries). The following reviews the major characteristics of both scheduled and unscheduled awards.

> **Scheduled PPD Awards** – The typical schedule covers injuries or losses involving specific body parts such as the eyes, ears, hands, arms, feet, and legs. The schedule prescribes that for the complete loss or loss of use of a stated member, compensation will be paid for a specified number of weeks. Where loss or loss of use is less than total, the maximum number of weeks is reduced in proportion to the percentage of the loss or loss of use. In a significant number of states, only the extent of physical impairment is considered when computing the scheduled award. For example, a 25 percent loss of a body member would be compensated based upon 25 percent loss of the complete body member. A fairly extensive list of body members is set forth in the **Alabama** law.
>
> > *"a. Amount and Duration of Compensation - For permanent partial disability, the compensation shall be based upon the extent of the disability. In cases included in the following schedule, the compensation shall be 66 2/3 percent of the average weekly earnings, during the number of weeks set out in the following schedule:*
> > *1. For the loss of a thumb, 62 weeks.*
> > *2. For the loss of a first finger, commonly called the index finger, 43 weeks.*
> > *3. For the loss of a second finger, 31 weeks.*
> > *4. For the loss of a third finger, 22 weeks.*
> > *5. For the loss of a fourth finger, commonly called the little finger, 16 weeks.*

---

[150] Ibid.

6. *The loss of the first phalange of the thumb or of any finger shall be considered as equal to the loss of one half of the thumb or finger, and compensation shall be paid at the prescribed rate during one half of the time specified above for the thumb or finger.*

7. *The loss of two or more phalanges shall be considered as the loss of the entire finger or thumb, but in no case shall the amount received for more than one finger exceed the amount provided in this schedule for the loss of a hand.*

8. *For the loss of a great toe, 32 weeks.*

9. *For the loss of any of the toes other than the great toe, 11 weeks.*

10. *The loss of the first phalange of any toe shall be considered to be equal to the loss of one half of the toe, and compensation shall be paid at the prescribed rate during one half the time prescribed above for the toe.*

11. *The loss of two or more phalanges shall be considered as the loss of an entire toe.*

12. *For the loss of a hand, 170 weeks.*

13. *For the loss of an arm, 222 weeks.*

14. *For the loss of a foot, 139 weeks.*

15. *Amputation between the elbow and wrist shall be considered as the equivalent to the loss of hand, and the amputation between the knee and ankle shall be considered as the equivalent of the loss of a foot.*

16. *For the loss of a leg, 200 weeks.*

17. *For the loss of an eye, 124 weeks.*

18. *For the complete and permanent loss of hearing in both ears, 163 weeks.*

19. *For the complete and permanent loss of hearing in one ear, 53 weeks.*

20. *For the loss of an eye and a leg, 350 weeks.*

21. *For the loss of an eye and one arm, 350 weeks.*

22. *For the loss of an eye and a hand, 325 weeks.*

23. *For the loss of an eye and a foot, 300 weeks.*

24. *For the loss of two arms, other than at the shoulder, 400 weeks.*

25. *For the loss of two hands, 400 weeks.*

26. *For the loss of two legs, 400 weeks.*

27. *For the loss of two feet, 400 weeks.*

28. *For the loss of one arm and other hand, 400 weeks.*

29. *For the loss of one hand and one foot, 400 weeks.*

30. *For the loss of one leg and the other foot, 400 weeks.*

31. *For the loss of one hand and one leg, 400 weeks*

32. *For the loss of one arm and one foot, 400 weeks.*

33. *For the loss of one arm and one leg, 400 weeks.*

d. Loss of Use of Member. -- The permanent and total loss of the use of a member shall be considered as equivalent to the loss of that member, but in such cases the compensation specified in the schedule for such injury shall be in lieu of all other compensation, except as otherwise provided herein. For permanent disability due to injury to a member resulting in less than total loss of use of the member not otherwise compensated in this schedule, compensation shall be paid at the prescribed rate during that part of the time specified in the schedule for the total loss or total loss of use of the respective member which the extent of the injury to the member bears to its total loss."[151]

Notwithstanding the fact that most states have established statutory schedules, there is no consistent number of weeks of compensation payable for the loss of a scheduled body member. For example, while **Alabama** schedules the complete loss of the arm at 222 weeks, other states like **South Carolina, Virginia** and **Louisiana** schedule the complete loss of the arm at 200 weeks. In **Connecticut**, complete loss of the master arm entitles the injured worker to 208 weeks of compensation in addition to the benefits paid during the healing or recovery period.

As with the period of entitlement, the amount of weekly compensation payable for PPD may be different than the benefit paid during the period of TTD. In the majority of states, benefits for a scheduled award are paid at the same rate as those payable during the period of TTD. In several states, the PPD rate for a scheduled loss is less than the TTD rate. In 2020, the **Wisconsin** maximum weekly benefit for a scheduled award is $362 per week whereas the maximum TTD weekly benefit is $1,051.

In lieu of compensation based on pre-injury earnings, **Idaho** and **North Dakota** compute the PPD benefit as a percentage of the statewide average weekly wage (SAWW). Idaho prescribes the payment to be 55 percent of the SAWW, and North Dakota provides that the impairment benefit is one-third of the SAWW. In these states, all injured workers are entitled to the same PPD weekly benefit amount without consideration for their own individual level of pre-injury earnings.

To further complicate the issue of scheduled PPD benefits, certain states permit the awarding of discretionary benefits which are designed to afford the adjudicator some leeway in the awarding of scheduled permanent partial awards. There may be occasions where the schedule does not serve to adequately compensate for the resulting disability and the discretionary provisions permits some latitude in the amount of compensation that may be awarded. For example, the economic consequences for a concert pianist who suffers the loss of his/her little finger would be different than for a construction laborer suffering the same loss. The concept behind the awarding of discretionary benefits is to adjust the compensation to address these atypical situations.

Five jurisdictions – **Connecticut, Kansas, New Mexico, New York,** and **Ohio** – have added provisions to their scheduled injuries to permit the payment of additional compensation. The following examples set forth the statutory provision as found in Connecticut:

---

[151] Ala. Code § 25-5-57 (a)(3)

"In addition to the compensation benefits provided by section 31-308, for specific loss of a member or use of the function of a member of the body, or any personal injury covered by this chapter, the commissioner, after such payments provided by said section 31-308 have been paid for the period set forth in said section, may award additional compensation benefits for such partial permanent disability equal to seventy-five percent of the difference between the wages currently earned by an employee in a position comparable to the position held by such injured employee prior to his injury, after such wages have been reduced by any deduction for federal or state taxes, or both, and for the federal Insurance Contributions Act in accordance with section 31-310, and the weekly amount which such employee will probably be able to earn thereafter, after such amount has been reduced by any deduction for federal or state taxes, or both, and for the federal Insurance Contributions Act in accordance with said section 31-310, to be determined by the commissioner based upon the nature and extent of the injury, the training, education and experience of the employee, the availability of work for persons with such physical condition and at the employee's age, but not more than the maximum provided in section 31-309. If evidence of exact loss of earnings is not available, such loss may be computed from the proportionate loss of physical ability or earning power caused by the injury. The duration of such additional compensation shall be determined upon a similar basis by the commissioner, but in no event shall the duration of such additional compensation exceed the lesser of (1) the duration of the employee's permanent partial disability benefits, or (2) five hundred twenty weeks. Additional benefits provided under this section shall be available only to employees who are willing and able to perform work in this state.
(b) Notwithstanding the provisions of subsection (a) of this section, additional benefits provided under this section shall be available only when the nature of the injury and its effect on the earning capacity of an employee warrant additional compensation."[152]

Unscheduled PPD Awards – The second form of PPD entitlement involves the unscheduled awards. Whereas scheduled awards are usually confined to the body extremities and senses, unscheduled awards focus on injuries to the back, psychiatric ailments, heart and vascular ailments, and other conditions not normally found within the schedule. These conditions are simply harder to evaluate, or measure compared to the complete loss, or even 50 percent loss, of the thumb. Furthermore, a condition that is unscheduled in one state may be a scheduled loss in an adjacent state.

Before discussing the various approaches to unscheduled PPD awards, it is important to distinguish between the terms disability and impairment. Again, Professor Barth provides a distinction between the two terms which are frequently

---

[152] Conn. Gen. Stat. § 31-308a

used interchangeably. Professor Barth observed that *"An injury or illness, the aging process, or a chronic condition may result in impairment – a physiological or psychological result that can be evaluated in medical terms. The individual may have lost some portion of his or her sight or hearing, may have limited range of motion in the back, or may have had a finger amputated. The key to understanding impairment is that the loss is thought to be best described and evaluated by medical professionals.*

"A disability, unlike impairment, represents the socioeconomic loss that an individual sustains as a result of an injury, illness, or condition. If a worker is injured and as a result cannot ever return to work, the disability is a very serious one. Another worker, with precisely the same injury and the same degree of impairment, may be able to return to work quickly with little or no impact on his or her earnings. The injury to that worker would result in a much lower degree of disability. Disability evaluation can include some assessment of the worker by a medical professional but should also take some account of the person's occupation and employment history, education and training, and probably other demographic and labor market variables."[153]

A number of theories of entitlement have evolved relative to the appropriate method for compensating for PPD. Some theories focus solely on the economic consequences resulting from the injury, while other approaches strive to compensate for the reduction in functional ability or the impact on the quality of life. Professor Barth describes the four approaches found in the states to address unscheduled PPD as follows:

> **Impairment-Based** – The most common approach that states use can be categorized as impairment based. In these states, the worker with an unscheduled permanent partial disability receives a benefit based entirely on the degree of impairment and the worker's pre-injury wage level. The extent of impairment is usually based on an estimate provided by a medical practitioner who uses an impairment rating guide. The most commonly employed source is the latest edition of the *American Medical Association's Guides to the Evaluation of Permanent Impairment*. In the interest of consistency, many states actually mandate which rating guide (and edition, in some cases) must be used. Even with a uniform source of reference, it is not unusual for disputes to occur over the estimated degree of impairment and, thereby, the size of the unscheduled PPD award. Even medical raters who are not perceived as worker-friendly or pro-employer or insurer friendly can disagree about the presence of and the extent of an unscheduled PPD.
>
> There is an important parallel between the application of a schedule for certain losses and the impairment-based approach for unscheduled conditions. In both,

---

[153] Barth, Peter, Phd. *Compensating Workers for Permanent Partial Disabilities*, Social Security Bulletin • Vol. 65 • No. 4 • 2003/2004 (pg. 19-20)

the state opts to use some type of average justice rather than determine the degree of disability that the injury caused a particular worker. Regardless of the labor market consequences of the worker's impairment, the benefit amount is unaffected. Under the impairment-based approach, the worker is entitled to a benefit even if the condition results in no loss of employment or earnings. Yet minor permanent impairments will result in low benefit levels, even if the disabling effects of the injury are catastrophic to the worker. Not surprisingly, this approach is especially vulnerable to the dueling-doc syndrome, where the claimant's medical evaluator assesses a higher level of impairment than does the employer or insurer's expert or where the latter may argue that there is no permanent, work-caused impairment at all.

In a few states, benefits for unscheduled injuries are paid for the period of the disability with no limitation on the number of weeks or the total maximum benefits. Several other states place no limitation on the number of weeks but restrict total benefits to a specified amount. Under other laws, there are a specific number of weeks for which payments may be made.

There are two exceptions to the strict application of the impairment-based method. First, in the states of **Colorado** and **Nevada,** the benefit amount is adjusted by a factor to take account of a worker's age. Both states adjust benefits so that the adjustment factor is greater for a younger worker than for an older worker. These adjustments are not very large, and it is reasonable to classify these two jurisdictions as using an impairment-based approach, even if their application of it differs from that of other states.

In the second exception, a few states set the benefit strictly on the basis of the degree of impairment. However, when the weeks of permanent partial disability benefits have expired, the worker may be eligible to be considered for an additional benefit. These supplemental benefits are paid only for limited periods of time and are awarded if the worker has not returned to employment or to employment near the pre-injury wage. Still, these states can be classified as impairment based. Simply put, very few workers ever receive these supplemental benefits because most workers with a permanent impairment are not sufficiently impaired to demonstrate loss earnings. Most workers with impairments are able to return to employment before any impairment benefits have expired.

Although this approach is best characterized as impairment based, it represents an attempt to provide some individual justice where the application of average justice is found to be inadequate. Although the most common method for setting benefits is to agree as to the number of weeks of entitlement, in practice there are common alternatives. The parties may agree on a lump-sum settlement that will usually include an agreement on the part of the worker to waive any right to further indemnity or medical benefits. The amount of the lump sum may reflect some discounting for the advance payment. It may also include something that reflects the possible medical needs that the worker will continue to have. The usual practice is to use recent practices in similar settlements as a template for the negotiated settlement amount.

Loss-of-Wage-Earning-Capacity (LWEC) – About a third of the states use the LWEC approach which links the benefit to the worker's ability to earn or to compete in the labor market. One can say that this is an *ex ante* approach, that is, it is a forecast of the economic impact that the impairment will have going forward. In the absence of actual estimates of such losses, the parties try to reach some agreement as to what the impact on earnings will be, using some variables that may be specified in the law.

The starting point is customarily the degree of impairment, with the operating premise that the more severe the impairment, the greater will be the potential impact on future earnings. The worker's occupation, work history, education, training, and age can also be important components in the calculation by the parties or by the agency charged with determining the level of the LWEC. In contrast to the impairment-based approach, this approach appears to apply individual justice in claims for an unscheduled permanent partial disability, but in practice, there are reasons why this characterization may not be correct.

First, the parties may find it simpler to settle using some customary and informally determined value for an unscheduled loss rather than litigate it. Adding to the likelihood of such an outcome, many jurisdictions find their dispute resolution process severely backed up, resulting in lengthy delays before a hearing will held. Second, the difference between the amount that the employer or insurer is prepared to pay and the amount that the worker is prepared to accept may be small enough to discourage the parties from waging a protracted dispute and agree to settle the claim.

The LWEC approach purports to predict the impact – presumably the earnings losses – of a permanent impairment. As such, there is necessarily some uncertainty or subjectivity in estimating these losses, which can be the source of disagreement. Supporters of this approach can point to the individual justice that it allows. Others ask whether the approach can deliver a good prediction of future losses. Another criticism of this approach is that it may encourage workers to delay returning to employment because a long period of temporary disability can help support the argument that the worker's future earnings prospects are meager.

Wage-Loss – In those states that use wage loss as the method to compensate for an unscheduled permanent partial disability, benefits are paid for the actual or ongoing loss in earnings that a worker incurs. Stated differently, to receive a permanent partial disability cash benefit, the worker must demonstrate some actual loss of earnings. Since the loss of earnings that follows from a permanent impairment can continue indefinitely, some jurisdictions establish a maximum potential duration for the payment of benefits. Alternatively, some states limit the duration of benefits if an impairment rating is below a given threshold. The duration of benefits can also be limited by ceasing entitlement when the worker reaches retirement age or by offsetting the benefits for old-age benefits paid under Social Security.

If the purpose of unscheduled permanent partial disability benefits is to compensate for earnings lost as a result of impairment, then unlike the methods based on impairment or the loss of earning capacity, the wage loss approach would appear to do precisely that. It also can be characterized as providing individual justice.

One might wonder why so few states embrace this approach. The likely answer is that this method is probably the most difficult to administer. In particular, it is difficult to determine with certainty why a worker's income may have declined after a work injury resulting in impairment. Was the wage-loss the result of the workplace injury or was it a result of some unrelated economic factor(s)?

Consider the following scenario. After losing time because of a work injury, the worker returns to employment. Six months later, the worker becomes unemployed for any of several reasons. The worker experiences difficulty finding other employment. From the worker's perspective, this is a result of the permanent impairment, which may limit the types of employment that the worker feels qualified to take or which renders him or her less attractive to a prospective employer. A determination must be made about the degree to which earnings losses are due to the work-caused condition and how much is due to the overall state of the labor market, the worker's motivation, any preexisting condition that the worker might have, or the worker's qualifications to take alternative employment.

The wage-loss approach may also serve to induce some beneficiaries to delay or postpone returning to employment. In response to this perception, some employers or insurers may seek to settle and close out cases as quickly as possible, thereby avoiding the possibility of paying permanent partial disability benefits over a long period.

Bi-furcated Approach – In a few jurisdictions, the benefit for a permanent disability depends on the worker's employment status at the time the assessment is made. If the worker has returned to employment with earnings at or near the pre-injury level, the benefit is based on the degree of impairment. In most cases, the worker will receive weekly benefits – or a lump sum payment – that supplements current earnings from employment. However, if the worker has not been able to return to work or has returned but is earning less than before the pre-injury, the worker will be rated on the basis of the loss of earning capacity. The impairment benefit that the worker would have received if he or she successfully returned to work is the lower bound of what the disabled worker will receive.

The bi-furcated approach can be thought of as a partial accommodation to using individual justice. Most workers will receive benefits based on the degree of impairment, resulting in some disparities in outcome in the future. However, some individual justice is given to those who are unable to return to pre-injury earnings, at least in the short run. The benefits paid will always be higher if the worker is compensated for the loss of earning capacity in a state using a bi-furcated approach.

At the margin, this method can provide a financial incentive to an employer to reemploy the worker. If the employer self-insures, the lower compensation costs are a direct gain for the business. If the employer purchases insurance, as most do, and is subject to experience rating with regard to the premium that is paid, a lower compensation benefit can also give the employer an incentive to retain the worker. No such direct incentive exists for the many small employers who are not covered under experience rating."[154]

With recognition for the theoretical forms of compensating for unscheduled PPD, state legislators and other interested parties continue to search for the ideal means by which to compensate for such loss. At this point it is beneficial to look at how unscheduled PPD is addressed in a number of prominent states following years of study and deliberation.

Texas, through a major law change enacted in 1991 and subsequent amendments, has adopted the bi-furcated approach. The Texas code provides that an injured worker may be entitled to Impairment Income Benefits (IIBs) following maximum medical improvement (MMI). Maximum medical improvement (MMI) is defined as *"(A) the earliest date after which, based on reasonable medical probability, further material recovery from or lasting improvement to an injury can no longer reasonably be anticipated; (B) the expiration of 104 weeks from the date on which income benefits begin to accrue; or (C) the date determined as provided by Texas Labor Code §408.104.*[155]

Following MMI, the health care provider determines if there is any permanent physical damage and will assign an impairment rating (IR) (the degree of permanent damage to the body as a whole) using the fourth edition, or the latest edition, of the *American Medical Association (AMA) Guides to the Evaluation of Permanent Impairment*. Where the injured employee has not yet reached MMI, the compensation law establishes MMI at 104 weeks (with the caveat for a longer period

---

[154] Barth, Peter, Phd. *Compensating Workers for Permanent Partial Disabilities,* Social Security Bulletin • Vol. 65 • No. 4 • 2003/2004 (pg. 19-22)
[155] Texas Administrative Code 130.1 (b.)(1)

where the claim involves a spinal surgery) from the date that income benefits began to accrue.

Three weeks of impairment benefits are paid for each percentage of impairment.[156] For example, if the injured worker receives an eight percent impairment rating, the worker will be entitled to receive 24 weeks of IIBs because three weeks of IIBs are paid for each percentage of impairment (8 x 3 = 24 weeks of IIBs). IIBs are paid at 70 percent of the worker's average weekly wage subject to the state maximum weekly benefit. IIBs end after the employee has received a total of three weeks of payments for each percentage of impairment.

In addition to IIBs, Supplement Income Benefits (SIBs) are available for those having an impairment rating of 15 percent or more and have not returned to work or have returned to work earning less than 80 percent of their pre-injury average weekly wage as a direct result of the impairment.[157] These benefits are paid monthly and are equal to 80 percent of the difference between 80 percent of the worker's average weekly wage (earned prior to the work-related injury) and any current earnings after the work-related injury.

If eligible for a SIB, benefits begin with the conclusion of payment for IIBs. Entitlement is denied for any filing period where the worker earns wages that are at least 80 percent of the worker's average weekly wage for at least 90 days. Entitlement to SIBs ends at 401 weeks (approximately seven and a half years) from the date of the injury or, in the case of an occupational illness; entitlement ends at 401 weeks from the date the injured worker first became eligible to receive income benefits. This maximum period of benefit entitlement is inclusive of temporary disability and impairments benefits.

Florida is also an example of the bi-furcated approach. In 1993, following a number of attempts to structure a workable "wage loss" program beginning in 1979, the Florida legislature enacted a compensation scheme similar to the Texas model. Following attainment of maximum medical improvement, impairment benefits based upon the degree of impairment as demonstrated by objective findings are payable at the rate of 75 percent of the employee's temporary total benefit. For injuries after July 1, 1990, pending the adoption by rule of a uniform disability rating agency schedule, the Minnesota Department of Labor and Industry Disability Schedule shall be used unless that schedule does not address an injury. In such case, the Guides to the Evaluation of Permanent Impairment by the American Medical Association shall be used. Three weeks of impairment compensation are payable for each percentage point of impairment. The employee's eligibility for temporary benefits, impairment

---

[156] Texas Labor Code Sec. 408.121
[157] Texas Labor Code Sec. 408.142

income benefits, and supplemental benefits terminates on the expiration of 401 weeks after the date of injury.

The impairment benefit is reduced by 50 percent for each week in which the worker earns income equal to or in excess of the worker's average weekly wage. Entitlement to impairment income benefits begins the day after the injured worker reaches maximum medical improvement or the expiration of temporary benefits, whichever occurs earlier. The duration of entitlement to impairment benefits is payable in accordance with the following schedule:

1. Two weeks of benefits are to be paid to the employee for each percentage point of impairment from 1 percent up to and including 10 percent.
2. For each percentage point of impairment from 11 percent up to and including 15 percent, 3 weeks of benefits are to be paid.
3. For each percentage point of impairment from 16 percent up to and including 20 percent, 4 weeks of benefits are to be paid.
4. For each percentage point of impairment from 21 percent and higher, 6 weeks of benefits are to be paid."[158]

In addition to the impairment benefit, supplemental benefits (wage loss) were payable monthly following the expiration of the period of impairment benefits when the impairment was greater than 20 percent. Effective with reforms enacted in 2003, Florida no longer provides for a supplemental benefit as found in Texas.

In **Kentucky**, which also does not have a scheduled award benefit, the maximum benefit for permanent partial disability is 75 percent of the state's average weekly wage. Recognizing that limited education and advancing age impact an employee's after-injury earning capabilities, special consideration such as education and age factors can be added to the income benefits, if the employee lacks the physical capacity to return to the work being performed at the time of injury.

When an injured worker improves to the point where he/she can return to work, but still has a permanent impairment as determined by the AMA Guides to Evaluation of Permanent Impairment, permanent partial disability benefits are available. The number of PPD payments depends on the disability rating. With a permanent disability rating of 50 percent or less, benefit payments will extend to 425 weeks while a permanent disability rating greater than 50 percent will be paid for 520 weeks.

The amount of benefit payments is dependent on the impairment rating, which is then multiplied by an education or age factor if applicable. The impairment rating multiplied by the factor establishes the permanent disability rating. A lower impairment rating results in a lower education or age factor used in the computation. The following illustrates the influence of the factors in Kentucky:

---

[158] Fla. Stat. Ann. § 440.15 (3)

AMA Impairment Rating	Factor
0-5%	0.65
6-10%	0.85
11-20%	1.00
21-25%	1.15
26-30%	1.35
31-35%	1.50
36% and above	1.70 [159]

For example, if the worker received a 30 percent impairment rating for a back injury and previously earned $600 per week, the weekly benefits under this formula would be $162 (2/3 x 600 = $400; $400 x .3 = $120; $120 x 1.35 (the statutory factor for a 30 percent rating) = $162). If the worker is not physically able to return to the same type of work done before your injury, the worker will receive three times the formula amount, subject to the same maximum and minimum that applies to TTD benefits. For those able to return to work and are earning the same or more than their pre-injury wages, the maximum benefits are lower (for most people, $734.25 for 2020 injuries). Kentucky law also adjusts the amount of PPD benefits for injured workers who have limited education and are older, because those factors can affect the ability to earn a living.

Professor Barth concluded his Social Security Bulletin article by noting that *"Administering a state's permanent partial disability benefit program is challenging. Perhaps the strongest evidence of difficulties is that after about nine decades of workers compensation in most of the states, no single 'best' approach has emerged. Systems that depend solely on impairment as a way to set benefits can run the risk of creating a serious inequity if the impairment is relatively low and the disability is severe. They may also discourage workers from obtaining prompt medical restoration until after the impairment has been rated, thereby increasing the potential cash benefit but jeopardizing the recovery of health.*

With few exceptions, systems that rely on schedules to pay benefits represent an approach that is similar to the impairment-based method, at least for applicable injuries. States that compensate for the loss of earning capacity, in contrast to impairment, risk encouraging litigation over the unknown, that is, the impact of the injury on the worker's future labor market experience. They may also encourage workers to delay returning to work as a way to raise the potential indemnification for the injury. The wage-loss approach is difficult to administer. It too may discourage prompt return to employment. And because the bifurcated method depends on elements of both the impairment and the disability approaches, it has the same potential vulnerabilities as those systems." [160]

---

[159] Ky. Rev. Stat. Chapter 342.730
[160] Barth, Peter, Phd. *Compensating Workers for Permanent Partial Disabilities,* Social Security Bulletin • Vol. 65 • No. 4 • 2003/2004 (pg. 22)

BENEFITS IN THE CASE OF DEATH

The Bureau of Labor Statistics (BLS) reported in 2019 that there were 5,333 fatal work injuries recorded in the United States, a two percent increase from the 5,250 in 2018. The fatal work injury rate was 3.5 fatalities per 100,000 full-time equivalent (FTE) workers, which was the same rate as reported in 2018.[161] Drivers accounted for 1,480 of all work-related deaths in 2019 and more than 1,060 deaths occurred in the private construction industry. Workers in the fishing and hunting industry had the highest mortality rates among full-time workers with 145 deaths per 100,000 people. They were followed by loggers, pilots, and flight engineers and roofers.[162]

Where the workplace injury or illness results in the death of the employee, the spouse and/or dependents of the deceased are entitled to survivor benefits. The purpose of survivor benefits is to provide financial support to surviving members of the deceased because the death of the employee also means economic loss to the dependents. Benefits payable in the event of death generally include a replacement of a portion of the worker's average weekly wages as well as a burial allowance.

Dependency benefits are calculated in a manner similar to that for temporary or permanent disability but vary according to the number of eligible dependents and may cease for dependent children at age 18 (or older if they are a full-time student) and for a spouse two years after remarrying. In most jurisdictions, a spouse's benefits will continue for life unless he or she remarries, but a number of states have a maximum time period for which these benefits are paid. For example, death benefits are payable for a maximum of 25 years in **Illinois**, 500 weeks in **Alabama, Idaho, Indiana, Michigan, South Carolina,** and **Virginia**; and only 250 weeks in **Massachusetts** (time limit does not apply to children in Massachusetts).

Dependency is frequently determined according to statutory law. Generally, dependency is determined as of the date of the injury or the date of death. Changes that occur after this date do not usually affect the dependency status. In some situations, a state law may specifically set forth the categories of dependents entitled to death benefits while in other states, it may be necessary to look to the state domestic relations law to determine the identity of eligible dependents. Still other states include only immediate family members such as the spouse and children, while a number of other states allow parents and other dependents to receive benefits. There are, however, certain broad generalizations that may be made with respect to workers compensation laws and the question of dependency.

Most states provide that a surviving spouse is a dependent entitled to death benefits. Frequently, however, the law contains limitations. For instance, some states require that, in order to be eligible for death benefits, the spouse must have been living with the deceased employee at the time of death or injury. Another common

---

[161] BLS National Census of fatal Occupational Injuries in 2019
[162] https://www.bls.gov/news.release/pdf/cfoi.pdf

requirement is that the spouse be financially dependent upon the deceased employee at the time of death or injury.

Sometimes certain family members, such as a spouse and/or children, are presumed to be dependent without having to provide proof. However, if there has been a severance of the marital relationship, such as a voluntary separation with financial independence, a surviving spouse may not be assumed dependent.

Many states look at family relationships or household makeup. For example, states may prescribe lists of familial relationships eligible for death benefits. Where states look to household membership, unmarried co-habiting partners, in-laws, stepchildren or stepparents, or even unrelated persons may qualify for death benefits, so long as they were living in shared households with the deceased workers, especially where financial dependence was present. Generally, states are liberal in determining who should be named a beneficiary, consistent with the liberal nature of the compensation law.

Dependent children of the deceased are generally entitled to death benefits, subject to certain limitations. The age of the child or children is one such limitation. Benefits are almost always paid to or on behalf of dependent children who are:

- Under the age of 18 years or who are still in high school.

- Under the age of 21 or 22 and are enrolled in an accredited educational institution.

- Any age, but who suffer from a physical or mental handicap that prevents the child or children from becoming self-supporting.

In each of these cases, the benefit period extends until the dependency is removed or the maximum time limit is reached. Thus, a child who does not attend college or some other advanced educational program will have his or her benefits terminated at the time he or she attains majority, or at a specific age (usually 18) if so provided by state law. Similarly, a physically or mentally handicapped child's benefits will be terminated if and when the handicap no longer prevents the individual from self-support.

The dependent's right to death benefits is separate and apart from the deceased worker's right to compensation. Thus, the rights of the dependents to death benefits are not affected by actions or conduct of the worker while he or she was living. This issue arises when the injured worker, before the date of death, executes a release of liability or enters into a settlement agreement that includes a waiver of death benefits. In the majority of states, dependents are not bound to the terms of the release or agreement with respect to their claim for death benefits. Similarly, if the deceased worker failed to file a notice of injury or claim for compensation within the statutory time period, the late filing would probably not have an effect on the dependent's claim for death benefits.

Some states allow common law spouses to receive benefits. Others specifically prohibit them from receiving benefits. Currently, only nine jurisdictions (**Colorado, Iowa, Kansas, Montana, Oklahoma Rhode Island, South Carolina, Texas,** and **Utah**) along with the **District of Columbia** recognize common-law marriages contracted within their borders. In addition, five states have "grandfathered" common law marriage (**Georgia, Idaho, Ohio, Oklahoma** and **Pennsylvania**) allowing those established before a certain date to be recognized. **New Hampshire** recognizes common law marriage only for purposes of probate. **Utah** recognizes common law marriages only if they have been validated by a court or administrative order.

Ordinarily, where death benefits are payable, the spouse will receive such benefits only until he or she remarries. A number of states provide that, upon remarriage, a lump sum be paid to the surviving spouse as a final settlement of the death benefit. This lump sum is usually calculated as a lesser sum of the total amount of benefits the spouse would have been entitled to had he or she not remarried.

Funeral/burial expense benefits vary widely across the country. The national funeral expense benefit average is a little more than $5,200. **Mississippi** provides the lowest benefit at $2,000 and **Minnesota** has the highest at $15,000.

DISFIGUREMENT BENEFITS

Disfigurement benefits are somewhat of an anomaly within the workers compensation program. Most other disability benefits focus, in one way or another, on replacing a portion of income lost because of the work-related injury or disease. In most instances, income replacement benefits operate as a safety net by providing some money for living expenses, but the amounts paid are sufficiently reduced (at least in theory) to provide the employee with an incentive to return to work as soon as possible. Similarly, expenses for medical treatment, physical rehabilitation, and vocational rehabilitation or retraining help the employee attain a state of health or a level of skill that allows a return to full employment. Disfigurement benefits, by contrast, neither provide a safety net nor actively facilitate return to work.

Disfigurement benefits – generally associated with awards for scarring – are usually paid in a lump sum in recognition of a permanent physical impact on the person. While workers compensation benefits generally do not include payments for pain and suffering, benefits for disfigurement may take this into account, and because pain and suffering cannot be easily calculated by a schedule of compensation, disfigurement benefits are often the subject of negotiation.

A number of states restrict disfigurement benefits for scarring by requiring that scars be in certain areas of the body to be compensable. For example, compensable scars often must be on the face, neck, or hands. Scars on parts of the body normally covered by clothing are generally not compensated. Similarly, scars on the lower extremities, which are less likely to draw the attention of observers, may also be excluded from compensation.

Awards for disfigurement vary from one jurisdiction to the next, but there is a predominant theme that runs through most states' methods of calculating benefits, with the amounts commonly based on a percentage of either the employee's average weekly wage or the state's average weekly wage. In most jurisdictions, there are tables that delineate a schedule of benefits based on specific criteria.

Several states place a maximum limit on the amount of disfigurement benefits, while others limit the period during which the award may be made to a specified number of weeks. For example, in **Hawaii**, the workers compensation law allows the director of workers compensation to award compensation not to exceed $30,000 for disfigurement. Disfigurement includes scarring and other disfiguring consequences caused by medical, surgical and hospital treatment of the employee.[163]

In **Illinois**, the amount of compensation a worker is eligible to receive for disfigurement is to be determined by agreement at any time or by arbitration at a hearing not less than six months after the date of the accidental injury. The amount may not exceed 150 weeks at the applicable rate of compensation. Illinois also specifically provides that members of the fire department are eligible for compensation for disfigurement only if the disfigurement results from burns.

BENEFIT ESCALATION AND OFFSET PROVISIONS

Benefit escalation refers to the periodic adjustment of income replacement benefits to compensate for changes in the cost-of-living. In the case of a disability extending over many years, the benefits payable at the time of injury may become inadequate with the passage of time. In response to that situation, certain programs such as the Social Security Old Age, Survivors and Disability Insurance (OASDI) program provide for an automatic cost-of-living adjustment or COLA, also referred to as benefit escalation. With similar recognition for the potential inadequacy of benefits payable over an extended period of time, many states enacted provisions designed to escalate certain workers compensation disability or death benefits.

This automatic benefit adjustment for Social Security benefits has been in effect since 1975 and is based on the percentage change in the consumer price index (CPI) from the third quarter of the prior year to the corresponding quarter of the current year. The purpose of these adjustments is to ensure that an individual's benefits are not eroded by inflation. For benefit payments issued beginning in January 2021, the Social Security COLA was 1.3 percent. At the same time, the maximum amount of earnings subject to the Social Security tax (taxable maximum) will increase to $142,800. There was no COLA for the years 2009 and 2010.

---

[163] Hawaii Rev. Stat. § 386-32

In contrast with Social Security, many state workers compensation laws do not provide an annual automatic increase for recipients of disability benefits based on changes in the cost of living. Of the sixteen jurisdictions that have enacted some form of benefit adjustment, there is a wide variance in terms of what disability benefits are subject to an adjustment, the maximum percentage increase that may be applied and the number of total adjustments permitted. For example, **Maryland** and **Massachusetts** provide for an annual cost of living increase but limit the adjustment to permanent total disability cases and further limit the maximum amount of the annual increase to 5 percent.

In **Oregon** and **Vermont**, all disability benefit recipients receive an annual cost of living increase effective July 1 of each year. Other examples of workers compensation cost of living increases include **Montana**, where the number of adjustments is limited to a maximum of 10 and the percentage increase may not exceed three percent; **Minnesota**, where the annual increase may not exceed two percent and the first adjustment takes place on the fourth anniversary of the injury; and **Illinois**, where the adjustment is limited to permanent total disability cases and the first adjustment occurs on July 15 following the second year after the injury.

For those states that have legislated some form of benefit escalation provision for claims remaining open beyond a minimum time duration, there is a wide variation in the pattern of these provisions with some being extremely limited in scope. For example, the escalation factor in **California** applies only to temporary total awards continuing for more than two years. A number of other states are limited as to the time when the original injury occurred.

In most instances, the benefit escalation clauses are restricted to total disability – often only permanent total disability – and death. Adjustments are frequently annual and automatic, and generally tied to the percentage increase in the statewide average weekly wage. In a few instances – especially where the escalation feature is designed to address dated cases – the escalated amount is financed through a special fund or sometimes the second injury fund.

While the escalation feature periodically adjusts benefits upwards, an offset provision is designed to prevent a duplication of benefits when an injured worker may be eligible for benefits from more than a single income replacement program. A typical example would be where the worker is receiving workers compensation disability benefits and is also entitled to Social Security disability or retirement benefits. Were the claimant to receive both workers compensation benefits and social security disability or retirement benefits, it would be possible for the combined benefits to exceed the amount of the wages the worker earned prior to becoming disabled.

In 1965, the Social Security law was amended to require Social Security Disability Insurance (SSDI) benefits to be reduced when the worker was also eligible for periodic or lump-sum workers compensation payments. The offset was to be applied so that the combined amount of workers compensation and SSDI benefits did not exceed eighty percent of the worker's "average current earnings".[164] In no case were the combined payments after the reduction to be less than the amount of total SSDI benefits before the reduction.

Under the 1965 law, the SSDI benefit was not subject to reduction if the state workers compensation law already provided for a reduction of the workers compensation benefit of a worker also receiving SSDI. This is referred to as a reverse offset. Among other major changes, the Omnibus Reconciliation Act of 1981 ended the opportunity for additional states to enact offset provisions. At the time of the 1981 legislation, 16 states had reverse offset statutes meaning that the workers compensation disability benefit could be reduced to reflect SSDI benefits.

Today, the approved states where a reverse offset applies when SSDI benefits are payable include: **Alaska, California, Colorado, Florida, Louisiana, Minnesota, New Jersey, New York, North Dakota, Ohio, Oregon, Washington,** and **Wisconsin** where temporary total benefits are subject to a reduction. In Louisiana, Minnesota and Oregon, the reduction for SSDI is limited to permanent total disability cases.

Once a worker reaches the age of normal retirement, various forms of economic security are available to the majority of workers. The primary benefit to which most retired workers are entitled is Social Security Retirement Insurance (SSRI) benefits. While the offset at the federal level is limited to SSDI benefits, there is no similar provision at the federal level allowing for an offset of state workers compensation benefits when SSRI or survivor benefits are being paid. At the same time, there is no restriction on the ability of states to provide for an offset of compensation benefits for SSRI or survivor benefits being paid.

At present, ten states permit some form of reduction in workers compensation disability benefits when Social Security retirement or survivor benefits are being paid. **Connecticut** allowed an offset for SSRI benefits between 7/1/1993 and 5/29/2006 after which the provision was repealed. **Louisiana** also stopped offsetting benefits as of 2002.

States have, over the years, enacted various approaches to accomplish an offset for Social Security retirement benefits. For example, **Maine** reduces total or partial incapacity benefits by 50 percent of the SSRI.[165] In another interesting approach, **Michigan** reduces the workers compensation payments by five percent until a maximum of a 50 percent reduction is realized following receipt of SSRI benefits.[166] And **Pennsylvania** confines

---

[164] The "average current earnings" is usually calculated as the average monthly earnings from a single calendar year, either the year the person's disability began or any one of the five calendar years before that year.
[165] Me. Rev. Stat. Ann. Title 39-A, § 221
[166] Mich. Stat. Ann. § 418:354

the offset to total disability benefits provided that the offset does not apply if Social Security Old-Age benefits were received prior to the compensable injury.[167]

West Virginia enacted a similar approach to that found in Pennsylvania but the provision was ruled unconstitutional by the West Virginia Supreme Court of Appeals.[168] The Court held that any statute that reduces workers compensation permanent total disability benefits by reason of receipt of Social Security Old Age benefits bears no reasonable relationship to proper governmental purpose of avoiding duplication of benefits and, therefore, the statute violated equal protection guarantees under the state constitution. Legislation enacted in **Arkansas** in 1996 which attempted to limit the reduction in benefits only to permanent partial disability was similarly found unconstitutional by the Arkansas Supreme Court[169]

In another approach, for injuries occurring after 1993, **South Dakota** prescribes that permanent total benefits are subject to offset where the employee is receiving Social Security Old Age benefits.[170] The amount payable after the offset is to equal 150 percent of the compensation to which the employee is entitled less the Social Security Old Age benefit. Also, this offset is not applicable where the employee was entitled to or receiving Social Security Old Age benefits at the time of injury.

Once a worker attains the age of normal retirement, various forms of economic security are available to the majority of workers. The primary benefit to which most retired workers are entitled is Social Security Old Age benefits. In addition, many workers are eligible for pension benefits funded in whole or part by employer contributions. (The following chapter covering benefit coordination will address in greater detail the offsets when Social Security benefits and other programs for which the worker is eligible are payable.)

While not an offset provision *per se*, a small number of states terminate entitlement to certain income replacement benefits when the injured worker becomes eligible or begins to receive Social Security retirement benefits. **Florida, Kentucky, Montana,** and **Tennessee** terminate the payment of permanent total disability once the injured worker qualifies for old-age federal benefits. **Minnesota** discontinues permanent total disability benefits at age 67 because the employee is presumed retired from the labor force.

---

[167] Pa. Stat. Ann. Title 77 § 71
[168] *Golden v. Westark Community College* 969 S.W.2d 154 (1998)
[169] *State of West Virginia vs. Richardson* 482 S.E.2d 162 (1996)
[170] S.D. Codified Laws Ann. § 62-4-7

Chapter Seven

CLAIMS MANAGEMENT, FRAUD AND SUBROGATION

CLAIMS MANAGEMENT

The observed increase in workers compensation claim liabilities and ultimate losses are attributable to a combination of external factors – those factors outside the control of risk management such as rate levels and medical inflation – and internal factors such as those associated with the investigation and management of claims. This chapter focuses on how claims practices can influence claims costs and contribute to the increase or decrease of such liabilities.

The first critical step following any workplace accident is for the employer to shut down any machinery or operation that presents an immediate hazard to other workers or property and to ensure appropriate medical care for the injured worker. This is the responsibility of the employer, and management should be properly instructed in the methods and procedures to follow in the case of a work-related incident.

Once the employer takes these initial steps and ensures that the injured worker is in receipt of appropriate medical attention, the next responsibility is to notify the insurance carrier or third-party administrator (hereafter those two entities are referred to as benefit administrator) of the incident. The injury should be immediately reported to the benefit administrator when the claim involves a serious or catastrophic injury.

For the benefit administrator, the entire workers compensation claim process begins with the employer's filing of the First Report of Injury (FROI). The FROI documents the basic information concerning the employer, the injured worker, and the particulars surrounding the accident. These particulars include when and how the accident happened, the part or parts of the body injured, and the type of injury.

A copy of the ACORD Workers Compensation First Report of Injury can be found on the following pages. (ACORD is a non-profit organization in the insurance industry that is widely recognized for the publication and maintenance of an extensive archive of standardized forms.) Pages two and three of the FROI form are not included as they are state specific requiring an employee signature. While individual states have designed their own FROI, the ACORD form is accepted for usage in virtually every jurisdiction.

WORKERS' COMPENSATION - FIRST REPORT OF INJURY OR ILLNESS

EMPLOYER
- EMPLOYER (NAME & ADDRESS INCL ZIP)
- CARRIER / ADMINISTRATOR CLAIM NUMBER *
- REPORT PURPOSE CODE *
- JURISDICTION *
- JURISDICTION LOG NUMBER *
- INSURED REPORT NUMBER
- OSHA CASE NUMBER
- EMPLOYER'S LOCATION ADDRESS (IF DIFFERENT)
- LOCATION #:
- PHONE #
- INDUSTRY CODE
- EMPLOYER FEIN

CARRIER / CLAIMS ADMINISTRATOR
- CARRIER (NAME AND ADDRESS)
- POLICY PERIOD   TO
- CLAIMS ADMINISTRATOR (NAME AND ADDRESS)
- PHONE (A/C, No, Ext):
- CHECK IF APPROPRIATE   SELF INSURANCE
- PHONE (A/C, No, Ext):
- CARRIER FEIN *
- POLICY / SELF-INSURED NUMBER
- ADMINISTRATOR FEIN *
- AGENT NAME:
- AGENT CODE NUMBER:

EMPLOYEE / WAGE
- NAME (LAST, FIRST, MIDDLE)
- DATE OF BIRTH
- SOCIAL SECURITY NUMBER
- DATE HIRED
- STATE OF HIRE
- ADDRESS (INCL ZIP)
- SEX: MALE / FEMALE / UNKNOWN
- MARITAL STATUS: UNMARRIED/SINGLE/DIVORCED / MARRIED / SEPARATED / UNKNOWN
- OCCUPATION / JOB TITLE
- EMPLOYMENT STATUS
- E-MAIL ADDRESS:
- PHONE
- # OF DEPENDENTS
- NCCI CLASS CODE *
- RATE   PER: DAY / WEEK / MONTH / OTHER
- AVERAGE WEEKLY WAGES
- # DAYS WORKED / WEEK
- FULL PAY FOR DAY OF INJURY? (Y / N)
- DID SALARY CONTINUE? (Y / N)

OCCURRENCE / TREATMENT
- TIME EMPLOYEE BEGAN WORK   AM / PM
- DATE OF INJURY / ILLNESS
- TIME OF OCCURRENCE   CANNOT BE DETERMINED   AM / PM
- LAST WORK DATE
- DATE EMPLOYER NOTIFIED
- DATE DISABILITY BEGAN
- CONTACT NAME
- TYPE OF INJURY / ILLNESS
- PART OF BODY AFFECTED
- PHONE (A/C, No, Ext):
- DID INJURY / ILLNESS EXPOSURE OCCUR ON EMPLOYER'S PREMISES? (Y / N)
- TYPE OF INJURY / ILLNESS CODE *
- PART OF BODY AFFECTED CODE *
- DEPARTMENT OR LOCATION WHERE ACCIDENT OR ILLNESS EXPOSURE OCCURRED
- ALL EQUIPMENT, MATERIALS, OR CHEMICALS EMPLOYEE WAS USING WHEN ACCIDENT OR ILLNESS EXPOSURE OCCURRED
- SPECIFIC ACTIVITY THE EMPLOYEE WAS ENGAGED IN WHEN THE ACCIDENT OR ILLNESS EXPOSURE OCCURRED
- WORK PROCESS THE EMPLOYEE WAS ENGAGED IN WHEN ACCIDENT OR ILLNESS EXPOSURE OCCURRED
- HOW INJURY OR ILLNESS / ABNORMAL HEALTH CONDITION OCCURRED. DESCRIBE THE SEQUENCE OF EVENTS AND INCLUDE ANY OBJECTS OR SUBSTANCES THAT DIRECTLY INJURED THE EMPLOYEE OR MADE THE EMPLOYEE ILL
- CAUSE OF INJURY CODE *
- DATE RETURN(ED) TO WORK
- IF FATAL, GIVE DATE OF DEATH
- WERE SAFEGUARDS OR SAFETY EQUIPMENT PROVIDED? (Y / N)
- WERE THEY USED? (Y / N)
- PHYSICIAN / HEALTH CARE PROVIDER (NAME & ADDRESS)
- HOSPITAL OR OFFSITE TREATMENT (NAME & ADDRESS)
- INITIAL TREATMENT:
  - NO MEDICAL TREATMENT
  - MINOR: BY EMPLOYER
  - MINOR CLINIC / HOSP
  - EMERGENCY CARE
  - OVERNIGHT HOSPITALIZATION
  - FUTURE MAJOR MEDICAL / LOST TIME ANTICIPATED
- WITNESS NAME:
- WITNESS NAME:
- PHONE (A/C, No, Ext):
- PHONE (A/C, No, Ext):
- PHONE NUMBER
- DATE ADMINISTRATOR NOTIFIED
- DATE PREPARED
- PREPARER'S NAME
- TITLE

ACORD 4 (2013/01)
IAIABC 1A-1 (1/1/02)
© 1993-2013 ACORD CORPORATION. All rights reserved.
REPRINTED WITH PERMISSION OF IAIABC
The ACORD name and logo are registered marks of ACORD

EMPLOYER'S INSTRUCTIONS

DO NOT ENTER DATA IN FIELDS MARKED *

DATES:
Enter all dates in MM/DD/YY format.

INDUSTRY CODE:
This is the code which represents the nature of the employer's business which is contained in the Standard Industrial Classification Manual or the North American Industry Classification System published by the Federal Office of Management and Budget.

OSHA CASE NUMBER:
Transfer the case number from the OSHA 300 log after you record the case there.

CARRIER:
The licensed business entity issuing a contract of insurance and assuming financial responsibility on behalf of the employer of the claimant.

CLAIMS ADMINISTRATOR:
Enter the name of the carrier, third party administrator, state fund, or self-insured responsible for administering the claim.

AGENT NAME & CODE NUMBER:
Enter the name of your insurance agent and his/her code number if known. This information can be found on your insurance policy.

OCCUPATION / JOB TITLE:
This is the primary occupation of the claimant at the time of the accident or exposure.

EMPLOYMENT STATUS:
Indicate the employee's work status. The valid choices are:

Full-Time	On Strike	Unknown	Volunteer
Part-Time	Disabled	Apprenticeship Full-Time	Seasonal
Not Employed	Retired	Apprenticeship Part-Time	Piece Worker

DATE DISABILITY BEGAN:
The first day on which the claimant originally lost time from work due to the occupation injury or disease or as otherwise deigned by statute.

CONTACT NAME / PHONE NUMBER:
Enter the name of the individual at the employer's premises to be contacted for additional information.

TYPE OF INJURY / ILLNESS:
Briefly describe the nature of the injury or illness, (eg. Lacerations to the forearm).

PART OF BODY AFFECTED:
Indicate the part of body affected by the injury/illness, (eg. Right forearm, lower back).

DEPARTMENT OR LOCATION WHERE ACCIDENT OR ILLNESS EXPOSURE OCCURRED:
(eg. Maintenance Department or Client's office at 452 Monroe St., Washington, DC 26210)

If the accident or illness exposure did not occur on the employer's premises, enter address or location. Be specific.

ACORD 4 (2013/01)

ALL EQUIPMENT, MATERIAL OR CHEMICALS EMPLOYEE WAS USING WHEN ACCIDENT OR ILLNESS EXPOSURE OCCURRED:

(eg. Acetylene cutting torch, metal plate)

List all of the equipment, materials, and/or chemicals the employee was using, applying, handling or operating when the injury or illness occurred. Be specific, for example: decorator's scaffolding, electric sander, paintbrush, and paint.

Enter "NA" for not applicable if no equipment, materials, or chemicals were being used. NOTE: The items listed do not have to be directly involved in the employee's injury or illness.

SPECIFIC ACTIVITY THE EMPLOYEE WAS ENGAGED IN WHEN THE ACCIDENT OR ILLNESS EXPOSURE OCCURRED:

(eg. Cutting metal plate for flooring)

Describe the specific activity the employee was engaged in when the accident or illness exposure occurred, such as sanding ceiling woodwork in preparation for painting.

WORK PROCESS THE EMPLOYEE WAS ENGAGED IN WHEN ACCIDENT OR ILLNESS EXPOSURE OCCURRED:

Describe the work process the employee was engaged in when the accident or illness exposure occurred, such as building maintenance. Enter "NA" for not applicable if employee was not engaged in a work process (eg. walking along a hallway).

HOW INJURY OR ILLNESS / ABNORMAL HEALTH CONDITION OCCURRED. DESCRIBE THE SEQUENCE OF EVENTS AND INCLUDE ANY OBJECTS OR SUBSTANCES THAT DIRECTLY INJURED THE EMPLOYEE OR MADE THE EMPLOYEE ILL:

(Worker stepped back to inspect work and slipped on some scrap metal. As worker fell, worker brushed against the hot metal.)

Describe how the injury or illness / abnormal health condition occurred. Include the sequence of events and name any objects or substance that directly injured the employee or made the employee ill. For example: Worker stepped to the edge of the scaffolding to inspect work, lost balance and fell six feet to the floor. The worker's right wrist was broken in the fall.

DATE RETURN(ED) TO WORK:

Enter the date following the most recent disability period on which the employee returned to work.

In most instances, the FROI is completed by the employer but may be completed and filed by the injured employee, or a representative filing on behalf of that individual. Those responsible for completing the FROI – usually a manager or supervisor at the employer's place of business – should conduct a basic, factual inquiry of the details of the accident and complete the initial accident report in keeping with the company's safety policies. This initial investigation is an opportunity to identify any unsafe work conditions and identify any witnesses who can support or contradict an alleged claim. Questions at this point should be limited to verifiable facts and conditions and not speculation or personal opinion.

All managerial and supervisory personnel should be trained in conducting a basic accident investigation. Ideally, management should also be involved in reviewing the injury report before it is sent to the benefit administrator to ensure that it is accurate, thorough, and completed in accordance with company and benefit administrator guidelines. However, it is important not to delay the submitting of the FROI as such delay may result in an unnecessary interruption in the payment of benefits where the injury is properly related to the employment.

Many companies have plant safety committees review accident reports on a regular basis to determine whether the accident arose as a result of human or mechanical error and to decide whether further action is required (additional training and education, safety reinforcement, adjustments to machinery or processes, etc.). Internal investigations are often conducted to determine the actual cause of the accident and to implement remedial action to prevent a recurrence of a similar injury in the future.

Once the supervisor's report is completed and reviewed by company management, it is forwarded to the benefit administrator. Establishment by the benefit administrator of a workers compensation claim begins with receipt of the FROI from the employer or the employee's representative. The benefit administrator will have a case manager (CM) assigned to handle the claim. Claims involving only medical payments and certain short-term lost-time claims may be handled by a member of the clerical staff. Any claim involving questions as to compensability and periods of extended lost time should be assigned to a CM. Where permitted by the state, the benefit administrator will file a copy of the FROI with the appropriate administrative agency on behalf of the employer.

ROLE OF CASE MANAGER

The case manager is the individual responsible for handling a claim following receipt of the FROI. The value of communication skills is an important attribute of the case manager. Today, CMs interact with injured workers who may not understand even the most rudimentary entitlements available to them through the workers compensation program. In addition, they must be proficient in managing human relations on a number of different levels. On the surface, they must be able to relate to the injured worker and possibly the worker's attorney. In addition, they must also interact with medical providers, legal representatives, and establish a relationship with the employer.

Following verification of coverage, a responsibility of the CM is the determination as to whether or not an investigation of the accident is required. This determination can be based on the CM's instinct and experience or, in certain instances, specific categories of claims that have been designated for further investigation as a matter of routine (e.g., heart claims, stress claims, injuries occurring in the parking lot, recreational and social injuries, or claims involving the potential for fraud or subrogation). There is a wide gamut of claim situations that may require investigation and, in some instances, the employer may be the one to "flag" a questionable case and request an investigation when submitting the FROI.

For many benefit administrators, the CM is responsible at the outset of the claim to ensure that immediate contact is made with the employer, the injured claimant, witnesses, and medical providers to verify information related to the claim. Equally important is the need for the CM to listen carefully to the answers and follow up on unusual or inconsistent information. Inexperienced claim handlers often appear to be following a list of predetermined questions and may hesitate to deviate from the script. Claims that in retrospect could have been properly denied if certain information been collected and had the investigation been thoroughly completed and thoughtfully assessed prior to making a determination accepting the claim as compensable.

Proper management of a workers compensation claim by the CM incorporates several key areas, all of which interact and combine to influence the claim's outcome (e.g., initial handling, investigation, reserving, medical management, etc.). With today's technology, some of these activities may be handled electronically or delegated to specific individuals or departments for completion. However, the CM should be the one responsible who ensures that the following steps are taken timely and completed accurately:

COVERAGE VERIFICATION

While a final determination of the compensability of a claim must await the results of the claims investigation, the CM must make a threshold determination regarding the potential for coverage issues. The initial question following receipt of a FROI is whether the accident is covered under a particular policy of insurance. This determination depends on a number of factors, including:

- Correct identification of the employer. Errors can arise in any situation, and it is important to be aware of situations involving dual employment, former employees, employee leasing, temporary hires, contractors and subcontractors and independent contractors.

- Is the employee protected by workers compensation? As a general rule, workers compensation is provided for employees who work full-time, for wages, although there are generally special provisions for volunteers, trainees, part-time workers, casual employees, etc.

- Is there a workers compensation policy in force that covers the date of the injury?

It is important to keep in mind that this initial step in the claim process is designed only to eliminate those claims where there is no potential for coverage. The determination of the compensability of the claim is determined once coverage has been verified.

ESTABLISHMENT OF THE CLAIM FILE

The CM commonly receives and evaluates the employers FROI and related documentation that serves to initiate the claim and opens a claim file. The type of documentation the file will eventually need is reflected in the checklist below. In most states, the benefit administrator files the FROI for cases where the loss time extends beyond the statutory waiting period for benefits with the industrial accident board or commission on behalf of the employer. OSHA will accept its own form, or a form filed with the insurer or state that contains the same information.

As the information is compiled, a file should be created. A checklist of file documentation may include:

- First Report of Injury form

- Supervisor or manager's incident report that may contain additional information regarding the accident

- Employee wage and compensation rate documentation

- Preliminary and follow-up medical reports indicating type and severity of the injury along with the estimated period of disability

- Witness statements (as required) along with any follow-up investigation reports

Activities undertaken by the case manager following the reporting of a claim are oftentimes viewed as administrative tasks – simply following a checklist of scripted items. The checklist may include such items as assessing immediate medical treatment needs, making three-point contact (contact with the employer, the injured worker, and the medical provider), assigning the claim to the appropriate adjuster for additional investigation, reviewing statements, and gathering documents (e.g., medical authorizations, photos, police reports, and wage statements).

Following these basic steps that take place in the early stages of a claim may not be of significance for the majority of reported claims that resolve quickly, but for that small percentage of claims upon which the majority of the benefit dollars are ultimately expended, proper claims management from the outset is crucial to achieving optimal claims results.

Another key initial activity is adjuster assignment. For example, claims where the injured employee reports injuries to non-specific or multiple body parts, such as "neck, shoulder, leg or arm" may present an element of subjectivity, uncertainty, and potential complexity. It is important that the adjuster thoroughly investigate precisely how the injury occurred – including statements from any witnesses – and communicate with the medical providers about the types of injuries that can result from that activity.

BENEFIT INITIATION AND MONITORING

Once the CM has determined the claim to be compensable, the CM establishes the appropriate payments required for wage reimbursement, medical services and other expenses and ensures that these payments are properly documented. There is the additional responsibility to ensure that initial payments are made promptly in line with state laws and regulations and that subsequent payments are also paid timely.

Wage replacement benefits are generally determined as a percentage of the worker's average weekly wage (AWW) subject to state maximum and minimum benefit amounts. In those states where the maximum weekly benefit is based on a percentage of the statewide average weekly wage (SAWW); this maximum amount is subject to change annually. In addition, some benefits may be subject to an annual cost-of-living adjustment. The CM needs to be aware of the most current level of benefit entitlement that the injured worker is entitled to and ensure that benefits are being paid accordingly.

In many companies today, supervision of the medical treatment along with the determination of the need for vocational rehabilitation services is provided by specialists in those areas. These specialists will make a determination as to the proper medical treatment and whether rehabilitation services are warranted. Medical bill review and medical bill adherence to a state fee schedule may be handled internally through staff or by an outside vendor.

Once initial payments have begun, the work of day-to-day management begins. For claims of extended duration, the CM, within acceptable guidelines, must order periodic medical reports, surveillance if appropriate, rehabilitation or return-to-work evaluations, etc. In addition to medical management, there is the need to deal with outside vendors and the legal management of the case where an attorney is involved. In some organizations, functions such as medical oversight, rehabilitation evaluations, litigation management along with other unique functions may be handled by other specialists either inside or outside the organization.

Finally, there is a further element to claims management that is not directly related to handling individual claims. This is the area of program improvement ensuring that the claims process itself is efficient, cost effective and meets acceptable standards. Recurring problems need to be recognized and addressed timely.

CASE RESERVING

The goal of reserving is to have the ultimate (final) value of the claim established as soon as practical, with the understanding that the ultimate value of the most serious claims is subject to change. The reserve amount is the number of dollars necessary to pay the financial and legal obligations associated with the claim. Accurate reserving is very important to the employer. If claim file reserves are set too high, the dollar amounts used in the calculation of future insurance rates are overstated causing the insurance premiums to be higher than it should be. When reserves are set too low, there is an opposite effect resulting in lower insurance rates than needed to cover the exposure.

The information needed to establish a precise reserve is normally not available upon initial receipt of the claim. In many instances, necessary medical information will not be available for some time after the claim has been reported. There are two primary approaches used in setting the initial reserve early when the necessary medical information is not available. The first approach is for the CM to "guesstimate" (a combination of guessing and estimating) based on what claims with similar injuries have cost in the past. The second approach is to use a statistical reserve where all claims have the same initial reserve amount based on the historical average of past closed claims.

Reserving, while formerly done manually by an adjuster or CM is today often times electronically computed on the basis of a formula. With the computerization of the claims process, there is a wide spectrum of data that may be incorporated for purposes of establishing an individual claim reserve. However, for ease of reflecting what goes into the reserving process, it is beneficial to view it in terms of how a reserve would be established manually.

In manually computing a reserve – even when referred to as a "guesstimate" – the CM will in most instances utilize a worksheet that is broken down into three categories – medical, indemnity and expense.

> **Medical** - To establish the amount of the medical reserve, the CM will need to review the medical reports to provide an informed estimate of the ultimate cost in the following sub-categories:
>
> Physicians
> Specialists
> Diagnostic Testing
> Hospitals
> Physical Therapy
> Occupational Therapy
> Pharmacy
> Transportation
> Attendant Care

Few work comp claims will require an estimated amount in every medical reserve sub-category so only those applicable in a particular claim would be completed.

Indemnity - To establish the amount of the indemnity reserve, the adjuster will analyze the medical reports and discuss with the employer any planned modified duty options in order to establish an informed estimate of the claim cost based on if and when the injured worker will be able to return to work. Consideration would also be made for any permanent residuals that may be associated with the injury along with the need for vocational rehabilitation. Dollar values would be assigned in the appropriate following sub-categories:

> Temporary Total Disability
> Temporary Partial Disability
> Permanent Partial Disability
> Permanent Total Disability
> Vocational Rehabilitation
> Death Benefits
> Dependent

Most files will have only two or three of the indemnity sub-categories completed. For example one file might have only reserve amounts for temporary total disability and permanent partial disability, while another file might have only the category of death benefits completed.

Expenses – All aspects of the claim need to be considered when estimating the ultimate dollar amount for the various sub-categories of the expense reserve. Expense reserves include:

> Defense Attorneys
> Surveillance Court Costs
> Medical Reports
> Court Reporters
> Independent Medical Examinations
> Experts
> Any Other Expense

Once the reserve worksheet is completed, the dollar amounts for medical, indemnity and expenses are totaled to produce the overall dollar reserve for the claim.

Completion of the initial reserve worksheet is not the end of the responsibility when reserving the claim. When new medical information or legal information is obtained that changes the medical prognosis, extent of the indemnity payment or the legal responsibility on the claim, the CM should review the reserves in each of the categories of medical, indemnity and expense and make any necessary adjustments, whether they are increases or decreases in the reserve amount.

One of the most prominent short-comings of manual reserving is the tendency to under-reserve. This involves taking the most optimistic view toward the claim outcome and setting the reserve based on "best-case scenario." This approach will often lead to "step-laddering" of reserves whereby reserves are periodically adjusted upward over the life of the claim as new information develops or as open reserves exceeded the amount of money already expended.

Formula reserving, while not perfect, through its wide usage of available information and broad-based prior experience will set a reserve at the most probable amount of ultimate exposure, and adjust that figure up or down as new information is received.

INFORMATION COMPILATION AND DATA COLLECTION

The collection and compilation of information pertinent to the claim is essential for efficient case management. Where an investigation is required for the determination of compensability, it is important that that function is done timely. A delay in the investigation may lead to delays in the payment of benefits that are due thereby resulting in unnecessary attorney involvement and litigation. Furthermore, even where an investigation is completed timely and thoroughly, if pertinent information captured from that investigation is not entered into discrete data fields in one location in the file system, the ability to identify claims with the potential for substantial dollar exposure may be missed.

Depending on the complexity of the claim, the following may be included in the file:

- Copy of any investigation report(s) along with witness statements

- Copies of signed agreements to compensation

- Ongoing medical reports

- Initial and quarterly claim status evaluation

- Independent medical exam report and rehabilitation evaluations

- Letters from the employer extending offer of return-to-work or restricted duty employment

- Copies of accident board/commission decisions and/or requests for hearings or appeals

- Copies of (subrogation) notice letters sent to third parties

In addition to the above, file "notes" may include entries such as the date of a reserve review, an adjuster's failed attempt to contact a party, the payment of a bill, comments by the medical and vocational rehabilitation specialists, the date a processing decision was made, the scanning of a document into the file, or the receipt of a police report with no substantive commentary, or other information pertinent to the handling of the claim.

Finally, in the process of compiling information and conducting an investigation concerning a claim, it is critical to keep in mind an adjusters' code of conduct or code of ethics.

CODE OF ETHICS FOR ADJUSTERS

All states have a code of conduct or code of ethics for claim adjusters. Many states' codes of ethics are based on **Florida's** Ethical Requirements for All Adjusters and Public Adjuster Apprentices (the "Ethical Requirements").[171]

The work of adjusting insurance claims engages the public trust. An adjuster shall put the duty for fair and honest treatment of the claimant above the adjuster's own interests in every instance. The following are standards of conduct that define ethical behavior, and shall constitute a code of ethics that shall be binding on all adjusters:

(a) An adjuster shall not directly or indirectly refer or steer any claimant needing repairs or other services in connection with a loss to any person with whom the adjuster has an undisclosed financial interest, or who will or is reasonably anticipated to provide the adjuster any direct or indirect compensation for the referral or for any resulting business.

(b) An adjuster shall treat all claimants equally. An adjuster shall not provide favored treatment to any claimant. An adjuster shall adjust all claims strictly in accordance with the insurance contract.

(c) An adjuster shall not approach investigations, adjustments, and settlements in a manner prejudicial to the insured.

(d) An adjuster shall make truthful and unbiased reports of the facts after making a complete investigation.

(e) An adjuster shall handle every adjustment and settlement with honesty and integrity and allow a fair adjustment or settlement to all parties without any compensation or remuneration to himself or herself except that to which he or she is legally entitled.

(f) An adjuster, upon undertaking the handling of a claim, shall act with dispatch and due diligence in achieving a proper disposition of the claim.

(g) An adjuster shall not negotiate or effect settlement directly or indirectly with any third-party claimant represented by an attorney, if the adjuster has knowledge of such representation, except with the consent of the attorney. For purposes of this subsection, the term third-party claimant does not include the insured or the insured's resident relatives.

---

[171] Florida's Administrative Code 69B-220.201

(h) An adjuster shall not advise a claimant to refrain from seeking legal advice, nor advice against the retention of counsel or the employment of a public adjuster to protect the claimant's interest.

(i) An adjuster shall not attempt to negotiate with or obtain any statement from a claimant or witness at a time that the claimant or witness is, or would reasonably be expected to be, in shock or serious mental or emotional distress as a result of physical, mental, or emotional trauma associated with a loss. The adjuster shall not conclude a settlement when the settlement would be disadvantageous to, or to the detriment of, a claimant who is in the traumatic or distressed state described above

(j) An adjuster shall not knowingly fail to advise a claimant of the claimant's claim options in accordance with the terms and conditions of the insurance contract.

(k) An adjuster shall not undertake the adjustment of any claim concerning which the adjuster is not currently competent and knowledgeable as to the terms and conditions of the insurance coverage, or which otherwise exceeds the adjuster's current expertise.

(l) No person shall, as a company employee adjuster or independent adjuster, represent him- or herself or any insurer or independent adjusting firm against any person or entity that the adjuster previously represented as a public adjuster.

ACCIDENT INVESTIGATION

Following establishment of a claim file, where there is a question of compensability, an accident investigation should be conducted. The accident investigation will usually be assigned to a claims adjuster by the CM. This investigation is geared toward determining the cause of the accident, the type and scope of injuries involved, and to identify any third-party recovery opportunities.

In addition to following the code of ethics in conducting an accident investigation, an adjuster must demonstrate good communication skills, be a good listener, and possess a basic understanding of human nature and motivation principles. The adjuster must be comfortable not only dealing with people, but dealing with them in times of stress, and sometimes in a climate of conflict or adversity

As regards cases for investigation, at one end of the spectrum are incidents involving no lost-time or situations where the injured employee has already returned to work. These claims may be handled under the company's safety procedures and may require little investigation beyond the employer's accident report and the completion and submission of the FROI.

At the other end of the spectrum are those accidents that result in serious injury or the potential for litigation, which should be handled under a company's special investigation procedure. Situations that almost always warrant the involvement of a special investigation along with perhaps the guidance of counsel include:

- Serious injury or death cases.

- Claims alleging an occupational disease.

- Accidents caused by or involving third parties.

- Accidents occurring off-premises, or while the employee is off-duty.

- Accidents involving exposure to chemicals or environmental hazards, which may affect a great number of employees.

- Intentional injuries or actions, including those involving the allegation of intentional infliction of emotional distress and bad faith/unfair claims practices.

- Cases involving injuries by one employee to another.

- Dual capacity cases, in which the employer occupies an additional legal status besides employer, such as landowner, physician or product manufacturer.

- Accidents that involve a third party or where the accident is the result of a defect in a third-party product.

CONDUCTING THE INVESTIGATION

In conducting the investigation, the adjuster must decide whether to interview the claimant and witnesses by telephone, or in person. The advantage to an in-person interview is that the adjuster can make a better appraisal of character and truthfulness and there is also a greater opportunity to control the testimony in a written statement. On the other hand, in-person interviews are costly and, in many cases, impractical. Adjusters can handle a larger volume of cases more efficiently by telephone, especially when the claimant or witness is located a significant distance from the claim office of the benefit administrator.

The purpose of the claim investigation is to obtain detailed information regarding the occurrence of the accident, the time and location, how the event happened, the names of any witnesses to the event, and to whom was the injury reported. The type of claim involved will dictate the format to follow and the particular questions that need to be answered. The important thing is to obtain as much detailed information as possible that pertains to the particular claim. This information should be developed using the wording expressed by the person being interviewed.

Whether an in-person or telephone interview is conducted, the interview should be done as soon as possible following establishment of the claim file so that details are neither forgotten nor obscured and there is less chance for fabrication. The adjuster must use good listening and analytical skills to get all the pertinent information out of an interview, evaluating each aspect as it is heard, directing the balance of the interview so that the necessary information is developed.

The adjuster needs to keep the interview on track and guide the process. Throughout the process, the adjuster should avoid questions that are too broad, leading, argumentative, or that have multiple parts. The nature of information needed in a workers compensation claim is the same whether the interview is taken in person or recorded by telephone.

The signed statement – usually the result of an in-person interview – is used for those cases that may later be the subject of controversy and subsequent litigation. In such cases, the statement should follow a definite format such as the following:

- **Identification** – Note the date, time, and place of the statement at the upper part of the first page with the number and date on each of the following pages.

- **No Open Spaces** – Avoid any open space on the page, including margins or indentations, to prevent the addition of other information at a later time.

- **No Erasures** – Mistakes or errors are to be crossed out instead of erasing. Any corrections should be inserted in the space above the cross-outs, and all cross-outs, additions, or changes should be initialed by the person being interviewed.

- **No Shortcuts and Shorthand** – Refrain from using abbreviations, shorthand, or acronyms. All words, including names, should be spelled out in full.

- **Phrasing** – To the extent possible, write the statement using the language of the person being interviewed.

- **Acknowledgment and Certification** – The person who is interviewed should read the statement in its entirety and make any necessary changes. At that point, a certification line is to be added to the statement indicating that the interviewee has read the statement and that it is true. The statement is endorsed by the interviewee's signature at the end. In addition, all statement pages should be individually numbered and signed.

- **Witness Signature** – The signature of the person being interviewed should be formally witnessed (by signature) and dated on each page. Ideally, the witness should be someone other than the adjuster, but if this is not possible, the adjuster can sign as a witness.

A properly conducted telephone interview will take less time than an in-person interview and should be prefaced with a pre-interview call where a mutually convenient time for the recorded interview is arranged. In the pre-interview call, the adjuster should walk through the recorded interview format and give the person some time to secure the necessary information and possibly complete a brief sketch for reference purposes. It should be clear that the format will be a question-and-answer interview, dealing only with the facts and circumstances of the accident and not addressing coverage or ultimate responsibility for the claim.

While similar in format to that for a signed statement, the following guidelines are appropriate for recorded interviews:

- **Date, Time, and Location** – The recorded interview should begin with the date, time, and location where the interview is being conducted.

- **Identify all Parties** – The interviewee (the person being interviewed) should be identified along with information concerning his employment and activity with the employer.

- **Establish Permission to Record** – The person being interviewed should acknowledge on the record that he/she understands the interview is being recorded and that it is done with the person's full knowledge, consent, and permission.

- **Obtain Complete Record of Event** – Like the written statement, the crux of the recording should be directed toward obtaining all the detailed information regarding the occurrence of the accident, the time and location, how the event happened, who were a witness, and any events that followed after the accident occurred.

- **Ensure Proper Spelling** – All proper names and locations and anything other than ordinary terms or words should be spelled out.

- **Avoid or Explain Interruptions** – Those in the room with the interviewee should be discouraged from interrupting while the conversation is being recorded. If necessary or useful to the investigation, the other parties can be interviewed later. Any interruptions that do occur should be explained on the tape. Notations should also be made if there is a break made to change tapes and the interviewee should be identified again.

- **Changes or Corrections** – Any offer to make changes by the interviewee should be made on the record and necessary changes referenced.

- **Closing Acknowledgment** – As with an in-person statement, the interviewee needs to be asked if he/she understood the questions asked and has answered them truthfully. This exchange should also be on the record.

- **Termination of Interview** – The interview should conclude with the interviewee's permission and acknowledgement that all information relevant to the claim has been provided. As a precaution, it is recommended that, while the person is still on the phone, the adjuster should play back the end of the interview to ensure that it was recorded.

Once the interview is concluded, the recording may be filed or transcribed. In routine cases, the recording is usually filed, with a summary of the interview along with the interviewer's impression of the person interviewed. In more serious cases, the recording is transcribed and sent to the person interviewed so as to provide an opportunity to note any corrections or changes. In such case, the interviewee is also requested to sign a written acknowledgment that the transcript accurately reflects the recorded conversation; and that the statements included in the transcript are true and correct.

A complete accident investigation, whether conducted in-person or via a telephone interview, includes the objective development and evaluation of all facts, observations, opinions, statements of both the injured employee and any witnesses to the event. The accuracy and thoroughness with which information and data is obtained and recorded will largely determine the quality of the final report and the ultimate determination of compensability. Raising the basic questions of who, what, why, when, where, and how helps to focus the investigation in the right direction and to cover critical aspects of the claim.

TIMELY CLOSURE OF CLAIM

Following the completion of all compensation payments – medical and indemnity – on the file, along with the assurance that the injured worker has returned to his/her former employment, or some alternative form of employment, the claim file is ready for closure. This type of conclusion occurs in the majority of workers compensation claims. Where required by the state administrative agency, necessary reports concerning the period of disability along with a breakdown of medical payments are to be reported.

In a small percentage of cases, claims are closed through a settlement process known generically referred to as lump sum settlements. All but a handful of states permit the indemnity portion of the claim to be resolved through a lump sum settlement, but a dozen states do not permit settlement of the medical portion of a claim. In many instances, injured workers appear to prefer to take their benefits in a lump sum and put the compensation process behind them, even if some of the benefit is paid at a discounted rate.

Under a lump sum settlement, attorneys can collect their fees more promptly and easily. More significant, perhaps, is that in many jurisdictions the amount that the attorney is able to charge is directly related to the size of the lump-sum payment. Thus, with the insurer, the worker, and the worker's attorney are typically supportive of lump sum settlements. Their frequent use is common in certain jurisdictions.

Lump-sum settlements can create problems in those jurisdictions that permit settlement of the medical portion of the claim. For example, benefits under Social Security Disability Insurance limit the combined benefits of the two programs to 80 percent of the worker's average current earnings. The issue becomes how to compute the lump sum benefit, net of attorney fees, for purposes of the offset, where a portion of the settlement represents an amount to pay for future medical costs associated with the injury.

In the past, many settlements were negotiated on the basis that a sizable portion of the settlement was for future medical so that the offset would be established against a smaller amount of the lump sum settlement. This is no longer appropriate since Medicare has taken steps to ensure that any medical associated with the work-related injury is not passed on to Medicare. Medicare requires approval of all settlements over a certain dollar threshold. (The subject of coordination between workers compensation benefits and Social Security and Medicare will be covered in greater detail in the final chapter.)

ATTORNEY-CLIENT PRIVILEDGE AND WORK PRODUCT DOCTRINE

Attorney-client privilege is based on the theory that people will not seek legal advice if there is a chance that their communications with the lawyer may be revealed to other parties. In addition, a lawyer can only provide effective representation if he or she is aware of all the pertinent facts known to the client. The elements required to establish the existence of the privilege include: a communication made between privileged persons; the communication is in confidence; and, the communication is for the purpose of seeking, obtaining, or providing legal assistance for the client.

Note that the communication must be for the purpose of obtaining legal assistance. Routine reports of corporate or business decisions that are relayed to counsel for purposes of information are generally not protected under the privilege. Thus, communications to attorneys conducting special investigations are not generally privileged unless the investigation serves as a basis for legal advice to the corporation. The retention letter or internal memo to counsel asking that the investigation be initiated should specifically request counsel's legal advice based on the ultimate results of the litigation.

There is no question that the attorney client privilege extends to corporations as well as individuals; the only issue is which corporate employees are included within the scope of the privilege. In answering this question, the Supreme Court has adopted the "Subject Matter" that requires that the following elements must be present for the attorney client privilege to apply: (1) a communication was made for the purpose of seeking and rendering legal advice to the corporation; (2) the communication was made by an employee at the direction of his superior; and, (3) the subject matter is within the scope of the employee's duties.[172] An issue left unresolved in the *Upjohn* decision is whether communications between former employees and counsel are covered by the privilege. Judicial opinions on this issue are varied. In those cases where the privilege has been extended, the key factors include:

Knowledge – Was the former employee the person with the best knowledge of the facts?

Confidentiality – Did the attorney and former employee treat the communication as confidential?

Common Interest – Was there any evidence that the former employee's loyalties or interests were significantly opposed to those of the corporation?

Once established, the attorney client privilege can be waived by the client or through disclosure. Where the privilege is asserted by a corporation as a client, it can be waived by a person or persons in a position of control. The work-product doctrine was adopted to protect the files and mental impressions of an attorney, and to provide a certain limit of privacy for an attorney to properly prepare the case. First espoused in the United States Supreme Court decision in *Hickman v. Taylor,* 329 U.S. 495 (1947), the work-product doctrine is based on the following three elements:

---

[172] *Upjohn Co. v. United States,* 449 U.S. 383 (1981)

- Material collected by an attorney in preparing for anticipated litigation is protected from disclosure.

- With certain exceptions, the protection provided in discovery under the work-product doctrine is not absolute; an opponent may overcome the privilege with a showing of substantial need and undue hardship in obtaining it.

- The attorney's mental impressions, thoughts, theories and analysis (termed "opinion" work-product) *are* afforded the greatest protection under the doctrine.

As later codified in the Federal Rules of Civil Procedure, the work product doctrine is limited to materials prepared in anticipation of litigation or trial. While there is no acid test as to what constitutes a likelihood of litigation, most courts require more than a mere possibility of litigation for application of the privilege. But the more liberal view supports extending the privilege if the motivation for creating the material was the possibility of future litigation, however likely the possibility is.

While the opposing party must show undue hardship and substantial need to overcome the privilege afforded by the work-product doctrine, an exception is made in the case of expert witnesses. Under the Federal Rules, a party is entitled, without showing need, to learn:

- The identity of (opposing) experts to be called at trial.

- The facts and opinions on which they are expected to testify.

- The grounds for their opinions.

Like the attorney-client privilege, the privileges afforded by the work-product doctrine can be waived or otherwise denied protection by disclosure or use of the materials at trial. The attorney's notes and other memoranda revealing his or her mental processes or opinions in evaluating the case, witnesses, and communications have an absolute privilege under the work-product doctrine. Since the privilege is absolute, it should survive a showing of substantial need by the other party.

WORKERS COMPENSATION FRAUD

The subject of fraud in the context of workers compensation frequently elicits the image of a worker making a claim for compensation benefits where the injury actually occurred as a result of some non-occupational cause or activity, or the worker continues to receive disability benefits while working for remuneration paid under the table. Related to this image is the secondary notion that a sizeable portion of the benefit dollars available through the system are going to those who perpetuate fraud.

Actually, no one has a good grasp of the extent of fraud in the workers compensation system. The first thing lacking is a uniform definition of what constitutes fraud so as to ensure that when people discuss the topic, they are making "apples to apples" comparisons. To some, fraud constitutes any form of abuse including malingering that delay the period of recovery, while for others, a deliberate and intentional act of deception must take place before the activity is considered fraudulent.

Notwithstanding the above, workers compensation fraud is a serious offense and is not a victimless crime. Workers compensation fraud translates into lower wages, lost jobs, higher premiums and higher prices for products and services. All consumers ultimately pay the price of fraud and whether that price is three percent or 20 percent, steps need to be taken to reduce its impact on the system.

When discussing the subject of insurance fraud, or more specifically for purposes here, workers compensation fraud, it is important to place the term in its proper context. As defined in Black's law Dictionary, *"Fraud consists of some deceitful practice or willful device, resorted to with intent to deprive another of his right, or in some manner to do him an injury."* Stated another way, fraud is the intentional perversion of truth in order to induce another to part with something of value or to surrender a legal right, or an act of deceiving or misrepresenting.

Thus, fraud is an intentional misrepresentation of material existing fact made by one person to another with knowledge of its falsity and for the purpose of inducing the other person to act, and upon which the other person relies with resulting injury or damage. In the case of workers compensation, a fraudulent act would result in the payment of benefits or the payment or reimbursement of expenses when the same are not warranted, or the affording of insurance coverage or protection in exchange for the payment of inadequate premium.

This general description of fraud is intended to distinguish the completely fraudulent situations from those scenarios where the system is being abused. While there is the potential for overlap between the instances of fraud and those of abuse, it is important to attempt to distinguish between the two. In the simplest terms, fraud occurs when someone knowingly and with intent, presents or causes to be presented, any written statement that is materially false and misleading to obtain some benefit or advantage, or to cause some benefit that is due to be denied. If there is no material written or verbal lie, there may be abuse, but the discretion does not rise to the level of fraud. In contrast, workers compensation abuse is any practice that uses the compensation system in a way that is contrary to either the intended purpose of the system or the law. This may include some behavior that is not criminal and some that is, most significantly, fraud.

Merely filing a claim that is not warranted or violating the rules of the workers compensation system, in the absence of fraud (a lie) or kickbacks, may be abuse, but it is not criminal. The specific elements of fraud must be present. Similarly, over-treatment by a physician might represent a difference in opinion where, although it may appear excessive and possibly abusive, it does not necessarily constitute fraud.

The presence or absence of a specific, provable false statement is the deciding factor. To separate fraud from abuse, it is necessary to look for the material written or verbal lie that was presented or caused to be presented. For example, engaging in some form of employment while receiving temporary disability payments might be an abuse or it might be fraud, depending upon the circumstances. If temporary disability benefits continue when the claimant has returned to work, and no one ever asks the claimant "are you working?" there is an abuse of temporary disability benefits, but there is no written or verbal lie and therefore no action that attains the level of employee fraud.

In separating criminal workers compensation fraud from abuse, the **New York** Workers Compensation Fraud Inspector General has identified the following key elements:

- There is always a false representation – the lie.

- The lie must be intentional or knowingly made.

- The lie must be made for the purpose of obtaining a benefit the claimant is not due, denying a benefit that is due, or obtaining insurance at less than the proper rate.

- The lie must be material, that is, it must make a difference. *"If the truth had been told, would you have done anything differently?"*

Questions relative as to what activities represent fraud and what represent abuse will always be difficult to distinguish but each serves to add costs to the system. Suffice to say that there is a difference between fraud and abuse, and that the difference is generally associated with the happening of a written or verbal false representation.

PERPETRATORS OF WORKERS COMPENSATION FRAUD

Who are the potential perpetrators of workers compensation fraud? Virtually any person or party associated with the program has the potential to engage in one type of fraud or another. As seen in the following, no party to the workers compensation program is immune:

- Employees who obtain improper benefits through intentional deception.

- Employers who avoid payment of proper insurance premiums through a variety of schemes; often to gain a competitive advantage in the marketplace.

- Medical care providers, who bill for services not rendered, misrepresent their services, receive kickbacks for referrals and/or contribute to a worker receiving improper benefits.

- An extreme form of fraud occurs where organized workers compensation fraud rings make a practice of recruiting people to file phony work injury claims. Workers are sent to medical clinics or legal referral centers (commonly known as "claim mills"), which in turn refer them to a doctor or lawyer who is in on the scheme

- Employers, carriers, and medical agents/experts who knowingly act to deny or dispute legitimate claims by workers; and, probably in the most extreme case

- Attorneys, usually in conjunction with a group of medical providers, who organize medical "mills" to treat non-existent injuries and attempt to resolve claims through quick lump sum settlements

The following describes in greater detail the various principal parties in the workers compensation program and how fraud may be perpetrated:

Fraud Perpetrated by Workers – When it comes to fraud in the workers compensation program, we are usually drawn to employers, doctors, and lawyers because those are the cases that tend to involve large dollar amounts. While there are opportunities for ordinary workers to exploit the system, it must be recognized that most workers decline to do it. Employee fraud occurs when an employee knowingly, either verbally or in writing, lies about, or causes another to lie about a material fact to obtain or continue workers compensation benefits to which she/he are not entitled. The following are examples of several different types of employee fraud.

Self-inflicted or intentional injury – Most state workers compensation laws preclude the payments of benefits where the injury is a result of an intentional act. To illustrate this type of fraud, two cases – ironically one from the East and the other the West coast – provide a couple of interesting examples.

In the first example, the manager of a **Massachusetts** service station reported to local police that he had been assaulted and robbed while taking cash receipts to the bank. To authenticate the assault, the manager sported a bruised face and a seriously injured eye. Under police questioning, his story did not hold up and the manager eventually confessed to stealing the deposit money. In 2007 the manager was charged with larceny and making a false report of a crime. In April he pled guilty to both charges and was sentenced to one year of probation and was also required to reimburse the insurance company for stolen payroll.[173]

The interesting sidebar to this case involves the question as to what about the supposed work-related injury to the employee's eye. The manager confessed that he had a friend give him a hard punch to the face, to make his story more credible. This hard punch had permanently damaged his vision. Because, initially, the injury appeared to arise out of and in the course of employment, the workers compensation insurer paid both medical expenses and indemnity benefits. Following the filing of charges for larceny, the insurer sought reimbursement and referred the matter to the Massachusetts Fraud Bureau. Following his indictment, the service station manager was required to reimburse the workers compensation insurer for the medical and indemnity payments.

So along with committing workers compensation fraud, the service station manager demonstrated a unique form of incompetence. He not only botched the fake robbery, had to repay the medical expenses and ill-gotten indemnity benefits, and, due to his friends' competence in mashing him in the face, has permanent impaired vision.

---

[173] A press release from MA Attorney General Martha Coakley dated July 23, 2008.

The "Monday" morning injury – The Monday morning injury has long been suspected of being a significant problem for the workers compensation program. This issue has tended to increase rather than lessen as more employers have discontinued employee access to non-occupational health and disability benefits. This problem is centered in the employee sustaining some form of injury over the weekend but waiting until returning to work on Monday morning and then reporting the injury as work-related. For example, the employee while skiing over the weekend or after work sustains a strain or sprain of the knee. Rather than having the knee injury treated at the time and paid for through the non-occupational health insurance, the employee waits until the following work shift and reports a work-related injury to the employer shortly after reporting for work.

Back injuries that involve a delay in reporting or unwitnessed events are other potential signs of a possible fraudulent claim.

Malingering or working while allegedly disabled – In addition to the forms of employee fraud noted above, there is also the potential for fraud following the occurrence of a legitimate work-related injury where the purpose of the fraud is to retain or continue the payment of compensation benefits when they should terminate. This type of fraud is represented in the scenario where the injured worker is receiving compensation benefits for a legitimate work-related injury and begins to work and denies any written or verbal inquiries from the employer or insurer regarding present work status. This sometimes occurs in relatively minor injury claims where there is an extended period of recovery or inability to return to work. In some instances, the treating physician, who is furnishing medical care to the injured worker, may abet this type of fraud.

In one example of this type of fraud, a **Connecticut** correction officer injured his back while lifting a box of toilet paper and soap at the New Haven Correctional Center. While collecting workers compensation benefits, the claimant decided that he wanted tickets to see a Hannah Montana concert. In an attempt to win tickets, he entered a contest that required him to dress as a woman, wear high heels, and run a 40-yard dash carrying an egg in a spoon. News crews and photographers filmed him running the dash and thousands of people – including his boss – saw him on TV. The officer was subsequently charged with one count of workers compensation fraud and faced up to 20 years in prison if convicted. And, to make the story complete, he did not win the race for those tickets.[174]

An important question to consider is what do employers, insurers and other benefit administrators need to be looking at to prevent the various forms of worker fraud. The list could be long, but the following provides just a partial list of some of the more common items on which to focus:

- Delayed reporting of the injury.

- Strains or sprains reported at the beginning of a work shift without witnesses.

---

[174] Story carried on the morning news on Channel 7 WABC-TV out of New York on March 26, 2008.

- The worker's account of the cause of the injury is vague or contradictory.

- Subjective complaints of injury are not medically diagnosed.

- The worker "shops" for caregivers and/or is non-compliant.

- The worker has a history of multiple workers compensation claims.

- The worker is aware that he/she may be "laid off" in the near future.

- The worker's employment status was in jeopardy prior to injury.

Fraud on the part of covered employees cannot be completely eliminated, but careful scrutiny surrounding the type of employees hired can be an important factor in controlling for fraud in the future.

Employer Fraud – Employer fraud occurs when the employer knowingly misrepresents the truth in order to avoid or deny compensation for legitimate work-related injuries, or falsifies policy-related information. Another form of employer fraud involves the employer who alleges to have purchased insurance coverage, but in fact has taken no such action. This type of employer fraud may entail the employer falsifying the Proof of Insurance and posting notice to employees indicating that insurance coverage is in force.

State compensation laws, with the exception of **Texas**, require employers to secure their workers compensation exposure either from some form of insurance or through self-insurance. Failure on the part of the employer to secure such coverage for their workers compensation exposure can result in serious fines or penalties. Many of the state workers compensation administrative agencies or insurance departments are becoming more proficient in monitoring this area of coverage to ensure that when a policy expires – or is cancelled – by one insurer, that there is another legitimate contract of insurance. Workers who are injured during the period when no coverage is in force are the ones most at risk. Unless the employer is financially able to provide benefits for the injured worker, the injured worker is left without compensation and medical care. In several states, there is no recourse for the worker of an uninsured employer except the courts.

But failure to obtain insurance is not the only way for employers to cheat the system. One of the areas of concern is the effort by employers to designate certain employees as independent contractors so as to remove those workers from the employer's responsibility to provide workers compensation coverage, afford coverage for periods of unemployment, and for the withholding of social security, federal and state taxes. In Chapter Two, the situation involving the ongoing saga with independent contractors in **California** represents a continuing issue that is likely to be extended into other jurisdictions.

But failing to obtain insurance, or designing employees as independent contractors, are not the only means by which employers can defraud the system. Other types of fraud are of particular concern to the insurance carrier since the act is nearly always perpetuated in order to circumvent payment of the appropriate amount of premium. In some instances, the agent or broker may assist the employer in engaging in this type of fraud.

Under reporting of payroll – The most obvious form of employer fraud is that of concealing payroll from consideration in the determination of insurance premium. For purposes of determining an employers' workers compensation premium, the system relies upon the employer reporting fully the amount of wages paid. This reporting of payroll is not done on an individual employee basis, but rather the cumulative wages of all employees by classification of employment.

The employer may submit financial statements that reflect only a portion of the actual payroll or may provide an estimate of payroll that is knowingly understated. While this form of fraud is often detected at the time of payroll audit, it is not unusual for the delay factor to result in inadequate premiums paid by the employer for a couple of years.

Misclassification of payroll – The NCCI has developed a classification system for workers compensation. The classification system is the insurance industry's way of lumping together employers with a similar likelihood of claims. The rate that is assigned to each classification anticipates the ultimate cost of all claims in that classification, plus insurance company overhead and profit. Since rates anticipate future claims, they must come from a base large enough to provide statistically valid conclusions. If that base is too small the rates will not closely match the ultimate cost of claims in that classification. The only way to insure a large enough rate base is to limit the number of classifications that are available. This is the underlying rationale for the workers compensation classification system.

Because rates vary by classification, the potential exists for employer fraud involving the misclassification of payroll. The classification for each form of employment determines the insurance rate that should be paid for each $100 of payroll. Where the employer has workers engaged in more hazardous occupations – and those occupations carry a higher rate per hundred dollars of payroll – there is the potential to manipulate the system in this fashion.

While there are many examples of employer fraud, the misclassification of payroll is the most frequent. To insure a roofer, the employer may have to pay ninety dollars in workers compensation premium for every hundred dollars in payroll. In other words, the cost to the honest employer is more than twice as much per hour (when all employer obligations are added together) to send the worker unto the roof than that worker's paycheck would suggest. But to obtain coverage for a clerical person working for that same employer, the rate is only a few cents per hundred dollars of payroll.

For the dishonest employer, the solution is obvious - classify the roofer as a clerical person. That worker's cost, instead of adding substantially to the employer's workers compensation premium, would increase it only slightly. But, if the "fake" clerk falls off the roof, the insurer is still responsible for all of the bills associated with the medical care and income replacement benefits.

Medical Provider Fraud – The following snip is taken from an article prepared by Associated Press correspondent Kelli Kennedy from the December 24, 2008 edition of the Miami Herald.

> *"Three days a week, Philip Audette sat in a cushy white chair at the St. Jude Rehab Center, a needle pumping HIV drugs into his arm. He talked and laughed with a dozen other patients, all in good health, all receiving drugs they didn't need. All for the money. Audette says he made $100 to $200 every visit, nearly $10,000 over several months, selling his Medicare number to the clinic's three owners, the Benitez brothers, who were later indicted on charges of bilking $119 million from Medicare.*

Authorities say there are thousands in South Florida like Audette, and federal officials say they play a large role in the fraud overwhelming the national Medicare system. While authorities are successfully cracking down on clinic owners, they disagree over whether prosecutors should go after the patients who get the phony treatments in addition to the clinics that provide them.

While the above is reflective of Medicare fraud, one can see how easily it may be transferred to the workers compensation program – especially where the workers compensation program affords first dollar coverage without deductibles or co-insurance and is prompted by the system to reimburse medical providers timely.

Medical provider fraud occurs when the provider falsifies – either in written or verbal form – information regarding the basis of any billing for services or benefits alleged to have been provided. Provider fraud is also identified with the furnishing of inappropriate treatment or rendering of unnecessary services in order to inflate fees and seek recovery for services over and above those provided. This frequently entails the ordering of multiple tests or x-rays that are unnecessary and may in actuality be detrimental to the health of the patient. This type of fraud may occur with legitimate work-related injuries without the knowledge or consent of the injured worker.

Attorney Fraud – The more typical example where attorney fraud occurs is when either an attorney or licensed representative knowingly participates in the misrepresentation of the truth in order to secure or deny compensation for their clients and/or themselves. This type of fraud may involve simply the acts of the attorney or may be conducted in conjunction with an unscrupulous benefit administrator or medical provider facility.

In one of the more outrageous cases captured by a television station in **California**, recruiters known as "cappers" solicited workers to file workers compensation claims while they were in the line for unemployment benefits. These workers were told that they could receive higher weekly benefits by filing for workers compensation rather than unemployment. Many of these claims alleged mental stress and other soft tissue injuries difficult to deny. Following a series of expensive tests by the medical treating mills, the attorneys sought to resolve the claim through negotiated lump-sum settlements. Here was a case of fraud being perpetuated by the alleged employees, medical providers, and attorneys.

Indicators of potential fraud from medical providers and attorneys are combined because of the similarity of practices and the potential for coordinated activities between the two groups. Some of these indicators include:

- Bills from a health care provider or attorney that present an unreasonable number of hours per day.

- Extensive medical treatments for relatively minor or subjective injuries. This often entails unnecessary x-rays and testing.

- Boilerplate reports coming from the same physician's office for more than one injured worker.

- Treatment being directed to a separate facility in which the referring physician has a financial interest.

- A relationship between an attorney and health care provider that appears to be a partnership in the handling of workers compensation cases.

- A specific firm has a high incidence of claims without evidence of a legitimate dispute or work history.

Benefit Administrator Fraud – Having identified the part played by other major workers compensation program participants; it would not be fair to ignore the potential of benefit administrator fraud. Insurance carriers and benefit administrators may also be guilty of fraud when a claims handler purposely misrepresents the truth in order to deny or support a claim, or where the claims handler accepts any form of consideration in exchange for the referral or settlement of a claim.

Benefit administrators are in a somewhat unique position when it comes to fraud. In the first place, when benefits are not properly and timely tendered, many states allow for the imposition of fines and penalties. In the second place, a number of states permit the injured party to bring a direct action for damages based on the theory of bad faith against the benefit administrator.

The two principle elements of a bad faith claim are that an unreasonable claim decision has been made and that knowledge on the part of the insurer or benefit administrator that the decision was unreasonable or that the entity failed to conduct an adequate investigation in order to determine whether its decision was reasonable or not. The subject of insurer and benefit administrator bad faith is discussed more fully in Chapter 11.

Before leaving the subject of insurer fraud there is an additional aspect to consider. Fraud may also be identified in the insurance agent or broker community. In a **New Jersey** case, an insurance broker was among seven individuals and eleven corporations charged for their alleged roles in a pair of workers compensation scams. The defendants were accused of lying on insurance applications and failing to remit insurance premiums to the insurance companies. As a result, many people were allegedly left without workers compensation coverage.

FRAUD PREVENTION

Approaching the subject of fraud from the perspective of the various system participants is not meant to imply that fraud is rampant in the system or even that a high percentage of claims are fraudulent. Rather, it is important to recognize where the potential for fraud may exist as the first step toward uncovering and addressing that type of activity. Each type of fraud involves certain warning signs of the potential existence of fraud and these signs should be recognized and taken seriously.

When contemplating the subject of fraud in the workers compensation program, the famous line by Willie Sutton seems appropriate. When asked by a newspaper reporter, "Why do you rob banks?" Willie justified his activity by responding, "Because that's where the money is."

The same response applies when addressing fraud in the workers compensation system. It may appear to be a good use of available funds to go after the individual claimants who are taking advantage of the system, but to be truly effective, the focus should be directed at the areas where big money is being siphoned out of the system. Catching and punishing individual claimants may provide amusing newspaper headlines, but real dollars can be saved when employers, medical providers working in conjunction with attorneys, cheating the system are identified, closed down, and brought to justice.

As has been identified in the foregoing, virtually every participant of the program has the potential to perpetuate fraud in some form or fashion. Just the limited illustrations noted above are sufficient to demonstrate that all aspects of the workers compensation program have the potential for fraud. While the list could go on at some length, the following provides a short list of 10 ways for employers and benefit administrators to prevent employee fraud.

1. Have in place a clear and concise written policy statement about the importance of promptly reporting all accidents and injuries to the appropriate personnel. Have in writing that the filing of a false claim is grounds for immediate termination.

2. Require prompt reporting of claims and convey that report immediately to your carrier or claims administrator along with any suspicious conditions that may require further investigation. Late reporting of claims increases lost time and medical cost, fosters abusive claims, and increases the probability of expensive litigation.

3. Re-enact accidents to determine what happened and how the hazard can be avoided in the future. The emphasis of the reenactment should be safety and injury prevention but may serve to uncover any fraud or abuse.

4. Have a supervisor accompany the injured worker to the provider for emergency or, with the employee's permission, to initial non-emergency treatment. Getting the injured worker treated by a high-quality doctor is one of the best means of avoiding exaggerated claims.

5. The employer should remain in contact with the medical provider and injured worker to discuss return to work options. Be wary of employees that miss medical appointments and are not available when you call.

6. Review all renewal applications to determine if current payroll being reported is consistent with any business expansion or contraction.

7. Review all renewal applications to identify any substantial changes in employee classifications that may improperly reflect a lowering of insurance exposure.

8. Determine if a new business or renewal application has any workers deemed by the employer to be independent contractors.

9. Scrutinize all medical and vendor billings to ensure that the services rendered are consistent with the injury being treated or service requested.

10. Be alert for multiple claims of the same or similar nature coming through a particular medical facility and/or firm of attorneys.

SUBROGATION

In insurance law, the principle of subrogation dictates that an insurer who has paid a loss under an insurance policy is entitled to all the rights and remedies belonging to the insured against a third party with respect to any loss covered by the policy. Essentially, subrogation allows an insurer who has indemnified an insured to stand in the shoes of the insured as regards the insured's claim for compensation against a third party, usually a tortfeasor.

Subrogation serves a number of purposes. One of the principal reasons underscoring the support for subrogation provisions is that they serve to preclude a double recovery. A double recovery occurs when the injured party files a claim on a single loss event with more than one insurer and obtains full reimbursement from each insurer. Double recovery violates the principle of indemnity which states that an insurance contract should not result in a profit for the insured. The primary purpose of insurance is to restore the injured party to their pre-loss condition.

A second important purpose for subrogation is to place the ultimate cost associated with the loss with the negligent third party or tortfeasor who caused the loss in the first place. Courts have repeatedly expressed that a goal of subrogation is to place the burden for a loss on the party ultimately liable or responsible for it and by whom it should have been discharged, and to relieve entirely the insurer or surety who indemnified the loss and who in equity was not primarily liable for the loss.

More than almost any other area of personal injury subrogation, workers compensation subrogation is fraught with traps and obstacles for those responsible for claims handling in this area. Every state compensation law recognizes the right of subrogation, but this is where the similarity ends. Upon review of state laws and their application, there are very few areas in which the laws of each individual state vary more and are applied as differently, than in the area of workers compensation subrogation. While the basic parameters of workers compensation claims from state to state remain somewhat constant, the laws regarding subrogation and their application vary greatly. Some of the specific areas where state laws differ in terms of addressing workers compensation subrogation issues include.

Time Frame for Seeking Recovery – Many states grant the insurer a right to independently, and apart from the worker, file a third-party action and pursue it. In other states, the injured worker is the true party in interest, and the workers compensation carrier is granted only a lien on the proceeds of any third-party recovery.

Some states grant the employee the exclusive right to bring an action within a certain period of time after which period the party paying compensation benefits may proceed with an action to recover such payments. For example, in **Maine**, if the employee fails to pursue a claim for recovering against a negligent third party within 30 days of the written demand by the employer, the right to subrogate is transferred to the employer. In **North Dakota**, the period is 60 days after which the employer may exercise an action in its own name as trustee of the injured worker. In **Hawaii, Massachusetts,** and **New Hampshire**, the time period is extended to a matter of months.

In a significant number of states, the injured party assigns his or her cause of action for third party damages against the third party to the employer or workers compensation carrier. Through such action the employer or insurance carrier is placed in the shoes of the injured worker. For example, under **Georgia** law, the employee retains his right to sue the third-party tortfeasor, but in the event that the employer's liability has been fully or partially paid, the employer or the employer's insurer is subrogated to the employee's right of action against a third party.

Allocation of Expenses – When an injured worker pursues an action for damages against a negligent third party, the workers compensation insurer may file a lien against any recovery realized by the injured worker. The amount of the lien is based on the indemnity payments and medical payments made by the insurer, and depending on the state, may include other benefits paid or to be paid such as vocational rehabilitation benefits. Also, depending on the state, the insurer may be given a credit for indemnity and medical payments to be paid in the future to the extent that the employee's net recovery exceeds the lien for payments already made.

What is found in virtually every state is that the employer's or carrier's lien is reduced by its pro rata share of the attorneys' fees and litigation expenses incurred by the employee in prosecuting the claim for recovery of damages. The **New Hampshire** law provides that after recovery on third party claims, expenses, and costs in the action, including attorneys' fees, is divided between the employer and the insurance carrier and employee as justice may require. In similar fashion, **Kansas** law sets forth that the court is to fix attorneys' fees which are to be paid proportionately by the employer and employee.

The issue of the proper allocation of expenses can become extremely complex in cases involving severe, long-term, and permanent injuries. This requires the computations of future payments of medical and indemnity benefits and translating that into present value dollars. This oftentimes becomes very subjective and another issue for possible litigation. Often times the carrier may simply agree to reduce its lien by one-third, ignoring both the future economic benefit it will receive and the litigation expenses incurred by the injured employee.

Distribution of Recovery – The original rule was that the employer or workers compensation insurer, after reduction of the number of damages collected minus expenses and attorney fees, is entitled to full reimbursement of compensation benefits paid out of any third party recovery. Not so surprisingly, numerous exceptions to this general rule have developed with the passage of time so that it is no longer appropriate to refer to it as a general rule.

The first exception for consideration is those jurisdictions in which the made whole doctrine has been introduced. The made whole doctrine is an equitable principle which generally limits the ability of an insurer to exercise its right of subrogation until the insured has been fully compensated or made whole. Under this doctrine, in the event of a subrogation dispute between the injured party and its insurer, the injured party has priority of rights to collect from the responsible third party. Thus, where the recovery from both the insurer and tortfeasor is less than or equal to its loss, the insurer forfeits its right to subrogation.

While **Georgia** is the sole state to legislatively incorporate the made whole doctrine into their workers compensation law, a number of other states, by judicial decision, have extended the doctrine into the workers compensation program. In **Indiana** the right of subrogation cannot be enforced until the whole debt is paid and the insured is thereby made whole.

Another example is found in the state of **Montana** where in 1977 the Montana Supreme Court rendered its opinion integrating the made whole doctrine into its insurance law.[175] The case involved a property insurance policy containing an expressed subrogation provision, which provided that *"the company may require from the insured an assignment of all right of recovery against any party for loss to the extent that payment therefore is made by the company."* The parties agreed that the insured's loss exceeded the policy limits, and that the insured would not be made whole when this amount was added to the tort recovery.

---

[175] *Skauge v. Mountain States Telephone & Telegraph Co.,* 565 P.2d 628 (1977)

The Supreme Court, following a review of the objectives of subrogation, adopted the rationale that when the sum recovered by the injured party from the tortfeasor is less than the total loss and thus either the injured party or the insurer must to some extent go unpaid, the loss should be borne by the insurer for that is a risk the injured party has paid it to assume. The *Skauge* holding has since been extended to workers compensation claims.[176]

In **Florida**, If the claimant recovers from a third-party tortfeasor either before or after the filing of suit, before accepting compensation or other benefits, or before filing a written claim for benefits, the amount recovered from the tortfeasor must be set off against any benefits other than for remedial care, treatment, and attendance or for rehabilitative services. In **Alabama**, the carrier is entitled to be reimbursed out of any judgment recovered by the employee or its representatives in a suit against the third party for all payments made by the employer which were included within the meaning of the word "compensation". Therefore, there can be situations when payments other than indemnity, medical, and death benefit payments can be recovered.

In **Oklahoma** there is no right of subrogation by the employer or the insurer for compensation paid for death caused by a third party. In the case of *McBride v. Grand Island Express,* the Oklahoma Supreme Court upheld a trial court opinion that insurers have no right to subrogation for workers compensation insurance death benefits paid to a deceased employee's beneficiaries.[177] Insurers who paid workers compensation death benefits can no longer intervene in third-party actions to recover under principles of subrogation.

The multiple complexities associated with the distribution of any subrogation recovery cannot be over-stated. Careful attention must be directed toward statutory provisions in effect at the time of the loss along with developing case law.

Excess Recovery Distribution – Following reimbursement of the benefit administrator's lien, if the injured party realizes a net recovery that is free and clear of attorneys' fees and costs, most states consider that recovery, or some portion of it, to constitute a credit to the benefit administrator, relieving it of paying future benefits until the credit is exhausted. In many instances, a recovery of a benefit administrator's credit or advance is more significant than reimbursement of its workers compensation lien. However, once again, the many different approaches of workers compensation subrogation in our country require a familiarity with the various state laws regarding such credits or advances.

In **Arizona**, the credit acts like a deductible and must be exceeded before the benefit administrator is obligated to make further benefit payments. The benefit administrator's future credit applies to all amounts recovered, including post-judgment interest. In Arizona, subrogating entities experience something unique since Arizona is one of the few states where the law does not allow a lien to be subject to a collection fee. Therefore, the worker's attorney's fees are deducted first from the gross recovery before reimbursement of the benefit administrator's lien. The remainder is the amount against which the benefit

---

[176] *State Comp. Ins. Fund v. McMillan*, 31 P.3d 347, 350 (2001)
[177] *McBride v. Grand Island Express* 2010 WL 5080933 (2010)

administrator has a lien, is reimbursed, and out of which any future credit it receives must originate

In some jurisdictions such as **Massachusetts**, once the benefit administrator has paid it's pro rata share of attorneys' fees and costs and is subjected to future claims for benefits; the employee's future claims for benefits are paid on a fractional basis. The law in the Commonwealth of Massachusetts provides that *"In determining the amount of "excess" that shall be subject to offset against any future compensation payment the board, the reviewing board, or the court in which the action has been commenced shall consider the fair allocation of amounts payable to and amongst family members who may have claims arising from the injury for which said compensation is payable."*[178]

In **Nebraska**, a benefit administrator must give notice to the worker's attorney and also to the third-party tortfeasor of its intent to take a credit. If it's a practical matter, the amount of any credit would then be negotiated with the employee as a part of the lump sum settlement of the workers compensation claim. After receiving its credit, the workers compensation benefit payments are suspended until the amount of compensation owed to the employee exceeds the amount of the employee's net recovery from the third-party tortfeasor.

In **Louisiana**, when a worker settles a third-party action, the benefit administrator is entitled to a credit or advance against future benefit payments. The benefit administrator has no right to any credit against any amount recovered by the plaintiff against the third-party for future medical expenses, unless there is an award for future medical expenses, and then only to the extent of the award for that item.

COMPARATIVE AND CONTRIBUTORY NEGLIGENCE

The foregoing has illustrated some of the issues associated with recovery of the amount that the benefit administrator paid to the injured worker in the form of workers compensation benefits. When addressing the subject of subrogation in any line of insurance – including workers compensation – it is important to keep in mind the issue of contributory negligence. While contributory negligence is not a factor when considering the payment of workers compensation benefits, contributory negligence is an issue of major consideration when an injured worker is seeking damages from a negligent third party.

When a claim for damages stemming from an accident is filed with a court, the factfinder (either a judge or a jury in the majority of situations) must first establish who caused the accident. This is followed by a determination of the extent of damages. In a typical situation, it is the party whose negligence caused the accident that is the one responsible for any resulting damages. Where more than one party or person caused the damage, then negligence may be distributed between the parties based on apportionment laws enacted in each state. The factfinder will be the one called upon to determine whether it was the actions of the defendant, the plaintiff, or both, that caused the accident. Based on the evidence submitted, a judge or jury will then allocate the

---

[178] Mass. Gen. Laws Ann. Ch. 152 § 15

amount or percentage that each party was negligent. Depending on the jurisdiction, this allocation will directly impact the amount of damages ultimately awarded.

Throughout the United States, there is essentially what can be described as four different systems used in establishing damage awards. These systems include pure contributory negligence, (pure comparative negligence, modified comparative negligence – 50 percent bar rule and modified comparative negligence – 51 percent bar rule.

The following briefly describes each of the different approaches along with identifying those states generally associated with that approach.

Pure Contributory Negligence – Historically, contributory negligence was a common law defense available in tort actions. Under the contributory negligence theory for recovery, if two people were involved in an accident, the injured person could only recover for his/her injuries and damages if that person had not contributed to the accident in any way. This approach was based on a policy originally established in England that stated a person who negligently causes harm to another cannot be held liable if that injured individual contributed to his own suffering and injury, even if it was only a very slight factor. [179]

To illustrate the impact of the contributory negligence defense, if two individuals were involved in an accident where one was injured, and if the injured party was only 5 percent at fault, that person would

> The *Butterfield* case is an interesting example inasmuch as Forrester (the defendant), while making repairs to his house, placed a pole across the road next to his house. Butterfield (the plaintiff), while riding at high speed at twilight, did not see the pole and struck same suffering personal injuries when he fell off his horse. A witness testified that visibility was 100 yards at the time of the accident and Butterfield might have observed and avoided the pole if he had not been riding at such a high speed. At trial, the jury returned a verdict for Forrester and Butterfield appealed. On appeal, it was held that if a plaintiff's conduct falls below the standard established by law for the protection of self against an unreasonable risk of harm, that plaintiff is contributorily negligent and cannot recover for personal injuries caused by a resulting accident. The court stated that in this case Butterfield would have seen the obstruction if he had used ordinary care. The accident was Butterfield's fault and due to his contributory negligence he may not recover. The court ruled that no injured plaintiff may recover damages against a negligent defendant if that plaintiff did not exercise reasonable and ordinary care to avoid the injury.

recover nothing. Any degree of negligence would be sufficient to preclude any recovery for damages. This method of calculating damages continues to be followed in only a small minority of jurisdictions.

While the defense of contributory negligence appears harsh, it must also be recognized that in certain cases, the contributory negligence defense can be overcome. If the plaintiff can

---

[179] *Butterfield v. Forrester,* 11 East 60, 103 Eng. Rep. 926 (1809)

prove that the defendant's willful and wanton acts caused the injury, then the defendant cannot claim contributory negligence as a bar to the plaintiff's recovery. Likewise, if the plaintiff can show that the defendant had the last clear chance to avoid an accident and did not do so, then the defendant can still be held accountable even if the plaintiff is found contributorily negligent.

Pure Comparative Negligence – Considering the potentially harsh result identified with the pure contributory negligence system, the majority of states have moved away from that strict approach to a form of a comparative negligence. In the United States, comparative negligence has been adopted as the basic rule of tort liability, principally by legislation but with a minority of states adopting the rule by judicial decision. Pure comparative negligence works in virtually the opposite way that pure contributory negligence operates. Under a comparative negligence system, the injured party may still recover some damages even if the injured party was partially at fault for the accident.

In states using a comparative negligence system, the factfinder determines the proportion of fault to be assigned to each responsible party. Currently, 13 states are generally recognized as following the pure comparative negligence system.

Modified Comparative Negligence - In addition to the pure comparative negligence systems, there the modified comparative negligence doctrine is a legal principle whereby the negligence is apportioned in accordance with the percentage of fault that the factfinder assigns to each party. According to this doctrine the plaintiff's recovery will be reduced by the percentage of negligence assigned to the plaintiff. In some states the plaintiff's recovery is barred if the plaintiff's percentage of fault is 50 percent or more. For example, the accident victim must be less than 50 percent responsible for the accident in order to recover damages. This is also known as 50 percent rule. A total of 33 states use some form of the modified comparative negligence system.

In nearly one-half the states, recovery is not barred so long as the injured party's negligence does not exceed the combined negligence of the party or parties from which recovery is being sought. In the states of **Illinois, Pennsylvania,** and **Texas,** the injured party's claim is barred if his/her negligence exceeds fifty percent of the combined fault of all the actors. Similar to the foregoing grouping, any recovery by the injured party is reduced in proportion to his/her negligence. **South Dakota** provides a slightly subjective approach on the subject. In South Dakota, a plaintiff's negligence does not bar recovery when it is slight in comparison with the negligence of the defendant.[180] However, it is to be noted that the term "slight" is a question of fact that varies with the facts and circumstances of each individual case.

NEGLIGENCE ON THE PART OF THE EMPLOYER

---

[180] S.D. Codified Laws Ann. § 20-9-2

A number of the state workers compensation statutes also address directly the subject of the reduction of the amount of any subrogation recovery based on the degree or percentage of the employer's fault. For example, **California** requires that the workers compensation carrier's subrogation recovery be reduced by a percentage representing the percentage of the employer's negligence. Therefore, a California carrier is only reimbursed for the amount by which its compensation liability exceeds its proportional share of the injured employee's recovery.

In **Louisiana**, the subrogation recovery allowed is identical in percentage to the recovery of the employee or his dependents against the third person, and where the recovery of the employee is decreased because of comparative negligence, the recovery of the person who has paid compensation or has become obligated to pay compensation is reduced by the same percentage.[181]

It is obvious from the foregoing material that the allocations of recovery schemes vary from state to state about as much as they possibly can. Knowing in which state the accident occurred or where an action for recovery has been filed is critical for purposes of maximizing any workers compensation subrogation recovery. These scenarios do not even take into consideration the possibility that the workers compensation carrier pays benefits under the laws of one state and vies for apportionment of a third-party recovery where suit has been filed in another state. This raises the ugly specter of conflict of laws in extraterritorial jurisdiction which would require a legal analysis to lie out and describe all the various scenarios.

As confusing and as variegated as the workers compensation subrogation laws are in this country, they become even more confusing and obfuscated when overlaid with other related subrogation issues such as lien reduction statutes, no-fault laws, tort reform and varying statutes of limitations, for both the worker and the benefit administrator. While the subrogation rights of a workers compensation insurer are many and varied, so are the possible ways of losing them, through inaction or ignorance. Every subrogation program owes it to educate its staff on not only the laws of the various states within its jurisdiction, but also the subrogation laws in any state in which it operates.

WAIVER OF SUBROGATION

Waivers of subrogation are a necessary aspect in the complex world of commerce and insurance. However, their application and effect on subrogation are frequently misunderstood. Some contractual arrangements, most frequently found in the construction industry, require the employer to waive their right of subrogation (and therefore the right of that of the benefit administrator) against them in the event of an accident.

One of the ways that have been developed to avoid subrogation is through the implementation and enforcement of waivers of subrogation. Just as the employer and the insurer have a legal right to pursue subrogation, a party to a commercial transaction has the right to structure the transaction so that the legal rights of recovery of the employer and insurer against another party

---

[181] La. Rev. Stat. Ann. § 23:1101

are limited. Such clauses, known as exculpatory clauses, have as their intent and effect, to limit an employer or that employer's insurer from subrogating against another party to a transaction.

From an historical perspective, the use of waivers of subrogation arose due to the provisions in a number of the original workmen's compensation laws which required the injured worker to make an election to either accept workmen's compensation benefits or to or to pursue a direct action for damages against the negligent third-party (the tortfeasor), but not both. Under the theory supporting the enactment of the original workmen's compensation laws, injured workers would elect the medical and indemnity benefits available under the workmen's compensation statute and return to work, thereby forgoing the uncertainty of any third-party action for damages.

It is to be noted that following the payment of medical and/or indemnity benefits, even though the injured worker was precluded from instituting an action for damages against the negligent third party, the compensation insurer was not prevented from filing its own claim against the negligent third-party. Under the subrogation provisions found in many of the first state workmen's compensation laws, insurers, following the payment of compensation benefits, were permitted to proceed against the negligent third party.

To preclude the insurer from pursuing a subrogation claim against the negligent third party, the waiver of subrogation form was developed. Provisions found in waivers of subrogation take various forms in commercial lines property and casualty insurance policies, as well as in workers compensation policies. Because there are many instances when the workers compensation claim may be caused by negligent actions by some other employer or contracting entity, a place to begin is to examine how the subject is addressed under the general liability policy.

It is common to find a waiver of subrogation clause in construction contracts. In many projects, the owners, architects and building contractors each sign a waiver for any damages covered by insurance. These contracts also generally require all of the parties to purchase hazard insurance to minimize risk and make certain that the project proceeds without financial loss to anyone if an accident should occur. The primary purpose of such waivers is to create a cooperative environment and reduce potential lawsuits.

Most insurers write general liability insurance on the Insurance Service Offices, Inc. (ISO) Commercial General Liability (CGL) Form CG 00 01. Condition 8 of the CGL policy affirms the carrier's legal right to subrogation and reads as follows:

> ***Transfer of Rights of Recovery Against Others to Us.*** *If the insured has rights to recover all or part of any payment we have made under this Coverage Part, those rights are transferred to us. The injured must do nothing after the loss to impair them. At our request, the insured will bring "suit" or transfer those rights to us and help us enforce them."*

A waiver of subrogation prior to a loss is permitted by the CGL coverage form. Condition 8 of CGL policy implicitly (though not expressly) permits an insured to waive recovery against a third party prior to loss. That waiver depends upon a contract separate from the CGL policy. It is possible that the contract language waiving the subrogation is flawed in some way thereby allowing an insurer to subrogate despite the wording of the contract.

Notwithstanding the use of waivers of subrogation in construction contracts, these waivers also play an important role in workers compensation insurance. As discussed in the chapter covering the standard Workers Compensation and Employers Liability Insurance Policy, the policy is designed under Part One to pay the statutory benefits specified by the compensation law of the states covered by the policy and under Part Two to cover the liability arising from a workplace injury when legal action is brought seeking damages other than the benefits provided under the compensation law.

Under the policy, the phrase "recovery from others" is used in place of the term "subrogation." The phrase can be found in both Part One and Part Two of the policy. The provision in subsection G. of Part One of the policy reads as follows: *"Recovery From Others We have your rights, and the rights of persons entitled to the benefits of this insurance, to recover our payments from anyone liable for the injury. You will do everything necessary to protect those rights for us and to help us enforce them."*

This clause simply describes the insurer's right to succeed to the same rights as the insured employer and the rights of those who have been the recipient of covered benefits. The policy provision also cautions the insured to do everything necessary to protect those rights.

The Recovery From Others provision found in Part Two of the policy is similar but more limited than the clause found in Part One. Unlike Part One, Part Two does not give the insurer the injured employee's rights, but only the rights of the employer against third parties. This difference is necessary because contractually, for Part Two coverage, the employer and not the injured worker are a party to the contract

Workers compensation policies require an endorsement to be added to the policy whenever there is a change requested from the standard policy coverage. Like the commercial general liability policy, an endorsement may be added to the standard workers compensation policy that waives the right of the insurer to subrogate. Such an endorsement may be written so as to apply to all contracts with a particular contractor or only to one contractor for one particular project.

Since the insurer is agreeing to pay claims without seeking reimbursement from the party or parties responsible for the injury, there is a cost or premium charge associated with the attachment of this endorsement to a policy. While the premium charge for the endorsement may vary by state, the insurer may charge up to two percent of the policy premium for blanket coverage or two to five percent of the project's premium for individual coverage.

The centralized organization responsible for policy forms and endorsements along certain rate-making activities in the majority of states is the National Council on Compensation Insurance (NCCI). The NCCI has developed form WC 00 03 13 (04/84), the Workers Compensation Waiver of Our Right to Recover from Others Endorsement, for purposes of waiving the insurers right to subrogation. States insurance departments may also promulgate special endorsements for the purpose of waiving subrogation rights. The wording for NCCI form WC 00 03 13 is as follows:

"We have the right to recover our payments from anyone liable for an injury covered by this policy. We will not enforce our right against the person or organization named in the Schedule. (This agreement applies only to the extent that you perform work under a written contract that requires you to obtain this agreement from us.) This benefit shall not operate directly or indirectly to benefit anyone not named in the Schedule."

Including the waiver of subrogation endorsement with a policy requires consideration for a number of factors. The biggest concern is that the waiver applies only to those firms that are listed on the schedule in the endorsement.

Most state workers compensation laws or case laws construing them, allow the employer and the insurer to waive its right to subrogate against a third party. Only about one-quarter of the states recognize the enforceability of waivers of subrogation. At the same time, states such as **Kentucky** and **Missouri** do not allow waivers of subrogation in the workers compensation setting and declares them contrary to public policy and void. These prohibitions against waivers of subrogation are the exception rather than the rule

There is some divergence in state law with regard to whether a waiver of subrogation merely prevents a carrier from filing a subrogation lawsuit against a third-party or whether it also prevents a benefit administrator from recovering its statutory right to reimbursement from the injured third party's recovery. In states such as **Texas**, they are construed to prevent both. Other states, such as **Alaska, Maine,** and **Wisconsin**, recognize the importance of workers compensation subrogation and allow recovery of the lien notwithstanding the existence of a waiver of subrogation endorsement.

The workers compensation waiver of subrogation is extremely common in today's contracts, particularly construction contracts. What is less clear is why. The reason could be that the contracting party is under the impression that the waiver will provide immunity from a third-party claim arising out of their subcontractor's workers compensation claim. If this is the hope, it's a false one. Again, to restate, a waiver of subrogation does not prevent the injured worker from bringing a direct action for damages against a third party responsible for the worker's injury. The waiver of subrogation only precludes the injured worker's employer and workers compensation benefit administrator from initiating a subrogation action and/or from enforcing its lien on a third-party claim. Thus, the only real winner from the use of the waiver is the injured worker who might receive a double recovery when the workers compensation lien does not have to be repaid to the employer. The contracting party loses or at least doesn't win since the waiver did not have the desired effect of preventing a third-party claim. The workers compensation benefit administrator loses because its right of recovery was forfeited.

Chapter Eight

COST CONTAINMENT STRATEGIES, MEDICAL RECORDS PRIVACY AND THE AFFORDABLE CARE ACT

In addition to the various types of income replacement benefits to which an injured worker may be entitled, when a covered employee has suffered a work-related injury, compensable hernia or occupational disease, the employer or its insurer is required to promptly provide all medically necessary and appropriate medical treatment. Such care and treatment include all medical services and surgical care including hospital and nursing services, medicine, orthopedic appliances and prostheses.

As noted in the chapter covering mandated medical benefits, medical care costs in the workers compensation program have continued an upward trend, growing faster than the overall Consumer Price Index measuring medical care costs. According to the National Council on Compensation Insurance (NCCI), medical care costs accounted for 58 percent of total workers compensation claim costs in 2008, compared with 42 percent for lost income payments. In 1987 the medical component represented only 46 percent of total costs.

CAUSES OF MEDICAL COST INCREASES

From the time of the passage of the original workers compensation laws until the early 1980s, policymakers paid little attention to the cost of the medical benefit component of workers compensation primarily because medical costs were a relatively small part of total expenses. In most states, medical costs represented one-third of the benefit dollar with benefits payable for indemnity and disability representing the remaining two-thirds.

However, beginning in the 1980s, workers compensation medical costs, along with medical benefits available from other sources (i.e., group health insurance, Medicare, Medicaid, etc.) began to rise. According to a report compiled by NCCI, during the last two decades of the 20th century, the medical severity of workers compensation claims cumulatively increased at a substantially faster pace than other healthcare costs in this country.

Rising medical costs continue to be recognized as a key cost driver in the workers compensation system. State legislatures, regulators and benefit administrators continue to look for ways to address rising medical costs and enact laws that alleviate the impact of healthcare costs on the workers' comp industry. However, caring for a worker injured as a result of a work-related injury is typically more expensive than general medicine, and as a result, workers compensation requires innovative cost-saving strategies while maintaining a high level of care.

Medicine, surgical procedures, drugs, and other forms of medical care have made incredible advances and health care now drives the cost of both wage replacement and medical care in many workers compensation cases. The treating physician's opinion of the case determines the duration of the disability, and in that portion of cases involving permanency, the extent of the permanent physical residuals of that injury.

At the same time, the individual's expectations of medical care may far outstrip anyone's ability to resolve the complex interactions between a worker's injury/illness, job satisfaction, labor relations, family and personal reactions to disability, and the legal system. Furthermore, there are differences in the way workers compensation patients are treated and who treats them that magnify the problem. Employers, benefit administrators, administrative state workers compensation boards, lawyers, and some other employee advocates all share a growing concern about the costs and quality of care rendered under the workers compensation system.

Before examining some of the medical cost containment strategies developed at the state level, it is well to examine some of the major factors that operate to drive general health care costs.

Cost Shifting – Total health care expenditures in the United States appears to have stabilized in recent years even though the rate of increase remains far in excess of inflation. Health care spending in this country grew 4.6 percent in 2019, reaching $3.8 trillion or $11,582 per person. As a share of the nation's Gross Domestic Product (GDP), health spending accounted for 17.7 percent. Health care cost, in their various forms, can be compared to a balloon – squeeze it in one place and it expands somewhere else.

Under current law, national health spending is projected to grow at an average rate of 5.5 percent per year for 2018-27 and to reach nearly $6.0 trillion by 2027. Health care spending is projected to grow 0.8 percentage point faster than Gross Domestic Product (GDP) per year over the 2018-27 period. As a result, the health share of GDP is expected to rise to 19.4 percent by 2027.[182] If the economy experiences an extended slowdown on the heels of COVID-19, health care could consume a much larger share and crowd out other needs, like education. Health care spending, excluding the impact of the pandemic, is projected by the government to continue to outpace economic growth, reaching 19.7 percent of the economy in 2028.[183]

In response to rising health care costs, Medicare has instituted the diagnostic related group (DRG) system of reimbursement which involves paying a set fee for an episode of a given illness. Medicare has also restricted the rate of increase for DRG's and other fees to a few percent a year. This pay schedule has been significantly below the rate of medical inflation. State and local programs have also resorted to reimbursement caps or discounted payment schedules in order to cope with rapid medical inflation and revenue shortfalls.

---

[182] https://www.cms.gov/Research-Statistics-Data-and-Systems/Statistics-Trends-and-Reports/NationalHealthExpendData/Downloads/ForecastSummary.pdf
[183] https://www.chcf.org/blog/health-care-costs-accounted-17-7-percent-gdp-2018/

Most group health insurance programs – designed to protect the worker and his/her family against the economic consequences of an injury or illness resulting from a non-occupational cause – contain large deductibles and/or co-payment arrangements that require the patient to exercise some judgment before purchasing medical/chiropractic services. As insurance costs increase for the employer, coverage is being discontinued in some instances, while in others, higher deductibles, higher co-payments, and more benefit caps have been introduced.

Workers compensation typically pays the full cost of medical care without application of deductibles or co-payments. Additionally, there is no maximum lifetime medical benefit under workers compensation nor are there a set of designed benefits. In workers compensation, all medical care or treatment necessary to realize a full and complete recovery is covered. Experience has shown that the group health plan design has served to moderate increases in insurance costs. The designed benefits plans are contrary to the philosophy of the workers compensation system, but they clearly reflect today's macro-economic aspects of health providers and health consumer behavior.

While cost constraints are being applied in the group health insurance programs, government programs such as Medicare and Medicaid pay for services at a set fee which is usually well below the cost of delivering those services. To compensate for these known lower reimbursements rates, providers typically set higher fees than they normally would if everyone paid the same amount. The drawback with this approach is that since workers compensation cases are paid at the level of first-dollar coverage, money "lost" on Medicare and Medicaid patients may be shifted to the workers compensation patient. Thus, the workers compensation program may end up paying an inflated fee for services. While it would not necessarily be a significant issue if the number of Medicare and Medicaid patients corresponded with the number of injured workers under worker compensation; Medicare and Medicaid patients far exceed the number of the full-pay workers compensation patients.

Prescription Drugs – Prescription drugs are a significant driver of the cost increases associated with medical care. According to the Centers for Medicare and Medicaid Services (CMS), while health care spending in the United States reached $3.8 trillion in 2019, retail prescription drug spending (10 percent of total health care spending) increased 5.7 percent in 2019 to $369.7 billion, accelerating from growth of 3.8 percent in 2018. Faster growth in use, or the number of prescriptions dispensed, contributed to the acceleration in total retail prescription drug spending, as prices for prescription drugs declined for the second consecutive year in a row, decreasing by 0.4 percent in 2019 after falling by 1.0 percent in 2018.[184]

As this impact of increasing drug costs relates to the workers compensation program, a recently released NCCI's research brief entitled, "Workers Compensation and Prescription Drugs - 2018 Update," breaks down the major factors that make up overall prescription drug costs for the industry. Among the findings:

---

[184] https://www.cms.gov/newsroom/press-releases/cms-office-actuary-releases-2019-national-health-expenditures

- The projected prescription drug share of total medical costs for Accident Year 2016 is 13.7 percent.

- Prescription drug costs per active claim have declined in 2015 and 2016 by two percent and four percent, respectively.

- Utilization is the main contributor to the decreases in 2015 and 2016.

- Prescription drug prices continue to rise, albeit at a slower rate than in previous years.

- Opioid costs per active claim have declined in 2015 and 2016 by three percent and seven percent, respectively. Such decreases are due to lower utilization.

- Physician dispensing and brand name costs per active claim have also declined in 2015 and 2016. These decreases are due to lower utilization as well.

- In-network prescription drug costs are lower than out-of-network drug costs.

- On average, brand name prescription drug prices have increased more than 10 percent per year in each of the last five years - with a cumulative increase of 80 percent since 2011.

- The top three drugs - Lyrica, OxyContin, and Gabapentin - account for more than 15 percent of prescription drug costs in 2016.[185]

Technology – The influence of technology operates to increase workers compensation medical costs in a number of ways. MRI's and other new medical technologies allow doctors to see inside the body and more accurately diagnose conditions. They also provide an opportunity to diagnose conditions earlier, leading to a more complete recovery for the patient, and in the case of workers compensation, a faster return to work. While the MRI, in some situations, replaced X-rays as a diagnostic tool there is always something new on the horizon. The use of PET/CT (positron emission tomography/ computerized tomography) scanners, which combine two types of radiological scans in one to create a highly accurate diagnostic tool, is growing fast in medicine. But like most new medical technology, the costs associated with the new technology are high. The PET/CT machines cost $2 million to $4 million to install, including structural renovations. The purchase and installation of this new equipment is justified only if there is sufficient utilization of the new device. That utilization transfers into additional costs for programs using the machine.

Similarly, new surgical techniques involving minimal cutting with fewer days in the hospital, or no in-patient stay at all, are also part of improvements in medical technology. Many of these new, less invasive procedures replace older, more complex procedures. Knee and hip replacement surgeries are more common and are likely to increase as the population

---

[185] https://www.workcompwire.com/2019/02/ncci-releases-2018-update-to-workers-comp-prescription-drugs-research-brief/

continues to age. Again, in many instances they serve to reduce the amount of time away from work, but at a significant medical cost.

New therapies and treatments improve the quality of life for patients suffering from chronic or terminal conditions. This includes drug therapies that allow people to lead normal, pain-free lives. Home health care has benefited from medical technologies, allowing for shorter hospital stays and more home-based care, as well as new types of equipment for home care.

While all of these advancements in medical technology allow patients to recover quicker and live longer, healthier lives, this advance comes with a price. Some experts suggest that medical technology when used in an out-patient hospital setting, physician's office and other out-patient settings actually decreases the cost of health care. This is because in general, treatment in an out-patient setting is less expensive than in-patient care. However, with workers compensation paying first dollar coverage with no cost for the patient and replacing a portion of income lost during the period of recovery, there is no way to study the actual savings (or increased costs) that may be realized due to the interrelationship and use of these more sophisticated tests and procedures.

Litigation – When originally enacted, the workers compensation program was intended to be a "self-administrating" program with a minimal need for attorney involvement and litigation. In exchange for the employer providing medical benefits and replacing a portion of pre-injury earnings, the injured worker gave up the right to sue the employer for damages for an injury "arising out of and in the course of" the employment. Notwithstanding the original intent, in actuality there has always been a significant degree of attorney involvement and litigation, with the amount of both increasing as disability benefits were adjusted to compensate a more adequate portion of the workers' pre-injury earnings.

Disputes arise over any number of issues including whether the injury arose out of and in the course of employment, whether the correct amount of benefits are being paid, whether the benefits have been paid timely, the existence and extent of permanent disability, and whether appropriate medical care is being provided. Each one of these issues carries a potential medical component. For example, differing medical opinions may exist as to whether a disease condition arose out of the employment. Medical consultations and tests required to determine the compensability of the claim can be expensive. The attorney involvement and litigation stemming from these disputes has served to increase both the amount of testing and treatment to prove the presence of an injury and to increase the amounts of settlements.

The above simply sets forth a few of the major factors that influence medical costs in the workers compensation system. The following will attempt to examine some of the more prominent efforts made at the state level to address these increasing medical costs.

COST CONTAINMENT STRATEGIES

In response to the costs associated with medical care and treatment, various methods have been introduced in the workers compensation program in an effort to control those costs. There are two strategies that have been in place for many years in a number of jurisdictions. The first is the matter of who is permitted to select the treating physician, and the second addresses the matter of medical fee schedules. These two strategies are discussed more fully in the following.

Choice of Medical Provider – Under many of the early workers compensation laws the injured employee was seldom permitted to select their own physician, except at his/her own expense. It seemed reasonable that the employer should select the treating physician since the employer was the one responsible for paying the bill. It is important to keep in mind that under those early compensation laws, medical benefits were frequently quite limited inasmuch as benefits were subject to a maximum time duration (90 days was the duration maximum in many states in 1940) or a maximum dollar amount ($100 or $200 dollar maximums were found in about half of the states in 1940).

With the passage of time and the growing concern for the inadequacy of medical benefits in the case of a serious work-related injury, states amended the compensation laws so as to extend the period of medical entitlement and also increased or eliminated any "cap" on the total amount of medical benefits payable for an individual claim. As compensation laws began to achieve the objective of unlimited medical care in terms of duration and amount, the subject of choice of provider became a matter of serious debate. The question arose as to who – the employer or the injured employee – should be able to select the treating provider. In an odd twist of concerns, both advocates of employer-choice and advocates for employee-choice raised essentially the same basic argument – if the choice of physician is controlled by the other party, quality of care will suffer.

Moving beyond the basic issue of quality of care that was of concern to both parties, the case for employee-choice of provider rested on three basic arguments.

- That an employee selected physician is less likely to sacrifice good care to the financial interest of the employer and is more likely to inspire in the employee the confidence needed to achieve a speedy recovery.

- That employers (or their insurance carrier) will select providers primarily for financial considerations that do little to enhance good medical care.

- Providers would be selected based on proximity to the employment location, their willingness to accept lower fees along with their willingness to accept direction from the employer/carrier.

The case for employer selection of the provider was usually made on the grounds that employees generally lacked the necessary knowledge to make an appropriate provider selection. It was frequently argued that many cases resulted in prolonged – or unnecessary –

disability because the worker, with little knowledge of the scope of a physician's practice, had the tendency to treat with a family practitioner rather than a specialist.

For those interested in a compromise between the two extremes of employer selection or employee selection of the treating provider, a third option arose which incorporated elements of the first two. The compromise took the form of having a panel of physicians maintained by the employer (thereby satisfying the issue of quality) with the employee having the right to make a selection from the panel or list (thereby affording the employee some range of choice, albeit a limited one). **Wisconsin** was the first state to enact legislation allowing for this type of selection process.

The National Commission that reported on the status of state workers compensation laws in 1972 explored the subject of choice of physician with recognition for both the employer and the employee interests. The Commission also recognized that the compensation administrative agency was interested in this issue inasmuch as the agency wanted to use physicians familiar with accurate reporting and evaluation of impairments. It was also recognized that few physicians combine in one person the qualities of interest to all of the parties. In their final report issued in 1972, the Commission recommended that the worker be permitted *"the initial selection of his physician, either from all licensed physicians in the State or from a panel of physicians selected or approved by the workmen's compensation agency."*[186]

As workers compensation medical payments continued to rise during the 1980s and 1990s, many states expanded their efforts to modify state laws so as to reduce medical costs while avoiding actions that might impair the outcomes experienced by injured workers. An issue often debated at the state level was giving employers more influence or direct control over the selection of providers.

Through the introduction of managed care arrangements (the subject of managed care will be covered later in this chapter) the employer and carrier were given more latitude in the selection of treating provider. However, not all states enacted managed care provisions, and even in those states where managed care arrangements were permitted, not all employers opted to utilize such arrangements.

While the debate continues to some extent and there remains an overlap within specific states in

> The Workers' Compensation Institute (WCRI) is an independent, not-for-profit research organization that provides objective data and analysis to those interested in making improvements to the workers compensation system. A recent publication *Workers' Compensation Medical Cost Containment: A National Inventory, 2021,* provides an update of statutory provisions, administrative rules, and administrative procedures used by states as of January 1, 2021. Medical cost containment falls into the categories of management and utilization with a goal of curbing the cost of particular services and reducing the amount of services provided. Copies of the inventory may be obtained by contacting the WCRI office located in Boston, MA.

---

[186] 1972 National Commission Recommendation 4.1

terms of provider choice, certain general observations can be made regarding the subject. It is important to recognize that states have introduced various caveats that make placing a particular state in any one distinct category difficult.

- Today, we find that in twenty jurisdictions[187] the employee is allowed to select the initial treating physician without restriction. **Arizona** permits the employee to select the treating physician if the employer is insured. However, if the employer is self-insured, the employer has the right to select the treating physician. In **New Mexico**, if the employee makes the first choice, the employer can make a change after 60 days. Where the employer makes the initial choice in New Mexico, the employee can make the change in provider after sixty days.

- In a smaller number of states the employee may select the initial treating provider unless the employer has an approved managed care arrangement in place. In **Nebraska**, the employer has the right to select the treating physician unless the employee selects a treating physician from whom he/she or a family member has received treatment in the past.

- Fifteen states continue to have provisions permitting the employer/insurer to select the initial treating physician, at least at some point. This selection would apply whether the employer or insurer has obtained approval for a managed care arrangement.

- While the concept of medical panels was found in a number of the early state compensation laws, only five states (**Georgia, Idaho, Pennsylvania, Tennessee,** and **Virginia**) continue to reference medical panels. In Idaho, the employee may select the treating physician if the employer does not designate the treating physician at the time of hire.

In **California**, the employee can select the treating provider if he/she predesignates. It depends upon what the employer is told in writing before the injury. To predesignate, the employer must be informed of the name and address of the workers personal physician or a medical group.

In **Pennsylvania**, the injured worker must go to a provider on the list of approved providers for the first 90 days of treatment but has the right to choose the provider if the employer fails to furnish a list of approved providers. In a recent law decision, it was held that if an employee did not receive adequate written notification of panel physicians from the employer, then the employee was not obligated to use a panel physician.[188] The court ruled that notification must be made on two occasion: first when the employee is hired, and second, "either immediately or as soon as practical" after the injury. Because the employer did not get the employee's acknowledgement of notification in writing after the injury, the

---

[188] *Pennsylvania Dep. Of Corrections v. Workers Compensation Appeals Board (Kirchner),* 805 A2d 633 (2002)

employee was permitted to select the treating physician and the employer was bound to pay for the treatment.

Notwithstanding the attention directed at the subject of the initial selection of treating provider, there is another – and perhaps equally important issue – associated with the right to change providers following initial treatment. In the majority of instances, workers compensation cases are of short duration involving only one or two medical visits followed by prompt return to work. For cases of short duration - commonly referred to as "medical only claims - there is no indemnity benefits payable and the medical costs represent the total cost associated with the claim.

Where treatment is rendered for a short duration – one or two visits – it may not be critically important as to who selects the treating physician so long as the outcome is appropriate and maximum recovery is realized. It is in that small percentage of workers compensation injuries where the injury is serious, and the disability extends for an extended period of time that the issue of appropriate treating provider becomes of critical importance. While the selection of the initial treating provider is critical for cases of extended duration, there also arises the subject of the ability of either the employer or the employee to change providers.

Where the employer has the initial right to select the provider, at what point in the recovery should the injured worker be able to change providers, or request a change in provider? Similarly, where the employee initially selects the treating provider, at what point should the employer be able to request a change of provider? And is this is subject left strictly for the employer and the employee to resolve, or is there a need for input and approval from the administrative agency?

The above are some of the basic questions that arise when considering the subject of the employee's ability to change providers. In addressing those questions, states have followed a number of different paths. In the first place, one of the determining issues is who has the right for the initial selection – the employer or the employee. This is further complicated where the employer is operating under a managed care arrangement. The following demonstrates some of the different approaches that have been introduced that enable the injured worker to change his/her medical provider:

- In **Delaware, Maryland,** and **Vermont,** the injured employee has an unrestricted right to change providers. The same right exists for the employee in **New Hampshire, New York, Rhode Island,** and **West Virginia** except where the employer has a managed care arrangement in place. In those instances, the managed care rules would determine under what conditions a change of provider can take place. In **Michigan**, the employer/insurer has the initial right of selection, but the employee can make unrestricted changes after the first ten days.

- **Arizona, the District of Columbia, Florida, Idaho, Louisiana, Montana, Nebraska, South Dakota, Texas,** and **Tennessee** require the employee to obtain the approval of the employer or the insurer before making a provider change. In addition to the employer or insurer, approval is required before the employee may change providers in **Colorado, Mississippi, North Carolina, Oklahoma, South Carolina,** and **Virginia.**

- A number of states permit the employee to make one change of providers before having to obtain approval. **Alaska, Hawaii, Illinois, Utah,** and **Wisconsin** follow this approach and then require approval from the employer or insurer. **Arkansas** and **Kentucky** permit one change before approval required from the administrative agency unless the employee is in a managed care arrangement. **Connecticut, Massachusetts,** and **Oregon** require approval of the employer/insurer and the administrative agency after the one change.

- **Indiana** and **New Jersey** do not permit the employee to make a change of providers, and **Missouri** permits a change of providers only within the managed care arrangement. In **Kansas**, an employer selection of treating provider state, the employee may request a change from a panel furnished by the employer and must have administrative agency approval.

- In the monopolistic funds states of **Ohio, North Dakota,** and **Wyoming,** the employee can change providers only with the approval of the state fund.

A small minority of states permit the employer to make a change in treating providers without restriction.

Medical Fee Schedules – In an effort to improve the performance of state workers compensation systems, the delivery and cost of workers compensation medical benefits is an area of major concern. In examining medical costs, it is well to consider that those costs reflect two components – the number of units of services rendered and the amount charged per unit of service. The medical fees charged by physicians, hospitals and other ancillary services thus represent one part of the equation that results in the total health care bill. It should be recognized at the outset that constraint on a single part of the equation (medical fees for example) will have minimal impact where the second part of the equation (in this case utilization) is left unchecked. While it is important to review the manner and operation of state workers compensation medical fee schedules, it is equally important to appreciate that it is simply one part of the equation.

One of the earliest efforts to constrain medical costs was the introduction of the medical fee schedule. In a number of states, workers compensation medical fee schedules go back nearly as far as the original enactment of the workers compensation law. For example, **Arizona** introduced the first medical fee schedule in 1925, followed by **North Carolina** in 1929.

Medical fee schedules are designed to establish the maximum reimbursement rate for health care services. Depending on the individual state, the medical fee schedule may address physician services, or may be designed to cover services by hospitals (in-patient and out-patient), surgical procedures, other practitioners such as osteopaths and chiropractors, ancillary services, and prescription drugs. Because of the limits placed on maximum reimbursement fees, the application of a medical fee schedule represents a popular cost containment strategy.

Currently found in the majority of jurisdictions, medical fee schedules dictate the maximum reimbursements that providers can receive for specified services. **Iowa, Missouri, New Hampshire, New Jersey,** and **Wisconsin** remain the only states without a workers compensation medical fee schedule while **Indiana** has a partial fee schedule. For jurisdictions that have in place a medical fee schedule, such schedules normally cover medical, surgical, radiology, chiropractic, and physical and occupational therapy with some of the schedules also covering anesthesiology, pathology, hospital charges and prescription drugs.

The designing or updating of fee schedules, often subject to political pressure from payers and providers, involves a delicate balance. If fees levels are set too high, their effectiveness as a cost savings tool may be limited because of the over utilization of services. At the same time, if fee levels are set too low, access to quality care may be in jeopardy.

For purposes of reviewing the potential impact of fee schedules, there are essentially three categories of services. These include medical services, hospital charges, prescription drugs. Not all states promulgate medical fee schedules, and within the states that do promulgate such reimbursement rates, fee schedules may not be promulgated for each of the categories denoted. The following provides an overview of the method of reimbursement that has developed for each of the general categories.

Fees for Medical Services – For reimbursement of medical services, states have come to use a variety of approaches. For example, a small number of states (**Alaska, Arizona, Arkansas, Connecticut,** and **Georgia**) base their provider fee schedule on the usual and customary provider charges as determined by insurance carriers. A number of states rely on Medicare rates for purposes of medical service reimbursements. States like **Hawaii** utilize the Medicare rate and then adjust that amount upward by 10 percent. Similarly, **Pennsylvania** reimburses providers at 113 percent of the Medicare rate.

A large number of states that originally enacted fee schedules employ a relative value scale for the purpose of establishing the level of reimbursable fees for physician services. First developed in **California**, the relative value scale attempted to price various procedures according to their demand on the physician's time. A sample of physicians was asked the amount of time required to conduct a specific procedure and the average fee charged for a list of specific procedures. Based on these replies, a cost per unit of physician's time was derived as the basis of the relative value scale. In effect, the scale serves to price one procedure relative to another. The agency then responsible for setting the medical fee applies a conversion factor or multiplier to the values in the relative value scale in order to arrive at a maximum fee for that service or procedure. As a result, over time fees in the schedule can be adjusted simply by changing the conversion factor or multiplier.

Over the past several decades, at least one-half of the states along with the **District of Columbia** have based their new or revised fee schedules on the Resource Based Relative Value Scale (RBRVS) instituted by Medicare in 1992. This is a system where differences in payment across types of service and across geographic areas are based on differences in the cost to providers. RBRVS determines prices based on three separate factors: physician work (54 percent), practice expense (41 percent), and malpractice expense (five percent).

The RBRVS system assigns a specific relative value to every unique medical procedure or service, as defined by the Current Procedural Terminology (CPT) coding scheme. The relative value assigned to a particular CPT code compares the resources required to provide the procedure or service involved to the average resources required for all services. The RBRVS also includes a geographic adjustment to reflect differences in prices in different areas of the country.

State regulators along with insurers have found that there are certain advantages to use of the RBRVS created by Medicare. First, the fee schedule covers a comprehensive range of services and provides an equitable reimbursement for all services and procedures. Secondly, the linking of the state fee schedule to the Medicare fee schedule shifts the administrative burden of ongoing fee schedule refinements and updates to the Centers for Medicare and Medicaid Services (CMS). Finally, Medicare fee schedules are more than just a set of prices. Coding standards and payment policies are implicit in the price, and finally; for most fee schedules, Medicare applies a dollar conversion factor to the relative value for a given service to convert that value into a payment amount.

Two states – **Illinois** and **Tennessee** – were among the most recent states to enact legislation permitting the establishment of medical fee schedules. Effective for treatment for work-related injuries rendered on or after February 1, 2006, Illinois joined the majority of states in establishing a medical fee schedule for workers compensation. The fee schedule includes payment rates, instructions, guidelines, and payment guides and policies regarding application of the schedule. The fee schedule is to be used in setting the maximum allowable payment for procedures, treatment, products, services or supplies for hospital inpatient, hospital outpatient, emergency room, ambulatory surgical treatment centers, accredited ambulatory surgical treatment facilities, prescriptions filled and dispensed outside of a licensed pharmacy, dental services, and professional services.

Beginning September 1, 2011, for covered procedures, treatments, services or supplies, the maximum allowable payment is set at 70 percent of the fee schedule amounts. This rate is to be adjusted yearly by the percentage change in the Consumer Price Index (CPI). The payment rates in the fee schedule are designated by geozip. A geozip is defined as a three-digit ZIP code based on data similarities, geographical similarities, and frequencies. The geozip distinction was later replaced with one based on regions. While the Illinois Medicare fee schedule has only four different rates throughout the state, under the workers compensation program, the state is divided into several regions. Where a particular region may not have the necessary number of charges and fees to calculate a valid percentile for a specific procedure, treatment or service, data from the region along with other regions demographically and economically similar can be used until nine charges or fees for that specific procedure are obtained

The **Tennessee** medical fee schedule – effective May 1, 2006, and applicable to all services provided after that date was last revised on September 10, 2019. This most recent version separates the fee schedule into three parts, called chapters. The first chapter contains specific information concerning impairment ratings, missed appointments, independent medical evaluations (IMEs) and other general information, as well as the overall purpose, scope, general guidelines, and procedures. The second chapter, is the medical fee schedule rules for outpatient services and addresses the proper conversion factor and percentages to use for calculating the maximum allowable amounts for physicians' professional services, according to specialty and CPT® codes, the maximum allowable amounts that may be paid to other providers for durable medical equipment, prosthetics, orthotics, therapy services, drugs and other outpatient services provided to injured employees The third chapter sets out the amount of in-patient reimbursements. The daily payments and the stop loss payments are not based on Medicare methods but reimburse hospitals on a per-day or *per diem* basis and include a method for extra payments for the most severe injuries.

For those states that do not utilize a medical fee schedule, when disputes over amounts payable for a medical fee arise, the dispute is referred to the administrative agency for purposes of resolution, In **Wisconsin,** after a fee dispute is submitted to the Workers Compensation Division, the insurer or self-insured employer must provide the Division with information on fees charged by other health service providers for comparable services. The insurer or self-insured employer is required to obtain the information on comparable fees from a database that is certified by the Division. If the insurer or self-insured employer does not provide the information required, the Division will determine that the disputed fee is reasonable and order that it be paid. If the insurer or self-insured employer provides the information required, the Division uses that information to determine the reasonableness of the disputed fee.

A Workers Compensation Research Institute's (WCRI) medical price index study released in May 2020 found that only seven states experienced substantial changes in overall prices paid as a result of major fee schedule changes during the study period. Virginia, which implemented a fee schedule in January 2018, saw professional services prices drop 13 percent between 2017 and 2018, and hold steady in 2019, according to the study.

The WCRI study also found that in states without fee schedules, including **Iowa, Missouri, New Hampshire, New Jersey,** and **Wisconsin**, prices paid for professional services were between 42 percent and 174 percent higher than the median of study states with fee schedules.

While the use of medical fee schedules demonstrates the extent the degree of potential savings, there are those who see problems with the application of medical fee schedules. Greg Krohm, former Executive Director of the International Association of Industrial Accident Boards and Commissions (IAIABC) and formerly administrator of the

Wisconsin Workers Compensation Division, has observed that from his perspective, *"it seems that workers compensation fee schedules are a bad idea."* His primary concern is that payment rules like fee schedules are devoid of financial incentives for good medicine and good treatment outcomes, including early return to work. In most states with fee schedules, the clinician automatically gets paid the lower of: (1) the charge stated on the bill; (2) a contractual rate (usually a percentage reduction from stated charge); or (3) the fee schedule amount.

Mr. Krohm notes that there is no reason for a clinician – other than one with professional and moral values – to put in the extra time it takes to counsel and manage patients on tricky issues like return to work, pain management, therapeutic programs, and the prevention of re-injury. The payment is a flat rate per billing code without regard to quality or care given.

Other concerns expressed by Mr. Krohm regarding the use of medical fee schedules include:

- The levels of compensation are set by political considerations which seldom have any relationship to the market rate for medical services in general, or for services provided to injured workers. In many markets, the fee schedule amount is quite generous relative to the amount paid by group health insurance, and higher still than Medicare payment levels.

- In many states, surgeons and other specialty providers have successfully lobbied regulators and lawmakers for payment advantages over evaluation and management CPT codes, i.e., office visits and primary care.

- Some states do not allow payment above the fee schedule. Many reason that payment above the fee schedule provides a financial incentive to offer treatment that favors the payer versus the injured worker.

- By making the maximum fee a public number, some providers (or their office managers) can set it as the target for charges. Thus, the ceiling becomes the floor.

Mr. Krohm concludes by noting that fee schedules might be rehabilitated, or their faults mitigated, if they paid a uniform percentage amount over Medicare (say in the range of a 25-40 percent premium). This target would be set to mimic the prevailing payment level for group health. A small extra margin could be justified by the increased paperwork and reporting that often goes with workers compensation cases.

Medical Provider Networks (MPNs) – For workers compensation, MPNs have become increasingly popular over the last several decades. A MPN is an entity or group of health care providers set up by an insurer or self-insured employer and subject to the approval of the state program administrator to treat workers injured on the job. In conjunction with increased market penetration, some MPNs have broadened their services: To improve outcomes, they do not just provide medical care, they manage the medical services on a claim, including interacting with the patient.

MPNs help employers manage their medical costs through a diverse network of qualified physicians, specialists, and providers that specialize in the treatment of occupational injuries. **California** requires that all MPNs must be approved by the Division of Workers Compensation's administrative director. California Workers Compensation Laws have very strict requirements for the establishment of an MPN by an insurer or employer:

Under California's regulations, each MPN must include a mix of doctors specializing in work-related injuries and doctors with expertise in general areas of medicine. MPNs are required to meet access to care standards for common occupational injuries and work-related illnesses. The regulations also require MPNs to follow all medical treatment guidelines established by the DWC and allow employees a choice of provider(s) in the network after their first visit.

Additionally, MPNs must offer an opportunity for second and third opinions if the injured worker disagrees with the diagnosis or treatment offered by the treating physician. If a disagreement still exists after the second and third opinion, an injured worker in the MPN may request an MPN independent medical review (MPN IMR). The MPN program became effective Jan. 1, 2005 and employees can be covered by an MPN once a plan has been approved by the DWC administrative director.[189]

Diagnosis-Related Groups (DRGs) – Services offered through a hospital facility have been the subject of dramatic changes designed to reduce overall medical costs. A diagnosis-related group (DRG) is a patient classification system that standardizes prospective payment to hospitals and encourages cost containment initiatives. In general, a DRG payment covers all charges associated with an **inpatient** stay from the time of admission to discharge.

Before the DRG system was introduced in the 1980s, hospitals would bill Medicare or the insurance provider charges for every Band-Aid, X-ray, alcohol swab, bedpan, and aspirin, plus a room charge for each day of hospitalization. Through this billing approach, hospitals were encouraged to keep the patient as long as possible and perform as many procedures as possible.[190]

With health care costs rising, the government sought a way to control costs while encouraging hospitals to provide care more efficiently. What resulted was the DRG. Starting in the 1980s, DRGs changed how Medicare pays hospitals. Instead of paying for each day of hospitalization along with incidentals, Medicare began to pay a single amount for hospitalization according to your DRG, which was based on the patient's age, gender, diagnosis, and the medical procedures involved in care.

The idea is that each DRG encompasses patients who have clinically similar diagnoses, and whose care requires a similar amount of resources to treat. The DRG system is intended to standardize hospital reimbursement, taking into consideration where a hospital is located, what type of patients are being treated, and other regional factors.[4]

---

[189] https://www.dir.ca.gov/dwc/mpn/dwc_mpn_main.html
[190] https://www.verywellhealth.com/drg-101-what-is-a-drg-how-does-it-work-3916755

To come up with DRG payment amounts, Medicare calculates the average cost of the resources necessary to treat people in a particular DRG, including the primary diagnosis, secondary diagnoses and comorbidities, necessary medical procedures, age, and gender. That base rate is then adjusted based on a variety of factors, including the wage index for a given area. A hospital in New York City pays higher wages than a hospital in rural Kansas, for example, and that's reflected in the payment rate each hospital gets for the same DRG. The baseline DRG costs are recalculated annually and released to hospitals, insurers, and other health providers through the Centers for Medicare and Medicaid Services (MS).

Attempts to date to control hospital costs in the workers compensation program have been to set the reimbursement rate using primarily the Medicare DRG, use a percentage discount below Medicare DRG charges, or apply the basis of the facility's cost to deliver that service. There are several states that reimburse hospitals based on some multiple of Medicare DRG. States using this methodology include **South Carolina** – which had seen rapidly rising medical expenses – and **Texas** who recently announced that it is moving in this direction.

Prescription Drug Monitoring Program (PDMP) – One of the factors frequently identified as contributing to the trend of higher prescription drugs costs is the absence of state control over the utilization and cost of drugs in workers compensation. Prescription drug monitoring programs (PDMPs) are statewide databases that gather information from pharmacies on dispensed prescriptions of controlled substances and, as such, are promising tools to help combat the prescription opioid epidemic. Prescribers, pharmacists, law enforcement agencies, and medical licensure boards are among the typical users of these databases. Prescription drug monitoring programs implemented since the late 1990s are all electronic allowing users, especially prescribers, access by means of an online portal.

Today, PDMPs cover a wide range of controlled substances. A new wave of implementation began in the early 2000s, and all states except **Missouri** have either implemented or upgraded their PMPs or have enacted legislation to do so. Effective PMPs help change prescriber behavior by identifying patients at a high risk of doctor shopping or diversion. They also allow law enforcement agencies and medical licensure boards to monitor aberrant prescribing practices.

A prescription drug monitoring program was associated with more than a 30 percent reduction in the rate of prescribing of Schedule II opioids. This reduction was seen immediately following the launch of the program and was maintained in the second and third years afterward. Increased utilization of these programs and the adoption of new policies and practices governing their use may have contributed to sustained effectiveness [191]

As a tool used by states to address prescription drug abuse, addiction, and diversion, PDMP may serve several purposes including:

---

[191] https://www.sciencedirect.com/topics/medicine-and-dentistry/prescription-drug-monitoring-program

- Support access to legitimate medical use of controlled substances.

- Identify and deter or prevent drug abuse and diversion.

- Facilitate and encourage the identification, intervention with and treatment of persons addicted to prescription drugs.

- Inform public health initiatives through outlining of use and abuse trends.

- Educate individuals about PDMPs and the use, abuse and diversion of, and addiction to prescription drugs.

PDMP's can be a powerful tool for doctors and pharmacists in identifying people potentially abusing opioids, knowingly or unknowingly. However, every state's PDMP functions differently, from what prescriptions drugs it collects information on, to when, and if, a doctor should check the PDMP. A problem associated with the program is that it is a tool that is only effective if applied. While currently almost every state has an active PDMP, a study revealed that only 16 states require use of the PDMP by providers (and then only in certain situations) and of those states, only one-half of those states require use of the PDMP before the initial dispensing of a controlled substance.

At the federal level, effective September 1, 2015, the Office of Workers' Compensation Programs (OWCP) Division of Federal Employees' Compensation (DFEC) began implementing changes to the calculation of the maximum allowable fee for brand name prescription drugs. The maximum allowable fee for brand name drugs is calculated at 85 percent of the average wholesale price (AWP – 15 percent) plus a $4.00 dispensing fee. The maximum allowable fee for generic drugs and non-drug items is not changing and is calculated at 70 percent of the average wholesale price (AWP – 30 percent) plus a $4.00 dispensing fee.

Pharmacy Benefit Management (PBM) – The workers compensation pharmacy benefit management (PBM) industry came into its own at the turn of the twenty-first century. While PBMs had long been active in the area of dug cost control, until drug costs exploded, many payers did not utilize PBMs. Those that used PBMs used them on a file-by-file basis. With the dramatic increases in drug costs in the early part of the last decade, payers scrambled to contract with PBMs and integrate them into their service offerings. Originally delivering value through lower prices, most PBMs implemented basic drug management programs, tightening drug formularies, promoting generic drugs, preventing early refills, and strengthening prior authorization processes over the years.

These clinical management programs have continued to become more sophisticated and more effective over time. Along with better script capture programs and more effective payer PBM working relationships, clinical management programs led to decreases in utilization. Combined with a decline in the number of new branded drugs, a large number of popular drugs going off patent, and extremely effective generic conversion programs, PBMs and payers were successful in not just managing, but actually reducing total pharmacy costs over the last few years.

One of the easiest and most effective means to control drug costs is by substituting generics for brand-name drugs where possible in the workers compensation system. Nonetheless, there are still many providers who prescribe brand name drugs unnecessarily. These prescribers – and their injured-worker patients – may be unaware of the cost differences involved. Many providers and injured workers believe brand name drugs are inherently of better quality than the generic versions. However, the generic drugs have the same active ingredients and work the same way as brand name drugs.

MANAGED CARE

The phrase "managed care" is often used to describe almost any attempt to limit health care expenditures in an increasingly competitive marketplace. In the period following World War II, the predominant American health insurance paradigm was one in which insurance companies sold coverage to employers, who provided coverage to employees as a benefit of employment. Health coverage became an element in contract negotiations between employers and employee unions during the middle of the 20th century when the American workforce was relatively young and healthy. At that time, many industries agreed to provide generous health benefits at little or no direct cost to the employee.

In this earlier unmanaged care environment, individuals seeking health care associated with a non-occupational injury or condition were free to select the provider of choice in a world of rapidly growing numbers of specialist physicians. With relatively few restrictions, payments were made by insurance companies and government programs to physicians, hospitals, and other health care providers on a fee-for-service or cost basis. Under this scenario, the higher the cost or charge, the larger the payment received by the treating provider.

Little thought was directed toward the predictable effects of the nation's changing demography (an aging population) or of financial disincentives that existed relative to the cost of care. Patients insulated from the costs of their care by insurance tended to increase their access to, and expectations for, health care; while physicians trained to go to extremes on patients' behalf developed increasingly effective and expensive, means of doing so. By the 1970s, these two dynamics led to a crisis of rapid and uncontrolled escalation in the cost of health care.

Although early examples of managed care programs can be identified as far back as the 1920s, the concept of managed care spread relatively slowly prior to the health care crisis in group insurance that arose in the 1970s and 1980s. When health care costs began to increase, it served as an impetus to encourage managed care as a means to contain or lower group health insurance costs. Increased competition in the group health insurance market led to the adaptation of managed-care techniques by for-profit health care firms, and at the same time a number of states changed their Medicaid plans to a managed-care approach.

As the corresponding experience of rising medical costs occurred also in the workers compensation system, managed care arrangements were introduced in a number of states as a method to address these rising costs. Prior cost containment generally focused on limiting employee choice of provider and putting in place medical fee schedules to establish maximum payments for medical services. With the introduction of managed care to workers compensation, significant challenges to the effective implementation of this type of system improvement were presented. Those challenges resulted from the fact that other health care delivery systems focus on medical recovery as the ultimate goal, while in workers compensation, the ultimate goal is to return injured workers to productive employment as quickly and safely as possible.

Taking their cue from the employee group health insurance programs, workers compensation reformers began in the early 1990s to actively experiment with various forms of managed care. During the early half of the 1990s, 23 states introduced some form of managed care either through specific enabling legislation or through administrative regulation. In **Florida** and **South Dakota** legislation was enacted that mandated the use of managed care for all work-related injuries. In **New Hampshire** and **Vermont**, managed care was mandated for all work-related injuries that occurred to employees where the employer was in the residual market.

It is important to recognize that managed care in the workers compensation program means different things to different people. Managed care as it is most broadly defined constitutes a comprehensive set of medical services provided by a network of health care providers and controlled by some type of medical organization. In an ideal environment, managed care seeks to provide quality medical care while controlling or managing excessive and unnecessary medical costs. For others, managed care simply represents the opportunity for the employer/insurer to determine the facility from which medical treatment will be provided to the injured worker and to negotiate discounted fees with providers. Between those two extremes, there are a multitude of approaches, all falling under the umbrella of managed care.

MANAGED CARE NETWORKS

Because of the complexity of managed care, it is appropriate to begin by reviewing the objectives of a managed care network along with a description of the major types of medical networks found in the group health insurance arena. It is beneficial to start from this foundation inasmuch as many workers compensation approaches were based to some degree on the group health insurance model.

The concept of what constitutes managed care has been evolving for many years and now contains a laundry list of techniques employers and insurers use to cut excess costs from health-care bills. These techniques include:

- Medical bill review to look for inappropriate charges and overcharges.

- Utilization review to prevent excessive testing and hospital stays.

- Provider networks such as Health Maintenance Organizations (HMOs) and Preferred Provider Organizations (PPOs) that guarantee discounts.

- Case management to control treatment for catastrophic cases. An employer assigns a case manager, usually a registered nurse, to oversee treatment, ensuring that the employee is receiving appropriate and cost-effective care, setting the stage for early return to work or disability management.

Stated simply, the basic objectives of a managed care network are threefold:

- Deliver high-quality care in an environment that manages or controls costs.

- Ensure that the care delivered is medically necessary and appropriate for the patient's condition.

- Ensure that the care is rendered by the most appropriate provider.

In the health insurance arena, a number of different medical managed care networks have evolved. Health Management Organizations (HMO) and Preferred Provider Organizations (PPO) are two of the more common types of network arrangements. A third type, the Point of Service (POS) model represents a blend between the HMO and PPO. A brief description of each of these network types serves to illustrate their similarities and differences:

Health Maintenance Organization (HMO) – An HMO is an organization that arranges to cover specific health care services at a fixed price for each insured patient (capitation). Under a capitated arrangement, a provider agrees to provide specified services to the plan members for this fixed, pre-determined payment for a specified length of time (typically, a year), regardless of how many times the member uses the service. If a provider spends more money to provide health care for a person than the contracted price per person (e.g., ordering certain tests or unnecessary tests), the provider loses money. If the participating provider does not see many of the persons under the contract and does not spend the allotted money on care per person, then the provider makes money. In other words, there may be a certain incentive to under-treat the patient that must be weighed against an incentive to treat in order to keep the patient healthy.

Under an HMO, members select a primary care physician (PCP), often called a gatekeeper, who provides, arranges, coordinates, and authorizes all aspects of the member's health care. PCPs are usually family doctors, internal medicine doctors or general practitioners. HMOs are the most restrictive type of health plan because they give members the least choice in selecting a health care provider. However, HMOs typically provide members with a greater range of health benefits for the lowest out-of-pocket expenses, such as either no or a very low co-payment.

Preferred Provider Organization (PPO) – In contrast to the HMO, a PPO is an insurance arrangement whereby the employer/benefit administrator (payer) has developed a network of preferred providers (hospitals, primary care providers, specialists, ancillary care providers, and home health care providers) who have agreed to care for the people covered by the PPO at a discounted rate for services provided and negotiated in advance. Unlike an HMO, the PPO does not generally utilize a gatekeeper, nor do they need to use an in-network provider for their care.

PPOs are reimbursed like traditional insurance programs. Once the deductible amount is met, the benefit administrator will pay a certain percentage of the health care bill. However, in the case of treatment outside of a network provider, the PPO pays a smaller percentage of the bill. For example, the insurance company may pay 80 percent of the costs where care is received from an in-network provider, but only 50-60 percent of the costs when care is obtained from a non-network provider.

Point of Service (POS) – A POS plan may be referred to as an HMO/PPO hybrid or an open-ended HMO. The reason it's called point of service is that members choose which option – HMO or PPO – they will use each time they seek health care. Like an HMO and a PPO, a POS plan has a contracted provider network. POS plans encourage, but don't require, members to choose a primary care physician. Members who choose not to use their PCPs for referrals (but still seek care from an in-network provider) still receive benefits but will pay higher co-payments and/or deductibles than members who use their PCPs. Members also may opt to visit an out-of-network provider at their discretion. If so, a member co-pays, and coinsurance and deductibles are substantially higher.

WORKERS COMPENSATION MANAGED CARE

Workers compensation health care networks are similar to managed care networks offered through health maintenance organizations (HMOs) and preferred provider organizations (PPOs). These networks provide cost-effective care for work-related injuries and illnesses. Because the networks specialize in treating injured workers, they also can provide better access to appropriate medical care and help injured workers get back on the job quickly and safely. The central component of these plans is the use of a provider network – an association of physicians, hospitals, and other providers who work cooperatively to provide patient care. The plans control costs by contracting with health care providers to perform health services at pre-negotiated rates and by closely supervising patient care and progress under treatment.

Because of the unlimited nature of workers compensation medical benefits both in terms of duration and benefit amount, plus the additional aspect of no deductible or co-payments arrangements, virtually every workers compensation managed care network took the form of a PPO. Capitated arrangements, whereby the employee would be covered for the injuries arising during the policy year at a fixed cost, were permitted under administrative regulations promulgated in a number of states. However, through discussions with medical providers, it became evident that the potential for having medical treatments continue for years into the future made the concept of capitation difficult if not impossible for benefit administrators to price.

Using PPOs, employers and benefits administrators were able to establish networks of providers who shared an expertise in handling work-related injuries and diseases. In some states the network providers were reimbursed based upon their usual and customary fees or, in those state with a medical fee schedule, in compliance with the fee schedule. In other situations, reimbursement to providers was negotiated on a percentage off of the existing medical fee schedule. The concept behind negotiation of fees below the medical fee schedule was that such action would increase patient volume through the channeling of more injured workers through a particular clinic or facility.

It should also be noted that prior to the enactment of laws either permitting or requiring the establishment of managed care arrangements, there was essentially nothing in the workers compensation statutes to preclude the implementation of a managed care network. The ability to establish managed care arrangements would have been especially appropriate in those states where the employer/insurer had the right to select the treating physician. However, in the instance of an employer choice of treating provider state, managed care was viewed as offering little beyond the ability of the employer/insurer to negotiate discounted fees with the provider.

Where the employer purchases a workers compensation insurance policy that requires the use of a certified network, the managed care network generally provides all the health care associated with any work-related injuries or illnesses suffered by the employer's workers. The benefit administrator pays for the cost of health care and any income benefits due to the worker for lost wages or permanent physical impairment.

Depending upon the individual states and the statute or regulations, benefit administrators may either operate networks directly or contract with independent networks to provide health care services to their policyholders' injured workers. Certified self-insured employers, groups of certified self-insured employers, and political subdivisions also may contract directly with a network or establish their own networks to treat their injured workers.

When a worker covered by a network suffers a work-related injury or illness, the worker selects a treating doctor from the network's list of participating health providers. The treating doctor takes the lead role in supervising the patient's workers compensation-related care. The treating doctor provides treatment for the patient's work injury and, if more extensive care is required, makes referrals to specialists.

Generally, patients are not allowed to see specialists without their treating doctor's approval. In most cases, an insurer will only pay for health care deemed medically necessary. State laws require networks to have a process to allow patients and doctors to appeal any adverse decisions regarding medical necessity. In addition, a network's treatment guidelines must be sufficient to provide necessary care and flexible enough to allow deviations from normal rules when justified.

All employees living within a network's service area are generally required to obtain treatment through the network for work-related injuries or illnesses. Except in certain circumstances, such as emergencies and authorized out-of-network care, the insurer may deny payment for care provided by a non-network provider.

As a rule, if an employer participates in a workers compensation managed care network, the employer is required to notify every employee in writing of the network's rules and procedures.

This notice includes information about the network's procedures for complaints and appeals of network treatment decisions, its service area, and a complete listing of network service providers

A network provider doctor is required to provide care in accordance with the network's rules, utilization review requirements, treatment guidelines, and return-to-work guidelines. In the event that expensive or non-routine medical care services are required, the network provider's treatment recommendations may require prior approval from the network to ensure the care is medically necessary.

It was in the early 1990s that workers compensation reformers first began to experiment with various forms of managed care. While some states mandated the development of managed care arrangements through both the enactment of legislation and the promulgation of specific regulations, other states permitted the operation of managed care arrangements without the benefit of legislation or administrative oversight.

Based upon the activity at the state level, essentially four different approaches can be identified. One of the major distinguishing features of these approaches centers on the issue of whether the employer/insurer or the injured worker had the right to select the initial treating provider. These four approaches include:

- **States where medical networks are permitted, and the employer/insurer has the right to select the initial treating provider.** States where the employer has the right to select the initial treating physician provide little incentive beyond the potential for medical bill discounting to create a managed care network. Nine states follow this approach whereby there is neither legislation nor specific regulations governing the operation of a network of medical providers.

- **States where medical networks are permitted, and the injured worker has the right to select the initial treating provider.** More prevalent in approach is the situation where the injured worker has the right to select the treating provider. In these jurisdictions, the common approach is that the employer/insurer may establish a managed care network, but the use of the network cannot impede the injured workers right to select the treating provider. Again, there are no specific statutes or regulations governing the operation of the medical network.

- **States where the managed care arrangements are regulated.** Early resistance to managed care networks within the state workers compensation systems was driven by concerns that injured workers would potentially receive lower quality medical care through network providers. It was feared that cost-cutting efforts (discounted fees for network providers) would minimize the number of services provided and adversely impact the quality of care. To address quality of care concerns, a significant number of states developed managed care network certification requirements that focused on customer service, financial stability and quality assurance capabilities. These states then use these certification requirements as a monitoring tool to ensure continuing quality of care. Nearly one-half of the states have some form of legislation and/or regulation establishing the criteria for managed care networks. It is to be noted that **Texas** is somewhat unique since it is the state and not individual employers or insurers that directly manage the regional health care delivery networks.

- **States where managed care is mandated.** **Florida**, with legislation enacted in 1993, initially mandated that all medical services for work-related injuries were to be provided through a managed care network beginning in 1997. This provision was subsequently repealed. In a similar manner, both **New Hampshire** and **Vermont** at one point required work-related injuries occurring to employees of employers in the residual market to be treated through managed care networks. These provisions were also subsequently repealed.

  The monopolistic state funds of **North Dakota** and **Ohio** contract with third-party vendors to provide managed care services for all claims of employers in the state fund. However, self-insured employers operating in North Dakota and Ohio are not required to have in place a managed care arrangement.

Currently, only **South Dakota** and **Colorado** have a mandate that all medical services be provided through a managed care network. The mandate in Colorado includes case management which is defined to include a system developed by the insurance carrier in which the carrier shall assign a person knowledgeable in workers compensation health care to communicate with the employer, employee, and treating physician to assure that appropriate and timely medical care is being provided.

COMPONENTS OF MANAGED CARE ARRANGEMENTS

Managed care networks, referring simply to the network of treating providers, represents only one aspect of managed care. A comprehensive managed care arrangement may include many additional functions which are not only designed to ensure that appropriate and timely medical care is being provided, but also that case management and review processes are in place to ensure compliance with proper medical standards.

The following highlights some of those specific managed care functions that are found in the majority of states that regulate the managed care process:

Medical Bill Review and Bill Repricing – In workers compensation, medical bills have traditionally been reviewed to determine if the medical bills were appropriate both in terms of relatedness to the injury/disease and the amount charged. In the past, the claims adjuster – the individual responsible for overseeing the activity on a particular claim – was responsible for conducting the medical bill and repricing. However, with the increase in the volume of medical bills received, the change in the specific areas of responsibility for a particular claims handler, and the sophisticated technology that has developed both to monitor and adjust medical bills, the subject of medical bill review and repricing has changed dramatically.

As the volume of medical bills continues to grow, employers/insurers are turning to advanced technology to control medical costs, automate routine administrative functions, and continue to increase productivity. On the front-end of the medical review process, electronic data interchange (EDI), scanning technology, and optical character recognition serve to eliminate – or at least reduce – manual data entry and paper shuffling. By the use of these electronic processes, reviewers can eliminate inefficient, labor intensive procedures that are prone to error and inefficiency.

Sophisticated bill review and repricing technology can automate and improve the bill review process and provide significant cost savings. By integrating an extensive library of fee schedules and robust databases of pricing parameters into the software, these systems can automatically apply appropriate fees and discounts to every bill, ensuring a consistent level of medical costs savings.

Decision management technology provides for another level of potential savings. Expertise once held by qualified claim handlers can now be incorporated into automated rules and edits. These rules and edits are integrated into the decision management engine as the conditions and policies warrant. The rules and decision engines then allow for the detection of bills that contain potentially excessive charges, over utilization of treatment, unnecessary service, or inappropriate care. Medical bills falling into one of these categories are then automatically red flagged and forwarded to the correct resource for further review.

Utilization Review – Utilization review is generally defined as a review of the medical necessity and appropriateness of medical treatment and services. It is defined for the workers compensation process as a review of the medical necessity and appropriateness of medical care and services for purposes of recommending payments for compensable injuries or diseases. In other words, the assessment of the medical necessity and appropriateness of medical treatment and services is ultimately for purposes of determining the availability of payment for those treatments or services. Medical necessity includes a review of the setting, frequency, and intensity of the treatment or service.

Utilization review may be performed by representatives from the health care network, the benefit administrator utilizing the network, or it may be contracted out to a third-party review specialist. In all cases, the review examines medical records to see if the patient was given an economical level of care consistent with their needs and the past needs of similarly-afflicted patients.

The review typically involves prospective, concurrent review, or inpatient evaluation of care and needs; and retrospective review, or the larger historical picture of how physicians, labs, or hospitals handled the care and treatment provided.

> **Prospective Review** is the process of confirming approval and collecting information prior to the admission of a patient. The prospective review process permits eligibility verification/confirmation, determination of coverage and communication with the physician and/or member in advance of the procedure, service, or supply.

Concurrent Review encompasses those aspects of case management that take place as contemporaneously as feasible during the provision of services at an inpatient level of care or during an ongoing outpatient course of treatment. Concurrent review is often conducted telephonically, and the process includes:

- Obtaining necessary information from appropriate facility staff as to progress and care being provided.

- Identifying continuing care needs early in the patients stay to facilitate discharge to the appropriate setting.

- Discharge planning is an integral part of inpatient concurrent review. Recognizing and planning for discharge needs begins at the time of notification and continues throughout the hospital stay.

Retrospective Review is the process of reviewing services after the service has been provided and the opportunity for a concurrent review has passed. The purpose of retrospective review is to identify and refer potential quality and/or utilization issues, and to initiate appropriate follow-up action, based on quality or utilization issues.

States have adopted various approaches in terms of conditions under which utilization review is either permitted or mandated. In many instances where managed care arrangements are subject to administrative certification, one of the primary requirements is having utilization review procedures in place. In other instances, utilization review is permitted, but if utilization review is to be conducted, the procedures are subject to administrative review and certification.

Treatment Guidelines – Most workers compensation systems strive to provide quality medical care to occupationally injured or ill workers at a reasonable cost to the employers subject to the statutory act. Treatment guidelines generally attempt to define treatment standards and ranges for specific injuries and/or disabilities.

The purposes of treatment guidelines are to:

- To improve outcomes and patient satisfaction by focusing on restoration of functional capacity through prompt, responsible delivery of healthcare based on the best medical evidence.

- To reduce excessive utilization of medical services (and corresponding medical costs).

- To identify and target ineffective and harmful procedures, thus reducing risk on injured workers.

- To reduce delayed recovery rates and indemnity costs with the concurrent management of treatment and time away from work.

- To improve clinical practice/utilization management by indexing procedures adjacent to a summary of their effectiveness based on supporting evidence.

- To automate approval for universally effective treatment methods, where appropriate, reducing friction and administrative delays on necessary medical care.

- To open the lines of communication among all parties in the return-to-work process by providing a common framework based on existing and emerging medical evidence.

- To help injured workers get back on their feet in good time, safely, easily, and effectively.

- To take evidence-based medicine to its logical endpoint, the convergence of health, wellness, productivity, efficiency, and responsible, cost-effective medical care.

It is generally believed that treatment guidelines are an effective tool with which to help accomplish the above public policy objective. Treatment guidelines can be state specific guidelines adopted by a state workers compensation agency or can be proprietary and used by the private sector to identify cases that may need additional attention. Not all state workers compensation agencies have adopted treatment guidelines, and even when they do, the condition for which they provide guidance and the level of enforcement vary.

Of the jurisdictions that have developed treatment guidelines, few have guidelines for more than the most common occupational injuries. The most common treatment guidelines in workers compensation are for low back, upper extremities, lower extremities, carpal tunnel injuries, and pain management.

Medical Case Management – Workers compensation medical case management focuses on returning an injured worker to work as quickly as possible since the direct and indirect costs of a claim can be high for an employer. The employer is paying not only for the medical and wage replacement benefits, but for lost productivity during the period that the employee is away from the employment.

In more concrete terms, **Vermont** defines the concept. *"Medical Case Management refers to the planning and coordination of health care services appropriate to achieve the goal of medical rehabilitation. Medical case management may include, but is not limited to, care assessment, including personal interview with the injured employee, and assistance in developing, implementing, and coordinating a medical care plan with health care providers, as well as the employee and his/her family and evaluation of treatment results. Medical case management is not the provision of medical care. The goal of medical case* *management should be to avail the disabled individual of all available treatment options to ensure that the client can make an informed choice."*[192]

Case management as a means of delivering services to injured workers has proven to save money, reduce litigation and return people to employment. Most medical case managers are registered nurses (RNs). Insurance carriers use nurse case managers in a variety of ways. The carrier may have its own nurse employees or hire a managed care organization to provide these services.

Case management services are provided either telephonically or on-site. Typically, the telephonic nurse obtains a medical history and current status of the injured worker, the physician's treatment plan, the employee's regular job duties, and a modified duty program, if one is in place. A call is made to the claim handler to provide an educated estimate regarding the anticipated length of disability, and any suggestions the nurse may have regarding the treatment plan.

During the time between office visits, the nurse may make calls to obtain the medical reports for review. When an employee is not progressing as planned, the nurse may suggest changing treating physicians, obtaining a second opinion, or requesting an independent medical examination (IME).

Establishing a working relationship with the injured worker and treating physician can be difficult over the phone. In addition, it can be difficult to obtain an accurate description of the full job duties. The employee's description of the job may differ significantly from that of the employer.

The up-front cost of on-site case management is more expensive than telephonic case management. However, on-site case management can provide a wealth of information that may be needed if the case becomes complicated by the necessity for surgery, home care services, or job accommodations. On-site case management enables and facilitates integrated treatment plans that for difficult cases are the only way to achieve the combined objectives of quality care, return to work, and cost effectiveness. For example, meeting with the injured worker, the case manager can establish a relationship and assess the workers' needs and understanding of the process. The patient is often more open to ask questions, discuss sensitive medical issues, and verbalize any fears they may have regarding their former employment.

By attending pivotal physician appointments with the employee, the case manager has a better chance of discussing the treatment and progress with the physician. If the patient is comfortable, then the physician is usually agreeable to discuss the plan and consider other options that may be available. If the case manager has the authority to authorize treatment, the approval for diagnostic tests or surgery can be done, thereby avoiding delays and lost time.

---

[192] Vermont Workers Compensation Rule 2.1295

Managed care along with all other forms of treating injured workers is changing dramatically presenting new challenges and new opportunities. As with all evolving situations, there exists the opportunity to improve upon what was done in the past. This holds equally true for those services being offered through a managed care arrangement.

The emergence of tele-medicine, a term often used interchangeably with tele-health, represents just one of those changes. The use of tele-medicine in offering managed care services has multiple advantages because it can break down geographical barriers - it can be used in both rural and urban settings -and the injured worker may receive treatment or follow-up care at the workplace, allowing for near-immediate return to work or reduced lost-time if appropriate.

This trend toward tele-medicine is being used particularly with relatively minor injuries, and it has the potential to further transform workers compensation care from the point of injury through rehabilitation and return to work. Using digital technologies, the insurers and third-party administrators (TPAs) are able to electronically connect injured workers to quality providers. This physician-patient interaction occurs via video conferencing on smart phones, tablets, and other devices.

Although tele-health costs the same as an in-person visit, there are many potential benefits, including reduced utilization, improved patient compliance, immediate triaging of injuries, improved access to care, high patient satisfaction with the care experience, faster claims closure, reduced likelihood of litigation, and eliminating travel and office wait times.

According to the American Medical Association, 70 percent of clinical encounters could successfully be performed through tele-medicine. Thus far, injured workers have reported a positive experience with tele-medicine. In addition, there are other forms of tele-services being implemented, including tele-rehabilitation, tele-physical therapy, remote patient monitoring and tele-interpretation – all with early signs of delivering value for workers compensation managed care.[193]

Some of the more prominent of these opportunities that can result in savings include:

- **Establish improved relationships with employers to test new models of prevention and recovery**. As employers struggle with rising premiums and increasing complexity in the healthcare ecosystem, some look to prevent illness and injury and promote wellness on their own. Employers are offering employees incentives to live healthier, contracting directly with healthcare facilities for healthcare at set prices, and partnering with other stakeholders to change the system. Workers compensation managed care arrangements, with their decades of experience and vast pools of data could be partners in building and testing these new models through specific insights and prevention-oriented interventions for workers.

- **Through the use of data, place a stronger focus on outcomes.** Unprecedented advances in the ability to collect, store, manipulate and analyze data is revolutionizing the

---
[193] https://www.workcompwire.com/2018/05/guest-post-innovations-in-workers-compensation-managed-care/

prevention and reduction of illness and injury and allowing providers to tailor comprehensive care for each patient. The more innovative managed care organizations could develop new analytical capabilities to track three outcomes: injury prevention, injury recovery, and successful return to work. Using a value-based analytical lens, they could compare outcomes and costs for each type of injury to uncover variability in utilization trends by condition, understand whether patients are receiving care aligned with evidence-based standards, and optimize provider networks for high-quality care.

- **Examine current networks to identify and select high-quality providers.** Leaders in the field of managed care could shift from using third-party networks with little to no performance management to value-based networks. Traditional networks seek to include providers that the payer already has advantageous rates with, while value-based networks are built around the highest-value providers and aim to concentrate as much care as possible in them. Insurance carriers have an opportunity to manage the performance of any third-party network providers' using the value-based approach — for example, by awarding higher compensation for improving utilization of high-value providers.

- **Embracing innovation and change.** As technological and medical advancements continue to emerge at a rapid pace, we will see ongoing developments in how health care is being delivered. As technological advances are being introduced, there is the need for a systematic approach to pilot new programs in a way that limits risk and optimizes benefits. While deploying the new developments, there is still the need to ensure the basics of quality care, by using physicians who have consistently demonstrated good outcomes. There are also cultural issues to consider and address, such as generational preferences and perceptions. Through it all, analytics is a core tool that can help ensure we're reaping value from our newly deployed capabilities.

The approach of adopting new treatment must be approached with care and consideration directed at limiting risk through well-defined pilot programs. It is interesting to consider that authorization of new treatments may be denied on the basis of being experimental, but then how is medical care to advance unless new treatments and therapies are given a try. This is where a well-defined pilot program can help advance our understanding of how and when to utilize or apply new treatment options.

A final situation worthy of more attention is the Medicare program that continues wielding its leverage to push the nation's medical systems away from fee-for-service arrangements toward alternative payment models expected to improve care quality. One of these alternative medical treatment modes is bundled care. Very few bundled care models have emerged for treating injured workers impediments to its implementation remain. Yet there are those in the workers compensation community that expect the bundled payment concept will eventually flow into more treatments for workplace injuries and illnesses.

Bundled care and bundled payment refers to the coordinated delivery of all medical provider services needed to address a specific illness or injury. A medical group or hospital, for example, would bundle all services including imaging, anesthesia, surgery, follow-up doctor visits and physical therapy for repairing a knee or hip. Bundled payment models can improve the quality and coordination of care while controlling costs by aligning financial incentives to the services delivered across the patient journey for a specific medical condition or injury. The financial structures of bundled payments vary from upside risk-only models, in which a provider's incentives are based on cost and quality performance, to full-risk models, in which insurers negotiate a set price for relevant care within an episode.

Under a bundled payment approach, payers move away from obsessing over unit costs and toward broadening their analysis of value. Within this approach, payers may consider new therapies that add cost but could improve outcomes when the whole claim's picture is considered. For example, genetic testing adds an expense, but it may also allow treating physicians to see how injured workers would respond to various opioid medications, including their risk of dependency to these drugs. Likewise, use of virtual reality might add costs, but it has the potential to revolutionize pain management.

MEDICAL RECORDS PRIVACY

As society continues to move forward in the Information Age, a significant segment of the population continues to express concern regarding the increased potential for abuse associated with unrestricted access to their personal records and associated health care information. A Lou Harris poll conducted in the mid-1990s found that three-quarters of Americans worried that health care information from a computerized national health information system could be used for non-health care reasons. In the same survey, nearly two-thirds of the respondents indicated that they did not want medical researchers to use their data for studies, even if the individual is never identified personally, unless researchers first obtained the individual's consent.

At a time when computer technology has developed to the point wherever increasing volumes of data can be collected and manipulated, there is this corresponding concern from those who do not want this data to be accessed or utilized for any purpose without their consent. These represent two very strong competing interests, and it is important to explore the issue from both perspectives so that appropriate procedures can be put in place to protect the privacy of the individual while realizing the advantages of this continually developing technology.

In considering the issue of medical records privacy, the first question that surfaces is: What constitutes health care information? Most health care information is taken from the medical record which, in addition to diagnostic, testing and charge information, may include a description of a person's family history, genetic testing, history of diseases and treatments, history of drug use, sexual orientation, and testing for sexually transmitted diseases. Subjective remarks about a patient's demeanor, character and mental state may also be a part of the medical record. Health care information thus consists of a wide range of medical information generated, gathered, and stored about an individual.

Computerization of health care information permits the storage of large volumes of data in a single small physical space. Rather than working with reams of paper files, computers allow for the entry of information contained in these records in a data format that can be manipulated and read via the computer. The linking of computer information systems allows the information to be accessible anywhere at any time to anyone who has authorized access. Utilizing the available data, new databases can be created and expanded with ease. This ability of the computer to manipulate large volumes of data instantaneously makes the potential dissemination of health care information virtually limitless.

There are significant advantages that can be realized from the current state of computerization. The accumulation of health care data in on-line systems can be utilized to improve the quality of patient care, advance medical science, lower health care costs, and enhance the education of health care professionals. One requires little imagination to see how access to on-line information can present the medical provider with the most current information on the identification and treatment of a medical problem. Similarly, such linkages also allow for the transfer of patient data from one health care facility to another to coordinate treatment plans.

Benefit administrators are primary users of health care data. Information has been collected since health insurance began, but the technology today has made it easier to collect and store large quantities of patient records in increasingly sophisticated ways. This permits data to be used to profile treatment practices and ensure that the most effective result is being obtained for each health care dollar expended. With the ever-evolving state of medical technology, the data can be used to identify effective new procedures and simultaneously measure outcome results. Timely access to the medical data can be a critical component for purposes of achieving early return to work. As such, health care data has become a valuable commodity both in terms of identifying new effective procedures and controlling costs.

A related use for health care data is medical research. Previously, virtually all information concerning the effectiveness of tests or treatments, if in health records at all, lie buried in large stores of paper files that could not be analyzed economically. Today, the search and retrieval capabilities of computerized medical records, in conjunction with on-line analysis tools, can enable much faster, more accurate analysis of data. This again is designed to benefit the patient by continually monitoring and measuring treatment outcomes and effectiveness.

While there are very distinct advantages to the compiling of medical information into large data bases, there also exists the opportunity for abuse. The concerns of privacy advocates are based on two underlying issues. The first is that individuals have a right to control the dissemination and use of their own personal health information. Because privacy is perceived as a fundamental right, advocates argue that organizations that may wish to use the information should be required to obtain explicit authorization for each instance of information collection, processing, or further disclosure.

The second concern is that information, revealed to another party without the explicit authorization of that individual, may be used to harm his or her interests. These may include economic or social interests or may extend into areas of personal or political embarrassment. Health care information can influence decisions about an individual's access to credit, admission to educational institutions, and the ability to secure employment or obtain insurance. While it is recognized by the advocates for privacy that the potential for unauthorized use of medical information exists in a paper-based environment, the argument was made that electronic health care information and computer networks compound the problem exponentially.

In a **Georgia** case, the employer/insurer's attorney wanted to meet with the treating physician to discuss the claim, but the doctor would not talk to the defense attorney without the express permission of the claimant, in spite of the fact that the claimant had executed a form authorizing the release of medical information. The Administrative Law Judge, Appellate Division and the Superior Court all agreed the hearing could not go forward until she consented to the doctor talking to the defense attorney, but the Court of Appeals reversed. In a 4 to 3 decision, the Court of Appeals reasoned that the phrase medical information was limited to tangible documentation.

In rendering their opinion, the majority determined the legislature did not contemplate ex parte communications when it drafted O.C.G.A. § 34-9-207. Therefore, the Court of Appeals held the Workers Compensation Act did not permit the employer/insurer's attorney to meet with or talk to the employee's authorized treating physician without the knowledge and consent of the employee. Nothing in Georgia law or HIPAA prohibits ex parte communications between the employer or its attorney and a treating physician in a workers compensation case as long as the communications relate to the job injury. The court also noted there was no requirement that a treating physician agree to be interviewed ex parte.

On appeal to the Georgia Supreme Court, in a unanimous decision, concluded that the Act's waiver was not so narrow. Under the plain and unambiguous language of the Act, it was noted that, *"any privilege the employee may have had in protected medical records and information related to a workers compensation claim is waived once the employee submits a claim for workers compensation benefits or is receiving weekly income benefits or the employer has paid any medical expenses."*[194] The conclusion reached in Georgia was that employers, insurers and their attorneys are permitted to meet with treating physicians to discuss their claims without the knowledge or approval of the claimant.

HEALTH INSURANCE PORTABILITY AND ACCOUNTABILITY ACT (HIPPA)

The system of protection for health care information that has developed to date can best be described as a patchwork of federal and state laws. At the federal level, the Privacy Act of 1974 specifically identified privacy as a fundamental constitutional right. Designed to protect individuals from government disclosure of confidential information, the Privacy Act prohibited federal agencies from disclosing information contained in a system of records to any person or agency without the written consent of the individual to whom the information pertains. This law further required that the agencies meet certain requirements for the handling of confidential information.

At the state level there is significant variation in terms of how health care information is being addressed. Among the states that have regulations, statutes, or case law recognizing medical records as confidential and limiting access to them, there is no consistency in the recognition of computerized records as legitimate documents under the law, and generally there is no recognition of the issues raised by the evolution to computerization. For example, virtually none

---

[194] *McRae v. Arby's Restaurant Group*, 313 Ga. App. 313 (721 SE2d 602) (2011)

of the laws address the practice of compiling medical information about patients for sale to businesses with a financial interest in the data.

At the federal level, the requirements about health care information privacy were addressed by Congress with passage of the 1996 Health Insurance Portability and Accountability Act (HIPPA). HIPAA is a federal law that required the creation of national standards to protect sensitive patient health information from being disclosed without the patient's consent or knowledge. The US Department of Health and Human Services (HHS) issued the HIPAA Privacy Rule to implement the requirements of HIPAA.

The Privacy Rule standards address the use and disclosure of individuals' health information (known as "protected health information") by entities subject to the Privacy Rule. These individuals and organizations are called "covered entities." The following types of individuals and organizations are considered covered entities:

- **Healthcare Providers:** Every healthcare provider, regardless of size of practice, who electronically transmits health information in connection with certain transactions. These transactions include claims, benefit eligibility inquiries, referral authorization requests, and other transactions for which HHS has established standards under the HIPAA Transactions Rule.

- **Health Plans:** Entities that provide or pay the cost of medical care. Health plans include health, dental, vision, and prescription drug insurers; health maintenance organizations (HMOs); Medicare, Medicaid, Medicare Choice, and Medicare supplement insurers; and long-term care insurers (excluding nursing home fixed-indemnity policies). Health plans also include employer-sponsored group health plans, government- and church-sponsored health plans, and multi-employer health plans. (An exception is a group health plan with fewer than 50 participants that is administered solely by the employer that established and maintains the plan is not a covered entity.)

- **Healthcare Clearinghouses:** Entities that process nonstandard information they receive from another entity into a standard (i.e., standard format or data content), or vice versa. In most instances, healthcare clearinghouses will receive individually identifiable health information only when they are providing these processing services to a health plan or healthcare provider as a business associate.

- **Business Associates:** A person or organization (other than a member of a covered entity's workforce) using or disclosing individually identifiable health information to perform or provide functions, activities, or services for a covered entity. These functions, activities, or services include claims processing, data analysis, utilization review, and billing.

A covered entity is permitted, but not required, to use and disclose protected health information, without an individual's authorization, for the following purposes or situations:

- Disclosure to the individual (if the information is required for access or accounting of disclosures, the entity MUST disclose to the individual).

- Treatment, payment, and healthcare operations.

- Opportunity to agree or object to the disclosure of PHI (Informal permission may be obtained by asking the individual outright, or by circumstances that clearly give the individual the opportunity to agree, acquiesce, or object.

- Incident to an otherwise permitted use and disclosure.

- Public interest and benefit activities—The Privacy Rule permits use and disclosure of protected health information, without an individual's authorization or permission.

- Limited dataset for research, public health, or healthcare operations.

While the HIPAA Privacy Rule safeguards protected health information (PHI), the Security Rule protects a subset of information covered by the Privacy Rule. This subset is all individually identifiable health information a covered entity creates, receives, maintains, or transmits in electronic form. To comply with the HIPAA Security Rule, all covered entities must do the following:

- Ensure the confidentiality, integrity, and availability of all electronic protected health information.

- Detect and safeguard against anticipated threats to the security of the information.

- Protect against anticipated impermissible uses or disclosures.

- Certify compliance by their workforce.

Covered entities should rely on professional ethics and best judgment when considering requests for these permissive uses and disclosures of medical information. The HHS Office for Civil Rights enforces HIPAA rules, and all complaints should be reported to that office. HIPAA violations may result in civil monetary or criminal penalties.[195]

HIPAA provides both civil and criminal penalties for any misuse of personal health information by covered entities. Civil penalties range from $100 per incident, up to $25,000 per person, per year, per standard. Criminal penalties are available for covered entities that knowingly and improperly disclose information, obtain information under false pretenses, or disclose or obtain information for actions designed to generate monetary gain. Violators are subject to penalties of up to $250,000 and 10 years in prison, depending on the particular offense.

---

[195] https://www.cdc.gov/phlp/publications/topic/hipaa.html

A data breach or security incident that results from any violation could see separate fines issued for different aspects of the breach under multiple security and privacy standards. A fine of $50,000 could, in theory, be issued for any violation of HIPAA rules; however minor. A fine may also be applied daily. For example, if a covered entity has been denying patients the right to obtain copies of their medical records and had been doing so for a period of one year, the OCR may decide to apply a penalty per day that the covered entity has been in violation of the law. The penalty would be multiplied by 365, not by the number of patients that have been refused access to their medical records.

Since the introduction of the HITECH Act[196] in February 2009, state attorneys general have the authority to hold HIPAA-covered entities accountable for the exposure of the personal health information of state residents and can file civil actions with the federal district courts. HIPAA violation fines can be issued up to a maximum level of $25,000 per violation category, per calendar year. The minimum fine applicable is $100 per violation.

A covered entity suffering a data breach affecting residents in multiple states may be ordered to pay HIPAA violation fines to attorneys general in multiple states. At present only a few U.S states have acted against HIPAA offenders, but since attorneys general offices are able to retain a percentage of the fines issued, more attorneys general may decide to issue penalties for HIPAA violations.[197]

From the perspective of workers compensation, it is important to recognize the critical role that health care information plays throughout the life of a claim. While medical information is not the sole source for benefit determination, the information is used to:

- Establish work-relatedness of the injury or disease.

- Determine whether a pre-existing condition is present to evaluate the potential impact on the treatment and recovery period.

- Comply with utilization review requirements which are designed to ensure that appropriate treatment is being afforded.

- Assist employers in the return-to-work process including the identification of situations where some form of job modification may be required.

Because workers compensation represents a statutory benefit, it contains some unique coverage exposures in terms of the amount and length of entitlement. Medical expenses are covered from the first dollar and are paid without benefit of co-payments or deductibles. Benefits for both medical and income replacement benefits are payable generally during the period of recovery without consideration for duration or dollar limits. Because of these unique characteristics, it is important that handlers of workers compensation claims continue to have access to necessary medical information in order to control costs while directing efforts at timely return-to-work.

---

[196] Section 13410(e) (1))
[197] https://www.hipaajournal.com/what-are-the-penalties-for-hipaa-violations-

The privacy of health care information is an important consideration and no one should minimize the potential for misuse. At the same time, it is critical to recognize the importance computerized records play in improving health treatment techniques and the ability to monitor and control health care costs. In the workers compensation arena, this health care data is a critical element throughout the life of a claim and continued timely access to appropriate information is essential for control of both the medical and indemnity payments. A patient's right to his/her own health care information needs to be established and processes developed for the patient to amend or supplement that information. Patients need to be able to access their own medical records and amend those records

THE AFFORDABLE CARE ACT (ACA)

The Patient Protection and Affordable Care Act, more commonly referred to as the Affordable Care Act (ACA) or "Obama care," was signed into law March 23, 2010. The Affordable Care Act is made up of the *Affordable Health Care for America Act, the Patient Protection Act*, and the health care related sections of the *Health Care and Education Reconciliation Act* and the *Student Aid and Fiscal Responsibility Act*. It also included amendments to other laws like the Food, Drug and Cosmetics Act and the Health and Public Services Act.

The ACA is a complex piece of legislation that attempted to reform the healthcare system by providing more Americans with affordable quality health insurance with an additional focus of curbing the growth in healthcare spending in this country. The law, as enacted, was intended to reform the healthcare system by giving more Americans access to quality, affordable health insurance and helps to curb the growth of healthcare spending. Under the ACA:

- All Americans with health insurance had have access to a number **of** new benefits, rights, and protections designed to ensure treatment when needed, including the bar against covering pre-existing conditions identified with many insurance policies.

- Insurance was to be made more affordable by reducing premium and out-of-pocket costs for tens of millions of families and small business owners who had been priced out of coverage in the past. The new law was intended to help over 32 million Americans afford health care that could not obtain coverage before and makes coverage more affordable for many more.

- Risks are to be spread equally to all insured to end discrimination. Previously, gender and health status discrimination existed, and health care costs could differ wildly due to factors like age. The ACA limits discrepancies in what can be charged and in order to accomplish this objective, all Americans are to maintain Minimum Essential Coverage beginning in 2014.

- **A** new competitive health insurance marketplace was established whereby millions of Americans will have access to group buying power and allowing them to compare plans and receive cost assistance.

Through 2016, about twenty million people were able to enroll and obtain coverage through the ACA. These people were eligible for government-subsidized, private health insurance or were able to sign-up – in some but not all states - through Medicaid, the government program for low-income families. The ACA also obligated insurers to cover sick people with pre-existing conditions and further obligated insurers not to charge them more than healthy people

On the day President Trump was sworn into office – January 20, 2017 – he signed an executive order instructing administration officials "to waive, defer, grant exemptions from, or delay" implementing parts of the Affordable Care Act while preparing to repeal and replace the health care law. After that, the administration began utilizing a piecemeal approach as they tried to take apart the Act. This was done through:

- The 2017 Republican-backed tax overhaul legislation that reduced the penalty for not having insurance to $0 thereby essentially eliminating the individual mandate.

- Permitting states to add "work requirements" to Medicaid.

- Ending payments from the federal government to insurers to motivate them to stay in the ACA insurance exchanges and help keep premiums down.

- The ACA initially established rules that health plans sold on HealthCare.gov and state exchanges had to cover people with preexisting conditions and had to provide certain "essential benefits." Short-term plans that did not include those benefits were limited to a maximum duration of three months. The Trump administration issued a rule that allowed these short-term plans to last 364 days and to be renewable for three years.

- Cutting funding to facilitate HealthCare.gov sign-ups such as the Navigator programs and an advertising budget were slashed.[198]

With the election of President Joe Biden in November 2020, along with Democratic control of both the House of Representatives and the United States Senate, it is likely that the issues will be revisited, and attempts made to address shortcomings in the original legislation and expand upon the original Affordable Care Act.

Following the original enactment of the Affordable Care Act, there was a great deal of speculation in terms of its potential impact on the health care delivery system in this country. Opinions were sharply divided on the application of various provisions of the ACA, and these differences are most evident as regards the inconsistency across state lines with the subject of health care exchanges, with some states opting for a state-based exchange system while others are relying on the federal initiative.

---

[198] https://www.npr.org/sections/health-shots/2019/10/14/768731628/trump-is-trying-hard-to-thwart-obamacare-hows-that-going

With the launching of the new law, questions arose as to how the Affordable Care Act was likely to impact the workers compensation program. One can only observe that at the point when the program was just beginning to unfold, the extent, nature and ultimate impact remained markedly unclear.

While many speculated as to the impact, Derek A. Jones, principal and consulting actuary at Milliman, wrote an article on the subject in July 2013. His article perhaps best articulates what could be projected at that time. Recognizing that there are likely to be certain changes associated with the new law, he observed in part:

"One clear intention of the ACA is that greater access to health insurance coverage should lead to a healthier population, which should have two direct effects on the workers compensation market. First, all else being equal, a healthier workforce is expected to lead to a reduction in claim frequency. Second, a healthier workforce could also lead to greater ability to recover from workplace injuries, which will accelerate the employee's return to work. If this occurs, or if healthier individuals are less inclined to continue on workers compensation with a combination of work-related and other medical conditions, the claim experience of the workers compensation market should improve.

Less clear, but perhaps more significant, is the potential shift of costs between the workers compensation and the health insurance markets. A common challenge for workers compensation providers is the tendency by a portion of the workforce that does not have health insurance to file for or to stay on workers compensation, with some health benefits being paid for medical conditions that may not be work-related. In practice, to the extent many of these claims are treated easily and closed quickly, the expanded availability of healthcare insurance by the general population may shift some of these claims to healthcare. To the extent they are small, there may not be a significant impact on either system. To the extent any of these claims are larger, there may be a significant cost shift from workers compensation to healthcare.

For workers with ailments that require regular treatments over a number of years, there is the issue of convenience in addition to the question of availability of insurance coverage—both workers and medical service providers (e.g., physicians, hospitals) generally prefer health insurance over workers compensation. Workers tend to dislike the lack of control they have in the workers compensation system, which is due to the requirements of dealing with claims handlers and medical claim payment systems and, in some states, having to select physicians from the employer's medical provider network. Workers also seek to minimize interaction with a carrier's claim handlers; this is a frequent driver of claimants' pursuits of workers compensation claim settlements. When a choice between health insurance and workers compensation coverage is available, many workers will opt for health insurance.

For physicians, the workers compensation system typically requires more justification of the treatment, as well as the preparation of reoccurring formal reports and other paperwork. In some cases, they may be required to testify regarding their treatments before receiving reimbursement from the insurance carrier. This administrative burden and low fee reimbursements are why many physicians do not accept workers compensation claimants as patients. Opportunities to direct patients to claim coverage under health insurance instead of workers compensation will be welcomed by the physician community.

While workers find the administrative requirements of workers compensation to be onerous, the increased use of deductibles and copayment requirements in the health insurance market could drive some users back to the workers compensation market. Another factor that could increase the costs of workers compensation is the current shortage of primary care physicians in the United States. A shortage of primary care physicians could delay the employee's medical evaluation(s) and thus impede carriers' ability to deny questionable claims as quickly as possible. More importantly, the lack of primary care physicians will prevent timely treatment of workers' medical conditions. Claims professionals commonly acknowledge that the first 90 days of a claim define the course for the claim while it remains open. Obstacles to timely initiation of a proper course of treatment will slow workers' ability to recover and to return to work, which could unnecessarily extend the medical cost and wage replacement components of workers compensation claims.

Another way the ACA has facilitated the shift from workers compensation to group health coverage is the creation of the Pre-existing Condition Insurance Plan (PCIP). The PCIP is a program to provide health coverage to people who have been denied coverage because of their health condition or who presently have a preexisting condition.[4] Before the ACA was enacted, workers compensation was used by many people to obtain at least some healthcare for a preexisting condition that was arguably associated with a work-related injury. In 2014, the ACA will prohibit health insurers from refusing coverage because of preexisting conditions and will maintain the spirit of the PCIP, which will no longer be needed."[199]

Now, with a new administration in office, some of the old questions regarding the Affordable Care Act will again surface and will bring with them new questions associated with the possible expansion of the original law.

So far in 2021, 10 states are presently considering legislation to establish a single-payer health insurance program. Five of those states - **California**, **Iowa**, **Maryland**, **Rhode Island**, and **Texas** – specifically mention workers compensation or injured workers medical benefits in their proposals. To date, no one has introduced federal single-payer health insurance legislation in the new Congress.

One other state to watch concerning the expansion of health care coverage is **Vermont** where, in January 2013, the state released a report, *"Integration or Alignment of Vermont's Workers Compensation System with Green Mountain Care,"* which describes how the state was considering moving toward its ultimate goal of integrating its new single-payer healthcare system with its workers compensation system. This requires further study, but if fully integrated, the medical coverage portion of workers compensation would be eliminated and ultimately the private system would be abandoned in favor of a monopolistic, publicly funded workers compensation system. The report also suggests that Vermont might select another route,

---

[199] *ACA: An Act of Unknown Consequences for Workers Compensation,* by Derek A. Jones at Milliman website

integrating only the healthcare portion, or it might reject integration in favor of some form of administrative alignment.

Chapter Nine

PROGRAM ADMINISTRATION, DISPUTE RESOLUTION AND SPECIAL FUNDS

Administration of the workers compensation law and the awarding of compensation benefits are under the jurisdiction of a workers compensation board, commission, or similar state administrative agency. In most jurisdictions, the administrative agency responsible for workers compensation operates under the supervision or direction of the state's department of labor or equivalent. **Nebraska** is the lone state where administration of the workers compensation law resides with the Workers Compensation Court.

Other approaches to the administrative agency include the four monopolistic states which are free standing state agencies. In **Texas** and **West Virginia,** the administration resides with the insurance commission, and in **Florida,** the Division of Workers Compensation under the Department of Insurance headed by the official in charge of financial regulation. Some agencies are set up as free standing commissions like **North Carolina** and **Arkansas**.

As originally developed, the workers compensation programs were intended to be a self-executing system in which benefits would flow directly to the injured worker without the need for attorney involvement and attendant litigation. As originally conceived, it was expected that, with elimination of the fault concept and the prescription of benefits by statute, injured employees would be able to protect their interests without external assistance. The original policymakers intended to make the system self-executing so that:

- Benefits would be delivered and terminated in a timely manner, thus minimizing economic and social hardships for workers, and providing reasonable cost to employers.

- Disputes would be resolved with a minimum of friction costs (including attorney fees, medical/legal costs, state agency administrative costs, and claims handling costs).

- Workers would return to work faster.

With the passage of time, it was recognized that the expectation for self-execution was overly optimistic. It had become clear that workers compensation laws and compensation claims are, in practice, much more complex than anticipated. Determinations of issues of compensability along with findings relative to the extent or degree of permanent disability are inherently controversial. At the same time, it came to be realized that good communication, clear laws and rules, mutual trust, and consistency of application contribute importantly to an effective delivery system.

The fifth objective of a modern workmen's compensation program, an effective delivery system, as delineated in the report compiled by the National Commission on State Workmen's Compensation Laws, is required in order to achieve the four basic objectives that include complete coverage, adequate income maintenance, necessary medical care and rehabilitation, and safety incentives.

An effective delivery system enlists a close working relationship between both private and public organizations including insurers, self-administered programs, workers compensation boards and commissions, and courts. To that end, a variety of individuals are also involved including employers, employees, benefit administrators, attorneys, and physicians. In other words, all program participants.

The role of an administrative agency can be divided into two fairly distinct, but clearly overlapping, functions. In the first place there is the day-to-day administrative oversight of the benefit delivery system. The monitoring of the delivery of benefits requires action to ensure their timely and proper delivery. The second function associated with benefit administration involves the more historic role of dispute resolution through informal and formal proceedings.

As indicated, these roles are distinct, but proactive administrative oversight can clearly be an effective mechanism for purposes of reducing the number of disputes, and ultimately the need for dispute resolution proceedings. While clearly a system without disputes may not be a reality, steps taken to reduce disputes and litigation is a goal that should be supported and acted upon by all program participants.

The following reviews those two important administrative agency functions with the recognition that there are differences in terms of how states approach each of those functions. The use of different terms for similar activities serves to add complexity to any attempt at comparisons among jurisdictions. Thus, while various jurisdictions may use different terms when referring to certain functions, for purposes of simplification, generic terms will be used. For example, while specific jurisdictions may have in place an industrial accident board or an industrial commission or a workers compensation division for purposes of administering their compensation law, the generic term of administrative agency (or just agency) will be used in describing those functions.

The material includes a number of tangential issues closely associated with the dispute resolution and the benefit administration process. As regards the dispute resolution process, the first is the subject of attorney fees and the second is the issue of lump sum settlements. In contrast to a contingency basis for determining attorney fees as found under most tort systems, states have enacted legislation with various approaches designed to restrict the amount of such fees. In the case of lump sum settlements, their expanded usage in certain jurisdictions raises questions of appropriateness in a system originally intended to be self-executing.

BENEFIT ADMINISTRATION AT THE STATE LEVEL

In 2013, two states became the most recent jurisdictions to join the majority of states where the workers compensation law is administered by an administrative agency. The **Oklahoma** Workers Compensation Commission (WCC) administrative system was changed from a system run by the courts to one administered by three commissioners appointed by the governor for six-year terms. In July 2014 the two systems began operating as stand-alone agencies. New claims were to be processed by the WCC until the old court-based system was phased out in 2020 as old claims were settled.

In the same year, the **Tennessee** system was changed through legislation that transferred all administrative oversight functions from the courts to a single independent state agency, the Tennessee Bureau of Workers' Compensation (BWC). The measure also created an ombudsman to hear complaints. With the changes in Oklahoma and Tennessee, **Nebraska** remains the last state with a court administered program.

Certain functions fall within the responsibility of an administrative agency. This is not to imply that all agencies undertake each one of the identified functions, but rather that when looking at the overall functions of an administrative agency in a generic sense, these activities are identified with a large number of agencies. In addition to those primary functions, the agency may be responsible for management of second injury or special funds and their assessments along with the administration and implementation of workplace safety programs. There is wide variance in terms of the level of activity undertaken by the different administrative agencies. In some instances, the agencies are quite pro-active in terms of system monitoring, while in other jurisdictions, the agency plays a less active role.

The primary administrative functions of a commission, bureau or workers compensation agency include:

> **Dissemination of Information** – Information is the keystone of any efficient administrative operation. Access to information is also a critical component in any effort to reduce disputes. The notion of dispute prevention has gained popularity in recent years as public policy makers have sought to make workers compensation systems more self-executing. As used in the field, the term dispute prevention actually encompasses a broad range of system features to ensure certainty, consistency, and communication in workers compensation, more than it is possible for us to convey here.
>
> The process of information dissemination starts with the proper distribution of written materials regarding the law and the rights and responsibilities of all of the system participants. Jurisdictions vary considerably in their approaches to providing information and assistance services. Following are a number of strategies that describe the information and assistance practices found in some jurisdictions:
>
> - Targeting written materials explaining the law and participants' rights and responsibilities under the law to all participants in the program. This distribution of information is done prior to the event of an injury and is usually located in an employers' place of business.

- Making available written information in other languages.

- Providing information regarding the program on the internet.

- Furnishing injured workers with a brochure detailing their rights and responsibilities following the reporting of a workplace accident.

- Advertising toll-free information lines available to various constituents.

All of these activities are designed to inform program participants of their rights and responsibilities and to provide a forum for answering questions in a non-adversarial atmosphere. Explaining how statutes and rules have been interpreted and collecting answers to "Frequently Asked Questions" are also useful. The more the injured worker understands regarding their rights and responsibilities under the law, and the earlier this information is provided, the less likely there will later be misunderstandings and disputes.

Monitoring the Benefit Delivery Process – Under most state laws, the injured employee is required to give the employer or insurer notice of an injury as soon as it is possible for the employee, or someone acting on his or her behalf, to do so. In some states, the time period for reporting the injury to the employer is specifically set forth in statute. For example, in **Maryland,** notice must be given within 10 days after injury or within 30 days after death. In **Kansas**, notice is to be given to the employer within 10 days and up to 75 days with "just cause." In other states, however, the time frame for reporting an injury is more ambiguous. **Arizona, Connecticut** and **Hawaii** require the notice to be given "forthwith." In **Indiana**, notice is to be given in writing "as soon as practical."

Most jurisdictions waive the notice requirement for the injured worker where a justified excuse is submitted. However, it is important to understand the rationale behind having the injured worker report the incident promptly. In the first place, the employer cannot commence the claim process until the claim is reported. Secondly, the facts surrounding the claim can be best investigated while still fresh. And finally, the later the report of a claim the costliest the claim tends to be, all else being equal. In addition, timely reporting of the claim allows the employer to commence an investigation into the circumstances surrounding the accident so that additional injuries might be avoided.

Once the employer has been made aware of a workplace injury, the employer is required to file an accident report with the administrative agency within a prescribed period of time. This initial report to the agency is generally referred to as the First Report of Injury (FROI). Only a minority of states require all injuries to be reported. For example, **Virginia** and **West Virginia** require the reporting of all injuries to the agency. The **Tennessee** Bureau of Workers Compensation requires all injuries requiring medical attention to be reported. The majority of states require only the reporting of injuries requiring the payment of lost-time benefits which includes those cases where the disability extends beyond the statutory waiting period.

Because many smaller employers may not be familiar with the reporting requirements and format, the insurance carrier or third party administrator (benefit administrator) frequently advise the employer to report the injury by telephone, fax or special web reporting tool to the benefit administrator for purposes of completing the report and submitting same to the administrative agency. Reporting electronically ensures that the proper information is collected immediately and that the payment of any benefits due will not be delayed.

Filing of the First Report of Injury (FROI) form with the agency places both the benefit administrator and the agency on notice of the claim. Where notice is to be filed only where the case involves lost-time benefits, the agency will generally receive notification of the injury concurrent with notification that income replacement benefits have been initiated.

Where the period of incapacity to work as a result of the injury extends beyond the statutory waiting period, benefit administrators are required to make payment within a specified period of time following the first date of disability. In uncontested cases – cases in which there is no dispute as regards to benefit entitlement – such payments may be initiated under either the direct payment system or by agreement.

Under the direct payment system, the benefit administrator takes the initiative and begins the payment of compensation benefits to the worker or his or her dependents. (Payment of benefits to dependents would be made in the case of the death of the employee.) The injured employee is not required to enter into any type of agreement and is not required to sign any documents before compensation payments begin. The compensation laws are specific in terms of the calculation of the amount of compensation benefits the employee should receive and the time period when payments are due. Where compensation payments are not initiated, the agency may step in, investigate the matter, and correct any errors.

Under the agreement system – in effect in the majority of states – the benefit administrator and the injured worker agree upon the amount of compensation benefits before payments may be initiated. In many instances, when the claim is uncontested, the benefit administrator will include the agreement form along with the first payment of compensation benefits. This serves to expedite the payment of replacement income and helps to remove any questions regarding possible benefit entitlement.

Following the filing of the FROI with the administrative agency, many states require the filing of supplemental forms and accident reports for various purposes. For example, virtually all jurisdictions require the filing of a report when making the initial payment of compensation benefits. Information included in this report would delineate the weekly or monthly earning of the injured employee along with the type and amount of periodic compensation benefits being paid. This information is reviewed by the agency to ensure that the proper type and amount of benefits are being paid.

In addition, upon termination of the payment of weekly benefits, upon any change in the amount or type of compensation benefits being paid, or when disability extends beyond a certain time period, the filing of a supplemental report is required in the majority of states. Some jurisdictions require the filing of a closing notice that captures information as to the amount and type of disability benefits paid, the duration of such benefits, along with a summarization of the medical or rehabilitation benefits paid. In virtually all instances, it is the benefit administrator and not the employer responsible for filing the supplemental reports. Exceptions are self-insured employers administering claims internally.

Filing of these various forms and documents provide the agency with the ability to monitor the benefit delivery process and to ensure the timely and correct payment of benefits. With today's electronic capability, these reports and forms are frequently transmitted electronically. This electronic data can then be collected and compiled by the agency as regards the type of accidental injuries occurring in a particular industry so steps may be taken to eliminate or reduce future occurrences. (The subject of data reporting will be discussed in detail in a subsequent section.)

Rehabilitation and Medical Oversight – Workers compensation laws vary regarding the necessity for physical and vocational rehabilitation. Generally, employers or their benefit administrators are required to provide rehabilitation or to make payments into a rehabilitation fund. In several states, injured employees must accept the rehabilitation services offered; if they do not, their compensation benefits may be suspended. Some states provide other penalties such as reducing the amount of the compensation award in such situations.

Most compensation laws provide for the payment of temporary total disability benefits during the period that vocational rehabilitation services are being provided. Some states mandate additional benefits in order to facilitate the rehabilitation process. These additional benefits may include payment of specific expenses for retraining such as books, tuition fees, board, and lodging (if away from home), childcare, and reimbursement of travel expenses. In most jurisdictions, rehabilitation costs and additional expenses are subject to a maximum dollar amount or limited to a maximum time period.

While the administrative agency may not actually furnish rehabilitation services, a proactive agency can provide helpful assistance and guidance including:

- A systematic approach to early case identification and referral to a disability management process.

- A thorough understanding of rehabilitation and of how to set objectives for cases referred.

- Continuous evaluation of the rehabilitation process to be certain the right people are making proper decisions.

- A tracking system to monitor the cost and effectiveness of the rehabilitation procedures used in bringing about a positive result.

The Federal Vocational Rehabilitation Act (FVCA), now effective in all states, includes federal funds to aid states in vocational rehabilitation of the industrially disabled. The FVCA is federal legislation that authorizes the formula grant programs of vocational rehabilitation, supported employment, independent living, and client assistance. It also authorizes a variety of training and service discretionary grants administered by the Rehabilitation Services Administration (RSA). The law includes a variety of provisions focused on rights, advocacy, and protections for individuals with disabilities.[1]

ELECTRONIC DATA REPORTING

Reliable data is a critical component of any system used to identify the causes and extent of work place injuries and illness. It is well recognized that reliable data can be used by employers to reduce the incidence and severity of workplace injuries and illnesses. Comparable data can be used by law makers to draw comparisons across jurisdictional lines and measure the impact of legislative and regulatory reform. Reliable data can measure and help determine the main system cost drivers.

The introduction of computer technology has assisted administrative agencies in their ability to fulfill their responsibility to collect reports and effectively monitor the benefit delivery process. The electronic means for reporting of specific claim and coverage data now provides the agency with the ability to receive information, formerly contained on various paper forms and documents, faster and more accurately. Through the use of these means, more information can be collected with quicker response in identification of any problems so that a wider scope of benefit monitoring can be realized.

In April of 1914, just three years following the enactment of the first workmen's compensation law in this country, regulators from federal and state programs gathered in Lansing, Michigan and formed an association. The next year, a Canadian province joined, and the International Association of Industrial Accident Boards and Commissions (IAIABC) was formed.

Even from that early point, the need for reliable information regarding the compensation program was recognized. It was in 1914 that the Commission on Workmen's Compensation Laws stated that, *"No real knowledge of the operation of Workmen's Compensation Acts can be acquired until complete statistics have been gathered ... injustices that may exist through the law cannot be remedied until the facts are known, and the facts cannot be known until complete statistics have been compiled."*

While the problem was recognized early on, little progress was made in the area of collecting reliable data for the next sixty years. Then, to assist program administrators in gathering the information necessary to answer questions and to evaluate how the workers compensation program was performing, the IAIABC adopted in 1975 a Basic Administrative Information System (BAIS). While identifying the type of information to be collected, the process itself was confined to the collection and compilation of data from paper forms.

---

[1] 29 U.S.C. § 701 et seq.

By the late 1980s, when the costs associated with workers compensation claims was rising rapidly, it became apparent that legislators and other policy makers were asking more and more questions and were equally persistent in their desire to obtain information as to how the workers compensation systems were working. Accordingly, in 1987, the Statistics Subcommittee of the IAIABC set out to reevaluate and update the BAIS system.

The process began with the collection and review of all paper report forms filed with the various state administrative agencies. These reports included copies of the First Report of Injury, wage statements, reports recording the initial payment of compensation, the claim closing notification, along with a host of other reports where information was collected by some, but perhaps not all, of the state agencies. Contents of these reports were categorized in order to provide for a coherent spectrum of what the various agencies were collecting.

Results of this first phase of the data collection project were compiled into a recommended list of data elements that agencies should be collecting in order to properly monitor the effective delivery of benefits. Concurrent with this first phase of the review project under the aegis of the IAIABC, the National Association of Insurance Commissioners (NAIC) established a subcommittee to review the subject of data collection. Based upon the similarity of purpose in terms of expanded workers compensation data collection, a joint working group composed of members of the IAIABC subcommittee and the NAIC subcommittee was formed.

The joint working group served to recognize that there were two forms of statistical data being requested. If the data collection process was to move forward and address the needs of all program participants, it would need to be in a position to gather both:

Rate-Setting Data – The data collected by rating organizations and insurance departments used for the purposes of setting rates and allocating costs to policy, class, etc. While utilized primarily for that purpose, rate-setting data is also collected by program administrators to monitor payments by injury type and establish the amounts paid or incurred for medical and vocational rehabilitation services.

Benefit Monitoring Data – Administrative agencies needed to be in a position to respond to questions such as: How many injured workers received compensation benefits in the prior year? How much was paid out in benefits by benefit type? How much was paid out in medical services? What was the timeliness of the first payment of compensation benefits? These and many more are all questions that a workers compensation program administrator should be able to answer. The ability to answer these and other questions requires the timely collection and organization of data about the workers compensation system.

In the early 1990s, several insurance carriers and associations representatives met with the IAIABC staff in an effort to standardize the data collection process and look for ways to efficiently collect the information. It was clear to many of these early participants of the need to collect and transmit this material through electronic means in lieu of the continued use of paper forms. The result of these discussions was the formation of the Electronic Data Interchange (EDI)[2] Steering Committee.

The mission of the IAIABC EDI project was to:

- To promote the advantages of exchanging the data between participant systems.
- To promote/recommend business and data interchange objectives.
- To assist participants to identify business data requirements.
- To establish data interchange standards.
- To provide a structure to accomplish these purposes.

EDI represents an extension of the first phase of the IAIABC data collection project which focused on the identification of data elements for system participants to collect. EDI, which stands for electronic data interchange, is the intercompany communication of business documents in a standard format. Simply defined, EDI is a standard electronic format that replaces paper-based documents such as purchase orders or invoices. By automating paper-based transactions, organizations can save time and eliminate costly errors caused by manual processing.

In EDI transactions, information moves directly from a computer application in one organization to a computer application in another. EDI standards define the location and order of information in a document format. With this automated capability, data can be shared virtually immediately instead of over the hours, days, or weeks required when using paper documents and mail to exchange information.

The commitment of the members of the IAIABC project to move in the direction of EDI simply moved the project to the next natural level. After first establishing a listing of recommended data elements for collection, the next issue to address was the identification of the most cost efficient and accurate manner in which to collect that data. EDI represented that next natural phase.

State workers compensation administrative agencies, responsible for monitoring the benefit delivery process, represent the most practical location for collecting that data. At that point, most state agencies utilized paper forms to collect incident information and monitor the claim process on each lost-time claim. Rather than utilizing those various forms (e.g. first injury reports, memorandum of payment, case progress reports, closed claim information, etc.), the EDI effort was intended to replace such forms through an

---

[2] Electronic Data Interchange is the exchange of standardized document forms between computer systems for business purposes. EDI is most often used between different companies ("trading partners") and uses some variation of the ANSI X12 standard (USA) or EDIFACT (UN sponsored global) standard.

electronic link whereby a standardized listing of data elements would be communicated electronically. EDI simply represented use of the most current technical capabilities to effectively transmit data.

When proposing EDI for workers compensation, it was important to first identify those features which favored its adoption. Those features have application whether discussing the role of the employer, the injured worker, the benefit administrator, or the administrative agency. Through a series of meetings and discussions, the following features were identified:

- The principal purpose in support of EDI is the cost efficiency. Reduced cost can be realized through the elimination of data entry at the state agency level when the state system is directly linked to an external data source. While state agencies would realize an immediate benefit through accepting first injury reports electronically, subsequent payment reports filed via electronic means would represent significant savings for employers and carriers. Additional savings are connected with reduced filing space requirements and reductions in the expenditures for postage and mail sorting time.

- Along with savings associated with the direct transfer of data through electronic means, there is the separate issue of improved data accuracy. Information entered or "keyed" a number of times is subject to error. The fewer times it is necessary to enter information, the greater will be the degree of accuracy. There is little value in collecting and utilizing data unless there is a strong assurance that the data is accurate.

- The ongoing collection of appropriate financial data in a timely fashion provides the opportunity to continually monitor and measure changes in the workers compensation environment. The electronic submission of data on all claims would permit comparison of experience at different points in time and across jurisdictional lines. This would afford the opportunity to identify systemic problems.

- A concluding reason in support of EDI was that it would culminate in the creation of comprehensive databases at the state level which would be standardized among states in the type and format of data being collected. This standardized format would assist benefit providers through the establishment of a single standard rather than developing systems to respond to the needs of fifty different states. Additionally, and perhaps most importantly, it would permit the comparison of experience across jurisdictional lines.

The potential for cost savings through the elimination of duplicative entry processes and the efficiencies associated with a single standard for data transfer made the project a key to controlling expenses in the rapidly rising workers compensation cost environment, both for the benefit administrator and the administrative agency.

The working group within the IAIABC proceeded with the concept of moving the data collection project into an implementation phase. At the same time, a technical working group was established — composed primarily of insurance carrier representatives, state agency personnel, and consultants — who focused on the details of defining the data elements and developing the format in which the data could be electronically transferred.

This group, after reviewing all the various forms presently filed with state agencies, identified distinct phases that the project would follow. These phases reflected the various generic categories into which the various state reporting forms fell and included:

First Report of Injury – The initial report completed by the employer, which notifies the parties of the occurrence of an occupational injury or illness.

Subsequent Payment Record – Forms designed to gather information on when benefit payments begin, case progress information, and paid amounts by benefit type when the claim is concluded.

Medical Data – Refined data pertinent to the dates of service, diagnostic and procedure codes, and costs associated with the providing of medical care.

Vocational Rehabilitation Data – Monitors the incidence of vocational rehabilitation, the outcomes, and the costs associated with it.

Litigation Data – Reflects the incidence of disputes, issues in dispute, outcome results at various adjudication levels, and system costs related to litigation.

Each of these categories represented a separate project phase for the technical working group. Focusing initially on the First Report of Injury, the working groups were able to create a standard reporting format that served the needs of virtually each one of the state agencies. Efforts were also directed at establishing the same standardized reporting formats for the proof of coverage, the reporting of medical information, and the subsequent payment report, which contains all those claim derivatives – including the level and type of benefit payments – that occur following the initial reporting of the claim.

The IAIABC has developed standards for three major products: claims, proof of coverage (POC), and medical. Implementation guides describing business rules for each product are available online to members that lay out all the relevant standards.

Claims – The EDI reporting format and transaction standard for Release 1 of the First Report of Injury ((FFROI) and the Subsequent Injury Report (SIR) were available for use beginning in 1995. This part of the project began with a series of pilot programs with select states. Since its inception, there have been subsequent releases, each progressively more comprehensive than its predecessor. The standards include business rules for electronic reporting of workers compensation claims information to jurisdictions, including both FROI and SROI.

Proof of Coverage (POC) – Filing of the proof of coverage via EDI is mandated in more than a quarter of the states. The POC product has three releases. The latest, Release 3.0, was published in 2012 for implementation for the first time in 2013.

Medical – Mandatory reporting of medical information is required only in the states of **California, Oregon,** and **Texas**. While many jurisdictions have talked about ultimately utilizing the medical product, they have indicated that the requirements and resources necessary to make the change were daunting.

Additional phases of the project reflect more complex issues. Collection of comparable data pertaining to vocational rehabilitation services has yet to be addressed. Similarly, variations in the way the state statutes are constructed will present unique problems to the collection of litigation data. However, even with recognition for these difficulties, the intent is to utilize EDI to the degree possible while seeking greater uniformity in order to make comparisons across jurisdictional lines.[3]

BENCHMARKING

As part of the decision-making process to collect data, one of the questions to be asked is – For what purpose is the data being collected? With advances in computer technology, it is quite easy to collect and store massive amounts of data. However, the question remains: What is to be done with all that data?

The general purposes of collecting data are to obtain information to keep on record, make decisions about important issues, and to make useful information available to others. Primarily, data is collected to provide information regarding a specific topic. One particularly useful use of data is for benchmarking system performance. Benchmarking is the practice of comparing one organization's data against data from other organizations. Benchmarks are most meaningful when the data set includes enough information to produce useful peer groups based on organizational characteristics.[4]

In a generic sense, benchmarking is the process of comparing the cost, cycle time, productivity, or quality of a specific process or method to another that is widely considered to be an industry standard or best practice. Essentially, benchmarking provides a snapshot of the performance of a particular operation and provides an answer in terms of how the operation compares in relation to a particular standard. The result of a benchmarking procedure is often a business case for making changes in order to make improvements.

Also referred to as "best practice benchmarking" or "process benchmarking", benchmarking is a process used in management and particularly strategic management, in which organizations evaluate various aspects of their processes in relation to best practice, usually within a peer group defined for the purposes of comparison. This then allows organizations to develop plans on how to make improvements or adopt best practice, usually with the aim of increasing some aspect of

---

[3] Information concerning the current status of the EDI project and state participation obtained from the offices of the IAIABC located in Madison, Wisconsin.
[4] https://www.asaecenter.org/resources/articles/foundation/2018/

performance. Benchmarking may be a one-time event but is often treated as a continuous process in which the effort is directed at continually seeking to challenge and improve existing practices.

Types of Benchmarking – Benchmarking can be internal (comparing performance between different groups or teams within an organization) or external (comparing performance with companies in a specific industry or across industries). There are a number of different forms of benchmarking which differ depending on the type of information being collected. The following types of benchmarking are identified in Wikepedia[5].

Process Benchmarking – The initiating firm focuses its observation and investigation of business processes with a goal of identifying and observing the best practices from one or more benchmark firms. Activity analysis will be required where the objective is to benchmark cost and efficiency; increasingly applied to back-office processes where outsourcing may be a consideration.

Financial Benchmarking – This performs a financial analysis and comparison of the results in an effort to assess overall competitiveness and productivity.

Performance Benchmarking – Allows a firm to assess their competitive position by comparing products and services with those of target firms.

Product Benchmarking – The process of designing new products or upgrades to current ones. This process will sometimes involve measuring the impact of new approaches against formerly accepted ways of doing business.

Strategic Benchmarking – Involves observing how others compete. This type of benchmarking is usually not industry specific, meaning it is best to look at other industries.

Best-in-class Benchmarking – Involves studying the leading competitor or the company that best carries out a specific function.

Operational Benchmarking – Embraces everything from staffing and productivity to office flow and analysis of procedures performed.

From the perspective of workers compensation, it is obvious that virtually each one of these different types of benchmarking may have application in some form in the program. For example, performance benchmarking permits the comparison of benefit administrators to that of other benefit administrators using objective and subjective criteria. Comparing how a benefit administrator performs a specific activity with the methods of a competitor or some other organization doing the same thing is a way to identify the best practice and to learn how to lower costs, increase productivity, or improve performance designed to realize overall excellence.

While there are many aspects of the workers compensation program that warrant benchmarking, probably the most common measure is the on-time payment performance among benefit administrators. By statute, most states require the first payment of compensation (income replacement) benefits to be made within fourteen days from the first date of disability. In most instances, the first payment of compensation benefits is due one week after completion of the statutory waiting period. The majority of states have a seven-day waiting period, and the first payment of compensation would be due on the 14th day following the date of the injury.

For lost-time claims where the disability extends beyond the statutory waiting period, it is generally accepted that benefit administrators make that first payment on-time approximately 80 percent of the time. This 80 percent threshold recognizes that some claims require fairly extensive investigation or medical documentation that may result in the delay of that initial payment. Similarly, the claim may be controverted or denied which will result in a case that is not eligible for any type of payment.

Through the monitoring and recording of the date of the injury along with the date of the first payment of compensation benefits, the administrative agency can maintain a running tabulation of a benefit administrator's on-time payment record. Through the process of maintaining such a record and comparing results across all of the benefit administrators operating in a particular state, the agency can identify and separate good performers from those who may require additional attention. This also provides an opportunity for the agency to identify specific practices that may assist other performers in improving their performance. This information may then be used by the organization or company to introduce change into its activities in order to improve performance so as to achieve the best practice standard.

A second example is in the area of workplace safety. The objective of expanded data collection should entail serious consideration for means to reduce the frequency and severity of workplace injuries. This can be accomplished through the collection of information that delineates the employer, the type of injury, and the cause of the injury.

The Occupational Safety and Health Act (OSHA) requires employers to maintain a log where workplace injuries and their severity (in terms of number of lost-time workdays) are recorded. OSHA publishes annually an exhibit demonstrating the number of lost-time injuries and workdays by employer classification. Employers are encouraged to compare their own experience against the industry norm. Where experience is worse than the norm, employers are encouraged to take steps to improve safety measures.

Administrative agencies, with the ability to collect and monitor more specific claim information, can similarly take steps to improve workplace safety. Again, identifying specific employers with specific types of injuries caused by a specific process can begin the process of identifying those employers who may require attention. Specific information on the amount of lost time and the number of claims involving permanent injuries also enhances the agency's ability to target safety efforts. Note, however, that injury rates for very small employers generally are not statistically meaningful and would be useless for targeting unsafe employers. Improved safety culminates in fewer injuries and ultimately lower costs for all employers.

While the focus of workers compensation benchmarking tends to be directed at the level of benefit payer or employer, there is also the opportunity for agencies to compare experience across jurisdictional lines. Issues regarding the length of disability by type of injury, the amount of medical payments by type of injury, the amount of compensation benefits paid for permanent disability, the amount of litigation along with the issues in dispute, and the number of lump-sum settlements are some of the ways experience in one jurisdiction may be compared with experience in another jurisdiction. Obtaining information as to how jurisdictions compare in a number of specific areas permits policymakers to focus on specific problem areas and to seek information from other jurisdictions in terms of steps taken that resulted in better outcomes or improved performance.

The goal of benchmarking is to improve performance and to identify the weaknesses within an organization and develop means to correct them. The benchmarking process helps identify gaps in performance and turn them into opportunities for improvement. Benchmarking enables companies to identify the most successful strategies used by other companies of comparable size, type, or regional location, and then adopt relevant measures to make their own programs more efficient. The results of benchmarking can be used as a guide for developing short-term plans in the organization and therefore prioritize the issues facing the organization. Program participant and policymakers can then make more informed decisions based on the best opportunities.

DISPUTE RESOLUTION

With recognition for the fact that all workers compensation systems are at best partially self-executing, public policymakers wrestle with how to design a dispute resolution system that resolves disputes promptly and efficiently while still protecting the due-process rights of all parties. Some recognize the value of resolving issues with the least amount of agency intervention, while others focus on how to dispose of formal hearing requests in the most efficient manner consistent with due-process considerations.

One of the most confounding issues in the workers compensation program is the frequency of litigation in the system. The impact of litigation is felt by both sides, primarily in terms of delay and cost. Litigation delay adds human cost when workers suffer economic and social hardships because benefits to which they are entitled are not paid timely. Delay in terminating benefits adds financial costs to the system when employers and insurers must pay benefits pending the outcome of litigation and cannot recoup the payments. Litigation also adds friction costs for both sides in terms of the legal and administrative costs of participating in formal dispute resolution. Finally, with recognition for financial accounting and management purposes, benefit administrators generally want to conclude claims with finality about future liability.

The majority of workers compensation claims are resolved without controversy. A claim is not considered contested if benefits – medical and income replacement – are paid voluntarily and the employee has no disagreement with the amount or type of benefits being paid. Nor would the case be considered contested if the state agency merely reviews the benefits voluntarily paid and accepted by the employee, or merely reviews the agreements reached by the parties on a voluntary basis.

A contested claim refers to any dispute regarding the level, type or duration of the benefits that are to be paid. It is well to restate the importance of the dissemination of information that was referenced earlier. While information brochures detailing the rights and responsibilities of all parties to the system cannot possibly cover every possible situation, the information brochures cover the majority of situations and provide guidance in terms of the level and type of entitlement. Proper information can go a long way in forestalling misunderstandings and at the same time preventing disputes.

In an attempt to limit the number of cases that reach the level of being contested, a number of states have included within the administrative structure a position referred to as an ombudsman. An ombudsman refers to an individual who investigates complaints and tries to deal with the issue or problem fairly. Examples of states that have incorporated the ombudsman program include **Alabama, Kentucky, Minnesota, New Mexico, Oklahoma, Tennessee, Texas,** and **Oregon.**

An ombudsman may assist injured workers in the following ways:

- Develop and provide clear and concise information regarding an employee's rights within the workers' compensation system.

- Assist unrepresented employees if they have problems in contacting a claim handler. They can also direct the employee to the correct representatives inside an employer when dealing with self-insured employers.

- Serve as a resource for additional human services an employee might need. This can include information on assistance with finding housing and medical care during disputes over primary liability and the reasonableness/necessity of medical treatment.

The objective of the ombudsman program is to work quickly and informally to allow the parties to take every possible step to settle their workers compensation differences before going to court. Through mediation, the ombudsman attempts to ensure that:

- Cases are handled quickly and professionally.

- Costs of litigation are reduced.

- Communication between all parties of the case is improved.

- Parties are allowed to continue their working relationships on the best terms possible by doing everything they can to settle their dispute quickly.

- Flexibility in being responsive to the needs of all parties of the case is a reality.[6]

It is important to recognize that the ombudsman program is not designed to provide legal advice. In most instances, the ombudsman is not an attorney and is not in a position to represent the injured worker in any legal proceedings. However, those working in that capacity have years of experience dealing with workers compensation issues, and they make every effort to provide accurate information regarding the operation of the workers compensation program and to resolve informally issues that might eventually rise to the level of a formal dispute.

A somewhat different ombudsman program exists in **California**. Created as part of the 1993 reforms, California employers have access to a workers compensation policyholder ombudsman within the Workers Compensation Insurance Rating Bureau (WCRIB). The policyholder ombudsman is an independent position who receives guidance from an oversight committee whose membership includes an insurer representative, an employer representative, and a representative from the California Department of Insurance. The position helps policyholders better understand the workers compensation system and their insurance policies, and the ombudsman can work directly with the policyholder to resolve disputes with their insurers.

As stated repeatedly, self-execution is a major objective of the workers compensation program. But no matter the effort made by all the parties, disputes will arise. In some instances, there are legitimate questions as to whether the injury arose out of and in the course of the employment. Frequently the issue in dispute is the degree of the permanent residual effects (i.e., permanent partial disability) of the compensable workplace injury. Legitimate disputes also arise as regards the ability of the employee to return to his/her former employment. A host of other potential issues may also arise.

INFORMAL DISPUTE PROCESSES

Jurisdictions have developed a number of very distinctive steps within the workers compensation programs in order to address these disputes. A complete litany of the various approaches is beyond the scope of this material and may be of questionable usefulness because of the different terms found in the different jurisdictions that are designed to accomplish essentially the same purpose. Rather than attempt to describe how the different terms may serve to operate in a particular system, a number of fairly generic terms will be used to describe what most systems are attempting to accomplish.

For purposes of simplicity, the four levels of dispute resolution will be discussed individually.

> **Informal Dispute Resolution** – While there is no single uniform approach adopted by the states, informal dispute resolution generally operates under the guise of few procedural rules – there are no rules governing the introduction of evidence, there is no sworn testimony or cross examination of witnesses, and no transcript or other written record of the proceedings is kept. The usual purpose of an informal dispute resolution conference is to give the parties

---

[6] dir.alabama.gov/wc/ombudsman.aspx

an opportunity to meet in the presence of an administrative representative (hearing officer) to exchange information, define issues, and to resolve disputed issues through discussion and by voluntary agreement. In many respects, the informal dispute process is similar to the ombudsman program identified in a number of jurisdictions.

Most informal proceedings are conducted through face-to-face meetings (conferences) with an agency representative who may be a specialist (non-attorney) or an adjudicator. Certain jurisdictions allow other approaches to resolve disputes informally. These approaches may be generally classified according to the planned outcome of the conference.

Mediation is defined as a conference where the mediator (a neutral third-party) assists the disputing parties to reach a voluntary agreement. The impartiality of the mediator is the key component that sets this process apart from other forms of dispute resolution. Because the mediator does not work for either party, he or she has no biased interest in the case outcome. Working toward the goal of an agreed-upon resolution of the case, the mediator meets with the parties together and, when necessary, will meet privately with one of the parties to attempt to reach an agreement.

Private mediation is permitted in 13 jurisdictions. As an example, **North Carolina** is notable for its extensive use of private mediation as an alternative to public agency sponsored informal dispute resolution. Starting in October of 1996, the industrial commission began a temporary test program of automatically referring dispute cases to outside mediation. Once a request for formal hearing was filed, the commission generated an order requiring the parties to participate in mediation and giving them 55 days to select a mediator or file a motion to be excused from mediation. The parties selected, either on their own or from a list supplied by the commission, a mediator. If they did not select a mediator, the commission appointed one from the list.

Because the rules of evidence and procedure are relaxed for mediation procedures, the parties are often better able to explain their positions resulting in a fair and timely resolution. Both time and money are saved because the issues can be agreed upon and concluded through mediation rather than through litigation.

Non-Binding Arbitration may be described as a conference wherein the arbitrator seeks to facilitate voluntary agreement but may issue an advisory opinion or non-binding recommendation. A few states permit arbitration in workers compensation cases wherein a neutral third party hears all sides and makes a determination of the contested issues.

In **Connecticut** for instance, informal hearings are mandatory before a formal hearing can be requested. At the end of the informal hearing, the commissioner makes a recommendation to the parties in writing. The same commissioner may or may not conduct any subsequent formal hearing. **New Mexico** uses a slightly different approach whereby mediators make written recommendations to the parties. If these recommendations are accepted by the parties, or the parties do not respond to the recommendation within a specified time period, the recommendation is considered to be a binding order.

Binding Arbitration is a conference wherein the convener attempts to facilitate a voluntary agreement but issues a binding decision at the end of the proceedings where no agreement can be reached. In this case, the decision of the convener is made a part of the case record. In **California**, arbitration is mandatory for certain disputed issues. These issues include insurance coverage and contribution by employers or carriers in certain occupational or cumulative trauma cases, cases with certain permanent disability ratings that cannot be set for hearing within a specified time, and vocational disputes that cannot be set for hearing within specified times.

Illinois and **North Dakota** allow for binding arbitration of workers compensation disputes. Disputed cases are decided by arbitration through an industrial commissioner in **Iowa. Kentucky** uses a hybrid mediation/arbitration approach. Once a case is assigned to an arbitrator, the arbitrator may try to mediate the case or schedule a benefit review conference. If no settlement is reached within 90 days after referral of the case to the arbitrator, the arbitrator is required to issue a written benefit determination. In **Texas,** if the dispute is still unresolved after the mediation conference, the parties may elect within 20 days after the conference to engage in binding, irrevocable arbitration by mutual agreement.

Informal dispute resolution forums may also be classified as multi-issue or specialized. Multi-issue informal dispute resolution forums address such issues as initial compensability, requests for a change of medical provider, disputes over medical bills, utilization review, rehabilitation benefits, average weekly wage, penalties, suspension or termination of temporary total disability, entitlement to permanent partial or permanent total disability benefits, reinstatement of benefits, and the amount of attorney fees.

The use of multi-issue informal conferences is prevalent among the jurisdictions. Nearly four-fifths of the jurisdictions have at least one forum. In three of the exclusive state funds states – **North Dakota, Washington,** and **Wyoming** – workers or employers can contest a benefit determination by the state fund by requesting administrative reconsideration by the claims examiner who made the original determination. Further recourse is to a formal hearing.

More than half of the jurisdictions have created some form of specialized informal dispute resolution forum. Most forums address disputes over medical benefits and related issues. Also significant are forums that address disputes over rehabilitation benefits and termination of temporary total disability benefits. The extent to which a given forum addresses these issues often depends on whether dispute resolution forums exist specialized and whether certain issues can only be addressed at formal hearings.

Specialized informal dispute resolution forums are designed to address one or more specified types of issues, such as medical bill disputes, utilization review and change of treating provider disputes, rehabilitation benefits and services disputes, suspension or termination of temporary total disability benefits disputes, disputes over the amount of permanency benefits, disputes over compromise lump-sum settlements, and disputes that are below a fixed dollar amount.

Administrative determinations are issued by specialists or adjudicators based on written submissions such as reports, questionnaires, written responses to questions, and summaries of issues and positions on the issues. They do not involve face-to-face meetings or telephone conference calls, but may involve telephone conversations between agency staff and a party to the dispute. The most common outcome is a binding decision, which usually can be contested by requesting a formal hearing. However, some jurisdictions attempt to resolve these disputes only by agreement.

FORMAL DISPUTE PROCESSES

Formal dispute resolution, the historic role played by many administrative agencies when the original workers compensation laws were first enacted, involves oral proceedings before an administrative agency adjudicator, consisting of argument or trial or both. Procedural rules are more relaxed at such hearings as contrasted with civil or criminal trials. Formal proceedings are distinguished from informal conferences by the following:

- Sworn testimony is taken.

- Cross-examination of witnesses is permitted.

- A record is kept of the proceedings.

- A written decision is issued if voluntary agreement is not reached.

Formal hearings usually consist of two separate stages. The first stage is typically called a prehearing conference or pretrial conference. These events involve face-to-face meetings or telephone conferences. The purposes of these forums are to: present written evidence and depositions, narrow the issues, dispose of motions, resolve issues by agreement, and schedule the formal hearing and schedule witnesses and depositions. In some jurisdictions the judge actively attempts to bring about voluntary agreement. In other jurisdictions, the primary purpose of the forum is to schedule the time and location of the formal hearing.

Despite the popularity of informal dispute resolution, 20 percent of the states seem to rely heavily on the formal hearing process to resolve disputes. **Oklahoma, Pennsylvania,** and **Utah** are three states that have historically relied heavily on formal hearings but have recently instituted informal dispute resolution.

The second stage, the formal hearing, may involve one session (meeting) or may take place in a series of sessions, spaced weeks, or months apart. Some jurisdictions have developed specialized types of formal hearings to address disputes over medical issues, termination of benefits, fines, penalties, and/or administrative rules. Some jurisdictions have developed specialized forums for reviewing and approving or disapproving compromise lump-sum settlements or commutations of benefits.

At the formal hearing, the proceedings are held by a single hearing officer who renders an opinion of the facts along with his/her decision relative to the claim. In nearly two-thirds of the jurisdictions, the typical formal hearing involves a single session. The remaining states typically hold multiple formal hearing sessions. This can occur because sessions are adjourned before the dispute is settled, or it can result from an established practice of holding serial-style formal hearings such as in **Pennsylvania** and **New Jersey**.

There is wide variation (from 10 minutes to seven hours) in the length of a typical formal hearing session. About half of the jurisdictions conduct formal hearing sessions that typically last from 30 to 90 minutes. **Idaho, Michigan, Vermont**, **Washington,** and **Wyoming** hold both multiple sessions *and* each session lasts more than three hours. **Maryland** typically holds one 20-minute formal hearing per case. **New York** commonly holds one or two, 20-minute formal hearing sessions.

In about 20 jurisdictions, medical evidence is usually introduced by medical report only. Another 20 jurisdictions rely on depositions (with or without reports) and five jurisdictions rely primarily on in-person or telephone testimony by medical providers (with or without reports). The remaining states use a combination of reports, depositions, and live testimony.

The outcomes of formal hearings may include a formal hearing decision, a settlement, or some other form of voluntary agreement. In many cases the parties settle immediately before trial, or even during a break in the trial. **Ohio** has a unique formal hearing process where parties who are dissatisfied with a formal hearing decision by a district hearing officer at the agency level can appeal the decision at a second formal hearing conducted by a staff hearing officer at the agency.

Administrative Appeals – A majority of jurisdictions have some sort of administrative body or an individual in the executive branch of state government to which either side or both can appeal a formal hearing decision. This is typically the first step in the appellate process. In most jurisdictions the appellate officer or panel reviews the formal hearing record and issues a decision based on a review of the law and the facts presented in the hearing record.

Statutory time frames for filing an appeal range from 10 to 45 days from issuance of the formal hearing decision with the most common interval being 30 days. Many jurisdictions hold that an appeal to an administrative appellate forum stays the formal hearing decision without qualification. In five jurisdictions, an appeal stays part of the formal hearing decision. In an additional nine jurisdictions the appeal does not stay the formal hearing decision.

In some jurisdictions the scope of review is limited to matters of law only. Oral argument may be permitted. In some jurisdictions a hearing *de novo* is held. Under a *trial de novo* process, the appellate authority is permitted to take additional testimony and/or review additional evidence before rendering a decision.

A significant number of jurisdictions have developed some form of administrative appellate forum to review formal hearing decisions upon request. Most commonly, these involve panels of three appellate judges, but other models exist such as review by other formal hearing judges, review by a single individual (for example, Industrial Commissioner), or review by a smaller or larger panel.

Thirty-one jurisdictions use panels to review appeals. Panel members are variously called commissioner, director, board member or judge. In **Connecticut, Nebraska, Oklahoma, Rhode Island**, and **South Carolina**, panels of judges or commissioners are constituted from among the ranks of those who issue formal hearing decisions. Naturally, the judge or commissioner who issued the formal hearing decision is not included on the panel to review the same case. In 34 jurisdictions the basis for review of appeals is law and fact. In some of these jurisdictions additional evidence may be introduced and oral argument may be heard. In **Connecticut** and **Massachusetts,** the basis of review is limited to matters of law.

In five jurisdictions a single individual reviews appeals. In **Connecticut, Nebraska, Oklahoma,** and **Rhode Island** the panel size is three; in **South Carolina** the panel is comprised of three or six commissioners. In the **District of Columbia**, appeals involving private-sector cases are reviewed by the director of the Department of Employment Services, while appeals involving public-sector cases go to a separate review board.

Appeals to the Judicial Level – All jurisdictions permit decisions issued by an administrative appellate body to be appealed to a state civil court. Again, the time to file an appeal with the courts varies from ten days in **Kansas** to file with the Court of Appeals, to 45 days in **California** to file with the Supreme Court of the District Court of Appeals. Most jurisdictions allow 30 days for filing an appeal with the courts.

The first level of appeal to the courts is generally with the Court of Appeals or the Superior Court. The appellate court name and appeals sequence depend on the civil court structure within each jurisdiction. In the state of **Idaho**, appeals from the Industrial Commission are taken directly to the Supreme Court.

Again, the court can review the appeal based on law and fact, law only, or, in some instances, it can conduct a trial *de novo*. In a few jurisdictions, either side can appeal to another court before taking the appeal to the state Supreme Court. The majority of jurisdictions permit appeal to the state Supreme Court or its equivalent. The final level of appeals in **Delaware** is to the Superior Court and in **Florida** to the First District Court of Appeals. In **Indiana, Kansas, New York, North Carolina, Utah,** and **Virginia,** the highest level of appeal is to the Court of Appeals.

As part of the workers compensation reforms enacted in 2013, **Oklahoma** established an expedited approach for resolving disputes. Where the claim is initially denied, the employer/insurer must notify the injured employee in writing of the decision within 15 days of the notice of the injury. The injured worker may appeal this denial to a three-member committee who must issue a written decision within 45 from the date the notice of contest was received. If any part of an adverse determination by the committee is upheld, the employee may file a petition for review in a proper state or federal district court. The district court is required to rely on the record established by the internal appeal process and use a deferential standard of review. This simple and direct dispute resolution process is intended to respond quicker than the traditional program found in Oklahoma.

ALTERNATE DISPUTE RESOLUTION (ADR)

Before leaving the discussion on dispute resolution, it is beneficial to recognize those jurisdictions where disputes may be resolved outside of the workers compensation program. About one-half of the jurisdictions permit dispute resolution to take place outside of the workers compensation system. An Alternative Dispute Resolution (ADR) program, also known as a "carve out," is designed to result in expeditious and equitable settlements between injured workers and their employer and/or insurance company outside of the state court system.

As noted in Chapter Three, a number of states permit management and labor to establish certain administrative mechanisms as part of the collective bargaining process. Such administrative mechanisms may include agreement between labor and management permitting the identification of certain medical providers to furnish medical care, establishing light-duty or return-to-work programs, and permitting the creation of an alternative dispute resolution (ADR) program designed to supplement, modify, or replace the provisions of the existing workers compensation law.

After an ADR program has been established, a labor management committee is formed to oversee it. As the name implies, this committee is usually comprised of an equal number of appointees from management and labor. The committee approves the lists of treating doctors, neutral evaluators, and other vendors that can provide services to injured workers, and approves the selection of the ombudsperson, mediators, and arbitrators.

An ADR must be approved by the state and cannot provide fewer benefits than the state system; it can, however, provide more benefits. The main goal of processing injured workers' claims through an ADR program is to provide better, faster medical care (with less denials), a timelier return to work and to minimize conflicts and delays, all while saving costs for the employers/insurance companies. An ADR can be designed to provide access to impartial doctors and mediators/arbitrators to resolve disputes concerning all classes of workers compensation benefits.[7]

---

[7] https://www.geklaw.com/workers-compensation/alternative-dispute-resolution.htm

Ten states have explicitly authorized by statute the establishment of ADR programs. In a number of other states such as **Connecticut, Georgia, Missouri,** and **Rhode Island**, it is possible to design a system, but workers cannot be required to use it. Other jurisdictions are considering the approach. In **Illinois**, a medical network can be established through collective bargaining agreements.

Alternative arrangements reflect compromise agreements that address the needs and concerns of both labor and management. As a means to address the length of time to reach resolution of disputed issues, alternative mechanisms may prove more time and cost effective. In the case of dispute resolution, to ensure prompt resolution with minimal need for attorney involvement, this may include approaches such as mediation and binding arbitration.

ATTORNEY FEES

In workers compensation proceedings, the injured worker may opt to be represented by an attorney of his or her own choice. Attorneys for injured workers usually perform legal work on a contingency basis. A contingency basis refers to the fact that the attorney is entitled to a percentage of any recovery if the claim is ultimately successful. If there is an award of benefits or settlement of the claim, the lawyer will take a percentage of that payout as his or her fee. The attorney receives nothing if the claim is unsuccessful. In some states, lawyers are compensated by the hour in workers compensation cases. However, they are typically still paid out of the proceeds of any award or our settlement at the end of your case.

To protect injured workers against excessive attorney fees, most states have established a cap – maximum amount to be paid in attorney fees – in workers compensation cases. The cap varies among states but is generally in the range of 10 percent to 25 percent. These limits are significantly lower than contingency fees in other types of cases, such as personal injury lawsuits, in which the standard fee is 33 percent. **Kansas** requires that the amount of attorney fees be fixed "pursuant to a written contract." This approach ensures that the injured worker is cognizant of the amount of fees that the attorney will receive if the claim is deemed ultimately successful. In contrast with Kansas, **Idaho** permits the amount of attorney fees to be set by the commission.

Caps on attorneys' fees can be structured in a number of different ways. In some states, the maximum contingency fee depends on how the case is resolved (for example, before or after a workers compensation hearing), which types of benefits are recovered, or the size of the award. For example, in 2018, **Kentucky** raised the maximum attorney fees to $18,000, with the following calculation: 20 percent of the first $25,000; 15 percent of the next $25,000; 10 percent of the remaining award with the fee capped at $18,000.[8]

In states where workers compensation attorneys are compensated by the hour, there is usually a cap on the hourly rate. This may be in addition to a maximum contingency fee. For example, a

---

[8] Ky. Rev. Stat. § 342.320

lawyer might be able to collect $150 per hour for every hour worked, but not more than 20 percent of the worker's total settlement or award.

In a minority of states, a cap on attorneys' fees in workers compensation cases does not exist. In such situations, attorneys are permitted to negotiate their own rates with clients so long as the fee is reasonable. In these states, it's not uncommon for lawyers to charge a 33 percent contingency fee.

In most states, attorneys' fees are subject to approval by a judge or an office within the workers compensation agency. Prior to conclusion of the claim, the attorney must submit his or her fee for approval. It is generally illegal for a lawyer to take a fee without getting the judge's or agency's approval first. In determining whether a fee is reasonable, the judge or agency will take into account multiple factors such as: the complexity of the case, the time and effort put in the attorney. and the rates customarily charged by attorneys in the immediate your area.

There may also legal costs that must be paid. These are the expenses that an attorney may incur in furthering the case, such as the cost of reproducing and filing of documents, copying medical records, and hiring expert witnesses (e.g., a medical specialist) to testify at a hearing. These costs will ultimately be the responsibility of the injured worker.

The general rule in workers compensation is that each party is responsible for payment of its own attorney. While that is true in the majority of jurisdictions, some laws call upon the employer/insurer to pay the workers attorney fees if the claim was initially controverted over the issue of compensability. Another situation where the employer/insurer may be responsible for the employee's attorney fees is in the case of "bad faith" in the handling of the claim.

A delicate balance must be set by the judge or the administrative agency to neither overpay or underpay attorneys for a particular type of case. Overly generous fees obviously promote increased litigation with a large body of attorneys' eager for cases. Under compensation would make attorneys less willing to represent injured workers with meritorious but difficult claims to prove as compensable.

LUMP SUM SETTLEMENTS

Workers compensation lump sum settlements represent an agreement between the benefit administrator and the injured employee who is generally represented by an attorney, along with the approval of the state administrative agency, to accept such a payment rather than paying cash benefits on a periodic basis and medical expenses as they are incurred.

In the workers compensation program, lump sum settlements are entered into for any number of reasons. In some cases, there are disputes regarding the initial question of compensability, subsequent entitlement to continuing benefits, permission to seek treatment from another provider, the degree of permanent disability, or a host of other potential reasons.

In a typical settlement involving the issue of initial compensability, the benefit administrator may dispute compensability and refuse to voluntarily pay for any of the medical costs relating to the alleged work-related injury. Normally there is no distinction between income replacement and medical costs. Furthermore, such settlements, rather than being based on a purely mathematical estimate of future lost earnings and medical expenses, reflect a compromise based on a portion of the amount that would have been payable if the claim were not in dispute. This percentage reflects the parties' mutual judgment or agreement about the injured worker's likelihood of prevailing taking into account factors such as whether there was a preexisting condition, the accident was really work related, the individual was acting as an employee or performing work-related activities at the time the injury occurred, as well as the cost and delays inherent in resolving the dispute through the adjudication process.

Lump sum settlements may also be utilized where the initial claim for compensation benefits has been accepted by the benefit administrator and questions subsequently arose as to continuing benefit entitlement. Medical opinions may differ as to the need for further treatment or regarding the ability of the injured worker to return to his/her former employment. Similarly, medical opinion may differ as regards the extent or degree of permanent disability that remains following medical recovery.

A significant number of lump-sum settlements involve what are frequently referred to by those familiar with workers compensation practices as commutations. As a rule, a commutation of benefits may occur once an award of permanent partial disability has been established and the worker has returned to full-time employment. The worker may then request the up-front payment of future permanent partial disability benefits that are still owed. The commuted amount is really a calculation based upon a discounted benefit amount the injured worker is entitled to receive under the workers compensation laws.

Commutations typically do not involve controversy between the injured worker and the benefit administrator over whether the carrier is actually liable to make payments. In such cases, the claim is settled simply for the purpose of receiving today, moneys that would otherwise be payable over an extended period of time. A workers compensation commuted claim does not typically involve the payment of any medical benefits. Medical treatment has generally been concluded and the commuted value of the claim involves the extent or degree of permanent disability.

For example, if an employee sustains a twenty percent loss of use of the arm as the result of a machine accident – in a jurisdiction where total loss of the arm entitles the worker to 250 weeks of permanent partial disability benefits – the 50 weeks of compensation (20 percent of 250) might be concluded at a discounted rate. The commutation of benefits serves to eliminate certain administrative expenses for the benefit administrator while providing the worker with a lump sum of cash to be used for other purposes. So long as the worker has returned to work and no further medical or disability benefits are anticipated, all program participants are well-served by the commutation.

On the other hand, a lump sum settlement – in some jurisdictions referred to as a compromise and release – is generally considered as a complete and final settlement of the claim. As originally intended, this was done only when considering the best interest of the injured worker. In practice however, lump sum settlements have become increasingly popular in a number of states. Benefit administrators find that a lump sum payment is an efficient way to dispose of problem claims since, once payment is made, any continuing responsibility for the claim is effectively concluded. Likewise, attorneys, system administrators and often times the injured worker, are similarly interested in resolving disputed claims via some form of lump sum settlement.

The problem with the over-utilization of lump sum settlements is that it defeats the basic purpose of the workers compensation program. Designed to replace a portion of the income lost during the period the injured worker is disabled, the laws provide for the periodic payment of benefits. Similarly, medical costs are compensated as the services or care is incurred. When payment is made in a lump sum, the money may be spent unwisely and the worker left in a position that these compensation laws were designed to avoid. Because of the unfortunate tendency for some claimants to dissipate or spend unwisely their settlements, some jurisdictions require that settlements be paid out over a span of time that corresponds with their disabling condition.

Situations do exist in which a lump sum settlement is in the best interest of the claimant and therefore, a viable alternative to periodic payments of compensation. For example, a pilot who loses an eye may not be regarded as suitable to engage in such employment, but the disability would not affect the individual's ability to find other forms of gainful employment. Thus, payment of a lump sum to enable the pilot to purchase a business enterprise or business equipment would not be unreasonable and could be in that person's best interest assuming, of course, that the individual has other financial means to address his or her daily living expenses.

There is another type of case where a lump sum settlement may represent a sound response for all involved parties. This involves the claim where legitimate questions exist relative to the compensability of a claim – where it is unclear whether an injury arose out of and in the course of employment – or where there are legitimate questions in terms of determining the amount of continuing benefits to which the injured worker may be entitled. Depending upon the strength or weakness of the case, a lump sum settlement may be in the best interest of all parties.

The primary goal of the administrative agency when reviewing a lump sum settlement proposal should be to design a compensation scheme that will best serve the needs of the injured worker. If those needs would be best served by a lump sum payment of benefits, the settlement should be approved. Suppose, however, that the claimant has no intention of investing the payment in some sound venture and the compensation benefits are needed by that individual to pay ordinary living expenses. Settlement of the claim by a lump sum payment is probably not in the best interests of that individual.

A variation of the lump sum settlement is the structured settlement. With a structured settlement, the employee agrees to a scheduled stream of payments that are tailored to meet the employee's future living and medical needs — as opposed to a single lump sum payment.

The employee can use the settlement as a way of ensuring that a certain amount of money comes in every month, quarter, or at whatever interval they desire. If the employee knows that certain medical expenses will be incurred at a specified time every year, for example, the agreement can be structured to ensure that the employee receives benefits in time to address those payments. It takes the worry and the risk out of managing a large sum of money and ensures that the settlement proceeds will serve the intended purpose: paying for medical and living expenses.

In addition to protecting the injured worker, the use of structured settlements benefits employers as well. Employers can assign the settlement amount to a third party financial institution, thereby removing the liability from the balance sheets and gaining significant tax benefits. Prior to the change in the law, employers were prohibited from assigning any liabilities in workers comp cases. Of course, a lot depends on the size of the settlement. The use of a structured settlement is not practical, for example, in a claim involving less than $10,000 because the risk of losing or mismanaging the money has much less severe consequences than squandering or mismanaging a $500,000 settlement.

Before concluding remarks on the subject of lump-sum settlements, it is important to recognize the role that Social Security and Medicare take in protecting their interest. When workers compensation disability benefits are resolved through payment of a lump sum, for purposes of calculating the Social Security offset, the workers compensation lump sum amount is treated as an amount which would otherwise have been paid periodically. Medicare regulations state that when a lump sum compensation award stipulates that the amount paid is intended to compensate for future medical care for a work injury, Medicare will not pay for any medical expenses associated with the work injury until the amount of the lump sum payment has been exhausted.[9] The subject of benefit coordination and adjustments pertaining to lump sum settlements was discussed earlier and will again be discussed in the final chapter.

SPECIAL FUNDS

Special funds serve a multitude of purposes for many of the state workers compensation programs. In an article entitled *Special Purposes for Some Special Funds*, Dr. Peter Barth (emeritus professor, University of Connecticut) noted that, *"In general, what most such funds have in common is that some certain socially determined ends needing financial support are perceived, for which no obvious and ineluctable source of funding exists. . . . The fund mechanism has the solid virtue, to some, of becoming a kind of dumping ground for good deeds."* In determining whether there is a continuing need for such funds, Dr. Barth observed that, *"There is need for some evaluation of the impact that these funds have on state compensation systems, how actual behavior of employers and workers is affected by them, and whether or not they are accomplishing their goals."*[10]

---

[9] 42 C.F.R §411.46
[10] NCCI Digest December 1986 Volume 1, Issue 3 (page 53)

While there is a tendency to identify the concept of the special fund with the individual state second injury fund (called by a variety of titles but essentially operating for the reimbursement of certain benefits when an injury occurs to a worker with a pre-existing injury or condition), review of state laws reveals a wide variety of other purposes that have come to be associated with special funds. The following examines those select special funds that have evolved for the purpose of addressing unique aspects in the workers compensation arena.

Second Injury Funds – In discussing second injury funds, it is well to acknowledge that states utilize various terms in identifying such funds (e.g. special fund, second injury fund, subsequent injury fund, and special disability trust fund). State second injury funds were originally created to encourage employers to hire and retain workers who had sustained prior physical impairments and to afford certain economic relief to those employers in those situations where a worker with a previous physical impairment sustained a second or subsequent injury. While states utilize various terms in identifying such funds (e.g. Special Fund, Subsequent Injury Fund, etc.) the generic term second injury fund provides an easy reference for purposes of describing state activity in response to this type of exposure.

Prior to states enacting second injury fund laws, when an injury in the course of employment occurred to a worker with a prior physical impairment – resulting in increased or perhaps permanent total disability – either the worker was penalized by having any compensation benefits limited to the disability directly associated with the second injury or, the employer was penalized by having to pay for the combined resulting disability. In the first instance, this concluded in an unfair result where the second injury may have had a far greater consequence than the initial disability. The best example of this inequity is found with a second injury resulting in the loss of the second eye. While the loss of one eye may not operate as a significant bar to employment, the loss of the second eye to that same worker would make that worker much harder to reemploy.

On the other hand, the approach whereby the employer would be responsible for the combined result of the prior and second injury provided a strong economic incentive for employers to refuse to hire or retain physically impaired employees. The significance of this economic incentive is best illustrated by a situation that arose in **Oklahoma** in the days before it enacted a second injury fund. In an opinion rendered by the Oklahoma Supreme Court, the employer was held liable for permanent total disability following the loss of the employee's second eye; the first eye having been lost previously in an earlier accident.[11]

Under prior rulings, the employer would have been responsible only for the new disability even though the combined effect of both resulted in permanent total disability. Because of the tremendous extra exposure, many employers laid off handicapped employees to avoid the potential liability for permanent total benefits in place of a scheduled permanent partial loss.

> A statement made by Mr. I. K. Huber of Oklahoma following the *Nease* decision observed that as a consequence of the decision "thousands of one-eyed, one-legged, one-armed, one-handed men were let go and were unable to find other employment in Oklahoma."

---

[11] *Nease v. Hughes Stone Co.*, 244 P 778 (1925)

The first second injury fund law, adopted by **New York** in 1916, provided that if a worker with one hand, arm, foot, leg, or eye lost a second such member in a work accident, the employer would be liable only for the second loss and any remaining compensation due for the combined injury would be paid from a special fund. While a number of states experimented with such legislation during the 1920s and 1930s, World War II served in a number of respects as the catalyst to establish such funds. It became evident that without such funds many veterans with debilitating war injuries would find it difficult to obtain meaningful employment. At the same time, employment of handicapped workers during the critical manpower shortage that existed during the war had shown that they could be suitably employed.

There was general agreement among groups of employers, employees, veterans' organizations, and other interested parties that second injury funds would be the best means to address the situation. In September of 1944, the International Association of Industrial Accident Boards and Commissions (IAIABC), approved draft legislation that provided for the establishment of a second injury fund to be supported by the payment of $500 in work-related no-dependency death cases. Following closely the New York approach, the model legislation provided that where an employee had sustained loss of one of two members in a prior work accident, so that loss of the other member would result in permanent total disability, an employer would be responsible only for the partial disability in case of subsequent loss of the second member with the balance of the claim to be paid from the second injury fund.

In the months that followed, many groups worked together to have second injury fund laws adopted in more states. In July of 1940, there were twelve states with some form of second injury fund legislation. By the end of 1945, that number had increased to 31 states. In the majority of instances, those laws, following the model legislation prepared by the IAIABC.

Following enactment of these initial second injury fund laws, criticism quickly developed regarding the narrowness of coverage, i.e., requiring the pre-existing disability to have been work-related and to involve the loss of a major body member followed by the combined effect to result in permanent total disability was a very steep threshold to overcome in order to obtain fund recovery. With the narrowness of coverage, very few claims qualified for fund relief. In response to mounting criticism, states began to experiment with broader legislative approaches.

Initial efforts at expansion of coverage involved the recognition of pre-existing impairment "from any cause or origin." A second area of concern was the matter of the combined effect. The requirement that the combined result culminate in permanent and total disability served to severely restrict the incidence of claims qualifying for second injury fund relief. In response to this concern, states began to simply require that the subsequent disability be, *"substantially greater by reason of the combined effect of the pre-existing impairment and the subsequent injury."*

With the shift toward the fund being responsible for the increased benefits stemming from the combined effect of the pre-existing disability and the second injury, disputes began to arise relative to the extent of the employer's responsibility. This action frequently resulted in litigation and unnecessary friction costs. The potential also existed for the fund to be drawn into claims involving disability of relatively minor impairments.

Recognizing the inefficiencies associated with the non-defined point at which the fund's responsibility could begin, and to preclude involvement in a multitude of relatively minor claims, the Model Act included a provision whereby, *"(T)he employer or his insurance carrier shall in the first instance pay all awards of compensation provided by this act, but such employer or his insurance carrier should be reimbursed from the special fund for all compensation payments sub-sequent to those payable for the first 104 weeks of disability."*[9]

During the period from the 1950s to the early 1990s, many states moved from fairly restrictive descriptions of what physical impairments constitute a pre-existing condition to a broadened perspective of what conditions would be subject to second injury fund relief. Whereas the second methodology relied upon a determination of the extent of the increased disability, a third methodology adopted by **Montana** and **Michigan** relies principally on a certification process. Where a vocationally handicapped person is certified, and subsequently suffers another injury, the employer is responsible for only 104 weeks of compensation. All additional benefits, without consideration of increased disability or permanent and total disability, are payable from the fund. This approach eliminates the substantiation of fact after the incident, but requires that proper procedures be followed at the time the handicapped worker is employed or retained in employment.

Funding and Financial Growth – There has never been a single method adopted by the various states for financing second injury funds. Many of the early laws secured financing through payments required in death cases where there were no surviving dependents. While a number of states continue to utilize that approach – adjusting the amount of payment to reflect increasing dollar exposures – many found that a single revenue source was insufficient for purposes of financing fund activity.

The Council of State Government's Model Act created a financing scheme that established a pro-rata sharing of the cost among all insurance carriers and self-insured employers based upon their proportionate share of total of workers compensation benefit payments made during the prior year.

Notwithstanding the method of financing adopted by a particular jurisdiction, second injury funds are financed based on pay-as-you-go. A pay-as-you-go funding scheme implies that the moneys collected each year are sufficient only to cover benefits that are payable that year. No moneys are set aside to pay future benefits where such obligations continue beyond the current year.

It is therefore important to recognize that in an environment dependent upon pay-as-you-go financing, even dramatic attempts to curb fund utilization will not result in immediate financial relief since funds will continue to require significant money infusion in order to finance the liabilities already in the system. This is often referred to as the unfunded liability. Over time, as the older liabilities expire, reduced financing may be realized, provided current access for new cases has been either terminated or substantially reduced.

State Efforts to Address Fund Growth – Beginning in the 1980s, the growth in the annual expenditures from state second injury funds prompted an effort in select states that was designed to restrain or control the growth in fund expenditures. Certain states followed the recommendation of the Model Act requiring the employer or insurance carrier to be responsible for the first 104 weeks of disability. Other states devised either shorter or longer time periods before the fund will respond, and have also adopted provisions permitting only a portion of payments beyond a specified number of weeks to be subject to reimbursement as a means to ensure appropriate administration by the party paying benefits. For example, prior to repealing access to the fund after July 1, 2007, in **New York**, for injuries occurring after August 1, 1994, the employer's responsibility was extended from the first 104 weeks of disability to the first 260 weeks in second injury fund cases.

A number of states sought to contain coverage through adoption of the Council of State Governments Model Act requiring knowledge of the pre-existing condition by the employer. Taking the subject of employer knowledge to a higher level, a few states established specific procedures whereby employers may register or certify with the administrative agency the existence of pre-existing conditions. Prior to repeal of their second injury fund provisions for newly arising claims, **Connecticut, Kansas, Minnesota**, and **New Mexico** permitted pre-existing conditions to be certified as an effort to expedite acceptance by the fund. However, while certification was intended to expedite the claim acceptance process, conditions that were not certified were not precluded from seeking acceptance through the traditional process.

Repeal of State Second Injury Fund Provisions – In response to the growing annual expenditure for certain second injury funds, the enactment of laws at the state and federal level that bar discrimination against persons with a handicap, along with the dearth of activity recognized in a number of other states, legislatures in a significant number of states took action to close their funds to claims arising after a certain date. For example, **South Carolina's** second injury fund, which was phased out by July 1, 2013, stopped considering claims from injuries that happened after June 2008 because of rising losses that resulted in surcharges to employers and insurers of nearly $200 million annually. **New York** closed its fund to all new claims in July 2010 when its outstanding liabilities topped $18 billion.

Since 1992, 20 states and the **District of Columbia** have passed legislation to abolish or phase out second injury funds, including **Alabama, Colorado, Connecticut, Florida, Georgia, Kansas, Kentucky, Louisiana, Maine, Minnesota, Nebraska, New Mexico, Rhode Island, South Dakota, Utah, Vermont, West Virginia** and, most recently in 2007, **Arkansas, New York,** and **South Carolina**.[12]

---

[12] https://www.shrm.org/hr-today/news/hr-magazine/pages/0709employmentlaw

It should also be noted that the above does not include the state of **Oklahoma,** which enacted legislation closing their Multiple Injury Trust Fund to permanent partial claims where the subsequent injury resulted in increased permanency occurred before November 1, 1999, and to cases where the subsequent injury resulted in permanent total disability with a date of injury prior to June 1, 2000. During the 2005 special legislative session, a substantive workers compensation reform bill was enacted that reinstated the fund's liability for permanent total disability claims involving a subsequent injury where the date of injury occurs on or after November 1, 2005.

As a final note, in a 2019 decision, the **Missouri** Supreme Court issued an opinion that permanent partial disability benefits would no longer be awarded from the second injury fund and that stricter rules would be applicable regarding permanent total disability cases for injuries occurring after January 1, 2014.[13]

Payment of Benefits for Uninsured Employers – Perhaps the most legitimate purpose for any special fund is the payment of disability and medical benefits to injured workers where the employer has failed to obtain insurance or to properly qualify as a self-insured employer. Without access to a special fund, the recourse of an injured worker in the case of failure of the employer to obtain insurance frequently involves litigation and a drawn-out recovery process. Often the offending employer is bankrupt or without financial resources for recovery of damages, in which case the injured worker would be left without any form of compensation or medical benefits.

In the majority of states, an uninsured employer or business is exposed to:

- Direct lawsuits by an injured employee
- Non-compliance penalties levied by the Workers' Compensation Board
- Stop-work orders until compliance is achieved
- Possible criminal sanctions
- Civil liability of the owners, partners or officers

A significant number of state laws have enacted specific statutes that call for the payment of benefits to injured employees of uninsured employers through either a specific uninsured employers fund or through the second injury fund. It is critical that a state introduce a rigorous monitoring routine to ensure that employers are in compliance with the law in terms of coverage, and to ensure that such coverage remains in force once a policy of insurance is purchased. At least 24 jurisdictions ensure protection for injured employees of uninsured employers through some form of special fund.[14]

---

[13] Missouri Supreme Court No. SC97317.
[14] Arizona, California, Connecticut, District of Columbia, Hawaii, Kansas, Kentucky, Maryland, Massachusetts, Minnesota, Missouri, Montana, Nevada, New Hampshire, New Jersey, New Mexico, New York, Oklahoma, Oregon, South Carolina, Tennessee, Utah, Virginia and Wisconsin.

There is general agreement that special funds, designed to pay benefits when the injury occurs to an employee of an uninsured employer, should be continued in those states where they exist and should be considered in those states where they have not yet been enacted. Such funds should also be charged with the responsibility of monitoring the workplace to ensure coverage compliance. Fines and penalties collected through the process of locating uninsured employers and associated violations may also be used to fund the operations of the special fund and should be applied to the payment of benefits to injured employees.

Payment of Supplemental Benefits – A by-product of the serious inflation experienced during the early 1980s was the movement to adjust weekly indemnity benefits to acknowledge the loss in purchasing power experienced by long-term benefit recipients. In order to overcome the influence of inflation on benefits, a number of states provided for an annual adjustment (increase) in the amount of weekly benefits paid – in some instances tied to the percentage increase in the statewide average weekly wage.

A number of different approaches evolved in terms of the payment of supplemental benefits. In general, when dealing only with existing claims, the response was for the state to either pay any supplemental benefit adjustment out of the existing second injury fund or special fund. In select states, like **Illinois** and **Wisconsin**, a separate fund was established for the purpose of supplemental benefit reimbursements.[15] In all, a total of 13 states provide for a supplemental benefit in some fashion, along with the vehicle available to reimburse benefit payers.

Rather than limiting supplemental benefits to aged cases, Oregon enacted a Retroactive Program for the purpose of providing workers or beneficiaries eligible to receive either death or permanent total disability benefits become eligible for Retroactive Program benefit increases when the benefits granted under the Retroactive Program bulletin exceed the benefits provided by the statute in effect at the time of the injury.[16]

Payment of Continuing Benefits on Time-Barred Claims – A variation on the theme of payment of supplemental benefits is the payment of continuing benefits where the workers compensation law imposed a limitation as to the duration or amount of either medical or disability benefits. While a significant percentage of state laws placed dollar or time limitations on medical benefits prior to 1970, virtually every state has removed such limitations through the legislative process. Similarly, most state laws have been adjusted to continue the payment of permanent total disability benefits for the duration of the disability.

A small number of states provide for the continuing of benefits from a special fund where benefit eligibility extends beyond the limit of time set forth in the statute. Examples of provisions of this nature include:

---

[15] Connecticut, Delaware, Florida, Hawaii, Illinois, Massachusetts, Michigan, Minnesota, Nevada, New Hampshire, New Jersey, New York and Wisconsin.
[16] Workers Compensation Division Rule **436-075-0010 (3)(a)**

- **Arkansas** pays weekly benefits from the Death and Permanent Total Disability Trust Fund to totally disabled workers or dependents of deceased workers after the insurer has paid indemnity liability of $50,000 or $75,000.

- The **Indiana** Second Injury Fund provides for an additional 150 weeks of total disability where benefits were exhausted by the statutory maximum of 500 weeks.

- **North Carolina** provides for life-time indemnity benefits for certain injuries prior to July 1, 1953, that were otherwise subject to a 500-week maximum.

- In **Rhode Island**, lifetime benefits are payable from the Second Injury Fund for cases occurring after 1940, which were subject to an aggregate maximum.

Addressing program limitations for medical benefits, **Colorado** established a Medical Disaster Fund for funding medical expenses of catastrophically injured workers with a date of injury occurring between 1965 and June 30, 1971. For the period between July 1, 1971, and June 30, 1981, the Major Medical Insurance Fund was created to again address the medical expenses of catastrophically injured workers and to assume the liabilities of the Medical Disaster Fund.

Indiana, New York, Oregon, and **Wisconsin** have each established special funds to address claims that are time-barred because of the statute of limitations. This situation arose most frequently when state laws applied a two or three-year statute of limitations for the reporting of occupational disease claims. In the states noted, these funds have also responded where claims have been closed and were precluded from being re-opened because of the passage of time.

With the extension of most states laws to include lifetime medical and disability entitlement, there is little merit – outside of the factor of addressing old cases – in establishing or maintaining special funds for this purpose. The same approach has application in terms of time-barred claims. Occupational disease laws have in most instances been amended to afford sufficient time for the reporting of claims following the onset of the disease and the knowledge of its relationship to the workplace.

Benefit Payments for Concurrent Employment – When an employee at the time of the injury is concurrently engaged in two or more employments, the question arises whether the wage basis for computing benefit entitlement should be limited to the earnings in the employment in which the injury occurred or should include the total earnings from all employments. This issue becomes especially important where the injury occurs in the lesser earning occupation or where the earnings in the job where the injury occurred are not sufficient to achieve the weekly maximum benefit.

The majorities of laws are silent on the issue of how earnings from concurrent employment should be considered and rely on the courts to make a determination. Six states have adopted the approach whereby a special fund (frequently the second injury fund) is to make payment for that portion of earnings not the responsibility of the employer at the time the injury occurred. States that address earnings from concurrent employment in this manner include **Connecticut, Hawaii, Michigan, Missouri, New Hampshire, New York,** and **Texas**.

The **Texas** law is the most recent state to enact such legislation with application to injuries occurring on and after July 1, 2004. The reimbursement provision states that, *"An insurance carrier is entitled to apply for and receive reimbursement at least annually from the subsequent injury fund for the amount of income and death benefits paid to a worker under this section that are based on employment other than the employment during which the compensable injury occurred. The commissioner may adopt rules that govern the documentation, application process, and other administrative requirements necessary to implement this subsection."*[17]

Benefits During Rehabilitation and Job Modifications – With the enactment of rehabilitation provisions in many states following the recommendations of the 1972 National Commission, laws were introduced to provide certain rehabilitation services or continuation of indemnity benefits during the period of rehabilitation through a special fund. Examples of states where a special fund provides benefits for vocational rehabilitation include:

- The **Massachusetts** Trust Fund may provide vocational rehabilitation services where the insurer and employee fail to agree on a program.

- The **Missouri** Second Injury Fund will pay $40 per week to the employee for a maximum of twenty weeks while undergoing rehabilitation.

- In **Nebraska**, vocational rehabilitation training costs are paid from the Workers Compensation Trust Fund. In addition, when vocational rehabilitation training requires residence at or near a facility or institution away from the employee's customary residence, whether within or without this state, the reasonable costs of board, lodging, and travel shall be paid from the Trust Fund.

- The **New York** Vocational Rehabilitation Fund provides additional compensation for injured employees during rehabilitation and provides for expenses of such rehabilitation. Using a somewhat different approach, but still attempting to encourage the re-employment of injured workers, the **New Hampshire** Second Injury Fund reimburses employers 50 percent of the expenses, not to exceed $5,000 of the costs employers incur for job modification in order to retain individuals for which plan modification plans have been approved by the Commission.

- In **Maine**, if an employer hires an employee after the employee has completed a rehabilitation program, that subsequent employer may apply for a wage credit from the Employment Rehabilitation Fund. Wage credits consist of a sum equal to

---

[17] Texas Labor Code Sec. 408.042 (g)

50 percent of the average weekly direct wages, not to exceed the amount of workers compensation benefits that the employee did not receive because of the employment. Total wage credit payments may not exceed a period of 180 days. The Fund also pays benefits if that worker sustains a subsequent injury that results in a reduction in earning capacity.

Miscellaneous Provisions - The foregoing describes some of the more generic purposes served by special funds. Special funds have frequently operated as facilities to address unusual or unique situations. While a complete listing of all the unique special funds might prove of interest to some, development of the list would require extensive review of all state laws and would add little to the ultimate consideration. The following provides a few examples of some of the more unique special funds that have been identified.

- The **Michigan** Silicosis Dust Disease and Logging Industry Compensation Fund was established for the purpose of apportioning the amount of disability between that due to silicosis or other dust disease, or to employment in the logging industry, and other compensable causes. The fund is responsible. *"In each case in which a carrier including a self-insurer has paid, or causes to be paid, compensation for disability or death from silicosis or other dust disease, or for disability or death arising out of and in the course of employment in the logging industry, to the employee, the carrier including a self-insurer shall be reimbursed from the silicosis, dust disease, and logging industry compensation fund for all sums paid in excess of $12,500.00 for personal injury dates before July 1, 1985, and for all compensation paid in excess of $25,000.00 or 104 weeks of weekly compensation, whichever is greater, for personal injury dates after June 30, 1985, ..."*[18]

- The **Pennsylvania Supersedeas Fund** - Under the Pennsylvania Workers Compensation Act, employers may request *supersedeas* in conjunction with petitions to terminate, suspend, and modify a worker's benefits. In cases in which supersedeas has been requested and denied, the carrier or self-insured employer insurer is entitled to reimbursement from the Workers Compensation Superseeseas Fund for payments of compensation benefits paid during the pendency of litigation, if upon final outcome, it is determined that such compensation was not payable.

- In **New York**, if an award requires payment of death benefits or other compensation by an insurance carrier or employer in periodic payments, the Board may, at its discretion, compute and require payment into the Aggregate Trust Fund. The Trust Fund had its origin prior to the creation of state guaranty or insolvency funds. Monies collected by the Aggregate Trust Fund are transferred to a separate account maintained by the state insurance fund which is responsible for the continued payment of benefits on those cases. Effective with a

---

[18] Michigan Statute Section 418.531

law change enacted in 2007, carriers must pay the "present day value" of any permanent partial disability directly into the Trust Fund. In addition to the Aggregate Trust Fund, there are two also the Black Car Operators Injury Compensation Fund - created to cover work-related injuries sustained by limousine drivers - and the New York Jockey Injury Compensation Fund which was created to provide coverage for work-related injuries to jockeys, apprentice jockeys and exercise persons.

Another twist on the special fund theme is found in **Minnesota** with the creation of the Workers Compensation Reinsurance Association. The reinsurance facility was created at a time when the availability of reinsurance was restricted by insurance pricing. The Reinsurance Association is a nonprofit, unincorporated association created to provide reinsurance protection for serious workers compensation losses to all insurers and self-insured employers in Minnesota. Members select one of three maximum per-loss occurrence retention levels (for 2004, these amounts were $360,000, $720,000 or $1,440,000). Once the per-loss maximum amount has been reached for a specific claim, further payments are reimbursed by the Association.

The creation and/or use of special funds to address very specific purposes merit attention on an individual basis. While one may adjudge that certain of the special funds were created as a subsidy for a select group of employers, it is not possible to make the same observation relative to certain other funds. In the case of certain funds, they were established in order to ensure that all of the workers were protected and the cost of that protection was internalized to those employers. Suffice to say for funds in this category that each must be examined individually for purposes of its current merit and its service to the community of employers. Where possible, the purpose of workers compensation should be to internalize the cost of the coverage and to ensure that rates charged for insurance are sufficient to pay for benefits now and in the future.

CHAPTER TEN

THE RATE-MAKING PROCESS

Workers compensation insurance is an obligation placed upon employers by state statute. Like all insurance, the concept of protection is quite straightforward: it is the sharing of risk. The purchaser of insurance pays a premium in lieu of facing a sizeable loss that may result in devastating financial consequences for the entity. In the case of workers compensation, an employer who does not qualify as a self-insurer pays a certain premium to an insurance company, and in return the insurance company assumes responsibility for paying prescribed benefits to workers, or their dependents, as a result of injury or fatality from work. Thus, through the mechanism of insurance, the employer is protected against a share of the financial consequences of a loss resulting in injury or death.

Today, every state establishes a fairly comprehensive list of benefits for those workers injured or killed as a result of their employment. These benefits include replacement of a certain portion of pre-injury earnings, full coverage of all medical costs – including prescription medications – associated with cure and recovery, death benefits to dependents following a fatal injury, along with rehabilitation benefits – both medical and vocational – to maximize and expedite recovery. Through the mechanisms of insurance or self-insurance, employers fulfill their statutory responsibilities. States are in a position to impose penalties on those employers who fail to meet these statutory obligations.

Whether coverage is obtained through an insurance carrier, a competitive or exclusive state fund, or the residual market, the method for determining how much the employer will pay for insurance is essentially the same. A rating organization, subject to the approval of the state insurance regulator, establishes the appropriate rate, or loss cost, for each work type classification. The insurance premium for a particular employer is computed by multiplying the appropriate rate for the employee's work classification times each one hundred dollars of the employee's remuneration (payroll along with certain adjustments).

In order to get beneath the rate-making process, it is beneficial to examine each one of the components involved in the rate-making process individually in order to understand how the entire process works. The place to begin is with the foundation of the rate-making process, the rating organization.

RATING ORGANIZATIONS

It was not long after the enactment of the first workmen's compensation laws that a number of state regulators pressured the insurance industry to standardize the rules for workmen's compensation insurance. It was in response to this request that the National Council on Compensation Insurance (NCCI) was formed in 1920. Although the NCCI is thought by many to be a governmental agency, it is not. The NCCI is an independent organization that operates as an interface between insurance companies and state insurance regulators.

The NCCI is a private corporation, technically owned by member insurance companies, that essentially operates as a centralized organization for workers compensation insurance rate-making, offering a large degree of standardization to the insurance industry. Most states require that the workers compensation policy and related administrative forms be filed with their insurance department for approval. NCCI files all required forms on behalf of its member companies. In addition to the issuance of forms, NCCI establishes the rules for classification and premium determination. Special rating plans, such as experience rating, retrospective rating, and other rating information are also developed by NCCI.

Not all states use the NCCI as their rating organization. Eleven states – **California, Delaware, Indiana, Massachusetts, Michigan, Minnesota, New Jersey, New York, North Carolina, Pennsylvania,** and **Wisconsin** – maintain their own independent rating bureaus. These independent rating bureaus are responsible for the promulgation of manual rules and rates, along with all other required functions, for their own particular jurisdiction. In addition, the four monopolistic fund states – **Ohio, North Dakota, Washington, and Wyoming** – function as their own rating organization. Ohio does use the NCCI classification codes.

Even though NCCI is the state approved rating organization, there may still be distinct differences between one NCCI state and another because each state can and often does enact distinct rules and statutes that may affect how premiums are computed. NCCI states operate under a uniform set of manual rules, but those rules include many exceptions for particular states.

While historically identified as a rating bureau or organization, NCCI is more recently identified as an advisory organization in recognition for its changing role in the development and promulgation of workers compensation rates. In most states, the NCCI and other rating organizations no longer file final recommended rates. Instead of filing recommended rates, they file actuarially determined loss costs. (NCCI does continue to file full rates in **Arizona, Florida, Idaho, Iowa,** and **Illinois**.) Companies are required to gross up loss costs for their own particular expenses and rating policies. These manual rates are subject to regulatory review and approval.

Outside of estimating the loss cost consequences of legislative reforms, NCCI does not engage in lobbying for workers compensation law changes. Industry efforts to improve state laws are left to other industry trade associations.

FUNCTIONS OF RATING ORGANIZATIONS

The basic method of pricing workers compensation insurance is to apply an approved classification rate per hundred dollar of exposure units or payroll. (The proper term is "remuneration" but because payroll is generally the largest component, the term payroll is more generally used.) The reason for using payroll is that fluctuations in payroll roughly match fluctuations in workplace exposure to injury. Also, payroll per worker tends to correlate with the standard for paying compensation benefits associated with lost wages. Payroll is also a verifiable number that can be confirmed or audited with minimum difficulty. Efforts have been made in recent years to allow certain types of employment – particularly construction related employment – to calculate premiums on an hours-worked basis. This approach has only been approved in the monopolistic fund state of **Washington**.

One of the fundamental aspects of pricing workers compensation insurance is the system of classifying different workplace exposures into a system of codes, each one with a rate commensurate with the risk of compensable injury associated with a particular type of employment. The theory is that rates should reflect to the degree possible the varying exposure to injury for different types of work. For instance, a clerical person is normally subject to a considerably smaller workplace risk of injury than is a steelworker or roofer. Based upon this difference in exposure to risk, the rate for the clerical classification code would be substantially lower than the rate for the steelworkers' or roofers' classification code.

Once you move beyond such an extreme example, the question of proper classification of workplace exposure becomes much more complicated. Is there a difference in workplace exposure to injury for a clerical person working within an office versus that of a grocery store manager? Experience demonstrates that there is, inasmuch as the grocery store manager may spend time in the aisles where canned goods may fall or near the checkout locations where an armed robbery may take place. Thus, rates are based on the loss experience for each work classification. Typically there are 600 or more different workplace classifications approved for use in a particular state.

For the majority of employers, only a few classification codes apply. The guiding classification principle is that the overall business enterprise of the employer determines the classification, not the individual workplace exposures of specific employees. For instance, in a manufacturing plant, the janitor isn't classified into a janitorial classification, but rather is placed into the classification used for the plant employees.

In most states, the classification system used is one devised and maintained by NCCI. NCCI has devised a system of approximately 600 classification codes, intended to cover a virtually comprehensive spectrum of workplace exposures. There are a handful of states that do not use the NCCI classification system. **California, New Jersey, New York, Delaware, and Pennsylvania** are states that have their own classification systems. Other states have some "state special" classifications that vary significantly from NCCI definitions for certain workplace exposures.

> **The Classification System** - It is apparent from the foregoing that the classification system is a critical component of the overall workers compensation rate-making process. Therefore, one of the most important functions of any rating organization is the development and

maintenance of an adequate and equitable classification system. Adequate in terms of recognizing all of the different occupational types and equitable in the sense that the computed manual rates for each classification are reflective of the degree of hazardous exposure for that occupation.

One of the primary functions associated with the pricing of workers compensation insurance is classifying a risk or exposure within the proper workers compensation class code. Incorrect risk classification by insurance agents and/or underwriters may result in premium for the employer that is too high, or conversely, lower premium that does not adequately reflect the exposure. In either instance, the exposure ought to be reclassified following an audit.

Subtle differences in products and operations frequently result in alternative interpretations of the proper classification. Since class rates often vary by 20 percent or more within related groups of businesses (e.g., cheese making and yogurt making), ambiguous classification calls are often contested among employers, agents, underwriters, and premium auditors.

Before describing the classification system used by workers compensation rating organizations, it is helpful to distinguish the NCCI classification system from the North American Industry Classification System (NAICS) used by the government to classify business establishments according to type of economic activity (process of production). The NAICS – used in Canada, Mexico, and the United States – released its first version in 1997 at which time it largely replaced the dated Standard Industrial Classification (SIC) system.

The NAICS of occupational classifications is found in virtually all governmental publications and often leads to the question as to why the insurance industry does not use the classification scheme for workers compensation purposes. While both the NCCI classification system and the NAICS do essentially the same function in terms of describing the different employment categories, their respective approaches to classifying the various employment categories does not lend itself to acceptance by the other organization. This can be demonstrated by briefly reviewing how the two classification systems operate.

Under NAICS, each establishment is assigned to an industry according to that establishment's primary business activity. The NAICS numbering system employs a six-digit code at the most detailed industry level. The first two digits designate the largest business sector, the third digit designates the subsector, the fourth digit designates the industry group, and the fifth digit designates particular industries. The sixth digit is for individual country differentiations.

Employers use the six-digit NAICS classification codes when reporting information to the federal government. For example, injury reporting information compiled for OSHA reporting purposes is based upon the NAICS coding system. To provide a thumbnail sketch of the classification system, the following illustrates the first two-digit as found in the NAICS 2012 version.

Sector Number	Description
11	Agriculture, Forestry, Fishing and Hunting
21	Mining
22	Utilities
23	Construction
31-33	Manufacturing
42	Wholesale Trade
44-45	Retail Trade
48-49	Transportation and Warehousing
51	Information
52	Finance and Insurance
53	Real Estate and Rental and Leasing
54	Professional, Scientific, and Technical Services
55	Management of Companies and Enterprises
56	Administrative and Support and Waste Management and Remediation Services
61	Education Services
62	Health Care and Social Assistance
71	Arts, Entertainment and Recreation
72	Accommodation and Food Service
81	Other Services (Except Public Administration)
92	Public Administration

Here are the six-digit codes for certain agricultural activities:

Six Digit Codes for Select Farming Activities

111140	Wheat Farming
111150	Corn Farming
111160	Rice Farming
111211	Potato Farming
111331	Apple Orchards
111332	Grape Vineyards
111335	Tree Nut Farming
111336	Fruit and Tree Nut Combination

The classification system used by most workers compensation rating organizations is set up quite differently than the NAICS classification system. NCCI devised a system of approximately 600 classification codes, intended to cover workplace exposures. NCCI manuals and rules regarding classification that are used in most states, and also is responsible for determining the correct classifications for particular employers in those states that use the NCCI system.

In the rating manuals, NCCI classifications are listed both alphabetically and numerically by code numbers. The code numbers on the rate pages in the manual are arranged in numerical order to facilitate reference to the rates and other values for each classification. The following are examples both of the NCCI classification codes in the alphabetic format and in the numeric format:

NCCI Classification Codes & Descriptions (Alphabetical)

1860	Abrasive paper or cloth preparation
1748	Abrasive wheel mfg. & drivers
4693	Absorbent cotton mfg.
8803	Accountant, auditor or factory cost or systemizer-traveling
2305	Acetate textile fiber

NCCI Classification Codes & Descriptions (Numeric)

0005	Bedding plant growers & drivers
0005	Christmas tree planting, cultivating and harvesting - & drivers
0005	Farm product – Christmas trees - & drivers
0005	Farm product – holly - & drivers
0005	Farm product – nursery, trees & shrubs - & drivers
0005	Farm product – trees - & drivers
0005	Farm-nursery employees & drivers (includes incidental landscape gardening)
0005	Shrub cultivation - & drivers
0005	Sod dealer – no farming - & drivers
0005	Tree planting for reforestation - & drivers
0008	Farm Product – asparagus - & drivers
0008	Farm product – beans, green - & drivers

It is evident from the above numeric descriptions that many different exposures to injury may be present for different employees all within the same classification code.

No matter which rating organization is used in a particular state, the rating organization establishes the rules regarding how certain business enterprises are classified for purposes of computing premiums. NCCI's "Basic Manual for Workers Compensation and Employers Liability Insurance (Basic Manual)" includes the filed and approved classifications applicable in each NCCI state. The NCCI also produces a manual that provides guidance on what is intended to be included in each classification code. This manual is the "Scopes® of Basic Manual Classifications," or the "Scopes® Manual" for short. With changes in industry, the NCCI continues to review its classification scheme but the workplace exposures in the real world continue to remain a moving target.

All of the classifications in the "Basic Manual" (other than the standard exception classifications) include certain operations that may appear to be separate operations. These so-called general inclusions are:

- Commissaries and restaurants for the insured's employees. (Such operations are assigned to a separate classification if conducted in connection with construction, erection, lumbering, or mining operations.)

- Manufacture of containers, such as bags, barrels, bottles, boxes, cans, cartons, or packing cases, for use in the employer's operations insured by the policy.

- Hospitals or other medical facilities operated by the employer for its employees.

- Maintenance or repair of the employer's buildings or equipment.

- Printing or lithographing onto the employer's own products.

Payroll for the above noted operations is included in the governing classification unless such operations are a separate and distinct operation; such operations are specifically excluded by the wording of the classification; or the principal business is described by a standard exception classification.

At the same time, certain operations are always subject to a separate classification unless the classification wording specifically includes such operations. These include:

- Aircraft operations (all members of the flying crew).

- All new construction or alterations.

- Stevedoring, including tallying and checking incidental to stevedoring.

- Sawmill operations (sawing logs into lumber by equipment such as circular carriage or band carriage saws).

Certain classifications on the rate pages are followed not by a rate, but by the symbol "a". These are known as "a-rated" classifications. (It should be noted that there are few "a-rated" classifications.) The rate or loss cost, as well as the minimum premium and other factors for such risks, must be obtained directly from the rating organization. If a risk includes an "a-rated" classification, the policy must be written on a rate-to-be-determined basis. Upon receipt of such a policy, the rating organization takes the necessary action required to establish the rate or loss cost. Often, this involves a physical inspection, so that all of the elements required for a composite rate may be established. These include the operations performed by each separate group of employees, as well as the average total number of employees engaged.

The workers compensation governing classification is the classification that applies to the majority of the insured's payroll other than one of the standard exception classes. It is the classification that usually identifies the type of work being performed by the insured's business. The governing classification will be used to properly determine how certain employees within a business are classified. Certain managers and miscellaneous employees will be classed within the governing classification. Executive officers who regularly perform duties of a manager, superintendent, foreman or worker will be included within the governing classification code.

Governing classifications, when properly applied, will represent the normal activities of any particular business operation. As an example, consider a metal goods manufacturing plant. Individual work processes found within this type of business may include:

- The processing of raw materials.

- Use of metal presses for stamping metal parts.

- Welding parts together.

- Cleaning process oil from completed parts.

- Packaging and distribution of completed parts.

When classifying this operation the governing classification would be metal goods manufacturing. All these individual work process would be contemplated by the governing class code.

A final note on classification of risks: With the exception of the construction industry, it's the business operation that is classified, not individual work processes within the business.

Collection of Statistical Data – A second critical function of a rating organization is the collection and compilation of rate-making data. In order to collect the information necessary to file for rate changes, rating organizations rely upon statistical information provided by member companies. The statistical information provided is primarily of three types.

Aggregate Financial Call Data is gathered from each company and includes company-wide standard premium, net premium after discounts and credits to policyholders, overall indemnity and medical losses paid, an estimate for losses incurred but not yet reported, claim counts, case reserves, and the value of adjustments for safety and specialty programs. This data is collected from each private insurance carrier and state fund (if appropriate) on a policy year and accident year basis.

Policy year data includes all premiums and losses for policies written during a specific time period. For example, policy year 2021 data would include premiums earned for all policies written between January 1, 2021 and December 31, 2021, and all losses associated with those same policies. Accident year data includes all premiums earned during a specific year and the losses incurred for accidents that occurred during that year, regardless of when the policy was written. For example, 2021 accident year data would include all premiums collected in 2021 and the losses incurred for all accidents that occurred during 2021. Policy year data is considered the most reliable and requires two years to collect.

Another form of loss related data that insurance carriers and state funds (if appropriate) are required to submit is Unit Statistical Data which consists of the audited exposure, premium, and loss information for a policy, and is reported separately for each exposure state covered on the policy. Unit Statistical Data is initially valued 18 months after the policy effective date. The first report is due 18 to 20 months after policy effective date. Subsequent reports for open, reopened and newly arising claims are due in 12 month intervals, with up to a total of 10 report levels required. As an example, a one-year policy written as of January 1, 2021 would be valued as of July 2022, with the first report due between July and September 2022. Unit Statistical data is used to determine classification relativities for state loss cost/ratemaking, develop experience modifications for insured employers, and fulfill actuarial analyses.

Unit Statistical Data includes a wide-range of information which is reported in accordance with the Statistical Plan used by each Workers Compensation Rating Organization. Examples of the data elements included are:

1. Policy Number
2. Exposure State in which the insured employer conducts its business and for which information is being reported
3. Carrier Code
4. Name of the insured employer
5. Classification code(s) describing the type of business or operations in which the insured engages
6. Exposure for each classification code
7. Manual rate for each classification code (usually a rate per $100 of payroll [exposure]) before the application of experience rating or other rate modification.
8. Manual premium, obtained by multiplying the units of exposure (generally payroll divided by $100) by the manual rate.
    a. Claim Number
    b. Accident date.
    c. Classification code associated with the claim.
    d. Injury Type Code.
    e. Incurred loss amount for indemnity.
    f. Incurred loss amount for medical.
    g. Claims status — open (designated by the numeral "0") or closed (designated by the numeral "1").

A third category of data collected by rating organizations is general expense data. As the name suggests, general expense data relates to an individual carrier's taxes, commissions, general overhead, and administrative and underwriting costs. Expense data is used by the rating bureau to determine average carrier expenses, which are incorporated into the manual rates. This expense loading is not included in those states where the rating organization is limited to the filing of loss costs.

Filing for Rate Changes – Once the classification system has been approved and the statistical data from member insurers has been compiled, the rating organization is in a position to fulfill its third and perhaps most critical function. Rating organizations are responsible for putting together – usually on an annual basis – a rate filing for submission to the state insurance department or insurance regulator. It is the state insurance regulator who is responsible for reviewing the rate filing and either approving, altering, or disapproving the filing.

The statutory purpose of rate regulation is to assure that rates are not excessive, inadequate, or unfairly discriminatory. This may be interpreted as preventing insurers from making too large of a profit on the business written, not making enough in premium to cover actual losses, or discriminating in how various rates and rating plans are applied. However, these criteria may not prevent, in some instances, the regulatory process from being exploited by special interest or politically powerful groups to seek rates that are insufficient to cover expected loss costs.

Manual Rates and Loss Costs – Traditionally, rating organizations, such as NCCI and state independent rating organizations developed manual rates for all available classifications. Those rates were the basis of the manual premiums. Regulation of workers compensation insurance rates in most states historically required all insurers to use the same rates, rating classes, and experience-rating plans. Rating organizations – in most instances, the NCCI – collected loss and expense data from all member companies and compiled that data to develop and file class-level advisory rates on behalf of the industry. A manual rate filing includes expected loss costs, loss adjustment expenses, insurer expenses and a factor for profit and contingencies. Manual rates are usually revised annually.

The mood of the country toward government regulation began to change in the 1970s, and many industries were deregulated. In 1980, the National Association of Insurance Commissioners (NAIC) bowed to this movement by adopting its first model competitive rating law. While this new model law did not explicitly mandate competitive rating for workers compensation, states began to rely on competition to set final rates for workers compensation class codes. At present, more than two-thirds of the states have in place some form of open competition rating law.

In those states with competitive rating laws, the NCCI or other rating organizations file loss costs instead of rates. Loss costs are the expected costs of actual losses and loss adjustment expenses, but do not include other insurer expenses or profits. Insurers must then file loss cost multipliers that, when multiplied by the loss costs, produce a final rate to include their expenses and profits. The loss cost multiplier is the competitive component, as a lower multiplier produces a final lower rate and premium than a higher loss cost multiplier would. Other pricing variables include insurers filing for deviation from published rates or filing their own rates. Loss cost multipliers, rate deviations and insurer-filed rates must generally be submitted to the insurance regulator of each jurisdiction for approval.

Even though advisory organizations will not promulgate rates in open rating states, insurers are generally expected to adhere to a mandatory classification system and unit statistical plan reporting, as well as an experience or merit rating plan. They are also expected to adhere to manual rules promulgated by the advisory organization and approved by the state's insurance commissioner. In addition, the standard policy form is required.

DEVELOPMENT OF THE EMPLOYER'S PREMIUM

The basic method of pricing a manual workers compensation rate for an employer is to compute a rate per hundred dollars of remuneration (more fully defined below). There are different classifications which apply to different work exposures, and each classification will carry its own particular rate per hundred dollars of payroll. Rates need to vary in order to reflect the varying exposure to injury of different kinds of work. For example, a bank teller is normally subject to considerably less workplace risk of injury than is a steelworker resulting in a lower rate per hundred dollars of payroll for the bank teller.

For the majority of employers, only a few classification codes will apply. The guiding classification principle in workers compensation is that the overall business enterprise of the employer is classified, not the individual workplace exposures of employees. The classification used for the business is called the governing classification. This is generally the classification that generates the most payroll for an employer.

There are also a number of workplace exposures that are normally broken out into their own classifications: clerical, outside salespeople, and often, but not always, drivers. These are referred to as standard exceptions. In addition, there are also exceptions made for certain kinds of employers. Generally, employers in construction-type classifications are not subject to this governing classification rule. Instead, the individual exposures of the workers are classified, according to the classification rules that apply in that particular state.

Taking the rate for a specific classification and multiplying it by each one hundred dollars of remuneration for employees in that classification develops an employers' manual premium. Because remuneration is such an important part of determining an employers' insurance premium, it is important to examine the issue of remuneration in greater detail.

In most instances, the premium for a workers compensation policy is computed on the entire remuneration paid or payable by the employer. However, classifications which address domestic workers are rated on a different basis.

> **Remuneration Inclusions** – Remuneration is defined as money or substitutes for money. Subject to state exceptions, NCCI's "Basic Manual" specifies that remuneration includes:
>
> a. Wage or salaries, including retroactive wages or salaries.
> b. Total cash received by employees for commissions and draws against commission.
> c. Bonuses, including stock bonus plans.
> d. Extra pay for overtime work.
> e. Pay for holidays, vacations, or periods of sickness.
> f. Payment by an employer of amounts otherwise required by law to be paid by

employees to statutory insurance or pension plans, such as the federal Social Security Act.
- g. Payment to employees on any basis other than time worked, such as piecework, profit sharing, or incentive plans.
- h. Payment or allowance for hand tools or power tools used by hand, provided by employees either directly or through a third party and used in their work or operations for the insured.
- i. The rental value of an apartment or a house (particular requirements apply).
- j. The value of lodging, other than an apartment or house (particular requirements apply).
- k. The value of meals (particular requirements apply).
- l. The value of store certificates, merchandise, credits, or any other substitute for money received by employees as part of their pay (with certain exceptions).
- m. Payments for salary reduction, retirement, or cafeteria plans (Internal Revenue Code Chapter 125) made through deductions from the employee's gross pay.
- n. Davis-Bacon wages paid to employees or placed by an employer into third party pension trusts.
- o. Annuity plans.
- p. Expense reimbursements to employees to the extent that an employer's records do not substantiate that the expense was incurred as a valid business expense.
- q. Payment for filming commercials, excluding subsequent residuals earned by the commercial's participant(s) each time the commercial appears in print or is broadcast.

It is to be noted that some employers voluntarily pay certain amounts of wages over and above the amount of any workers compensation or non-occupational disability benefits. The employer may supplement such benefits, either by continuing to pay full wages and obtaining the awarded benefits as reimbursement or by granting the employees some amount in addition to the awarded benefits. Such supplements to workers compensation or disability benefits awards are included as remuneration. However, a premium is charged only on the net amounts in excess of the benefits provided by law.

In addition, remuneration can include pay to employees for extra time not worked. The entire wages paid for idle time is included as payroll and is assigned to the classification that applies to work normally performed by an employee under the following conditions.

- a. Suspensions or delays of work caused by weather conditions.
- b. Delays while waiting for materials.
- c. Delays while waiting for another contractor to complete certain work.
- d. Delays arising from breakdown of equipment.
- e. Stand-by times where employees are on the job, but their active services are not continuously required.
- f. Special union requirements or agreements calling for pay for idle time under specified circumstances.
- g. Other causes of similar nature.

When payroll audits are made for premium computation purposes, a reduction in payroll is not allowed for any taxes withheld by the employer.

Remuneration Exclusions – Subject to state exceptions, the following items are excluded in the computation of remuneration:

a. Contributions made by the employer to a group insurance or pension plan.
b. Special rewards for individual invention or discovery.
c. Payments to an employee upon dismissal are not included in the premium computation unless they are for previous time worked or accrued vacation.
d. Itemized expenses such as those incurred by outside salesmen. Reimbursed expenses and flat expense allowances are excluded from the premium computation if such expenses were incurred in connection with the employer's business, the amount of each employee's expenses is separately recorded, *and* such amounts approximate the actual expenses incurred by the employee.
e. Payments made by an employer to a union to serve as vacation funds for union member or for welfare, medical, hospitalization, or other similar purposes.
f. Reinstatement wages resulting from rulings of the National Labor Relations Board.
g. Employer contributions to federally approved group savings plans provided the employer is not required to report these amounts as current income.
h. In most states, remuneration does not include residual payments to theatrical and similar performers made after termination of employment. Such payments are made for the right to subsequent use of the performer's work rather than arising from an employer-employee relationship.
i. Tips or gratuities: Remuneration excludes all tips and other gratuities received by employees in the course of their work from patrons, customers or sources other than the employer.
j. Veteran's subsistence allowance: Subsistence allowance paid to the veteran-in-training does not constitute wages for premium or benefit purposes.

Other Considerations in Computing Remuneration – In the computation of the premium where the employee receives meals, the value of such meals received by employees as part of their pay, if furnished by the employer, is included to the extent shown in the employer's records. As regards lodging, if lodging is furnished by the employer, the value of lodging (other than an apartment or house), is included to the extent shown in the employer's records. And, if an apartment or house is received as part of the pay, it is to be included at the value of comparable accommodations in the same building or neighborhood.

The subject of overtime has special rules. Overtime means those hours worked for which there is an increase in the rate of pay earned by employees. However, in the case of guaranteed wage agreements under which the employee receives a guaranteed wage for actually working any number of hours up to a specified number of hours per week, overtime includes only those hours worked in excess of the specified number. In almost all jurisdictions, overtime remuneration can be deducted if the insured maintains books and records that indicate separately the additional remuneration for overtime paid to employees over and above their regular rates of pay.

DIVISION OF PAYROLL RULES

It is generally not permissible to divide the payroll of any one employee between two or more classifications. The entire payroll of each employee not eligible for one of the standard exception classifications must usually be assigned to the highest-rated classification representing any part of his or her work. An exception to this is the provision allowing for the interchange of labor. In the event that there are employees who perform duties directly related to more than one job classification that has been assigned to a policy, their payroll may be divided between the two classifications, subject to certain conditions.

- The classifications must be properly assigned to the employer in accordance with the rules of the classification system.

- The employer must maintain proper payroll records that disclose the actual payroll by classification for each individual employee performing such duties. In other words, the division or allocation of payroll between two or more classifications cannot be estimated or calculated as a percentage. The employer's records must show the actual time spent working within each job classification.

If all of these conditions are not met, the entire payroll of individual employees performing duties for two or more job classifications is assigned to the classification on the policy that bears the highest authorized rate.

Total Payroll Rule – The exposure to liability insured under a workers compensation policy is the sum of the exposures to injury of each employee while on the job. This exposure is measured by the amount of payroll expended. The payroll provides a direct reflection of the time exposed to the hazard of the job and is readily available as a definite premium base. Total payroll is the most practicable and verifiable basis for determining the premium. Therefore, the premium for a workers compensation policy is computed on the basis of the entire remuneration paid by the insured to employees after deductions have been made in accordance with the overtime rule.

If a payroll limit applies to a classification, that part of the remuneration of each employee which exceeds the applicable average may be excluded from the premium computation. To use this exclusion, the employer's books and records must indicate separately the total remuneration earned by all employees whose average weekly remuneration exceeded the applicable limit during the total time they were employed while the policy was in force.

Payroll Limitation Rule – Highly paid workers (e.g., executive officers) and classifications with notes that so indicate often have payroll capped to reflect limitations in indemnity payment per claim. Under the payroll limitation rule, bonuses paid during the policy period are considered as earned during the policy term and prorated over the entire period of the recipient's employment during the policy term. A number of states have the payroll limitation rule applicable to certain classifications. For example, in **New York**, the rule is designed to provide a more equitable distribution of premium between high wage paying and low wage paying employers in the construction industry.

The payroll limitation rule is invoked after deductions from the employee's remuneration have been made under the overtime rule (explained above). It is applied only on a single-policy basis. If an employer has two or more concurrent policies (which may occur where different jobs or locations are separately insured), it is not permissible to combine them for the purpose of determining deductions under the payroll limitation rule.

FURTHER MANUAL RATE ADJUSTMENTS

When the rate for a particular classification is multiplied by remuneration (per hundred dollars) in that classification, the result is referred to as the manual premium. The manual premium may then be adjusted by an experience modification factor, based on prior loss experience of an employer. (The method for calculating the experience modification factor will be discussed later in this chapter.) The manual premium may be subject to a premium discount which is a discount based simply on the size of the premium.

Because it's impossible to know ahead of time exactly how much payroll will be generated over the term of the policy, workers compensation insurance is written initially on an estimated premium basis. Thus, after the policy ends there will normally be some kind effort made by the insurer to determine the actual payroll for the policy period, and to adjust the premium based on these revised payroll numbers. If the policy premium is relatively small, the insurance company might just ask the employer to report the actual payrolls. If the policy premium is larger, the insurance company will probably want to send out a premium auditor to determine actual payrolls.

Large firms are generally of a size that their rates, after application of their experience modification factor are reflective of their own experience. The larger the risk, the more of its own experience can be used in the computation of the modification factor. Medium-sized firms pay a weighted average based on their own experience and class rates, and very small firms pay pure class rates. In addition, insurers may compete through dividends to above average-risk employers and through service quality. In the 1980s and early 1990s, increasingly stringent regulation of NCCI manual rates led to fewer downward deviations, smaller schedule-rating credits and dividends, and larger residual markets and residual-market deficits.

The manual rate for a classification is the rate per hundred dollars of payroll that a particular insurance company has filed to use in a particular state. As stated previously, a few states require that all insurance companies use the same schedule of manual rates within the jurisdiction, but today, most states allow competing insurance companies to use filed loss costs and then develop their own schedule of manual rates.

A typical manual rate page includes the code number, the rate or loss cost per $100 of payroll, the loss constant (if applicable), and the minimum premium. The following illustrates the information found on a manual rate page:

Code No.	Rate per $100 of Payroll	Loss Constant	Minimum Premium

1009	$23.22	$26	$100
1463	9.44	28	100
7207	11.35	26	100
7313	4.76	74	100
8233	13.89	26	100
9061	2.13	26	100

A typical workers compensation insurance policy for a large manufacturing firm might have multiple classifications, each with its own manual rate, due to separate and distinct operations. Some employers may have dozens or even hundreds of different classifications on their policies. Each classification will be listed, with a brief written description along with a four-digit code number and the manual rate for each.

Minimum Premium – The annual premium may not be less than the minimum premium. The minimum premium applying to the policy is inserted by the insurer on the Information Page under Item 4. Where a minimum premium applies to a policy, it generally may not exceed a specific dollar amount for any classification. The minimum premium for each classification is indicated on the rate pages. Only one minimum premium is applicable, regardless of the number of classifications or the number of states in which operations are covered. Where the policy includes two or more classifications, generally the minimum premium for the policy is the highest minimum premium for any classification on the policy. Where the policy covers operations in more than one state, the minimum premium is determined by taking the highest minimum premium of any one of the states involved.

On final audit of every policy, the minimum premium to be retained by the insurer is recomputed in accordance with the foregoing rules on the basis of the actual audited payrolls of the classifications applicable to the policy.

The minimum premium applies only to basic coverage. Additional minimum premiums for higher Employer's Liability Insurance (Part Two of the policy) limits represent the lowest charges for providing the higher limits and are charged in addition to the regular minimum premiums. Furthermore, there are special minimum premiums for maritime risks (i.e., masters and members of crews of vessels) and interstate railroad risks (the Federal Employers' Liability Act), due to the high hazard involved in such operations.

Premium Discount – A premium discount is a size discount that is applied to workers compensation insurance premiums that exceed $10,000. It's also a sliding scale discount, so that as the premium grows larger, so does the percentage of the discount. These increasing discounts are figured by brackets, much like income tax brackets. The premium discount reduces premiums both on the policy and on the audit of the policy based on which bracket the premium fits in. If the premium on the audit is different than that originally on the policy, the percentage of premium discount can change.

Merit Rating – Several states (e.g. **Alabama, Hawaii, Massachusetts,** and **Pennsylvania)** have programs in place that offer credits or debits on premiums for employers too small to qualify for experience rating. These programs are known as merit rating. For example, an employer that is not experience rated and whose annual premium is less than $5,000 may qualify for merit rating as follows:

No claims in most recent year	**10% credit**
No claims in most recent two years	**15% credit**
One claim in most recent year	**No credit**

In the case where the employer has had two or more claims in the most recent year, there is a ten percent debit

Schedule Rating Credits or Debits – Many states also allow discretionary credits or debits by insurers. These are generally known as schedule rating credit or debit programs and they work much like experience modification factors. They are percentage discounts or surcharges that further adjust the modified premium. A 25 percent schedule credit would further reduce an employer's premium charges by 25 percent. Conversely, a 25 percent schedule debit would increase an employer's premium by 25 percent. Twenty-eight jurisdictions permit schedule rating.[19] Both **New York** and **New Jersey** permit scheduled rating under their own promulgated rules.

These schedule credits and debits are filed by insurers, or by the rating organization on behalf of the insurers, with state regulators and are intended to be used on a rational and specified basis. An insurance company will file with the state insurance regulator a request to be approved for a maximum overall limit of credit and debit charges. If approved, the insurer can then apply up to that maximum credit or debit for a particular policyholder. Schedule rating permits the premium for a risk to be modified in accordance with a table that accounts for characteristics of the risk that are not reflected in its experience.

Within those overall limits, insurers also file sub-limits for particular criteria they propose for these adjustments.

Schedule rating premium adjustments must be reported under unique statistical codes on unit statistical reports submitted to the NCCI. All schedule debits and credits are to be based on evidence that is contained in the file of the insurer at the time the schedule debit or credit is applied. The effective date of any schedule debit or credit shall not be any date prior to the receipt in the insurer's office of the evidence supporting the debit or credit.

A number of states have enacted other premium credits that can apply to certain employers within their jurisdictions. Certain states have enacted contractor premium adjustment plans which can give employers in construction-related field's credits if their average hourly wages are relatively high. This can give some premium relief to construction businesses that

---

[19] Alabama, Arizona, Colorado, Connecticut, District of Columbia, Idaho, Indiana, Iowa, Kansas, Kentucky, Maryland, Minnesota, Mississippi, Montana, Nevada, New Hampshire, New Mexico, North Carolina, Oklahoma, Rhode Island, South Carolina, South Dakota, Tennessee, Texas, Utah, Vermont, Virginia, and West Virginia.

pay high hourly wages. Other states allow credits for employers that maintain drug-free workplaces, for employers that elect to utilize managed care networks, for employers with safety committees, or for employers that engage in certain safety audit programs.

Other Premium Credits or Debits – There can be other, relatively small charges that contribute to an employer's final workers compensation premium. An expense constant is often added, which is a flat charge that essentially is a surcharge for the expense of producing the policy. There may be a terrorism charge to reflect the risk of catastrophic loss from a terrorist attack, which is a rate time's total payroll. If applicable, terrorism and catastrophic loss rating factors are usually a fraction of one percent of premium. Interest may be charged on installment payments of premium.

Some states have introduced surcharges to fund the operations of the state workers compensation commission or bureau (agencies that monitor claim activity and adjudicate claims.) In certain states, second injury or special fund assessments are included within the manual rates. In a number of jurisdictions where such assessments were becoming a sizeable expense factor, such assessments were allowed to be a separately stated line item in the computation of insurance rates.

GUARANTEED COST PLANS

A workers compensation policy with a fixed or guaranteed cost premium is the most conservative and the easiest to understand. Such programs are stable in regard to cost. A company that chooses a guaranteed cost plan knows what the insurance will cost at policy inception because the policy premium is the cost. The premium varies only as a factor of payroll and experience modifier, if applicable. It does not vary directly as the result of loss experience and cannot be increased retrospectively.

The guaranteed cost premium is the manual, or standard, premium. If an account qualifies for an experience modifier, it is applied to the standard premium. The guaranteed cost program is the starting point for all workers compensation programs and can be reduced by discounts, dividends, and deductibles or increased by loss or expense constants. Even though it is the easiest to understand, it may not be the most desirable – or even available in the marketplace.

Estimated Premium – At the time a policy is issued, an estimated manual premium is determined by multiplying the estimated annual remuneration for each classification by the corresponding manual rate. After the total manual premium is computed, any experience rating or retrospective rating modification is applied to the total manual premium. The terrorism premium is added after other premium calculations have been completed. No discounts apply to the terrorism premium. The policy is subject to an audit upon its expiration or cancellation for the purpose of determining the final earned premium, at which time the same procedure is followed, i.e., the experience rating or retrospective rating modification is applied to the total earned manual premium.

If more than one classification applies to a policy, miscellaneous employees such as, janitors, porters, cleaners, maintenance workers, receiving and shipping clerks, packers, and general superintendents, are assigned to the governing classification. The basic classification is defined as the classification which describes the operations of the employer. However, if a risk (or that part of a risk which is conducted at a specific location) is described by two or more classifications, that classification which develops the largest amount of payroll is the governing classification. Generally, a standard exception classification is not considered in determining the governing classification.

Where there is only one basic classification applicable to a risk, all employees, including miscellaneous employees such as those described above, must be assigned to that single basic classification. However, any employee described by any of the Standard Exception Classifications is assigned to the appropriate standard exception classification.

Premium Audits – After the policy has expired, it is subject to a final premium adjustment as indicated above, and this may result in the payment of an additional premium or a return premium, depending upon whether the final premium is more or less than the total of previous premium payments.

For some insurers, if the annual premium is $15,000 or more, an actual payroll audit must be made at least once a year. If the annual premium is less than $15,000, an actual payroll audit must be made during the first year the risk is written, and at least once every three years thereafter while it is insured by the same insurance carrier, in which case, a signed statement indicating the payroll must be obtained from the employer for each year the risk is not audited.

It is very common for carriers to use mail audits for smaller employers. In such cases a form is sent to the policyholder for verification of payroll. In some instances, such as a private residence or a janitorial risk with only one or two employees, actual audits may be waived, and signed payroll statements may be accepted. If a risk is subject to interim audits, signed payroll statements may be accepted from the insured in lieu of all except the final audit, which must include an actual audit for all periods for which payroll statements were accepted.

OTHER POLICY CONSIDERATIONS

A policy may not be written to cover more than one risk. In applying this rule, a risk is defined as one legal entity or two or more legal entities in which the same person, group of persons, or corporation owns a majority of the voting stock. If voting stock does not exist, as in the case of associations or partnerships, a risk would comprise those entities in which the same group of persons constitutes the majority of the memberships.

Under no circumstances may a policy be written to cover only a part of a specific location of a given risk, leaving another part of the same location uninsured. The entire operations of any one employer at a specific location must be covered by a single policy.

Policies must be written on the basis of the entire payroll for the operations of the employer which are the subject of insurance. However, it is permissible to exclude from the coverage, any person, or group of persons, who are exempted from the provisions of a law (e.g., persons engaged in a clerical or teaching capacity in a religious, charitable, or educational institution which is not operated for profit).

An employer is required to keep a true and accurate record of the number of his employees and the wages paid to them for four years after each policy period. Such records must be available for inspection during regular business hours and as often as necessary by investigators of the workers compensation board or by auditors or inspectors of the insurer or administrative workers compensation insurance rating board. In addition, any and all records required by any law on which the employer files or reports information concerning wages must be open for inspection. Failure to keep such records or falsification of such records generally constitutes a misdemeanor.

EXPERIENCE RATING

The object of the experience rating plan (ERP) is to recognize the differences between individual insured's through the use of the insured's own loss experience. In effect, the ERP adjusts for the fact that the hazards of a particular employer may not perfectly fit the hazards of operations contemplated in the classification plan.

The experience rating process serves as a means of using a history of past losses to predict the future losses of an insured. This is done by comparing the experience of an individual insured to the expected losses of an average insured in the same classification. Therefore, using the insured's past experience, the experience modification is determined by comparing the actual losses to expected losses.

Experience rating offers the prospect of a premium reduction thereby providing the employer with an incentive to develop safety programs, accident prevention procedures and implementation of early return to work programs. Thus, experience rating benefits employers by promoting occupational safety and returning workers to their former level of employment.

In addition, because experience rating represents a refinement of the premium determination process, it benefits employers by producing a net premium cost that is a better indicator of the employer's own potential for incurring claims. This means that the insurance premium will be more appropriate for the protection being provided and neither more nor less than is appropriate using sound insurance principles.

Manual rate determination covered in the previous section reflects only the average conditions found in each classification. The purpose of assigning an employer to a classification is to ensure that the rates reflect the costs of all employers with similar characteristics. The determination of the manual rate for each classification includes the experience of both the less risky and the riskier insured's. If the rating system went no further than manual rating, then the insurance underwriter would aggressively seek the better than average, more desirable insured's, while the less desirable insured's would have difficulty obtaining coverage. Obviously, the pricing program must be further refined beyond developing classification manual rates.

In experience rating, the actual loss patterns of the individual employer are determined over a period of time, usually the past three years. This experience is then compared with the expected losses used for and as reflected by the manual rate or rates which apply to the employer's business. A modification factor greater than 1.0 indicates a loss experience that has been worse than expected while a modification factor less than 1.0 indicates a loss experience that has been better than expected. In a hard market where insurers are looking to identify the best risks, an experience modification factor under 1.0 is far more attractive to an insurer than a similar risk with an experience modification factor greater than 1.0.

For employers subject to experience rating, an employer with better than expected losses is awarded a credit, while poorer than expected loss experience carries a debit rating. Experience rating takes the average loss experience (manual rates), and modifies it by the loss experience incurred by the individual risk. Consequently, the two primary benefits of experience rating are:

- It tailors the cost prediction and, hence, the final net premium cost to the individual insured more closely than does the manual rating.

- It provides an incentive for loss prevention which is absent in manual rating.

The NCCI experience rating plan, first introduced in the 1940s, is an evolving procedure. In its long history, the rating plan has been changed infrequently. The most recent change took place in 2013 when the rating split point (the dollar value between primary and excess losses) was increased from $5,000 to an indexed value of $15,000 over a three year phase-in period. The indexed value would serve to adjust the split-point in future years.

CHARACTERISTICS OF EXPERIENCE RATING

Experience rating is mandatory for all insured's who qualify. The experience rating calculation is not made by the insurer, but rather is computed by the appropriate rating organization, such as the NCCI, according to a fixed formula designed to measure how the performance of an employer differs predictably from employers of his own type of business. Experience rating is therefore a standard measure that applies to nearly all risks.

A common misconception is that experience rating modification factors are calculated by the state. In most states, this is not true. Experience modification factors are calculated by rating organizations and most states use the NCCI for this computation. As noted previously, **California, Delaware, Indiana, Massachusetts, Michigan, Minnesota, New Jersey, New York, North Carolina, Pennsylvania,** and **Wisconsin** have their own separate rating bureaus. Modification factors calculated for California, Delaware, Pennsylvania, Michigan, and New Jersey are stand-alone modifiers, meaning that they are used only on premium charges for those individual states, even if the company also has operations in other states. But rating data from Indiana, Massachusetts, and Minnesota are integrated into a single multi-state modifier when a company has operations in other states.

Several general items are worth setting forth regarding experience rating:

- Loss data in the computation is used to adjust future premiums thus making the process prospective.

- Experience modification is recomputed on an annual basis and is effective for a twelve-month period.

- Only a single modification factor is applied to a particular risk at any one time. The experience modification factor applies to all operations of the risk. A risk is defined as all entities eligible for combination under the plan, regardless as to whether one or more insurance policies are used to insure the risk.

- The expected losses used to develop the experience modification factor are based on the losses that are expected for all business in the insured's classification code. To illustrate, the expected losses for a specific manufacturer would be compared with the expected losses for all manufacturers as a class.

- Schedule rating is usually permitted in addition to experience rating.

- With experience rating, there is a direct correlation between claims history and premium to be charged. Poor claim experience will affect the amount of compensation premium an employer will be required to pay.

It is to be noted that the experience modification factor is not applied to the loss constant, expense constant, policy minimum premium, premium developed by the occupational disease rates for risks subject to the Federal Coal Mine Health and Safety Act, premium under the National Defense Projects Rating Plan, the seat surcharge for aircraft operations, premium under atomic energy, premium developed under three year fixed rate policies, or premium for Migrant and Seasonal Worker Protection Act coverage.

The employer's experience modification factor includes all businesses under common ownership and the injury history developed in all states where coverage may be provided by private insurers. A single interstate experience modification applies in all states except **California, Delaware, Michigan, New Jersey, Pennsylvania, Texas,** and the monopolistic fund states, where interstate experience rating has not been adopted due to state laws.

EXPERIENCE IN MODIFICATION CALCULATION

NCCI experience rating calculations are based on no more than 45 months of workers compensation policy information. For data to be included in the calculation, the policy effective date must be at least 21 months prior to the rating effective date and no more than 57 months prior to the rating effective date.

To illustrate, the experience used is determined as follows:

1. Start with the effective date of the policy to which the experience modification will apply. (For purposes of this example, we will use January 1, 2021.)

2. Add three months to that date (April 1, 2021).

3. Subtract two years (April 1, 2019).

4. Subtract an additional three years (April 1, 2016).

5. The experience period used in the calculation will include policies effective on or after April 1, 2016, through policies effective on or before April 1, 2019. The insured's new rating modification will reflect experience for policy periods effective January 1, 2016, January 1, 2017, and January 1, 2018 – assuming continuing annual renewals during that time.

Note that 2019 data will not be included in determining the experience modification factor. There are two reasons for this. First, the 2019 data would not be available until the policy expired and the insurer conducted a payroll audit and submitted the payroll and loss information to NCCI. The information would not be complete until well into the 2020 policy year. Second, loss information includes open claims; to the extent that loss reserves are amended more in the first year than later as claims age, it is fairer to both insurer and insured to use mature data.

Once the employer meets the qualifications for rating (the dollar thresholds established by each state, typically between $5,000 and $10,000 in premium), the experience rating plan formula is applied, and a credit or debit modification is published by the rating organization that generally must be used by any insurer insuring the business. The modification will apply for one year, and a new modification will be calculated and issued for the succeeding year. The payroll and claims information used in experience rating comes from Unit Statistical Reports. (Contents of the Unit Statistical Report were covered previously.)

Insurers are required to file a unit report with NCCI, or with the applicable state rating bureau or monopolistic fund, for each policy they issue. The format for reporting is on file with the regulatory authorities in each state. As many as four subsequent annual reports are required if any changes in payroll, premium, or claims take place after the initial report.

EXPERIENCE MODIFICATION FORMULA

The experience modification formula is designed to tailor the cost of coverage to a particular employer. It accomplishes this by a formula modification of the manual rate. Two basic statistical laws underlie the formula:

- First, the larger the base, the more reliable is the actual loss record. Integral to the plan is a credibility scale so that the actual historical record is used to a greater degree as the size of the employer increases. The loss experience of small employers has almost no predictive power for losses in the upcoming rating period. For example, out of 100 florists with one or two employees, 90 or more will have no claims in a given year.

- Second, the cost of an injury varies over a very large range and is therefore less predictable than the fact that an injury occurred. This fact is incorporated through the use of the primary and excess components.

This second point regarding the cost of an injury is best illustrated when setting a reserve – monies to be paid into the future – following a fatal injury. Survivor benefits for a young worker in their 20's, leaving a surviving spouse and three children, would be considerably greater than the survivor benefits for a worker in their 50's, leaving no dependents. The important fact is that the accident did occur. Thus, the experience rating plan gives greater weight to accident frequency than to accident severity.

This reliance on accident frequency also measures risk desirability. Compare the employer with one loss of $50,000 during the rating period with another employer of about the same size with 15 accidents, each of $3,000 per claim, totaling $45,000. Which business is a better insurance risk, and which one would be expected to develop more claims in the future? Obviously, the risk with the one large claim is relatively more desirable, particularly when you consider that any one of the 15 small accidents could have, under slightly different conditions or circumstances have exceeded the $50,000 amount. However, the fact that an employer incurred a small number of very costly injuries may be an important characteristic and must be taken into consideration.

The formula is as follows:

(Actual Primary Losses + Stabilizing Value + Actual Ratable Excess)

divided by

(Expected Primary Losses + Stabilizing Value + Expected Ratable Excess)

The first step in the experience rating process is the transfer of payroll and loss information from the Unit Statistical Reports to the Experience Rating Form, which requires the same information as the Unit Statistical Report and indicates the policy for which the experience modification is being calculated.

Payroll and loss information is shown separately for each policy year under review. The form lists the payroll exposure for each classification code, actual incurred losses, the indicator of whether the claim is open or closed, and the claim number for losses over $2,000. In transferring the losses from the Unit Statistical Report to the Experience Rating Form, indemnity and medical amounts are combined, since rating requires only the total amount of the claim. For example, an individual claim with an indemnity cost of $40,000 and medical costs of $32,500 would be reflected as $72,500 on the experience rating form.

Primary and Excess Values – The next step is to separate the actual losses between what is referred to as the primary value and the balance, which is referred to as the excess value. In most states, under the NCCI rating plan, all losses valued at $18,000 or less are primary losses. (It is to be noted that the $18,000 primary loss amount is subject to periodic adjustment.) For medical-only claims, (claims involving only medical expenses and no lost-time) the primary amount is reduced by seventy percent.

As mentioned previously, an important consideration in experience rating is the frequency of injuries or, stated another way, how often injuries occur. Another component is severity – the monetary seriousness of the injuries. The severity has little or no rating significance for small employers, but gains in importance as the size of the employer increases. A small employer may continue for years without a claim and then see an injury for which cost exceeds by many times the total premium paid. An equitable experience rating plan must recognize this fact and temper the debit due to such a loss as well as the credit for no losses.

Using the example described previously where primary losses are capped at $18,000: An employer with 15 small injuries will have a much larger primary loss total than the single-loss employer. The primary losses in this case would be all of the $45,000 in total claim losses, assuming no claim exceeded the $18,000 primary loss limitation. The employer with a single claim would have $18,000 in primary loss, with all the rest excess. Because of the relative weightings, the 15 injury employer will receive a much higher modification, even though the total losses are less than for the risk with one $50,000 loss.

This methodology permits a blend of the frequency of occurrence and the individual cost of each injury. The experience rating plan thus recognizes both accident frequency and accident severity through this method known as split rating. The split within individual losses is made as follows: The dollar cost of each claim up to $18,000 is included as a primary loss or value in the formula. For claims greater than $18,000, only $18,000 is included as the primary value. The balance of the claim is excess loss or excess value, and is used in the formula in a reduced capacity based on the size of the employer. Claim amounts that are over a value called the state accident limit are excluded from the formula.

Although severity of losses is recognized in experience rating, large losses are more infrequent and are considered as more fortuitous than small claims. In fact, very large losses are so infrequent that including the entire portion of the claim beyond a certain dollar threshold in the experience period reduces the reliability of the experience rating plan. One very large claim does not imply a pattern of claim frequency and therefore each individual claim is capped by a state accident limitation.

For many states, the state accident limitation is approximately $100,000. As a result, an individual claim reserved at $733,655 would be capped at $100,000 for experience rating purposes. These limited losses used in the experience rating plan are referred to as ratable losses. The amount of loss above the state accident limitation (in the above example $633,655) is excluded from the calculation of the employer's experience rating modification and is referred to as a non-ratable loss.

Under the split rating formula, the total of all the primary values of each loss has a larger weight in the formula than the rest of the loss dollars. The total ratable excess has some weight in the formula, while the non-ratable losses have no weight at all because they are excluded from the rating. The weight or credibility assigned to a primary or excess loss is established so that the modification will best reflect the quality of the particular insured relative to its business classification. These credibilities vary by size of insured so that the modified rate of the larger employer is more influenced by its own experience. The larger employer is statistically more reliable and is, thus, more likely to show its true colors than the smaller employer.

Expected Loss Rate (ELR) – Having determined actual primary and excess losses, the next step is to obtain the expected losses for the insured. Actual losses will be compared with the expected losses to determine if a credit (decrease) or debit (increase) modification is in order to adjust the basic manual rate premium.

The expected loss rate is determined from rating tables for each state. It is the amount of expected losses for the classification for each $100 of payroll and is used to determine total expected loss. The ELR is a portion of the manual rate for each classification. For illustration purposes we will assume an acceptable level of losses is 65 percent of the premium. Thus, if the manual rate for a particular classification is $5.00 per $100 of payroll, the ELR will be $3.25 per $100 of payroll. Therefore, to obtain the expected losses, the ELR is multiplied by the payroll divided by $100. For example, with an ELR of 3.25 and payroll of $250,000, the calculation is 3.50 x ($250,000 ÷ 100) = $8,125. This figure is then entered in the Expected Losses column.

The formula makes a further division of the expected losses into expected primary and expected excess losses. The percentage of total expected losses which are expected primary losses is known as the discount or D-ratio, also found in state rating tables. The expected losses are then multiplied by the D-ratio to obtain the dollar figure for expected primary losses. Expected excess losses are then obtained by subtracting the expected primary losses from the total expected losses

Expected losses are based on payroll during the experience period. Each individual payroll amount is divided by $100 and then multiplied by the expected loss rate (ELR) for the specific classification, within each policy year. This results in the expected losses per $100 of payroll for each classification. Expected losses for the experience period for all classifications are then totaled.

The expected primary losses – losses that do not exceed $18,000 each – are determined by multiplying the total expected losses for each classification by a discount ratio (D-ratio). The total of the expected losses minus the total of the expected primary losses equals the expected excess losses.

On the experience rating worksheet, the losses valued at less than $18,000 are listed as both primary and actual. Losses that have a dollar value in excess of $18,000 are shown at $18,000 in the primary actual loss column and at their total dollar value in the total actual loss column. Primary actual losses are subtracted from total actual losses for the experience period. The difference is labeled "actual excess".

While the primary losses are included for their full dollar value, 30 percent of the full amount for medical-only claims, only a portion of the excess losses is included. How much depends on how large the business is, as measured by its total expected losses. The larger the business, the more statistically credible the loss experience and the more heavily the excess losses are counted in the formula.

Stabilizing Values – Once the basic components have been developed, the individual components are combined to calculate the experience modification using the following formula mentioned above. The basic procedure for calculating the experience rating modification is to divide the actual losses by the expected losses for each insured.

To limit the effect of wide fluctuations that may occur from year to year for any given insured, a stabilizing value is added to both the actual and expected losses. Also, to recognize that the loss experience of larger employers is more credible than that of smaller employers, both the actual excess losses and the expected excess losses are multiplied by a weighting (W) factor to obtain the ratable excess.

The prior discussion covered in detail how the actual and expected primary losses are determined. The Stabilizing Value includes the following elements:

- Excess Losses includes those claims valued over $18,000.

- Expected Excess Losses is the total expected losses minus total expected primary losses.

- Weighting Value is a factor (obtained from a state rating table) applied to actual excess losses and expected excess losses. The factor determines how much of the value of excess losses are used. The weighting value increases as the expected losses increase. The larger a business (and hence, its expected losses), the more statistically credible (reliable) its loss experience and the more heavily its actual experience is counted in the formula.

- Ballast Value represents a stabilizing element designed to limit the effect of any single loss. This is a dollar amount obtained from a table, based on the total expected losses. The ballast factor in the experience rating formula helps prevent the mod from shifting too far above or below unity. It is a stabilizing element designed to limit the impact of any single loss on the mod. The ballast value increases as expected losses increase. The higher the total expected losses, the higher the ballast.

The Stabilizing Value is calculated by multiplying (one minus Weighting Value) times Expected Excess Losses and adding the Ballast Value. This value is added to both the numerator and the denominator, resulting in a quotient much closer to one than would otherwise occur.

Ratable Excess Losses are calculated by multiplying the Weighting Value times the Actual (in the numerator) and Expected (in the denominator) Excess Losses. Again, the Weighting Value takes into account actual past loss experience, to the extent that it is credible.

The experience modification is obtained by plugging the numbers from the worksheet and rating tables into the formula described above. The calculation is carried out to two decimal places. A modification less than unity (1.00) is considered a credit; a modification greater than unity is referred to as a debit. The resulting factor is applied to the employer's manual premium at the renewal.

Issuance of Experience Modification Factors - In most states where NCCI is the designated rating or advisory organization, NCCI will automatically send an experience rating worksheet to the employer on an annual basis. Access to the experience rating worksheet, in most states, is also permitted to the insurer of record and the producer (agent or broker) of record. An employer may elect to allow access to the experience rating worksheet by written notification to NCCI. Such notification must be on the employer's stationery and must be signed by an owner or officer of the company.

Insured employers should receive a copy of its experience rating calculation from the rating organization. In most instances this is now available electronically. When the employer receives the rating calculation, it is important for the employer to check the components to make sure they are correct. There are generally at least two or three pages to an experience rating calculation. If the employer has multiple operations in multiple states, there may be more pages. In all cases, the experience modification itself appears toward the bottom of the first page of the experience rating calculation worksheet. In some instances there will be the terms such as preliminary or contingent next to the experience modification.

LOSS SENSITIVE PROGRAMS

Workers compensation pricing programs involve both the front and back end. The front end is the cost of the policy at the start of the policy term. The back end is the way in which claim experience may affect the ultimate cost of the policy. In other words, in the second instance, the ultimate premium charged for a policy is sensitive to the amount of losses experienced (paid and/or incurred) during the policy period.

Establishment of the manual rate represents the starting point in determining the cost of a workers compensation insurance policy. For employers over a certain premium threshold, the manual premium is amended by application of the experience rating modification factor. The result is referred to as the total modified premium. Additional premium adjustments, which vary by state, may apply after application of the experience modification factor. However, it is the total estimated annual premium, after the applicable premium adjustments that is displayed on the policy Information Page and is considered the front end cost.

Some workers compensation programs start and end with the total estimated annual premium. In these, there are no back end premium adjustments. The insured pays the computed premium, the policy is issued, claims are reported to the insurance company, and no more money changes hands between the employer and insurer unless audited payrolls differ from the estimated payrolls used at policy inception. The entire risk of the workers compensation exposure is transferred to the insurance company. Such programs are called fully insured or guaranteed cost plans. Only a change in classification codes, payroll, or a revision in the experience rating modification factor can generate a premium change.

Under a loss sensitive program, market conditions, account size, and account claims history affect program availability. A greater variety may be offered, but when the market is soft employers are less motivated to retain more loss potential. When the market hardens, however, fewer options are available and a company's loss history may have a greater impact on the type of programs available. In addition, smaller companies may not be eligible for certain programs. They may only be eligible for a fully insured, or guaranteed cost, program.

The various types of loss sensitive programs to be discussed in the following are retrospective rating (incurred loss and paid loss), dividend plans (sliding scale and standard) and deductible programs (small and large). NCCI manual rules permit companies to offer incurred loss retrospective plans to companies with premiums of $25,000 or more. Since there is the risk of paying more with a retrospective rating plan than a guaranteed cost program, businesses need to be sure they can financially assume that risk. Adverse market conditions may cause insurers to refrain from offering dividend plans to all but the best accounts, however, so businesses may be forced to purchase a guaranteed cost program.

RETROSPECTIVE RATING PLANS

For many firms, reducing workers compensation premiums involves assuming more risk themselves. One means for an employer to assume greater workers compensation risk is through development of a traditional self-insurance program. However, another option, retrospective rating, combines some advantages of self-insurance with the security and convenience of traditional insurance. Retrospective rating plans (hereinafter also referred to as retro plans) are more responsive to loss experience than manual or experience rating. Retro plans also offer a significant amount of flexibility. The insured and insurer can negotiate terms that will suit their respective needs. So, a retro plan can be structured to the requirements of an insured with good loss experience as well as protect an underwriter from poor experience within certain parameters.

Unlike traditional self-insurance or captives, retro plans are available to most firms and are relatively easy to use. Participation under the NCCI retro plan requires that an insured have an estimated standard annual premium of at least $25,000 ($75,000 for a three-year plan). The premium included in a retro plan does not need to be all workers compensation – it may include other commercial casualty lines. However, the other commercial casualty lines are rated under a manual developed and maintained by Insurance Services Office, Inc. (ISO).

In recent years, changes to the workers compensation retrospective rating plan manual of the National Council on Compensation Insurance (NCCI) have made retrospective rating more flexible. Qualifying risks may negotiate certain retrospective rating plan elements under these flexible plan rules. A big reason for these changes was to make retrospective rating more competitive with self-insurance, especially for large insureds.

Retrospective means "looking back on," and that is exactly how a retrospective rating plan works. Under a retro plan, the employer pays the policy premium to the insurance company at the beginning of the term. The ultimate premium is calculated after the policy expires, based on the loss experience of the policy year. As time elapses, the premium is adjusted upward or downward as claims develop and mature. This continues until all claims are closed – a time frame that may stretch for years into the future.

A retro plan provides a simple manner of making premium cost loss sensitive. Expenses remain the responsibility of the insurance company. For those employers that effectively control their losses, the premium is lower than on a guaranteed cost plan. However, there are also disadvantages to this type of plan. If the loss experience exceeds expectations, the ultimate cost is greater than the guaranteed cost plan. In addition, rather than closing out the premium cost after one year, the final premium is not determined for several years. This can be quite costly as serious losses develop over a period of years.

An employer's workers compensation premium, developed through the application of manual rates, reflects that employer's loss experience to a degree. The manual premium may be increased or decreased by an experience modification factor. It may also be subject to a premium discount. This type of premium calculation is commonly referred to as a guaranteed-cost, fixed-cost, or premium-discount plan.

But experience rating fails to reflect experience fully. For one thing, the rating process dilutes the actual record to eliminate wide premium fluctuations. Also, the experience rating process uses a three-year loss and payroll history as the basis for adjusting a future premium. As the operative history begins four years prior to the effective date of the experience modification, and ends one year prior, it takes four years for a loss to work its way into and out of the experience modification.

> **Basics of Retrospective Rating** – The retrospective rating process begins with the standard premium as defined in the workers compensation manual. The standard premium reflects the experience modification, but not the premium discount because this is taken into consideration by the retro plan formula. The standard premium estimated at the inception of a policy may be paid monthly, quarterly, semi- annually, or entirely in advance. It is adjusted after expiration of the policy, using actual payrolls developed during the policy period. The standard premium is adjusted later based on loss experience during the policy period. The first retrospective premium calculation is based on losses as valued six months after the end of the policy period.
>
> If loss experience is favorable, the insurance company may owe the employer a return premium. On the other hand, additional premium may be due to the insurer if experience is

not favorable. That adjustment may be the final premium, or it may be recalculated 12 months later and in subsequent years at 12-month intervals until all claims have been adjusted or the insured and insurer agree to a final adjustment based on the valuation of open cases at that time.

Retrospective Rating Formula – The following is designed to demonstrate the methodology used in computing the basic premium factor and is not intended to explore all the nuances of retro plans necessary for those who wish to become proficient in this area of account pricing. It should also be emphasized that this discussion is limited to NCCI's retro plan. While ISO procedures are similar for other lines of insurance, they are somewhat more complex, particularly when more than one line of insurance is included in a plan.

The basic formula for the adjustment of retrospective rating premiums, while appearing deceptively simple, has remained the same for many years and is expressed as follows:

Retrospective Rating Premium = [Basic Premium + Excess Loss Premium + Retrospective Development Premium + Converted Losses] x Tax Multiplier

This calculation is subject to minimum and maximum premium factors that reflect the amount of risk the employer desires to assume. This straightforward concept masks the complex mechanics of retrospective rating. A number of computations underlie the development of each component of the formula. The following will not go into the detailed computations, but, rather, focus on the principals involved.

The formula includes three elements: determination of the basic premium, the establishment of converted losses, and the application of the tax multiplier. Development of these three elements is often times a complex process and may be the subject of negotiation with the insurer.

The Basic Premium Factor is the percentage of the standard premium that is necessary to issue the policy and operate the program. It includes the insurers underwriting expenses, producer commission if applicable, insurance charges, and a contingency for profit. The Basic Premium Factor generally ranges between 15 to 35 percent depending upon the size of the risk, the amount of insurance being provided, and other factors. The Basic Premium Factor multiplied by the standard premium derives the basic premium.

The Loss Conversion Factor (LCF) is a percentage that represents the cost to adjust claims and generally ranges between eight and 15 percent of losses. (The LCF may be calculated based upon a dollar amount per claim instead of a percentage.) The LCF is then applied to the total value of claims (losses) which are then referred to as converted losses. Some claims may account for unusual adjusting costs such as special surveillance or expert witness testimony which are allocated to a specific claim. Such unusual adjusting costs are referred to as Allocated Loss Adjustment Expense (ALAE). The ALAE is added directly to the converted losses and is not subject to the LCF.

The tax multiplier covers the licenses, fees, assessments, and taxes that insurers pay on the premium they collect. Assessments include payments for funding the workers compensation administrative agency or commission, along with assessments to cover payments to second injury funds and other associated system costs. The tax multiplier is taken from the rating organizations manual and varies from state to state, ranging from under one to more than 20 percent. The tax multiplier also reflects any residual market loading.

At this point in the computation of the retrospective rating premium, two limitations come into play: the minimum and maximum premium. The insured and the insurer negotiate and agree on the amount of these two limitations.

Maximum premium is stated in the retrospective rating plan as a percentage of standard premium. Should the employer select a maximum factor of 1.25, the final premium, including converted losses, cannot exceed 125 percent of standard premium, including the tax multiplier. Even if losses amount to many times the standard premium, the employer will not pay more than 125 percent of standard premium.

The employer also selects a minimum premium which is the lowest possible premium that will be paid, should there be no losses at all. It also is stated in the retrospective rating plan as a percentage of standard premium. The premium will never be less than the basic premium multiplied by the tax multiplier. That money pays the insurer to run the insurance operation, even if there are no losses.

Excess Loss Coverage – If the standard premium that is subject to retrospective rating is at least $100,000, an employer may elect to purchase excess loss coverage. Excess loss coverage limits the amount of incurred loss arising from one accident that will be included in the retrospective rating premium calculation. Excess loss coverage also is referred to as buying a loss limitation. This type of plan is very similar to large deductible insurance, discussed below.

For example, a retro plan may incorporate only the first $100,000 in the cost of each worker's accident in the claims portion of the retrospective premium formula. This type of plan caps losses at $100,000 per accident. Only the first $100,000 of incurred losses from each accident is used in the retrospective rating premium calculation. To protect against a loss in excess of $100,000, the employer may purchase excess loss coverage.

Retrospective Development Factor – As previously noted, the employer is charged with all losses incurred during the policy year. However, when the first retrospective rating calculation is made, it is likely that there will still be open claims. Because the insurer does not know what the ultimate cost of these claims will be, an estimate must be made of their final value. If the employer and the insurer agree, the first computation, based on valuation six months after the end of the policy period, can become the final adjustment. But since the insurer's estimate may be higher than the ultimate payout, the employer may not want to close the books at that time.

In this case, a second computation will be made one year later, and every 12 months after that until both the employer and the insurer agree that the latest computation represents an accurate picture of the policy year losses. After each computation, the employer will receive a return premium or have to pay additional premium, depending on whether the loss computation has gone up or down from the previous adjustment. Obviously, this process can take years. The retrospective development premium option provides a way for the insurer to anticipate future increases in loss costs. It is computed as follows:

Retrospective Development Premium Equals
Standard Premium x Retrospective Development Premium Factor x Loss Conversion Factor

Two sets of retrospective development factors are provided for each state. The lower of the two sets of factors applies when the retrospective rating plan has a loss limitation. The lower factor is justified because the retrospective premium cannot include the portion of any claims that exceeds the limitation. The retrospective development factors are applied to the first three calculations of the retrospective rating plan. Their purpose is to reduce the likelihood that subsequent annual calculations will result in additional premium.

DIVIDEND PLANS

Dividend plans are basically guaranteed cost plans that offer the potential for a financial reward if the employer has better than expected claims experience. The two most common types of dividend plans available are a flat-dividend plan and a sliding-scale dividend plan. A flat-dividend plan returns a flat percentage of the premium back to the eligible policies. Under a sliding-scale dividend plan, the size of the dividend returned depends on the insured's loss ratio. The lower the loss ratio is at the expiration date; the higher the dividend payment will be.

Sliding scale dividend plans typically base claim experience on the losses of a particular group to which the insured belongs or to an individual insured business. Since dividend programs have an upside in the potential for a dividend, but no downside in the form of the employer having to pay additional premium if claims are higher than expected, dividend plans typically are reserved for those businesses that have better than average loss experience.

Many workers compensation insurers use premium size guidelines in determining what type of loss sensitive program a business may qualify. Small businesses with workers compensation premiums of $25,000 or less may not be offered any choice other than a guaranteed cost or dividend plan. Since there is no down side to a dividend plan for the insured, it is an attractive option for small businesses.

Dividends are never guaranteed and are paid only if declared by the insurance company's board of directors after the policy period has ended. If declared, they are paid at various intervals following expiration of the policy, sometimes in a lump-sum and sometimes in a series of payments. Dividends usually are not computed earlier than 12 months or more after the expiration date of the policy.

Policies with back-end dividend plans are subject to experience rating. Therefore, if a company qualifies for an experience modifier, it is used to develop the standard premium. These plans are designed so that an insured may receive a dividend if workplace injuries are less expensive than anticipated. They are designed to reward companies that do a good job in preventing and managing workplace injuries.

There are essentially two types of dividend programs. The first type is tied directly to the underwriting results of an individual insured. Instead of relying on the experience of the entire group, an individual company stands on its own claims experience for purposes of dividend calculation. These are called sliding scale dividend plans. These plans start with the expectations of a particular loss ratio. Insured's who develop a lower loss ratio may be rewarded with a dividend. Those who develop a higher than expected loss ratios lose any dividend.

For example, a plan might assume that the incurred loss ratio for a manufacturer will be sixty-five percent. The incurred loss ratio is determined by dividing incurred losses by the earned premium. Incurred losses include both paid and reserved claim amounts. If the loss ratio is less than 65 percent, a dividend may be declared. If the loss ratio is higher than 65 percent, the insured is not responsible to pay additional premium – the insurance company has to absorb the excess losses. However, the insured forfeits the dividend. This plan provides a financial incentive to prevent worker injuries and to manage any claims that do occur.

The second type of dividend program is referred to as the standard or flat dividend. If a dividend is declared, the standard dividend is paid a year or more after the policy expires. They are most often used with affinity or group programs. Affinity programs are designed around similar types of business. For example, a trade group of manufacturers, grocery stores, schools, or other business type may develop a workers compensation group program that is open to association members. Since the group represents a large amount of premium, insurance companies may be willing to offer a dividend plan to members of the group. Even though an insured receives the benefit of a possible dividend, the insured will not have to pay additional premium unless such additional premium is developed through the payroll audit.

Dividend plans work because the employer is rewarded when the insurer makes an underwriting profit on a homogeneous group of accounts. Since the insured does not risk having to pay additional premium in the event of bad losses, the potential return is lower than in riskier plans. There is a trade-off between risk and potential benefit. For example, an association of manufacturers may go to one carrier to purchase workers compensation insurance.

Individual group members are underwritten separately, and the amount of premium for each is reviewed as a whole to provide the insurer with an incentive to write the coverage. Individual workers compensation policies are issued to each group member and each pays its own premium. After the policies expire, the claims experience of all members is combined to determine whether an underwriting profit was made. If so, the insurer may declare a dividend.

However, if claims costs are higher than a pre-determined amount, no dividend is payable. Again this is discretionary on the part of the insurer and influenced by competitive pressures.

DEDUCTIBLE PROGRAMS

Deductible programs are a form of self-insurance that permit the employer to reimburse an insurance company for workers compensation losses, up to a stated deductible amount, in return for a lower premium. As with the other loss-sensitive programs, it is critical for the employer to be in a position to estimate future losses, by size of loss, in order to determine if a deductible program makes sense. However, an account that has had problems in the past, but has since corrected those problems, may benefit greatly from a deductible program.

With a deductible program, the insurance company issues a workers compensation policy similar to that of a guarantee cost plan. Like a guaranteed cost plan, the insurance company remains responsible for all claim payments along with other administrative functions associated with a workplace injury or death. Many plans allow for direct payment by the policyholder for losses under the deductible. Where payments are made by the insurer or TPA, only following the payment of benefits is the insurer permitted to seek reimbursement from the insured employer.

Following payment by the insurer, the employer would be responsible for the first portion of any loss up to the agreed deductible figure, including claim-handling expenses. The policy would also contain an aggregate deductible, which limits the maximum exposure during the policy term. These plans require collateral, usually in the form of a letter of credit. Some employers may find the collateral requirements burdensome, especially since collateral is required year after year, with letters of credit frequently stacking atop each other.

However, the up-front costs in this plan may be greatly reduced – from 25-40 percent of the normal premium – and the possibility for a lower overall cost is substantially greater than a retrospective rating plan.

Of course, there are also disadvantages with a deductible program. Poor loss experience can generate costs that would exceed that payable under a guaranteed cost plan. In addition, some claims may involve payment over an extended period of time and the employer may need to make payments over many years.

> **Small Deductible Programs** – Historically, those employers who were not eligible for experience or retrospective rating plans lacked programs that provided incentives to control losses and lower their insurance costs. During the late 1980s and early 1990s, the Small Business Association began an initiative to encourage state insurance regulators to review this dilemma and implement programs that would address this issue. As a result, small deductible programs were born. These programs give employers the opportunity to gain some premium relief through deductible premium credits by electing to pay a selected deductible amount.

Currently, most states have implemented a Workers Compensation Small Deductible Program. Small deductibles are those ranging from $100 to $10,000 or more, depending on the particular state's laws. They might apply to medical benefits, indemnity benefits (which compensate an injured worker for lost wages), or both, again depending on the laws of the state. For example, **Colorado** permits small deductibles of $500 to $5,000 applied to both types of claims, while **Hawaii** allows $100 to $10,000 applied only to medical benefits. Employers who opt for the small deductible program receive a small premium discount.

In several states, insurance companies are under no obligation to offer the small deductible program while in others they are. However, the rules are not clear as to what exactly constitutes an offer. Some states interpret the term offer very loosely meaning that as long as the employer is aware that the program is available, then that constitutes an offer. Other states hold the wording to its strictest terms and interpret that if a carrier is providing any type of quote to an employer, then one of the options must be the small deductible program. In some states insurance companies are obligated to provide the deductible program to their customers only when they receive a written request from the customer.

While there are currently a number of different approaches to the issue of what constitutes an offer, the following provides a number of examples:

- States such as **Delaware, Georgia, Hawaii. Illinois, Massachusetts, Montana, New Hampshire, New York, Oklahoma,** and **Texas** mandate that the insurer must offer an employer a small deductible program.

- In the states of **Alabama, Arkansas, Colorado, Kentucky, Maine, Minnesota, Nebraska, New Mexico, Oregon,** and **South Carolina**, the insurer is required to offer a small deductible only if the insurer determines that the customer is financially stable to be responsible for the deductible amount.

- In **Pennsylvania**, the insurer must offer the small deductible only if the customer requests same.

The size of the deductible that constitutes a small deductible varies by state. However, most states that permit small deductibles initiative the program at a minimum deductible amount of $100. Under the small deductible program, the maximum of the deductible permitted is in the range between $5,000 and $10,000 with a few states permitting higher deductible amounts.

Large Deductible Programs – Large deductibles are designed to offer the insured a method for increasing its retention without incurring unlimited liability. The program is designed for large employers usually with multistate exposures. The size of deductibles for these plans is generally in a range from $100,000 to $1,000,000 per occurrence. The insurer makes all payments as it would under a standard workers compensation policy. The insured then reimburses the insurer. The insured also puts up a security for the deductible exposure Many large deductible programs allow for the policyholder to manage their own claims to use the services of a third party administrator (TPA) they have selected to handle some or all of their claims.

One of the original incentives for large deductible programs was in the area of taxation and state assessments. Since the deductible amount of claims is not actually premium, premium taxes and assessments were not levied against it. This offered some tax relief to the insurer and possibly the insured employer. In the 1980s, the impetus for assessment relief was particularly great in states with large, underfunded assigned risk pools. However, some states have revised their taxation so that this incentive may no longer apply.

Large deductible programs are popular because they offer most of the advantages of a self-insurance plan, but are typically insured by a licensed insurer, which reduces red tape of applying for self-insurance rights. Deductibles can range from $5,000 to $1 million per any one loss. Insurance companies charge a deductible premium, which is often discounted as much as 80 percent from the manual premium – depending upon the deductible amount selected – and the actual cost of claims as paid.

Deductibles may be applicable to medical payments, indemnity payments, or both. It is intended to provide the same coverages and services as a fully insured policy, yet allowing the insured to retain the liability for the loss dollars under the deductible limit. Under most endorsements, the insurance company agrees to handle all claims under the policy, and usually advances payment and seeks reimbursement for amounts paid under the deductible limit. In some instances, the policyholder is permitted to contract directly with a TPA for claim adjustment and the payment of benefits.

Most services are included in the deductible plan on a bundled basis. Because the insurer is statutorily responsible for paying claims, a letter of credit or other acceptable liquid collateral is usually required to secure the insured employer's payments of its share of expected ultimate losses. However, while there are many advantages of large deductible plans, risk financing for the deductible can be problematic.

While some states do not allow large deductible policies, most states just have minimum premium requirements for companies to qualify. These requirements are based on standard premium size, and most start at $100,000 in standard premium. A number of states – **California, Colorado, Florida, Nebraska,** and **New Hampshire** – require up to $500,000 in premium to be eligible for a large deductible program. If a company has operations in multiple states, some of which don't allow the large deductible program, multiple insurance policies can be written. Typically, a guaranteed cost policy is written for the states of operation that don't allow the large deductible. All remaining states will be included on the deductible policy. As long as the same insurer is writing both policies, the claims administration is relatively seamless.

Under an insured program where the insurance company is advancing claims payment and seeking reimbursement afterwards, many large deductible policies are secured through some form of escrow account and/or letter of credit. An escrow is cash typically equal to an estimated amount of two months-worth of claims payments. The escrow account is the insured's money, and is refundable at the termination of the policy and subsequent closure of all claims. A letter of credit is a document issued by a bank that guarantees the payment of a customer's draft. It substitutes the bank's credit for the customer's credit. The amount of the letter of credit is set by the insurance company and is usually equal to the amount of expected losses for the entire policy period.

Chapter Eleven

EXCLUSIVE REMEDY AND BAD FAITH

The exclusive remedy doctrine, a cornerstone upon which the workers compensation system was built, provides the basis for a give-and-take arrangement for addressing work-related injuries and disease: the employee relinquishes the right to sue the employer in exchange for a guaranteed, yet limited, set of benefits without regard to the issue of fault. Thus, workers compensation becomes the employee's exclusive remedy for addressing work-related injuries.[20]

When first enacted, the concept of no-fault protection was new and it was the decision of some legislative bodies to describe the legislative intent of the new law. These original concepts remain a part of several statutes and continue to reflect the thinking that existed when the laws were first enacted. The State of **Washington's** law clearly demonstrates legislative intent and was a part of the original law adopted in 1911. The provision reads as follows:

"The common law system governing the remedy of workers against employers for injuries received in employment is inconsistent with modern industrial conditions. In practice it proves to be economically unwise and unfair. Its administration has produced the result that little of the cost of the employer has reached the worker and that little only at large expense to the public. The remedy of the worker has been uncertain, slow and inadequate. Injuries in such works, formerly occasional, have become frequent and inevitable. The welfare of the state depends upon its industries, and even more upon the welfare of its wage worker. The state of Washington, therefore, exercising herein its police and sovereign power, declares that all phases of the premises are withdrawn from private controversy, and sure and certain relief for workers, injured in their work, and their families and dependents is hereby provided regardless of questions of fault and to the exclusion of every other remedy, proceeding or compensation, except as otherwise provided in this title; and to that end all civil actions and civil causes of action for such personal injuries and all jurisdiction of the courts of the state over such causes are hereby abolished, except as in this title provided."[21]

The extent of the immunity associated with the exclusive remedy under those early workmen's compensation laws was initially confined to that solely of the employer. Over time, amendments were introduced to extend that immunity to certain classes of individuals who bore some special relationship to the employer.

---

[20] *"The Continued Erosion of the Exclusive Remedy Doctrine"* published by McAnany, Van Cleave & Phillips, P.A. and *New York Workers' Compensation* (23rd edition) *West's New York Malpractice Series* by Martin Minkowitz Chapter 8.
[21] Wash. Rev. Code § 51.04.010

A significant group recognized as an extension of the employer, entities such as insurers and those providing engineering or safety services to the employer. The insurer entity received considerable attention after an **Illinois** court held that, under **Florida** law, an insurer could be sued by an injured worker for negligent performance of safety inspections.[22] In response to this action, a number of states amended their statutes to grant immunity to the insurer of the employer and to other entities having some direct relationship with the employer.

Another group frequently determined to be immune to actions at common law consists of fellow employees who, in the course of employment, may be the cause of a compensable injury or death. Roughly half of the states have extended the immunity provisions to fellow employees.

States have made various changes to the exclusive remedy provisions in their compensation laws, but the essential ingredient of employer immunity from suits by injured employees in exchange for prescribed income and medical benefits has remained the cornerstone of the workers compensation program. But as with every rule, there are exceptions that eventually develop and this is true for the rule of exclusive remedy. These exceptions that have developed can be roughly grouped into four general categories: claims for intentional injury, dual capacity claims, claims involving third party action-over, and injuries outside the scope of the law.

As with other issues, there is overlap between these groups and certain situations fall outside these specific categories. The following serves to describe some of the more common situations within these categories, along with a few examples of case, where a worker may bring a cause of action against his or her employer.

CLAIMS FOR INTENTIONAL INJURY

An intentional act on the part of the employer is a direct action with intent to cause harm or injury to the employee. The public policy reason for allowing an exception to the exclusive remedy for intentional acts is self-evident. The employer, merely because of the status as an employer, should not be allowed to commit intentional torts such as assault, battery, false imprisonment, or the intentional infliction of emotional distress without suffering the appropriate legal and economic consequences.

Traditionally, the majority of states followed the specific intent test that required an employer to truly intend both the act and the result – in this case an injury or death – before the exclusive remedy exception for intentional injury was lost. Under the specific intent test, as noted by in Larson's Law of Workmen's Compensation, the liability of the employer could not be, *"stretched to include accidental injuries caused by the gross, wanton, willful, deliberate, intentional, reckless, culpable, or malicious negligence, breach of statute, or other misconduct of the employer short of conscious and deliberate intent directed to the purpose of inflicting an injury."*[23]

---

[22] *Nelson v. Union Wire Rope Corp.*, 199 N.E. 2d 769 (1964)
[23] Arthur Larson, *The Law of Workmen's Compensation* § 68.13

While not the only state to be active in this regard, **California** can be viewed as a leader in terms of intentional injury claims. In 1982, the California legislature amended the workers compensation law codifying three implied exceptions to the exclusive remedy provision that had been recognized at common law: the dual capacity doctrine, intentional physical assaults by the employer, and fraudulent concealment.

This action in part followed the decision in the *Magliulo* case where a physical assault by an employer upon an employee has been held to justify an action at law against the employer.[24] Five years after the *Magliulo* case was decided, the California Supreme Court, in *Johns-Manville Products Corp.* accepted the defendant's argument that the term willful misconduct as used in the statute included intentional wrongdoing.[25]

But not all cases go in favor of the employee as illustrated by a 2002 decision where an employee and his wife brought an action against the employer and supervisors for assault and battery and loss of consortium, alleging that the employer deliberately instructed the employee to enter a building while knowing, or substantially certain to know, that he would be seriously injured. The Superior Court, Los Angeles County, entered summary judgment in favor of the employer and the employee appealed. The Court of Appeals held that employer's alleged conduct was not outside boundaries of the compensation bargain, and thus, employee's action was barred by exclusivity provision of workers compensation act, and employee's admission that there was no intent by anyone at employer to injure or cause him harm would not permit recovery under intentional assault exception to exclusivity provision.[26]

Arriving at the opposite result was a more recent **California** case where the employer suspected the employee of stealing supplies and the employer's staff physically threatened and harassed the employee by preventing him from entering his home, disregarded his instructions to leave his property, and attempted to intimidate him. The California Second District Court of Appeals ruled that an employee may pursue civil remedies against the employer outside of the workers compensation system where the conduct causing such injury exceeded the normal risks of the employment relationship. The jury's finding that the defendants used intimidation and harassment, including intruding into the employee's home and attempting to coerce him into a confession, was supported by the evidence. The employee's injuries fell outside the scope of the normal risks of employment and the employee was entitled to pursue civil remedies.[27]

Another state that was a forerunner in the broadening of the interpretation of deliberate intent to injure came from **West Virginia** where an employee was injured by a saw where a safety guard had been removed with the knowledge of the employer. In its decision, the West Virginia Supreme Court determined that "willful, wanton, or reckless misconduct" satisfied a state statute requiring *"deliberate intent to produce such injury or death on the part of the employer."*[28]

---

[24] *Magliulo v. Superior Court* (1975) 47 Cal. App.3d 760
[25] *Johns-Manville*, 27 Cal. 3d at 473, 612 P.2d at 953
[26] *Brutz v. CalMat Co., West Law* 265175 (2002)
[27] *Levin v. Canon Business Solutions*, 2010 WL 731645 (Cal.App. 2 Dist., March 4, 2010)
[28] *Mandolitis v. Elkin Industries, Inc.*, 246 S.E. 2d 907 (1978)

Following the *Mandolitis* decision, the West Virginia legislature – in an attempt to restrict exposure – amended the statute by establishing a five-fold test under which a separate cause of action could be supported. In an abbreviated format, the requirements whereby a cause of action could be supported included the existence of a specific unsafe working condition, that the employer was aware of and realized this unsafe working condition, that the unsafe working condition was a violation of a state or federal safety statute, the employer intentionally exposed the employee to the unsafe working condition, and the unsafe working condition resulted in injury or death to the worker.

In a subsequent ruling, the West Virginia Supreme Court in the *Mayles* decision recognized that the legislature amended the deliberate intention statute with the intent to make it more difficult for an employer to lose the immunity provided by the workers compensation act. Despite the statutory amendment, the Supreme Court upheld a significant tort award for an injured employee making it easier for creative plaintiffs to defeat the immunity the legislature intended.[29] This prompted further legislative action designed to address the five elements that serve to define what constitutes an intentional injury.

The West Virginia Labor Code § 23-4-2 was amended in 2015 to clarify the underpinnings of a deliberate intention claim in a number of key ways.

- "Actual knowledge" is not presumed and must be proven through direct evidence. Examples of previous accidents or speculation of what management should have known are insufficient. Documents or other credible evidence are required.

- A "commonly accepted and well-known safety standard" must be based on consensus in the relevant industry of the employer and must be memorialized in a written rule or standard.

- A "serious compensable injury" must meet the requirements set forth regarding permanent impairment or disfigurement, total whole person workers' compensation impairment ratings, or physician certifications of imminent death or occupational pneumoconiosis.

- Complaints not asserting specific intention of injury must be accompanied by a verified statement from a person knowledgeable in workplace safety and industry-specific standards.

In a 2018 case, the Supreme Court of Appeals reversed a trial court's denial of post-trial motions following an adverse jury verdict in a deliberate intention action. The plaintiff suffered permanent injuries after falling through a grating that had been left open by a maintenance crew and landed on a concrete floor. The maintenance workers had left the grate open because dust conditions inside the silo had reduced visibility inside the silo to nearly zero. The court held there was no evidence that the employer had "actual knowledge" of the unsafe working

---

[29] *Mayles v. Shoney's, Inc.*, 405 S.E. 2d 15 (1990)

condition, as the maintenance crew had not communicated the grate's status to anyone, nor was there evidence that the employer intentionally exposed the employee to the specific unsafe working condition.[30]

Following much the same path as West Virginia, the **Ohio** Supreme Court in the 1982 *Blankenship* decision held that an employee and his/her spouse could sue the employer in tort for the intentional use of chemicals if the employer knew they were harmful, and for failure to warn and to report the dangerous conditions to federal and state agencies as required.[31]

Following the *Blankenship* decision, the judiciary proceeded to expand on the decision in virtually every conceivable direction. A legislative fix was enacted in 1986 wherein the statute was amended so that "intentional tort" was redefined as an act committed with the belief that the injury was "substantially certain" to occur. Following some preliminary decisions consistent with the intent of the statutory reform, the Ohio Supreme Court subsequently ruled the 1986 amendment unconstitutional. In finding the legislation unconstitutional, the Court opined that, *"the legislature cannot enact legislation governing intentional torts arising out of the workplace because, by their very nature, intentional torts always take place outside of the employment relationship."*[32]

In a subsequent case before the Ohio Supreme Court, the Court clarified that in order to establish intent for the purpose of proving the existence of an intentional tort committed by an employer against his employee, the following must be demonstrated:

(1) Knowledge by the employer of the existence of a dangerous process, procedure, instrumentality, or condition within its business operation.

(2) Knowledge by the employer that if the employee is subjected by his employment to such dangerous process, procedure, instrumentality, or condition, then harm to the employee will be a substantial certainty.

(3) That the employer, under such circumstances, and with such knowledge, did act to require the employee to continue to perform the dangerous task.

The Court went on to clarify that:

"[I]n order to establish an intentional tort of an employer, proof beyond that required to prove negligence and beyond that to prove recklessness must be established. Where the employer acts despite his knowledge of some risk, his conduct may be negligence. As the probability increases that particular consequences may follow, then the employer's conduct may be characterized as recklessness. As the probability that the consequences will follow further increases, and the employer knows that injuries to employees are certain or substantially certain to result from the process, procedure or

---

[30] *Firstenergy Generation, LLC v. Muto*, 2018 W. Va. LEXIS 185 (Mar. 12, 2018)
[31] *Blankenship v. Cincinnati Milacron, Inc.*, 433 N.E. 2d 572 (1982)
[32] *Brady v. Safety-Kleen Corp.*, 576 N.E. 2d 722 (1991)

condition and he still proceeds, he is treated by the law as if he had in fact desired to produce the result. However, the mere knowledge and appreciation of a risk - something short of substantial certainty - is not intent."[33]

This decision served to reduce the amount of litigation alleging intentional injury in Ohio.

The key phrase in the Ohio decision was one requiring the resulting injury to be one of substantial certainty. Taking the lead from that decision, a growing number of states have adopted the substantially certain rule in terms of recognizing what constitutes an intentional injury.

One of those states is **New Jersey** where the Supreme Court has affirmed the substantial certainty test for intentional injury whereby an injured employee may bring a tort action against an employer if the employee can prove that the employer had knowledge that its actions were substantially certain to cause injury.[34] In addition, the resulting injury and the circumstances of its infliction must be more than a fact of life of industrial employment and plainly beyond anything the legislature intended for the workers compensation act to immunize.

It is important to recognize that negligence is not the same as an intentional act. In a case from **Connecticut,** it was held that an employee could not sue his employer for injuries suffered when a machine malfunctioned. The employee argued that the employer knew the machine was defective because it had malfunctioned previously and the employer did not repair it. The employee thus argued that his injury fell within the intentional act exception to the exclusive remedy because the employer created a dangerous condition that made the employee's injury substantially certain to occur. The Court disagreed, holding that the employer's actions may have been negligent but did not rise to the level of intentional harm.[35]

However, arriving at a different conclusion, the Superior Court of Connecticut denied an employer's motion for summary judgment where the plaintiff's assertion raised an issue of material fact as to the presence of an intentional tort. In bringing a wrongful death action after her husband was killed in a truck accident, the widow alleged that the employer had knowledge of the truck's limited or inadequate braking system, and that the employer allowed the deceased to use the truck and provided no special instructions. The court held that no proof of deliberate purpose to injure is required to prove an intentional tort, because such a requirement *"allows employers to injure and even kill employees and suffer only workers' compensation damages so long as the employer did not specifically intend to hurt the worker ... Prohibiting a civil action in such a case would allow a corporation to 'cost-out' an investment decision to kill workers"*[36]

In **Iowa**, the state Supreme Court held that an employee could not sue his employer and co-employees for the intentional torts of false imprisonment and battery for injuries inflicted during an on-the-job prank. Under Iowa law, workers compensation is the exclusive remedy against a

---

[33] *Fyffe v. Jenoe's Inc.* 570 N.E. 2d 1108 (1991)
[34] *Laidlow v. Hariton Machinery Co., Inc.,* 170 *N.J.* 602 (2002)
[35] *Sorban v. Sterling Engineering Corp.* 830 A. 2d 372 (2003)
[36] *Tracy v. Sterling Superior Services,* 2009 Conn. Super. LEXIS 93 (2009)

co-employee if the injury arose out of the course of employment and was not caused by the co-employee's "gross negligence amounting to such lack of care as to amount to wanton neglect for the safety of another." The court looked at the following factors to determine gross negligence: (1) knowledge of the peril to be apprehended; (2) knowledge that the injury is a probable result of the danger; and (3) a conscious failure to avoid the peril. Because the employee's injury was not a probable result of the co-employees' conduct, the employee could not sue them in tort. In addition, the employee was barred from suing the employer in tort because his injuries were clearly covered by the Workers Compensation Act.[37]

Similarly, it has been held by the **Nebraska** Supreme Court that the Workers Compensation Act was the exclusive remedy for workers where the alleged injuries arose out of and in the course of the worker' employment, regardless of allegations of intentional torts. The employee was asked by his supervisor to enter a grain bin and to shovel grain into the center of the bin's conical base in order to facilitate removal of grain. The employee died of asphyxiation after being engulfed in the grain. The Supreme Court affirmed the lower court decision holding that despite the egregiousness of the employer's conduct, the injury was still an accident as defined by the Act and the Act does not thereby unconstitutionally discriminate between employees and non-employees or employee victims of employer willful negligence and employee victims of their own willful negligence.[38]

In **South Dakota,** only injuries intentionally inflicted fall outside the scope of the Workers Compensation Act. In order to recover in tort, a worker must demonstrate that the employer had actual knowledge that the dangerous condition would cause illness and still required the employee to perform the hazardous work. Although the supervision of the employee may have been negligent or reckless, it was not outrageous enough to demonstrate intent to injure.[39]

In a recent decision, the **New Jersey** Supreme Court reaffirmed the high burden of proof required to prove an intentional work injury and overcome the exclusive remedy. In this case, the worker was injured while involved in relocating a dewatering pump for a retention pond. The sump relocation involved digging a sloped trench and laying down layers of filter fabric and stone, along with piping. Eventually, the deepest part of the trench reached a depth of 18-20 feet. OSHA safety regulations mandate that workers cannot enter a trench that is deeper than five feet if protective systems are not in place. The laborer was injured when, in the deepest part of the trench, the sides collapsed burying the worker up to his chest. The Supreme Court's decision affirmed that even where an avoidable accident occurs, through reckless behavior or willful violation of OSHA safety requirements, the workers compensation bar may not necessarily be pierced. The injured party must be able to prove that the employer's pre-accident conduct was essentially fraudulent and substantially certain to lead to injury or death.[40]

Another state that adheres to the substantial certainty test is **Louisiana**. At a bench trial, a Louisiana court permitted the testimony of the plaintiff's expert witness on the subject of

---

[37] *Nelson v. Winnebago Industries* 619 N.W. 2d 385 (2000)
[38] *Estate of Teague ex rel. Martinosky v. Crossroads Cooperative Association,* 834 N.W.2d 236 (2013)
[39] *Fryer v. Kranz*, 616 N.W.2d 102 (S.D. Sep. 6, 2000)
[40] *Van Dunk v. Reckson Associates Realty Corp., et al.*, 2012 N.J. LEXIS 678 (2012)

whether an injury or death was substantially certain to occur, and found that an intentional tort was present. The employee at a manufacturing plant died when he became caught between a pipe and a conveyor belt. The plant had recently removed and an altered part of the machinery after another employee had previously been caught in the machinery and was thrown to the ground. The employer was unable to determine a way to add the guards to the machinery to prevent this type of incident in the future. The trial court awarded more than $2.7 million to the various plaintiffs. On appeal the Third Circuit Court concluded that the employer's supervisory personnel knew that the accident was substantially certain to occur from the failure to guard the conveyor process and allowing the hazardous activity to continue. The award of the trial court was upheld.[41]

In 1991, the **North Carolina** Supreme Court carved out an exception for intentional injury and held that if the employer "intentionally engaged in misconduct knowing it was substantially certain to cause serious injury or death to employees", that employee, or the personal representative of the estate in case of death, may pursue a civil action against the employer. That exception developed from an egregious set of facts in which an employee died when a ditch caved in on him.[42] Since that time, the North Carolina courts have interpreted the *Woodson* exception very narrowly and have generally denied employee claims. In a recent case, a 17-year-old Guatemalan national legally in the United States was killed when, while working alone, he was caught inside a large pallet shredder. The North Carolina Court of Appeals upheld the trial court's order granting summary judgment for the employer where the employer's removal of a safety guard and assigning an underage employee to operate dangerous equipment did not render injury or death substantially certain to occur.[43]

Other states than those previously mentioned that have adopted the substantially certain rule include **Alaska, Connecticut, Michigan, Missouri, South Carolina, South Dakota, Texas,** and **Vermont.** Some have done this through the enactment of specific legislative language while others have accomplished the same end through case law.

Beyond the substantial certainty rule, the intentional exception to the exclusive remedy of workers compensation can take other forms. Taking the concept to an extreme interpretation, in **New York** it was held that the widow of a prison employee who was killed by a state trooper during an assault to retake a prison from rioting prisoners could maintain an action for damages against prison authorities under the intentional exception to the exclusive remedy provision in the law. In this case, the assault on the prison, including the use of deadly force, was an intentional plan prepared and carried out by state police and prison authorities with the approval of the highest officers in the state government.[44]

A recent ruling by the **Oklahoma** Supreme Court has the potential to substantially expand what constitutes an intentional injury leaving certain safety-indifferent employers facing greater exposure to lawsuits when an employee is injured or killed. The case involved an employee of

---

[41] *Rhine v. Bayou Pipe Coating,* 11-724 (La. App. 3d Cir. 11/02/11)
[42] *Woodson v. Rowland,* 407 S.E.2d 222 (1991)
[43] *Valenzuela v. Pallet Express, Inc.,* 700 S.E.2d 76 (2010)
[44] *Jones v. State of New York* 468 N.Y.S 2d 223 (1983)

Oklahoma Roofing and Sheet Metal who was working on the roof of a three-story building and died from a fall after his employer required him to unhook his fall protection. The decision with the Supreme Court was whether the directive from the employer to remove the safety device was an "intentional" act and therefore the result was not an accident. The Supreme Court ruled the employer knew the injuries were substantially certain to occur and, therefore, rose to the level of an intentional act. The decision means that under no circumstances should employees ever be put in a position where an injury is substantially certain to occur. Employers must establish appropriate safety protocols and require those protocols be followed.[45]

As stated at the outset, establishing that an employer engaged in an intentional injury is frequently difficult to prove in many jurisdictions, and the courts are inclined to find for the employer. The individual facts in an individual case will always be the determinative factor. However, it is also important to recognize that there are always exceptions to the rule and individual cases are frequently determined based on the interpretation of the facts and allegations surrounding the event. Nonetheless, the rule of substantial certainty does represent a higher threshold for the injured worker to overcome.

FRAUDULENT CONCEALMENT

A separate category or grouping of intentional acts that has at times been considered outside the scope of the exclusive remedy is the subject of fraudulent concealment. Fraudulent concealment means the employer is aware of something that could potentially harm an employee. The employer does not disclose the existence of the potential harm, and the employee becomes injured, or an illness or injury is aggravated as a result. The three elements that are needed to prove fraudulent concealment claim are: (1) the employer concealed the existence of the unsafe condition, (2) the employer concealed the connection between the potential harm and employment, and (3) the injury to the employee was aggravated following the employer's concealment.

Fraudulent concealment claims frequently arise in situations involving exposure to asbestos, mold, or toxic chemicals. Key elements of a claim are that the employer has actual knowledge and that the employee is unaware of the potential for harm and its relationship to his or her employment. These claims are limited to damages caused by the aggravation of the injury that results from the employer's failure to disclose.

California led the foray into this exception to the exclusive remedy in the *Johns-Manville* case – referenced in the prior section) that came before the California Supreme Court. In that case it was held that while the workers compensation law barred the employee's action at law for the initial injury, the allegation that the employer fraudulently concealed from him, from his doctors, as well as from the state, that he was suffering from a disease caused by ingestion of asbestos, thereby preventing him from receiving treatment for the disease and inducing him to continue to work under hazardous conditions, were sufficient to state a cause of action for aggravation of the disease, as distinct from the hazards of the employment, which caused him to contract the

---

[45] *Oklahoma Roofing & Sheet Metal v. Wells* 457 P. 3d 1020 (2019)

disease. Based on the decision, the employee was entitled to bring an action at law against his employer for such aggravation.[46]

In a more recent decision, a hazardous waste treatment plant employee had worked for a storage plant for 29 years. In 2013, the plant was shut down due to its discharge of illegal amounts of lead into the air, water and soil. Before operations at the facility were halted, the employee claimed he experienced two health-related incidents at work. In June 2016, more than three years after these two alleged incidents and suspension of operations at the plant, the plaintiff sued the company seeking damages for injuries he claimed were caused by exposure to lead and other hazardous chemicals and that his health had been slowly deteriorating since operations at the facility were suspended in 2013.

The trial court dismissed the lawsuit before trial, ruling that the claim was precluded by workers compensation exclusivity principles. On appeal, the appeals court noted that the fraudulent concealment exception is extremely limited, and that to maintain a civil action against an employer under the fraudulent concealment exception, a plaintiff must show that the employer knew of the plaintiff's work-related injury, the employer concealed the knowledge from the plaintiff, and the injury was aggravated as a result of such concealment.

Allegations that the company knew there were risks to employees from lead and other chemicals was not enough to show fraudulent concealment. There also was no evidence that the company concealed its supposed knowledge of the plaintiff's injury and that this injury was aggravated as a result of such concealment. Therefore, the plaintiff could not maintain his lawsuit under the state labor code ruling that the trial court was correct to dismiss the lawsuit before trial.[47]

Other decisions regarding the issue of fraudulent concealment have resulted in differing opinions. A **Nebraska** decision involved a workplace incident where employees at a smelting plant and the personal representative of the estate of a deceased employee, sued to recover for bodily injuries allegedly arising from exposure to lead, cadmium, and arsenic at the plant. The employer and the employer's contract physician demurred based on the exclusivity provisions of the workers compensation act. On appeal the Supreme Court held that the exclusivity provisions of the workers compensation act prevented the employees from bringing a personal injury action for work-related injuries, even though the injuries allegedly arose from the employer's intentional concealment of dangers inherent in work environment.[48]

A later decision in **Washington** arrived at the opposite conclusion. A number of employees brought action against their employer for deliberately exposing them to toxic chemicals. The Superior Court denied summary judgment for the employer and, on appeal, the Court of Appeals held that the employees provided evidence that their employer may have known that injury was certain to occur from the employees' exposure to chemicals and willfully disregarded that knowledge, and the employees alleged facts supporting inference that their employer willfully disregarded knowledge that the working environment at the employer's plant would cause

---

[46] *Johns-Manville Products Corp. v. Superior Court,* 165 Cal. Rptr. 858 (1980)
[47] *Deville v. Bloch*, Calif. Ct. App., No. B291099 (Nov. 21, 2019).
[48] *Abbott v. Gould, Inc.,* 443 N.W. 2d 591 (1989)

continuing injury to the employees. In this case, the employees were permitted to proceed with a direct action for damages against their employer.[49]

DUAL CAPACITY

It may be generally summarized that the fraudulent concealment exception applies where an employer fraudulently conceals a worker's injury and its connection to the employment whereby the concealment results in an aggravation of the injury. Like all claims associated with the workers compensation act being the exclusive remedy for an injured worker, the facts of each individual case along with the intent of the various parties, will ultimately influence the outcome.

When an injury occurs on the job, under most circumstances, the employee's only recourse is to file a claim through the workers compensation system. However, the employer also has a duty to provide a safe environment for the public, and that same duty would extend to an employee whether he or she is on the job. For instance, if a restaurant employee slipped and fell while dining (not during the ordinary course of his or her employment), the employee could sue the owners of the restaurant for failure to provide a safe environment.

Dual capacity or dual persona claims involve those situations where the employer occupies, coincidentally, a role independent of that associated with the original cause of the injury. As stated in an Oklahoma decision, *"an employer who is generally immune from tort liability may become liable to his employee as a third- party tortfeasor; if he occupies, in addition to his capacity as employer, a second capacity that confers on him obligations independent of those imposed on him as an employer."*[50] Physicians have been specific targets of this doctrine, based on their independent license and duties to the patient where the patient also happens to be an employee.

EMPLOYER FURNISHED MEDICAL

It is to be recognized that while there have been widespread and varied attempts to invoke the dual capacity doctrine, it has been successful in only a limited number of states, and even there, generally for only a limited period of time. The doctrine is generally considered to have had its genesis in **California** in the case of *Duprey v. Shane* and subsequently was extended to a few other states where the doctrine came into full bloom when pressed into service in product liability cases.

In *Duprey*, a nurse suffered on the job injuries and was treated by her employer, a chiropractor. After that initial injury, the employer's negligent treatment caused further injury. The Supreme Court held that even though the nurse's initial injury was industrial (and therefore covered by workers compensation), she could bring a separate lawsuit against her employer for medical malpractice because her employer was acting in another capacity – as a doctor, not as her

---

[49] *Baker v. Schatz,* 912 P. 2d 501 (1996)
[50] *Weber v. Armco, Inc.*, 663 P.2d 1221 (Okla. 1983)

employer - when he caused the second injury.[51] The Court noted that the doctor had a "dual legal personality," that of a doctor and that of an employer.

In 1982, the California legislature abrogated much of the dual capacity doctrine by amending Labor Code section 3602, subd. (a) The amendment reiterated the exclusivity rule and states, in relevant part, "*the fact that either the employee or the employer also occupied another or dual capacity prior to, or at the time of, the employee's industrial injury shall not permit the employee or his or her dependents to bring an action at law for damages against the employer.*" The change was designed to limit the dual capacity doctrine to a narrow set of clearly defined circumstances represented by the facts in *Duprey*. Subsequent court decisions have upheld this position.

Following the activity in California, **Ohio** adopted the rationale underlying the earlier California decision in *Duprey*. In so doing, the Ohio Supreme Court stated, "*We find no compelling reason why an action should be less viable merely because the traditional obligations and duties of the tortfeasor spring from the extra-relational capacity of the employer, rather than a third party.*"[52]

Courts in several other jurisdictions have applied the dual capacity theory in medical malpractice cases. The **Colorado** Supreme Court disallowed co-employee immunity under the Workers Compensation Act in a suit against a doctor who was employed by Adolph Coors Company to render medical services to employees. The Supreme Court reasoned that the statute did not require Coors to maintain a clinic. "*When an employer voluntarily undertakes to directly render medical treatment to its injured employees, it assumes a function which is not required by the Act and, what is most significant, which is not an integral part of its business.*"[53]

Notwithstanding the decisions in several jurisdictions – primarily **California** and **Ohio** – to recognize the dual capacity doctrine in medical malpractice cases, the apparent numerical weight of authority among jurisdictions holds that a compensation act provides the exclusive remedy for the aggravation of a compensable injury by the medical malpractice of a co-employee. Typically, the compensation act confers immunity on co-employees as well as on employers.

A leading case reflecting the exclusivity defense is found in **Tennessee** in a case where the employee argued that the hospital acted in two capacities: as an employer and as a hospital, and that, had she been treated at another hospital, she could have maintained a tort action. The Supreme Court held that, as a matter of law, the initial compensable injury is the cause of any aggravation or additional injuries received during the course of treating the original compensable injury. The court succinctly stated, *"Nothing in [the Tennessee Act] may be construed to evince a legislative intent that an employer may ever be classified as a 'third person,' without doing violence to the plain language which permits common lawsuits against 'some person other than the employer.' The employer is the employer; not some person other than the employer. It is that*

---

[51] *Duprey v. Shane*, 241 P. 2d 78 (1951)
[52] *Guy v. Arthur H. Thomas Co.*, 378 N.E.2d 488 (1978)
[53] *Wright v. District Court for the County of Jefferson*, 661 P2d 1167 (1983)

simple. The injured workman is confined to the benefits provided by the Workmen's Compensation Act and may not sue his employer in tort."[54]

In a **Maryland** case, a hospital patient who was also a nurse employed by the hospital, brought a negligence action against the hospital and several personnel, alleging that she was injured when she fell in her hospital room. The Circuit Court entered judgment on a jury verdict for the patient. On appeal, the Court of Appeals held that the dual capacity theory, viewing the hospital in its capacity as employer and in its capacity as health care provider as discrete legal entities with no necessary relationship to each other, was not compatible with Maryland law, and thus, the workers compensation exclusivity defense applied to the hospital with respect to the medical malpractice action brought by the patient.[55]

A review of case law concerning the dual capacity doctrine in a medical malpractice context was undertaken by the **Texas** Supreme Court. In that case the hospital's pharmacy had negligently filled prescriptions for medication to treat the work-related back pain of a nurse who was continuing to work and who was not a patient admitted to the hospital. The pharmacy did not dispense prescriptions to the public, nor to hospital employees, unless they had been injured on the job. Under those facts the court held that dual capacity could not apply.[56]

Cases in **New York** have distinguished between a health clinic open solely to employees and one furnishing health services to the general public. In the former context, an employee's exclusive remedy for medical malpractice is workers compensation while in the latter context a tort action was permitted. The following quote summarizes the New York distinction:

> *"Where an employee of a hospital is admitted as a patient [to treat an injury compensable under the workers compensation law], and is negligently treated at that hospital, the injuries which result have been held not to arise out of the injured person's employment, so that an action at law to recover for such injuries may be brought. These cases are to be distinguished from those in which malpractice is committed by a co-employee of the plaintiff, and where the medical services rendered by that co-employee were not available to the public, but were exclusively available to co-employees, so that a nexus exists between the plaintiff's employment and the occurrence of the malpractice."*[57]

EMPLOYER MANUFACTURED PRODUCTS

Taking the concept of dual capacity to another level, an employee injured in the course of employment by a product or instrumentality manufactured by the employer, may be able to sue his or her employer based on its separate capacity as manufacturer of the product. A lead case with this outcome was found in **Ohio** where an employee of a stevedoring company, was driving

---

[54] *McAlister v. Methodist Hosp. of Memphis*, 550 S.W. 2d 240 (1977)
[55] *Suburban Hospital, Inc. v. Kirson*, 763 A. 2d 185 (2000)
[56] *Payne v. Galen Hosp. Corp.*, 28 S.W. 3d 15 (2000)
[57] *Milashouskas v. Mercy Hospital* 64 A.D. 2d 978 (1978)

a truck for the tire company (Uniroyal) pursuant to an arrangement between the tire company and the stevedoring company. The employee brought action against the tire company to recover for injuries sustained when a tire on the truck blew out. The tire had been manufactured by Uniroyal. The Court of Appeals held that the employee of the stevedoring company was also an employee of the tire company for workers compensation purposes. Where an employer occupies a second or dual capacity which confers upon it obligations unrelated to and independent of those imposed upon it as an employer, the employee injured as result of the violation of the employer's second or dual capacity obligation is not barred by the workmen's compensation law from recovering from the employer.[58]

About the same time that Ohio rendered the *Mercer* decision, **California** produced a similar interpretation of a manufacturers' exposure. The employee was injured when the elevator scaffolding device on which he was working collapsed. The defective scaffolding was identical in design to equipment manufactured by the employer for market to the public. Following suit by the employee alleging several causes of action based upon negligent manufacture and product liability, the lower court ruled that the employee's sole remedy was under the workers compensation law. The court of appeals reversed that opinion and held that under the dual capacity doctrine, a plaintiff may state a cause of action based on the manufacturer's liability even though the defendant is also the employer, provided that the product involved is manufactured by the employer for sale to the general public rather than for the sole use of the employer.[59]

For a time, both **California** and **Ohio** drew a distinction between products manufactured by the employer solely for its own use, and those that were also available to the general public. In a subsequent California decision, the courts went beyond that narrow interpretation and stated that the exclusiveness defense applied only if the duty involved in the accident arose solely from the employment relationship. In the *Bell* decision, a route salesman who was injured while delivering gas brought an action based upon strict products liability against his employer, employer's customer, and others alleging that he was injured as a proximate result of defects in a tank truck and other equipment. The Los Angeles County Superior Court granted summary judgment in favor of the employer.

Appeal was taken and the California Supreme Court held that employee's pleading alleged a cause of action against both the employer and the customer on the basis of their being manufacturers of defective product; interpreting workers compensation law in harmony with products liability doctrine, a manufacturer will not escape liability to its employees for defective products where there would be liability to any other injured person; and coincidental employment relationship will not shield the employer from common-law liability where concurrent cause of injury is attributable to the employer's separate and distinct relationship to an employee and which invokes a different set of obligations than an employer's duties to its employees.[60]

---

[58] *Mercer v. Uniroyal, Inc.* 361 NE2d 492 (1976)
[59] *Douglas v. E.J.Gallo Winery* 137 Cal Rptr 797 (1977)
[60] *Bell v. Industrial Vangas Co.*, 637 P2d 266 (1981)

The turning point in **Ohio** relative to the dual capacity exposure for employers came with a Supreme Court ruling in a case where an employee was permanently blinded when a fellow employee inadvertently sprayed chemical fertilizer in his eyes. The court held that the exclusive remedy portion of the compensation law barred employee's action against his employer. In order to support the employee's dual capacity theory, the employee would have had to have been working in an unrelated and independent capacity from that of the employer.[61]

In looking to decisions in other states, the Ohio Supreme Court specifically referenced **Oklahoma** and an earlier 1983 decision where the Oklahoma courts held that, *"The decisive dual-capacity test is not concerned with how separate or different the second function of the employer is from the first, but whether the second function generates obligations unrelated to those flowing from the employer. This means that the employer must step outside the boundaries of the employer-employee relationship, creating separate and distinct duties to the employee; the fact of injury must be incidental to the employment relationship."*[62] This opinion was supported by earlier decisions in both **Massachusetts** and **Michigan**.

LEGISLATIVE RESPONSE TO DUAL CAPACITY ACTIONS

In response to the plethora of suits seeking recovery under the dual capacity doctrine, a number of states initiated legislative action to address the subject. **Arkansas,** while not faced with any serious claims stemming from the dual capacity doctrine, amended the exclusive remedy provisions in their workers compensation law to specifically state that the remedies under the chapter were to be the exclusive entitlement "regardless of the multiple roles, capacities or persons the employer may be deemed to have."[63]

Following a number of troubling dual capacity cases, in 1982 the **California** legislature limited the circumstances under which an action under the dual capacity doctrine could be brought by amending the exclusive remedy provision as follows:

> *"An employee, or his or her dependents in the event of his or her death, may bring an action at law for damages against the employer, as if this division did not apply, in the following instances:*
> *(1) Where the employee's injury or death is proximately caused by a willful physical assault by the employer.*
> *(2) Where the employee's injury is aggravated by the employer's fraudulent concealment of the existence of the injury and its connection with the employment, in which case the employer's liability shall be limited to those damages proximately caused by the aggravation. The burden of proof respecting apportionment of damages between the injury and any subsequent aggravation thereof is upon the employer.*
> *(3) Where the employee's injury or death is proximately caused by a defective product manufactured by the employer and sold, leased, or otherwise transferred for valuable*

---

[61] *Bakonyi v. Ralston Purina Co.* 478 N.E. 2d 241 (1985)
[62] *Weber v. Armco, Inc.* 663 P. 2d 1221 (1983)
[63] Ark. Code Ann. § 11-9-105 (a)

consideration to an independent third person, and that product is thereafter provided for the employee's use by a third person."[64]

Louisiana was another state to address the subject legislatively. Since its original enactment, Louisiana law provided that workers compensation was the exclusive remedy against an employer for an employee injured on the job. However, in 1988, on appeal, the Louisiana Supreme Court adopted the dual capacity doctrine in *Ducote v. Albert*.[65] The court held that a company physician who treated an employee a for work-related injury and whose alleged misdiagnosis and treatment resulted in worsening of the injury, under dual-capacity doctrine, was not a co-employee entitled to immunity from tort, and liability was governed by general tort law.

In response to the *Ducote* decision, the legislature quickly amended the law to foreclose the opportunity for an injured employee to sue his/her employer under any dual capacity doctrine or theory. A new subsection was adopted that provided, *"This exclusive remedy is exclusive of all claims, including any claims that might arise against his or her employer, or any principal or any officer, director, stockholder, partner, or employee of such employer or principal under any dual capacity theory or doctrine."*[66]

While not going so far as to bar or severely limit dual capacity actions through the enactment of legislation, slightly more than one-third of the states have rejected the doctrine through case law.

In a further attempt to address some of the activity surrounding the dual capacity doctrine, a new, more limiting doctrine, evolved. In some jurisdictions, an employer may be vulnerable to a direct suit for damages if the employer has a second persona completely independent and unrelated to its status as an employer that is legally recognized as a separate legal entity. This doctrine of dual persona is distinguished from the earlier form of dual capacity by its requirement that the employer have a completely unrelated and legally recognized identity other than as employer to be held liable to a suit brought by an injured employee.

DUAL PERSONA

The clearest example of a separate legal identity for purposes of the dual persona rule is that of a separate corporation. This rule was demonstrated in **New York** where an action was instituted against the corporate employer, its parent and subsidiaries for fatal injuries sustained by plaintiff's decedent. The fact that the employee was killed when struck by a broken part from a machine manufactured by his employer was held not to entitle the surviving widow to sue the employer in tort in its capacity as a participant in the manufacture and design of the machine. Noting that the theory advanced by the widow was commonly known as the dual capacity doctrine, the court concluded that the doctrine, as it had been applied to permit suits against employers in their capacity as manufacturers of plant equipment, was fundamentally unsound.[67]

---

[64] Cal. Labor Code § 3602 (b)
[65] *Ducote v. Albert*, 521 So. 2d 399 (1988)
[66] La. Rev. Stat. Ann. § 1032. A (b)
[67] *Billy v. Consolidated Machine Tool Corp.* 412 N.E. 2d 934 (1980)

A subsequent decision involved an employee of a broadcasting company who was injured while working on a television transmitter. The employee brought a personal injury action against the broadcasting network that was affiliated with the company he worked with, and its employee, whose actions in accidentally pushing a switch had caused injuries. The network moved for summary judgment based on affirmative defense of workers compensation exclusivity, and employee cross-moved to dismiss defense. The District Court held that under **New York** law, workers compensation benefits paid by the broadcasting company did not provide a defense to the network, since the company and the network, while affiliated, remained separate entities for legal and tax purposes.

In **New Jersey**, the Superior Court of the Appellate Division ruled that an injured worker's products liability lawsuit against his employer failed because of the exclusive remedy doctrine, even though the worker based his suit on the dual capacity argument. The employee was injured when his hands and arms were caught in a conveyor, causing severe and permanent injuries. After receiving compensation benefits, the employee filed a premises liability lawsuit against the employer alleging that the employer had altered the machine and removed a safety device. A trial court dismissed the suit citing exclusive remedy, and the employee appealed.

The appeals court noted that the employer had earlier purchased the plant in question from another firm which included the conveyor machine that caused the injuries. The appellate judges noted that the action was based on the dual capacity doctrine, and explained that the dual capacity doctrine stands for the proposition that, *"an employer normally shielded from tort liability by the exclusive remedy principle in workers compensation may be liable in tort to its own employee if it occupies, in addition to its capacity as an employer, a second capacity that confers on it obligations independent of those imposed on him as an employer."*

Specifically, the employee argued that when the employer purchased the plant containing the machine, liability (for the defective conveyor) now attached to the new owner as a matter of law. However, New Jersey courts have held that the doctrine "is disfavored, if not outright disapproved." The appellate judges ruled that the fact that the defendant bought the conveyor along with the plant did not "create a cause of action that survives the exclusivity bar." While the court ruled that the suit was barred by exclusive remedy, it was noted that the worker could pursue a products liability claim against the original owner of the plant.[68]

In a **Wisconsin** case it was held that an employer may become a third person, vulnerable to tort suit by an employee, if – and only if – the employer possesses a second persona so completely independent from and unrelated to his status as employer that by established standards the law recognizes it as a separate legal person.[69] The dual persona exists where the duality is firmly entrenched in common law or where the duality is one created by modern statute.

---

[68] *Habashi v. Interbake Foods, Inc.*, No. A-0912-07T3, (2008)
[69] *Riccitelli v. Broekhuizen*, 595 N.W. 2d 392 (1999)

In a case decided by the **Michigan** Supreme Court, it was noted that the dual capacity doctrine was recognized in Michigan. However, in defining this doctrine, the Court adopted a definition consistent with the concept of dual persona. The Supreme Court stated:

> *Since the term "dual capacity" has proved to be subject to such misapplication and abuse, the only effective remedy is to jettison it altogether, and substitute the term "dual persona doctrine." The choice of the term "persona" is not the result of any predilection for elegant Latinisms for their own sake; it is dictated by the literal language of the typical third-party statute, which usually defines a third party, in the first instance, as "a person other than the employer." This is quite different from "a person acting in a capacity other than that of employer." The question is not one of activity, or relationship - it is one of identity.* [70]

THIRD PARTY ACTION-OVER

In a limited number of states, there are circumstances under which an employer may be required to pay damages to an employee injured in the course of his/her employment. A statement, first pronounced by Dr. Arthur Larson in 1953, has frequently been cited as the preamble to opinions and articles on the subject. *"Perhaps the most evenly balanced controversy in all of compensation law is the question whether a third party in an action by the employee can get contribution or indemnity from the employer, when the employer's negligence has caused or contributed to the injury."*

A third party action-over involves a claim made against the employer by a third party who has been sued by an injured employee. For example, an employee injured at work by a defective punch press manufactured by a third party, may be entitled to receive workers compensation benefits from the employer and may also bring an action for damages against the third party manufacturer who produced the punch press. A third party action-over claim results when the producer of the product is sued and in turn, sues the employee's employer for contribution or indemnification as a joint tortfeasor based on some alteration of the product made by the employer.

The basic issue is whether the employer should have immunity against an action brought by the third party because the employer furnished compensation benefits to the injured employee, or should the employer continue to have a responsibility beyond that of compensation benefits for damages based upon the extent of the employers' negligence because the claim comes from the third party and not the employee?

Before proceeding with an examination of the topic, it is well to review the difference between contribution and indemnification. Black's dictionary defines contribution as the *"[r]ight of one who has discharged a common liability to recover of another also liable, the aliquot portion which he ought to pay or bear."*[71] Stated in simpler terms, one who is compelled to pay more

---

[70] *Herbolsheimer v. SMS Holding Co., Inc.*, 608 N.W. 2d 487 (2000)
[71] Black's Law Dictionary 328 (6th ed.1990)

than a just share of a common liability is entitled to recover from another who is also liable, the proportionate share that the other should pay.

In some respects, contribution is construed as a form of indemnity, or indemnity may be perceived as an extreme form of contribution. Contribution and indemnity are variant common-law remedies used to secure restitution and fair apportionment of loss among those whose activities combine to produce injury. Both spring from the need to shift the burden among tortfeasors. However, indemnity springs from a contractual relationship or agreement between the parties which give rise to a duty, whereas contribution rests on the theory of equity and the idea that, where there is a common obligation, those that share in that common obligation should share in any subsequent liability.

Indemnification – The clearest exception to the exclusive remedy doctrine is the right of a third party to enforce an express contract or agreement in which the employer specifically or implicitly agrees to indemnify the third party for the type of loss sustained by the employee. An example of this is the landlord/tenant relationship in which an employer promises in the lease to hold the landlord harmless in the case of injury. Thus, if an employee is injured and recovers damages from the landlord, the landlord is in a position to recover from the employer any damages the landlord was called upon to pay.

However, the right to indemnification may also be enforced outside the existence of an express agreement or contract. This can be accomplished where the third party can demonstrate that the third party and the employer stood in a special legal relationship which carried with it the obligation of indemnification. An example of this is the bailee/bailor relationship. Generally these cases reflect the additional factor of the degree of negligence or the minor (passive) negligence of the third party versus the major (active) negligence of the employer.

To clarify the intent that an employer is responsible to a third party when a written agreement has been entered into prior to the injury, a number of states have specific legislation addressing the subject. The following example is found in **California** –

"Liability to reimburse or hold third person harmless on judgment or settlement. If an action as provided in this chapter prosecuted by the employee, the employer, or both jointly against the third person results in judgment against such third person, or settlement by such third person, the employer shall have no liability to reimburse or hold such third person harmless on such judgment or settlement in absence of a written agreement so to do executed prior to the injury."[72]

Contribution – The great majority of jurisdictions, relying on the rationale that the employer's sole liability is through the providing of workers compensation benefits, hold that the employer cannot be sued or joined by a third party as a joint tortfeasor, either under a contribution statute or at common law. In the ordinary case, when an employee is injured by the joint negligence of the employer and a third party, any bid for contribution will fail.

---

[72] Cal. Labor Code § 3864

Furthermore, the employer will generally be relieved entirely of any liability since compensation payments made by the employer will be subject to reimbursement after judgment is assessed against the third party.

However, the courts in a minority of states have arrived at an opposite conclusion. The following addresses both the case law that served as the genesis for and the subsequent legislation adopted to address this exposure. This review will be limited to the select states of **New York, Illinois, Minnesota,** and **North Carolina** and three additional states where any third-party recovery from the employer is limited to the extent of compensable benefits paid or payable.

One of the earliest cases concerned with the subject of third party over suits occurred in **New York** in 1972, in *Dole v. Dow*[73]. In the case, Dow Chemical Co. was the defendant in an action brought following the death of the plaintiff's (Dole) husband. The plaintiff brought an action for damages against Dow Chemical for negligently causing the death of her husband. Dole had died while cleaning his employer's grain storage bin, which he had been fumigating with a poisonous fumigant, manufactured by Dow Chemical. Dow was alleged to have been negligent in failing to properly label the fumigant.

Dow Chemical, asserting its own right of recovery for breach of an alleged independent duty owed to it by the employer (owner of the grain storage bin), brought a third-party claim over against the employer. The lower court dismissed the third-party complaint and Dow appealed. The Supreme Court, Appellate Division reversed and further appeal was taken. The Court of Appeals held that the action against the employer by the third party could proceed. In defending its elimination of employer immunity, the court stated that the chemical company was not suing for damages on account of the worker's death but was asserting its right of recovery for breach of an independent duty owed to it by the employer.

The *Dole* decision placed the employer in the position of not only being responsible for the workers compensation death benefits, but could, if the extent of liability exceeded the amount of compensation benefits, be responsible for any award over and above the amount of workers compensation benefits paid and payable. This exposure would be covered under the Employers Liability section (Part Two) of the workers compensation policy.

In 1996, following numerous legislative attempts to address the issue, the liability of an employer for contribution or indemnity created by the *Dole* decision was restricted. Legislation was enacted that confined the employer's exposure to those cases where the employee's injury rose to the level of a grave injury.

A portion of the New York statute pertaining to the workers compensation exclusive remedy along with what constituted a grave injury reads as follows:

> *"For purposes of this section the terms "indemnity" and "contribution" shall not include a claim or cause of action for contribution or indemnification based upon a*

---

[73] *Dole v. Dow Chemical*, 282 N.E. 2d 288 (1972)

provision in a written contract entered into prior to the accident or occurrence by which the employer had expressly agreed to contribution to or indemnification of the claimant or person asserting the cause of action for the type of loss suffered.

An employer shall not be liable for contribution or indemnity to any third person based upon liability for injuries sustained by an employee acting within the scope of his or her employment for such employer unless such third person proves through competent medical evidence that such employee has sustained a "grave injury" which shall mean only one or more of the following: death, permanent and total loss of use or amputation of an arm, leg, hand or foot, loss of multiple fingers, loss of multiple toes, paraplegia or quadriplegia, total and permanent blindness, total and permanent deafness, loss of nose, loss of ear, permanent and severe facial disfigurement, loss of an index finger or an acquired injury to the brain caused by an external physical force resulting in permanent total disability." [74]

Following enactment of this legislation, any action against a third party for injuries occurring on or after September 10, 1996, which did not rise to the level of grave injury, could no longer serve as the basis for a third party bringing an action against the employer for either contribution or indemnity. Where a grave injury did exist, the legislation did not operate to limit the employer's exposure to the amount of compensation payments paid or payable. The employer could be responsible for damages more than the workers compensation benefits paid or payable. In this fashion, the New York solution differed from the approach found in a number of other states.

The rather comprehensive list of grave injuries essentially removed any discretion on the part of the adjudicator in terms of whether the employer may be brought into the action. It should also be noted that if the employer has entered a contract prior to the accident, in which the parties agree to indemnify or contribute to payment for a loss in case of an injury, that contract or agreement was not affected by the grave injury statute.

Decisions have been rendered that examined the issue of grave injury. In one case, the worker lost the tips of five fingers while operating a die cutting machine and sued the machine's manufacturer. In turn, the manufacturer asserted a third-party claim against the worker's employer. Following denial of the employer's motion for summary judgment, the employer appealed and the Supreme Court, Appellate Division, reversed. After leave to appeal was granted, the Court of Appeals held that the loss of multiple fingertips did not constitute a "loss of multiple fingers," and thus was not a grave injury under provision of the workers compensation law. This decision was affirmed at the Appellate Division.[75]

In **Illinois**, arriving at a result similar to that found in New York. The decision involved an employee injured while working on an injection-molding machine who brought an action against the manufacturer of the machine on a strict tort liability theory. The manufacturer filed a third-party complaint seeking contribution from the employer. The Circuit Court

---

[74] N.Y. Con. Law Art. 3 § 11
[75] *Castro v. United Container Machinery Group, Inc.*, 761 NE2d 1014 (2001)

granted a motion by the employer to dismiss the third-party complaint, and the Appellate Court affirmed. The Illinois courts held that if the defendant manufacturer's third-party complaint alleged that the employer's misuse of a product or assumption of risk inherent with the use of a product, contributed to the employee's injuries, the manufacturer had stated a sufficient cause of action for contribution.[76]

On allowance of the manufacturer's petition for leave to appeal, the Illinois Supreme Court held that (1) where the Supreme Court has created a rule or doctrine which, under present conditions, it considers unsound and unjust, the court has not only power, but duty, to modify or abolish it, and (2) governing equitable principles required that, if the manufacturer was held liable on the basis of strict liability in tort, and if the employer-buyer was negligent in respect to use of the product, the manufacturer could recover on its third-party complaint against the employer-buyer for contribution based on the latter's relative degree of fault contributing to the plaintiff employee's injuries.

In response to the *Skinner* decision, the Illinois legislature enacted legislation designed to maintain the employer's responsibility to a third party, but to limit that responsibility to the amount of compensation benefits paid or payable. This was accomplished through the placement of a limitation on the amount of the employer's subrogation recovery.

The **Minnesota** Supreme Court achieved a somewhat similar result to that realized in Illinois initially without the benefit of statute. The Minnesota District Court upheld an award of $35,000 in damages to an injured worker, but denied the defendant manufacturer contribution from the employer which was partly at fault for the accident. On appeal, the Supreme Court held that the manufacturer failed to demonstrate an abuse of discretion with respect to admission of evidence of safety standards, that there was no evidence of assumption of risk requiring submission of the issue to a jury, that the award of damages was not excessive, and that the manufacturer was entitled to contribution from the employer in an amount not to exceed compensation benefits paid or to be paid by employer to employee because of the accident.[77]

In 2000, the Minnesota statute was amended to clarify that the maximum responsibility to a third party was to be established as the amount of workers compensation benefits paid or payable.

Three states have amended their exclusive remedy provisions to address the responsibility of the employer where the injured employer brings an action against a negligent third party. In **Idaho**, the legislature approved language whereby:

> *"The liability of an employer to another person who may be liable for or who has paid damages on account of an injury or occupational disease or death arising out of and in the course of employment of an employee of the employer and caused by the breach of any duty or obligation owed by the employer to such other person,*

---

[76] *Skinner v. Reed,* 374 N.E. 2d 437 (1978)
[77] *Lambertson v. Cincinnati Corp.,* 257 NW2d 679 (1971)

shall be limited to the amount of compensation for which the employer is liable under this law on account of such injury, disease, or death, unless such other person and the employer agree to share liability in a different manner."[78]

The provision was followed where an employee brought an action against a third-party truck owner alleging that as a result of the third party's failure to supply a chain guard and other protective devices on a grain auger on the truck, employee's left thumb was severed from his hand. The District Court entered judgment on jury verdict awarding employee $20,000, reduced by amount representing employee's negligence, 40 percent, and by amount of workers compensation benefits he had received, $5,638.52, resulting in judgment of $6,361.48. The employee appealed and the Supreme Court held that determination of negligence of employer was not necessary before reduction of the judgment by the amount of workers compensation benefits, the reduction of judgment to prevent double recovery was appropriate, and the damage award was not inadequate.[79]

In **Kansas**, action taken by the legislature in 1982 resulted in a situation where the subrogation interest of the employer was reduced by the percentage of the recovery attributed to the negligence of the employer. The amended statute provides:

"If the negligence of the workers employer or those for whom the employer is responsible, other than the injured worker, is found to have contributed to the party's injury, the employer's subrogation interest or credits against future payments of compensation and medical aid, as provided by this section, shall be diminished by the percentage of the recovery attributed to the negligence of the employer or those for whom the employer is responsible, other than the injured worker."[80]

And in **Kentucky**, except in the case of a written indemnification agreement, the employer's responsibility to a third party is limited to the compensation benefits for which the employer is liable. The law was amended to provide:

"The liability of an employer to another person who may be liable for or who has paid damages on account of injury or death of an employee of such employer arising out of and in the course of employment and caused by a breach of any duty or obligation owed by such employer to such other shall be limited to the amount of compensation and other benefits for which such employer is liable under this chapter on account of such injury or death, unless such other and the employer by written contract have agreed to share liability in a different manner."[81]

INJURIES OUTSIDE SCOPE OF THE LAW

---

[78] Idaho Code § 72-209. (2)
[79] *Schneider v. Farmers Merchant, Inc.*, 678 P. 2d 33 (1983)
[80] Kan. Rev. Stat. Ch.44-504 (d)
[81] Ky. Rev. Stat. Ann. § 342.690 (1)

A review of the early literature regarding state workmen's compensation laws reveals that it was never the intent of those laws to cover claims that fell outside of the typical states coverage. In all but a few jurisdictions, the exclusive remedy doctrine applied only to those injuries or diseases which were compensable under the applicable compensation law. If the employee's injury or disease did not qualify as compensable for reasons such as failure to arise out of and in the course of the employment, the employer-employee relationship became irrelevant and the employee retained his/her common law right to file negligence suit and seek recovery of damages. Failure on the part of the employer to provide workers compensation coverage as required by law also served to expose the employer to a direct action for damages.

Under rare occasions, situations still arise where employment events may be construed to fall outside the scope of the employment. In a case eventually heard at the U.S. District Court for the Northern District of **Florida**, the employee alleged that she was exposed to toxic mold from a contaminated work environment. She filed several workers compensation claims, which were consolidated and scheduled for a hearing. The employer denied the claims, arguing that the alleged exposure did not occur in the course and scope of the employment.

Before the hearing, the employee withdrew her claims without prejudice and then commenced a common law action alleging that the employer was negligent in its maintenance and operation of the building. The employer moved for summary judgment arguing that, *"to the extent the employee's injuries were caused by an on-the-job accident or toxic exposure, her remedies are limited to those benefits payable under Florida's Workers Compensation Law, and she should be required to litigate her claims to conclusion in the workers compensation proceedings before proceeding with her civil action."* The U.S. District Court ruled in favor of the employee, denying the motion for summary judgment and holding that the employee was not required to litigate her claim to completion in the workers' compensation system, and the common law action could be maintained.[82]

In another example, in **Vermont,** an employee was working for a moving company when an acetylene tank fell on his hand and crushed it. Although the employer did not have workers compensation insurance, the employer paid workers compensation benefits claimed by the injured employee. After exhausting these benefits, the employee brought suit seeking damages for the employers' negligence. The superior court granted summary judgment for the employer concluding that the employee had made a binding election to claim compensation benefits and was, therefore, barred from bringing a civil action for damages.

The injured employee appealed to the Vermont Supreme Court arguing that acceptance of compensation benefits did not waive his right to a civil suit because he never completed a signed, written agreement approved by the Commissioner. The Supreme Court held that the employer is still able to force an election by the worker as long as it is voluntary pursuant to the terms of the statute. Thus, before making any compensation payments, whether voluntarily or under the direction of the department, the employer can insist that the worker waive the right to sue. In this case, the employer never did take such action. In fact, even when the employee s

---

[82] *Rush v. BellSouth Telecommunications, Inc.*, 2011 WL 691617 (2011)

lawyer informed the employer that he intended to bring suit, the employer continued to pay benefits without addressing the election issue. In the absence of a waiver that complied with the terms of the statute, the employee never made a binding election that precluded his right to bring a civil suit against his employer. The case therefore was reversed and remanded.[83]

L　　　　　　　L　　　L

Allegations of sexual harassment and sexual assault are other phenomena falling outside the scope of workers compensation coverage. A cause of action for sexual discrimination – the forerunner of sexual harassment – was created through state legislative human rights laws and by the enactment the Federal Civil Rights Law of 1964. While the original laws recognized only a cause of action for sex discrimination, by the late 1970s, both state and federal courts came to recognize sexual harassment as a form of sexual discrimination.

In an **Arizona** case dealing with a number of issues associated with emotional distress, an employee filed a tort action against her employer in federal court alleging harassment, intentional infliction of emotional distress, and negligent infliction of emotional distress. With respect to the negligent infliction of emotional distress, the employer argued that the compensation act was her sole remedy for work-related injuries. The United States District Court for the District of Arizona disagreed, refusing to grant the employer's motion to dismiss. The workers compensation system is designed to compensate accidental injuries, and the plaintiff's allegations, if true, would constitute injuries that should have been expected. Specifically, the opinion relied upon a section of the Arizona law which states that *"[a] mental injury ... shall not be considered a personal injury by accident."* Without ruling on the merits of the claim, the District Court held that the plaintiff's negligent infliction of emotional distress claim was not precluded by the exclusive remedy bar.[84]

A claim arose in **Florida** that directly addressed the issue of sexual harassment in the workplace. Several female employees alleged claims against their employer for assault and battery, intentional infliction of emotional distress, and negligent hiring and retention of employees, based upon claimed instances of sexual harassment. The circuit court dismissed the complaint on the grounds that workers compensation provided the exclusive remedy for employees and the decision was affirmed at the District Court of Appeal.

On appeal, the Florida Supreme Court reversed the lower court decision. In reaching their decision, the court emphasized that sexual harassment does not generally involve physical injury arising out of an accidental occurrence and there is a strong public policy argument for permitting tort remedies for sexual harassment, as expressed in the Federal Civil Rights Act. That public policy would be abrogated if the exclusivity rule were applied to prevent employees from bringing such an action. Furthermore, workers compensation was designed to provide economic recovery for a worker's loss of resources and earnings. The concerns expressed by

---

[83] *Smith v. Desautels*, 953 A.2d 620 (2008)
[84] *Lombardi v. Copper Canyon Academy, LLC*, 2010 WL 3775408 (2010)

sexual harassment law involve loss of personal dignity. To the extent that these two types of injuries are separable, the court concluded that they should be enforced separately.[85]

Following the same rationale enunciated by the Florida Supreme Court, a number of other states established case law permitting the victim of sexual harassment or assault to bring an action for damages against the employer. In **Alaska,** the Supreme Court held that an employer could be held liable in tort for a supervisor's sexual harassment even though the supervisor was acting outside the scope of employment. However, the court ruled that the employer could not be subject to punitive damages because it would be "unfair to punish an employer for acts committed by employees who are in no sense pursuing objectives of the employer." The trial court had awarded plaintiff $1.5 million in punitive damages.[86]

In **California**, an employee sued her employer for emotional distress alleging the employer's sexual misconduct. The trial court held that the exclusive remedy barred the employee's claim and dismissed the case. The Court of Appeal reversed, holding that the exclusive remedy defense does not bar emotional distress claims when the employer's conduct falls outside the normal risks of an employment relationship, such as when the employer engages in harassment or discrimination.[87]

Similarly, the **Colorado** Supreme Court ruled that an employee may pursue a tort action against a co-worker and employer for the co-worker's sexual harassment. The Supreme Court resolved a split of authority in the lower courts, holding that because such harassment tends to be inherently private and personal in nature, there is an insufficient nexus between the employment and the injury to find that the conduct arose out of the employment. In addition, the court reasoned that because there is no redress for sexual harassment claims in the workers compensation system, the legislature intended that harassment claims be addressed outside of the system. Barring a sexual harassment claim under the exclusive remedy provisions would thwart the strong public policies against sexual harassment.[88]

While the trend has been in the direction of permitting employees to sue their employers directly for damages where the allegation is one of sexual harassment, a few jurisdictions have concluded that claims for sexual harassment are barred by the exclusivity doctrine. For example, the **South Carolina** Supreme Court held that workers compensation was the exclusive remedy and barred an employee's lawsuit for assault, battery, and intentional infliction of emotional distress based on sexual harassment by a co-employee. The court noted that the employee could not argue that her employer failed to provide protection for her and at the same time maintain that her injury did not arise out of the employment.[89]

---

[85] *Byrd v. Richardson-Greenshields Securities, Inc.,* 552 So. 2d 150 (1989)
[86] *VECO Inc. v. Rosebrock,* 970 P. 2d 906 (1998)
[87] *Hill v. Columbia TriStar Television* Court of Appeals decision rendered April 2003
[88] *Horodyskyj v. Karanian,* 33 P. 3d 470 (2001)
[89] *Loges v. Mack Trucks*, 417 S.E. 2d 538 (1992)

In addition to South Carolina, it appears that **Delaware** [90] and **Maine** [91] apply the exclusivity bar across the board. This general holding is based on the premise that the "injuries complained of occurred at the place of employment and arose out of and in the course of the employment." Because they arose out of a covered situation, the workers compensation law is the appropriate forum for response.

A slight variant on the theme of direct actions brought in the case of sexual harassment can be found in those cases where the allegation of intentional infliction of emotional distress has been raised. This perhaps stems from the fact that when suit is filed, generally multiple allegations of misconduct are raised. For example, where there is an allegation of sexual harassment and/or sexual assault, there may well be an allegation of intentional infliction of emotional distress.

In a **New Mexico** case, a co-employee alleged numerous incidents of sexual harassment by a supervisor. Management was aware of the situation and did nothing other than transfer the supervisor to a different department. Two employees sued the employer alleging negligent supervision and intentional infliction of emotional distress. At trial, the jury awarded the victims compensatory damages along with a punitive damage award of $1,200,000 to the first employee and $550,000 to the second employee.

On appeal, the New Mexico Supreme Court held that a claim falls outside the act if the injuries are not compensable under the Workers Compensation Act. The employees had psychological problems because of the harassment. In New Mexico, only primary (mental-physical) and secondary (physical-mental) mental impairments are compensable. Because neither of these criteria was met, the employees did not have compensable work related injuries and the court held that they were free to sue their employer in court.[92]

Another example of a claim brought alleging intentional infliction of emotional distress is a case **in Louisiana where the** employee appealed from the decision of the District Court dismissing her emotional distress claims against the employer. The Court of Appeals held that the exclusive remedy provision of the workers compensation act did not bar all negligent infliction of emotional distress claims filed in tort against an employer.[93]

EMOTIONAL DISTRESS

In a **Texas** decision, **several e**mployees sued their employer for intentional infliction of emotional distress based on the workplace conduct of their supervisor. The district court entered judgment on jury verdict for employees and awarded damages and this decision was affirmed by the court of appeals. The employer appealed and the Texas Supreme Court held that severe emotional distress caused by a supervisor's continuing abuse was not a compensable injury under the workers compensation act, and thus the employee's suit was not barred by the act, the

---

[90] *Konstanopoulos v. Westcao Corp.*, 690 A. 2d 936 (1996)
[91] *Green v. Wyman-Goron, Co.*, 664 N.E. 2d 808 (1996)
[92] *Coates, etal v. Wal-Mart Stores*, 976 P2d 999 (1999)
[93] *Richardson v. Home Depot USA*, 808 So2d 544 (2001)

supervisor's conduct was extreme and outrageous, the employer was vicariously liable for the supervisor's intentional conduct, and evidence supported a finding that the emotional distress suffered by the employees was severe.[94]

However, notwithstanding the apparent trend permitting employees to sue their employer for intentional infliction of emotional distress, there are also judicial decisions where workers compensation remains the exclusive remedy despite the allegation. The **Massachusetts** District Court held that Massachusetts law does not recognize a common-law action for discharge in violation of public policy against age discrimination, and a claim for intentional infliction of emotional distress was barred by the exclusivity provision of the Massachusetts workmen's compensation act. In this case the plaintiff brought a multi-count action based on the claim that he was wrongfully discharged because of his age.[95]

And in **North Carolina**, a former client sued her vocational rehabilitation specialists for negligent infliction of emotional distress. The Durham County Superior Court granted summary judgment for the rehabilitation specialists and the former client appealed. The Court of Appeals reversed and the vocational rehabilitation specialists petitioned for discretionary review. The North Carolina Supreme Court remanded the decision with directions. The Court of Appeals held as matter of first impression that the workers compensation act provided the exclusive remedy for claimant's negligent infliction of emotional distress claim.[96]

RETALIATORY DISCHARGE

In other situations involving workplace events, the majority of states recognize, either by case law or by statute, the tort of retaliatory discharge for filing a claim for workers compensation benefits. A ruling by the Supreme Court of **Indiana** is generally recognized as the judicial precedent wherein discharge of an employee in retaliation for filing a workers compensation claim was actionable at law resulting in both actual and punitive damages. The employee had injured her arm on the job and had received compensation benefits, including permanency benefits for the partial loss of use of her arm. A month following her return to work, although capable of performing her job, she was fired without reason or cause.

Following her termination, the employee filed an action for both actual and punitive damages. The Indiana Supreme Court reversed an order for dismissal and remanded the case for trial. At the trial level, the court invoked the following passage from the Workers Compensation Act. *"No contract or agreement, written or implied, no rule, regulation or other device shall, in any manner operate to relieve any employer in whole or in part of any obligation created by this act."*[97] The court viewed the threat of discharge as a device under this clause. The court acknowledged the common law rule that, under ordinary circumstances, an employee at will may

---

[94] *GTE Southwest, Inc. v. Bruce,* 998 SW2d 605 (1999)
[95] *Crews v. Memorex Corp.,* 588 F. Supp. 27 (1984)
[96] *Riley v. Debaer* 562 S.E. 2d 69 (2002)
[97] Ind. Stat. Ann. § 22-3-2-15

be fired without cause, but concluded, *"[W]hen an employee is discharged solely for exercising a statutorily conferred right an exception to the general rule must be recognized."*[98]

Following the decision in *Frampton*, the courts in a significant number of states confronted the same issue. Most of these decisions ruled in favor of the employee although a number of the southern states – notably **Alabama, Mississippi, North** and **South Carolina**, and **New Mexico** – clung to the rigid employment at will doctrine which permits the employer to terminate an employee with or without cause.

In a number of instances, state legislative bodies attempted to resolve the issue. **Texas** enacted a reasonably comprehensive provision in response to the employer practice of terminating employees who filed for workers compensation benefits. Other states with similar provisions limited strictly to the situation where the employee is terminated from employment for filing a compensation claim include **Alabama, Hawaii, Louisiana, Oklahoma, South Carolina,** and **Virginia. South Carolina** provides that the burden of proof is upon the employee and the employer has an affirmative defense to the action.[99]

Today, the typical statutory provision found in the majority of states is no longer limited only to the discharge of an employee for filing a workers compensation claim. In an effort to address any form of workplace discrimination, the typical provision addresses both discharge of the employee or any other manner of discrimination because the employee filed a claim for benefits. This type of statutory language is found in **Connecticut** law that provides, *"No employer who is subject to the provisions of this chapter shall discharge, or cause to be discharged, or in any manner discriminate against any employee because the employee has filed a claim for workers compensation benefits or otherwise exercised the rights afforded to him pursuant to the provisions of said chapter."*[100]

An additional type of claim that generally falls within the normal scope of workers compensation coverage is that involving loss of consortium. A claim for loss of consortium arises when one of the marriage partners has lost the companionship (consortium) of the other partner as the result of someone else's negligence or intentional conduct. Loss of consortium is broadly defined to include such things as the loss of society, affection, assistance, and the impairment of sexual relations in a marital relationship. The general rule in the majority of jurisdictions is that no common law action for damages may be maintained for the loss of services and consortium due to a compensable injury to his or her spouse.

LOSS OF CONSORTIUM

Based on the language in a number of the early workmen's compensation laws, it was initially recognized that the exclusive remedy of the compensation law did not bar suits by persons other than the employee. In contrast to that limited approach, most jurisdictions subsequently

---

[98] *Frampton v. Central Indiana Gas Co.*, 297 N.E. 2d 425 (1975)
[99] S.C. Code Ann. § 41-1-80
[100] Conn. Gen. Stat. § 31-290a (a)

extended the scope of coverage to include the employee's spouse, dependents, next of kin, or anyone else entitled to recover damages from the employer.

The case that is generally recognized as setting the stage for loss of consortium suits arose in **Massachusetts** when the plaintiff and her children filed suit against the employer alleging that the plaintiff's husband and father was seriously injured as a result of the negligent, willful, wanton, and reckless conduct of the employer. Ferriter had been paralyzed after a wooden beam fell fifty feet and struck him on the neck.

On appeal from the trial court, the Supreme Judicial Court of Massachusetts held that the children's claim for loss of consortium was a claim upon which relief could be granted, dismissal of the negligent infliction of emotional distress claim was improper since the wife and children could arguably establish that they satisfied the proximity requirements of the tort claim, and the previous recovery of the injured worker under the workers compensation statute did not serve to bar the wife's and children's claim.[101]

Subsequent to the judicial action, the Massachusetts legislature amended the pertinent section to provide that, *"... the employee's spouse, children, parents and any other member of the employee's family or next of kin who is wholly or partly dependent upon the earnings of such employee at the time of injury or death, shall also be held to have waived any right created by statute, at common law, or under the law of any other jurisdiction against such employer, including, but not limited to, claims for damages due to emotional distress, loss of consortium, parental guidance, companionship or the like, when such loss is a result of any injury to the employee that is compensable under this chapter."*[102]

This amendment was intended to forestall a proliferation of suits brought by a spouse or dependents for loss of consortium and consequential bodily injury suits. In doing so, Massachusetts followed the lead of the majority of other states that previously had expanded the coverage to include those with some dependency or direct association with the employee.

TORT RECOVERY FOR NON-COMPENSABLE CONDITIONS

---

[101] *Ferriter v. Daniel O'Connell's Sons, Inc.,* 413 N.E. 2d 690 (1980)
[102] Mass. Gen. Laws Ann. Ch. 152, § 24

Closely akin to the subject of exposure for injuries outside the scope of the law are those situations where claims to circumvent the exclusive remedy are prompted by the enactment of provisions designed to limit the scope of coverage or to further limit benefit entitlement.

Following the recommendations of the National Commission in 1972, virtually all states worked to broaden the extent of their coverage while at the same time increasing the level of benefit entitlement. While the question of increasing benefits has its appeal for those interested in ensuring adequate protection against the economic consequences of a work-related injury, there eventually arises the question as to whether the coverage and/or benefit pendulum has swung too far in favor of the injured worker.

Without making any judgment as to whether the pendulum has swung too far in one direction or the other, there is little question that employers have, in the interest of controlling workers compensation costs, taken steps to limit the circumstances under which claims are considered compensable, and have also cut back – or further refined – the benefits to which the injured are entitled. Beginning in the 1980s and continuing into the current century, many legislative efforts have been directed at either one or both of these factors.

Changes in statutory language enacted by state legislatures beginning in the late 1980s, were designed to raise the threshold in terms of what constituted a compensable injury or occupational disease. An excellent example of this type of court activity can be found in the state of **Washington**. Having earlier extended coverage to include occupational disease, by the 1980s, the Washington courts began to more narrowly interpret the causation standard for occupational disease claims. In a case eventually heard by the Washington Supreme Court, an employee of the Department of Social and Health Services was required to work in an office environment that continuously exposed her to tobacco smoke. After two years of exposure to smoke, the employee developed chronic obstructive pulmonary disease, which was totally disabling, forcing her termination of employment.

The employee filed a workers compensation claim that was denied as not compensable under either an industrial injury or occupational disease. In response to denial of her claim, the employee sued her employer based on the argument that the employer breached its duty to provide a working environment reasonably free from smoke. The trial court dismissed the suit, but both the Court of Appeals and Supreme Court disagreed with the trial court. The Supreme Court held that a worker cannot be barred from suing an employer for negligence at common law unless a substitute remedy has been provided under the workers compensation act. There must be one remedy or the other, otherwise the employers' end of the bargain that is at the heart of the creation of the workers compensation system has not been held up.[103]

While challenges to the exclusive remedy of workers compensation was not new, the topic has taken on a more serious nature following some of the more recent reforms. It was noted in an earlier chapter that in a continuing attempt to define more clearly what constitutes a compensable injury, a number of jurisdictions enacted provisions requiring the compensable injury to be the

---

[103] ***McCarthy v. Department of Social and Health Services,*** 759 P. 2d 351 (1988)

major cause of any resulting disability. Because of the potential for an injury to be substantially the result of non-occupational causation, with perhaps only minimal workplace contribution to the disability, **Arkansas** enacted legislation addressing injuries resulting from repetitive motion, back injury and hearing loss. The reform legislation established the burden of proof to be a *preponderance of the evidence,* and the law went on to further provide that, *"the resultant condition is compensable only if the alleged compensable injury is the major cause of the disability or need for treatment."*[104] The law in Arkansas goes on to explicitly define the term major cause to mean more than 50 percent of the cause.

A few states have enacted a provision requiring the employment to be the major contributing cause of the injury or occupational disease. These states include **Montana, Oregon,** and **South Dakota**. Prior to 1990, Oregon had a compensability standard that required that work must be a material cause in order for the claim to be compensable. This requirement was slightly more restrictive than the standard of compensability found in most jurisdictions at that time. In 1990, in response to rising workers compensation costs, the Oregon legislature enacted language whereby, *"No injury or disease is compensable as a consequence of a compensable injury unless the compensable injury is the major contributing cause of the consequential condition."*[105]

Following adoption of the new standard, a steelworker who had a pre-existing condition of chronic paranasal sinusitis, was denied compensation benefits because his work was not a major cause of his condition, and thus, he did not sustain a compensable injury within the meaning of the exclusivity provision. The steelworker sought treatment for his symptoms and filed a workers compensation claim. The insurer denied the claim, explaining that it did not appear the condition was worsened by or arose out of and in the course of the employment, either by accident or occupational disease. At a hearing, the referee denied the claim and on appeal to the Workers Compensation Board, the ruling was upheld.

The employee then brought a direct action for damages in circuit court against his employer, based on inhalation and exposure to particulates in the workplace, alleging statutory and common law claims. Ultimately reaching the Oregon Supreme Court, it was held that the exclusive remedy provisions in the workers compensation law did not preclude workers whose compensation claims had been denied from bringing civil actions against their employers in an effort to recover damages for their work-related injuries. In examining the legislature's intent when it enacted the exclusive remedy provisions, the Court concluded that the legislature had not intended to prevent a worker whose workers compensation claim had been denied for failure to meet the major contributing cause standard from pursuing civil negligence claims against the employer in the effort to receive at least some damages for work-related injuries. [106]

Responding promptly to this decision, the 1995 Oregon legislature amended the law so that the exclusive remedy was applicable to all "injuries, diseases, symptom complexes or similar conditions arising out of and in the course of employment," not just compensable injuries.[107] In

---

[104] Ark. Code Ann. § 11-9-102 (4)(A)
[105] Or. Rev. Stat. § 656.005 (7)(a)
[106] *Errand v. Cascade Steel Rolling Mills, Inc.*, 888 P2d 544 (1995)
[107] Or. Rev. Stat. §§ 656.012 and 656.018

response to the new law, advocates for workers argued that the new language violated the Oregon Constitution which provides that, "every man shall have remedy by due course of law for injury done in his person, property, or reputation."[108]

In due course the issue again came before the courts for adjudication. This case involved a lube technician for a trucking company who, in the course of his employment, was exposed to chemical mists and fumes. The administrative law judge denied the claim because the employee failed to prove that his exposure at work was the major contributing cause of his lung condition. The employee then sued his employer alleging negligence in exposing him to "acid mist and fumes at work" resulting in permanent injury. The employer moved for dismissal based on the 1995 amendment to the exclusive remedy provision. The trial court granted the motion to dismiss and the Court of Appeals affirmed.

The case was appealed to the Oregon Supreme Court where the court reversed the earlier rulings and held that the major contributing cause standard, combined with the exclusive remedy of the workers compensation law, violated the Oregon Constitution's remedy clause, which provides that there must be a remedy for every harm recognized by the law. The court provided a lengthy and scholarly dissertation that traced the development of the remedy clause from the Magna Carta through adoption of the Oregon Constitution in 1859 to the present. The court found that the major contributing cause standard applied in workers compensation occupational disease cases is higher than the causation standard applied in common law tort theories. This standard, coupled with the exclusive remedy provision, created a situation where the plaintiff was left without any remedy for injury to a constitutionally protected right. The court deemed this lack of redress to be unconstitutional and allowed the employee to proceed with an action for damages against his employer.[109]

While not using the explicit term of major contributing cause, provisions such as major cause, predominate cause, or prevailing cause can be found in a number of other statutes. In 2005, the **Missouri** legislature enacted a provision whereby an injury by occupational disease is compensable only *"if the occupational exposure was the prevailing factor in causing both the resulting medical condition and disability. The 'prevailing factor' is defined to be the primary factor, in relation to any other factor, causing both the resulting medical condition and disability."*[110]

The constitutionality of the prevailing factor standard was raised when the Missouri Supreme Court considered a challenge brought by a group of labor organizations regarding amendments to the workers compensation statute that were designed to accomplish a more restrictive definition of accident, the heightened burden on employees to prove causation, and the complete denial of compensation for particular injuries. These labor organizations claimed that the amendments violated due process, violated the Missouri Constitution's open courts provision, and lacked a rational basis for the reduction in benefits available to employees.

---

[108] Oregon Constitution Article I §10
[109] *Smothers v. Gresham Transfer, Inc.*, 332 Or. 83 (2001)
[110] Mo. Rev. Stat. § 287.067

Upon review, the Supreme Court of Missouri found that the labor organizations had legally protectable interests but the Court also held that because the plaintiffs could not show that any person had actually been injured by the new amendments, the constitutional and due process claims were not ripe for judicial review. The court, however, did find the employees' request for declaratory judgment regarding the exclusivity requirements of the Act to be justiciable. On this claim the court ruled in favor of the labor organizations, holding that employees exempted from recovery under the workers' compensation statute because of the amended definitions of accident and injury were not bound by the Act's exclusivity clause. For this reason, the court held that these employees were entitled to pursue recovery for their injuries under common law negligence.[111]

As can be seen above, those efforts at cutting back on benefit entitlement has prompted legal challenges as to whether such actions negate the original *quid pro quo* of workers compensation. The *quid pro quo* being the injured worker foregoing the right to sue his or her employer for negligence following an industrial injury in exchange for which the injured worker is entitled to adequate benefit compensation without consideration for the issue of fault. As long as there is some benefit payable, is that sufficient to represent adequate benefit compensation?

Florida is also among those states that introduced provisions designed to place the burden on the injured workers to prove that the industrial accident was the major contributing cause of the injury. To be compensable the employee must prove that the nature of the employment was the major contributing cause of the occupational disease and that the major contributing cause must be shown by medical evidence only, as demonstrated by physical examination findings and diagnostic testing.[112] Fortunately, the Florida First District Court of Appeal carved out an important exception to the major contributing cause provision. The court ruled that an employee need not meet the rigorous major contributing cause standard when there is a pre-existing condition that is occupationally related.[113] In other words, pre-existing conditions resulting from compensable work-related accidents are not a factor in the denial of workers compensation benefits under the major contributing cause standard.

However, a Circuit Court ruling in Florida went much farther and challenged the constitutionality of the entire Florida workers compensation law. Not confined to the issue of major contributing cause, the ruling addressed the lack of certain disability benefits available to injured workers in certain instances, and included the provision requiring the injured worker to pay for a portion of medical costs once maximum medical improvement had been reached. The opinion was in response to an amendment to a request for Declaratory Relief where the Circuit Court had been requested to declare the exclusive remedy provision of the Florida Workers Compensation Act invalid because, among a series of other reasons, it violated the Florida Constitution.[114]

---

[111] *Missouri Alliance for Retired Ams. v. Dep't of Labor and Indus. Relations*, 277 S.W. 3d 670 (MO 2009)
[112] Fla. Stat. Ann. § 440.151
[113] *Pearson v. Paradise Ford*, 951 So.2d 12 (2007)
[114] *Padgett v. State of Florida, Office of the Attorney General,* Case No. 11-13661 CA 25. (2014)

The facts in the Florida case were uncontested. Elsa Padgett, an account clerk, tripped in a walkway in January 2012 when a co-worker left boxes on the floor. Already at retirement age, Padgett fell on her hip and sustained serious damage to her shoulder. Following shoulder replacement surgery, she remained in significant pain and was eventually forced to retire. She did not qualify for permanent total disability benefits and impairment benefits were not available. Because maximum medical improvement had been reached, Padgett was also responsible for a portion of the cost for her medical treatment.

In his ruling, Circuit Court Judge Cueto declared Florida's long-controversial workers' compensation law unconstitutional. The ruling noted that successive state legislatures had so diminished medical care and wage-loss benefits for injured workers that the statute now violated employees' fundamental rights. Judge Cueto went on to observe that the nearly 80-year-old law forces injured workers into a legal system so flawed it does not provide adequate medical care or dollars to replace lost wages. Except under rare circumstances, injured workers cannot sue their employers. "The benefits in the act have been so decimated," Cueto wrote, "that it no longer provides a reasonable alternative" to filing suit in civil court.

In the *Padgett* case, the issue of compensability was not in question. Rather, it was the issue of further benefits after maximum medical improvement had been reached. Unlike the cases mentioned previously in **Oregon** and **Missouri**, under the reforms adopted by the Florida legislature in 2003, an injured worker would have to wait until maximum medical improvement was reached before they knew if they were entitled to any continuing benefits. This precluded their ability to opt for either a tort or workers compensation recovery at the outset of the claim.

Though the Florida Attorney General chose not to intervene in the case, her office defended the statute, saying, "while some individual workers may be worse off with workers' compensation in a particular instance, others benefit greatly." The decision of the Circuit Court of Miami was appealed to the Florida Supreme Court and in a brief order dated December 22, 2015 the Florida Supreme Court denied the petition to review the *Padgett* decision and further added that no motion for rehearing will be entertained by the court.[115].

About 60 years ago, writing for the United States Supreme Court in Brown v. Allen (1953), Justice Jackson observed that, "we are not final because we are infallible, but we are infallible only because we are final." A paraphrase of this has been a favorite of Supreme Court scholars ever since: "The Court is not last because it is always tight, but it is always right because it is last." As a general rule, the Supreme Court is the end of the road for litigation. Its decision is the final word.[116]

EXPOSURE FOR NON-SUBSCRIBERS IN TEXAS

Texas remains the sole elective state for workers compensation coverage. (While Oklahoma has enacted a law designed to permit alternative coverage, this law still requires the employer to

---

[115] Fla. R. App. P. 9.330(d)(2)
[116] http://flojcc.blogspot.com/2015/12/the-florida-court-declines-review-of.html

provide benefits at least equal to those found in the state's workers compensation law.) In Texas, employers who purchase workers compensation insurance are identified as subscribers, while employers who elect not to purchase insurance from a licensed carrier or qualify as a self-insured entity are referred to as non-subscribers. While a subscriber is required to provide workers compensation benefits, the non-subscriber may choose to provide some form on occupational injury coverage where medical and income replacement benefits are generally limited, or to forgo any coverage for workplace injuries. The Texas Code clarifies that a non-subscriber is not entitled to the defenses that "the employee was guilty of contributory negligence, the employee assumed the risk of injury or death, or the injury or death was caused by the negligence of a fellow employee."[117]

A Texas Supreme Court ruling rendered in 2000 addressed the issue of comparative responsibility for a non-scribing employer. In the case before the Supreme Court, an employee suffered injuries as a result of a fall while descending a ladder. She sued her non-subscribing employer alleging that the store's negligence proximately caused her injuries. The employer contended that her conduct either caused or contributed to the incident which therefore entitled the employer to protection under the comparative responsibility statute. The court wrote that, *"comparative responsibility is the legislative successor to, and a natural subset of, contributory negligence, which section 406.033 precludes non-subscribers from relying on as a defense."* The court further noted, *"that allowing a comparative responsibility question would remove the very penalty – the abrogation of certain common-law defenses – that the Legislature intended would encourage employers to subscribe to workers compensation insurance."*[118]

To avoid negligence lawsuits stemming from workplace incidents, some non-subscribing employers developed a liability waiver to be signed by the employee in lieu of entitlement to workers compensation benefits. Following the introduction of these waivers, various courts in Texas have rendered a number of decisions. The Texas Court of Appeals in San Antonio rendered the first substantive decision holding in *Reyes v. Storage & Processors, Inc.* that the non-subscribing employers benefit plan was void and unenforceable because it violated public policy.[119]

Two subsequent decisions by the Court of Appeals in Amarillo were then rendered. In the first case cited as *Lawrence v. CDB Services, Inc.* the court upheld the use of a waiver contained in a non-subscriber's employee benefit plan. In the second decision, cited as *Lambert v. Affiliated Foods, Inc.*, the Affiliated Foods Employee Disability Plan provided coverage for both occupational and non-occupational injuries sustained by employees and the court determined that the two plans were not capable of comparison as was done in the *Reyes* decision.

The decisions in *Lawrence* and *Lambert* were combined for purposes of appeal to the Texas Supreme Court. In rendering their decision, the Supreme Court first commented on the earlier Court of Appeals decision in *Reyes* and then noted that the appeals court engaged in a substantive comparison of the respective benefits and concluded that the employer provided

---

[117] Tex. Code Ann. § 406.033
[118] *Kroger Stores v. Keng,* 23 S.W. 3d 347 (2000)
[119] *Reyes v. Storage & Processors, Inc.,* 995 S.W. 2d 722 (1999)

benefits were inferior to those provided under the law and were therefore void. The Supreme Court opined that engaging in such a qualitative, plan-by-plan evaluation is ill advised. Such an analysis is premised on the questionable presumption that the various benefits can in fact be compared. Furthermore, practical concerns arise when trying to determine whether one set of benefits is substantially equivalent to another.

In rendering their decision, the Supreme Court concluded that:

> *"The Texas Workers Compensation Act neither clearly prohibits nor clearly allows voluntary pre-injury employee elections to participate in non-subscribing employers' benefit plans in lieu of exercising common law remedies. And whether or not such elections should be held void on the theory that they contravene the general statutory scheme and thus violate public policy is a decision that we believe, absent clear legislative guidance and in light of numerous competing public policy concerns, is better left to the Legislature. Accordingly, we decline to invalidate the petitioners' elections on public policy grounds and affirm the court of appeals' judgments."*[120]

Another variant to limit the litigation rights of an injured employee of a non-subscriber is through the use of an arbitration clause. In a case stemming from a 1995 workplace injury, the employer was a non-subscriber. Prior to the injury, the employee had signed an Election and Agreement Form. This form allowed an employee to select a comprehensive coverage program in the event of an accident. In exchange for receipt of this comprehensive benefit package, any disputes were to be submitted to binding arbitration. Employees had the choice of a more basic benefit package which did not contain an arbitration provision. In this case, the employee signed up for the comprehensive coverage package, thus agreeing to binding arbitration. Following his work related injury, the employee filed suit against his employer. The trial court stayed the litigation ordering the parties to submit to arbitration. When the employee refused to submit to arbitration, the trial court dismissed the case.

On appeal, the employee argued that the contract requiring arbitration of claims for personal injury against the non-subscriber was not enforceable because it was unconscionable and against public policy. The Beaumont Court of Appeals disagreed and held that the arbitration agreement was properly obtained, was not unconscionable, and was not against public policy. Because the arbitration agreement was properly obtained, the trial court was required to compel arbitration and stay its own proceedings. The employee's only recourse against his employer was through arbitration.[121]

Recent estimates by the Texas Association of Non-subscribers indicate that approximately 114,000 employers – representing nearly one-half of all employers – operate as non-subscribers in Texas. It is also recognized that a responsible non-subscriber can implement a comprehensive program that provides occupational injury benefits to their employees even though such benefit plans may not be equal to the benefits available through the workers compensation program. In today's market, there are a multitude of insurance programs to choose from that provide medical

---

[120] *Lawrence v. CDB Services, Inc.*, 44 S.W. 3d 544 (2001)
[121] *Smith v. H. E. Butt Grocery Co.*, 18 S.W.3d 910 (2000)

benefits, wage replacement benefits, disability benefits and death benefits. While these programs are available, there are none that provide medical benefits without a dollar cap or indemnity benefits comparable to those available under virtually every other state workers compensation program.

In addition to purchasing an occupational accident insurance plan, which provides workplace injury benefits, a responsible non-subscriber also needs to consider workplace safety. This very important element is a must for any employer who elects to become a non-subscriber. It is also important to file the proper forms with the Texas Workers Compensation Commission (TWCC) and post the appropriate signs required when an employer becomes a non-subscriber.

In concluding this review of the subject of exclusive remedy, it is important to keep in mind that the exclusive remedy doctrine represents the cornerstone of the original workmen's compensation laws. The rationale was simple. The employee gave up the right to sue the employer at common law seeking a potentially large verdict in favor of a system that allowed the employee to receive benefits, albeit on a smaller scale, more quickly and without having to demonstrate fault on the part of the employer. Similarly, employers benefited inasmuch as their liability was limited and they no longer had the threat that a large damage award would devastate their business.

In certain limited instances, the exclusive remedy doctrine is anything but exclusive. Although the doctrine was designed to protect employers from having to defend costly lawsuits for work-related injuries, over the years the courts have managed to carve out a number of exceptions to the rule. The attacks on the doctrine are not new or surprising. Almost since its inception, there have been determined attempts in dozens of jurisdictions to circumvent the doctrine. The motivation is obvious – the common law system generally affords a more lucrative recovery for both the injured party and the attorney. With the erosion of the rule, some employers may be wondering whether they have lost the benefit of the original bargain.

BAD FAITH AND UNFAIR CLAIM PRACTICES

As stated previously, the workers compensation system was basically designed to be non-adversarial and for the insurer and/or benefit administrator to deliver benefits both timely and in the proper amount. The intent was for benefits to be delivered to an injured employee for covered and compensable injuries with a minimum of hassle and/or delay.[122] Insurance law is clear that a workers compensation insurer cannot wrongfully deny or delay the payment of workers compensation benefits. Despite this, many benefit administrators engage in bad faith practices such as:

- Disputing or delaying benefits without providing the injured worker a valid reason.

- Forcing an injured worker to compromise and accept a low-ball offer.

---

[122] Hrendon, Everette Lee, Jr., "Workers' Comp and Bad Faith" located at the National Underwriter website - propertycasualty360.com.

- Refusing to pay benefits or stopping paying for necessary medical care.

- Holding back benefits even as you go through the appeals process and ultimately win your claim[123].

Bad faith may be defined as "the fraudulent deception of another person; the intentional or malicious refusal to perform some duty or contractual obligation."[124]

In the instance where benefits are not properly (and promptly) rendered, many states provide for penalties and fines while still retaining the exclusive remedy provision for those responsible for providing the benefits. In nearly half the states and the **District of Columbia**,[125] the courts have held that the workers compensation insurer is entitled to immunity under the exclusive remedy provisions of the relevant state workers compensation act.

For example, **California** can and will impose fines and penalties but does not allow bad faith claims. The California Workers Compensation Law provides that, *"When payment of compensation has been unreasonably delayed or refused, either prior to or subsequent to the issuance of an award, the amount of the payment unreasonably delayed or refused shall be increased up to 25 percent or up to ten thousand dollars ($10,000), whichever is less.*[126]

In a case before the California Supreme Court, it was held *"that the only satisfactory excuse for delay in payment of disability benefits, whether prior to or subsequent to an award, is genuine doubt from a medical or legal standpoint as to liability for benefits, and that the burden is on the employer or his carrier to present substantial evidence on which a finding of such doubt may be based."*[127] Thus, the key elements for purposes of establishing a penalty remain a genuine medical or legal doubt and substantial evidence produced by the employer or carrier to support the doubt.

In **New Mexico**, If unfair claim processing or bad faith has occurred in the handling of a particular claim, the claimant is to be awarded, in addition to any benefits due and owing, a benefit penalty not to exceed 25 percent of the benefit amount ordered to be paid. [128]

---

[123] https://doylelawfirm.com/workers-compensation-bad-faith/
[124] The Free Dictionary by Farlex
[125] Alabama, Arkansas, California, Connecticut, District of Columbia, Georgia, Idaho, Illinois, Indiana, Kentucky, Louisiana, Massachusetts, Minnesota, Missouri, Nebraska, New Mexico, New York, Pennsylvania, Rhode Island, South Carolina and Washington.
[126] Cal. Labor Code § 5814
[127] *Kerley v. Workmen's Comp. App. Bd.*, 4 Cal. 3d 223 (1971)
[128] N.M. Stat. Ann. § 52-1-28.1 B.

During the 2013 legislative session, the **Tennessee** legislature, among a number of other administrative and procedural changes, enacted a provision whereby a bad faith penalty may be assessed against an employer for failure to reimburse medical expenses paid by the employee or failure to provide reasonable and necessary medical expenses and treatment. Such penalty shall be a sum not exceeding 25 percent of such expenses.

The general rule in **New Jersey** allows no direct action available to an injured employee against the employer, or against the employer's insurer when the insurer does what is required under the law. The New Jersey Appellate Division has repeatedly concluded that there are no damages for pain or suffering under the New Jersey workers compensation law. In a recent claim before the Appellate Division, the insurer had stipulated that the employee's injuries were compensable, and began paying compensation, eventually providing payments totaling over $500,000. Years after compensation benefits began, the employee alleged that the insurer had failed to comply with a judicial order to pay certain outstanding medical expenses and other fees. According to the allegations, the persistent refusal to pay these amounts resulted in delays of possible medical treatment and a worsening of his medical condition.

Affirming the rulings of two lower courts, the Supreme Court of New Jersey ruled that a tort action could not be maintained. Assuming that the insurer's failure to pay comply with judicial orders was wrongful and wanton, New Jersey law does not permit a tort action to be maintained for the insurer's failure to comply with an order to pay benefits. The Supreme Court noted that recent legislative amendments specifically address the problem of non-compliance by insurance carriers. These amendments added new remedies, including contempt orders that may be issued by workers compensation courts and the possibility of additional compensation. These new remedies did not, however, in their final form, authorize workers compensation courts to refer such situations for adjudication in civil courts. Therefore, the workers compensation system, and its additional penalties and remedies for an insurer's unlawful non-compliance, are the exclusive remedy in this case.[129]

The **Alabama** Supreme Court has held on a number of occasions that bad faith claims are barred by the exclusive remedy provisions in the Alabama Workers Compensation Act. However, the Supreme Court has allowed the tort of outrage to proceed but only in very limited, fact specific situations. In order to establish a claim for outrage, a plaintiff must prove that the defendant's conduct was intentional or reckless, that it was extreme and outrageous, and that it caused emotional distress so severe that no reasonable person could be expected to endure it. The Supreme Court has said that a plaintiff must demonstrate that the defendant engaged in *"conduct so outrageous in character and so extreme in degree as to go beyond all possible bounds of decency, and to be regarded as atrocious and utterly intolerable in a civilized society."* This test is applied strictly, *"thereby allowing an outrage claim to go to the jury only in egregious cases."* The court has also noted that, *"in order to create a jury question on the tort of outrage, there must exist 'sufficient evidence from which permissible inferences could be drawn to support a finding of the extreme conduct necessary to constitute outrageous conduct.'"*[130]

---

[129] *Stancil v. ACE USA,* 211 N.J. 276 (N.J., Aug. 1, 2012)
[130] *Davis v. Liberty Mutual Ins. Co.,* 2007 U.S. Dist. LEXIS 49685 (2007)

In a **Kentucky** case, an injured worker, after settling his claim for workers compensation benefits with the insurer, sued the insurer for bad faith in refusing to pay and delaying payments for medical treatment. The injured worker also alleged that the insurer's bad faith had worsened his injuries requiring additional medical treatment. The insurer moved to dismiss for lack of jurisdiction, arguing that the suit was barred by the workers' compensation exclusive remedy provisions. The trial court summarily denied the motion and the Kentucky Supreme Court held that the workers compensation law shielded a covered employer and its insurer from any liability outside of the workers compensation remedy to a covered employee for damages arising out of a work-related injury. [131]

Many courts have ruled that the workers compensation carrier has a duty of good faith and fair dealing to the injured worker under the workers compensation policy in the same manner as to the named insured under any other insurance policy or contract. If and when these legislative measures fail, some of the legislatures or the courts may conclude that a stronger measure must be taken; namely to allow bad faith tort claims to be filed outside of the workers comp administrative system. The rationale expressed by some courts has been that the injury or damage caused by the claims handling arouse out of handling the claim as opposed to arising out of or in the course of the injured workers' employment.

In a number of states, the courts have reasoned that subsequent to the workers compensation accident and injury, if the unreasonable claims handling causes additional pain, suffering, distress or damages in addition to the initial comp injury, the responsible party can be sued under a tort theory for knowingly, wilfully, or recklessly inflicting injury or damage. Certain states will allow the tort claim for bad faith only if the injured worker prevails within the workers compensation system, whereas other states will allow suit for damages because of unreasonable delay and or denial even if the claim is ultimately held to be non-compensable.

The fifteen states that do allow bad faith claims generally require that the acts of the employer/carrier rise above the level of mere negligence. Acts require a level of both negligence and knowing unreasonableness, such as wilful, wanton, conscious, or reckless disregard of the consequences of the action. Some states, **Hawaii** for example, will allow bad faith tort claims to be pursued if the actions of the claim's personnel meet the negligence standard of unreasonably denying or delaying benefits.

In **Arizona**, if a claim that a compensation carrier acted in bad faith is made in the Industrial Commission, penalties may be imposed by the Commission upon the carrier of 25 per cent of the benefit amount ordered to be paid or $500, whichever is more. A history or pattern of violations can result in a penalty of up to $1,000 per violation. If instead, a lawsuit alleging bad faith is filed in court, the injured employee may seek substantial damages in addition to the cost of his/her medical care and lost wages, including compensatory damages for pain, exacerbation of the injury, emotional distress etc., as well as costs and attorneys' fees. By filing a workers compensation bad faith action in court, the injured employee may also seek an award of punitive damages. To win in court, an injured worker suing for bad faith must effectively prove the objective unreasonableness of a carrier's conduct and the carrier's subjective awareness of the

---

[131] *Kentucky Employers Mutual Ins. v. Coleman*, 2007 KY LEXIS 167 (2007)

unreasonableness of its conduct. Bad faith may exist if in the investigation, evaluation, and processing of the claim, the insurer acted unreasonably and either knew or was conscious of the fact that its conduct was unreasonable.[132]

In an article appearing in the January 22, 2004 edition of the *Black Hills Pioneer,* a former nursing home worker was awarded more than $12 million in a judgment against three insurance companies that denied her workers compensation claim. A Rapid City, **South Dakota** jury returned its verdict awarding $60,000 in compensatory damages and $12 million in punitive damages following a four-day trial in federal court. Suit was originally filed in U.S. District Court in Rapid City in July 2001. Her attorneys accused the companies of bad-faith dealing with Torres, barratry, abuse of process, and interference with business and contract relations.

The case centered around the insurance carriers incentive program that offered bonuses to claims workers who lowered payouts on claims. The program offered workers end-of-year bonuses of as much as 20 percent of their pay if they reduced overall payouts from one year to the next. Her attorneys argued that the program created an improper conflict of interest for claims adjusters, who are supposed to be motivated by fairness to claimants, not cost control for insurance companies. While the $12 million jury verdict received a great deal of attention, the decision was not the final say inasmuch as jury verdicts involving punitive damages must be reviewed by a federal court and judges have the authority to reduce or eliminate the awards.[133]

> **Avoiding Bad Faith** – The two principal elements of a bad faith claim are an unreasonable claim decision, and knowledge on the part of the company or administrator that the decision was unreasonable, or demonstration that the company failed to conduct an adequate investigation to determine whether its decision was reasonable or not.
>
> The workers comp system in the various states will work if all participants are honest and trustworthy. When parties to the system forget and depart from the philosophy and purpose of the workers compensation system is when problems arise which can lead to fines, penalties, audits or bad faith claims.
>
> **The Duty to Investigate** – If the worker makes a claim for a non-existent, inflated or non-work-related injury, then the defendants – the employer, carrier, and claims adjuster – hold the purse strings, most of the power and have a huge bank account with which to investigate and prove that the claim is bogus. There is a definite disparity of bargaining power between the employer/carrier and the injured worker. The employer/carrier must, as many courts have ruled, act in good faith and deal fairly with the parties to the insurance contract, including the injured worker.
>
> If there is a reasonable basis to believe that the claim does not arise out the employment and/or did not occur in the course of employment, then the defendants have a duty to investigate and deny if appropriate. Delaying or denying benefits is appropriate if and

---

[132] *Zilisch v. State Farm Mutual Auto Ins. Co.*, 995 P.2d 276, 280 (2000)
[133] *Torres v. Travelers Insurance Co., et al.*, No. 01-5056 (2004)

only if the defendants promptly, properly, and objectively investigate and evaluate the claim and document the basis for delay or denial.

The defendants should not force the injured worker to file for a hearing to collect benefits, unless the defendants have a genuine and reasonable belief, based on a proper and timely investigation, and have documented a reasonable basis to contest the claim as non-compensable.

Paying Claims, Not Bolstering Profits – The temptation on the part of one or more of the defendants to delay or deny comp benefits to further their own financial gain can lead to the mishandling of legitimate claims. The employer, carrier or adjusting outfit may have an incentive or bonus program tied to the reducing the number of comp claims or reducing the benefits paid.

In the article, "Slouching to Gomorrah: Adjuster Pay Plans and Bad Faith," Kevin Quinley, CPCU, stated "The job of the claims department is to pay claims . . . The adjuster's job is not to turn a profit, to advance a company's A.M. Best rating or to max out on the incentive compensation plan. Once these factors start seeping into the adjuster's consciousness at the file-handling level, mischief creeps in. Dysfunctional incentives drive suspect claim practices."

The delay or denial of benefits may result from an understaffed claims office, an overworked adjuster, a poorly trained adjuster, a vindictive employer, an improper incentive program, or any of a number of other unacceptable reasons. Some of the claims handling issues that have resulted from these reasons and others led legislatures to impose fines and penalties and audits on defendants in an attempt to convince the defendants to properly adhere to the intent of the workers' comp system. A problem with the use of fines and penalties is that some states have the fines and penalties payable to the governmental body and not to the injured worker.

In addition to the two principal elements of bad faith denoted above, the unfair claims act upon which most state laws are modeled prohibits the following actions by an insurer (or self-insured employer):

- Misrepresentation of coverage.

- Failure to communicate promptly on claims.

- Procrastination of good faith settlements when liability is clear.

- A history of appealing awards in order to pressure claimants into accepting smaller settlements.

In the handling of a claim, if there is a reasonable basis or red flag indicating possible non-compensability, then an investigation should be promptly initiated and completed. The adjuster should give at least equal consideration to the injured worker and try as hard to prove compensability as the steps taken to prove non-compensability. The claims handler should not focus solely on finding an excuse or basis for denial or delay. It would be bad faith to ignore facts supporting compensability while trying to find facts to support a denial. In the same fashion, a denial or delay in providing benefits should not be based on speculation, rumor, or ambiguous information.

CHAPTER TWELVE

OTHER ECONOMIC SECURITY PROGRAMS

The development of our present system of social insurance has been pragmatic and incremental. Proposals for change generally have been formulated in response to specific problems rather than a broad national agenda. A second characteristic of our system has been its high degree of decentralization. While certain programs are almost entirely federal with respect to administration, financing, or both, others are limited to only state or local control. The private sector has also served to play a significant role in the provision of health and medical care and income maintenance benefits.

In this country, as with most industrial countries, social insurance had its genesis with the enactment of workmen's compensation laws. While the workmen's compensation programs served as a model for social insurance at the state level, the severe Depression of the 1930's prompted action for some form of social insurance at the federal level. In 1935, President Roosevelt proposed to Congress economic security legislation that ultimately came to fulfillment with passage of the Social Security Act in 1936. This law established two social insurance programs on a national scale to help address the financial risks associated with old age.

While initially of a fairly limited scope, the old-age program was barely in full operation before significant changes were adopted. The second major component of the original Social Security law was a system of unemployment insurance. Taking the lead from a program already in operation in **Wisconsin**, the Social Security Act included a coordinated unemployment program designed to provide partial income replacement to regularly employed members of the labor force who became involuntarily and temporarily unemployed.

World War II also served as an impetus among employers to provide various forms of employer provided group insurance including life insurance and non-occupational health and disability protection. As legislation enacted during and following the war froze wages, private employers began to offer such forms of protection as an inducement to hire and retain workers. While these forms of insurance were voluntarily provided by the employer, many larger employers were encouraged by the competitive forces of the marketplace to provide and expand such protection.

During the 1940s, again in response to the perceived need for protection against the economic consequences of non-occupational events, four states adopted legislation providing for weekly cash benefits to workers who were temporarily disabled because of non-occupational injury or illness. It was not until 1969 that a fifth state joined this select group.

Other social insurance programs developed during the last century were designed to address and expand upon the medical and economic needs of the retired, the poor and the disabled. In 1956, disability insurance was added to the Social Security program in order to protect against the loss of income in cases of total disability. In 1965, the Medicare and Medicaid programs were introduced.

The development and expansion of each of these benefit programs, designed to replace a portion of prior earnings or address the need for health care, has resulted in potential duplication of benefits where the coverage under one program may serve to overlap or duplicate the coverage available through another program. This was not the original intent or design of the various programs but arose as a by-product of the extension of benefits within individual programs.

This potential overlap of benefits was not confined to those benefit programs designed to provide some form of income replacement. The potential for benefit duplication also exists in the area of medical care. While perhaps of less significance, duplication of coverage may also exist under other coverage's such as unemployment insurance, short and long term disability programs, and other programs. This occurs where the work-relatedness of a particular injury or disease is not precisely defined or the program applies different legal tests in determination of the inability to work. Unless the potential for benefit duplication is recognized and addressed directly, situations will exist where unnecessary benefit duplication will occur when workers compensation benefits are being paid.

Examination of the roles and interplay between existing economic security programs demonstrates the difficulty of looking at any single program in a vacuum. Each program represents an individual pillar in the multitude of pillars that serve to support the American system of social insurance. The system has been shaped both by long-standing tradition and by changing economic and social conditions. At both the state and federal level there has been recognition that certain risks in an increasingly industrial economy could best be met through a social insurance approach to public welfare. In other words, contributory financing of social insurance programs serves to ensure that protection is available as a matter of right as contrasted with a public assistance or welfare approach whereby only those in need qualify for benefits.

The following serves to provide a high level review of the more prominent programs along with examining the interface between these programs and the workers compensation program.

OLD AGE, SURVIVORS AND DISABILITY INSURANCE (OASDI)

The Old Age, Survivors, and Disability Insurance (OASDI) program – referred to by most Americans as Social Security - is the largest income-maintenance program in the United States. Based on several social insurance principles, the program provides monthly benefits designed to replace, in part, the loss of income following retirement, disability, or death.

Today, Social Security coverage is virtually universal, with nearly 96 percent of the workforce in this country covered. Employers and workers finance the program through a payroll tax that is levied under the Federal Insurance Contribution Act (FICA) and the Self-Employment Contribution Act (SECA). Tax deposits are formally entrusted to the Federal Old-Age and Survivors Insurance Trust Fund, the Federal Disability Insurance Trust Fund, the Federal Hospital

Insurance Trust Fund, or the Federal Supplementary Medical Insurance Trust Fund. The annual report by the program's Board of Trustees noted the following: in 2019, 54 million people were receiving Social Security benefits, while 157 million people were paying into the fund. Of those receiving benefits, 44 million were receiving retirement benefits and 10 million disability benefits.

Social Security benefits are financed through a dedicated payroll tax - Federal Insurance Contribution Act (FICA) – where employers and employees each pay 6.2 percent of wages up to the taxable maximum of $142,800 in 2021. The self-employed pay 12.4 percent of wages up to the taxable maximum of $142,800.

Benefit eligibility for Social Security benefits requires fully insured status, which is obtained by acquiring a certain number of credits (also called quarters of coverage) from earnings in covered employment. The number of credits needed depends on the worker's age and the type of benefit. Workers may acquire up to four credits per year, depending on their annual covered earnings.

The Social Security Administration (SSA) uses a complex weighted formula to calculate benefits for each person. In 2021, the maximum monthly benefit is $3,148 for someone filing at full retirement age (age 62 years and two months). A higher maximum monthly amount of $3,895 applies to someone who files at age 70, while a lower maximum monthly amount of $2,324 applies to someone filing at age 62.

Social Security bases an individual's retirement and disability benefit on the amount of income on which paid Social Security taxes have been paid. This amount is referred to as covered earnings and workers average covered earnings over a period of years is the workers average indexed monthly earnings (AIME). A formula is applied to the AIME to calculate a primary insurance amount (PIA) -the base figure used in setting the benefit amount. The formula consists of fixed percentages of different amounts of income (called bend points, which are adjusted each year). For example, in 2020, 90 percent of the first $960 of a worker's AIME is added to the worker's PIA, plus 32 percent of the AIME from $960 to $5,785, plus 15 percent of the AIME over $5,785. These amounts are added up to come up with the worker's PIA. A special minimum PIA is payable to persons who have had covered employment or self-employment for many years at low earnings.

As a simple rule-of-thumb, workers who retire at their normal retirement age, with average earnings (the national average wage index for the current year), have 45 percent of their prior year's earnings replaced by Social Security benefits. For those with maximum earnings (160 percent of the national average wage index). the replacement rate is 25 percent. For minimum earners (45 percent of the national average wage index), the replacement rate is 61 percent.

Social Security benefits are subject to an annual cost-of-living adjustment. The amount of the annual adjustment is based on the percentage increase in the Consumer Price Index (CPI) in the third quarter of the current year relative to the corresponding quarter in the preceding year. Benefits are adjusted effective October 1 of each year.

Social Security Old Age and Retirement Benefits – Widespread unemployment and financial destitution stemming from the Great Depression operated as a catalyst prompting federal legislators to establish a program of social protection. The original Social Security law, enacted August 14, 1935, provided for retirement benefits and lump sum death payments for workers in commerce and industry. Monthly benefits to retired workers were limited to those ages 65 and older. In 1939, the original law was expanded to provide benefits for dependents of the retired worker - including a surviving wife age 65 or older. Survivorship benefits for widows and orphaned children also became part of that legislation.

Individuals are fully insured for retirement and survivor insurance if they have at least as many credits as the number of full calendar years elapsing after age 21 and before age 62, disability, or death, whichever occurs first. For persons reaching age 62 after 1990, 40 credits are needed to qualify for retirement benefits. For workers who die before acquiring fully insured status, certain survivor benefits are payable if they were currently insured – that is, they have acquired six credits of coverage in the 13-quarter period ending with the quarter in which they died.

The normal retirement age (the age of eligibility for unreduced benefits) began to increase gradually from 65 to 67, beginning with workers who reached age 62 in the year 2000. The scheduled normal retirement age increased by two months per year in two stage increments until, beginning in 2022, the normal retirement age will be 67.

For workers retiring before their normal retirement age, monthly benefits are actuarially reduced to take account of the longer period during which benefits will be paid. Workers retiring before the normal retirement age will have benefits reduced by 5/9 of one percent for the first 36 months of receipt of benefits immediately preceding age 65, plus 5/12 of one percent for months in excess of 36 months resulting in a maximum reduction in benefits of 30 percent for those retiring at age 62. Benefits may also be recomputed if, after retirement, the worker has additional earnings that would result in a higher PIA.

Social Security retirement benefits are not subject to be reduced where the retired employee is also receiving workers compensation benefits. Where a worker receiving income replacement benefits through the workers compensation retires and is eligible and receiving Social Security retirement benefits, there will be no offset of benefits unless the state has enacted legislation providing for such an offset.

To this end, a number of jurisdictions have enacted legislation designed to terminate or reduce entitlement to certain workers compensation benefits following either the injured employee reaching retirement age or where the claim for benefits is filed following retirement. Probably the most explicit approach to benefit termination at the time of retirement can be found in **Kentucky**. For injuries occurring on and after December 12, 1996, all income benefits payable for disability terminate on the date on which the employee qualifies for normal old-age Social Security retirement benefits, or after two years, whichever occurs last. Similarly, all income benefits payable to spouses and dependents will terminate when they qualify for Social Security retirement benefits.[134] A similar provision which discontinued workers compensation benefits "after the employee became eligible for normal old age benefits under the Federal Old Age" program was held to be a constitutionally valid attempt to prevent the duplication of wage loss.[135]

A number of other states have enacted provisions designed to terminate entitlement to select disability benefits once the injured worker attains retirement age. In some instances, where the workplace injury with accompanying disability is sustained during the period of retirement, the worker remains eligible for certain types of disability along with necessary medical.

> **Montana** – Where the claimant is receiving, or is entitled to receive, Social Security retirement benefits, the claimant is considered to be retired. When the claimant is retired, he/she is no longer entitled to workers compensation benefits for permanent partial disability (except for an impairment award), permanent total disability and rehabilitation benefits. The claimant continues to be entitled to temporary total compensation, any award for impairment and medical benefits.[136] If a retired worker is gainfully employed and sustains a work-related injury, the worker is entitled to temporary total disability benefits, any impairment award, and medical benefits.
>
> **Minnesota** – Permanent total disability benefits cease at age 67 because the employee is presumed retired from the labor force.[137] In the case of those entitled to temporary total disability benefits, such benefits are to cease at retirement.[138] In both instances, the employee may rebut these presumptions.
>
> **Arkansas** – Permanent total disability benefits are payable during the period of continuing total disability until the employee reaches the age of 65. For those who sustain a workplace injury resulting in disability after age 60, permanent total disability benefits are payable for a period not to exceed 260 weeks.[139] The constitutionality of this provision was affirmed by the courts in 1997.[140]
>
> **Florida** – Entitlement to permanent total disability benefits, where the presumption of permanent total disability is not listed in the statute, cease when the employee reaches age 75, unless the employee is not eligible for Social Security disability or retirement benefits because the employee's compensable injury has prevented the employee from working sufficient quarters to be eligible for such benefits, notwithstanding any age limits. If the accident occurred on or after the employee reaches age 70, benefits are

---

[134] Ky. Rev. Stat. Ann. § 342.730
[135] *Brooks v. Island Creek Coal Co.* 678 SW2d 791 (1984)
[136] Mont. Code Ann. § 39-71-710
[137] Minn. Stat. Ann. § 176.101 Subd. 4
[138] Minn. Stat. Ann. § 176.101 Subd. 8
[139] Ark. Code Ann. § 11-9-522 (f)(1)
[140] *Golden v. Westark Community College* 948 SW2d 108 (1997)

payable during the continuance of permanent total disability, not to exceed five years following the determination of permanent total disability. [141]

Tennessee – The law limits permanent total disability benefits to age 65 and further specifies that permanent total disability claims filed after age 60 are limited to a maximum of 260 weeks and are further reduced by any Social Security retirement benefits.[142] The Tennessee Supreme Court, after reviewing the holdings in a number of other states, held that the provision did not violate the claimant's equal protection rights.[143]

While not necessarily terminating entitlement to worker's compensation benefits upon retirement, **Massachusetts** allows that any employee (at least 65 years of age) who has been out of the workforce for at least two years and is eligible for federal Social Security old-age benefits is not entitled to compensation for total incapacity or partial incapacity.[144] This is a presumption of non-entitlement that may not be overcome by the employee's uncorroborated testimony.

Social Security Disability Insurance (SSDI) – In 1956, disability insurance was added to the Social Security program to protect against the loss of income in cases of total disability. When initially enacted, disability benefits were payable only to persons age 50 or older. Subsequent amendments allowed for disability benefits to be payable to younger employees

To be eligible for SSDI benefits, a worker must be fully insured and must meet a test of substantial recent covered work — that is, they must have credit for work in covered employment for at least 20 of the 40 calendar quarters ending with the quarter the disability began. Younger workers disabled before age 31 may qualify for benefits under a special insured status requirement. They must have credits in one-half the calendar quarters after age 21, up to the date of their disability, or, if disabled before age 24, one-half the quarters in the three years ending with the quarter of disability

For purposes of entitlement, disability is defined as *"the inability to engage in any substantial gainful activity by reason of any medically determinable physical or mental impairment that can be expected to result in death or that has lasted or can be expected to last for a continuous period of not less than 12 months".* [145] A person's age, education, and work experience are considered along with medical evidence in making a determination of disability. The impairment must be of a degree of severity that renders the individual unable to engage in any kind of substantial gainful work that exists in the national economy. Consideration is not taken as to whether such work exists in the immediate area in which the individual lives, if a specific job vacancy exists, or if that individual would be hired upon application for the work.

---

[141] Fla. Stat. Ann. § 440.15 (1)(b) 5
[142] Tenn. Code Ann. § 50-6-207
[143] *Vogel v. Wells Fargo Guard Services* 937 SW2d 856 (1996)
[144] Mass. Gen. Laws Ann. Ch. 152, § 35E
[145] 42 USC § 423(d)(1)

Although Social Security disability benefits and workers compensation are the nation's two largest disability benefit programs, the two programs are quite different. Workers are eligible for workers compensation benefits from their first day of employment, but Social Security disability benefits begin after a five-month waiting period and are paid only to workers who have a substantial work history. Workers compensation provides benefits for both short-term and long-term disabilities and for partial as well as total disabilities. These benefits cover only disabilities arising out of and in the course of employment. In contrast, Social Security disability benefits are paid only to workers who have long-term impairments that preclude any gainful work, regardless of whether the disability was work-related.

The current federal statute requires that the amount of Social Security disability insurance (SSDI) benefits be reduced when the combined amounts of SSDI benefits and state workers compensation benefits exceed 80 percent of the employee's average current earnings.[146] This offset of state workers compensation benefits against federal disability benefits prevents a disabled employee who is receiving both Social Security disability benefits and workers compensation disability benefits from receiving more than eighty percent of his/her pre-injury wages. At the same time, the coordination provision allows for SSDI to supplement benefits in those cases where the workers compensation benefit is less than 80 percent of pre-injury pay.

An example illustrating the computation for an average wage earner may serve to clarify how the offset provision operates. (For purposes of this example, the workers compensation benefit is shown as a monthly sum even though in the majority of states, compensation benefits are computed on a weekly basis.) Employee X is entitled to a monthly Social Security disability primary insurance amount (PIA) of $1,024 and a monthly workers compensation benefit of $1,652 based on monthly earnings of $2,478. In this example the monthly earnings correspond to the workers average current earnings (ACE). 80 percent of that ACE is $1,982. Because the $1,982 is higher than the monthly Social Security disability benefit ($1,024), the monthly workers compensation benefit ($1,652) is subtracted from the $1,982. This leaves the employee with a combined monthly benefit of $1,982 made up of the $1,652 workers compensation benefit plus a reduced Social Security disability benefit of $330.

The reduction in the Social Security disability benefit will continue until the month the worker reaches his/her normal retirement age (or the worker applies for early retirement), or the month workers compensation disability benefits are discontinued, whichever comes first.

There are several ways, depending upon specific state legislation, in which an offset can be applied where Social Security benefits and periodic workers compensation benefits are being paid concurrently. In addition to the federal offset provision in the instance of concurrent periodic benefits, the Social Security program has adopted specific provisions that address the resolution of a workers compensation claim through a lump sum settlement.

---

[146] 42 USC § 424a(a)

As a starting point, itt is important to recognize that prior to February 1981, only a minority of the states had enacted reverse offset provisions whereby workers compensation benefits were reduced when the worker was also receiving Social Security disability benefits. The Omnibus Reconciliation Act of 1981 ended the opportunity for additional states to enact such an offset provision. While the offset at the federal level is limited to Social Security disability benefits, no similar provision at the federal level operates to offset state workers compensation benefits when Social Security retirement or survivor benefits are being paid.

So long as the state had a reverse offset provision in place prior to 1981, an offset may be taken against Social Security disability benefits. States that apply a reverse offset might not apply it to all types of worker's compensation benefits. Fifteen states have some kind of reverse offset rule, even if it does not apply to all types of worker's compensation benefits.

- Three states provide for the reduction of certain compensation benefits by one-half the federal retirement benefit. **Maine** applies the reduction to total or partial incapacity benefit[147]. **Michigan** applies the reduction to cases involving total incapacity, partial incapacity, and lump sums[148]. **Pennsylvania** confines the offset to total disability benefits provided that the offset does not apply if Social Security old age benefits were received prior to the compensable injury.[149]

- In a unique approach, for injuries occurring after 1993, **South Dakota** prescribes that permanent total benefits are subject to offset where the employee is receiving Social Security old age benefits.[150] The amount payable after the offset is to equal 150 percent of the compensation to which the employee is entitled less the old-age insurance benefit. This offset is not applicable where the employee was entitled to or receiving old-age benefits at the time of injury.

- In an interesting twist in approach, **Minnesota** enacted what might be described as a threshold prior to the application of any benefit offset. Minnesota requires that $25,000 in permanent total benefits be paid before further benefits can be reduced by the federal disability, retirement or survivors benefit.[151] In the case of death, combined benefits from workers compensation and government survivor benefits may not exceed 100 percent of the weekly wage earned by the deceased worker at the time of the injury causing death.[152]

- Another unique approach is found in **Utah** where, through the introduction of a threshold, 312 weeks of permanent total disability must transpire before continuing benefits will be reduced by one-half the federal old-age benefit. In the case of death,

---

[147] Me. Rev. Stat. Ann. Title 39-A, § 221
[148] Mich. Stat. Ann. § 418:354
[149] Pa. Stat. Ann. Title 77 § 71
[150] S.D. Codified Laws Ann. § 62-4-7
[151] Minn. Stat. Ann. § 176.101 Subd. 4
[152] Minn. Stat. Ann. § 176.111 Subd. 21

benefits payable to a wholly dependent person, following an initial 312 week period, are to be reduced by one-half of any federal Social Security death benefit.[153]

As observed when reviewing Social Security offset provisions, when workers compensation benefits are being paid periodically, the general rule is that the injured worker may not receive combined workers compensation and Social Security disability benefits that are more than 80 percent of his/her average current earnings in the highest of the last five years before becoming disabled. Furthermore, through reference to periodic benefits, the Social Security Act encompasses virtually every conceivable form of workers compensation indemnity benefit. To that end, a lump sum settlement (e.g., stipulation, compromise and release, commutation) is regarded as a form of periodic payment.

A lump sum settlement can be in the form of a commutation or compromise agreement whereby the insurer is released from future liability. Such a settlement is a substitute for periodic payments and is subject to the offset. In this situation, the lump sum is prorated to reflect the monthly rate that would have been paid had the lump sum award not been made. Medical and legal expenses incurred by the worker in connection with the workers compensation or public disability benefit claim may be excluded in computing the offset. A payment representing past-due periodic payments which simply brings payments up to date is not considered a lump sum settlement for purposes of calculating the Social Security disability offset.

For purposes of calculating the Social Security offset, the workers compensation lump sum amount is treated as an amount which would otherwise have been paid periodically. To obtain a reasonable and equitable result, current law permits the Social Security Administration to substitute a reasonable periodic payment rate for the lump sum. Where the settlement agreement does not establish the amount of the periodic payment, the rate paid prior to the settlement payment is used. If no periodic payments were made prior to the settlement, the state's maximum benefit schedule is applied. The state's maximum benefit rate may also be used pending verification of the weekly rate or the rate specified in the settlement agreement.

As a general rule, benefits that serve to bring the injured worker up to date are not considered as part of the lump sum amount for offset purposes, but are rather deemed a substitute for periodic payments and are subject to the same offset provisions as apply to workers compensation periodic benefits.

SUPPLEMENTAL SECURITY INCOME (SSI)

The Social Security Administration offers two types of benefits for disabled workers, Social Security Disability Insurance (SSDI) and Supplemental Security Income (SSI). While SSDI is available to those who have paid into the system through taxable income, SSI serves as a safety net for those who do not qualify for SSDI. SSI is for people who are 65 or older, as well as for

---

[153] Utah Code Ann. § 34A-2-413 and 34A-2-702

those of any age, including children, who are blind or who have disabilities, or have a condition that keeps them from working and is expected to last at least one year or result in death. There are different rules for children.

To qualify for the SSI benefit program, all of the following requirements must be met:

- Be at least age 65 OR be blind or disabled.

- Have limited income and resources.

- Be a citizen or a national of the United States or an alien who meets certain applicable requirements.

- Reside in one of the 50 states, District of Columbia, or the Northern Mariana Islands, except for a child of military parent(s) assigned to permanent duty anywhere outside the United States or certain students temporarily abroad.

Other factors that may affect eligibility include the persons marital status, monthly income from work and his/her bank balance.

The basic monthly SSI payment for 2021 is the same nationwide. It is $794 for one person and $1,191 for a couple. Recipients may be eligible for more if they live in a state that adds money to the federal SSI payment. If the family has other income, the amount received may be reduced. Seeing that SSI benefits are available to those who do not have a work history and qualify for SSDI, it is unlikely that these benefit recipients would be eligible for and receiving workers compensation benefits.

MEDICARE

Title XVIII of the Social Security Act, designated as Health Insurance for the Aged and Disabled, is commonly referred to as Medicare. As part of the Social Security amendments enacted in 1965, the Medicare legislation created a health insurance program for aged persons to complement the retirement, survivors, and disability insurance benefits available under the Social Security Act. When originally implemented in 1966, Medicare was limited to coverage of most persons age 65 or older. It was later amended to include those entitled to Social Security or Railroad Retirement disability benefits for at least 24 months, those persons with end-stage renal disease, and certain otherwise non-covered aged persons who elected to pay a premium for coverage.

Medicare has traditionally been composed of two parts – Part A and Part B. It was later expanded to include Part C and D. The following summarizes the protection under each Part:

Part A Coverage – Covers hospital services. Hospital services include inpatient hospital care, up to 100 days of care in a skilled nursing facility (not custodial or long-term care), home health care services, and hospice care. In 2020, Part A coverage afforded protection to

60.9 million people (52.3 million aged and 8.7 million disabled enrollees).[154] Part A benefit payments totaled $167.6 billion for 2004. Insurance companies are contracted to examine and pay claims and ensure the accuracy of payments. There are no monthly premiums payable for Part A coverage.

Part B Coverage – The medical insurance portion of Medicare that serves to cover medically necessary physicians' and surgeons' services, including some covered services provided by chiropractors, podiatrists, dentists and optometrists, and outpatient care. Other covered services include laboratory services, medical equipment, and outpatient medical services. Almost all those entitled to Part A coverage elect to enroll in Part B. Like Part A coverage, insurance companies are contracted to examine and pay claims and ensure the accuracy of payments. Part B coverage is obtained through payment of a standard monthly premium – $148.50 for 2021.

Part C Coverage – Also referred to as the Medicare Advantage Plans, Part C is an additional insurance option for people with original Medicare. Part C plans are offered by private companies approved by Medicare. With original Medicare, an individual is covered for Part A and Part B. Part C offers coverage for Medicare Parts A and B plus additional services, such as prescription drugs, dental, vision, and more. Medicare Advantage Plans may offer extra coverage, such as vision, hearing, dental, and/or health and wellness programs. Most include Medicare prescription drug coverage (Part D). Medicare pays a fixed amount for care every month to the companies offering Medicare Advantage Plans.

Part D Coverage – Beginning January 1, 2006, a new Medicare prescription drug coverage was made available to all beneficiaries who qualified for Medicare. Part D coverage is provided by a broad range of private plans. All plans must cover a wide range of listed prescription drugs (called a formulary where drug coverage plans place drugs into different levels called tiers). These tiers reflect different price ranges for the drugs. There is a monthly premium for all plans. Beneficiaries have the option of having the premium taken from their Social Security check, paying the premium directly, or having the premium taken directly from a bank account.

It should be noted that certain health care services are not covered by either Parts A or B. Non-covered services include dental care and dentures, eyeglasses, and hearing aids. However, some of these services may be covered under a Part C Medical Advantage Plan. In addition, long-term nursing care and custodial care are not covered under Medicare Plan. These last items are of increasing importance in the context of potential long-term and high-end costs for older individuals without long-term care insurance.

The United States spent nearly 800 billion dollars on the Medicare program in 2019. Medicare, however, has also significant income, which amounted also to some 800 billion dollars in 2019. It is estimated that almost 80 percent of this income was generated by general revenue and payroll taxes.[155] The current tax rate for Medicare is 1.45 percent for the employer and 1.45

---

[154] https://www.ncpssm.org/our-issues/medicare/medicare-fast-facts/
[155] https://www.statista.com/topics/1167/medicare/

percent for the employee, or 2.9 percent total. For those on Medicare there is a monthly premium for Part B coverage. Most people will pay the standard premium amount of $148.50 for 2021. An Income Related Monthly Adjustment Amount (IRMAA) is applied to those with high incomes.

The Medicare program is administered by the Centers for Medicare and Medicaid Services (CMS) within the federal Department of Health and Human Services. CMS has regional offices located in major cities throughout the United States. CMS contracts with private companies known as Medicare intermediaries which process Medicare claims. It also contracts with a private company to review and provide recommendations to the regional offices regarding proposed allocations of funds set aside out of workers compensation settlements to pay for future medical care.

Since its inception in 1965, Medicare coverage is secondary to other forms of medical insurance benefits, specifically including medical benefits available through workers compensation. The Social Security Act states that Medicare does not cover any medical items or services for which "payment has been made or can reasonably to be expected to be made under a workmen's compensation law or plan of the United States or a state…."[156]

However, Medicare may make a conditional payment where a workers compensation payer "has not made or cannot reasonably be expected to make payment with respect to such item or service promptly (as determined in accordance with regulations)."[157] A conditional payment is a payment that Medicare makes for services where another payer may be responsible. If a conditional payment has been made by Medicare and the benefit recipient or payer refuses to repay Medicare for care covered by workers compensation, there are four ways that Medicare can seek reimbursement of its conditional payments:

- Medicare has the right of a direct legal action against any entity that has the primary responsibility to pay for medical expenses as a result of a work injury.

- Medicare can intervene in any ongoing litigation. Through the right of intervention, Medicare can argue its entitlement to reimbursement within the actual workers compensation case.

- Medicare can claim an offset against any sums owed the entity who was responsible for refunding any conditional payments made by Medicare. If a medical provider accepted conditional payments and then failed to reimburse Medicare, Medicare can withhold future payments to offset any amount that is due Medicare.

- Finally, Medicare has the right of subrogation which means that it can be placed in the legal position of the beneficiary to recover conditional payments made from third parties (e.g., the employer or insurance carrier) who are responsible to pay benefits as a result of the work injury.[158]

---

[156] 42 USCA §1395y(2)(b)(2)(A)(ii)
[157] 42 USCA §1395y(2)(b)(2)(B)
[158] 42 U.S.C.§1395y (b)(2)(B)(iii)

Medicare Secondary Payer (MSP) is the term used when the Medicare program does not have primary payment responsibility on behalf of its beneficiaries - that is, when another entity has the responsibility for paying for medical care before Medicare. Until 1980, the Medicare program was the primary payer in all cases except those involving workers compensation or for care that was the responsibility of another government entity. With the addition of the MSP provisions in 1980 along with subsequent amendments, Medicare is secondary payer to group health plan insurance in specific circumstances, but is also secondary to liability insurance (including self-insurance), no-fault insurance, and workers compensation.

Where the responsibility for a workers compensation claim is in dispute and benefits will not be paid promptly, the provider, physician, or other supplier may bill Medicare as primary payer. If the item or service is reimbursable under Medicare rules, Medicare may pay conditionally, subject to later recovery if there is a subsequent settlement, judgment, award, or other payment.[159]

The settlement of a workers compensation claim through a lump sum settlement is addressed under Medicare provisions.[160] The law provides that the burden of future medical expenses in workers compensation cases may not be shifted to Medicare, and further provides that Medicare's interest must be considered in workers compensation settlements when future medical expenses are a component of the settlement.[161]

To this end, a Workers' Compensation Medicare Set-Aside Arrangement (WCMSA) is a financial agreement that allocates a portion of a workers' compensation settlement to pay for

---

[159] 42 C.F.R. § 411.21

[160] 42 CFR 411.46 - *(a) Lump-sum commutation of future benefits. If a lump-sum compensation award stipulates that the amount paid is intended to compensate the individual for all future medical expenses required because of the work-related injury or disease, Medicare payments for such services are excluded until medical expenses related to the injury or disease equal the amount of the lump-sum payment.*

(b) Lump-sum compromise settlement.

(1) A lump-sum compromise settlement is deemed to be a workers' compensation payment for Medicare purposes, even if the settlement agreement stipulates that there is no liability under the workers' compensation law or plan.
(2) If a settlement appears to represent an attempt to shift to Medicare the responsibility for payment of medical expenses for the treatment of a work-related condition, the settlement will not be recognized. For example, if the parties to a settlement attempt to maximize the amount of disability benefits paid under workers' compensation by releasing the workers' compensation carrier from liability for medical expenses for a particular condition even though the facts show that the condition is work-related, Medicare will not pay for treatment of that condition.

(c) Lump-sum compromise settlement: Effect on services furnished before the date of settlement. Medicare pays for medical expenses incurred before the lump-sum compromise settlement only to the extent specified in § 411.47.
(d) Lump-sum compromise settlement: Effect on payment for services furnished after the date of settlement.—

(1) Basic rule. Except as specified in paragraph (d)(2) of this section, if a lump-sum compromise settlement forecloses the possibility of future payment of workers' compensation benefits, medical expenses incurred after the date of the settlement are payable under Medicare.
(2) Exception. If the settlement agreement allocates certain amounts for specific future medical services, Medicare does not pay for those services until medical expenses related to the injury or disease equal the amount of the lump-sum settlement allocated to future medical expenses.

[161] 42 CFR § 411.47

future medical services related to the workers' compensation injury, illness, or disease. These funds must be depleted before Medicare will pay for treatment related to the workers compensation injury, illness, or disease.

The amount of the WCMSA is determined on a case-by-case basis and is subject to review by CMS, when appropriate. The amount of money required to be allocated to the set-aside account differs with each claim. As is typical in any negotiated settlement, the value of future medical expenses requires consideration of the individual's current health status, the age of the individual, the seriousness of the injury or illness, current healthcare needs, future expected healthcare needs, life expectancy, and prospects for the future (e.g., work, insurance, pain, etc.)

In situations where it is expected that the injured workers life expectancy may be shortened due to the workplace injury or some unrelated health problem or condition, written documentation may be submitted to CMS from an annuity company as to the injured workers rated age. A reduced life expectancy may serve to shorten the duration of medical care to be provided and, in turn, serve to reduce the amount of the set-aside arrangement. Once the CMS determined set aside amount is exhausted and accurately accounted for to CMS, Medicare will be the primary payer for future Medicare covered expenses related to the work-related injury."

While there are no statutory or regulatory provisions requiring that a WCMSA proposal be submitted to CMS for review, submission of a WCMSA proposal is a recommended process. CMS will only review WCMSA proposals that meet the following criteria.

- The claimant is a Medicare beneficiary, and the total settlement amount is greater than $25,000.00.

- The claimant has a reasonable expectation of Medicare enrollment within 30 months of the settlement date and the anticipated total settlement amount for future medical expenses and disability/lost wages over the life or duration of the settlement agreement is expected to be greater than $250,000.00

CMS continues to stress that this is a CMS workload review threshold and not a substantive dollar or "safe harbor" threshold. Medicare beneficiaries must still consider Medicare's interests in all workers compensation settlement negotiations and ensure that Medicare is secondary to workers compensation in such cases. In other words, if the total settlement amount is $25,000 or less, the parties to the settlement are still required to consider Medicare's interests.

CMS has determined that an individual has a reasonable expectation of Medicare enrollment if any of the following situations apply.

- The individual has applied for SSDI benefits.

- The individual has been denied SSDI benefits but anticipates appealing that decision.

- The individual is in the process of appealing and/or re-filing for SSDI benefits.

- The individual is 62 years and six months old (i.e., may be eligible for Medicare based upon his/her age within 30 months).

- The individual has an End Stage Renal Disease (ESRD) condition but does not yet qualify for Medicare based upon ESRD.

To the extent a workers compensation settlement meets both of the criteria (i.e., the settlement is greater than $250,000 and the claimant is reasonably expected to become a Medicare beneficiary within 30 months of the settlement date), then a CMS-approved Medicare set-aside arrangement is appropriate.

According to CMS, a WCMSA is not recommended if all of the following apply:

- The facts of the case demonstrate that the injured individual is only being compensated for past medical expenses (i.e., for services furnished prior to the settlement).

- There is no evidence that the individual is attempting to maximize the other aspects of the settlement (e.g., the lost wages and disability portions of the settlement) to Medicare's detriment.

- The individual's treating physicians conclude in writing that to a reasonable degree of medical certainty the individual will no longer require any Medicare-covered treatments related to the work-related injury.

Additionally, failure to obtain CMS approval and Medicare subsequently deems the settlement an intentional attempt to shift the burden of treatment to Medicare, Medicare may apportion the entire settlement to future Medicare expenses and refuse to pay any Medicare covered medical expense until the entirety of the settlement is exhausted on the treatment of the injury.[162]

MEDICAID

The question frequently arises as to what is the difference between Medicare and Medicaid. Medicare is a federal insurance program wherein medical bills are paid from trust funds which those covered have paid into. It serves people over 65 primarily, whatever their income, and serves younger disabled people and dialysis patients. On the other hand, Medicaid is a federal-state assistance program serving low-income people of every age. Patients usually pay no part of the cost for covered medical expenses. The program varies from state to state and is run by both state and local governments within federal guidelines.[163]

Medicaid is a cooperative program funded and administered jointly by the federal and state governments. Subject to federal standards, states administer Medicaid programs and have

---

[162] 42 CFR 411.46
[163] https://www.hhs.gov/answers/medicare-and-medicaid/what-is-the-difference-between-medicare-medicaid/index.html

flexibility to determine covered populations, covered services, health care delivery models, and methods for paying physicians and hospitals. Under the original 1965 Medicaid law, Medicaid eligibility was tied to cash assistance (either Aid to Families with Dependent Children (AFDC) or federal Supplemental Security Income (SSI) for parents, children and the poor aged, blind and people with disabilities. States could opt to provide coverage at income levels above cash assistance.

Over time, Congress expanded federal minimum requirements and provided new coverage options for states especially for children, pregnant women, and people with disabilities. Congress also required Medicaid to help pay for premiums and cost-sharing for low-income Medicare beneficiaries and allowed states to offer an option to buy-in to Medicaid for working individuals with disabilities. Other coverage milestones included enacting the Children's Health Insurance Program (CHIP) in 1997 to cover low-income children above the cut-off for Medicaid with an enhanced federal dollar match.

States have broad discretion in determining which groups will be covered under their Medicaid program along with the financial criteria for eligibility. However, to be eligible for federal funds, states are required to provide coverage for certain individuals. Medicaid coverage is automatically extended to persons receiving cash assistance under the Temporary Assistance for Needy Families (TANF) program and generally to Supplementary Security Income (SSI) recipients. Under the welfare reform legislation of 1996, TANF replaced the old welfare programs known as Aid to Families with Dependent Children (AFDC), the Job Opportunities and Basic Skills Training (JOBS) program and the Emergency Assistance (EA) program. Medicaid coverage is also mandatory for many pregnant women and children where family income is at or below 133 percent of the federal poverty level.

Medicaid covers both required and optional services. Some required services include inpatient and outpatient hospital services, prenatal care and vaccines for children, physician services, nursing facility services for persons aged 21 or older, and laboratory and X-ray services. Optional services under a state program include intermediate care facilities for the mentally retarded, prescription drugs and personal care. In addition, services provided may include personal care services, chore services, respite care services, and adult day care.

Within broad federal guidelines and certain limitations, states determine the amount and duration of services offered under their Medicaid programs. States may limit, for example, the number of days of hospital care or the number of physician visits covered. Two restrictions apply. First, limits must result in a sufficient level of services to reasonably achieve the purpose of the benefits. Second, limits on benefits may not discriminate among beneficiaries based on medical diagnosis or condition.

Three Medicaid services important for people with disabilities include:

- Nursing facilities (i.e., nursing homes).

- Home health services.

- Personal care services.

Nursing facilities are mandatory for people aged 21 or over who receive cash payments from SSI or TANF, but they are optional for everyone else. Home health services are, in effect, mandatory for the same Medicaid recipients for whom nursing facility services are provided. Personal care services are provided in a person's home by a qualified person under the guidance of a registered nurse. These services can include bathing, dressing, ambulation, feeding, grooming, meal preparation, cleaning, laundry, and shopping.

States have the option to establish a medically needy program for individuals with significant health needs whose income is too high to otherwise qualify for Medicaid under other eligibility groups. Medically needy individuals can still become eligible by spending down the amount of income that is above a state's medically needy income standard. Individuals spend down by incurring expenses for medical and remedial care for which they do not have health insurance. Once an individual's incurred expenses exceed the difference between the individual's income and the state's medically needy income level (the spend down amount), the person can be eligible for Medicaid. The Medicaid program then pays the cost of services that exceeds the expenses the individual had to incur to become eligible.

In 2010, as part of a broader health coverage initiative, the Affordable Care Act (ACA) expanded Medicaid to non-elderly adults with income up to 138 percent FPL ($17,236 for an individual in 2019) with enhanced federal matching funds. The ACA changes effectively eliminated categorical eligibility and allowed adults without dependent children to be covered; however, as a result of a 2012 Supreme Court ruling, the ACA Medicaid expansion is effectively optional for states. .
It is important to recognize that Medicaid does not provide medical assistance for all persons with low income. The ACA established a new methodology for determining income eligibility for Medicaid, which is based on Modified Adjusted Gross Income (MAGI). MAGI is used to determine financial eligibility for Medicaid, CHIP, and premium tax credits MAGI is the basis for determining Medicaid income eligibility for most children, pregnant women, parents, and adults. The MAGI-based methodology considers taxable income and tax filing relationships to determine financial eligibility for Medicaid.

Medicaid operates as a vendor payment program. States may pay health care providers directly on a fee-for-service basis, or pay for services through various prepayment arrangements such as health maintenance organizations. Within federally imposed upper limits and specific restrictions, each state has broad discretion in determining the payment methodology and payment rate for services. Generally, payment rates must be sufficient to enlist enough providers so that covered services are available at least to the extent that comparable care and services are available to the general population within that geographic area. Providers participating in Medicaid must accept Medicaid payment rates as payment in full.

Some Medicaid beneficiaries may be required to pay a deductible, co-insurance, or a co-payment for certain services. Pregnant women, children under age 18, and hospital or nursing home patients who are expected to contribute most of their income to institutional care are excluded from any form of cost-sharing. All Medicaid beneficiaries are exempt from any co-payment for emergency services and family planning services.

Although the states are primarily responsible for policing fraud and abuse in the Medicaid program, the Centers for Medicare & Medicaid Services (CMS) within the federal Department of Health and Human Services provides technical assistance, guidance and oversight in these areas. Fraud schemes often cross state lines, and CMS strives to improve information sharing among the Medicaid programs and other stakeholders.

Like Medicare, the Medicaid program is intended to be the payer of last resort; that is, all other available third-party resources must meet their legal obligation to pay claims before the Medicaid program pays for the care of an eligible individual. As a condition of eligibility, individuals are required to assign to the state Medicaid agency their rights to any third-party payments.[164]

States are authorized to take all reasonable measures to determine whether there is any legal liability on the part of a third party to pay for care and services available under the state plan. Third parties which may be liable to pay for services include private health insurance, Medicare, employment-related health insurance, court judgments or settlements from a liability insurer, workers compensation, first party probate-estate recoveries, long-term care insurance, and other state and federal programs (unless specifically excluded by federal statute).

Once states have determined that a potentially liable third party exists, the state is required to either cost avoid or pay and chase claims. Cost avoidance is where the provider of services bills and collects from liable third parties before sending the claim to Medicaid. Pay and chase is utilized when the state Medicaid agency pays the medical bills and then attempts to recover from liable third parties. States are generally required to cost avoid claims unless they have a waiver approved by CMS which allows them to use the pay and chase method.

In a number of instances, state workers compensation laws address the responsibility of a carrier where medical expenses have been paid by some other healthcare provider. For example, **Georgia** law provides that a workers compensation carrier may be held liable for medical expenses incurred by an employee and paid by a group insurance company or other healthcare provider, where an employee subsequently files a workers compensation claim and is subsequently determined to be entitled to benefits.[165] Even in those instances where the compensation carrier has no knowledge of an employee's entitlement to Medicaid benefits, the carrier may still be liable for payment of past or future medical bills.

Two additional examples are found in the state laws of **Louisiana** and **California**. In Louisiana, there is specific reference to Medicaid and the fact that any payment made by Medicaid or any other state medical assistance programs of medical expenses would not extinguish the claim against the employer or insurer for those medical expenses.[166] Like many other states,

---

[164] 42 USC § 1396k(a)(1)(A)
[165] Ga. Code Ann. § 34-9-206
[166] La. Rev. Stat. Ann. § 1212

California recognizes any liens filed where any benefits have been paid or services provided by a health care provider, a health care service plan, a group disability policy, including a loss of income policy, a self-insured employee welfare benefit plan, or a hospital service contract. Any awards or approved settlements are to provide for reimbursement for benefits paid or services provided under such plans.[167]

STATE TEMPORARY DISABILITY INSURANCE (STDI)

Five states along with Puerto Rico have social insurance programs that partially compensate for the loss of wages caused by temporary non-occupational disability or maternity. Because of the temporary nature of the benefit duration, those programs are known as state temporary disability insurance (STDI).

During the severe depression of the 1930s, this country began to introduce its national social insurance programs to provide protection against cyclical unemployment and old-age dependency. Following the establishment of the federal-state system of unemployment compensation insurance, it was recognized that there was no comparable program for responding in the case of short-term disability resulting from non-occupational causes. As a partial incentive to create such programs at the state level, in 1946, Congress amended the Federal Unemployment Tax Act (FUTA) permitting states, where employees made contributions under the unemployment insurance program, to use some or all of these contributions for the payment of temporary disability benefits.

Of the nine states that could have benefited from this provision for initial funding for temporary disability insurance, five states took advantage of the program. **Rhode Island** had already enacted the first state law in 1942. **California** and the railroad industry followed in 1946, then **New Jersey** in 1948, and **New York** in 1949. A two-decade hiatus followed before **Hawaii** passed their program in 1969.

The methods used for providing this protection vary. In **Rhode Island**, the coverage is provided through an exclusive, state-operated fund into which all contributions are paid and from which all benefits are disbursed. In addition, covered employers may provide supplemental benefits in any manner they choose.

In **California** and **New Jersey**, coverage is provided through a state-operated fund, but employers are permitted to contract out of the state fund by purchasing group insurance from commercial insurance companies, by self-insuring, or by negotiating an agreement with a union or employees' association. Coverage by the state fund is automatic unless or until an employer or the employees take positive action by substituting a private plan that meets the standards prescribed in the law and is approved by the administering agency.

Both **Hawaii** and **New York** operate special funds to pay benefits to workers who become disabled while unemployed or whose employers have failed to provide the required protection. In

---

[167] Cal. Labor Code § 4903.1

other jurisdictions, benefit payments for the disabled unemployed are made from the regular state-operated funds. In both Hawaii and New York, the law requires employers to provide their own disability insurance plans for their workers by setting up an approved self-insurance plan, by reaching an agreement with employees or a union establishing a labor-management benefit plan, or by purchasing group insurance from a commercial carrier. In New York, the employer may also provide protection through the State Insurance Fund, which is a state-operated competitive carrier.

The temporary disability insurance laws of the five states cover most commercial and industrial wage and salary workers in private employment where the employer has at least one worker. Principal occupational groups excluded from coverage are domestic workers, family workers (parent, child, or spouse of the employer), government employees, and the self-employed. State and local government employees are included in Hawaii, and the other state programs generally provide elective coverage for some or all public employees.

STDI laws, like state unemployment insurance and workers compensation programs, cover most commercial and industrial wage and salary workers in private employment. Principal occupational groups excluded include domestic workers, family workers, government employees, and the self-employed (except in **California** where the law permits elective coverage for self-employed persons). State and local government employees are included in **Hawaii**, and the other state laws permit some or all public employees to elect coverage. Only **California**, Hawaii and **New Jersey** cover agricultural workers.

To qualify for benefits, a claimant must have a specified history of past employment or earnings and be disabled. In general, the laws define disability in terms of the inability of an individual to perform the regular or customary work because of the individual's physical or mental condition. In most states, the term sickness has been defined to include pregnancy.

In **Hawaii, New Jersey,** and **Rhode Island**, the maximum weekly benefit is recomputed annually so that it equals a specified percentage of the state's average weekly wage in covered employments.

The following describes the basic components found in each of the state programs:

- **California** – Eligible workers include those who earned at least $300 in the previous year. The program is funded by a deduction of one percent of the worker's wages up to a maximum of $1,229.09 in 2020. Following a seven-day waiting period, benefits are payable for a maximum of 52 weeks. The program is designed to replace about 60-70 percent of the workers base salary up to a maximum of $1,300 per week.

- **Hawaii** – Employees who earned $400 or more per week for a minimum of 14 weeks in the previous year are eligible for benefits. Employers are required to maintain private coverage or to self-insure. The employer may deduct up to 0.5 percent of the workers' wages up to a maximum of $5.60 per week. Benefits are payable for a minimum of 26 weeks following a seven-day waiting period. Beneficiaries are entitled to a maximum of $650 which is about 58 percent of the workers average weekly wage in 2020.

- **New Jersey** – Eligible employees include those who earned $200 or more per week for a minimum of 20 weeks in the prior year. Funding provided through employee contribution of 0.26 percent of wages (up to $350.74 annually) and employer contribution of between 0.1 percent and 0.75 percent of wages up to a maximum of between $35.30 and $264.75 per week. Benefit entitlement continues for 26 weeks (or however long it takes for benefits to equal 1/3 of wages in previous year), after an initial seven-day waiting period. Beginning July 1, 2020, employees receive 85 percent of their average wage of the previous year, up to a maximum of $881 per week

- **New York** – Employees entitled to benefits include those who had worked four or more consecutive weeks for a covered employer immediately prior to disability Program funded through employee contributions of 0.05 percent of wages up to 60¢ per week. Any amount required more than this must be provided by employers. Benefits are approximately 50 percent of the worker's salary up to $170 per week and are payable for up to 26 weeks in a year following a seven-day waiting period.

- **Rhode Island** – Eligible employees include those who earned $12,600 in the previous year. Program funded by employee wage deductions of 1.3 percent up to a maximum of $939.90 per year (attributable to a wage base of $72,300 for 2020). A maximum weekly benefit equal to 4.62 percent of monthly salary is payable up to a maximum of $867 per week. Eligibility for benefits begins after seven days and may continue up to 30 weeks depending on the level of the workers previous earnings.

All STDI laws restrict payment of benefits when the claimant is also entitled to or receiving workers compensation benefits. However, the statutes generally provide some exceptions to this rule – for example, if the workers compensation is for partial disability or for previously incurred work disabilities.

In **California** an employee receiving or entitled to workers compensation benefits for the same period of temporary disability is not eligible for STDI benefits unless the STDI benefit is higher than the compensation benefit. If the STDI benefit is higher, the claimant is entitled to the difference to be paid from the disability fund. Where the compensability of the workers compensation claim has not yet been established, the claimant may receive STDI benefits subject to reimbursement from any workers compensation benefits subsequently awarded for that corresponding week.

Hawaii does not allow for the duplication of benefits unless a claimant is receiving workers compensation benefits for permanent partial or total disability previously incurred. Like **California**, Hawaii allows for the payment of STDI benefits where a claimant's right to workers compensation has not yet been determined. Where the claimant is ultimately successful in pursuing the workers compensation claim, payments are proportionately allocated among the employer or insurer according to the amount of STDI benefits they have paid.

In **New Jersey**, both the definition of disability and eligibility conditions exclude the payment of STDI benefits for any week for which workers compensation, other than permanent total or partial disability, are payable. Where the workers compensation claim is contested, STDI benefits may be paid until the disability becomes compensable under the workers compensation law.

The **New York** law defines disability under STDI to exclude illnesses or accidents arising out of or in the course of employment, whether workers compensation benefits are payable. It further provides that no benefits are payable for any period for which workers compensation benefits, other than permanent partial benefits for a prior disability, are paid or payable.

In **Rhode Island,** a worker may receive STDI benefits if there is doubt as to the claimant's eligibility for workers compensation. If the worker later becomes entitled to workers compensation benefits, the worker is liable for the repayment of the STDI benefits.

UNEMPLOYMENT COMPENSATION (UC)

Through federal and state cooperation, unemployment compensation (UC) programs are designed to provide benefits to regularly employed members of the labor force who become involuntarily unemployed and who are able and willing to accept suitable employment. Workers in all 50 states, the **District of Columbia**, Puerto Rico, and the Virgin Islands are covered under unemployment insurance programs.

Generally, employers must pay both state and federal unemployment taxes if: (1) they pay wages to employees totaling $1,500, or more, in any quarter of a calendar year; or, (2) they had at least one employee during any day of a week during 20 weeks in a calendar year, regardless of whether or not the weeks were consecutive.[168] The federal unemployment compensation law is called the Federal Unemployment Tax Ac (FUTA).[169] The law authorizes the collection of federal unemployment insurance taxes. For 2019, the FUTA tax rate is 6 percent. The federal tax applies to the first $7,000 you pay to each employee as wages during the year. Each state determines their own unemployment insurance tax rate.

With the exception of **Alaska, New Jersey**, and **Pennsylvania,** unemployment benefits are funded exclusively by a tax imposed on employers. The three exceptions require both employer and (minimal) employee contributions. For more established employers (usually those in business for at least three years), states will assign a tax rate based, at least in part, on the history of unemployment charges to that employer's account. Where an employer has been in operation for a relatively short time, and does not qualify for an experience rating, the state may assign a new account rate to the employer. State tax rates are also subject to the overall condition of the unemployment insurance fund.

Government agencies, Indian tribes, religious schools, and most non-profit employers are not required to participate in the unemployment program. However, these employers may elect to reimburse the cost of benefits paid to their workers rather than pay payroll taxes.

---

[168] https://oui.doleta.gov/unemploy/pdf/partnership.pdf
[169] 26 USCA 3301-3311

For those employers participating in the program, a requirement is that all contributions collected under state laws be deposited in the Unemployment Trust Fund of the United States Treasury Department. The fund is invested as a whole, but each state has a separate account to which its deposits and its share of interest on investments are credited. At any time, a state may withdraw money from its account but only to pay unemployment benefits. Thus, unlike the situation in the majority of states having workers compensation and temporary disability insurance laws, unemployment insurance benefits are paid exclusively through a public fund. Private plans cannot be substituted for the state plan.

Aside from a limited number of federal standards, each state has the major responsibility for determining the amount and duration of benefits (except for certain federal requirements concerning Federal-State Extended Benefits), the contribution rates (with limitations), and, in general, the eligibility requirements and disqualification provisions. The states also directly administer their programs: collecting contributions, maintaining wage records (where applicable), taking claims, determining initial and continuing eligibility, and paying benefits to unemployed workers.

Unemployment benefits are available as a matter of right, without a means test, to unemployed workers who have demonstrated their connection to the labor force by a specified amount of recent work or earnings in covered employment. Workers whose employers are covered by the unemployment insurance program are eligible for benefits if they are involuntarily unemployed, able to work, available for work, and actively seeking work. Workers must meet the initial eligibility and qualifying requirements of the state law and be free from disqualifications.

There are also circumstances that may serve to disqualify a worker from collecting unemployment benefits. These include:

- Having been fired for misconduct.

- Quit without good cause.

- Resigned because of illness.

- Left to get married.

- Self-employed.

- Involved in a labor dispute.

- Attending school.

- Frequent unexcused absences.

- Insubordination or harassment.

A worker's rights to monetary benefit are based on wages in covered work over a prior reference period called the base period. Such benefit rights remain fixed for a benefit year. In most states, the base period is the first four quarters of the last five completed calendar quarters preceding the claim for unemployment benefits. A minority of states allow for additional benefits based on more recent earnings.

The UC program operates counter-cyclically to economic trends, paying out more benefits during recessionary times and building solvency during recovery periods. For fiscal year 2019, the estimated number of covered workers totaled 144.8 million. For the same period, the total amount of benefits paid for all programs totaled $27.3 billion.[170]

On March 18, 2020, the Families First Coronavirus Response Act (FFCRA) was signed into law which provided additional flexibility for state unemployment insurance agencies and additional administrative funding to respond to the COVID-19 pandemic. Later that month, the Coronavirus Aid, Relief, and Economic Security (CARES) Act was signed into law expanding a states' ability to provide unemployment insurance for many workers impacted by the COVID-19 pandemic, including for workers who were not ordinarily eligible for unemployment benefits.

The COVID-19 pandemic has had a significant effect on unemployment in every state, industry, and major demographic group in the United States. The unemployment rate peaked at an unprecedented level, not seen since data collection started in 1948, in April 2020 with the unemployment rate reaching a high of 14.8 percent before declining to a still elevated level in December 2020 of 6.7 percent.

Each state establishes a ceiling on the weekly benefit amount and no worker may receive an amount greater than the ceiling. Mississippi pays the lowest maximum weekly amount of $235, while Massachusetts has the highest maximum weekly amount of $823 and an amount of $1,234 where there are dependents. For 2020 to 2021, 10 states provide additional allowances for certain dependents. Additional funds were available to the unemployed during 2020 and for those eligible, there was an additional $300 per week from the Pandemic Unemployment Compensation (PUC) program starting December 27, 2020 and ending on March 13, 2021.

All but 12 states require a waiting period of one week of total unemployment before benefits can begin. Four states pay benefits retroactively for the waiting period if unemployment lasts a certain period or if the employee returns to work within a specified period.

In general, states provide a statutory maximum duration of 26 weeks of benefits in a benefit year. However, certain employment conditions may affect the duration of benefits. For example, extended benefits may be available for workers who exhaust their entitlement to regular state benefits during periods of high unemployment. The COVID-19 pandemic has also prompted increases in the duration for which unemployment benefits are payable. As of December 27, 2020, workers are eligible for a 24-week extension through the Pandemic Emergency Unemployment Compensation (PEUC) program. However, the last 11 weeks can only be for

---

[170] https://oui.doleta.gov/unemploy/pdf/partnership.pdf

weeks that start on or after December 27, 2020. This means as of December 27, 2020, for those eligible, the period of entitlement may be a total of 50 weeks.

As business and industry slowly recover from the COVID-19 pandemic, further federal assistance will likely continue to be necessary as millions of out-of-work Americans are depending on UC benefits to cover their housing costs, groceries, and other expenses.

Federal law requires that weekly unemployment benefits be reduced by taking into account the weekly amount of retirement income based on the previous work of an individual for the same base period employer.[171] Most states reduce UC benefits when the worker receives wages and other wage replacement income, either on the grounds that it is a substitute for wages, or duplicative of unemployment compensation benefits. The most common types of deductible income are wages paid in lieu of notice, dismissal payments, Social Security payments, severance pay, and workers compensation benefits.

A number of states treat receipt of workers compensation benefits – particularly benefits payable for permanent total disability – as automatically disqualifying, while other states consider it deductible income. This is because receipt of workers compensation benefits – payable because the worker is disabled – prompts questions about the individual's availability for and ability to work.

In several states, entitlement to workers compensation benefits for temporary total disability and permanent total disability is suspended during the period the employee is receiving UC benefits. In addition to claims involving payment for temporary total and permanent total disability, **Arkansas** also permits compensation for temporary partial disability to be suspended while UC benefits are being paid.

A separate approach identified in a number of states allows for the reduction of workers compensation benefits when the employee is also entitled to and receiving UC benefits. **California, Colorado, Kentucky, North Carolina**, and **Pennsylvania** allow for the workers compensation total disability benefits to be reduced by the amount of the UC benefit being received. **Maine** takes the same approach but excludes lump sums and permanent partial disability benefits. **Michigan** does allow for the offset of permanent partial disability benefits when UC benefits are being paid.

Rhode Island recognizes the receipt of UC benefits only when the employee is entitled to reinstatement following a work-related injury. When the employee is entitled to reinstatement but the position sought is not available or does not exist, the employee may file for UC benefits as if he/she had been laid off from that employment. At that point, the employee cannot collect both workers compensation and UC benefits.

FAMILY MEDICAL LEAVE ACT (FMLA)

---

[171] 42 USCA §3304 (a)(15)

The Family and Medical Leave Act (FMLA) became effective on August 5, 1993, for most employers. It was with recognition for the lack of employment policies to accommodate working parents in their choice between job security and parenting and the inadequate job security that existed for employees with serious health issues that FMLA was enacted. The purpose of the law was designed to entitle employees to take reasonable leave for medical reasons for the birth or adoption of a child, and for the care of a child, spouse, or parent who has a serious health condition.

Under FMLA, covered employers are required to provide up to 12 weeks of unpaid, job-protected leave to eligible employees for certain family and medical reasons. Employees are eligible if they have worked for their employer at least 12 months, have worked at least 1,250 hours over the past 12 months, and work at a location where the company had at least 50 employees at the location or within 75 miles of the location.

FMLA applies to all public agencies, including state, local, and federal employers, local education agencies (schools) private sector employers who employ 50 or more employees for at least 20 work weeks in the current or preceding calendar year, including joint employers and successors of covered employers. For FMLA purposes, most Federal and Congressional employees are under the jurisdiction of the U.S. Office of Personnel Management (OPM) or the Congress.

The law provides employees with up to 12 weeks of protected leave each year, provided they take leave for a qualifying reason. Qualifying reasons for FMLA include:

- The birth of a new child or to care for a newborn.

- The placement of a child for adoption or foster care with the employee, or to provide care for the newly placed child.

- To provide care for the spouse, child, or parent of an employee who has a severe health condition.

- For an employee to attend to a severe health condition that makes them unable to perform their job.

- Any qualifying exigency arising out of the fact that the employee's spouse, son, daughter, or parent is a military member on covered active duty.

- To care for a covered service member with a serious injury or illness if the employee is the spouse, son, daughter, parent, or next of kin of the service member (military caregiver leave).

The definition of what constitutes a serious health condition, which is defined to mean an illness, injury, impairment, or physical or mental condition that involves:

- Any period of incapacity or treatment connected with inpatient care (i.e., an overnight stay) in a hospital, hospice, or residential medical care facility.

- A period of incapacity requiring absence of more than three calendar days from work, school, or other regular daily activities that also involves continuing treatment by (or under the supervision of) a health care provider.

- Any period of incapacity due to pregnancy, or for prenatal care.

- Any period of incapacity (or treatment therefore) due to a chronic serious health condition (e.g., asthma, diabetes, epilepsy, etc.).

- A period of incapacity that is permanent or long-term due to a condition for which treatment may not be effective (e.g., alzheimer's, stroke, terminal diseases, etc.).

- Any absences to receive multiple treatments (including any period of recovery therefrom) by, or on referral by, a health care provider for a condition that likely would result in incapacity of more than three consecutive days if left untreated (e.g., chemotherapy, physical therapy, dialysis, etc.).

Upon return from FMLA leave, an employee must be restored to the employee's position of employment when the leave commenced, or to an equivalent job with equivalent pay, benefits, and other terms and conditions of employment. In addition, an employee's use of FMLA leave cannot result in the loss of any employment benefit that the employee earned or was entitled to before using FMLA leave.

It is important to recognize that the FMLA is a federal program that serves different purposes than the workers compensation program. Although there are significant differences between the two programs, there are also times when both are applicable to an employee's situation. For example, when an employee needs to attend to a severe health condition such as a work-related injury or illness, the employee may qualify for both workers compensation and the FMLA program.

Aside from the fact that workers compensation is a state-run program while the FMLA is a federal law, these programs differ in other ways as well. First of all, FMLA leave is available to any employee who develops a serious health condition – regardless of whether the condition is work-related. Another difference is that time off under the FMLA is unpaid (although employers do have the option to provide paid leave) while workers compensation benefits provide income replacement and coverage for medical bills.

A third difference is that the FMLA provides protected leave, meaning the employer must allow the employee to return to his or her previous job (or an equivalent) after the 12 weeks is up. No such protection exists for employees who are out of work while receiving workers compensation benefits.

Where the employee is eligible for leave under the FMLA and the injury is considered a serious health condition, the time lost because of the work-related injury is subject to be treated under the FMLA. The FMLA defines serious health condition broadly to include any illness, injury, impairment, or physical or mental condition that involves either inpatient care or continuing treatment by a health care provider. The statute does not distinguish between work-related and non-work-related injuries. Thus, a work-related injury or illness that requires an employee to take leave to seek inpatient care or continuing treatment likely will be covered by the FMLA.

If an employee is eligible for time off under both the FMLA and workers compensation, the two programs *can* run concurrently, meaning that both would be in effect at the same time. This does not happen automatically, however, an employer must inform an employee in writing that their FMLA leave has begun, and FMLA cannot be charged retroactively prior to the date the written notice was provided. An employer is not allowed to force an employee to take FMLA leave when the employee is eligible for workers compensation benefits.

Accordingly, whenever an employee is injured on the job and needs time off to recover, the employer should immediately determine if the employee also is eligible for leave under the FMLA. If the employee is eligible for FMLA leave, the employer should notify the employee in writing that the leave is covered under the FMLA so that the leave time may be counted against the employee's 12-week FMLA entitlement. If the employer does not run the workers compensation period of disability leave concurrently with the FMLA leave, the employee may still have the full 12-week FMLA entitlement available to use after the workers compensation disability has concluded.

In order to deduct the time spent on workers compensation from an employee's annual FMLA leave entitlement, the employer must notify the employee in writing that the workers compensation is designated as FMLA leave and will count against, and run concurrently with, the employee's 12-week entitlement. The notice to the employee must detail the specific obligations of the employee while on FMLA leave and explain the consequences of a failure to meet these obligations. Most employers use the Department of Labor's Form WH-381 to comply with such notice requirements. If the employer does not provide the notice, it cannot count the workers compensation towards the 12-week FMLA entitlement.

If the employee is receiving workers compensation benefits without being placed specifically on FMLA leave, the employer should promptly send notice to the employee so that the FMLA clock starts running. However, the employer may then only designate the leave from the date written notice to the employee is provided. It cannot retroactively designate the time spent on WC leave against the FMLA entitlement.

AMERICANS WITH DISABILITIES ACT (ADA)

At this time, more than 55 million Americans, or roughly 18 percent of our population, have disabilities, and like all Americans, they participate in a variety of programs, services, and activities provided by their state and local governments. This includes those who have become disabled while serving in the military. It is also estimated that by the year 2030, approximately

71.5 million baby boomers will be over age 65 and will need services and surroundings that meet their age-related physical needs.[172]

The ADA protects the rights of people who have a physical or mental impairment that substantially limits their ability to perform one or more major life activities, such as breathing, walking, reading, thinking, seeing, hearing, or working. It does not apply to people whose impairment is unsubstantial, such as someone who is slightly nearsighted or someone who is mildly allergic to pollen. However, it does apply to people whose disability is substantial but can be moderated or mitigated, such as someone with diabetes that can normally be controlled with medication or someone who uses leg braces to walk.

It is also applicable to people who are temporarily substantially limited in their ability to perform a major life activity. In addition, the ADA also applies to people who have a record of having a substantial impairment (e.g., a person with cancer that is in remission) or are regarded as having such an impairment (e.g., a person who has scars from a severe burn).

Enacted July 26, 1990, the Americans with Disabilities Act (ADA) is a wide-ranging civil rights law that prohibits, under certain circumstances, discrimination based on disability. It affords similar protections against discrimination to Americans with disabilities as the Civil Rights Act of 1964, which made discrimination based on race, religion, sex, national origin, and other characteristics illegal.

Disability is defined by the ADA as "...a physical or mental impairment that substantially limits a major life activity." The determination of whether any condition is considered a disability is made on a case-by-case basis. Certain specific conditions are excluded as disabilities, such as current substance abuse and visual impairment that is correctable by prescription lenses. ADA prohibits discrimination on the basis of disability in employment, state and local government, public accommodations, commercial facilities, transportation, and telecommunications.

As enacted, the law applies to employers with 15 or more employees and private businesses of any size, which operate facilities such as restaurants, hotels, retail stores, doctors' offices, laundromats, etc. The law also covers state and local government entities including school districts and other instrumentalities of state and local government and all programs, activities and services they provide or operate such as law enforcement, judicial facilities and voting facilities.

As originally enacted, the ADA legislation was composed of five titles. The law was later amended to focus on three titles which include:

> **Title I Employment** – Prohibits private employers, state and local governments, employment agencies and labor unions from discriminating against qualified individuals with disabilities in job application procedures, hiring, firing, advancement, compensation, job training, and other terms, conditions, and privileges of employment. The ADA covers

---

[172] https://www.ada.gov/regs2010/titleII_2010/title_ii_primer.html

employers with 15 or more employees, including state and local governments. It also applies to employment agencies and to labor organizations.[173]

Title II: State and Local Government Activities – Protects qualified individuals with disabilities from discrimination on the basis of disability in services, programs, and activities provided by state and local government entities. Title II extends the prohibition on discrimination established by section 504 of the Rehabilitation Act of 1973, as amended, 29 U.S.C. 794, to all activities of state and local governments regardless of whether these entities receive Federal financial assistance.[174]

Title III Public Accommodations – Prohibits discrimination on the basis of disability in the activities of places of public accommodations (businesses that are generally open to the public and that fall into one of 12 categories listed in the ADA, such as restaurants, movie theaters, schools, day care facilities, recreation facilities, and doctors' offices) and requires newly constructed or altered places of public accommodation — as well as commercial facilities (privately owned, nonresidential facilities such as factories, warehouses, or office buildings) — to comply with the ADA Standards.[175]

The ADA contains certain terms and phrases that serve to define who is covered and the form of accommodation(s) required. ADA protection applies primarily, but not exclusively, to disabled individuals. An individual is disabled if he/she meets at least any one of the following tests.

- He/she has a physical or mental impairment that substantially limits one or more of his/her major life activities.

- He/she has a record of such an impairment.

- He/she is regarded as having such impairment.

The term "qualified individual with a disability" means an individual with a disability who, with or without reasonable accommodation, can perform the essential functions of the employment position that such individual holds or desires. For the purposes of the Act, consideration is given to the employer's judgment as to what functions of a job are essential, and where an employer has prepared a written description before advertising or interviewing applicants for the job, such description shall be considered evidence of the essential functions of the job.

In 2008, the Americans with Disabilities Act Amendments Act (ADA Amendments Act) was signed into law. This law change emphasized that the definition of disability should be construed in favor of broad coverage of individuals to the maximum extent permitted by the terms of the ADA and rejected earlier holdings in several Supreme Court decisions. The effect of these changes made it easier for an individual seeking protection under the ADA to establish that he or she had a disability within the meaning of the ADA.

---

[173] https://www.ada.gov/ada_title_II.htm
[174] ibid
[175] ibid

As part of ADA, an employer may not inquire into an applicant's workers compensation history before making a conditional offer of employment. After making a conditional job offer, an employer may then inquire about a person's workers compensation history in a medical inquiry or examination that is required of all applicants in the same job category. Also, an employer may not base a decision to hire based on an applicant's workers compensation history. However, an employer may refuse to hire, or may discharge an individual, who is not currently able to perform a job without posing a significant risk of substantial harm to the health or safety of the individual or others, if the risk cannot be eliminated or reduced by reasonable accommodation.[176]

Filing a workers compensation claim does not prevent an injured worker from filing a charge under the ADA. "Exclusivity" clauses in state workers compensation laws bar all other civil remedies related to an injury that has been compensated by a workers compensation system. However, these clauses do not prohibit a qualified individual with a disability from filing a discrimination charge with the Equal Employment Opportunity Commission (EEOC) or filing a suit under the ADA if issued a "right to sue" letter by EEOC.

An employer may refuse to hire or may fire a person who knowingly provides a false answer to a lawful post-conditional job offer inquiry about his or her condition or workers' compensation history. An employer may also submit medical information and records concerning employees and applicants (obtained after a conditional job offer) to state workers' compensation offices and "second injury" funds without violating ADA and HIPAA confidentiality requirements.

The ADA is a federal law and all claims associated with ADA violations are filed in federal district courts. Some prominent decisions handed down include:

- A court decision in **New York** affirmed that the exclusive remedy bar under the workers compensation program does not preclude an employee from bringing a claim under the ADA even if the disability arises from an injury compensable only through workers compensation. The employee was injured while working in a store and underwent a medical examination and was told she could return to work under certain restrictions. The employer refused part of employee's accommodation request, stating that certain acts the employee said she could not perform were a vital part of her job function. The employee brought an action for damages, claiming a violation of the ADA.

  The employer argued that the exclusive remedy provision barred this action, inasmuch as the employee was injured while on the job, and had already begun to receive workers compensation benefits for the injury. The United States District Court for the Northern District of New York denied the motion for summary judgment finding that the payment of workers compensation benefits does not preclude a later action brought under a federal law such as the ADA. Moreover, the Workers' Compensation Board only awarded the employee partial benefits based on a mild to moderate disability, meaning the employee did not need to answer the question of how she would continue to perform the essential

---

[176] https://adata.org/faq/how-does-ada-affect-workers-compensation-programs

functions of her job with the injury in question (a question which she would have had to answer had she been awarded benefits for total disability).[177]

- An employer's failure to accommodate an injured worker to return to the workplace can prove to be quite costly. In a 2009 decision, the Equal Employment Opportunity Commission (EEOC) announced that Sears Roebuck and Co. was required to distribute $6.2 million to 235 former employees as a result of ADA related litigation. The monetary distribution stemmed from a consent decree resolving a class lawsuit against the retail giant. At that point, it was the largest ADA settlement in a single lawsuit in EEOC history. The litigation was in response to a refusal on the part of Sears to provide proper accommodations to workers following injuries.

- In a 2020 case involving the question of reasonable accommodation, a jury in **Wisconsin** determined that the employer (Walmart) had let go of a long-time disabled employee – an employee who had a developmental disability, was deaf and visually impaired and worked as a cart pusher – arguing that he was unable to perform essential job functions without a job coach and that a full-time job coach was an unreasonable accommodation. In awarding $5.2 million in damages, the District court ruled that a full-time job coach is a reasonable accommodation and does not create an undue hardship.[178]

- In 2018, the 6th circuit ruled that a full-time presence at work is not an essential job function. This case involved a woman who returned to her job after maternity leave with a requested reduced schedule due to postpartum and separation anxiety. The woman was temporarily granted this request, but her employer fired her for not returning to a full-time schedule. In the decision, the judge rejected the idea that working full time is an essential job function asserting that if employers were allowed to refuse reduced or modified schedules, that would further disability discrimination for countless employees who needed to attend medical appointments and treatment.[179]

Case law continues to evolve around provisions found in the ADA law. Employers are encouraged to follow the developments on these cases and to respond accordingly.

EMPLOYER SPONSORED PENSION, DISABILITY AND MEDICAL PROGRAMS

A century ago, employer-provided benefits such as time away from employment with pay or medical insurance were uncommon. Today, by contrast, these and other benefits are often an important part of how workers are compensated. The availability of these various forms of economic security continues to evolve. For example, in addition to the many basic forms of economic security, many employers offer an increasing array of options that provide workers with greater flexibility in balancing work with other facets of life.

---

[177] *Fowler v. Kohl's Dept. Stores, Inc.*, 2009 WL 2155481 (N.D.N.Y.,2009)
[178] (*EEOC v. Walmart*, Inc., Case No. 6:20-cv-00163-KKC) on Aug. 3, 2020,
[179] *Hostettler* v. *College* of *Wooster*, 895 F. 3d 844 - *2018*

An employer-sponsored plan is a type of benefit plan offered to employees at no or relatively low cost. These plans may cover an array of services including retirement savings and healthcare. Employees who enroll in such programs capitalize on the benefit of receiving discounted services. Employers offering these plans typically benefit from tax breaks.

Two of the primary forms of benefit security available to workers for time away from employment with pay are pension plans and disability income protection.

PENSION PLANS

Employers are not required to offer pension plans to their employees. The decision on the part of the employer is voluntary, and where the decision is made to offer such a plan, the employer is able to make decisions regarding the design, terms and features of the plan(s) being offered. While the offering of a pension program is voluntary, employers are motivated to provide such protection for a number of reasons. In a highly competitive labor market, the program represents a valuable tool for purposes of attracting and retaining a competent workforce. Secondly, there are certain tax advantages or preferences for the employer associated with the offering of a pension program.

A federal law, the Employee Retirement Income Security Act of 1974 (ERISA), sets minimum standards for most voluntarily established retirement and health plans in private industry to protect those individuals covered by these plans. The following demonstrates the requirements under ERISA:

(1) Requires plans to provide participants with plan information, including important information about plan features and funding.

(2) Sets minimum standards for participation, vesting, benefit accrual and funding; provides fiduciary responsibilities for those who manage and control plan assets.

(3) Requires plans to establish a grievance and appeals process for participants to get benefits from their plans.

(4) Gives participants the right to sue for benefits and breaches of fiduciary duty.

(5) If a defined benefit plan is terminated, guarantees payment of certain benefits through a federally chartered corporation, known as the Pension Benefit Guaranty Corporation (PBGC).[180]

ERISA covers two types of retirement plans: defined benefit plans and defined contribution plans. A defined benefit plan promises a specified monthly benefit at retirement. The plan may state this promised benefit as an exact dollar amount, such as $100 per month at retirement. Or, more commonly, it may calculate a benefit through a plan formula that considers such factors as

---

[180] https://www.dol.gov/general/topic/retirement/typesofplans

salary and years of service Typically, benefit amounts are calculated on the basis of the employee's final average pay multiplied by the number of years of employment times a percentage factor. For example, $70,000 (average salary during the final five years of employment) X 30 (number of years of employment) X 1.5 percent (the percentage factor) would result in an annual pension benefit of $31,500 starting at the normal retirement age.

On the other hand, a defined contribution plan does not promise a specific amount of benefits at retirement. In these plans, the employee or the employer (or both) contribute to the employee's individual account under the plan, sometimes at a set rate, such as five percent of annual earnings. These contributions are generally invested on the employee's behalf and the employee ultimately receives the balance in their account, which is based on contributions plus or minus investment gains or losses. The value of the account will fluctuate up or down consistent with changes in the value of the investments.

Following are examples of some defined benefit and defined contribution plans.

- A 401(k) Plan is a defined contribution plan that is a cash or deferred arrangement. Employees can elect to defer a portion of their salary which is instead contributed on their behalf, before taxes, to a 401(k) plan. The employer may match these contributions and there is a dollar limit on the amount an employee may elect to defer each year. An employer must advise employees of any limits that may apply. In some instances, employees may direct their own investments.

- A profit-sharing plan or stock bonus plan is a defined contribution plan under which the plan may provide, or the employer may determine, annually, how much will be contributed to the plan (out-of-profits or otherwise). The plan contains a formula for allocating to each participant a portion of each annual contribution. A profit sharing plan or stock bonus plan may include a 401(k) plan.

- A Simplified Employee Pension Plan (SEP) is a relatively uncomplicated retirement savings vehicle. A SEP allows employees to make contributions on a tax-favored basis to individual retirement accounts (IRAs) owned by the employees. SEPs are subject to minimal reporting and disclosure requirements. Under a SEP, an employee must set up an IRA to accept the employer's contributions.

- An Employee Stock Ownership Plan (ESOP) is a form of defined contribution plan in which the investments are primarily in employer stock.

- A Cash Balance Plan is a defined benefit plan that defines the benefit in terms characteristic of a defined contribution plan. In a typical cash balance plan, a participant's account is credited each year with a pay credit (such as five percent of compensation from the employer) and an interest credit (either a fixed rate or a variable rate that is linked to an index such as the one-year treasury bill rate). Increases and decreases in the value of the plan's investments do not directly affect the benefit amounts promised to participants. The investment risks and rewards on plan assets are borne solely by the employer.

Defined benefit plans and defined contribution plans typically pay out accrued benefits at the plan's specified normal retirement age, at the time of early retirement, or when the employee separates from the employment. Both defined benefit plans and defined contribution plans may pay benefits as an annuity – series of periodic payments for a specified number of years or the lifetime of the participant – or as a lump sum. Plans that permit lump sum distributions promote benefit portability by allowing participants to take their benefits when they terminate employment with the plan sponsor prior to retirement.

In addition to taking their benefits as an annuity or as a lump sum, defined contribution plans may permit participants to receive benefits at retirement in a series of periodic withdrawals (installments), determining both the amount and frequency of these withdrawals under terms set forth in the plan, until the balance in the account is exhausted.

Both defined benefit and defined contribution plans must offer married participants who elect to receive their benefits in the form of an annuity a joint and survivor annuity payment at retirement so that a surviving spouse of the covered participant continues to receive benefits in the case of the death of the participant. The income payable to the surviving spouse must be at least equal to one-half of the income originally received by the deceased plan participant.

The forfeiture provisions found in most pension plans may allow for the reduction of pension benefits in the case where workers compensation benefits are payable. In two actions initiated in **New Jersey** state courts, retired employees who had received compensation awards subsequent to retirement challenged the validity of provisions in their employers' pension plan that reduced their pension benefits by an amount equal to the compensation award for which the retirees were eligible. The state court held that the private plans were subject to ERISA. On appeal, the United States Supreme Court ultimately held that Congress had contemplated and approved the type of pension provisions challenged when ERISA was passed. Although neither ERISA or its legislative history mentioned integration of pension benefits with workers compensation benefits, the court found support for the practice in other ERISA provisions allowing the option of integrating pension benefits with Social Security and Railroad Retirement benefits, and in an Internal Revenue Service regulation permitting integration of benefits provided by federal or state law.[181] Accordingly, the statute relied upon by the retirees was held to be preempted by federal law since the statute eliminated an approved method for calculating pension benefits under plans governed by ERISA.

GROUP DISABILITY PROGRAMS

Employee benefit plans proliferated in the 1940s and 1950s. Strong unions bargained for better benefit packages, including tax-free, employer-sponsored health and disability insurance. Wage freezes imposed by the government during the Second World War served to accelerate the spread of group health care and income replacement programs. Unable by law to attract workers by paying higher wages, employers instead improved their benefit packages. Also, fear of federal

---
[181] *Alessi v. Raybestos-Manhattan, Inc.* 101 S. Ct. 1895 (1981)

expansion into short-term and long-term insurance provided an added incentive for employers to offer the coverage.

In contrast with the pension plans that pay benefits following an employee's working career, income protection for disability resulting from non-occupational causes is available through either short-term disability or long-term disability plans, or both. In 2007, 38 percent of all workers in private industry were participating in a short-term disability plan, while 30 percent of the workers were participating in a long-term disability program.[182]

The Bureau of Labor Statistics (BLS) reveals that benefits are not evenly spread among the workforce. Some workers are more likely than others to have access to benefits. Full-time workers, for example, have greater access to benefits than do part-time workers, and workers in large establishments usually have greater access to benefits than those in small establishments. Workers who belong to a labor union also are more likely to be offered benefits than those in non-union jobs. Moreover, having access to a benefit does not necessarily mean that workers choose to receive that benefit – it simply means that the employer may make the benefit available.

Short-Term Disability (STD) – STD benefits are designed to compensate an employee for income lost as a result of short-term absences from work from an accident or sickness that arises from a non-occupational cause. Under the majority of plans, STD benefits are not payable for any total disability covered by workers compensation or similar plan, even if the employee chooses not to claim such benefits.

To be eligible for STD benefits, the employee must be unable to perform the important duties of his/her own occupation and be under the personal care of a physician. Conditions resulting from participation in a riot, acts of declared war or armed aggression, or suicide are generally not covered. Typically, STD plans provide coverage on the first day following an accident or hospitalization and the 8th or 15th day of absence as a result of sickness. However, the waiting period for accident or hospitalization could be as long as 15 days.

The benefit schedule is generally based on a percentage of the employee's pre-disability weekly gross earnings subject to a maximum weekly benefit. Unless the plan member is paying the entire STD premium, the benefit will be taxable when received. A taxable STD plan will often be based on a schedule as high as 75 percent of pre-disability gross earnings whereas a non-taxable plan will generally not exceed 67 percent.

The benefit duration or period is the maximum amount of time for which STD benefits are payable. Common benefit periods are 15 weeks, 17 weeks, and 26 weeks. In many instances, the STD benefit period is integrated with the Long Term Disability benefit. For example, a STD plan with a benefit period of 17 weeks would usually be coordinated with a LTD plan with an elimination period of 17 weeks. An employee who suffers a long-term disability can

---

[182] Source: U.S. Bureau of Labor Statistics National Compensation Survey: Employee Benefits in Private Industry in the United States, March 2007 Tables 13 & 14

therefore receive benefits seamlessly as eligibility for the STD benefit ends and eligibility for LTD benefits begin.

Long-Term Disability (LTD) – For most workers, extended time away from the employment may create a significant financial hardship. LTD insurance serves to protect the financial well-being of employees against such an occurrence. For purposes of long-term disability, there are two basic definitions of disability, both relating to an individual's ability to work, own/regular occupation and any suitable occupation. The own/regular occupation definition is applied during the first two years of disability, and any suitable occupation is applied after the disability continues for two years.

Under the own/regular occupation definition, the individual is totally disabled if determined medically to be unable to perform the material duties of his/her own occupation. Under the any suitable occupation definition, the individual is considered totally disabled if determined medically to be unable to perform the material duties of any occupation for which he/she is reasonably suited by education, training, or experience.

Many employers will have a 90-day waiting period before LTD benefits begin, but some may offer shorter waiting periods. For plans that include a Short Term Disability (STD) benefit, the LTD plan is frequently structured so that the elimination period ends and benefits begin as soon as STD benefits cease.

The level of benefit entitlement is generally based on a percentage of the employee's basic monthly earnings, subject to a maximum cap. Each plan defines the earnings on which the benefit is based. A typical plan provides for a benefit in an amount equal to 60 percent of the worker's basic monthly earnings subject to a maximum monthly benefit. Payment of partial or residual benefits is not generally part of the standard LTD contract but is available as an option. LTD benefits are typically paid to age 65 although some plans will only pay for five years or other limited periods. As Social Security retirement is increasing to age 67, many plans are now paying benefits to normal retirement age.

The typical LTD plan does not pay full benefits if there are other disability payments being made. These are called offsets or simply other income. Only income listed in the policy can be used as an offset against payment of LTD benefits. Sources of income which can be applied as an offset include state-mandated disability payments including workers compensation, Social Security Disability Insurance (SSDI) and other government disability benefits, disability payments from a pension or retirement plan, and disability payments from another group LTD policy.

The workers compensation program is designed to replace a portion of the earnings lost when an injury or disease precludes an employee from engaging in gainful employment. As a general rule, an injured worker's receipt of benefits under an employer sponsored pension plan or disability insurance program will not affect the worker's entitlement to workers compensation benefits. Some states, however, provide for a reduction of compensation benefits to workers eligible for disability or wage loss benefits from an employer funded source.

A private pension agreement providing that any workers compensation benefits received by a retired employee will be deducted from his or her monthly pension payments is not against public policy, nor is it rendered invalid by reason of a statutory prohibition of waiver by employees of their rights to workers compensation. Similarly, a private long-term disability plan may provide for the offset of any workers compensation award against benefits due to the worker under the plan.[183]

Colorado permits temporary total, temporary partial, permanent partial and permanent total disability benefits to be reduced in cases where periodic disability benefits are payable from a pension or disability plan financed in whole or in part by the employer.[184] Where the employee has contributed to the pension or disability plan, workers compensation benefits are to be reduced in an amount proportional to the employer's percentage of total contribution to the pension or disability plan. This reduction in workers compensation benefits does not occur where the disability or pension plan includes an offset for workers compensation benefits.

Maine[185] and **Michigan**[186] have enacted similar provisions permitting an offset of workers compensation benefits where benefits are payable from a self-insurance plan, a wage continuation plan, a disability plan, a pension plan or a retirement plan. Where the employer makes the total contribution to any of these plans, the compensation benefit is reduced by the after-tax amount of the payments received from the plan. Where the employee contributes to the plan, the compensation benefit is to be reduced by the proportional amount based upon the employer's contribution to the total insurance premiums for the plan.

Three states, **Georgia, Kansas,** and **Louisiana**, recognize the employer's ability to reduce the workers compensation benefit by the proportionate amount that the employer paid for a disability plan or wage continuation program.[187] A number of states allow for benefit coordination where the employer has contributed in full for the plan or plans.

- In **Alabama**, workers compensation benefits may be reduced by the amount of benefits paid pursuant to a disability plan, retirement plan, or other plan providing for sick pay, if the employer provided the benefits or paid for the plan.[188]

- All income benefits payable in **Kentucky** are to be offset by payments made under an exclusively employer-funded disability or sickness and accident plan, except where the employer-funded plan contains an internal offset provision for workers compensation benefits.[189]

---

[183] Couch on Insurance 3D 173:62
[184] Colo. Rev. Stat. Ann. § 8-42-103 (1)(d)(I)
[185] Me. Rev. Stat. Ann. Title 39-A, §§ 212/213
[186] Mich. Stat. Ann. §§ 418:351, 354, 361 & 835
[187] Ga. Code Ann. § 34-9-243 (b)
Kan. Stat. Ann. § 5-44-01
La. Rev. Stat. Ann. § 23:1225
[188] Ala. Code § 25-5-57 (c)
[189] Ky. Rev. Stat. Ann. § 342.730 (6)

- Temporary total disability benefits payable in **Ohio** are to be reduced by the amount of temporary non-occupational accident and sickness program funded in full by the employer.[190] The offset of compensation benefits is to be made only upon the order of the bureau or industrial commission or agreement of the claimant.

The workers compensation law in **New Jersey** permits compensation benefits to be "set off against disability pension benefits or payments but shall not be set off against employees' retirement pension benefits or payments."[191] In **Pennsylvania,** severance benefits paid by the employer directly liable for the payment of compensation and the benefits from a pension plan to the extent funded by the employer which are received by an employee shall be credited against the amount of the award made for temporary total, temporary partial and permanent total disability. No offset is to be taken where the compensation benefits payable are for permanent partial disability.[192]

EMPLOYER SPONSORED GROUP HEALTH PLANS

Group health insurance in the United States has evolved during the 20th century. The idea of collective coverage first entered into public discussion during the First World War and the Great Depression. Soldiers fighting in the First World War received coverage through the War Risk Insurance Act, which Congress later extended to cover servicemen's dependents. In the 1920s, healthcare costs increased to the point that they exceeded most consumers' ability to pay.

The Great Depression exacerbated this problem dramatically, but resistance from the medical and insurance community defeated several efforts to establish any form of a national health insurance system. This opposition has continued into the 21st century.

Employer sponsored group health insurance plans first emerged in the 1940s as a way for employers to attract employees when wartime legislation froze wages. This was a popular tax-free benefit which employers continued to offer after the war's end, but it failed to address the needs of retirees and other non-working adults. Federal efforts to provide coverage to those groups led to the Social Security Amendments of 1965, which set the stage for Medicare and Medicaid.

The vast majority of group health insurance plans are employer-sponsored benefit plans. It is possible, however, to purchase group coverage through an association or other organizations. In 2019, employer-sponsored health plans provided some level of health coverage for approximately 160 million Americans – nearly half the total population of the country. Health insurance benefits are more likely to be provided by larger companies with an estimated 99 percent of companies with 200 or more workers offer health benefits.

---

[190] Ohio Rev. Code Ann. § 4123.56
[191] N.J. Stat. Ann. § 34:15-29
[192] Pa. Stat. Ann. Title 77 § 204

The primary advantage of a group plan is that it spreads risk across a pool of insured individuals. This benefits the group members by keeping premiums low, and insurers can better manage risk when they have a broader spectrum of participants they are covering.

Group health plans generally offer coverage through either a Health Maintenance Organization (HMO) or a Preferred Provider Organization (PPO). Insurers can exert greater control over costs through an HMO in which providers contract with insurers to provide care to members. The HMO model tends to keep costs low, at the cost of restrictions on the flexibility of care afforded to individuals. PPOs offer the patient greater choice of doctors and easier access to specialists but tend to charge higher premiums than HMOs.

Health Maintenance Organization (HMO) – An HMO is a type of managed care health insurance plan. While HMO plans typically have the advantage of lower premiums due to contracting with providers within a specific network, they provide less flexibility in terms of how members can receive medical care. HMOs typically provide a medical network made up of providers that have agreed to lower their rates for plan members and also meet quality standards. Medical care under an HMO plan is covered only if the patient sees a provider within that HMO's network. There are few opportunities to see a non-network provider. There are also typically more restrictions for coverage than other plans, such as allowing only a certain number of visits, tests or treatments. Some other key points about HMOs:

- Some plans may require the insured to select a primary care physician (PCP), who will determine what treatment you need.

- With some plans, a PCP referral is required in order to see a specialist or have a special test done.

- There is generally no coverage when opting to see a provider or specialist outside of an HMO network.

- Premiums are generally lower for HMO plans, and there is usually no deductible or a low one.

Preferred Provider Organization (PPO) – A PPO is defined as a type of managed care health insurance plan that provides maximum benefits for those who visit an in-network provider. Like HMOs, they also feature a network of providers, but there are fewer restrictions on seeing non-network providers. Additionally, a referral from a primary physician is usually not required to see an out-of-network provider. PPO plans usually have greater flexibility and options for seeing doctors and specialists at the expense of higher premiums. PPO plans provide that doctors or specialists can be scheduled without having to see a PCP first, and premiums tend to be higher, and it is common for there to be a deductible.

With group health insurance, the employer selects the plan, or plans, to offer to employees. The premium cost is often split between the employer and employee, and there is a minimum percentage rate the employer must contribute. Similar to coverages available through workers compensation, insurance plans must cover a set of essential benefits which include:

- Ambulatory care (outpatient) services
- Emergency services
- Hospitalization
- Maternity and newborn care
- Mental health and substance abuse services
- Prescription drugs
- Rehabilitative services and devices
- Laboratory services
- Preventive and wellness services, including annual physicals and mammograms
- Chronic disease management
- Pediatric services, including dental and vision

Requirements for offering group health insurance coverage are dependent on the size of the employer. Under federal law, small businesses – those with fewer than 50 employees - are not required to provide insurance to their employees under the Affordable Care Act. However, the employer has the option to offer coverage to full-time or part-time employees (those working fewer than 30 hours per week). If a small business employer offers coverage to one part-time employee, all part time employees must be offered coverage. Dependents of eligible employees are generally able to get coverage under a group plan.

The Affordable Care Act, which was signed into law in 2010, includes an employer mandate for large businesses, designed to increase participation by employers and by more of their employees. The large business mandate applies to all businesses with at least 50 full-time equivalent employees. Full-time employees are those who work 30 hours or more per week, part-time employees work less than 30 hours per week, figured on a monthly basis. The employer mandate was phased in for larger companies starting in 2015, and applied to all companies with 50 or more full-time equivalent employees by the start of 2016.

If a worker loses their job, either voluntarily or by the decision of their company (for any reason except gross misconduct), or if the worker has a reduction in the number of hours per week so as to no longer qualify for health care coverage, the employer may stop paying its share of the employee's health insurance premiums. In that case, COBRA allows the worker and his/her dependents to retain the same level of health insurance coverage provided they are willing to pay for it on their own. COBRA (Consolidated Omnibus Budget Reconciliation Act) is a federal law that permits workers to retain employee health care insurance for a limited time (18-36 months) after the employment ends or coverage is terminated. Continuation of coverage under COBRA requires the worker to pay the full monthly premium, including any part of the premium that was paid for by the employer, plus a two percent administrative charge.

As stated previously, a major difference between an employer sponsored group health plan and workers compensation is that workers compensation insurance applies only to workplace injuries and diseases while health insurance applies to non-work injuries and diseases. In fact, most health insurance policies contain language that excludes coverage for occupational injuries and illnesses.

An exception to this exclusion may occur where there is a dispute as to whether the injury or disease arose out of the employment. The group health insurer may be called upon to provide the medical care and related medical expenses until such time the issue of whether the claim is compensable has been determined. If the condition is found to be work-related, the workers compensation benefit administrator will be called upon to reimburse the group carrier for any expenses incurred along with the obligation to reimburse for any deductible and co-payment amounts that were incurred during the period the claim was in dispute.

TABLE OF CASES

A

Abbott v. Gould, Inc., 443 N.W. 2d 591 (1989)	423
Adams. v. Acme White Lead and Color Works, 148 N.W. 485 (1914)	199
Aetna Life Insurance Co. v. Industrial Comm'n, 254 P. 995 (1927)	172
Ahern v. Spier, 105 A. 340 (1918)	171
Albertson's Inc. v. WCAB (Bradley), 182 Cal. Rptr. 304 (1982)	205
Alessi v. Raybestos-Manhattan, Inc. 101 S. Ct. 1895 (1981)	492
Attorney General v. Insurance Commissioner of Michigan, 323 N.W. 2d 645 [Footnote 3]	140
Aucompaugh v. General Electric 111 A.D. 2d 1073 (1985)	175

B

Bachman Co. v. WCAB, 683 A. 2d 1305 (1996)	173
Bailey v. American General Insurance Company, 279 S.W. 2d 315 (1955)	207
Baker v. Schatz, 912 P. 2d 501 (1996)	424
Bakonyi v. Ralston Purina Co. 478 N.E. 2d 241 (1985)	428
Bass v. National Super Markets, Inc., 911 S.W.2d 617 (1995)	68
Bell v. Industrial Vangas Co., 637 P2d 266 (1981)	427
Bias v. Workers' Compensation Comm'r, 176 W. Va. 421 (1986)	211
Billy v. Consolidated Machine Tool Corp. 412 N.E. 2d 934 (1980)	429
Blake v. Grand Union Co., 98 N.Y.S. 2d 738 (1950)	183
Blankenship v. Cincinnati Milacron, Inc., 433 N.E. 2d 572 (1982)	418
Borgnis v. Falk Co. 133 N.W. 209 (1911)	12
Bradshaw v. Old Republic Insurance Company, 922 S.W. 2d 503 (1996)	130
Brady v. Safety-Kleen Corp., 576 N.E. 2d 722 (1991)	418
Brock v. Mr. W Fireworks, Inc., 814 F.2d 1042 (5th Cir. 1987	60
Brooks v. Island Creek Coal Co. 678 SW2d 791 (1984)	462
Brutz v. CalMat Co., West Law 265175 (2002)	416
Burrough's v. LCR-M 781 So. 2d 877 (2001)	211
Butterfield v. Forrester, 11 East 60, 103 Eng. Rep. 926 (1809)	291
Byrd v. Richardson-Greenshields Securities, Inc., 552 So. 2d 150 (1989)	439

C

Castro v. United Container Machinery Group, Inc., 761 NE2d 1014 (2001)	434
Chandris, Inc. v. Latsis, 515 U.S. 347 (1995)	164
Cherokee Industries, Inc. v. CNA Insurance Company 84 P3 798 (2004)	52
Circuit City Stores v. Illinois Workers' Comp. 391 Ill.App.3d 913 (2009)	182
Coates, etal v. Wal-Mart Stores, 976 P2d 999 (1999)	440
Cody v. Snider Lumber Co, 399 S.E. 2d 104 (1991)	188
Cohen et al. v. Cohen's Department Store, Inc., 198 S.E. 476 (Va. 1938)	172
Commissioners of State Insurance Fund v. Photocircuits Corp., N.Y. Misc. LEXIS 1388 (2003)	140
Cox v. Costal Products Company, Inc., 774 A. 2d 347 (2001)	181
Crews v. Memorex Corp., 588 F. Supp. 27 (1984)	441

D

Davis v. Liberty Mutual Ins. Co., 2007 U.S. Dist. LEXIS 49685 (2007)	453
Deerfield Plastics Co. v. Hartford Insurance Co., 536 N.E. 2d 322 (1989)	140
Design Kitchens and Bath v. Lagos 882 A. 2d 817 (2005)	52
Deville v. Bloch, Calif. Ct. App., No. B291099 (Nov. 21, 2019).	423
Dole v. Dow Chemical Company, 30 N.Y. 2d 143 (1972)	133

Dole v. Dow Chemical, 282 N.E. 2d 288 (1972) — 433
Dominick v. Houtech Inland Well Service, Inc., 718 F. Supp. 489 (E.D. La 1989) — 165
Douglas v. E.J.Gallo Winery 137 Cal Rptr 797 (1977) — 427
Ducote v. Albert, 521 So. 2d 399 (1988) — 429
Duprey v. Shane, 241 P. 2d 78 (1951) — 134, 425
Dynamex Operations West, Inc. v. Superior Court of Los Angeles (2018) — 23, 65

E

Easly v. D&O Contractors, 895 So.2d 23 (2005) — 202
EEOC v. Walmart, Inc., Case No. 6:20-cv-00163-KKC on Aug. 3, 2020 — 489
Empowerment Association v. WCAB (Porch), 962 A.2d 1 (2008) — 206
Errand v. Cascade Steel Rolling Mills, 888 P.2d 544 (1994) — 189
Errand v. Cascade Steel Rolling Mills, Inc., 888 P2d 544 (1995) — 445
Estate of Teague ex rel. Martinosky v. Crossroads Cooperative Association, 834 N.W.2d 236 (2013) — 420
Estrada v. Fedex Ground Package System, Inc., 154 Cal. App. 4th 1 (2007) — 65

F

Farrington v. Total Petroleum, Inc., 486 N.W. 2d 677 (1992) — 187
Ferriter v. Daniel O'Connell's Sons, Inc., 413 N.E. 2d 690 (1980) — 134, 443
Festa v. Teleflex, Inc., 382 S.E. 2d 122 (1980) — 193
Fine v. S.M.C. Microsystems Corp., 553 N.E. 2d 1337 (1990) — 185
Firstenergy Generation, LLC v. Muto, 2018 W. Va. LEXIS 185 (Mar. 12, 2018) — 418
Fowler v. Kohl's Dept. Stores, Inc., 2009 WL 2155481 (N.D.N.Y.,2009) — 489
Frampton v. Central Indiana Gas Co., 297 N.E. 2d 425 (1975) — 442
Fryer v. Kranz, 616 N.W.2d 102 (S.D. Sep. 6, 2000) — 420
Fyffe v. Jenoe's Inc. 570 N.E. 2d 1108 (1991) — 419

G

Gaetan H. Bourgoin v. Twin Rivers Paper Co. L.L.C., et. al.36 — 223
Gargiulo v. Gargiulo, 97 A.2d 593 (1953). — 173
Gilbert v. Publix Supermarkets, Inc., 790 So. 2d 1057 (2001) — 181
Gilbert v. Tyson Foods Inc. , 782 So. 2d 786 (2001) — 174
Gleason v. Samaritan and Church Mutual Insurance Co., 926 P. 2d 1349 (1996) — 204
Golden v. Westark Community College 948 SW2d 108 (1997) — 462
Golden v. Westark Community College 969 S.W.2d 154 (1998) — 257
Granados v Windsor Development Corp. 509 S.E.2d 290 (1999) — 52
Green v. Wyman-Goron, Co., 664 N.E. 2d 808 (1996) — 440
GTE Southwest, Inc. v. Bruce, 998 SW2d 605 (1999) — 441
Guy v. Arthur H. Thomas Co., 378 N.E.2d 488 (1978) — 425

H

Habashi v. Interbake Foods, Inc., No. A-0912-07T3, (2008) — 430
Hager v. M&K Construction, 2021 N.J. LEXIS 332 (April 13, 2021) — 224
Hammer v. Dagenhart, 247 U.S. 251 (1918) — 10
Harbor Tug & Barge Co.v. Papai, 520 U.S. 548 (1997) — 164
Harris v. Board of Education, 825 A. 2d 265 (2003) — 188
Heatherly v. Hollingsworth Co., Inc., No. COA10-994 (2011) — 175
Heirs v. John A. Hull & Co., 164 N.Y.S. 767 (1917) — 199
Held v. New York State Workers Compensation Board 58 A.D.3d 971 (2009) — 100
Held v. New York State Workers Compensation Board 85 A.D.3d 35 (2011) — 100
Herbolsheimer v. SMS Holding Co., Inc., 608 N.W. 2d 487 (2000) — 431

Hill v. Columbia TriStar Television Court of Appeals decision rendered April 2003	439
Holmes v. Gold Kist, Inc. 670 So. 2d 449 (1995)	170
Holmes v. Gold Kist, inc. 673 So. 2d 449 (1995)	209
Horodyskyj v. Karanian, 33 P. 3d 470 (2001)	439
Hostettler v. College of Wooster, 895 F. 3d 844 - 2018	489
Hulley v. Moosbrugger, 95 A. 1007 (1916)	174

I

Isaac Ortiz v. Cement Products No. S-05-437 (2005)	52
Ives v. South Buffalo Railroad 201 N.Y. 271 (1911)	12
Ives. V. South Buffalo Railway co. 94 NE 431 (1911)	43

J

Jamison v. Encarnacion, 281 U.S. 635, 640 (1930)	159
Johns-Manville Products Corp. v. Superior Court, 165 Cal. Rptr. 858 (1980)	423
Jones v. State of New York 468 N.Y.S 2d 223 (1983)	421

K

Kentucky Employers Mutual Ins. v. Coleman, 2007 KY LEXIS 167 (2007)	454
Kerley v. Workmen's Comp. App. Bd., 4 Cal. 3d 223 (1971)	452
Konstanopoulos v. Westcao Corp., 690 A. 2d 936 (1996)	440
Kroger Stores v. Keng, 23 S.W. 3d 347 (2000)	449

L

Laidlow v. Hariton Machinery Co., Inc., 170 N.J. 602 (2002)	419
Lambertson v. Cincinnati Corp., 257 NW2d 679 (1971)	435
Lawrence v. CDB Services, Inc., 44 S.W. 3d 544 (2001)	450
Levin v. Canon Business Solutions, 2010 WL 731645 (Cal.App. 2 Dist., March 4, 2010)	416
Lockwood v. Independent School Dist. No. 877 312 N.W.2d 924 (1981)	207
Loges v. Mack Trucks, 417 S.E. 2d 538 (1992)	439
Lombardi v. Copper Canyon Academy, LLC, 2010 WL 3775408 (2010)	438

M

Magliulo v. Superior Court (1975) 47 Cal. App.3d 760	416
Mandolitis v. Elkin Industries, Inc., 246 S.E. 2d 907 (1978)	416
Martin v. Wabash Railroad, 142 F. 650 (1905)	4
Matter of Quigley v. Village of E. Aurora, 2021 N.Y. App. Div. LEXIS 1223 (2021)	224
Mayles v. Shoney's, Inc., 405 S.E. 2d 15 (1990)	417
McAlister v. Methodist Hosp. of Memphis, 550 S.W. 2d 240 (1977)	426
McBride v. Grand Island Express 2010 WL 5080933 (2010)	289
McCarthy v. Department of Social and Health Services, 759 P. 2d 351 (1988)	444
McGriff v. Worsley Companies, Inc., 654 S.E.2d 856, 376 S.C. 103 (S.C. App. 2007)	184
McRae v. Arby's Restaurant Group, 313 Ga. App. 313 (721 SE2d 602) (2011)	329
Medellin V. Cashman KPA, etal, Mass. Dept. of Industrial Accidents (2003)	52
Mendoza v. Monmouth Recycling Corp. 672 A. 2d 221 (1996)	52
Mercer v. Uniroyal, Inc. 361 NE2d 492 (1976)	427
Milashouskas v. Mercy Hospital 64 A.D. 2d 978 (1978)	426
Missouri Alliance for Retired Ams. v. Dep't of Labor and Indus. Relations, 277 S.W. 3d 670 (MO 2009)	447

N

Nationwide Mutual Insurance Co. v. Ed Soules Construction Co., 397 So. 2d 775 (1981)	140

Nelson v. Union Wire Rope Corp., 199 N.E. 2d 769 (1964) — 415
Nelson v. Winnebago Industries 619 N.W. 2d 385 (2000) — 420

O

Oakes v. Workmen's Compensation Appeal Board, 445 A. 2d 838 (1982) — 191
Oklahoma Roofing & Sheet Metal v. Wells 457 P. 3d 1020 (2019) — 422
Olson v. Hartford Accident and Indemnity Company, 477 S.W.2d 859 (1972) — 207

P

Padgett v. State of Florida, Office of the Attorney General, Case No. 11-13661 CA 25. (2014) — 447
Payne v. Galen Hosp. Corp., 28 S.W. 3d 15 (2000) — 426
Pearson v. Paradise Ford, 951 So.2d 12 (2007) — 447
Pennsylvania Dep. Of Corrections v. Workers Compensation Appeals Board (Kirchner), 805 A2d 633 (2002) — 304
Potter v. McCulla, 288 Neb. 741, 2014 Neb. LEXIS 124 (2014) — 194
Priestley v. Fowler, 3 Mees & Wels. 1, 150 Eng. Rep. (1837) — 4

R

Ramos v. M&F Fashions, 713 A. 2d 486 (1998) — 180
Reinforced Earth Company v. Workers Compensation Appeal Board 749 A 2d 1036 (2000) — 53
Reyes v. Storage & Processors, Inc., 995 S.W. 2d 722 (1999) — 449
Rhine v. Bayou Pipe Coating, 11-724 (La. App. 3d Cir. 11/02/11) — 421
Riccitelli v. Broekhuizen, 595 N.W. 2d 392 (1999) — 430
Richardson v. Fiedler Roofing, Inc., 502 N.Y.S. 2d 125 (1986) — 179
Richardson v. Home Depot USA, 808 So2d 544 (2001) — 440
Riley v. Debaer 562 S.E. 2d 69 (2002) — 441
Robbins v. Original Gas Engine Co., 157 N.W. 437 (1916) — 190
Roberts v. J.F. Newcomb & Co., 138 N.E. 443 (1922) — 178
Rose v. Berry Plastics Corp. et al., 2019 OK Civ. App. 55 — 223
Ruiz v. Belk Masonry Co. 559 SE 2d 249 (2002) — 53
Rush v. BellSouth Telecommunications, Inc., 2011 WL 691617 (2011) — 437

S

Saunders v. Industrial Commission, 727 N.E. 2d 247 (2000) — 179
Schneider v. Farmers Merchant, Inc., 678 P. 2d 33 (1983) — 436
Sellers v. Venture Express, Inc., 2021 Ala. Civ. App. LEXIS 9 (2021) — 81
Sharon Vredenburg v. Sedgwick CMA and Flamingo Hilton-Laughlin. (2008) — 176
Shatto v. McLeod Regional Med. Ctr., 2013 S.C. LEXIS 339 (2013) — 64
Skauge v. Mountain States Telephone & Telegraph Co., 565 P.2d 628 (1977) — 288
Skinner v. Reed, 374 N.E. 2d 437 (1978) — 435
Smith v. Desautels, 953 A.2d 620 (2008) — 438
Smith v. H. E. Butt Grocery Co., 18 S.W.3d 910 (2000) — 450
Smothers v. Gresham Transfer, Inc., 332 Or. 83 (2001) — 446
Sorban v. Sterling Engineering Corp. 830 A. 2d 372 (2003) — 419
Southern Pacific Co. v. Jensen, 244 U.S. 205 (1917) — 14, 165
Stancil v. ACE USA, 211 N.J. 276 (N.J., Aug. 1, 2012) — 453
State Comp. Ins. Fund v. McMillan, 31 P.3d 347, 350 (2001) — 289
State Industrial Commissioner v. Leff, 265 N.Y. 533 (1934) — 172
State of West Virginia vs. Richardson 482 S.E.2d 162 (1996) — 257
Suburban Hospital, Inc. v. Kirson, 763 A. 2d 185 (2000) — 426
Sylvia Martin v. Virginia Beach (2020) — 175

T

Taylor v. City of Titusville, 288 So.3d 731 (2019)	202
Temple v. Denali Princess Lodge, 21 P .3d 813 (2001)	174
Terlecki v. Strauss, 89 A. 1023 (1914)	180
Testa v Sorrento Restaurant, 10 AD2d 133 (1960)	52
Thompson v. Keller Foundations, Inc., 883 So. 2d 356 (2004)	183
Torres v. Travelers Insurance Co., et al., No. 01-5056 (2004)	455
Tracy v. Sterling Superior Services, 2009 Conn. Super. LEXIS 93 (2009)	419
Trent v. Stark Metal Sales, Inc., 2015-Ohio-1115, 2015 Ohio App. LEXIS 1070 (2015)	223

U

United Airlines v. Walter, 482 S.E. 2d 849 (1997)	195
United States v. Silk, 331 U.S. 704 (1947),	60
Upjohn Co. v. United States, 449 U.S. 383 (1981)	275
US Bank Home Mortgage v. Schrecker, 2014 Ky. LEXIS 617 (2014)	182

V

Valenzuela v. Pallet Express, Inc., 700 S.E.2d 76 (2010)	421
Van Dunk v. Reckson Associates Realty Corp., et al., 2012 N.J. LEXIS 678 (2012)	420
Vasquez v. Dillard, Inc., 2016 OK 89 (Sept. 13, 2016)	23, 103
Vaughan Roofing & Sheet Metal, LLC v. Rodriquez 131 S. Ct. 1572 (2011)	53
VECO Inc. v. Rosebrock, 970 P. 2d 906 (1998)	439
Vogel v. Wells Fargo Guard Services 937 SW2d 856 (1996)	463

W

Weber v. Armco, Inc. 663 P. 2d 1221 (1983)	428
Weber v. Armco, Inc., 663 P.2d 1221 (Okla. 1983)	424
Wolfe v. Sibley, Lindsay & Curr Co., 36 N.Y.2d 505 (1975)	205
Woodson v. Rowland, 407 S.E.2d 222 (1991)	421
Wright v. District Court for the County of Jefferson, 661 P2d 1167 (1983)	425

Z

Zach v. Nebraska State Patrol, 727 N.W.2d 206 (Neb. 2007)	208
Zilisch v. State Farm Mutual Auto Ins. Co., 995 P.2d 276, 280 (2000)	455

Index

A

"A-rated" classifications – 382
ABC Test – 23, 62, 65
Abuse – 5, 277-278, 285, 312-313, 327-328, 431, 435, 440, 455, 475, 486, 498
Accidental Injury – 75, 184, 188, 190-192, 205-206, 216, 233, 254
Accident investigation – 262, 270, 273
Acord Workers Compensation First Report of Injury – 258
Acts of God – 8, 175
Actual-risk doctrine – 172
Administrative appeals – 358
Affordable Care Act (ACA) – 297, 333-336, 474, 498
Aggregate excess coverage – 96
Aggravation of pre-existing condition – 191, 193
Agreement system – 342
Aggregate financial call data – 383
Agricultural laborers – 15, 43, 45
Allocation of expenses – 287-288
Aliens – 51-53
Alternative benefit schemes – 44, 100-101
    Texas "opt-out" program – 22, 44, 102-103
    "Carve-out" programs – 44, 104
    Oklahoma Employee Injury Benefit Act (OEIBA) – 103
Alternate Dispute Resolution (ADR) – 104, 360
AMA Guides to Evaluation of Permanent Impairment – 247, 249
American Legislative Exchange Council (ALEC) – 101
Americans with Disabilities Act (ADA) – 226, 485-487
Average indexed monthly earnings – 460
Apportionment – 133, 203, 290, 293, 428, 432
"Arising out of" the employment – 169, et seq.
Artificial members – 217-218
Assault – 173-174, 279, 415-416, 421, 428, 437-440
Assumption of risk – 5, 7, 15, 43, 102, 166, 435
Attendant care – 217, 219, 266
Attorney-client privilege – 275-276
Attorney fees – 8, 274, 288, 338, 339, 356, 361-362
"Average current earnings" – 256, 274, 464, 466
Average weekly wage – 19-21, 230, 232-233, 241, 248-249, 254-255, 265, 356, 371, 477

B

Bad faith – 271, 284, 362, 414, 451-457
Barth, Peter, University of Connecticut – 17, 238, 365
Basic Administrative Information System (BAIS) – 344, 345
Basic Manual for Workers Compensation and Employers Liability Insurance – 381
Benchmarking – 349-352
Benefit escalation – 216, 254-255
Binders, renewals, and cancellations – 144
Binding arbitration – 356, 361, 450
Black Car Operators Injury Compensation Fund – 375
Burton, John – 17
Bureau of Labor Statistics (BLS) – 26, 34, 251, 493

C

Cancellation clause – 142
Carve-out program(s) – 44, 103, 104, 105
Case reserving – 266
Casual employment – 47
Centers for Disease Control and Prevention (CDC) – 38-39
Centers for Medicare and Medicaid Services (CMS) – 299, 308, 312, 469, 471-472, 475
Choice of medical provider – 302
Claims administration – 97, 412
Claims investigation – 97, 263
Classification of risks – 383
Code of ethics for adjusters – 269
Commission on Workmen's Compensation Laws – 344
Common law defenses – 9, 15, 43, 83, 102, 449
Commutations – 358, 363
Compensability Standards – 187-188
    Usual exertion rule – 187
    Unusual exertion rule – 188
Competitive state fund – 22, 83, 86-87
Compulsory law – 11
Concurrent employment – 372-373
Contribution – 2, 9, 126, 133, 356, 431-435, 445, 459, 478, 480, 490-492, 495
Contributory negligence – 4, 7, 15, 43, 159, 166, 290-292, 449
Controlled Substances Act of 1970 (CSA) – 222
Council of State Governments Model Act – 369
"Course of" the employment – 1, 4, 75, 126, 129, 132, 134, 147, 171, 174, 178-186, 190-192, 194, 196, 200-201, 206, 209-210, 279, 301, 364, 366, 374, 415, 420, 426, 435-436, 445, 455, 464, 479
Covered workers – 1, 15, 43, 126, 481
    Numeric exceptions – 44-45

       Agricultural laborers – 15, 43, 45
       Casual workers – 15, 18, 43, 47
       Domestics – 15, 17, 43, 48, 155
       Family members – 49, 57, 85, 251-252, 290
       Sole proprietors and partners – 49-50
       Illegal aliens – 51-53
       Real estate agents or brokers – 53-54
COVID-19 – 24-25, 38-39, 66, 183-184, 202, 212-214, 298, 481-482
COVID-19 presumption – 24, 212, 214
Cumulative injury – 75, 192, 193-195, 203

D

Data collection – 268, 345-347, 351, 481
Death benefits – 16, 19, 78, 106, 251-254, 267, 289, 373-374, 376, 433, 451
Deductible programs – 22, 92, 123, 404, 410-412
       Large deductible programs – 411-412
       Small deductible programs – 123, 410
Department of Health and Human Services (DHHS) – 330, 469, 475
Diagnosis Related Groups (DRG) – 298, 311-312
Direct payment system – 342
Disability benefit computation – 231
Disability benefit duration – 231
Disability benefits – 16-17, 19, 21, 62, 102, 104, 129, 145, 147, 158, 161, 215, 229, 231, 233, 235-236, 241, 244-246, 249, 253, 255-257, 276-278, 280, 301, 343, 356, 363, 365, 370-371, 387, 447-448, 451-452, 460, 462-467, 470, 476, 482, 494-496
       Temporary Total Disability (TTD) – 19-20, 214, 227, 230-231, 233, 236-237, 267, 343, 356, 462, 482, 496
       Permanent Total Disability (PTD) – 19, 231, 234-236, 255-257, 267, 356, 366-367, 370-372, 434, 448, 462-463, 465, 482, 495-496
       Temporary Partial Disability (TPD) – 237, 267, 482
       Permanent Partial Disability (PPD) – 21, 220, 234, 237-239, 242-246, 249-250, 257, 267, 354, 363, 370, 375, 462, 482, 496
             Scheduled PPD Awards – 239
             Unscheduled PPD Awards – 242
                 Impairment based – 243-245, 250
                 Loss of wage-earning capacity – 245
                 Wage-loss – 21, 125, 158, 160, 237, 245-246, 248-250, 448, 462, 494
                 Bi-furcated approach – 246-248
Disfigurement benefits – 215, 253-254
Dispute Resolution – 89, 104, 245, 338-339, 352, 354-357, 360-361
Dissemination of information – 340, 353
Dividend Programs – 123, 408-409
       Small deductible programs – 123, 410

        Large deductible programs – 411-412
Domestics – 15, 17, 43, 48, 155
DoorDash – 23, 65, 67
Dual capacity – 85, 134, 271, 415-416, 424-431
Dual persona – 424, 429-431
Dual purpose doctrine – 181

E

Eastman, Crystal – 7,10
Elective laws – 15, 17, 20
Electronic Data Interchange (EDI) – 321, 346-349
Employee Stock Ownership Plan (ESOP) – 491
Employers Liability Insurance – 126, 128, 132, 134-137, 145-152, 165-168, 295, 381
Employers' Liability Laws – 6-8
Energy Employees Occupational Illness Compensation Program Act of 2000 – 162
English Workmen's Compensation Act of 1897 – 169, 190
Ergonomic – 184
Excess Loss Coverage – 407
Exclusive Remedy – 14, 69, 75, 77, 85, 102, 126, 132, 135, 166, 187, 189, 414-416, 419-422, 424-426, 428-430, 432-433, 435, 437-442, 444-447, 451-454, 488
        Dual capacity – 85, 134, 271, 415-416, 424-431
        Dual persona – 424, 429-431
        Intentional injury – 133, 279, 415-417, 419, 421-422
        Fraudulent concealment – 416, 422-424, 428
        Third party action-over – 133, 415, 431
Exclusive state funds – 83-86, 88, 356,
Expected Loss Rate (ELR) – 401
Experience rating – 96, 99, 108, 122, 156, 247, 377, 384-385, 392-393, 395-405, 409, 479
Extraterritorial coverage – 72-73, 75, 130
        In-state worker/ Out-of-state injury – 74
        Out-of-state worker/ In-state injury – 76
        Express written agreements – 80
        Reciprocal agreements – 80-82

F

Fair Labor Standards Act (FLSA) – 10, 67
Family and Medical Leave Act (FMLA) – 482-485
Federal Compensation Programs – 158
        Federal Employees Compensation Act (FECA) – 11, 158
        Federal Employers' Liability Act (FELA) – 7, 147, 159-160, 391
        Federal Coal Mine Health and Safety Act – 32, 127, 147, 161, 397
        Radiation Exposure Compensation Act (RECA) – 162-163
        Energy Employees Occupational Illness Compensation Program Act – 162

    Death on the High Seas Act – 163
    Merchant Marine Act (Jones Act) of 1920 – 127, 163
    Longshore and Harbor Workers Compensation Act – 127, 129, 147, 165, 167
      Defense Base Act – 147, 167
       Non-Appropriated Fund Instrumentalities Act – 147, 167-168
       Outer Continental Shelf Lands Act – 147, 167-168
Federal Insurance Contribution Act (FICA) – 459-460
Federal Unemployment Tax Act (FUTA) – 55, 476
Federal Vocational Rehabilitation Act (FVCA) – 343
Fellow-servant rule – 4-5, 7, 15, 102
First Report of Injury (FROI) – 258, 264, 341-342, 345, 348
Formal dispute resolution – 352, 357
Fraud – (Chapter Seven) 52, 70-71, 258, 263, 276-285, 475
   Attorney fraud – 283
   Employee fraud – 278-280, 285
   Insurer fraud – 284
   Medical provider fraud – 283
Fraudulent concealment – 416, 422-424, 428

G
General Accounting Office (GAO) – 36
German Accident Insurance Law – 8
Gig economy – 25, 56, 65-67
"Going and coming" rule – 180-181
Governing classifications – 383
Gradual or cumulative injury – 193
Grave injury (New York) – 133, 433-434

H
Hazard control – 116-119
Health Insurance Portability and Accountability Act of 1996 (HIPPA) – 329-330
Health Maintenance Organization (HMO) – 316-317, 330, 497
Heart conditions – 191
Horseplay – 174

I
Illegal aliens – 51-53
Immigration Reform and Control Act (IRCA) – 53
Impairment income benefits – 247, 249
Income replacement benefits – 1, 102, 215-216, 228-234, 253-254, 257, 283, 297, 332, 342, 351, 449, 461
Increased risk doctrine – 170-172, 175
Indemnification – 96, 126, 133, 135, 250, 431-434, 436

Independent contractors – 23, 25, 54, 56-60, 62-65, 67, 263, 281, 286
Independent Medical Examination (IME) – 220-222, 267, 324
Independent rating bureaus – 127, 377
Informal dispute resolution – 354-357
Information Page – 126-130, 134, 136-138, 141-146, 148-152, 154, 167, 391, 403
Injury aggravation – 195
Injury by accident – 1, 77, 129, 134, 137, 145-146, 148, 151, 160, 165, 167, 169, 187, 190-192, 438
Inspections clause – 142
InstaCart – 23, 65
Intentional injury – 133, 279, 415-417, 419, 421-422
Intentional infliction of emotional distress – 271, 415, 438-441
International Association of Industrial Accident Boards and Commissions (IAIABC) – 309, 344-348, 367
In the course of employment – 1, 75, 126, 129, 132, 134, 147, 171, 174, 179-180, 182-186, 189-192, 194, 196, 200-201, 206, 209-210, 279, 301, 364, 366, 374, 415, 426, 435-436, 445, 455, 464, 479

J
Joint and several liability – 98-99
Jones Act – 127, 163, 165
Jones, Derek A. – 335-336

K
Keating-Owen Child Labor Act of 1916 – 10
Krohm, Greg – 309

L
Laissez-faire – 4, 7
Larson, Arthur – 2, 181, 204, 431
Longshore and Harbor Workers Compensation Act – 127, 129, 147, 165, 167
Loss control program – 26-27, 29, 118
Loss Conversion Factor – 157, 406, 408
Loss of consortium – 85, 133-134, 416, 442-443
Loss-of-wage-earning-capacity – 245
Lump sum settlements – 274, 279, 284, 339, 352, 357-358, 362-365
Lyft – 23, 56, 65, 67

M
Major contributing cause – 23, 189, 445-447
Malingering – 16, 277, 280
Managed care – 103, 303-306, 314-320, 322, 324-326, 393, 497

Marijuana – 24-25, 222-224
Master-servant relationship – 3, 4
Maximum medical improvement – 215, 217, 219-220, 233-234, 237, 247-249, 447-448
Mediation – 353, 355-356, 361
Medicaid – 297, 299, 308, 312, 314, 330, 334, 459, 469, 472-475, 496
Medical benefits – 2, 16, 102, 106, 154, 158, 161-163, 215-217, 219, 244, 297, 301-302, 306, 317, 336, 356, 363, 370-372, 411, 415, 451, 462, 469
Medical bill review and repricing – 320
Medical case management – 323
Medical fee schedules – 302, 306-310, 315
    Medical services – 21, 102, 214, 216-217, 220, 265, 297, 307, 310, 315, 320, 322, 345, 425-426, 468, 470-471
    Hospital services – 467, 473
Medical marijuana – 24, 222-224
Medical Provider Networks (MPNs) – 310-311
Medical records privacy – 297, 327
Medicare – 101, 274, 283, 297-299, 307-312, 326, 330, 365, 459, 467-473, 475, 496
Medicare Advantage Plans – 468
Medicare Secondary Payer (MSP) – 470
Mental stress claims – 205
    Physical-mental – 204-205, 270, 440
    Mental-physical – 204, 208, 440
    Mental-mental – 24, 204-208, 212
Merchant Marine Act of 1920 – (see Jones Act)
Merit rating – 385, 391-392
Michigan Silicosis Dust Disease & Logging Industry Compensation Fund – 374
Migrant and Seasonal Agricultural Worker Protection Act – 46, 147
Mine Safety and Health Administration – 32
Minimum premium – 144, 149, 151, 382, 390-391, 397, 407, 412
Misclassification of payroll – 282
Modified comparative negligence – 291-292

N
National Association of Professional Employer Organizations (NAPEO) – 70
National Association of Insurance Commissioners (NAIC) – 88, 345, 385
National Commission on State Workmen's Compensation Laws – 17, 26, 42-44, 72, 339
    Nineteen Essential Recommendations – 18, 72
National Council on Compensation Insurance (NCCI) – 91, 108, 114, 126-127, 211, 213, 216, 218, 295, 297, 377, 405
National Institute for Occupational Safety and Health (NIOSH) – 33
Newspaper Vendors – 54, 56
Non-Appropriated Fund Instrumentalities Act – 147, 167-168
Non-binding arbitration – 355

Non-Subscriber(s) – 44, 102-103, 448-451
North American Industry Classification System (NAICS) – 379-380

O

Occupational disease – 24, 50, 75-77, 80, 97, 120, 129, 131-132, 136, 145, 147, 167, 194, 196-203, 207-208, 216, 228, 271, 297, 372, 397, 435, 444-447
Occupational Safety and Health Act of 1970 – 33-34, 40, 351
Occupational Safety and Health Administration (OSHA) – 27, 32-41, 97, 119, 264, 351, 379, 420
    OSHA penalties and citations – 39
Occupational Safety and Health Review Commission (OSHRC) – 33
Odd-lot doctrine – 236-237
Office of Workers Compensation Programs (OWCP) – 158, 161, 168, 313
Offset provisions – 254, 256, 465-466
(Oklahoma) alternate benefit program – 22
Oklahoma Employee Injury Benefit Act (OEIBA) – 103
Old Age, Survivors, and Disability Insurance (OASDI) – 254, 459
Omnibus Reconciliation Act of 1981 – 256, 465

P

Patient Protection and Affordable Care Act – 333
Pandemic – 24-25, 38-39, 66, 183, 202, 213-214, 298, 481-482
Part A Coverage – 467-468
Part B Coverage – 468-469
Part C Coverage – 468
Part D Coverage – 468
Payroll limitation rule – 389-390
Peculiar or increased-risk doctrine – 170
Pennsylvania Supersedeas Fund – 374
Personal comfort doctrine – 181-182
Personal injury – 3, 5, 15, 190-192, 206-208, 210, 242, 287, 361, 374, 423, 430, 450
Personal injury by accident – 1, 77, 169, 190, 438
Personal Protective Equipment (PPE) – 28, 30, 35, 37, 39
Physical rehabilitation – 19-20, 165, 217, 221, 225, 253
Point of Service (POS) – 316-317
Policy Endorsements – 126, 143, 153
Positional risk doctrine – 172, 175, 177
Postmates – 23, 65
Post-Traumatic Stress Disorder (PTSD) – 24, 208, 211-212
Pre-existing injury – 191, 366
Preferred Provider Organization (PPO) – 316-317, 497
Premium (see rate-making)
Premium audits – 394

Premium discounts – 89, 92, 122-123
Prescription drug coverage – 468
Prescription Drug Monitoring Program (PDMP) – 312
Prescription Monitoring Program (PMP) – 312
Presumptions – 24-25, 202, 209-214, 462
Presumption of Injury – 209, 211
Primary insurance amount (PIA) – 460, 464
Private insurance – 2, 85-88, 90, 99, 108, 153, 383
Professional Employer Organization (PEO) – 70-72
Profit Sharing Plan – 491
Program Administration – 338
Proof of Coverage (POC) – 348
Pure comparative negligence – 291-292
Pure contributory negligence – 291-292

Q
Qualified Loss Management Program (QLMP) – 91
Quid pro quo – 14, 69, 209, 447

R
Radiation Exposure Compensation Act (RECA) – 162-163
Rate-Making – 97, 140, 295, 376-378, 383
    Classification systems – 378-379
    Estimated premium – 139-141, 149, 390, 393
    Expected loss rate – 401
    Experience rating – 96, 99, 108, 122, 156, 247, 377, 384-385, 392-393, 395-405, 409, 479
    Loss costs – 89, 377, 384-385, 390, 408
    Manual rate – 107, 122, 384-385, 390-391, 393, 395-396, 398, 401, 403
    Minimum premium – 144, 149, 151, 382, 390-391, 397, 407, 412
    Rating organizations – 345, 376-377, 379-380, 383-385, 396, 407
    Remuneration inclusions – 386
    Remuneration exclusions – 388
    Scheduled rating – 392
    Statistical data – 89, 345, 383
    Unit statistical data – 384
Real estate agents or brokers – 53-54
Reciprocal agreements – 80-82
Recovery from others (see also subrogation)
Reemployment Assistance Program (RAP) – 228
Recreational, social, and athletic activities – 185
Rehabilitation – 1, 17-21, 53, 83, 97, 103-104, 108, 158, 165, 215, 217, 221, 224-228, 253, 265, 267-268, 287, 323, 325, 339, 343-345, 348-349, 356, 373, 376, 441, 462, 487

Remuneration – 42, 53-54, 141, 144, 149, 151, 154-155, 157, 186, 232, 269, 276, 376, 378, 386-390, 393
Repetitive trauma (see cumulative injury)
Resource Based Relative Value Scale (RBRVS) – 308
Residual markets – 90, 390
Retaliatory discharge – 441
Retroactive periods – 229
Retrospective rating – 95, 123, 139, 157, 377, 393, 404-408, 410
Return to work programs – 360
Reverse offset – 256, 465
Risk pricing – 122
Role of Case Manager – 264
Roosevelt, President Theodore – 11

S
Safety violations – 46
Scheduled rating – 392
Scopes® of Basic Manual Classifications – 114, 381
Second injury funds (see special funds)
Self-Employment Contribution Act (SECA) – 459
Self-Insurance – 2, 22, 80, 83, 85, 92-95, 97, 99-100, 103, 107, 131, 136, 146, 148, 154, 281, 376, 404-405, 410, 412, 470, 477, 495
    Individual self-insurance – 94-95, 97, 100
    Self- insurance groups – 97
Sexual Harassment – 438-440
Simplified Employee Pension Plan – 491
Sole proprietors and partners – 49-50
Social Security Administration – 61, 460, 466
Social Security Disability Insurance – 234, 255, 274, 463-464, 466, 494
Special Funds – 146, 338, 340, 365-366, 371-372, 374-375, 476
    Second injury fund – 255, 366-373
    Uninsured employers fund – 370
Specific excess coverage – 95-96
Standard Workers Compensation Policy – 50, 82, 86, 96, 106, 126-127, 143, 165-166, 295, 411
    General Section – 128-129, 145, 166
    Part One – (Workers Compensation Insurance) – 126, 129-130, 134, 136-137, 145, 149, 151, 153-154, 166, 295
    Part Two – (Employers Liability Insurance) – 126, 132-138, 146, 151, 154, 167, 295, 391, 433
    Part Three – (Other States Insurance) – 138, 148, 151
    Part Four – (Your Duty If Injury Occurs) – 138-139, 148
    Part Five – Premiums – 139-140, 144, 149
    Part Six – Conditions – 142, 150

Information Page – 126-130, 134, 136-138, 141, 143-146, 148-152, 154, 167, 391, 403
State Temporary Disability Insurance (STDI) – 476
Statewide average weekly wage (SAWW) – 20-21, 230, 241, 255, 265, 371
Statutory employees – 68
Stop gap coverage – 86, 154
Structured settlement – 364-365
Subrogation – 131-132, 137, 139, 155, 258, 263, 268, 286-290, 293-296, 435-436, 469
Substance abuse – 486, 498
Substantial certainty test – 419-420
Suicide – 176-177, 205, 208, 493
Supplement Income Benefits (SIBs) – 248
Supplemental Security Income (SSI) – 466, 473

T

Telecommuting – 183-184
Temporary total disability (TTD) – 19-20, 214, 227, 230-231, 233, 236-237, 267, 343, 356, 462, 482, 496
Terrorism – 108, 120, 157, 177, 393
Terrorism Risk Insurance Act – 157
Texas "opt-out" program – (see non-subscriber program)
Third party action-over – 415
Time limitation (for filing claim) – 16
Total payroll rule – 389
Traveling employees – 182-183
Treatment guidelines – 23, 224, 311, 318-319, 322-323
Triangle Shirtwaist factory – 13
Twenty-four (24) hour coverage – 21, 101

U

Uber – 23, 56, 65, 67
Underwriting – (see Chapter Three) 31, 83, 91, 96, 105-106, 108-109, 114-116, 118, 120, 123, 125, 144, 384, 406, 409
    Risk classification – 114, 379
    Housekeeping – 117, 119, 125
    Hazard control – 116-119
    Loss history – 86, 90, 95, 114, 121-122, 404
    Risk Pricing – 122
Unit statistical data – 384
Unfair claim practices (see Bad Faith)
United States Bureau of Labor Statistics (BLS) – 26, 251, 493
Unusual exertion rule – 188
Unscheduled permanent partial disability – 243, 245-246
    Bi-furcated approach – 246-248

　　　　　Loss-of-wage-earning-capacity (LWEC) – 245
　　　　　Wage loss – 21, 125, 158, 160, 237, 245-246, 248-250, 448, 462, 494
Usual exertion rule – 187
Utilization review – 315, 319, 321-322, 330, 332, 356
　　　　　Prospective review – 321
　　　　　Concurrent review – 321-322
　　　　　Retrospective review – 321-322

V

Von Bismarck, Otto – 8
Vicarious liability – 3
Vocational or physical rehabilitation – 215, 225
Voluntary Protection Program (VPP) – 34-36

W

Wage loss – 21, 125, 158, 160, 237, 245-246, 248-250, 448, 462, 494
Waiting period – 15-16, 102, 228-229, 233, 237, 264, 341-342, 351, 464, 477-478, 481, 493-494
Waiver of subrogation – 293-294, 296,
War and terrorism (see terrorism)
Willful misconduct – 146, 179, 416
Workers' Compensation Medicare Set-aside Arrangement (WCMSA) – 470-472
Workers Compensation Research Institute (WCRI) – 228, 303, 309
Work at home – 185
Work product doctrine – 275-276
Workplace Safety and Loss Prevention – 26
World Trade Center (WTC) – 177

$250.00
ISBN 979-8-9858499-0-5

Copyright © AMCOMP 2011
Fourth Edition 2021
The American Society of Workers Comp Professionals, Inc.

Made in the USA
Columbia, SC
13 July 2023